THE UNWORRY BOOK

Written by Alice James

Designed and illustrated by Stephen Moncrieff

Additional illustration by
Cristina Martin Recasens
and Freya Harrison

Expert advice from
Dr Angharad Rudkin,
clinical psychologist,
University of Southampton

WE ALL WORRY

Worries are annoying, but they're also normal, and unfortunately pretty common. EVERYONE worries at some point, and some of us worry a lot.

Worrying isn't a bad thing, and often it can help you do a good job or be a better person. But it's important to be able to cope with worries so they don't stop you living your life.

SO... think of this book as a kind of unworry toolkit. It's full of things to calm you down and distract you, and places where you can put your worries, instead of letting them hang around in your head.

UNWORRY TOOLKIT

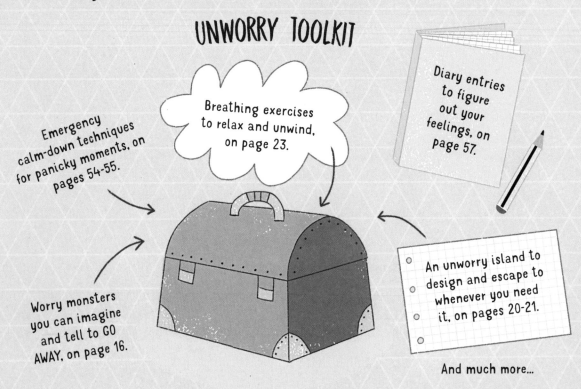

Emergency calm-down techniques for panicky moments, on pages 54-55.

Breathing exercises to relax and unwind, on page 23.

Diary entries to figure out your feelings, on page 57.

Worry monsters you can imagine and tell to GO AWAY, on page 16.

An unworry island to design and escape to whenever you need it, on pages 20-21.

And much more...

WHY DO WE WORRY?

Worries exist to help you manage risk and stay safe – like an ALARM SYSTEM that goes off when you're in danger. When you worry, chemicals are released in your body, so you're ready to react to danger:

YOUR BODY TEMPERATURE INCREASES

YOUR HEART PUMPS FASTER

YOUR HANDS GET SWEATY AND SHAKY

In extreme circumstances worrying can save your life – for example by stopping you running out in front of a car. But you don't need it to survive day-to-day. Most of the time when you worry, it's just your alarm system over-reacting. Some people's alarms go off more than others. The important thing is not how much you worry, but how you deal with it...

...AND THAT'S WHERE THIS BOOK COMES IN.

HOW THIS BOOK WILL HELP

This book will try to help you deal with worries, from little random ones to BIG overwhelming ones. It might not make them go away COMPLETELY, but here are three ways it might help a little.

1. BY HELPING YOU FIGURE OUT THE PROBLEM

It can be useful just to work out HOW you feel - are you worried, or is the feeling actually excitement or nerves? Being able to recognize how you feel is called EMOTIONAL AWARENESS, and you can find out about it on these pages:

There's a **map of emotions** to wander through on pages **8-9**.

Find out how to use **colours** rather than words to **express your feelings** on pages **26-27**.

There is also information about the **science** of worry and emotions, on pages **22, 44, 64 & 88**.

4

2. BY GIVING YOU A PLACE TO WORRY

Sometimes when you worry it can just build up and up, with nowhere to go. There are lots of places in this book where you can get worries out of your head and onto paper:

Divide your worries into ones you can and can't **control,** on pages **36-37.**

Fill in a **diary** for a few days, on pages **56-61.**

Break **big worries** down into **little chunks,** on pages **80-81.**

Write, draw or doodle anything **on your mind** on pages **76-77.**

If worries are **stopping you from sleeping,** get them out of your head on pages **90-91.**

Put your worries on a **worry shelf** on pages **92-93.**

3. BY DISTRACTING YOU

You don't always need to focus on the worry itself to feel better. It's often best just to think about something completely different - while your brain is occupied with other things, the worries get pushed out.

You might also find that while you're distracted, the worry disappears entirely, sorting itself out quietly in the back of your mind.

This book is full of stuff to distract you.

Stuff to make and create

Fiddle star, page **84**

Worry box, page **12**

Stuff to write and imagine

Stories, page **46**

Comics, page **70**

Limericks, page **40**

Stuff to decorate, scribble and design

Draw patterns, pages **32 & 72**

Decorate paint splats, page **66**

Follow a maze, page **38**

Scribble, pages **18 & 52**

Stuff to do with your body

Breathe, page **23**

Yoga, page **68**

Relax, page **65**

Move, page **34**

You might feel a bit awkward trying some of these things. It doesn't always come naturally to think about emotions, and doodling or designing worry monsters might feel a bit daft. But that's normal too, and OK. Just have a go and see how you get on.

Everything in the book has been checked and recommended by a psychologist - a brain and behaviour expert. Everything in here is designed to be helpful - there's a range of stuff to help all sorts of different people, so there should be something in here that helps YOU.

USBORNE QUICKLINKS

For advice, support, and
more unworry activities, go to
www.usborne.com/quicklinks
and type in the keyword UNWORRY.
Please follow the online safety guidelines
at the Usborne Quicklinks website.

HOW DO YOU FEEL?

Sometimes it's really helpful just to try putting your finger on exactly how you're feeling.

If you're struggling to name a feeling, take a wander through this EMOTIONS MAP. You can come back to this page again and again. Add words to the map if what you feel isn't here.

UPSET

EXCITED

HOPEFUL

HAPPY

CROSS

ANNOYED

FRIGHTENED

RELAXED

You might feel one, or two, or twenty emotions.

SCARED

TIRED

CHEERFUL

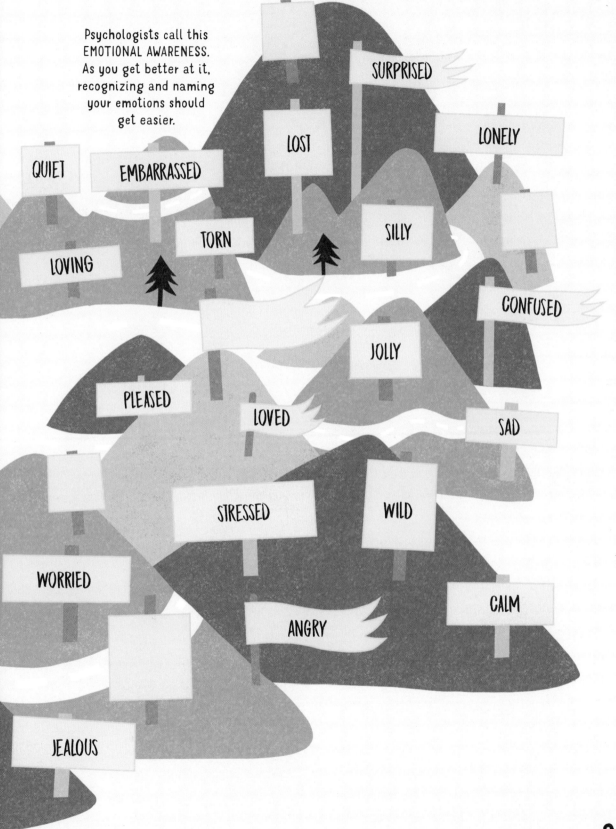

Psychologists call this EMOTIONAL AWARENESS. As you get better at it, recognizing and naming your emotions should get easier.

SURPRISED

LOST

LONELY

QUIET

EMBARRASSED

TORN

SILLY

LOVING

CONFUSED

JOLLY

PLEASED

LOVED

SAD

STRESSED

WILD

WORRIED

CALM

ANGRY

JEALOUS

PEACEFUL PENCILS

Psychologists often recommend a technique called MINDFULNESS for anyone who might be worrying.

Mindfulness is all about focusing on small details in the here and now. Colour in this pattern, and as you do, only think about the things you can feel, hear and smell, right now. Go slowly, and deliberately, and take time to wrap yourself up in it.

Listen to the sound the pen or pencil makes as it brushes across the paper.

Notice the glistening wet ink of your pen, or the grain of the paper as your pencil draws across it.

Smell the pages of the book.

Feel the ridges of your pencil, or the plastic barrel of your pen.

Smell the wood of your pencil, or the ink of your pen.

Feel the textures of this page under your fingers. Does it feel warm, or cool?

WORRY BOX

Writing down a worry helps to get it OUT OF YOUR HEAD. Try making a worry box to get rid of worries you're jotting down. Turn the box into a creature, and imagine it EATING up the worries.

YOU WILL NEED:

AN EMPTY ENVELOPE, JAR, TISSUE BOX OR TUB
PENS, DECORATIONS, GLUE

It can be made of anything you can put stuff in.

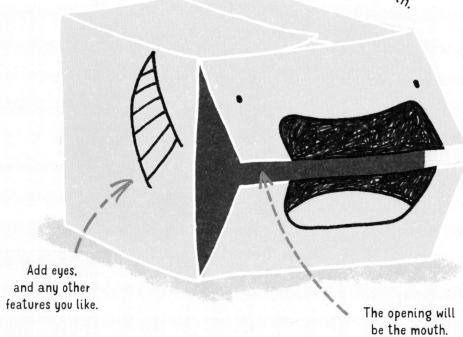

Add eyes, and any other features you like.

The opening will be the mouth.

Then start decorating.
Here are some ideas, but you
can use anything you find.

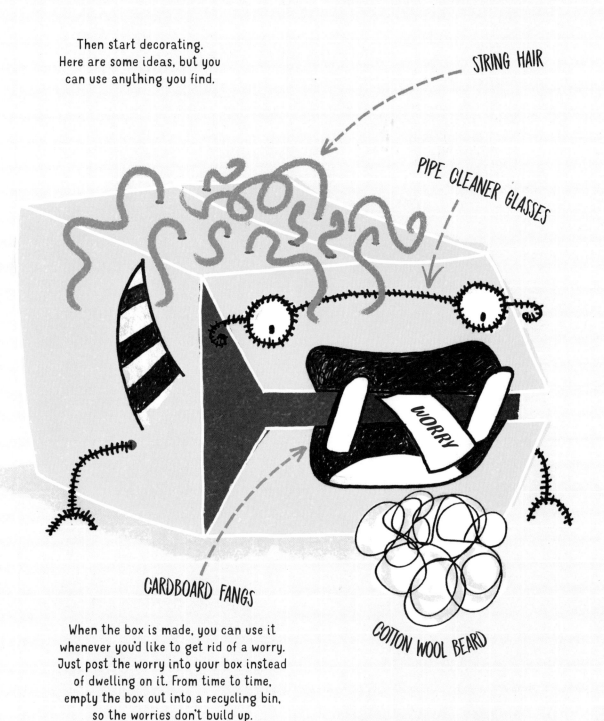

STRING HAIR

PIPE CLEANER GLASSES

WORRY

CARDBOARD FANGS

COTTON WOOL BEARD

When the box is made, you can use it
whenever you'd like to get rid of a worry.
Just post the worry into your box instead
of dwelling on it. From time to time,
empty the box out into a recycling bin,
so the worries don't build up.

WORRY

Alternatively, you could just
SCRUNCH them up and THROW them
away. Sometimes worries just need
to be chucked away entirely.

WHAT IFS

"WHAT IF I'M LATE?"

"WHAT IF IT GOES WRONG?"

"WHAT IF I CAN'T DO IT?"

A LOT OF OUR WORRIES START WITH THE WORDS 'WHAT IF...'

This is really normal. Our brains often jump to the WORST CASE SCENARIO - the worst possible thing you can think of happening.

Many worries are actually really simple to solve, but once you start to worry you get more and more anxious, and find it hard to see rational, sensible solutions.

"WHAT IF I FORGET TO BRING PENCILS TO A TEST?"

COULD BE SOLVED BY

Asking someone for a spare! You could ask a friend, a teacher, or borrow one from a classroom.

Some 'what if' worries can be a bit harder, because they are more emotional. That doesn't mean they don't have answers though.

"WHAT IF I FALL OUT WITH MY FRIEND?"

COULD BE SOLVED BY

Talking it through, apologizing if you need to, and working it out together. The falling out doesn't need to be permanent.

Making a new friend. People change over time, and friendships change with them.

It might not work for every worry, but thinking of some logical, simple answers to your 'what if' questions can be a really effective way of calming down. Try it for yourself, and see if it works. There's an activity to help you with 'what if' worries on the next page.

It can be really helpful to think about your worries as a character, completely separate from yourself. Psychologists call this unworry technique EXTERNALISING.

Use the space below to design a 'what if' creature. Whenever a worry pops into your head, just imagine the creature and tell it to go away, or turn its volume down – DIMINISH it, LOSE it, get RID of it...

You might find your creature looks silly, or ridiculous. That's actually really useful. It's good to remember your worries are just thoughts. You can beat them, and even laugh at them.

It can also help to create an ANTI-what-if creature – a wise, reasonable, logical character that can help you think of those simple solutions. Design yours here.

IT COULD BE A:

WIZARD   ANGEL   WISE OWL

It might feel silly to draw a worry gremlin, or anti-worry wizard, but psychologists think it's really helpful to externalise worries. If you don't want to draw them, you could describe them in words instead, or just draw a blob.

SCRIBBLE

Rather than shouting,
crying or getting angry when you're worried,
try SCRIBBLING the anxiety away. Scratch,
scrawl and scribble on this page until the
worry subsides and you feel calmer.

Whenever you feel worried,
you could get a piece of paper
out of the recycling bin and
scribble all over it. Then scrunch
it up and throw it away again.

UNWORRY
ISLAND

Design your own UNWORRY ISLAND, a place you can imagine and visit whenever you need to, especially at bedtime if worries are stopping you from sleeping.

What's the weather like?

Where do you stay?
A hut? A treehouse?
An igloo?

Who else is there with you? Or are you on your own?

What do you eat? Fruit from the trees? Fish from the sea? An endless supply of ice cream from a cafe?

It doesn't have to be realistic. This is YOUR unworry island - it can be absolutely anything you want, as long as there are no worries there.

The more you use your island to relax, the more helpful it'll be. Scientists call this process CONDITIONING. You train your body to RELAX whenever you imagine the island. So don't just visit the island once, pop back again and again, and add or change things whenever you like.

THE SCIENCE OF STRESS

Worrying causes a lot of physical changes in your body. When you get stressed, your body releases chemicals called HORMONES.

The most famous worry hormone is ADRENALINE. Adrenaline gets your body ready for what scientists call...

the
FIGHT OR FLIGHT
response.

In prehistoric times adrenaline prepared people to FIGHT dangerous animals, or FLEE from them, in order to save their lives. This is how it works...

Making your heart beat faster. This gets more blood flowing around your body to deliver vital stuff your muscles need to GO.

Making you breathe in short shallow gasps. It's trying to get more oxygen into your blood quickly, to FUEL the running or fighting.

Making you very ALERT, AWARE and ON EDGE, so you can respond really fast.

After a few minutes, or sometimes hours, adrenaline GOES AWAY - levels of the hormone go back down, and you feel normal again.

AND BREATHE...

Once you know what worry does to your body, it's easier to make yourself feel better.

Adrenaline makes you want to breathe in QUICKLY. This makes you more and more stressed, as if you're running out of air.

Keep both feet on the floor, shoulder-width apart.
This is called GROUNDING, and it makes you feel instantly more calm, reassured and in control.

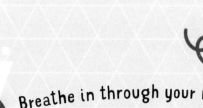

Breathe in through your nose for **3** seconds,

RIGHT INTO YOUR CHEST.

Breathe out for **3** seconds

through your mouth.

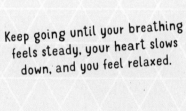

Keep going until your breathing feels steady, your heart slows down, and you feel relaxed.

LAUGH!

Scientists have found that when your muscles move and tense as you LAUGH, chemicals called ENDORPHINS are released in your brain. Endorphins make you feel happier and relaxed, and also reduce the amount of stress chemicals in your body. So chuckle, giggle, chortle or guffaw, and see if it helps your worries go away...

In this box write down or draw things that you find really funny.

Silly words

Animals doing human things

Think about the last time
 you laughed so much it
 hurt. What was it about?

Use this space to write down any jokes
you like - or you could make up your own.

SCRIBBLE YOUR FEELINGS

You don't have to write or talk about your worries to figure them out. Just try doodling in a way that reflects your mood, so you can see what your mood LOOKS LIKE. So, grab some colours and start SCRIBBLING.

If you're feeling quiet, or sad, you could use gentle, small movements with the pencil.

If you're feeling angry you might press hard, or if you're feeling anxious you might scribble and scrawl.

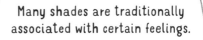

Many shades are traditionally associated with certain feelings.

RED   ANGRY ADVENTUROUS

ORANGE   FIERY WARM EXCITED

YELLOW   HAPPY CHEERFUL OPTIMISTIC

GREEN   JEALOUS EMBARRASSED PEACEFUL

BLUE   CALM SAD THOUGHTFUL

PURPLE   POWERFUL MAGIC CONFIDENT

BLACK   MOODY SCARED MYSTERIOUS

GREY   SAD GRUMPY QUIET

You could use these ideas, or make up your own.

You could use one colour for one emotion, or a range to represent a scramble of feelings.

RIP IT!

Find some paper, and tear it up into as many tiny pieces as you can. Stick them all over this page, and create a snowstorm of ripped paper.

When the page is full,
count the pieces. How
many are there?

Your brain isn't very good at
doing more than one thing at
once. If it's focusing on this, it's
NOT focusing on worries.

BUILD YOURSELF UP

Sometimes you might have worries that aren't about stuff going on around you, but about you yourself - "Can I do it?", "Am I good enough?", "I feel as if I failed."

You can FIGHT these worries by telling yourself GOOD things LOUDER than your brain tells you bad things. Psychologists call this POSITIVE SELF TALK. Fill this page with positive things about yourself, and reminders that you're doing a good job.

Things you're good at.

Things you're working on or improving at.

Things you like about yourself.

I look good in my new hat.

If you're struggling, think about things your friends think you're good at, or like about you. The things you write might feel a bit cheesy, but BUILDING YOURSELF UP can help banish worries. Come back to this page for a boost of confidence whenever you feel you need one.

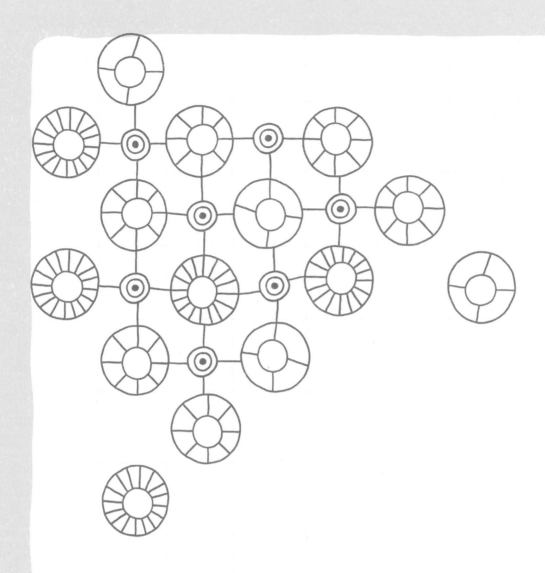

Sometimes, when you distract yourself
with something, you'll find that whatever
you were worrying about has just stopped
feeling like a problem without you noticing.

PATTERNS

Here's some more peaceful, focused distraction. Continue these patterns across the page, concentrating on the shapes you're making and using all the space. You could colour them in too.

MOVE IT, MOVE IT!

Being active releases chemicals called ENDORPHINS in your brain. Endorphins are feel-good chemicals that give you a big BOOST.

Here are some ideas for getting active that are quick and easy to do at home, or out and about. They may sound obvious and perhaps a bit silly, but don't worry – just GO FOR IT.

DANCE

Put some music on and DANCE for a few minutes.

Make your dance as...

BIG SMALL FUNKY or WILD ...as you like.

Just move!

JUMP

Star jumps

Big jumps

Hop jumps

Long jumps

STEP

Find some stairs and walk up and down them a few times, until you're out of breath.

UP

UP   UP

DOWN

DOWN

Phew!

Scientists have shown that being PHYSICALLY active can improve your MENTAL wellbeing. It can also improve your SELF-ESTEEM and give you a sense of ACHIEVEMENT, and provide a great DISTRACTION.

More moving = less worrying, so get to it!

UNDER CONTROL

Some worries and problems are within your control,
and have simple solutions you can find straight away. But
there are a lot of worries that are totally OUT of your control.

Learning the difference between those worries is really
important. Think about the things you worry about.
Write any you CAN control on this page, and any
you CAN'T control on the opposite page.

THINGS YOU CAN CONTROL

Things you say

THINGS YOU CAN'T CONTROL

Stuff on
the news

The weather

Things on this page might still be really worrying. But the fact
you can't change them means there's no point spending lots of
time thinking about them. Learning to LET GO of these things
is one of the greatest unworry techniques there is.

MAZE

Find your way through this maze to the finish.
Focus on keeping your pencil between the lines.
Think of it as finding your way through a tangle
of worries, and out the other side.

START

FINISH

39

LIMERICKS

Keep your brain busy and make yourself chuckle by writing some humorous poems called LIMERICKS. Limericks work like this:

The first, second and fifth lines rhyme, and each of these lines has 8 or 9 syllables.

1 An elderly fellow called Keith
2 Had mislaid his set of false teeth.
3 They'd been left on a chair,
4 He forgot they were there,
5 Sat down - and was bitten beneath.

The third and fourth lines are shorter, and have their own rhyme.

Each of these lines has 5 or 6 syllables.

Limericks are often silly and funny.

Try finishing off these limericks. Use a pencil so you can change it if you want to.

There was a young man made of tin,

- - - - - - - - - - - - - - - - - - - -

- - - - - - - - - - - - - - - - - - - -

- - - - - - - - - - - - - - - - - - - -

- - - - - - - - - - - - - - - - - - - -

There once was an alien called Zars,

_____

_____

_____

An old penguin was skating on ice,

_____

_____

_____

Try a whole limerick
with your own first line:

_____

_____

_____

_____

_____

CALM

Calm. Four letters, one little word, but a
big, brilliant feeling.

Write it out really small

Now really
BIG

In your swirliest, fanciest writing

Upside down

Backwards

Press as lightly as you can

Try writing it with the hand you don't normally use

Write it in a Thick chunky outline

Fill the letters in soothing shades

THE SCIENCE OF BEING NEGATIVE

Annoyingly, humans are built to notice and focus on NEGATIVES more than POSITIVES. Negative things like dangers, illnesses and bad weather could affect the survival of prehistoric people, so it was important to spot them and think about them. But our brains still do this today.

Scientists have a fancy term for this:

NEGATIVITY BIAS

When something bad happens, your brain BUZZES with more ELECTRICITY than it does for good stuff.

That means you are hard-wired to process negative things. This is one of the reasons people worry so much.

ON THE POSITIVE

The good news is you can do something about your brain's inbuilt negativity bias by thinking really hard about POSITIVE THINGS.

Think about things you're **REALLY LOOKING FORWARD TO** and write them here.

It could be a trip, lunch, a TV show, seeing a friend - anything you're EXCITED about.

ONCE UPON A TIME...

Try to forget about any worries by taking your mind somewhere completely different. This is sometimes called ESCAPISM. It might not solve the problem, but it can help you feel better for a while.

Use this story starter, and carry it on - immerse yourself in your story, in a land far, far away.

There were rustles and whispers coming from behind the door. Slowly, carefully, they pushed it open, and

gasped...

Where does the door lead?

A dragon's keep

A forest clearing

A deserted building

A secret garden

A space transporter

A laboratory

48

MOOD GRID

Pick colours for each of the moods below. Then colour in the first box in the grid on the right, depending on how you're feeling. Come back to this page once a day, filling in one more box each time.

This is about looking inside and seeing how you are - recognizing emotions, and LETTING YOURSELF feel them.

You could use the shades suggested on page 27, or choose the colours these emotions feel like to YOU.

Happy   Sad   Worried   Tired   Excited   Not sure

If some of these aren't emotions you feel very much, cross them out and write new ones. For example you might change "sad" to "confused", or "grumpy".

Most days you'll probably feel more than one thing, but colour in the mood you feel the MOST that day.

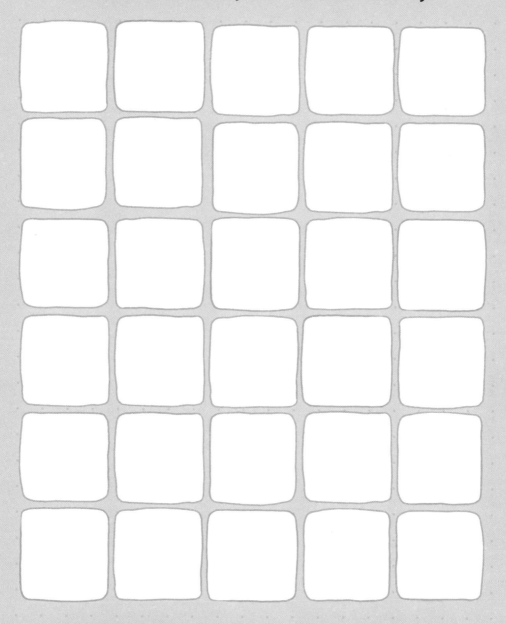

If you use "not sure" a lot, have a look at the emotions map on page 8-9 to see if any of those words help you put your finger on what you feel.

TAKE A LINE FOR A WALK

Take a few minutes to distract your brain from any worried wanders that it might be going on. Follow this line, and continue it ALL OVER the page. Try to make sure the pencil doesn't leave the paper.

You could draw something
in particular, or just let the
pencil walk randomly over the
page in a scribble or swirl.

IF YOU'RE IN A PANIC...

Sometimes, when worries build up a lot, you can start to panic. Your heart beats quickly, you feel breathless and shaky, and you get a heavy feeling in your chest.
If this happens, try this, the MINDFULNESS 5.

NOTICE **5** things you can see

LISTEN TO **4** things you can hear

FEEL **3** things you can touch

FIND **2** things you can smell

IS THERE **1** thing you can taste?

Have a go wherever you are now to see how it works. Focus on your senses to find a mindfulness 5, and write them here.

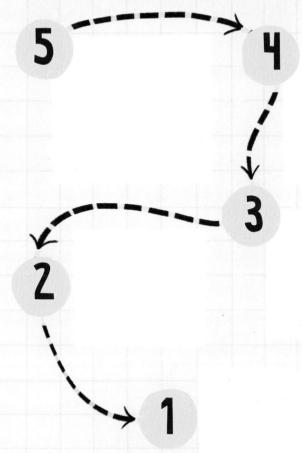

This is a useful tool to remember in really panicky moments. It will help to ground you, and reduce your anxiety. By the time you've found the things, you might even have forgotten what you were worrying about.

JUST REMEMBER

5 SEE
4 HEAR
3 TOUCH
2 SMELL
1 TASTE

FIVE-DAY DIARY

Jotting down what's going on in your life, and how you feel about it, can help you work out what you tend to worry about. It can also improve your EMOTIONAL AWARENESS - being able to identify your feelings.

Over the next five days, try filling in all the boxes on the next few pages. If you find it helpful, or enjoyable, you could use the simple layout to start keeping your own journal in a separate notebook.

DAY 1

In here you could draw a face of how you felt, or add a number from 1-10.

Date

Day

Weather

Overall mood

What happened today

Good stuff

Not so good stuff

Any worries on your mind

DAY 2

Date

Day

Weather

Overall mood

What happened today

Good stuff

Not so good stuff

Any worries on your mind

DAY 3

Date

Day

Weather

Overall mood

What happened today

Good stuff

Not so good stuff

Any worries on your mind

DAY 4

Date

Day

Weather

Overall mood

What happened today

Good stuff

Not so good stuff

Any worries on your mind

DAY 5

Date

Day

Weather

Overall mood

What happened today

Good stuff

Not so good stuff

Any worries on your mind

WHAT'S IMPORTANT?

Psychologists think you worry less if you focus on the stuff you VALUE in life, more than your aims or goals. You can't fail at a value, or get it wrong, and thinking about what's important to you can help you make decisions and work out who you are.

HERE'S A LIST OF VALUES. WHICH ONES MATTER MOST TO YOU?

Kindness
Be helpful and compassionate towards everyone

Power
Influence people and be in charge

Cooperation
Work well with others, and bring people together

Independence
Support yourself, and find your own way

comedy
Find the funny side, and make others laugh

Adventure
Explore, find, and experience new things

Honesty
Be truthful and open with yourself and others

Trust
Be loyal and reliable

Justice
Be fair, and aware of what is right and wrong

Equality
Treat everyone as equals, whoever they are

skills
Improve and develop your talents and abilities

courage
Be brave, fight negative things, and keep going

Spirituality
Feel connected to big ideas and beliefs

Creativity
Invent, design and make

Hard work
Be dedicated, committed, and graft

challenge
Make yourself do new or difficult things

curiosity
Discover, ask questions, explore and learn

If what you value most isn't here, write it in this box:

Choose the SIX of these values that are the MOST important to you, and write them here:

1. _____
2. _____
3. _____
4. _____
5. _____
6. _____

THE SCIENCE OF FEAR

Sometimes you worry even if there's no real reason to.

This pesky feeling of fear comes from a place in the brain called the

AMYGDALA.

The amygdala's response is AUTOMATIC – you have absolutely no control over it. That's why, even when REALLY you know there's nothing to be worried about or scared of, your body still reacts.

The amygdala is MUCH QUICKER than the rational, conscious decision-making part of your brain. So you feel fear before you can tell yourself there's nothing to worry about.

RELAAAAAX

BUT you can BEAT fearful feelings by
taking time to relax your body.
Relaxing gets rid of the tension caused by
your amygdala's automatic response.

Psychologists recommend something called

PROGRESSIVE MUSCLE RELAXATION.

That's a fancy way of saying you tense your
muscles, then relax them, one by one.

1
Start at your
toes, and clench
them downwards
for a few seconds.
Relax.

2
Then clench
your leg
muscles, and
relax them.

3
Pull in your bottom
muscles, stomach
muscles, and
continue, one by one,
right up through
your body to your
face, and RELAX.

Breathing slowly
as you do it will
help calm you
down more.

SPLAT

Immerse yourself in doodling and
drawing, and turn these splodges of paint
into other things – from creatures and
aliens to hats, cars and flowers.

STRETCH
AND
BREATHE

Have a go at this sequence of yoga poses. While you're doing it, focus on BREATHING steadily and deeply, in, and then out, to unwind gently and relax. Be MINDFUL - think about your body, how it's moving, and what you can feel under your hands and feet. As you do it, let any worries drift off.

This circular sequence is called a SUN SALUTATION.

START and
FINISH here.

1

Stand up
tall.

2

Breathe IN,
and raise
your hands
above your
head.

11

Breathe IN. Stand up
tall and raise your
hands above your head.

10

Breathe OUT. Bring
your right foot
forward and stand up,
keeping your chest
close to your knees.

9

Breathe IN. This time bring
your left foot forward.

3

Breathe OUT, and bend right over.

4

Breathe IN. Put your right foot back, and your left foot out in front of you. Place your hands on the floor. Breathe OUT.

5

Breathe IN. Bring your left foot back. Keep your legs and back straight.

6

Breathe OUT. Bend your elbows and slowly lower yourself till your legs and chest are on the floor.

7

Breathe IN. Raise your chest off the floor.

8

Breathe OUT. Lift your bottom straight into the air, so you're a v-shape.

The more you do this the easier it'll be.

STORY MAKER

Time for some more CREATIVE distraction and brain-stretching. Use the 'story board' here to create a story. You could draw, or write, or use a combination of both to make a cartoon strip.

Pick one of these characters to build a story around, or make up one of your own.

A mysterious spy who might be a double agent.

Someone who has been framed for a crime they didn't commit.

The sole survivor of a shipwreck.

A scientist who's discovered aliens, but hasn't told anyone else.

STORY BOARD

Putting yourself in someone else's shoes can
help you understand your own feelings more.

DOTS

Join the dots to reveal an intricate pattern. Start with dot 1, and connect them one by one in order, until they're all joined up. Concentrate on the numbers and pattern, and forget about anything else you're dwelling on.

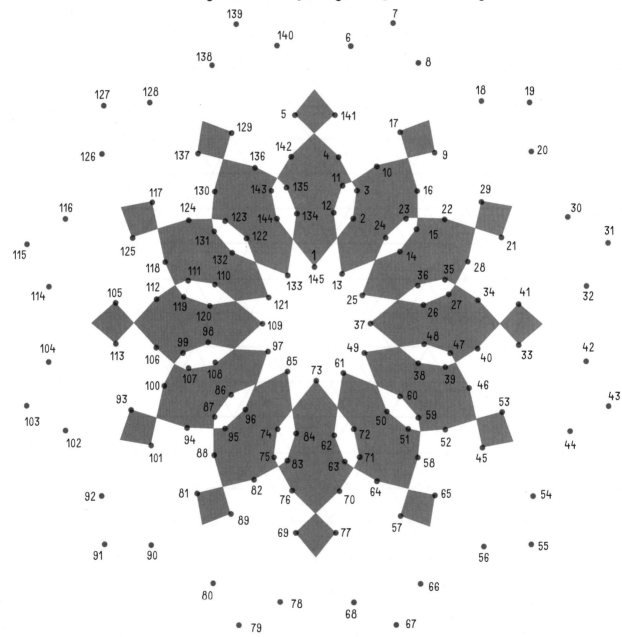

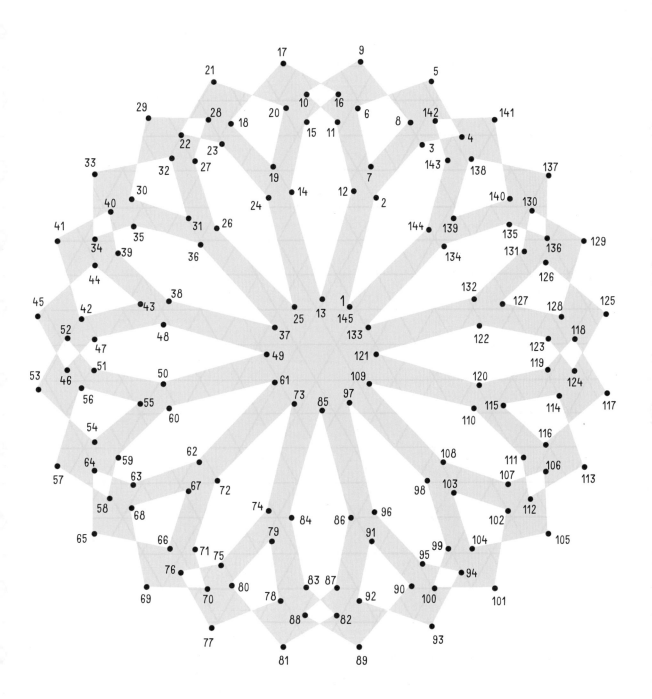

73

Gloopy

Cosmic

WONDERFUL WORDS

Fill this page with words you REALLY LIKE.
They could mean things that make you
smile, or just be really lovely to SAY.

Whopper

Maracas

Turnip

Thunderclap

Fork

Pickle

Gelato

Pickle

Serendipity

ON YOUR MIND

Fill in the outline with anything that's in your head today.
It can be WORRIES, ideas, INVENTIONS, hopes, DREAMS,
crushes, plans – anything you're thinking about.

You could draw, scribble, doodle, or write it out in words.

Here's another one for another day.

Getting stuff OUT of your head and onto paper can help
you declutter and untangle your thoughts.

BRAIN PUZZLES

Have a go at all the puzzles on this page.
Keep your brain focused on these, rather than on worries.

Crack this code to work out what the message says.

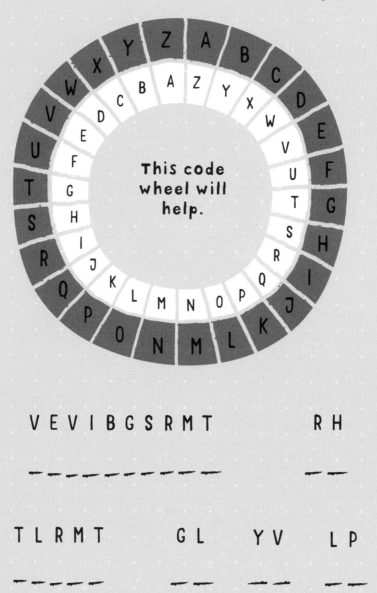

This code
wheel will
help.

V E V I B G S R M T   R H

_ _ _ _ _ _ _ _ _ _   _ _

T L R M T   G L   Y V   L P

_ _ _ _ _   _ _   _ _   _ _

WORDSEARCH

Look for all these unworry terms:

calm
unwind
Relax
unworry
Mindful
Breathe
Laugh
Rest

The words might be across, up, down or backwards.

T	E	S	B	C	L	A	M	R	G
S	C	A	L	M	A	T	I	R	N
E	E	X	A	X	U	N	N	W	O
R	X	U	N	W	I	N	D	H	E
W	O	R	R	R	E	L	F	X	H
X	A	L	E	R	C	O	U	N	T
B	R	A	T	H	F	O	L	E	A
N	U	C	L	A	U	G	H	R	E
U	N	W	O	R	R	Y	L	E	R
C	A	M	M	I	N	D	O	K	B

How many words can you make using the letters of

Relaxation

Only use each letter as many times as it appears in 'relaxation'. What's the longest word you can make?

Find the answers on page 96.

BREAK IT DOWN

It's often easier to write a worry down than to find the words to say it to someone out loud. Pop your worries onto these sticky notes in SHORT CHUNKS – they'll be easier to DIGEST than long, wordy, tangled thoughts.

DOODLE

Scribble freely with a pencil or pen, then doodle and draw to turn the scribble into something else, like this creature.

Use any paper in your recycling
bin for more doodling,
scribbling and scrunching.

FIDDLE STAR

When you get worried, and adrenaline builds up in your body, you often feel fidgety and nervous. But LETTING YOURSELF fidget can help you unwind, as it allows adrenaline to leave your body calmly. Follow these instructions to make an origami star, perfect for spinning, fiddling and fidgeting.

YOU WILL NEED:

A piece of paper

Scissors

A pen or pencil

1 Cut two strips of paper, each about 21cm (8 inches) long, and 5cm (2 inches) wide.

2 Strip 1   Strip 2

Fold each strip in half, down the middle, then open it up again.

3 Fold the top half of each strip to the side, like this, using the crease halfway down as a guide.

84

4

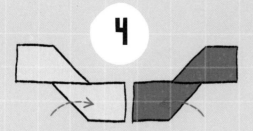

Fold the bottom half to the side, in the opposite direction.

5

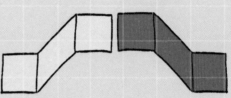

Flip each strip over, so they look like this.

6

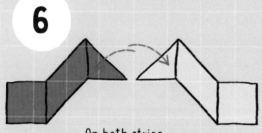

On both strips, fold the top corner down, forming a triangle.

7

Do the same at the bottom, folding the bottom corners up into triangles.

8

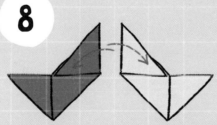

Fold the top triangles inwards.

Turn the page to finish the star.

85

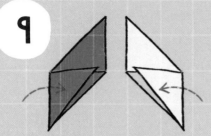

9

Fold the bottom triangles inwards too. They should overlap to form a diamond shape. Then unfold the bottom triangles again - you only need the creases.

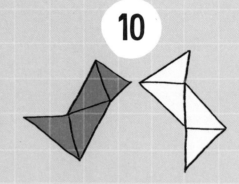

10

Flip the right hand strip over.

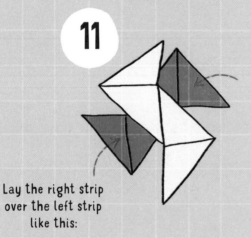

11

Lay the right strip over the left strip like this:

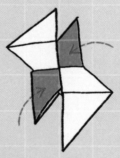

12

Tuck the corner sticking out on the left into the pocket in the right hand strip. Do the same for the right corner.

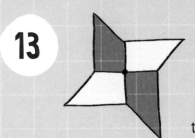

13

Flip the paper over, and do the same at the back. Tuck all four corners in, until you have a star shape.

Poke a hole through the middle with the pen or pencil, and push it through. Start spinning!

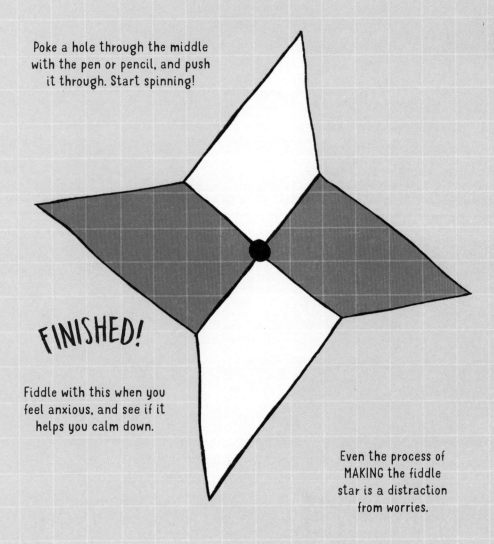

FINISHED!

Fiddle with this when you feel anxious, and see if it helps you calm down.

Even the process of MAKING the fiddle star is a distraction from worries.

THE SCIENCE OF WORRIED SLEEP

Worries often pounce when you're trying to get to sleep. They can make it hard to switch off, and sometimes give you nightmares.

Scientists still don't know exactly

HOW or WHY

people dream, but they think that bad dreams are your brain's way of trying to work out exactly what you are worrying about.

While you sleep, your brain digests and processes complicated thoughts and concerns, and that can turn into nightmares.

SLEEP TIPS

Sleep is really important for unworrying. During sleep, your brain clears and sorts out thoughts and worries that build up in the day, making you feel better in the morning.

Here are some tips for a calm, unworried night's sleep.

AVOID SCREENS

Try not to look at a TV, phone, computer or tablet before you get into bed.

The light of a screen **STIMULATES** your brain, and websites, messages and social media can feed worries you have.

GET WORRIES OUT

If particular worries pop into your head as you try to sleep, WRITE THEM DOWN. Then you can let them go until morning, or forget them completely.

WIND DOWN

RELAX before you settle down. A warm bath or shower, or milky drink, can help calm your body down and get it ready to sleep. You could also try smelling something scented with calming lavender.

Turn the page for a place to put night-time worries.

NIGHT WORRIES

Use the clouds to jot down any worries that come into your head while you're trying to sleep. Get them out and onto paper so you stop thinking about them, and start to SNOOOOZE instead.

WORRY SHELF

If you have a worry in your head, it can help to take
it out and put it onto an imaginary shelf, where it can sit while
you get on with other things. Pop your worries onto this shelf
whenever you need to, and keep them shut here, at the
back of this book.

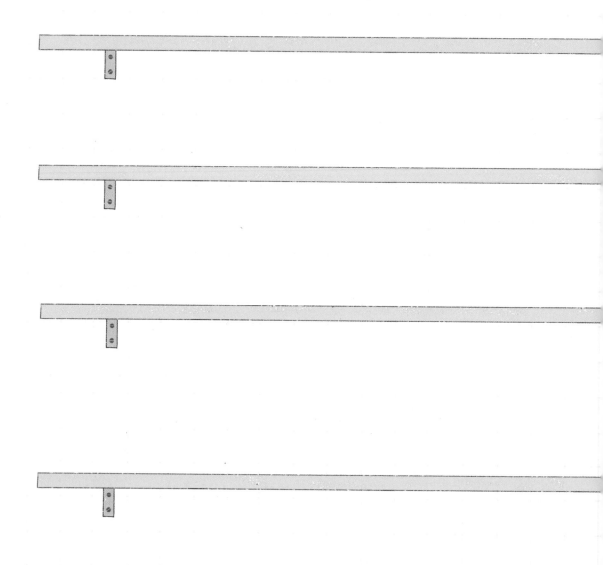

worry

You might find the worry sorts itself out while it is on the shelf, and when you come back to it, it's not a problem any more.

93

HELPING HAND

List five people you feel you can talk to about your worries, one on each finger. Psychologists call this your HELPING HAND – the five people who can help you feel better.

3

2

4

1

5

When you're really worried, look at this hand and find one of these people to talk to.

IF WORRIES OVERFLOW...

Most of the time worries will come and go. Taking simple steps such as breathing, relaxing, and keeping your brain focused on other things can help you feel better.

But if your worries become very overwhelming, or are making it hard for you to feel relaxed, it is really important that you TALK to someone about them. The person you talk to can comfort and support you, give you ideas to cope with your worries, or put them into perspective. Use the people on your helping hand, or any grown-up that you trust.

You could talk to your teacher at school, a counsellor or a nurse, if your school has one. They will be able to give you help, advice and support, especially if worries are affecting how you concentrate or behave at school.

If worries are seriously impacting on your life, it can be a good idea to go and see your doctor. Doctors can put you in touch with specialists called psychologists and psychiatrists who can help you cope with, and get rid of, worries.

For links to websites that offer tips, advice and support to young people and parents and carers, go to the Usborne Quicklinks website at www.usborne.com/quicklinks.

Answers for page 78-79: The message says "Everything is going to be OK"

```
T  E  S  B  C  A  L  M  R  G
S  C  A  L  M  A  T  I  R  N
E  E  X  A  U  N  N  N  W  O
R  X  U  N  W  I  N  D  H  E
W  O  R  R  E  L  F  X  H
X  A  L  E  R  C  O  U  T
B  R  A  T  H  F  O  L  A
N  U  C  L  A  U  G  H  E
U  N  W  O  R  R  Y  L  E  R
C  A  M  M  I  N  D  O  K  B
```

If you find 5-10 words in RELAXATION, good start.
If you find 11-20, great job. If you find more than 20, fantastic!

Additional design by Jenny Offley   Edited by Sam Taplin

First published in 2019 by Usborne Publishing Ltd.,
Usborne House, 83-85 Saffron Hill, London EC1N 8RT, England.

www.usborne.com Copyright © 2019 Usborne Publishing Ltd.

Bayes' Formula

$$P(F_i|E) = \frac{P(F_i) \cdot P(E|F_i)}{P(F_1) \cdot P(E|F_1) + P(F_2) \cdot P(E|F_2) + \cdots + P(F_n) \cdot P(E|F_n)}$$

Probability in a Bernoulli Experiment

If p is the probability of success in a single trial of a Bernoulli experiment, the probability of x successes and $n - x$ failures in n independent repeated trials of the experiment is

$$\binom{n}{x} \cdot p^x \cdot (1 - p)^{n-x}.$$

Variance; Standard Deviation

The **variance** of a set of n numbers $x_1, x_2, x_3, \cdots x_n$, with mean $\bar{x}$, is

$$\text{Var}(x) = \frac{\Sigma(x - \bar{x})^2}{n}.$$

The **standard deviation** of the set is

$$\sigma = \sqrt{\frac{\Sigma(x - \bar{x})^2}{n}}.$$

Binomial

Suppose an experiment is a series of n independent repeated trials, where the probability of a success in a single trial is always p. Let x be the number of successes in the n trials. Then the probability that exactly x successes will occur in n trials is given by

$$\binom{n}{x} p^x (1 - p)^{n-x}.$$

The mean μ and variance $\text{Var}(X)$ of this binomial distribution are respectively

$$\mu = np \quad \text{and} \quad \text{Var}(X) = np(1 - p).$$

The standard deviation σ is

$$\sigma = \sqrt{np(1 - p)}.$$

Compound Amount

If P dollars is deposited for n years with interest compounded m periods per year at a rate of interest i per year, the compound amount A is

$$A = P\left(1 + \frac{i}{m}\right)^{mn}.$$

Future Value of an Annuity

The future value, A, of an annuity of n payments of R dollars each at the end of each consecutive interest period, with interest compounded at a rate i per period, is

$$A = R\left[\frac{(1 + i)^n - 1}{i}\right], \quad \text{or} \quad A = R \cdot s_{\overline{n}|i}.$$

THIRD EDITION

FINITE MATHEMATICS

MARGARET L. LIAL / CHARLES D. MILLER

American River College

SCOTT, FORESMAN AND COMPANY

Glenview, Illinois   London, England

To the Student

A *Student Solutions Manual* to accompany this textbook is available from your college bookstore. The detailed step-by-step solutions in the manual can help you study and understand the course material by providing additional correct examples for the odd-numbered exercises.

Cover and chapter opener artworks are from *The Spirit of Colors: The Art of Karl Gerstner,* Henri Stierlin, editor. Photographs by Alexander von Steiger, Basel. © 1981 by The Massachusetts Institute of Technology. Reproduced with permission.

Cover: Karl Gerstner. *Color Lines C1/L9,* Intro Version 1957, 1976–77. Nitrocellulose on wood, 580 × 580 framed. **Extended application symbols:** artwork first appearing on page 41: Karl Gerstner. From the series *Aperspective 3* (The Large Sliding Mirror Picture), 1953/55; page 99: Karl Gerstner. *Color Sound 1C,* Intro Version, 1968–1972, 1973; page 102: Karl Gerstner. *Carro 64,* alterable object, 1956/61; page 112: Karl Gerstner. *AlgoRhythm 1,* alterable object of 7 plates, 1969–1970.

Library of Congress Cataloging in Publication Data

Lial, Margaret L.
    Finite mathematics.

    Includes index.
    1. Mathematics—1961–   .   I. Miller, Charles
David.   II. Title
QA37.2.L49   1985   510   84-23538
ISBN 0-673-18023-9

3 4 5 6—RRC—89 88 87 86 85

PREFACE

The third edition of *Finite Mathematics* gives a solid foundation in the non-calculus portions of mathematics needed by students majoring in the management, life, and social sciences. In addition to presenting the required techniques, the text supplies numerous applications to motivate students. The only prerequisite for this book is a previous course in algebra.

We have tried to produce a book that is useful to the student and helpful for the instructor. For the student we have written a book with explanations and examples that are clear, direct, and to the point. The exercises are carefully graded in difficulty with examples corresponding to the exercises. Abundant applied problems and extended applications show students how mathematics is used in realistic situations. For the instructor, we have produced a comprehensive instructional package.

The text is carefully laid out to match standard courses. Each section includes only those topics that an instructor would normally expect to find.

PEDAGOGICAL FEATURES

Exercise sets are extensive, with a wide range of difficulty from drill problems to the more challenging. Almost every exercise set includes applications to management and biology.

Examples clearly illustrate the techniques and concepts presented. Numbering more than 240, the examples prepare students for success with the exercises.

Applications are included in examples and exercise sets to motivate student interest. Our applications are practical, varied, and interesting.

Extended applications are included throughout the book in appropriate spots. These extended applications answer the question, "Why are we studying this?" Students can see the utility of the mathematics by seeing it used at Upjohn or Southern Pacific, for example.

A **second color** is used pedagogically. Important rules, definitions, theorems, and equations are enclosed in colored boxes and highlighted with a title in the margin. **Color** is also used to annotate equations, clarify troublesome areas, and in the artwork to clarify processes and procedures.

The idea of mathematical models for real-world applications is emphasized throughout the book, beginning in Chapter 1. Both the strengths and limitations of models are discussed.

Chapter 1 on linear functions is an **optional review chapter.** Well prepared students can go right to Chapter 2, on matrix theory, or to Chapter 5, leading to probability. For many students, Chapter 1 will be a convenient reference.

The book has **two complete chapters on linear programming,** one on the graphical method and one on the simplex method. A section on duality theory is new in this edition.

The chapter on **mathematics of finance** has been **updated** to reflect current interest rates. A section on sequences was added to allow more thorough coverage of annuities and amortization. There is a new application of present value to athletes' salaries.

Digraphs and networks are becoming more important in business applications and in data processing. **This new chapter** makes the text up-to-date and complete.

Systems of linear equations and their solutions are presented before matrices to better motivate matrix theory and demonstrate the power of matrix methods.

The book is designed throughout for **maximum flexibility.** It is not unusual to finish Chapter 6, on probability, only a few days before the end of a term, leaving time for only a brief treatment of Markov chains in Chapter 8, or decision theory in Chapter 9. For this reason, these chapters have been written so that the first sections of each provide a good introduction to the topic and to the types of problems for which the topic is useful.

Chapter interdependence is as follows:

Chapter 1, Linear Models, and Chapter 2, Matrix Theory, have no prerequisite.

Chapter 3, Linear Programming: The Graphical Method, requires Sections 1.1 and 1.2 of Chapter 1 (work which might have been done in an earlier course).

Chapter 4, Linear Programming: The Simplex Method, requires Chapters 2 and 3.

Chapter 5, Sets and Counting, has no prerequisite.

Chapter 6, Probability, requires Chapter 5.

Chapters 7, 8, and 9, the applications of probability, require Chapter 6.

Chapter 10, Mathematics of Finance, has no prerequisite.

Chapter 11, Digraphs and Networks, depends on Chapter 2.

SUPPLEMENTS

Instructor's Manual. This manual features answers to even-numbered exercises, as well as an extensive test bank.

Student Solutions Manual. This booklet, available for purchase by students, features complete solutions to all odd-numbered exercises.

Computer applications. Donald Coscia has prepared a softbound textbook packaged to include a diskette (in Apple II and IBM-PC versions). The programs allow students to solve meaningful problems without the difficulties of extensive arithmetic calculations. This book bridges the gap between the text and the computer by providing additional explanations and additional exercises for solution using a micro-computer. (Appropriate computer exercises in this text are identified with the symbol shown in the margin.)

Acknowledgments

Many instructors helped us prepare this revision. In particular, we would like to thank

Yousef Alavi, Western Michigan University
Steven Bellenot, Florida State University
Robert Blefko, Western Michigan University
Joseph Buckley, Western Michigan University
Ronald M. Davis, Northern Virginia Community College
David Hinde, Rock Valley College
Eleanor Kendrick, San Jose City College
Marty McCaskey, Western Michigan University
Curtis McKnight, University of Oklahoma
Nancy Shoemaker, Oakland University
Lee Witt, Western Michigan University.

Finally, we must thank Marge Prullage, Kayla Cohen, and Janet Tilden, editors who contributed a great deal to the finished book.

Margaret L. Lial
Charles D. Miller

CONTENTS

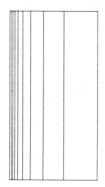
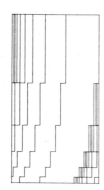
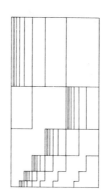
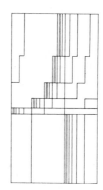

LINEAR MODELS

Karl Gerstner. Drawings from *The Golden-Sectioned Pillar*, alterable object, 1956/57.

To use mathematics in the solution of a real-world problem, it is usually necessary to set up a **mathematical model**—a mathematical description of the real-world situation. To construct a mathematical model of a given situation, a solid understanding of the situation to be modeled is needed. It is also necessary to have a good knowledge of the possible mathematical ideas that can be used in order to construct the model.

Much mathematical theory that is useful for model building has been developed over the years. Yet the very richness and diversity of contemporary mathematics often serves as a barrier between a person in another field and the mathematical tools that person needs. There are so many useful parts of mathematics that it is often hard to know which to choose.

One way around this problem is to have a thorough understanding of the basic and most useful mathematical tools that are available for model building. In this chapter we look at the mathematics of *linear* models—those used for data whose graphs can be approximated by a straight line.

1.1   Linear Equations and Inequalities in One Variable

We begin with a review of *linear equations,* because studying linear mathematical models involves solving linear equations. A **linear equation in one variable** is an equation that can be simplified to the form $ax = b,$ where a and b are real numbers, with $a \neq 0.$ For example,

$$2x = 5, \quad 3m + 7 = -12, \quad \text{and} \quad 6(a - 3) + 4 = 2a - 7$$

are linear equations.

The following two properties are used to solve linear equations.

Addition and Multiplication Properties	For real numbers a, b, and c: **1.** if $a = b$, then $a + c = b + c$; **2.** if $a = b$, then $ac = bc$, $(c \neq 0)$.

By these properties any number can be added to both sides of an equation, and any nonzero number can be used to multiply both sides of an equation. Since subtraction is defined as adding the negative of a number, subtracting the same number from both sides of an equation is justified by the addition property. Also, division on both sides of an equation by the same nonzero number is justified by the multiplication property.

EXAMPLE 1

Solve each equation.

(a) $\frac{3}{2}x = -12$

Multiply both sides of the equation by 2/3.

$$\frac{2}{3} \cdot \frac{3}{2}x = \frac{2}{3}(-12)$$

$$x = -8$$

Check the solution, -8, by substitution in the original equation.

(b) $-6m + 2 = 14$

First subtract 2 on each side of the equation, then divide both sides by -6.

$$-6m + 2 = 14$$

$$-6m = 12$$

$$m = -2$$

The solution is -2.

(c) $-3(k - 5) + 7 = 2(k + 1)$

Use the distributive property to clear parentheses.

$$-3(k - 5) + 7 = 2(k + 1)$$

$$-3k + 15 + 7 = 2k + 2$$

Now combine like terms on the left side of the equation to get

$$-3k + 22 = 2k + 2.$$

To get the variable terms on one side of the equation and the constants on the other side, subtract $2k$ on both sides of the equation, and then subtract 22 on both sides, which gives

$$-5k + 22 = 2$$

$$-5k = -20.$$

Finally, divide both sides by -5 to get

$$k = 4.$$

Check in the original equation to see that 4 is the correct solution. ▪

Sometimes a linear equation involves more than one letter. As a general rule, the first letters of the alphabet—a, b, c, and so on—are used to represent constants, while letters near the end of the alphabet, such as x, y, and z, are used for variables.

EXAMPLE 2

Solve each equation for x.

(a) $ax - b = c$

Here x is the variable; the other letters are treated as constants. Add b to both sides of the equation, then divide both sides by a. We must assume $a \neq 0$ for this step.

$$ax - b = c$$
$$ax = c + b$$
$$x = \frac{c + b}{a}$$

(b) $2x + y = 6(x - 3) + 12$

To solve for x, treat y as a constant. Get all terms with x on one side of the equation and all terms without x on the other side.

$$2x + y = 6x - 18 + 12$$
$$2x + y = 6x - 6 \qquad \text{Combine terms}$$
$$-4x + y = -6 \qquad \text{Subtract } 6x$$
$$-4x = -6 - y \qquad \text{Subtract } y$$
$$x = \frac{-6 - y}{-4} \qquad \text{Divide by } -4$$
$$x = \frac{6 + y}{4} \qquad \text{Simplify} \quad \blacksquare$$

The next example shows how a linear equation may actually occur.

EXAMPLE 3

Richard Calvin receives a $14,000 bonus from his company. He invests part of the money in tax-free bonds at 6% and the remainder at 10%. He earns $1060 per year in interest from the investments. Find the amount he has invested at each rate.

Let x represent the amount Calvin invests at 6%, so that $14,000 - x$ is the amount invested at 10%. Since interest is given by the product of principal, rate, and time, the interest earned in one year is

$$\text{interest at } 6\% = x \cdot 6\% \cdot 1 = .06x,$$
$$\text{interest at } 10\% = (14,000 - x)(10\%)(1) = .10(14,000 - x).$$

The total interest is $1060, so

$$.06x + .10(14,000 - x) = 1060.$$

Solve this equation.

$$.06x + 1400 - .10x = 1060$$
$$1400 - .04x = 1060$$
$$-.04x = -340$$
$$x = 8500$$

Check in the words of the original problem that $8500 was invested at 6%, and $14,000 - $8500 = 5500 at 10%. $\blacksquare$

Linear Inequalities   Many mathematical models involve inequalities rather than equations, so it is useful to review the solution of linear inequalities. A **linear inequality in one variable** is an expression that can be simplified to the form $ax < b$. (Throughout the discussion of linear inequalities, $<$ can be replaced with $>$, $\leq$, or $\geq$.) To solve a linear inequality, use the following properties, which are very similar to the addition and multiplication properties of equations.

Addition and

Multiplication

Properties of

Inequality

For real numbers a, b, and c,

1. if $a < b$, then $a + c < b + c$;
2. if $c > 0$ and $a < b$, then $ac < bc$;
3. if $c < 0$ and $a < b$, then $ac > bc$.

As with the corresponding properties for equality, the first property can be used with subtraction, while the second and third properties apply to division as well as to multiplication.

EXAMPLE 4

Solve the following inequalities.

(a) $3x - 5 < 7$

Use the properties as follows.

$$3x - 5 < 7$$
$$3x < 12 \qquad \text{Add 5}$$
$$x < 4 \qquad \text{Divide by 3}$$

The solution is $x < 4$.

(b) $4 - 3y \geq 7 + 2y$

Get the terms with y on one side, and the terms without y on the other side.

$$4 - 3y \geq 7 + 2y$$
$$4 - 5y \geq 7 \qquad \text{Subtract } 2y$$
$$-5y \geq 3 \qquad \text{Subtract 4}$$
$$y \leq -\frac{3}{5} \qquad \text{Divide by } -5$$

Note that dividing by -5 led to reversing the inequality from $\geq$ to $\leq$, so that the solution is $y \leq -3/5$. ▨

1.1 EXERCISES

Solve the linear equations in Exercises 1–16.

1. $4x - 1 = 15$

2. $-3y + 2 = 5$

3. $3m + 2 = -m + 7$

4. $-2k + 8 = 5k - 10$

5. $.2m - .5 = .1m + .7$

6. $.01p + 3.1 = 2.03p - 2.96$

7. $\frac{5}{6}k - 2k + \frac{1}{3} = \frac{2}{3}$

8. $\frac{3}{4} + \frac{1}{5}r - \frac{1}{2} = \frac{4}{5}r$

9. $2x - (x + 3) = 7 - x$

10. $4y + 3(1 - y) = 2 + y$

11. $3r + 2 - 5(r + 1) = 6r + 4$

12. $5(a + 3) + 4a - 5 = -(2a - 4)$

13. $5(3x - 2) = 7(x + 2)$

14. $3(2p + 5) = 5(p + 2)$

15. $\frac{x}{3} - 7 = x - \frac{3x}{4}$

16. $\frac{y}{3} + 1 = \frac{2y}{5} - 4$

Solve the linear inequalities in Exercises 17–32.

17. $2x - 5 \leq 15$

18. $-y + 10 \geq 18$

19. $6 - 4m \geq 12$

20. $8 + 3p \leq 20$

21. $5k + 2 < 2k - 3$

22. $6 - 4x > 14x + 10$

23. $9 - 3z > 8z + 12$

24. $2r - 12 < 5r + 10$

25. $\frac{4}{5}x + 3 \leq x - \frac{1}{5}$

26. $\frac{a}{3} - 4 \geq \frac{a}{4} + 7$

27. $3(t - 2) + 5 \geq t - 4$

28. $6 - 2(y + 1) \leq 6y + 1$

29. $5 - 3p + 2(p - 4) \leq 4p$

30. $-3 + 2(p - 1) + p \geq 4 - p$

31. $2(k - 5) + 3 < -(k + 1)$

32. $-x - (2x + 3) > 3x - 1$

Solve Exercises 33–38.

33. Ms. Prullage invests $20,000 received from an insurance settlement in two ways— some at 13%, and some at 16%. Altogether, she makes $2840 per year interest. How much is invested at each rate?

34. Grey Thornton received $52,000 profit from the sale of some land. He invested part at 15% interest and the rest at 19% interest. He earned a total of $9040 interest per year. How much did he invest at each rate?

35. Matt Whitney won $100,000 in a state lottery. He paid income tax of 40% on the winnings. Of the rest, he invested some at 8 1/2% and some at 16%, making $5,550 interest per year. How much is invested at each rate?

36. Mary Collins earned $48,000 from royalties on her cookbook. She paid a 40% income tax on these royalties. Part of the balance was invested at 7 1/2% and part at 10 1/2%. The investments produce $2550 interest income per year. Find the amount invested at each rate.

37. Janet Branson bought two plots of land for a total of $120,000. On the first plot, she made a profit of 15%. On the second, she lost 10%. Her total profit was $5500. How much did she pay for each piece of land?

38. Suppose $20,000 is invested at 12%. How much additional money must be invested at 16% to produce a yield of 14.4% on the entire amount invested?

Exercises 39 and 40 depend on the octane rating of gasoline, a measure of its antiknock qualities. The octane ratings of actual gasoline blends are compared with those of standard fuels. In one way to measure octane, a standard fuel is used that is made of only two ingredients, heptane and isooctane. For this fuel, the octane rating is its percentage of isooctane. For example, a gasoline with an octane rating of 98 has the same antiknock properties as a standard fuel that is 98% isooctane.

39. How many liters of 94 octane gasoline should be mixed with 200 liters of 99 octane gasoline to get a mixture that is 97 octane?

40. A service station has 92 octane and 98 octane gasoline. How many liters of each should be mixed to provide 12 liters of 96 octane gasoline for a chemistry experiment?

41. A business college charges a tuition of $6440 annually. Tom makes no more than $1610 per year in his summer job. What is the least number of summers that he must work in order to make enough for one year's tuition?

42. A nurse must make sure that Ms. Carlson receives at least 30 units of a certain drug each day. This drug comes from red pills or green pills, each of which provides three units of the drug. The patient must have twice as many red pills as green pills. Find the smallest number of green pills that will satisfy the requirement.

43. Bill and Cheryl Bradkin went to Portland, Maine, for a week. They needed to rent a car, so they checked out two rental firms. Firm A wanted $28 per day, with no mileage fee. Firm B wanted $108 per week and 14¢ per mile. Let x represent the number of miles that the Bradkins would drive in one week.

(a) Write an expression for the cost to rent for one week from Firm A.

(b) Write an expression for the cost to rent for one week from Firm B.

(c) Write an inequality in which the cost to rent from Firm A is less than the cost to rent from Firm B and solve the inequality to decide how many miles the Bradkins would have to drive before the Firm A car was the better deal.

44. A company that produces video cassettes has found that revenue from the sales of the cassettes is $5 per cassette less sales costs of $100. Production costs are $125 plus $4 per cassette. Let x represent the number of cassettes produced and sold.

(a) Write an expression for the revenue from the sale of x cassettes.

(b) Write an expression for the cost to produce x cassettes.

(c) Write an inequality in which the revenue expression is greater than the cost expression and solve it to find the minimum production level at which the company can make a profit.

Solve the following equations for x.

45. $2(x - a) + b = 3x + a$ **46.** $5x - (2a + c) = a(x + 1)$ **47.** $ax + b = 3(x - a)$

48. $4a - ax = 3b + bx$ **49.** $x = a^2x - ax + 3a - 3$ **50.** $2a = ax - a - 6x + 6$

51. $a^2x + 3x = 2a^2$ **52.** $ax + b^2 = bx - a^2$

1.2 Functions

A common problem in real-life situations is to describe relationships between quantities. For example, assuming that the number of hours a student studies each day is related to the grade received in a course, how can the relationship be expressed? One way is to set up a table showing the hours of study and the corresponding grade that resulted. Such a table might appear as follows.

Hours of Study	Grade
3	A
2 1/2	B
2	C
1	D
0	F

In other relationships, a formula of some sort is used to describe how the value of one quantity depends on the value of another. For example, if a certain bank account pays 12% interest per year, then the interest, I, that a deposit of P dollars would earn in one year is given as

$$I = .12 \times P, \quad \text{or} \quad I = .12P.$$

The formula, $I = .12P$, describes the relationship between interest and the amount of money deposited.

In this example, P, which represents the amount of money deposited, is called the **independent variable,** while I is the **dependent variable.** (The amount of interest earned *depends* on the amount of money deposited.) When a specific number, say 2000, is substituted for P, then I takes on *one* specific value—in this case, $.12 \times 2000 = 240$. The variable I is said to be a function of P. By definition,

Function

A **function** is a rule which assigns to each element from one set exactly one element from another set.

In almost every use of functions in this book, the "rule" mentioned in the box will be given by an equation, such as the equation $I = .12P$ above.

Domain and Range

The set of all possible values for the independent variable in a function is called the **domain** of the function: the set of all possible values for the dependent variable is the **range.**

The domain and range may or may not be the same set.

EXAMPLE 1

Do the following represent functions? (Assume x represents the independent variable, an assumption we shall make throughout this book.) Give the domain and range of any functions.

(a) $y = -4x + 11$

For a given value of x, calculating $-4x + 11$ produces exactly one value of y. (For example, if $x = -7$, then $y = -4(-7) + 11 = 39$.) Since one value of the independent variable leads to exactly one value of the dependent variable, $y = -4x + 11$ is a function. Both x and y may take on any real number values at all, so the domain and range here are both the set of all real numbers.

(b) $y^2 = x$

Suppose $x = 36$. Then $y^2 = x$ becomes $y^2 = 36$, from which $y = 6$ or $y = -6$. Since one value of the independent variable can lead to two values of the dependent variable, $y^2 = x$ does not represent a function.

(c) $y = 2x + 7$, $x = 1, 2, 3$, or 4

A given value of x produces exactly one value of y, making $y = 2x + 7$ a function. The independent variable x is restricted to the values 1, 2, 3, or 4, so the domain is the set $\{1, 2, 3, 4\}$. If $x = 1$, then $y = 2x + 7$ becomes $y = 2 \cdot 1 + 7 = 9$, while if $x = 2$, then $y = 2 \cdot 2 + 7 = 11$. If $x = 3$, then $y = 13$, while $x = 4$ produces $y = 15$. The range is the set of all possible values of y, or $\{9, 11, 13, 15\}$. ▪

f(x) Notation   Letters such as f, g, or h are often used to name functions. For example, we might use f to name the function

$$y = 5 - 3x.$$

To show that this function is named f, and to also show that x is the independent variable, it is common to replace y with $f(x)$ (read "f of x") to get

$$f(x) = 5 - 3x.$$

By choosing 2 as a value of x, $f(x)$ becomes $5 - 3 \cdot 2 = 5 - 6 = -1$, written

$$f(2) = -1.$$

In a similar manner,

$$f(-4) = 5 - 3(-4) = 17, \qquad f(0) = 5, \qquad f(-6) = 23,$$

and so on.

EXAMPLE 2

Let $g(x) = x^2 - 4x + 5$. Find $g(3)$, $g(0)$, and $g(a)$.

To find $g(3)$, substitute 3 for x.

$$g(3) = 3^2 - 4(3) + 5 = 9 - 12 + 5 = 2$$

Find $g(0)$ and $g(a)$ in the same way.

$$g(0) = 0^2 - 4(0) + 5 = 5$$
$$g(a) = a^2 - 4a + 5 \quad ▪$$

EXAMPLE 3

Suppose the sales of a small company have been estimated to be

$$S(x) = 125 + 80x,$$

where $S(x)$ represents the total sales in thousands of dollars in year x, with $x = 0$ representing 1984. Estimate the sales in each of the following years.

(a)   1984

Since $x = 0$ corresponds to 1984, the sales for 1984 can be found from $S(0)$; that is, by substituting 0 for x.

$$S(0) = 125 + 80(0) \qquad \text{Let } x = 0$$
$$= 125$$

Since $S(x)$ represents sales in thousands of dollars, sales would be estimated as 125×1000, or \$125,000 in 1984.

(b)   1988

To estimate sales in 1988, let $x = 4$.

$$S(4) = 125 + 80(4) = 125 + 320 = 445,$$

so that sales should be about \$445,000 in 1988.   ■

Graphs   Given a function $y = f(x)$, a given value in the domain of f produces a value for y. This pair of numbers, one for x and one for y, can be written as an **ordered pair,** (x, y).

For example, let $y = f(x) = 8 + x^2$. If $x = 1$, then $f(1) = 8 + 1^2 = 9$, producing the ordered pair (1, 9). (Always write the value of the independent variable first.) If $x = -3$, then $f(-3) = 8 + (-3)^2 = 17$, giving $(-3, 17)$. Other ordered pairs for this function include (0, 8), $(-1, 9)$, (2, 12), and so on.

A graph of these ordered pairs is drawn with the perpendicular number lines of a **Cartesian coordinate system,** shown in Figure 1. The horizontal number line, or **x-axis,** represents the first component of the ordered pairs, while the vertical or **y-axis** represents the second component. The point where the number lines cross is the zero point on both lines; this point is called the **origin.**

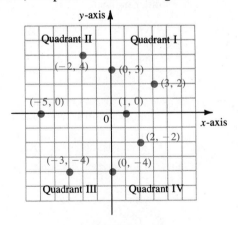

FIGURE 1

Locate the point $(-2, 4)$ on the graph by starting at the origin and counting 2 units to the left on the horizontal axis, and 4 units upward parallel to the vertical axis. This point is shown in Figure 1, along with several other sample points. The number -2 is the **x-coordinate** and 4 is the **y-coordinate** of the point $(-2, 4)$.

The x-axis and y-axis divide the graph into four parts or **quadrants.** For example, Quadrant I includes all those points whose x- and y-coordinates are both positive. The quadrants are numbered as shown in Figure 1. The points of the axes themselves belong to no quadrant. The set of points corresponding to the ordered pairs of a function is the **graph** of the function.

EXAMPLE 4

Let $f(x) = 7 - 3x$, with domain $\{-2, -1, 0, 1, 2, 3, 4\}$. Graph the ordered pairs produced by this function.

If $x = -2$, then $f(-2) = 7 - 3(-2) = 13$, giving the ordered pair $(-2, 13)$. In a similar way, other ordered pairs can be found to complete the following table.

x	-2	-1	0	1	2	3	4
y	13	10	7	4	1	-2	-5
Ordered pair	$(-2, 13)$	$(-1, 10)$	$(0, 7)$	$(1, 4)$	$(2, 1)$	$(3, -2)$	$(4, -5)$

These ordered pairs are graphed in Figure 2. ▪

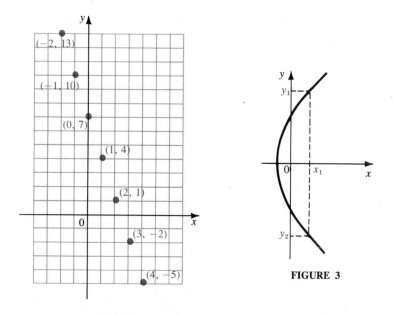

FIGURE 2

FIGURE 3

For a graph to be the graph of a function, each value of x in the domain of the function should lead to exactly one value of y. Figure 3 shows a graph. For the value $x = x_1$, the graph gives the two values of y, y_1 and y_2. Since the given value of x corresponds to two different values of y, this graph is not the graph of a function. The **vertical line test** for a function is based on this idea.

Vertical Line Test

If a vertical line cuts a graph in more than one point, then the graph is not the graph of a function.

1.2 EXERCISES

List the ordered pairs obtained in Exercises 1–22 if the domain of x for each exercise is $\{-2, -1, 0, 1, 2, 3\}$. Graph each set of ordered pairs. Give the range.

1. $y = x - 1$ **2.** $y = 2x + 3$ **3.** $y = -4x + 9$

4. $y = -6x + 12$ **5.** $y = -x - 5$ **6.** $y = -2x - 3$

7. $2x + y = 9$ **8.** $3x + y = 16$ **9.** $2y - x = 5$

10. $6x - y = -3$ **11.** $y = x(x + 1)$ **12.** $y = (x - 2)(x - 3)$

13. $y = x^2$ **14.** $y = -2x^2$ **15.** $y = 3 - 4x^2$

16. $y = 5 - x^2$ **17.** $y = \dfrac{1}{x + 3}$ **18.** $y = \dfrac{-2}{x + 4}$

19. $y = \dfrac{3x - 3}{x + 5}$ **20.** $y = \dfrac{2x + 1}{x + 3}$ **21.** $y = 4$

22. $y = -2$

Identify any of the following that represent functions.

23.
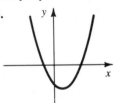

24.
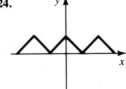

25.
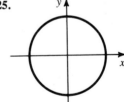

26.
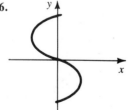

27.
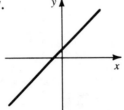

28.
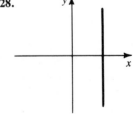

For each of the functions in Exercises 29–40, find **(a)** $f(4)$; **(b)** $f(-3)$; **(c)** $f(0)$; **(d)** $f(a)$.

29. $f(x) = 3x + 2$ **30.** $f(x) = 5x - 6$

31. $f(x) = -2x - 4$ **32.** $f(x) = -3x + 7$

33. $f(x) = 6$ **34.** $f(x) = 0$

35. $f(x) = 2x^2 + 4x$ **36.** $f(x) = x^2 - 2x$

37. $f(x) = -x^2 + 5x + 1$ **38.** $f(x) = -x^2 - x + 5$

39. $f(x) = (x + 1)(x + 2)$ **40.** $f(x) = (x + 3)(x - 4)$

41. Let $f(x) = 2x - 3$. Find each of the following.

   (a) $f(0)$ **(b)** $f(-1)$ **(c)** $f(-6)$ **(d)** $f(4)$ **(e)** $f(a)$

   (f) $f(-r)$ **(g)** $f(m + 3)$ **(h)** $f(p - 2)$ **(i)** $f[f(2)]$ **(j)** $f[f(-3)]$

42. Suppose the sales of a small company that sells by mail are approximated by

$$S(t) = 1000 + 50(t + 1),$$

where $S(t)$ represents sales in thousands of dollars. Here t is time in years, with $t = 0$ representing the year 1985. Find the estimated sales in each of the following years.

   (a) 1985   **(b)** 1986   **(c)** 1988   **(d)** 1990

43. A chain-saw rental firm charges $7 per day or fraction of a day to rent a saw, plus a fixed fee of $4 for resharpening the blade. Let $S(x)$ represent the cost of renting a saw for x days. Find each of the following.

   (a) $S\left(\dfrac{1}{2}\right)$ **(b)** $S(1)$ **(c)** $S\left(1\dfrac{1}{4}\right)$ **(d)** $S\left(3\dfrac{1}{2}\right)$

   (e) $S(4)$ **(f)** $S\left(4\dfrac{1}{10}\right)$ **(g)** $S\left(4\dfrac{9}{10}\right)$

   (h) A portion of the graph of $y = S(x)$ is shown here. Explain how the graph could be continued.

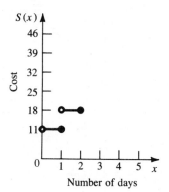

Cost

Number of days

44. To rent a midsized car costs $40 per day or fraction of a day. If you pick up the car in Boston and drop it off in Utica, there is a fixed $40 charge. Let $C(x)$ represent the cost of renting the car for x days, taking it from Boston to Utica. Find each of the following.

   (a) $C\left(\dfrac{3}{4}\right)$ **(b)** $C\left(\dfrac{9}{10}\right)$ **(c)** $C(1)$ **(d)** $C\left(1\dfrac{5}{8}\right)$

   (e) $C\left(2\dfrac{1}{9}\right)$ **(f)** Graph the function $y = C(x)$.

1.3   Linear Functions

In this section we begin a study of **linear functions,** which are very important in applications.

Linear Function

A function of the form

$$f(x) = ax + b,$$

for real numbers a and b, is a linear function.

Examples of linear functions include $y = 2x + 3$, $y = -5$, and $2x - 3y = 7$, which can be written as $y = (2/3)x - (7/3)$.

We can graph a linear function, such as $y = x + 1$, by finding several ordered pairs. For example, if $x = 2$, then $y = 2 + 1 = 3$, giving the ordered pair $(2, 3)$. Also, $(0, 1)$, $(4, 5)$, $(-2, -1)$, $(-5, -4)$, $(-3, -2)$, among many others, are ordered pairs which satisfy the equation.

To graph $y = x + 1$, begin by locating the ordered pairs obtained above. This graph is shown in Figure 4(a). All the points of this graph appear to be on one straight line, which can be drawn through the plotted points, as in Figure 4(b). This straight line is the graph of $y = x + 1$. Since any vertical line will cut the graph of Figure 4(b) in only one point, the vertical line test verifies that $y = x + 1$ is a function.

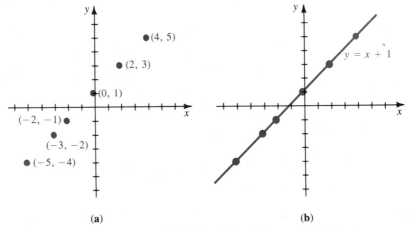

(a)   (b)

FIGURE 4

EXAMPLE 1

Use the equation $x + 2y = 6$ to complete the ordered pairs $(-6, \ )$, $(-4, \ )$, $(-2, \ )$, $(0, \ )$, $(2, \ )$, $(4, \ )$. Graph these points and then draw a straight line through them.

To complete the ordered pair $(-6, \ )$, let $x = -6$ in the equation $x + 2y = 6$.

$$x + 2y = 6$$
$$-6 + 2y = 6 \qquad \text{Let } x = -6$$
$$2y = 12 \qquad \text{Add 6 to both sides}$$
$$y = 6$$

Ordered pair: $(-6, 6)$.

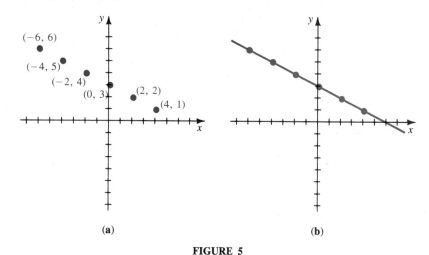

(a)   (b)

FIGURE 5

In the same way, if $x = -4$, then $y = 5$, giving $(-4, 5)$. Check that the remaining ordered pairs are as graphed in Figure 5(a). A line is drawn through the points in Figure 5(b). ▓

Intercepts   It can be shown that the graph of any linear function is a straight line. Since a straight line is completely determined by any two distinct points that it passes through, only two distinct points are needed for the graph. Two points that are often useful for this purpose are the x-intercept and the y-intercept. The **x-intercept** is the x-value (if one exists) where the graph of the equation crosses the x-axis. The **y-intercept** is the y-value (if one exists) at which the graph crosses the y-axis. At a point where the graph crosses the y-axis, $x = 0$. Also, $y = 0$ at an x-intercept. (See Figure 6.)

EXAMPLE 2

Use the intercepts to draw the graph of $y = -2x + 5$.

To find the y-intercept, the point where the line crosses the y-axis, let $x = 0$.

$$y = -2x + 5$$
$$y = -2(0) + 5 \qquad \text{Let } x = 0$$
$$y = 5$$

The y-intercept is 5, leading to the ordered pair $(0, 5)$. In the same way, the x-intercept may be found by letting $y = 0$.

$$0 = -2x + 5 \qquad \text{Let } y = 0$$
$$-5 = -2x$$
$$\frac{5}{2} = x$$

The x-intercept is 5/2, or 2 1/2, with the graph going through $(2\ 1/2, 0)$.

The two intercepts led to the graph of Figure 6. To check the work, a third point can be found by choosing another value of x (or y) and finding the corresponding value of the other variable. Check that $(1, 3)$, $(2, 1)$, $(3, -1)$, and $(4, -3)$, among many other points, satisfy the equation $y = -2x + 5$ and lie on the line of Figure 6. ▤

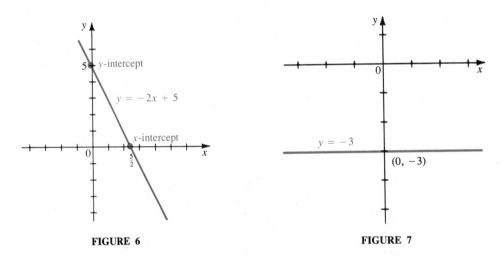

FIGURE 6   **FIGURE 7**

In the discussion of intercepts given above, we added the phrase "if one exists" when talking about the place where a graph crosses an axis. The next example shows a graph that does not cross the x-axis, and thus has no x-intercept.

EXAMPLE 3

Graph $y = -3$.

The equation $y = -3$, or equivalently, $y = 0x - 3$, always gives the same y value, -3, for any value of x. Therefore, no value of x will make $y = 0$, so the graph has no x-intercept. Since $y = -3$ is a linear function with a straight-line graph, and since the graph cannot cross the x-axis, the line must be parallel to the x-axis. For any value of x, the value of y is -3, making the graph the horizontal line parallel to the x-axis and with y-intercept -3, as shown in Figure 7. As the vertical line test shows, the graph is the graph of a function. In general, the graph of $y = k$, where k is a real number, is the horizontal line having y-intercept k. ▤

EXAMPLE 4

Graph $x = -1$.

   To obtain the graph of $x = -1$, complete some ordered pairs using the equivalent form, $x = 0y - 1$. For example, $(-1, 0), (-1, 1), (-1, 2)$, and $(-1, 4)$ are some ordered pairs satisfying $x = -1$. (The first coordinate of these ordered pairs is always -1, which is what $x = -1$ means.) Here, more than one second coordinate corresponds to the same first coordinate, -1. As the graph of Figure 8 shows, a vertical line can cut this graph in more than one point. (In fact, a vertical line can cut the graph in an infinite number of points.) For this reason, $x = -1$ is not a function. ▧

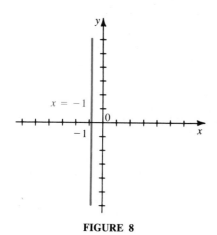

FIGURE 8

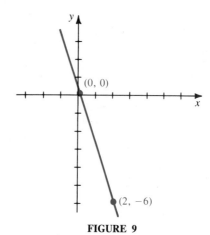

FIGURE 9

EXAMPLE 5

Graph $y = -3x$.

   Begin by looking for the x-intercept. If $y = 0$, then

$$y = -3x$$
$$0 = -3x \qquad \text{Let } y = 0$$
$$0 = x. \qquad \text{Divide both sides by } -3$$

   We have the ordered pair $(0, 0)$. Starting with $x = 0$ gives exactly the same ordered pair, $(0, 0)$. Two points are needed to determine a straight line, and the intercepts have led to only one point. To get a second point, choose some other value of x (or y). For example, if $x = 2$,

$$y = -3x = -3(2) = -6 \qquad \text{Let } x = 2$$

giving the ordered pair $(2, -6)$. These two ordered pairs, $(0, 0)$ and $(2, -6)$, were used to get the graph shown in Figure 9. ▧

Linear functions can be very useful in setting up a mathematical model for a real-life situation. In almost every case, linear (or any other reasonably simple) functions provide only approximations to real-world situations. However, these can often be remarkably useful approximations.

Supply and Demand   In particular, linear functions are often good choices for **supply and demand curves.** Typically, as the price of an item increases, the demand for the item decreases, while the supply increases. The following example shows this.

EXAMPLE 6

Suppose that Greg Odjakjian, an economist, has studied the supply and demand for aluminum siding and has come up with the conclusion that price, p, and demand, x, in appropriate units and for an appropriate domain, are related by the linear function

$$p = 60 - \frac{3}{4}x.$$

(a)   Find the demand at a price of $40.

$$p = 60 - \frac{3}{4}x$$

$$40 = 60 - \frac{3}{4}x \qquad \text{Let } p = 40$$

$$-20 = -\frac{3}{4}x$$

$$\frac{80}{3} = x$$

At a price of $40, 80/3 units will be demanded; this gives the ordered pair (80/3, 40). (It is customary to write the ordered pairs so that price comes second.)

(b)   Find the price if the demand is 32 units.

$$p = 60 - \frac{3}{4}x$$

$$p = 60 - \frac{3}{4}(32) \qquad \text{Let } x = 32$$

$$p = 60 - 24$$

$$p = 36$$

When the demand is 32 units, the price is $36. This gives the ordered pair (32, 36).

(c)   Graph $p = 60 - \frac{3}{4}x$.

Use the ordered pairs (80/3, 40) and (32, 36) to get the demand graph shown in Figure 10. Only the portion of the graph in Quadrant I is shown, since this function is only meaningful for positive values of p and x. ▧

EXAMPLE 7

Suppose that the economist of Example 6 concludes that the price and supply of siding are related by

$$p = \frac{3}{4}x,$$

where x now represents supply.

(a) Find the supply if the price is $60.

$$60 = \frac{3}{4}x \qquad \text{Let } p = 60$$

$$80 = x$$

If the price is $60, then 80 units will be supplied to the marketplace. This gives the ordered pair (80, 60).

(b) Find the price if the supply is 16 units.

$$p = \frac{3}{4}(16) = 12 \qquad \text{Let } x = 16$$

If the supply is 16 units, then the price is $12. This gives the ordered pair (16, 12).

(c) Graph $p = \frac{3}{4}x$.

Use the ordered pairs (80, 60) and (16, 12) to get the supply graph shown in Figure 10. ▨

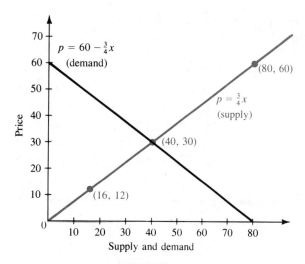

FIGURE 10

As shown in the graphs of Figure 10, both the supply and the demand graphs pass through the point (40, 30). If the price of the siding is more than $30, the supply will exceed the demand. At a price less than $30, the demand will exceed the supply. Only at a price of $30 will demand and supply be equal. For this reason, $30 is called the *equilibrium price*. When the price is $30, demand and supply both equal 40 units, the *equilibrium supply* or *equilibrium demand*. In general, the **equilibrium price** of a commodity is the price found at the point where the supply and demand graphs for that commodity cross. The **equilibrium demand** is the demand at that same point; the **equilibrium supply** is the supply at that point.

EXAMPLE 8

Use algebra to find the equilibrium supply for the aluminum siding. (See Examples 6 and 7.)

The equilibrium supply is found when the prices from both supply and demand are equal. From Example 6, $p = 60 - (3/4)x$; in Example 7, $p = (3/4)x$. Set these two expressions for p equal to each other to get the following linear equation:

$$60 - \frac{3}{4}x = \frac{3}{4}x$$

$$240 - 3x = 3x \qquad \text{Multiply both sides by 4}$$

$$240 = 6x \qquad \text{Add } 3x \text{ to both sides}$$

$$40 = x.$$

The equilibrium supply is 40 units, the same answer found above. ▪

1.3 EXERCISES

Graph each of the equations in Exercises 1–24. Identify any which are *not* linear functions.

1. $y = 2x + 1$
2. $y = 3x - 1$
3. $y = 4x$
4. $y = x + 5$

5. $3y + 4x = 12$
6. $4y + 5x = 10$
7. $y = -2$
8. $x = 4$

9. $6x + y = 12$
10. $x + 3y = 9$
11. $x - 5y = 4$
12. $2y + 5x = 20$

13. $x + 5 = 0$
14. $y - 4 = 0$
15. $5y - 3x = 12$
16. $2x + 7y = 14$

17. $8x + 3y = 10$
18. $9y - 4x = 12$
19. $y = 2x$
20. $y = -5x$

21. $y = -4x$
22. $y = x$
23. $x + 4y = 0$
24. $x - 3y = 0$

25. Suppose that the demand and price for a certain model of electric can opener are related by

$$p = 16 - \frac{5}{4}x,$$

where p is price and x is demand, in appropriate units. Find the price for a demand of

(a) 0 units;   (b) 4 units;   (c) 8 units.

Find the demand for the electric can opener at a price of

(d) $6;   (e) $11;   (f) $16.

(g) Graph $p = 16 - \dfrac{5}{4}x$.

Suppose the price and supply of the item above are related by

$$p = \frac{3}{4}x,$$

where x represents the supply, and p the price. Find the supply when the price is

(h) \$0; (i) \$10; (j) \$20.

(k) Graph $p = \dfrac{3}{4}x$ on the same axes used for 25 (g).

(l) Find the equilibrium supply.

(m) Find the equilibrium price.

26. Let the supply and demand functions for strawberry-flavored licorice be

$$\text{supply: } p = \frac{3}{2}x \qquad \text{and} \qquad \text{demand: } p = 81 - \frac{3}{4}x.$$

(a) Graph these on the same axes.

(b) Find the equilibrium demand.

(c) Find the equilibrium price.

27. Let the supply and demand functions for butter pecan ice cream be given by

$$\text{supply: } p = \frac{2}{5}x \qquad \text{and} \qquad \text{demand: } p = 100 - \frac{2}{5}x.$$

(a) Graph these on the same axes.

(b) Find the equilibrium demand.

(c) Find the equilibrium price.

28. Let the supply and demand functions for sugar be given by

$$\text{supply: } p = 1.4x - .6 \qquad \text{and} \qquad \text{demand: } p = -2x + 3.2.$$

(a) Graph these on the same axes.

(b) Find the equilibrium demand.

(c) Find the equilibrium price.

29. In a recent issue of *Business Week*, the president of Insta-Tune, a chain of franchised automobile tune-up shops, says that people who buy a franchise and open a shop pay a weekly fee of

$$y = .07x + \$135$$

to company headquarters. Here y is the fee and x is the total amount of money taken in during the week by the tune-up center. Find the weekly fee if x is

(a) \$0; (b) \$1000; (c) \$2000; (d) \$3000.

(e) Graph the function.

30. In a recent issue of *The Wall Street Journal*, we are told that the relationship between the amount of money that an average family spends on food, x, and the amount of money it spends on eating out, y, is approximated by the model

$$y = .36x.$$

Find y if x is

(a) \$40; (b) \$80; (c) \$120.

(d) Graph the function.

1.4   Slope and the Equation of a Line

As mentioned in the previous section, the graph of a straight line is determined by two different points on the line. We can also draw the graph of a straight line knowing only *one* point on the line *if* we also know the "steepness" of the line. The number which represents the "steepness" of a line is called the *slope* of the line.

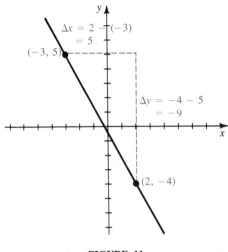

FIGURE 11

To see how slope is defined, start with Figure 11, which shows a line passing through the two different points $(x_1, y_1) = (-3, 5)$ and $(x_2, y_2) = (2, -4)$. The difference in the two x values,

$$x_2 - x_1 = 2 - (-3) = 5$$

in this example, is called the **change in x.** The symbol Δx (read "delta x") is used to represent the change in x. In the same way, Δy represents the **change in y.** In our example,

$$\Delta y = y_2 - y_1 = -4 - 5 = -9.$$

These symbols are used to define the slope of a line:

Slope of a Line

> The **slope** of a line through the two different points (x_1, y_1) and (x_2, y_2) is defined as the change in y divided by the change in x, or
>
> $$\text{slope} = \frac{\text{change in } y}{\text{change in } x} = \frac{\Delta y}{\Delta x} = \frac{y_2 - y_1}{x_2 - x_1}.$$

The slope of the line in Figure 11 is

$$\text{slope} = \frac{\Delta y}{\Delta x} = \frac{-4 - 5}{2 - (-3)} = \frac{-9}{5}.$$

Using similar triangles, it can be shown that the slope is independent of the choice of points on the line. That is, the same slope will be obtained for *any* choice of two different points on the line. (See Exercise 66 below.)

EXAMPLE 1

Find the slope of the line through the points $(-7, 6)$ and $(4, 5)$.

Let $(x_1, y_1) = (-7, 6)$. Then $(x_2, y_2) = (4, 5)$. Use the definition of slope:

$$\text{slope} = \frac{\Delta y}{\Delta x} = \frac{5 - 6}{4 - (-7)} = \frac{-1}{11}. \qquad \blacksquare$$

In finding the slope, we could have let $(x_1, y_1) = (4, 5)$ and $(x_2, y_2) = (-7, 6)$. In that case,

$$\text{slope} = \frac{6 - 5}{-7 - 4} = \frac{1}{-11} = \frac{-1}{11},$$

the same answer. The order in which coordinates are subtracted does not matter, as long as it is done consistently.

The slope of a line is a measure of the steepness of the line. Figure 12 shows examples of lines with different slopes. Lines with positive slopes go up from left to right along the x-axis, while lines with negative slopes go down from left to right.

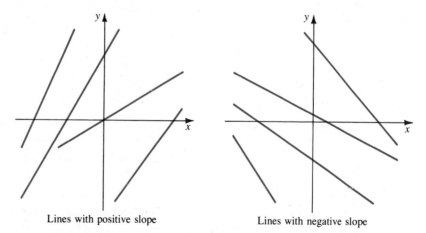

Lines with positive slope   Lines with negative slope

FIGURE 12

EXAMPLE 2

Find the slope of the line $3x - 4y = 12$.

Find the slope with two different points on the line. Find two such points here by finding the intercepts. First let $x = 0$ and then let $y = 0$.

If $x = 0$,	If $y = 0$,
$3x - 4y = 12$	$3x - 4y = 12$
$3(0) - 4y = 12$	$3x - 4(0) = 12$
$-4y = 12$	$3x = 12$
$y = -3$	$x = 4$

This gives the ordered pairs $(0, -3)$ and $(4, 0)$. Now the slope can be found from the definition.

$$\text{slope} = \frac{0 - (-3)}{4 - 0} = \frac{3}{4}$$

In the last section, we saw that the graph of a linear function is a line. The equation that describes a linear function may take many different forms. In the rest of this section we look at some of these forms for the equation of a line.

Slope-Intercept Form A generalization of the method of Example 2 can be used to find the equation of a line given its y-intercept and slope. Assume that a line has y-intercept b, so that it goes through $(0, b)$. Let the slope of the line be represented by m. If (x, y) is any point on the line *other* than $(0, b)$, then we can use the definition of slope with the points $(0, b)$ and (x, y) to get

$$m = \frac{y - b}{x - 0}$$

$$m = \frac{y - b}{x}$$

or

$$mx = y - b,$$

from which

$$y = mx + b.$$

This result, called the slope-intercept form of the equation of a line, can be summarized as follows.

If a line has slope m and y-intercept b, then the equation of the line is

$$y = mx + b,$$

the **slope-intercept form** of the equation of a line.

EXAMPLE 3

Find an equation for the line having y-intercept 7/2 and slope $-5/2$.

Use the slope-intercept form with $b = 7/2$ and $m = -5/2$.

$$y = mx + b$$

$$y = -\frac{5}{2}x + \frac{7}{2}$$

Multiply both sides by 2 to get an equation without fractions.

$$2y = -5x + 7 \quad \blacksquare$$

The slope of a line can be found from its equation by solving the equation for y. Then the coefficient of x is the slope and the constant term is the y-intercept. (See Exercises 67 and 68.) For example, we found in Example 2 above that the slope of the line $3x - 4y = 12$ is 3/4. This slope also could be found by solving for y.

$$3x - 4y = 12$$

$$-4y = -3x + 12$$

$$y = \frac{3}{4}x - 3$$

As the coefficient of x shows, the slope is 3/4.

EXAMPLE 4

Find the slope and y-intercept for each of the following lines.

(a) $5x - 3y = 1$

Solve for y: $5x - 3y = 1$

$$-3y = -5x + 1$$

$$y = \frac{5}{3}x - \frac{1}{3}.$$

The slope is 5/3 and the y-intercept is $-1/3$.

(b) $-9x + 6y = 2$

Solve for y: $-9x + 6y = 2$

$$6y = 9x + 2$$

$$y = \frac{3}{2}x + \frac{1}{3}.$$

The slope is 3/2 and the y-intercept is 1/3. $\blacksquare$

The slope and y-intercept of a line can be used to draw the graph of the line as shown in the next example.

EXAMPLE 5

Use the slope and y-intercept to graph $3x - 2y = 2$.

Solve for y:
$$3x - 2y = 2$$
$$-2y = -3x + 2$$
$$y = \frac{3}{2}x - 1$$

The slope is 3/2 and the y-intercept is -1.

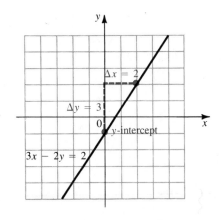

FIGURE 13

To draw the graph, first locate the y-intercept of -1, as shown in Figure 13. To find a second point on the graph, use the slope. If m represents the slope, then

$$m = \frac{\Delta y}{\Delta x} = \frac{3}{2}$$

in our example. If x changes by 2 units ($\Delta x = 2$), then y will change by 3 units ($\Delta y = 3$). To find the second point, start at the y-intercept graphed in Figure 13 and move 3 units up and 2 units to the right. Once this second point is located, the line can be drawn through it and the y-intercept.   ▨

Point-Slope Form   The slope-intercept form of the equation of a line involves the slope and the y-intercept. Sometimes, however, the slope of a line is known, together with one point (perhaps *not* the y-intercept) that the line goes through. The *point-slope form* of the equation of a line is used to find the equation in this case. Let (x_1, y_1) be any fixed point on the line and let (x, y) represent any other point on the line. If m is the slope of the line, then, by the definition of slope,

$$\frac{y - y_1}{x - x_1} = m,$$

or
$$y - y_1 = m(x - x_1).$$

Point-Slope Form

> If a line has slope m and passes through the point (x_1, y_1), then an equation of the line is given by
> $$y - y_1 = m(x - x_1),$$
> the **point-slope form** of the equation of a line.

EXAMPLE 6

Find an equation of the line going through the given point with the given slope.

(a) $(-4, 1)$, $m = -3$

Use the point-slope form, since we know a point the line goes through, together with the slope of the line. Substitute the values $x_1 = -4$, $y_1 = 1$, and $m = -3$ into the point-slope form.

$$y - y_1 = m(x - x_1)$$
$$y - 1 = -3[x - (-4)]$$
$$y - 1 = -3(x + 4)$$
$$y - 1 = -3x - 12$$
$$y = -3x - 11$$

(b) $(3, -7)$, $m = 5/4$

Use the point-slope form.

$$y - y_1 = m(x - x_1)$$
$$y - (-7) = \frac{5}{4}(x - 3) \qquad \text{Let } y_1 = -7, m = 5/4, x_1 = 3$$
$$y + 7 = \frac{5}{4}(x - 3)$$
$$4y + 28 = 5(x - 3) \qquad \text{Multiply both sides by 4}$$
$$4y + 28 = 5x - 15$$
$$4y = 5x - 43 \quad \blacksquare$$

The point-slope form also can be used to find an equation of a line given two different points that the line goes through. The procedure for doing this is shown in the next example.

EXAMPLE 7

Find an equation of the line through $(5, 4)$ and $(-10, -2)$.

Begin by using the definition of slope to find the slope of the line which passes through the two points.

$$\text{slope} = m = \frac{-2 - 4}{-10 - 5} = \frac{-6}{-15} = \frac{2}{5}$$

Use $m = 2/5$ and either of the given points in the point-slope form. If $(x_1, y_1) = (5, 4)$, we get

$$y - y_1 = m(x - x_1)$$

$$y - 4 = \frac{2}{5}(x - 5) \qquad \text{Let } y_1 = 4, \ m = \frac{2}{5}, \ x_1 = 5$$

$$5y - 20 = 2(x - 5) \qquad \text{Multiply both sides by 5}$$

$$5y - 20 = 2x - 10$$

$$5y = 2x + 10.$$

Check that we get the same result if $(x_1, y_1) = (-10, -2)$. ▣

EXAMPLE 8

Find an equation of the line through $(8, -4)$ and $(-2, -4)$.
Find the slope.

$$m = \frac{-4 - (-4)}{-2 - 8} = \frac{0}{-10} = 0$$

Choose, say, $(8, -4)$ as (x_1, y_1).

$$y - y_1 = m(x - x_1)$$

$$y - (-4) = 0(x - 8) \qquad \text{Let } y_1 = -4, \ m = 0, \ x_1 = 8$$

$$y + 4 = 0 \qquad \qquad 0(x - 8) = 0$$

$$y = -4 \quad ▣$$

As we saw in the previous section, $y = -4$ represents a horizontal line, with y-intercept -4. Generalizing from this example, every horizontal line has a slope of 0.

EXAMPLE 9

Find an equation of the line through $(4, 3)$ and $(4, -6)$.
Find the slope.

$$m = \frac{-6 - 3}{4 - 4} = \frac{-9}{0}$$

Division by 0 is impossible, so the slope is undefined. Graphing the given ordered pairs $(4, 3)$ and $(4, -6)$ and drawing a line through them gives a vertical line. In the last section, we saw that vertical lines have equations of the form $x = k$, where k can be any real number. Since the x-coordinate of the two ordered pairs given above is 4, the desired equation is

$$x = 4. \quad ▣$$

A vertical line has undefined slope.

A summary of the types of equations of lines discussed in this section follows.

Equations of Lines

Equation	Description
$ax + by = c$	if $a \neq 0$ and $b \neq 0$, line has x-intercept c/a and y-intercept c/b
$x = k$	**vertical line,** x-intercept k, no y-intercept, undefined slope
$y = k$	**horizontal line,** y-intercept k, no x-intercept, slope 0
$y = mx + b$	**slope-intercept form,** slope m, y-intercept b
$y - y_1 = m(x - x_1)$	**point-slope form,** slope m, line passes through (x_1, y_1)

1.4 EXERCISES

In Exercises 1–10, find the slope, if it exists, of the line going through the given pair of points.

1. $(-8, 6), (2, 4)$

2. $(-3, 2), (5, 9)$

3. $(-1, 4), (2, 6)$

4. $(3, -8), (4, 1)$

5. The origin and $(-4, 6)$

6. The origin and $(8, -2)$

7. $(-2, 9), (-2, 11)$

8. $(7, 4), (7, 12)$

9. $(3, -6), (-5, -6)$

10. $(5, -11), (-9, -11)$

Find the slope and y-intercept of each of the lines in Exercises 11–26.

11. $y = 3x + 4$

12. $y = -3x + 2$

13. $y + 4x = 8$

14. $y - x = 3$

15. $3x + 4y = 5$

16. $2x - 5y = 8$

17. $3x + y = 0$

18. $y - 4x = 0$

19. $2x + 5y = 0$

20. $3x - 4y = 0$

21. $y = 8$

22. $y = -4$

23. $y + 2 = 0$

24. $y - 3 = 0$

25. $x = -8$

26. $x = 3$

Graph the line going through the given point and having the given slope in Exercises 27–38.

27. $(-4, 2), m = 2/3$

28. $(3, -2), m = 3/4$

29. $(-5, -3), m = -2$

30. $(-1, 4), m = 2$

31. $(8, 2), m = 0$

32. $(2, -4), m = 0$

33. $(6, -5)$, no slope

34. $(-8, 9)$, no slope

35. $(0, -2), m = 3/4$

36. $(0, -3), m = 2/5$

37. $(5, 0), m = 1/4$

38. $(-9, 0), m = 5/2$

In Exercises 39–44, find an equation for each line having the given y-intercept and slope.

39. $4, m = -3/4$

40. $-3, m = 2/3$

41. $-2, m = -1/2$

42. $3/2, m = 1/4$

43. $5/4, m = 3/2$

44. $-3/8, m = 3/4$

Find equations for each of the lines in Exercises 45–58.

45. Through $(-4, 1)$, $m = 2$

46. Through $(5, 1)$, $m = -1$

47. Through $(0, 3)$, $m = -3$

48. Through $(-2, 3)$, $m = 3/2$

49. Through $(3, 2)$, $m = 1/4$

50. Through $(0, 1)$, $m = -2/3$

51. Through $(-1, 1)$ and $(2, 5)$

52. Through $(4, -2)$ and $(6, 8)$

53. Through $(9, -6)$ and $(12, -8)$

54. Through $(-5, 2)$ and $(7, 5)$

55. Through $(-8, 4)$ and $(-8, 6)$

56. Through $(2, -5)$ and $(4, -5)$

57. Through $(-1, 3)$ and $(0, 3)$

58. Through $(2, 9)$ and $(2, -9)$

Many real-world situations can be approximately described by a straight-line graph. One way to find the equation of such a straight line is to use two typical data points from the graph and the point-slope form of the equation of a line. In Exercises 59–63, assume that the data can be approximated fairly closely by a straight line. Use the given information to find an equation of the line. Find the slope of each of the lines.

59. A company finds that it can make a total of 20 solar heaters for $13,900, while 10 solar heaters cost $7500. Let y be the total cost to produce x solar heaters.

60. The sales of a small company were $27,000 in its second year of operation and $63,000 in its fifth year. Let y represent sales in the x-th year of operation.

61. When a certain industrial pollutant is introduced into a river, the reproduction of catfish declines. In a given period of time, three tons of the pollutant results in a fish population of 37,000. Also, 12 tons of pollutant produce a fish population of 28,000. Let y be the fish population when x tons of pollutant are introduced into the river.

62. According to research done by the political scientist James March, if the Democrats win 45% of the two-party vote for the House of Representatives, they win 42.5% of the seats. If the Democrats win 55% of the vote, they win 67.5% of the seats. Let y be the percent of seats won, and x the percent of the two-party vote.

63. If the Republicans win 45% of the two-party vote, they win 32.5% of the seats (see Exercise 62.) If they win 60% of the vote, they get 70% of the seats. Let y represent the percent of the seats, and x the percent of the vote.

64. A person's tibia bone goes from ankle to knee. A male with a tibia 40 cm in length will have a height of 177 cm, while a tibia 43 cm in length corresponds to a height of 185 cm.

   (a) Write a linear equation showing how the height of a male, h, relates to the length of his tibia, t.

   (b) Estimate the height of a male having a tibia of length 38 cm; 45 cm.

   (c) Estimate the length of the tibia for a height of 190 cm.

65. The radius bone goes from the wrist to the elbow. A female whose radius bone is 24 cm long would be 167 cm tall, while a radius of 26 cm corresponds to a height of 174 cm.

   (a) Write a linear equation showing how the height of a female, h, corresponds to the length of her radius bone, r.

   (b) Estimate the height of a female having a radius of length 23 cm; 27 cm.

   (c) Estimate the length of a radius bone for a height of 170 cm.

66. Use similar triangles from geometry to show that the slope of a line is the same, no matter which two distinct points on the line are chosen to compute it.

67. Show that b is the y-intercept in the slope-intercept form $y = mx + b$.

68. Suppose that $(0, b)$ and (x_1, y_1) are distinct points on the line $y = mx + b$. Show that $(y_1 - b)/x_1$ is the slope of the line, and that $m = (y_1 - b)/x_1$.

1.5 Linear Mathematical Models

In this section, we discuss mathematical models in more detail; then we look at some mathematical models using the equations we have discussed in the last two sections.

If we completely understand the principles causing a certain event to happen, then the mathematical model describing that event can be very accurate. As a rule, the mathematical models constructed in the physical sciences are excellent at predicting events. For example, if a body falls in a vacuum, then d, the distance in feet that the body will fall in t seconds, is given by

$$d = \frac{1}{2}gt^2,$$

where g is a constant (number) representing gravity. (As an approximation, $g = 32$ feet per second per second.) Using this equation, d can be predicted exactly for a known value of t.

The situation is different in the fields of management and social science. Mathematical models in these fields tend to be less accurate approximations, and often gross approximations at that. So many variables come into play that no mathematical model can ever hope to produce results comparable to those produced in physical science.

In spite of the limitations of mathematical models, they have found a large and increasing acceptance in management and economic decision making. There is one main reason for this—mathematical models produce very useful results.

Let us look at some mathematical models of real-world situations.

EXAMPLE 1

Sales Analysis It is common to compare the change in sales of two companies by comparing the rates at which these sales change. If the sales of the two companies can be approximated by linear functions, the work of the last section can be used to find rates of change. For example, the chart below shows sales in two different years for two different companies.

Company	Sales in 1985	Sales in 1988
A	$10,000	$16,000
B	5000	14,000

The sales of Company A increased from $10,000 to $16,000 over this 3-year peri-od, for a total increase of $6000. The average rate of change of sales is

$$\frac{\$6000}{3} = \$2000.$$

(a)   If we assume that the sales of Company A have increased linearly (that is, that the sales can be closely approximated by a linear function), then we can find the equation describing the sales by finding the equation of the line through $(-3, 10,000)$ and $(0, 16,000)$, where $x = 0$ represents 1988 so that $x = -3$ represents 1985. The slope of the line is

$$\frac{16,000 - 10,000}{0 - (-3)} = 2000,$$

the same as the annual rate of change found above. Using the point-slope form of the equation of a line gives

$$y - 16,000 = 2000(x - 0)$$
$$y = 2000x + 16,000,$$

the equation describing sales.

(b)   Assume that the sales of Company B also have increased linearly. Verify that the equation giving its sales is

$$y = 3000x + 14,000,$$

and the average rate of change of sales is $3000.

As the example suggests, the average rate of change is the same as the slope of the line. This is always true for data that can be modeled with a linear function. ▪

EXAMPLE 2

Suppose that a researcher has concluded that a dosage of x grams of a certain stimu-lant causes a rat to gain

$$y = 2x + 50$$

grams of weight, for appropriate values of x. If the researcher administers 30 grams of the stimulant, how much weight will the rat gain?

Let $x = 30$. The rat will gain

$$y = 2(30) + 50 = 110$$

grams of weight.

The average rate of change of weight with respect to the amount of stimulant is given by the slope of the line. The slope of $y = 2x + 50$ is 2, so that the differ-ence in weight when the dose is varied by 1 gram is 2 grams. ▪

Cost Analysis   In manufacturing, it is common for the cost of manufacturing an item to be made up of two parts: one part is a **fixed cost** for designing the product, establishing a factory, training workers, and so on. Within broad limits, the fixed cost is constant for a particular product and does not change as more items are made. The second part of the cost is a **variable cost** per item for labor, materials, packing, shipping, and so on. The variable cost may well be the same per item, with total variable cost increasing as the number of items increases.

EXAMPLE 3

Suppose that the cost of producing clock-radios can be approximated by the linear model

$$C(x) = 12x + 100,$$

where $C(x)$ is the cost in dollars to produce x radios. The cost to produce 0 radios is

$$C(0) = 12(0) + 100 = 100,$$

or $100. This amount, $100, is the fixed cost.

Once the company has invested the fixed cost into the clock-radio project, what then will be the additional cost per radio? To find out, let's first find the cost of a total of 5 radios:

$$C(5) = 12(5) + 100 = 160,$$

or $160. The cost of 6 radios is

$$C(6) = 12(6) + 100 = 172,$$

or $172.

The sixth radio itself thus costs $172 − $160 = $12 to produce. In the same way, the 81st radio costs $C(81) − C(80) = \$1072 − \$1060 = \$12$ to produce. In fact, the $(n + 1)$st radio costs

$$C(n + 1) - C(n) = [12(n + 1) + 100] - [12n + 100] = 12$$

dollars to produce. Since each additional radio costs $12 to produce, $12 is the variable cost per radio. The value 12 is also the slope of the cost function, $C(x) = 12x + 100$. ■

In economics, the cost of producing an additional item is called the **marginal cost** of that item. In the clock-radio example, the marginal cost of each radio is $12.

Cost

> If a cost function is given by a linear function of the form $C(x) = mx + b$, then m represents the **variable cost** per item and b the **fixed cost.** Conversely, if the fixed cost of producing an item is b and the variable cost is m, then the **cost function,** $C(x)$, for producing x items, is given by $C(x) = mx + b$.

EXAMPLE 4

In one city, a taxi company charges riders $1.80 per mile plus a fixed fee of $1.50. Write a cost function, $C(x)$, which is a mathematical model for a ride of x miles.

Here the fixed cost is $b = 1.50$ dollars, with a variable cost of $m = 1.80$ dollars. The cost function, $C(x)$, is

$$C(x) = 1.80x + 1.50.$$

For example, a taxi ride of 4 miles will cost $C(4) = 1.80(4) + 1.50 = 8.70$, or $8.70. For each additional mile, the cost increases by $1.80. ■

EXAMPLE 5

The variable cost for raising a certain type of frog for laboratory study is $12 per unit of frogs, while the cost to produce 100 units is $1500. Find the cost function, $C(x)$, given that it is linear.

Since the cost function is linear, it can be expressed in the form $C(x) = mx + b$. The variable cost of $12 per unit gives the value for m in the model. The model can be written $C(x) = 12x + b$. To find b, use the fact that the cost of producing 100 units of frogs is $1500, or $C(100) = 1500$. Substituting $x = 100$ and $C(x) = 1500$ into $C(x) = 12x + b$,

$$C(x) = 12x + b$$
$$1500 = 12 \cdot 100 + b$$
$$1500 = 1200 + b$$
$$300 = b.$$

The desired model is given by $C(x) = 12x + 300$. The fixed cost is $300. ▪

Depreciation Because machines and equipment wear out or become obsolete over a period of time, business firms must take into account the amount of value that the equipment has lost during each year of its useful life. This lost value, called **depreciation,** may be calculated in several ways. The simplest way is to use **straight-line,** or **linear,** depreciation, in which an item having a useful life of n years is assumed to lose a constant $1/n$ of its value each year. For example, a typewriter with a ten-year life would be assumed to lose 1/10 of its value each year, and 4/10 of its value in 4 years.

A machine may have some **scrap value** at the end of its useful life. For this reason, depreciation is calculated on **net cost**—the difference between purchase price and scrap value. To find the annual straight-line depreciation on an item having a net cost of x dollars and a useful life of n years, multiply the net cost by the fraction of the value lost each year, $1/n$. The annual straight-line depreciation, $D(x)$, is then

$$D(x) = \frac{1}{n}x.$$

EXAMPLE 6

An asset has a purchase price of $100,000 and a scrap value of $40,000. The useful life of the asset is 10 years. Find each of the following for this asset.

(a)   net cost

Since the net cost is the difference between purchase price and scrap value,

$$x = \text{net cost} = \$100,000 - \$40,000 = \$60,000.$$

(b)   annual depreciation

The useful life of the asset is 10 years. Therefore, 1/10 of the net cost is depreciated each year. The annual depreciation by the straight-line method is

$$D(x) = \frac{1}{10}x = \frac{1}{10}(60,000) = 6000,$$

or $6000.

(c)   undepreciated balance after 4 years

The total amount that will be depreciated over the life of the asset is $60,000. In four years, the depreciation will be

$$4(\$6000) = \$24,000,$$

and the undepreciated balance will be

$$\$60,000 - \$24,000 = \$36,000. \quad \blacksquare$$

Straight-line depreciation is the easiest method of depreciation to use, but it often does not accurately reflect the rate at which assets actually lose value. Some assets, such as new cars, lose more value annually at the beginning of their useful life than at the end. For this reason, two other methods of depreciation, the *sum-of-the-years'-digits* method, discussed in Exercises 33 and 34 below, and *double declining balance,* discussed in Section 1.6, often are used.

Break-Even Analysis   A company can make a profit only if the revenue it receives from its customers exceeds the cost of producing its goods and services. The point at which revenue just equals cost is called the **break-even point.**

EXAMPLE 7

A firm producing chicken feed finds that the total cost, $C(x)$, of producing x units is given by

$$C(x) = 20x + 100.$$

The feed sells for $24 per unit, so that the revenue, $R(x)$, from selling x units is given by the product of the price per unit and the number of units sold, or

$$R(x) = 24x.$$

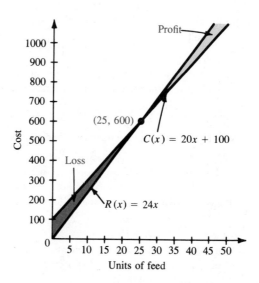

FIGURE 14

The firm will just break even (no profit and no loss), as long as revenue just equals cost, or $R(x) = C(x)$. This is true whenever

$$R(x) = C(x)$$
$$24x = 20x + 100 \qquad \text{Substitute for } R(x) \text{ and } C(x)$$
$$4x = 100$$
$$x = 25.$$

The break-even point is at $x = 25$.

The graphs of $C(x) = 20x + 100$ and $R(x) = 24x$ are shown in Figure 14. The break-even point is shown on the graph. If the company produces more than 25 units (if $x > 25$), it makes a profit; if $x < 25$ it loses money.   ▨

1.5 EXERCISES

1. Suppose the sales of a particular brand of electric guitar satisfy the relationship
$$S(x) = 300x + 2000,$$
where $S(x)$ represents the number of guitars sold in year x, with $x = 0$ corresponding to 1984. Find the sales in each of the following years.

   (a) 1986   (b) 1987   (c) 1988   (d) 1984

   (e) Find the annual rate of change of the sales.

2. If the population of ants in an anthill satisfies the relationship
$$A(x) = 1000x + 6000,$$
where $A(x)$ represents the number of ants present at the end of month x, find the number of ants present at the end of each of the following months. Let $x = 0$ represent June.

   (a) June   (b) July   (c) August   (d) December

   (e) What is the monthly rate of change of the number of ants?

3. Let $N(x) = -5x + 100$ represent the number of bacteria (in thousands) present in a certain tissue culture at time x, measured in hours, after an antibacterial spray is introduced into the environment. Find the number of bacteria present at each of the following times.

   (a) $x = 0$ (b) $x = 6$ (c) $x = 20$

   (d) What is the hourly rate of change in the number of bacteria? Interpret the negative sign in the answer.

4. Let $R(x) = -8x + 240$ represent the number of students present in a large business mathematics class, where x represents the number of hours of study required weekly. Find the number of students present at each of the following levels of required study.

   (a) $x = 0$ (b) $x = 5$ (c) $x = 10$

   (d) What is the rate of change of the number of students in the class with respect to the number of hours of study? Interpret the negative sign in the answer.

(e) The professor in charge of the class likes to have exactly 16 students. How many hours of study must he require in order to have exactly 16 students?

5. Assume that the sales of a certain appliance dealer are approximated by a linear function. Suppose that sales were $850,000 in 1980 and $1,262,500 in 1985. Let $x = 0$ represent 1980.

(a) Find the equation giving the dealer's yearly sales.

(b) What were the dealer's sales in 1983?

(c) Estimate sales in 1988.

6. Assume that the sales of a certain automobile parts company are approximated by a linear function. Suppose that sales were $200,000 in 1978, and $1,000,000 in 1985. Let $x = 0$ represent 1978 and $x = 7$ represent 1985.

(a) Find the equation giving the company's yearly sales.

(b) Find the sales in 1980.

(c) Estimate the sales in 1987.

7. Suppose the number of bottles of a vitamin, $V(x)$, on hand at the beginning of the day in a health food store is given by

$$V(x) = 600 - 20x,$$

where $x = 1$ corresponds to June 1, and x is measured in days. If the store is open every day of the month, find the number of bottles on hand at the beginning of each of the following days.

(a) June 6   (b) June 12   (c) June 24

(d) When will the last bottle from this stock be sold?

(e) What is the daily rate of change of this stock?

8. In psychology, the just-noticeable-difference (JND) for some stimulus is defined as the amount by which the stimulus must be increased so that a person will perceive it as having just barely been increased. For example, suppose a research study indicates that a line 40 centimeters in length must be increased to 42 cm before a subject thinks that it is longer. In this case, the JND would be $42 - 40 = 2$ cm. In a particular experiment, the JND is given by

$$y = 0.03x,$$

where x represents the original length of the line and y the JND. Find the JND for lines having the following lengths.

(a) 10 cm   (b) 20 cm

(c) 50 cm   (d) 100 cm

(e) Find the rate of change in the JND with respect to the original length of the line.

Write a cost function for each of the models in Exercises 9–12. Identify all variables used.

9. A chain saw rental firm charges $12 plus $1 per hour.

10. A trailer-hauling service charges $45 plus $2 per mile.

11. A parking garage charges 50¢ plus 35¢ per half-hour.

12. For a one-day rental, a car rental firm charges $44 plus 28¢ per mile.

Assume that Exercises 13–20 can be expressed as a linear cost function. Find the appropriate cost function in each case.

13. Fixed cost, $100; 50 items cost $1600 to produce.

14. Fixed cost, $400; 10 items cost $650 to produce.

15. Fixed cost, $1000; 40 items cost $2000 to produce.

16. Fixed cost, $8500; 75 items cost $11,875 to produce.

17. Variable cost, $50; 80 items cost $4500 to produce.

18. Variable cost, $120; 100 items cost $15,800 to produce.

19. Variable cost, $90; 150 items cost $16,000 to produce.

20. Variable cost, $120; 700 items cost $96,500 to produce.

21. The manager of a local restaurant told us that his cost function for producing coffee is $C(x) = .097x$, where $C(x)$ is the total cost in dollars of producing x cups. (He is ignoring the cost of the coffee pot and the cost of labor.) Find the total cost of producing the following numbers of cups.

  (a) 1000 cups   **(b)** 1001 cups

  (c) Find the marginal cost of the 1001st cup.

  (d) What is the marginal cost for *any* cup?

22. In deciding whether or not to set up a new manufacturing plant, company analysts have decided that a reasonable function for the total cost to produce x items is

$$C(x) = 500{,}000 + 4.75x.$$

  (a) Find the total cost to produce 100,000 items.

  (b) Find the marginal cost of the items to be produced in this plant.

Let $C(x)$ be the total cost to manufacture x items. Then the quotient $(C(x))/x$ is the average cost per item. Use this definition in Exercises 23 and 24.

23. $C(x) = 800 + 20x$; find the average cost per item if x is

  (a) 10;   **(b)** 50;   **(c)** 200.

24. $C(x) = 500{,}000 + 4.75x$; find the average cost per item if x is

  (a) 1000;   **(b)** 5000;   **(c)** 10,000.

For each of the assets in Exercises 25–30 find the straight-line depreciation in year 4, and the amount undepreciated after 4 years.

25. Cost: $50,000; scrap value: $10,000; life: 20 years

26. Cost: $120,000; scrap value: $0; life: 10 years

27. Cost: $80,000; scrap value: $20,000; life: 30 years

28. Cost: $720,000; scrap value: $240,000; life: 12 years

29. Cost: $1,400,000; scrap value: $200,000; life: 8 years

30. Cost: $2,200,000; scrap value: $400,000; life: 12 years

31. Suppose an asset has a net cost of $80,000 and a four-year life.

  (a) Find the straight-line depreciation in each of years 1, 2, 3, and 4 of the item's life.

  (b) Find the sum of all depreciation for the four-year life.

32. A forklift truck has a net cost of $12,000, with a useful life of 5 years.

 (a) Find the straight-line depreciation in each of years 1, 2, 3, 4, and 5 of the forklift's life.

 (b) Find the sum of all depreciation for the five-year life.

Some assets, such as new cars, lose more value annually at the beginning of their useful life than at the end. By one method of depreciation for such assets, called the **sum-of-the-years'-digits** method, the depreciation in year j, which we call D_j, is given by

$$D_j = \frac{n - j + 1}{n(n + 1)} \cdot 2x$$

where n is the useful life of the item, $1 \le j \le n$, and x is the net cost of the item.

33. For a certain asset, $n = 4$ and $x = \$10,000$.

 (a) Use the sum-of-the-years'-digits method to find the depreciation for each of the four years covering the useful life of the asset.

 (b) What would be the annual depreciation by the straight-line method?

34. A machine tool costs $105,000 and has a scrap value of $25,000, with a useful life of 4 years.

 (a) Use the sum-of-the-years'-digits method to find the depreciation in each of the four years of the machine tool's life.

 (b) Find the total depreciation by this method.

For each of the assets in Exercises 35–38, use the sum-of-the-years'-digits method to find the depreciation in year 1 and year 4.

35. Cost: $36,500; scrap value: $8500; life: 10 years

36. Cost: $6250; scrap value: $250; life: 5 years

37. Cost: $18,500; scrap value: $3900; life: 6 years

38. Cost: $275,000; scrap value: $25,000; life: 20 years

39. The cost to produce x units of wire is $C(x) = 50x + 5000$, while the revenue is $R(x) = 60x$. Find the break-even point and the revenue at the break-even point.

40. The cost to produce x units of squash is $C(x) = 100x + 6000$, while the revenue is $R(x) = 500x$. Find the break-even point.

You are the manager of a firm. You are considering the manufacture of a new product, so you ask the accounting department to produce cost estimates and the sales department to produce sales estimates. After you receive the data, you must decide whether or not to go ahead with production of the new product. Analyze the data in Exercises 41–44 (find a break-even point) and then decide what you would do.

41. $C(x) = 85x + 900$; $R(x) = 105x$; not more than 38 units can be sold.

42. $C(x) = 105x + 6000$; $R(x) = 250x$; not more than 400 units can be sold.

43. $C(x) = 70x + 500$; $R(x) = 60x$ (Hint: what does a negative break-even point mean?)

44. $C(x) = 1000x + 5000$; $R(x) = 900x$.

45. The sales of a certain furniture company in thousands of dollars are shown in the chart below.

x Year	y Sales
0	48
1	59
2	66
3	75
4	80
5	90

(a) Graph this data, plotting years on the x-axis and sales on the y-axis. (Note that the data points can be closely approximated by a straight line.)

(b) Draw a line through the points (2, 66) and (5, 90). The other four points should be close to this line. (These two points were selected as ''best'' representing the line that could be drawn through the data points.)

(c) Use the two points of 45(b) to find an equation for the line that approximates the data.

(d) Complete the following chart.

Year	Sales (actual)	Sales (predicted from equation of 45(c))	Difference, Actual Minus Predicted
0			
1			
2			
3			
4			
5			

(We will obtain a formula for the ''best'' line through the points in Section 1.6.)

(e) Use the result of (c) to predict sales in year 7.

(f) Do the same for year 9.

46. Most people are not very good at estimating the passage of time. Some people's estimations are too fast, and others, too slow. One psychologist has constructed a mathematical model for actual time as a function of estimated time: if y represents actual time and x estimated time, then

$$y = mx + b,$$

where m and b are constants that must be determined experimentally for each person. Suppose that for a particular person, $m = 1.25$ and $b = -5$. Find y if x is

(a) 30 minutes;   (b) 60 minutes;   (c) 120 minutes;   (d) 180 minutes.

Suppose that for another person, $m = .85$ and $b = 1.2$. Find y if x is

(e) 15 minutes;   (f) 30 minutes;   (g) 60 minutes;   (h) 120 minutes.

For this same person, find x if y is

(i) 60 minutes;   (j) 90 minutes.

47. Find the depreciation by the straight-line and sum-of-the-years'-digits methods for items with the following characteristics:

(a) Cost $12,482, life 10 years; (b) Cost $29,700, life 12 years;

(c) Cost $145,000, life 30 years; (d) Cost $258,000, life 15 years.

EXTENDED APPLICATION

Estimating Seed Demands—The Upjohn Company

The Upjohn Company has a subsidiary which buys seeds from farmers and then resells them. Each spring the firm contracts with farmers to grow the seeds. The firm must decide on the number of acres that it will contract for. The problem faced by the company is that the demand for seeds is not constant, but fluctuates from year to year. Also, the number of tons of seed produced per acre varies, depending on weather and other factors. In an attempt to decide the number of acres that should be planted in order to maximize profits, a company mathematician created a model of the variables involved in determining the number of acres to plant.*

The analysis of this model required advanced methods that we will not go into. We can, however, give the conclusion; the number of acres that will maximize profit in the long run is found by solving the equation

$$F(AX + Q) = \frac{(S - C_p)X - C_A}{(S - C_p + C_c)X} \tag{1}$$

for A. The function $F(z)$ represents the chances that z tons of seed will be demanded by the marketplace. The variables in the equation are

A = number of acres of land contracted by the company,
X = quantity of seed produced per acre of land,
Q = quantity of seed in inventory from previous years,
S = selling price per ton of seed,
C_p = variable cost (production, marketing, etc.) per ton of seed,
C_c = cost to carry over one ton of seed from previous year,
C_A = variable cost per acre of land.

To advise management of the number of acres of seed to contract for, the mathematician studied past records to find the values of the various variables. From these records and from predictions of future trends, it was concluded that S = $10,000 per ton, X = .1 ton per acre (on the average), Q = 200 tons, C_p = $5000 per ton, C_A = $100 per acre, C_c = $3000 per ton.

The function $F(z)$ is found by the same process to be approximated by

$$F(z) = \frac{z}{1000} - \frac{1}{2}, \text{ if } 500 \le z \le 1500 \text{ tons.} \tag{2}$$

*Based on work by David P. Rutten, Senior Mathematician, The Upjohn Company, Kalamazoo, Michigan.

EXERCISES

1. Evaluate $AX + Q$ using the values of X and Q given above.
2. Find $F(AX + Q)$, using equation (2) and your results from Exercise 1.
3. Solve equation (1) for A.
4. How many acres should be planted?
5. How many tons of seed will be produced?
6. Find the total revenue that will be received from the sale of the seeds.

EXTENDED

APPLICATION

Marginal Cost—Booz, Allen, and Hamilton

Booz, Allen, and Hamilton is a large management consulting firm.* One of the services they provide to client companies is profitability studies, in which they show ways in which the client can increase profit levels. The client company requesting the analysis presented in this case is a large producer of a staple food. The company buys from farmers, and then processes the food in its mills, resulting in a finished product. The company sells both at retail under its own brands, and in bulk to other companies who use the product in the manufacture of convenience foods.

The client company has been reasonably profitable in recent years, but the management retained Booz, Allen, and Hamilton to see whether its consultants could suggest ways of increasing company profits. The management of the company had long operated with the philosophy of trying to process and sell as much of its product as possible, since, they felt, this would lower the average processing cost per unit sold. However, the consultants found that the client's fixed mill costs were quite low, and that, in fact, processing extra units made the cost per unit start to increase. (There are several reasons for this: the company must run three shifts, machines break down more often, and so on.)

In this case, we shall discuss the marginal cost of two of the company's products. The marginal cost (cost of producing an extra unit) of production for product A was found by the consultants to be approximated by the linear function

$$y = .133x + 10.09,$$

where x is the number of units produced (in millions) and y is the marginal cost. For example, at a level of production of 3.1 million units, an additional unit of product A would cost about

$$y = .133(3.1) + 10.09 \approx \$10.50.†$$

At a level of production of 5.7 million units, an extra unit costs $10.85. Figure 1 shows a graph of the marginal cost function from $x = 3.1$ to $x = 5.7$, the domain over which the function above was found to apply.

---

*This case was supplied by John R. Dowdle of the Chicago office of Booz, Allen, and Hamilton.
†The symbol $\approx$ means *approximately equal to.*

The selling price for product A is $10.73 per unit, so that, as shown on the graph that follows, the company was losing money on many units of the product that it sold. Since the selling price could not be raised if the company was to remain competitive, the consultants recommended that production of product A be cut.

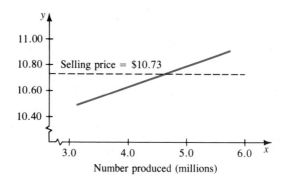

Number produced (millions)

For product B, the Booz, Allen, and Hamilton consultants found a marginal cost function given by

$$y = .0667x + 10.29,$$

with x and y as defined above. Verify that at a production level of 3.1 million units, the marginal cost is about $10.50; while at a production level of 5.7 million units, the marginal cost is about $10.67. Since the selling price of this product is $9.65, the consultants again recommended a cutback in production.

The consultants ran similar cost analyses of other products made by the company, and then issued their recommendation to the company: The company should reduce total production by 2.1 million units. The analysts predicted that this would raise profits for the products under discussion from $8.3 million annually to $9.6 million—which is very close to what actually happened when the client took the advice.

EXERCISES

1. At what level of production, x, was the marginal cost of a unit of product A equal to the selling price?

2. Graph the marginal cost function for product B from x = 3.1 million units to x = 5.7 million units.

3. Find the number of units for which marginal cost equals the selling price for product B.

4. For product C, the marginal cost of production is
$$y = .133x + 9.46.$$
   (a) Find the marginal cost at a level of production of 3.1 million units; of 5.7 million units.
   (b) Graph the marginal cost function.
   (c) For a selling price of $9.57, find the level of production for which the cost equals the selling price.

1.6   Constructing Mathematical Models (Optional)

In this section we actually construct two different mathematical models—one for double declining balance depreciation and one showing the relationship between the number of stores owned by U.S. Shoes and the sales for this same company for the last few years.

As we develop these two models, notice the fundamental difference between them. To develop the model for depreciation, we start with the basic principles, apply some of the mathematics we have learned in this course, and come up with a model which gives the depreciation of an item *exactly*.

On the other hand, the model we develop for U.S. Shoes sales cannot go back to basic principles. (What are the basic principles for shoe sales? How do we write equations for them?) Rather, we construct a mathematical model for shoe sales by gathering data on past sales and using it to predict future sales. Such methods can never give exact answers. The best we can expect is an approximation; if we are careful and lucky we can get a good approximation.

Double Declining Balance Depreciation   As we said in the last section, when a business buys an asset (such as a machine or building) it doesn't treat the total cost of the asset as an expense immediately. Instead, it *depreciates* the cost of the asset over the lifetime of the asset. For example, a machine costing $10,000 and having a useful life of 8 years, at which time it is worthless, might be depreciated at the rate of $10,000/8 = $1250 per year. As noted in the previous section, this method of depreciation is called straight-line depreciation, and assumes that the asset loses an equal amount of value during each year of its life.

This assumption of equal loss of value annually is not valid for many assets, such as new cars. A new car may lose 30% of its value during the first year. For assets that lose value quickly at first, and then less rapidly in later years, the Internal Revenue Service permits the use of alternate methods of depreciation. In Exercise Set 1.5, we discussed the sum-of-the-years'-digits method of depreciation, one alternate method.

Another common method is **double declining balance** depreciation. To find the depreciation in the first year, multiply the cost of the asset, x, by the fraction $2/n$, where n is the life of the asset in years. That is, the **depreciation in year 1** is

$$\frac{2}{n} \cdot x.$$

The number 2 in this formula is the origin of the word "double" in the name of this method.

EXAMPLE 1

A forklift costs $9600 and has a useful life of 8 years. Find the depreciation in year 1 using the double declining balance method.

By the formula above,

$$\text{depreciation in year 1} = \frac{2}{n} \cdot x$$

$$= \frac{2}{8} \cdot 9600 \qquad \text{Let } n = 8 \text{ and } x = 9600$$

$$= 2400,$$

that is, $2400. ◾

The depreciation in later years of an asset's life can be found by multiplying the depreciation from the previous year by $1 - 2/n$. For example, an asset costing $5000 with a life of 5 years would lead to a depreciation of 5000(2/5), or $2000, during the first year of its life. To find the depreciation in year 2, multiply the depreciation in year 1 by $1 - 2/5$, as follows.

$$\textbf{depreciation in year 2} = \textbf{(depreciation in year 1)} \times \left(1 - \frac{2}{n}\right)$$

$$= 2000\left(1 - \frac{2}{5}\right) \qquad \text{Let } n = 5$$

$$= 2000\left(\frac{3}{5}\right)$$

$$= 1200,$$

or $1200. To find the depreciation in year 3, multiply this result by $1 - 2/5$, or 3/5, again.

The depreciation by the double declining balance method in each of the first four years of the life of an asset is shown in the following table.

Year	1	2	3	4
Amount of depreciation	$\frac{2}{n} \cdot x$	$\frac{2}{n} \cdot x \cdot \left(1 - \frac{2}{n}\right)$	$\frac{2}{n} \cdot x \cdot \left(1 - \frac{2}{n}\right)^2$	$\frac{2}{n} \cdot x \cdot \left(1 - \frac{2}{n}\right)^3$

As the table suggests, each entry is found by multiplying the preceding entry by $1 - 2/n$. Based on this, the depreciation in year j, written D_j, is the amount

$$D_j = \frac{2}{n} \cdot x\left(1 - \frac{2}{n}\right)^{j-1} \qquad \text{or} \qquad D_j = \frac{2}{n}\left(1 - \frac{2}{n}\right)^{j-1} x.$$

This result is a general formula for the entries in the table. This formula even gives the correct result for year 1, since $j - 1$ then equals $1 - 1 = 0$, and $(1 - 2/n)^0 = 1$. It is a mathematical model for double declining balance depreciation. If double declining balance depreciation were to be used for each year of the life of an asset, then the total depreciation would be less than the net cost of the asset. For this reason, it is permissible to switch to straight-line depreciation toward the end of the useful life of the asset.

EXAMPLE 2

Oxford Typo, Inc., buys a new printing press for $39,000. The press has a life of 6 years. Find the depreciation in years 1, 2, and 3 using the double declining balance method.

Use the mathematical model given above for D_j; replace j in turn by 1, 2, and 3.

$$D_j = \frac{2}{n}\left(1 - \frac{2}{n}\right)^{j-1} x$$

$$D_1 = \frac{2}{6}\left(1 - \frac{2}{6}\right)^{1-1}(39{,}000) \qquad \text{Let } j = 1,\ n = 6,\ x = 39{,}000$$

$$= 13{,}000\left(1 - \frac{2}{6}\right)^{0} \qquad \frac{2}{6} \cdot 39{,}000 = 13{,}000$$

$$= 13{,}000(1) \qquad \left(1 - \frac{2}{6}\right)^{0} = 1$$

$$D_1 = 13{,}000$$

Find D_2 and D_3 in the same way.

$$D_2 = \frac{2}{6}\left(1 - \frac{2}{6}\right)^{2-1}(39{,}000) \qquad D_3 = \frac{2}{6}\left(1 - \frac{2}{6}\right)^{3-1}(39{,}000)$$

$$= 13{,}000 \cdot \left(1 - \frac{1}{3}\right)^{2-1} \qquad = 13{,}000 \cdot \left(1 - \frac{1}{3}\right)^{2}$$

$$= 13{,}000 \cdot \left(\frac{2}{3}\right)^{1} \qquad = 13{,}000 \cdot \left(\frac{2}{3}\right)^{2}$$

$$= 13{,}000 \cdot \left(\frac{2}{3}\right) \qquad = 13{,}000 \cdot \left(\frac{4}{9}\right)$$

$$D_2 \approx 8667 \qquad D_3 \approx 5778$$

Note that we have used the symbol "$\approx$" in the last line of the example above. This symbol means "is *approximately* equal to", and will be used throughout the book.

The methods of depreciation presented earlier were based on the *net cost,* the difference between actual cost and scrap value. On the other hand, double declining balance depreciation uses only the actual cost, not the net cost. However, total depreciation can never exceed the net cost. For this reason, adjustments sometimes must be made in the results produced by the formula above. This is shown in the next example.

EXAMPLE 3

An item costs $14,000 and has a 5-year life with a scrap value of $2000. The double declining balance depreciation in each of the first three years of the life of the item is found as follows.

$$D_1 = \frac{2}{5}\left(1 - \frac{2}{5}\right)^{1-1}(14{,}000) = 5600$$

$$D_2 = \frac{2}{5}\left(1 - \frac{2}{5}\right)^{2-1}(14{,}000) = 3360$$

$$D_3 = \frac{2}{5}\left(1 - \frac{2}{5}\right)^{3-1}(14{,}000) = 2016$$

This formula would produce the following result for D_4:

$$D_4 = \frac{2}{5}\left(1 - \frac{2}{5}\right)^{4-1}(14{,}000) = 1209.60.$$

However, the depreciation in the first three years totals $5600 + $3360 + $2016 = $10,976. The net cost of the item is $14,000 − $2000 = $12,000, so that only $12,000 in depreciation may be claimed. This means, therefore, that only $12,000 − $10,976 = $1024 in depreciation may be claimed in year 4, with $0 in year 5. ▨

Curve Fitting—The Least Squares Method   In the past few years, U.S. Shoes, which owns many different shoe stores including Red Cross, Pappagallo, and other well known stores, has increased the number of its stores rapidly. This growth has naturally led to increased sales. In the rest of this section, we develop a mathematical model showing the relationship between the number of stores and sales. To begin, we gather data on the number of stores and the sales for each of the past five years. This data is shown in the following chart.* (The numbers are rounded for simplicity.)

Number of Stores	Sales (billions of $)
900	.75
1000	.90
1100	.95
1300	1.05
1350	1.20

Clearly, we cannot use this data to obtain a precise, exact mathematical model, such as the one for depreciation. There are too many variables here; the state of the economy, prices, and other factors affect shoe sales. For example, when the number of stores increased from 1100 to 1300, an increase of 200, sales increased by .1 billion dollars, or $100,000,000. However, an increase of only 50 stores, from 1300 to 1350, corresponded to increased sales of .15 billion, or $150,000,000.

We want an equation that describes the relationship between the number of stores and the sales as closely as possible. Figure 15 shows a graph of the data from the chart. Since we want to predict sales from the number of stores, let sales be the

*From "What Makes U.S. Shoe Shine" in *Fortune,* Vol. 108, #7, October 3, 1983.

dependent variable, y, and the number of stores be the independent variable, x. The points in the graph of Figure 15 appear to lie approximately along a line, which means that a linear function may give a good approximation to the data. Many lines could be drawn on the graph that would be "close" to all the points of the graph. How do we decide on the "best" possible line? The line used most often in applications is that in which the sum of the squares of the vertical distances from the data points to the line is as small as possible. Such a line is called the **least squares line.**

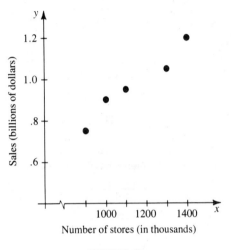

FIGURE 15

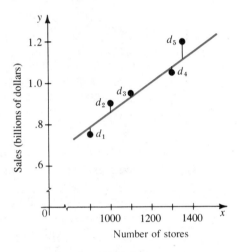

FIGURE 16

In Figure 16 a line has been drawn which seems to lie close to the points which represent the data. The distances from these points to the line are indicated by d_1, d_2, d_3, d_4, and d_5. For n points, corresponding to the n pairs of data, the least squares line is found by minimizing the sum $(d_1)^2 + (d_2)^2 + (d_3)^2 + \ldots + (d_n)^2$.

For the points $(x_1, y_1), (x_2, y_2), \ldots, (x_n, y_n)$, if the equation of the desired line is $y' = mx + b$, then

$$d_1 = y'_1 - y_1 = mx_1 + b - y_1$$
$$d_2 = y'_2 - y_2 = mx_2 + b - y_2$$

and so on. The sum to be minimized becomes

$$(mx_1 + b - y_1)^2 + (mx_2 + b - y_2)^2 + \ldots + (mx_n + b - y_n)^2,$$

where $(x_1, y_1), (x_2, y_2), \ldots, (x_n, y_n)$ are known and m and b are to be found.

The method of minimizing this sum requires calculus and is not given here. The result gives equations for finding the slope and y-intercept of the least squares line. We used y' instead of y in the equation of the line to distinguish the predicted y-values on the line from the y-values of the given pairs of data points.

Least Squares Line

The least squares line $y' = mx + b$ that gives the best fit to the data points $(x_1, y_1), (x_2, y_2), \ldots, (x_n, y_n)$ has

$$\text{slope } m = \frac{n(\Sigma xy) - (\Sigma x)(\Sigma y)}{n(\Sigma x^2) - (\Sigma x)^2}$$

and y'-intercept $b = \dfrac{\Sigma y - m(\Sigma x)}{n}$.

The symbol Σ indicates "the sum of:" Σxy means the sum $x_1 y_1 + x_2 y_2 + \ldots + x_n y_n$, Σx means $x_1 + x_2 + \ldots + x_n$ and so on. Note that n is the number of data points.

To find the least squares line for the U.S. Shoe data, first find the required sums. Let x represent the number of stores (in thousands) and y represent the sales (in billions of dollars) and fill in a chart as shown in the table.

x	y	xy	x^2	y^2
.90	.75	.6750	.8100	.5625
1.00	.90	.9000	1.0000	.8100
1.10	.95	1.0450	1.2100	.9025
1.30	1.05	1.3650	1.6900	1.1025
1.35	1.20	1.6200	1.8225	1.4400
5.65	4.85	5.6050	6.5325	4.8175

(The column headed y^2 will be used later.) Now calculate m and b; here $n = 5$.

$$m = \frac{n(\Sigma xy) - (\Sigma x)(\Sigma y)}{n(\Sigma x^2) - (\Sigma x)^2}$$

$$= \frac{5(5.605) - (5.65)(4.85)}{5(6.5325) - (5.65)^2}$$

$$= .84 \quad \text{(rounded)}$$

$$b = \frac{\Sigma y - m(\Sigma x)}{n}$$

$$= \frac{4.85 - (.84)(5.65)}{5}$$

$$= .02 \quad \text{(rounded)}$$

Substitute m and b into the least squares line equation, $y' = mx + b$; the least squares line which best fits the five data points has equation $y' = .84x + .02$. This is the mathematical model of the relationship between number of stores and sales. The equation can be used to predict y from a given value of x, as shown in Example 1. However, it is not a good idea to use the least squares equation to predict data points that are not close to those points on which the equation was modeled.

Suppose the company opens 50 new stores for a total of 1400 or 1.4 thousand stores. Estimate the total sales.

Use the least squares line from above with $x = 1.4$.

$$y' = .84x + .02$$
$$y' = .84(1.4) + .02$$
$$= 1.196$$

Sales for the 1400 stores will be about $1.2 billion. ▢

EXAMPLE 5

How many stores would be needed to increase sales to $2 billion?

Let $y' = 2$ in the equation above.

$$2 = .84x + .02$$
$$1.98 = .84x$$
$$x = 2.36$$

The number of stores must increase to about 2360 to produce sales of $2 billion. ▢

Correlation   Once an equation is found for the least squares line, we might well ask, "Just how good is this equation for prediction purposes?" If the points from the data fit the line quite closely, then we can expect future data pairs to do so. Also, if the points are widely scattered about even the "best fitting" line, then predictions are not likely to be accurate.

In order to have a quantitative basis for confidence in our predictions, we need a measure of the "goodness of fit" of the original data to the prediction line. One such measure is called the **coefficient of correlation,** denoted r.

Correlation Coefficient

$$r = \frac{n(\Sigma xy) - (\Sigma x)(\Sigma y)}{\sqrt{n(\Sigma x^2) - (\Sigma x)^2} \cdot \sqrt{n(\Sigma y^2) - (\Sigma y)^2}}$$

The coefficient of correlation, r, is always equal to or between 1 and -1. Values of exactly 1 or -1 indicate that the data points lie *exactly* on the least squares line. If $r = 1$, the least squares line has a positive slope; $r = -1$ gives a negative slope. If $r = 0$, there is no linear correlation between the data points. (However, some other nonlinear function might provide an excellent fit for the data.) Graphs which correspond to these values of r are shown in Figure 17.

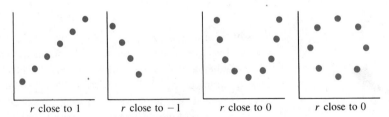

r close to 1   r close to -1 r close to 0   r close to 0

FIGURE 17

EXAMPLE 6

Find r for the U.S. Shoe Company data.

From Table 1 $\Sigma x = 5.65$, $\Sigma y = 4.85$, $\Sigma xy = 5.6050$, $\Sigma x^2 = 6.5325$, and $\Sigma y^2 = 4.8175$. Also, $n = 5$. Substituting these values into the formula for r gives

$$r = \frac{5(5.6050) - (5.65)(4.85)}{\sqrt{5(6.5325) - (5.65)^2} \cdot \sqrt{5(4.8175) - (4.85)^2}}$$

$$= \frac{.6225}{\sqrt{.74} \cdot \sqrt{.565}}$$

$$= .96.$$

This is a very high correlation, as one would expect. Increasing the number of stores clearly would increase sales, so it is not surprising that the coefficient of correlation indicates a close relationship. ▪

1.6 EXERCISES

1. An apartment house costs $180,000. The owners decide to depreciate it over 6 years (it isn't built very well). Use the double declining balance method to find the depreciation in each of the following years.

   (a) year 1   (b) year 2
   (c) year 3   (d) year 4

2. A new airplane costs $600,000 and has a useful life of 10 years. Use the double declining balance method of depreciation to find the depreciation in each of the following years.

   (a) year 1   (b) year 2
   (c) year 3   (d) year 4

Complete the tables in Exercises 3 and 4, which compare the three methods of depreciation. [Recall: For straight line and the sum-of-the-years'-digits methods, x is the net cost of an asset; $x = $ cost minus scrap value. Also, the formula for depreciation in year j, by the sum-of-the-years'-digits method, is

$$D_j = \frac{n - j + 1}{n(n + 1)}(2x).]$$

3. Cost: $1400; life: 3 years; scrap value: $275

Depreciation in Year	Straight-line	Double Declining	Sum-of-years'-digits
1			
2			
3			
Totals			

4. Cost: $55,000; life: 5 years; scrap value: $0

Depreciation in Year	Straight-line	Double Declining	Sum-of-years'-Digits
1			
2			
3			
4			
5			
Totals			

5. In a study to determine the linear relationship between the size (in decimeters) of an ear of corn (y) and the amount (in tons per acre) of fertilizer used (x), the following data were collected.

$$n = 10 \qquad \Sigma xy = 75$$
$$\Sigma x = 30 \qquad \Sigma x^2 = 100$$
$$\Sigma y = 24 \qquad \Sigma y^2 = 80$$

(a) Find an equation for the least squares line.

(b) Find the coefficient of correlation.

(c) If 3 tons per acre of fertilizer are used, what length (in decimeters) would the equation in (a) predict for an ear of corn?

6. In an experiment to determine the linear relationship between temperatures on the Celsius scale (y) and on the Fahrenheit scale (x), a student got the following results.

$$n = 5 \qquad \Sigma xy = 28,050$$
$$\Sigma x = 376 \qquad \Sigma x^2 = 62,522$$
$$\Sigma y = 120 \qquad \Sigma y^2 = 13,450$$

(a) Find an equation for the least squares line.

(b) Find the reading on the Celsius scale that corresponds to a reading of 120° Fahrenheit, using the equation of part (a).

(c) Find the coefficient of correlation.

7. To determine if high school grade-point averages and college grade-point averages can be closely approximated by a linear function, a college registrar randomly selected 10 students, finding the averages shown in the chart.

High School GPA x	2.5	2.8	2.9	3.0	3.2	3.3	3.3	3.4	3.6	3.9
College GPA y	2.0	2.5	2.5	2.8	3.0	3.0	3.5	3.3	3.4	3.6

(a) Find the equation of the least squares line for this data.
Using the results of (a), estimate the college grade-point average of students with high school grade-point averages of **(b)** 2.7   **(c)** 3.5.

(d) What high school grade-point average does the least squares equation require for a college grade-point average of 2.5?

(e) Find the coefficient of correlation.

8. A sample of 10 adult men gave the following data on their heights and weights.

Height (inches)	(x)	62	62	63	65	66	67	68	68	70	72
Weight (pounds)	(y)	120	140	130	150	142	130	135	175	149	168

(a) Find the equation of the least squares line.

Using the results of (a), predict the weight of a man whose height is

(b) 60 inches;   **(c)** 70 inches.

(d) Compute the coefficient of correlation.

9. The following table shows the percent profit at a typical fast food restaurant in a recent year.

Annual Store Sales in Thousands, x	250	375	450	500	600	650
Percent Pretax Profit, y	9.3	14.8	14.2	15.9	19.2	21.0

(a) Find the least squares line for this data.

(b) Use the results of (a) to estimate the percent of profit for sales of $400,000.

(c) Use the results of (a) to determine what level of sales would produce profit of 15%.

(d) Find the coefficient of correlation.

10. Records show that the annual sales of the EZ Life Company in 5-year periods for the last 20 years were as follows.

Year (x)	Sales (in millions) (y)
1960	1.0
1965	1.3
1970	1.7
1975	1.9
1980	2.1

The company wishes to estimate sales from these records for the next few years. Code the years so that $1960 = 0$, $1961 = 1$, and so on.

(a) Plot the 5 points on a graph.

(b) Find the equation of the least squares line, and graph it on the graph of part (a).

(c) Predict the company's sales for 1984 and 1985.

(d) Compute the correlation coefficient.

11. U.S. West is the largest regional holding company created by the AT&T divestiture. The company includes Mountain Bell, Northwestern Bell, and Pacific Northwest Bell. The table below shows the number of customer lines (in millions) serviced by U.S. West over a six-year period.

Year (x)	1978	1979	1980	1981	1982	1983
Number of Lines (y)	5	7.8	8.9	9.8	9.6	10.4

Let 1978 represent year 1, 1979, year 2, and so on.

(a) Use the data to find a least squares line.

(b) Use the results of (a) to predict the number of customer lines that will be serviced by U.S. West in 1985.

(c) Use the results to determine in what year there will be 15 million customer lines.

(d) Find the coefficient of correlation.

12. The following data furnished by a major brewery were used to determine if there is a relationship between repair costs and barrels of beer produced. The data in thousands are given for a 10-month period.

Month	Barrels of Beer X	Repairs y
Jan	369	299
Feb	379	280
Mar	482	393
April	493	388
May	496	385
June	567	423
July	521	374
Aug	482	357
Sept	391	106
Oct	417	332

(a) Find the equation of the least squares line.

(b) Find the coefficient of correlation.

(c) If 500,000 barrels of beer are produced, what will the equation from part (a) give as the predicted repair costs?

13. (This problem is appropriate only for those who have studied common logarithms.) Sometimes the scatter diagram of the data does not have a linear pattern. This is particularly true in biological applications. In these applications, however, often the scatter diagram of the *logarithms* of the data has a linear pattern. A least squares line then can be used to predict the logarithm of any desired value from which the value itself can be found. Suppose that a certain kind of bacterium grows in number as shown in Table A. The actual number of bacteria present at each time period is replaced with the common logarithm of that number (Table B).

Table A

Time in Hours	0	1	2	3	4	5
Number of Bacteria	1000	1649	2718	4482	7389	12182

Table B

Time x	0	1	2	3	4	5
Log y	3.0000	3.2172	3.4343	3.6515	3.8686	4.0857

We can now find a least squares line which will predict y, given x.

(a) Plot the original pairs of numbers. The pattern should be nonlinear.

(b) Plot the log values against the time values. The pattern should be almost linear.

(c) Find the equation of the least squares line. (First round off the log values to the nearest hundredth.)

(d) Predict the log value for a time of 7 hours. Find the number whose logarithm is your answer. This will be the predicted number of bacteria.

It is sometimes possible to get a better prediction for a variable by considering its relationship with more than one other variable. For example, one should be able to predict college GPAs more precisely if both high school GPAs and scores on the ACT are considered. To do this, we alter the equation used to find a least squares line by adding a term for the new variable as follows. If y represents college GPAs, x_1 high school GPAs, and x_2 ACT scores, then y', the predicted GPA, is given by

$$y' = ax_1 + bx_2 + c.$$

This equation represents a **least squares plane.** The equations for the constants a, b, and c are more complicated than those given in the text for m and b, so that calculating a least squares equation for three variables is more likely to require the aid of a computer.

14. Alcoa* used a least squares plane with two independent variables, x_1 and x_2, to predict the effect on revenue of the price of aluminum forged truck wheels, as follows.

$x_1 =$ the average price per wheel

$x_2 =$ large truck production in thousands

$v =$ sales of aluminum forged truck wheels in thousands

---

*This example supplied by John H. Van Denender, Public Relations Department, Aluminum Company of America.

Using data for the past eleven years, the company found the equation of the least squares line to be

$$y' = 49.2755 - 1.1924x_1 + 0.1631x_2,$$

for which the correlation coefficient was .902. The following figures were then forecast for truck production.

1982	1983	1984	1985	1986	1987
160.0	165.0	170.0	175.0	180.0	185.0

Three possible price levels per wheel were considered: $42, $45, and $48.

(a) Use the least squares plane equation given above to find the estimated sales of wheels (y') for 1984 at each of the three price levels.

(b) Repeat part (a) for 1987.

(c) For which price level, on the basis of the 1984 and 1987 figures, are total estimated sales greatest?

(By comparing total estimated sales for the years 1982 through 1987 at each of the three price levels, the company found that the selling price of $42 per wheel would generate the greatest sales volume over the six-year period.)

Find the least squares line and the coefficient of correlation for the sets of data pairs in Exercises 15–18.

15.

x	2.1	3.2	4.6	4.9	5.3	5.8
y	10.3	12.7	11.9	13.2	14.0	14.8

16.

x	143	152	169	175	178	185	190	202
y	43	58	55	62	69	71	78	83

KEY WORDS

mathematical model
linear equation in one variable
independent variable
dependent variable
function
domain
range
ordered pair
x-intercept
supply curve
demand curve
equilibrium price
slope
change in x
fixed cost
variable cost
marginal cost

Cartesian coordinate system
x-axis
y-axis
origin
quadrant
graph
vertical line test
linear function
y-intercept
depreciation
straight-line depreciation
scrap value
net cost
sum-of-the-years'-digits depreciation
double declining balance depreciation
least squares line

Chapter 1 REVIEW EXERCISES

Solve each of the linear equations in one variable in Exercises 1–8.

1. $3x + 2 = 8$

2. $-m + 7 = 12$

3. $2k - 3 = 6 - k$

4. $4p - 2p + 3 = 3p$

5. $5n - (n + 1) = 3(n + 2)$

6. $4(y + 3) - 2y = -(y - 1)$

7. $\frac{3}{2} + 3z = 5 + \frac{2z}{4}$

8. $\frac{x}{5} - \frac{3}{5} = 2x + 1$

In Exercises 9–18 solve each of the linear inequalities in one variable.

9. $4m + 2 \le 12$

10. $3z + 5 \le 8$

11. $5 - 2m > 7$

12. $9 - 5p > 12$

13. $2k + 3 \le 5k - 4$

14. $4 - 3z \le 2z + 1$

15. $\frac{2}{3}x + 4 \ge x - \frac{1}{3}$

16. $\frac{a}{5} - 3 \ge 2a + \frac{2}{5}$

17. $2(k + 5) - 3k < k + 4$

18. $5 - 4b < 2(b + 3) - b$

Solve Exercises 19 and 20.

19. Virginia Wallace invested an inheritance of $30,000 in two ways; part at 8 1/2% interest, and the rest at 10%. Her total annual interest on the money is $2820. How much was invested at each rate?

20. To manufacture x thousand computer chips requires fixed expenditures of $352 plus $42 per thousand chips. Receipts from the sale of x thousand chips amount to $130 per thousand.

  (a) Write an expression for expenditures.

  (b) Write an expression for receipts.

  (c) For a profit, receipts must be greater than expenditures. How many chips must be sold to produce a profit?

List the ordered pairs obtained from each of the following functions, if the domain of x for each exercise is $\{-3, -2, -1, 0, 1, 2, 3\}$. Graph each set of ordered pairs. Give the range.

21. $2x - 5y = 10$

22. $3x + 7y = 21$

23. $y = (2x + 1)(x - 1)$

24. $y = (x + 4)(x + 3)$

25. $y = -2 + x^2$

26. $y = 3x^2 - 7$

27. $y = \dfrac{2}{x^2 + 1}$

28. $y = \dfrac{-3 + x}{x + 10}$

29. $y + 1 = 0$

30. $y = 3$

For each of the functions in Exercises 31–34, find **(a)** $f(6)$, **(b)** $f(-2)$, **(c)** $f(-4)$, **(d)** $f(r + 1)$.

31. $f(x) = 4x - 1$

32. $f(x) = 3 - 4x$

33. $f(x) = -x^2 + 2x - 4$

34. $f(x) = 8 - x - x^2$

35. Let $f(x) = 5x - 3$ and $g(x) = -x^2 + 4x$. Find each of the following.

(a) $f(-2)$

(b) $g(3)$

(c) $g(-4)$

(d) $f(5)$

(e) $g(-k)$

(f) $g(3m)$

(g) $g(k - 5)$

(h) $f(3 - p)$

(i) $f[g(-1)]$

(j) $g[f(2)]$

36. Assume that it costs 30¢ to mail a letter weighing one ounce or less, with each additional ounce, or portion of an ounce, costing 27¢. Let $C(x)$ represent the cost to mail a letter weighing x ounces. Find the cost of mailing a letter of the following weights.

(a) 3.4 ounces

(b) 1.02 ounces

(c) 5.9 ounces

(d) 10 ounces

(e) Graph C.

(f) Give the domain and range for C.

Graph each of the linear functions in Exercises 37–44.

37. $y = 4x + 3$

38. $y = 6 - 2x$

39. $3x - 5y = 15$

40. $2x + 7y = 14$

41. $x + 2 = 0$

42. $y = 1$

43. $y = 2x$

44. $x + 3y = 0$

45. The supply and demand for a certain commodity are related by

$$\text{supply: } p = 6x + 3;$$
$$\text{demand: } p = 19 - 2x,$$

where p represents the price at a supply or demand, respectively, of x units. Find the supply and the demand when the price is

(a) 10;   **(b)** 15;   **(c)** 18.

(d) Graph both the supply and the demand functions on the same axes.

(e) Find the equilibrium price.

(f) Find the equilibrium supply; the equilibrium demand.

46. For a particular product, 72 units will be supplied at a price of 6, while 104 units will be supplied at a price of 10. Write a supply function for this product.

Find the slope for each of the lines in Exercises 47–54 that have slope.

47. through $(-2, 5)$ and $(4, 7)$

48. through $(4, -1)$ and $(3, -3)$

49. through the origin and $(11, -2)$

50. through the origin and $(0, 7)$

51. $2x + 3y = 15$

52. $4x - y = 7$

53. $x + 4 = 9$

54. $3y - 1 = 14$

Find an equation for each of the lines in Exercises 55–60.

55. through $(5, -1)$, slope $2/3$

56. through $(8, 0)$, slope $-1/4$

57. through $(5, -2)$ and $(1, 3)$

58. through $(2, -3)$ and $(-3, 4)$

59. undefined slope, through $(-1, 4)$

60. slope 0, through $(-2, 5)$

Find each of the following linear cost functions.

61. eight units of paper cost $300; fixed cost is $60

62. fixed cost is $2000; 36 units cost $8480

63. twelve units cost $445; 50 units cost $1585

64. thirty units cost $1500; 120 units cost $5640

65. The cost of producing x units of a product is $C(x)$, where
$$C(x) = 20x + 100.$$
The product sells for $40 per unit.

(a) Find the break-even point.

(b) What revenue will the company receive if it sells just that number of units?

66. An asset costs $21,000 and has a six-year life with no scrap value. Find the first year depreciation for this asset by each of the following methods.

(a) straight line

(b) sum-of-the-years'-digits

(c) double declining balance

67. Complete the following table for an asset costing $79,000, having a scrap value of $11,000 and a four-year life.

Depreciation in Year	Straight-line	Double Declining	Sum-of-the-years'-digits
1			
2			
3			
4			

68. Complete a table similar to the one of Exercise 67 for an asset costing $430,000, having a five-year life, and a scrap value of $70,000.

69. Find the least squares line for the following data.

x	3	5	7	8
y	4	11	20	23

70. Use your equation from Exercise 69 to predict y when x is 6.

71. Find the coefficient of correlation for the data in Exercise 69.

72. The following data show the connection between blood sugar levels, x, and cholesterol levels, y, for 8 different patients.

Patient	1	2	3	4	5	6	7	8
Blood sugar level, x	130	138	142	159	165	200	210	250
Cholesterol level, y	170	160	173	181	201	192	240	290

For this data, $\Sigma x = 1394$, $\Sigma y = 1607$, $\Sigma xy = 291{,}990$, $\Sigma x^2 = 255{,}214$, and $\Sigma y^2 = 336{,}155$.

(a) Find the equation of the least squares line, $y' = mx + b$.

(b) Predict the cholesterol level for a person whose blood sugar level is 190.

(c) Find r.

SYSTEMS OF LINEAR EQUATIONS AND MATRICES

Karl Gerstner. From the series *Aperspective 3* (The Large Sliding Mirror Picture), 1953/55.

Many mathematical models involve more than one equation that must be satisfied. A set of equations related in this way is called a **system of equations.** Any solutions of the equations in the set that satisfy all the equations are solutions of the system. After discussing systems, this chapter introduces the idea of a **matrix,** and shows how matrices are used to solve systems of linear equations.

2.1   Systems of Linear Equations

An animal feed is made from three ingredients: corn, soybeans, and cottonseed. One unit of each ingredient provides the number of units of protein, fat, and fiber shown in the table. For example, the entries in the first row, .25, .4, and .3, mean that one unit of corn provides twenty-five hundredths (one fourth) of a unit of protein, four tenths of a unit of fat, and three tenths of a unit of fiber. Suppose we need to know the number of units of each ingredient that should be used to make a feed which contains 22 units of protein, 28 units of fat, and 18 units of fiber.

	Protein	*Fat*	*Fiber*
Corn	.25	.4	.3
Soybeans	.4	.2	.2
Cottonseed	.2	.3	.1

To find out, let x represent the number of units of corn; y, the number of units of soybeans; and z, the number of units of cottonseed which are required. Since the total amount of protein is to be 22 units,

$$.25x + .4y + .2z = 22.$$

Also, for the 28 units of fat,

$$.4x + .2y + .3z = 28,$$

and, for the 18 units of fiber,

$$.3x + .2y + .1z = 18.$$

To solve the problem, values of x, y, and z must be found that satisfy this system of equations. Verify that $x = 40$, $y = 15$, and $z = 30$ is a solution of the system, since these numbers satisfy all three equations. In fact, this is the only solution of this system. Many practical problems lead to such systems of equations. In this chapter, we consider methods for solving these systems of first-degree equations.

A **first degree equation** in n unknowns is any equation of the form

$$a_1x_1 + a_2x_2 + \cdots + a_nx_n = k,$$

where a_1, a_2, $\cdots$, a_n and k are all real numbers. Each of the three equations from the animal feed problem is a first degree equation in 3 unknowns. The **solution** of the first degree equation

$$a_1 x_1 + a_2 x_2 + \cdots + a_n x_n = k$$

is a sequence of numbers s_1, s_2, $\cdots$, s_n, such that

$$a_1 s_1 + a_2 s_2 + \cdots + a_n s_n = k.$$

The solution may be written between parentheses as $(s_1, s_2, \cdots, s_n)$. For example, $(1, 6, 2)$ is a solution of the equation $3x_1 + 2x_2 - 4x_3 = 7$, since $3(1) + 2(6) - 4(2) = 7$.

A first-degree equation in two unknowns has a graph which is a straight line. For this reason, first-degree equations are also called **linear equations.** In this section we develop a method of solving a system of first degree equations. Although our discussion will be confined to equations with only a few variables, the methods of solution can be extended to systems with many variables.

Because the graph of a linear equation in two variables is a straight line, there are three possibilities for the solution of a system of two linear equations in two variables.

1. The two graphs are lines intersecting at a single point. The coordinates of this point give the solution of the system. [See Figure 1(a).]
2. The graphs are distinct parallel lines. When this is the case, the system is **inconsistent;** that is, there is no solution common to both equations. [See Figure 1(b).]
3. The graphs are the same line. In this case, the equations are said to be **dependent,** since any solution of one equation is also a solution of the other. There are an infinite number of solutions. [See Figure 1(c).]

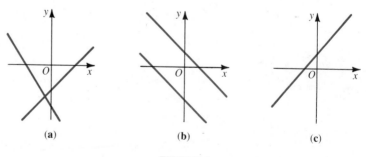

FIGURE 1

In larger systems, with more equations and more variables, there also may be exactly one solution, an infinite number of solutions, or no solution. In any system, if all the equations are dependent, the system will have an infinite number of solutions. If no solution satisfies every equation in the system, the system is inconsistent.

Transformations   To solve a linear system of equations, properties of algebra are used to change the system until a simpler equivalent system is found. An **equivalent system** is one that has the same solutions as the given system. Three transformations can be applied to a system to get an equivalent system:

Transformations

of a System

1. **exchanging any two equations;**
2. **multiplying both sides of an equation by any nonzero real number;**
3. **adding to any equation a multiple of some other equation.**

Use of these transformations leads to an equivalent system because each transformation can be reversed or "undone," allowing a return to the original system.

EXAMPLE 1

Solve the system

$$3x - 4y = 1 \tag{1}$$
$$2x + 3y = 12. \tag{2}$$

We want to get a system of equations which is equivalent to the given system, but simpler. If the equations are transformed so that the variable x disappears from one of them, the value of y can be found. First, use the second transformation to multiply both sides of equation (1) by 2. This gives the equivalent system

$$6x - 8y = 2 \tag{3}$$
$$2x + 3y = 12. \tag{2}$$

Now, using the third transformation, multiply both sides of equation (2) by -3, and add the result to equation (3).

$$(6x - 8y) + (-3)(2x + 3y) = 2 + (-3)(12)$$
$$6x - 8y - 6x - 9y = 2 - 36$$
$$-17y = -34$$
$$y = 2$$

The result of these steps is the equivalent system

$$3x - 4y = 1 \tag{1}$$
$$y = 2. \tag{4}$$

To find the value of x, substitute 2 for y in equation (1) to get

$$3x - 4(2) = 1$$
$$3x - 8 = 1$$
$$x = 3.$$

The solution of the given system is (3, 2). The graphs of both equations of the system are shown in **Figure 2**. The graph suggests that (3, 2) satisfies both equations of the system. ■

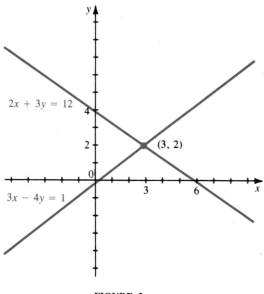

FIGURE 2

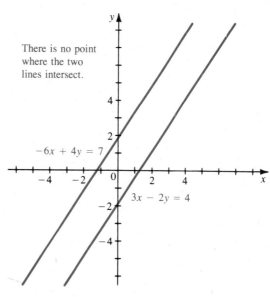

FIGURE 3

Since the method of solution in Example 1 results in the elimination of one variable from an equation of the system, it is called the **elimination method** for solving a system.

EXAMPLE 2

Solve the system

$$3x - 2y = 4$$
$$-6x + 4y = 7.$$

Eliminate x by multiplying the first equation by 2 and adding the result to the second equation.

$$2(3x - 2y) + (-6x + 4y) = 2(4) + 7$$
$$6x - 4y - 6x + 4y = 8 + 7$$
$$0 = 15$$

The new system is

$$3x - 2y = 4$$
$$0 = 15. \quad \textbf{False}$$

In the second equation, both variables have been eliminated with the result a false statement, a signal that these two equations have no common solution. This system is inconsistent and has no solution. As Figure 3 shows, the graph of the system is made up of two distinct parallel lines. ▪

EXAMPLE 3

Solve the system

$$-4x + y = 2$$
$$8x - 2y = -4.$$

To eliminate x, multiply both sides of the first equation by 2 and add the result to the second equation.

$$2(-4x + y) + (8x - 2y) = 2(2) + (-4)$$
$$-8x + 2y + 8x - 2y = 4 - 4$$
$$0 = 0$$

This true statement indicates that the two equations have the same graph, which means that there is an infinite number of solutions for the system. In this case, all the ordered pairs that satisfy the equation $-4x + y = 2$ (or $8x - 2y = -4$) are solutions. See Figure 4. ▓

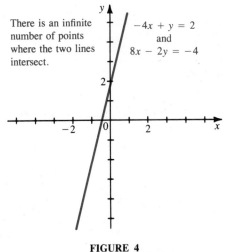

There is an infinite number of points where the two lines intersect.

$-4x + y = 2$
and
$8x - 2y = -4$

FIGURE 4

Several steps are needed to use the elimination method to solve a system of three equations with three variables, as shown in Example 4.

EXAMPLE 4

Solve the system

$$2x + y - z = 2 \tag{1}$$
$$x + 3y + 2z = 1 \tag{2}$$
$$x + y + z = 2. \tag{3}$$

Begin by eliminating one variable from one pair of equations. Suppose we choose to eliminate x from equations (2) and (3) by multiplying both sides of equation (3) by -1 and then adding the two equations vertically.

$$x + 3y + 2z = 1 \tag{2}$$
$$\underline{-x - y - z = -2}$$
$$2y + z = -1 \tag{4}$$

Now eliminate x from another pair of equations, say (1) and (2). This can be done by multiplying both sides of equation (2) by -2 and adding the result to equation (1).

$$
\begin{array}{rr}
2x + y - z = 2 & \textbf{(1)} \\
-2x - 6y - 4z = -2 & \\
\hline
-5y - 5z = 0 & \textbf{(5)}
\end{array}
$$

Equations (4) and (5) are now used to eliminate another variable. Multiplying both sides of equation (5) by 1/5 and adding the result to equation (4) eliminates z.

$$
\begin{array}{rr}
2y + z = -1 & \textbf{(4)} \\
-y - z = 0 & \textbf{(6)} \\
\hline
y = -1 &
\end{array}
$$

Now substitute for y in equation (6) to get

$$-y - z = 0$$
$$-(-1) - z = 0$$
$$1 - z = 0$$
$$z = 1.$$

Finally, substituting $y = -1$ and $z = 1$ into one of the original equations, say equation (1), gives

$$2x + (-1) - (1) = 2$$
$$2x - 2 = 2$$
$$2x = 4$$
$$x = 2.$$

The solution is $(2, -1, 1)$. ▪

The Echelon Method   Although the elimination method can be used to solve systems with more than two equations, it is a complicated process even for systems of three variables. A more systematic approach, using matrix notation (discussed later in this chapter), makes it possible to solve systems of equations by computer. In the next example we solve the system of Example 4 again to illustrate the new method.

EXAMPLE 5

Solve the system

$$
\begin{array}{rr}
2x + y - z = 2 & \textbf{(1)} \\
x + 3y + 2z = 1 & \textbf{(2)} \\
x + y + z = 2. & \textbf{(3)}
\end{array}
$$

We want to replace the given system with an equivalent system from which the solution is easily found. In the new system, the coefficient of x in the first equation should be 1. Use the first transformation to exchange equations (1) and (2). (We could have multiplied both sides of equation (1) by 1/2 instead.) The new system is

$$x + 3y + 2z = 1 \qquad \text{(2)}$$
$$2x + y - z = 2 \qquad \text{(1)}$$
$$x + y + z = 2. \qquad \text{(3)}$$

To get a new second equation without x, multiply each term of equation (2) by -2 and add the results to equation (1). This gives

$$-5y - 5z = 0. \qquad \text{(4)}$$

Multiply both sides of equation (4) by $-1/5$ to make the coefficient of y equal to 1.

$$y + z = 0 \qquad \text{(5)}$$

We now have the equivalent system

$$x + 3y + 2z = 1 \qquad \text{(2)}$$
$$y + z = 0 \qquad \text{(5)}$$
$$x + y + z = 2. \qquad \text{(3)}$$

Get a new third equation without x by multiplying both sides of equation (2) by -1 and adding the results to equation (3). The result is

$$-2y - z = 1. \qquad \text{(6)}$$

Now multiply both sides of equation (5) by 2 and add to equation (6) to get

$$z = 1. \qquad \text{(7)}$$

The original system has now led to the equivalent system

$$x + 3y + 2z = 1 \qquad \text{(2)}$$
$$y + z = 0 \qquad \text{(5)}$$
$$z = 1. \qquad \text{(7)}$$

From equation (7) we know $z = 1$. Substitute 1 for z in equation (5) to get $y = -1$. Finally substitute 1 for z and -1 for y in equation (2) to get $x = 2$, and the solution of the system, $(2, -1, 1)$. ▪

This method, where the system is rewritten in the form suggested by equations (2), (5), and (7), is sometimes called the **echelon method.** In summary, to solve a linear system in n variables by the echelon method, perform the following steps using the three transformations.

The Echelon Method of Solving a Linear System	1. Make the coefficient of the first variable equal to 1 in the first equation and 0 in the other equations. 2. Make the coefficient of the second variable equal to 1 in the second equation and 0 in all remaining equations. 3. Make the coefficient of the third variable equal to 1 in the third equation and 0 in all remaining equations. 4. Continue in this way until the last equation is of the form $x_n = k$, where k is a constant.

Parameters   The systems of equations discussed so far have had the same number of equations as variables. Such systems have either one solution, no solution, or an infinite number of solutions. However, sometimes a mathematical model leads to a system of equations with fewer equations than variables. Such systems always have an infinite number of solutions or no solution.

EXAMPLE 6

Solve

$$2x + 3y + 4z = 6 \tag{1}$$
$$x - 2y + z = 9 \tag{2}$$
$$3x - 6y + 3z = 27. \tag{3}$$

Since the third equation here is a multiple of the second equation, this system really has only the two equations

$$2x + 3y + 4z = 6 \tag{1}$$
$$x - 2y + z = 9. \tag{2}$$

Exchange the two equations so that the coefficient of x is 1 in the first equation of the system. This gives

$$x - 2y + z = 9 \tag{2}$$
$$2x + 3y + 4z = 6. \tag{1}$$

To get a new second equation without x, multiply both sides of equation (2) by -2 and add to equation (1). The result is

$$7y + 2z = -12.$$

Multiply both sides of this equation by 1/7. The new system is

$$x - 2y + z = 9 \tag{2}$$
$$y + \frac{2}{7}z = \frac{-12}{7}. \tag{3}$$

Since we have only two equations, we can go no further. To complete the solution, solve equation (3) for y.

$$y = \frac{-2}{7}z - \frac{12}{7}$$

Now substitute the result for y in equation (2), and solve for x.

$$x - 2y + z = 9 \tag{2}$$
$$x - 2\left(\frac{-2}{7}z - \frac{12}{7}\right) + z = 9$$
$$x + \frac{4}{7}z + \frac{24}{7} + z = 9$$
$$7x + 4z + 24 + 7z = 63$$
$$7x + 11z = 39$$
$$7x = -11z + 39$$
$$x = \frac{-11}{7}z + \frac{39}{7}$$

We now have both x and y expressed in terms of z. Each choice of a value for z leads to values for x and y. For example,

if $z = 1$,   then $x = -\dfrac{11}{7} \cdot 1 + \dfrac{39}{7} = 4$ and $y = -\dfrac{2}{7} \cdot 1 - \dfrac{12}{7} = -2$;

if $z = -6$,   then $x = 15$ and $y = 0$;

if $z = 0$,   then $x = \dfrac{39}{7}$ and $y = \dfrac{-12}{7}$.

Since x and y are both given in terms of z, the variable z is called a **parameter.** There is an infinite number of solutions for the original system, since z can take on an infinite number of values. The set of solutions may be written

$$\left\{ \left(\frac{-11}{7}z + \frac{39}{7}, \ \frac{-2}{7}z - \frac{12}{7}, \ z \right) \right\}.$$

By solving the original system in a different way, we could make x or y the parameter. ▪

Example 6 discussed a system with one more variable than equations. If there are two more variables than equations, there usually will be two parameters, and so on. What if there are fewer variables than equations? For example, consider the system

$$2x + 3y = 8 \tag{1}$$
$$x - y = 4 \tag{2}$$
$$5x + y = 7, \tag{3}$$

which has three equations and two variables. Since each of these equations has a line as its graph, there are various possibilities: three lines that intersect at a common point, three lines that cross at three different points, three lines of which two are the same line so that the intersection would be a point, three lines of which two are parallel so that the intersection would be two different points, three lines which are all parallel so that there would be no intersection, and so on. As in the case of n equations with n variables, the possibilities result in a unique solution, no solution, or an infinite number of solutions.

To solve the system using the echelon method, begin by exchanging equations (1) and (2) to get a 1 for the coefficient of x in the first equation.

$$x - y = 4 \tag{2}$$
$$2x + 3y = 8 \tag{1}$$
$$5x + y = 7 \tag{3}$$

Now multiply both sides of equation (2) by -2 and add the result to equation (1) to get $5y = 0$. The new system is

$$x - y = 4 \tag{2}$$
$$5y = 0 \tag{4}$$
$$5x + y = 7. \tag{3}$$

Multiply both sides of equation (4) by 1/5 to get $y = 0$. Substituting $y = 0$ leads to $x = 4$ in equation (2) and $x = 7/5$ in equation (3), a contradiction. This contradiction shows that the system has no solution.

Applications   If the mathematical techniques of this text are to be useful, you must be able to apply them to practical problems. To do this, always begin by reading the problem carefully. Then identify what must be found. Each unknown quantity should be represented by a variable. It is a good idea to *write down* exactly what each variable represents. Then reread the problem, looking for all necessary data. Write that down, too. Finally, look for one or more sentences which lead to equations or inequalities. The next example illustrates these steps.

EXAMPLE 7

A bank teller has a total of 70 bills, of five-, ten- and twenty-dollar denominations. The number of fives is three times the number of tens, while the total value of the money is $960. Find the number of each type of bill.

Let x be the number of fives, y the number of tens, and z the number of twenties. Then, since the total number of bills is 70,

$$x + y + z = 70.$$

Also the number of fives, x, is 3 times the number of tens, y.

$$x = 3y$$

Finally, the total value is $960. The value of the fives is $5x$, of the tens is $10y$, and of the twenties is $20z$, so that

$$5x + 10y + 20z = 960.$$

Rewriting the second equation as $x - 3y = 0$ gives the system

$$
\begin{aligned}
x + \quad y + \quad z &= 70 & \textbf{(1)} \\
x - \quad 3y \quad\quad &= 0 & \textbf{(2)} \\
5x + 10y + 20z &= 960. & \textbf{(3)}
\end{aligned}
$$

To solve by the echelon method, first eliminate x from equation (2). Do this by multiplying both sides of equation (1) by -1 and adding to equation (2). Then multiply both sides of the result by $-1/4$. The new system is

$$
\begin{aligned}
x + \quad y + \quad z &= 70 & \textbf{(1)} \\
y + \tfrac{1}{4}z &= \tfrac{35}{2} & \textbf{(4)} \\
5x + 10y + 20z &= 960. & \textbf{(3)}
\end{aligned}
$$

Use a similar procedure to eliminate x from equation (3) to get the system

$$
\begin{aligned}
x + y + \quad z &= 70 & \textbf{(1)} \\
y + \tfrac{1}{4}z &= \tfrac{35}{2} & \textbf{(4)} \\
5y + 15z &= 610. & \textbf{(5)}
\end{aligned}
$$

To eliminate y from equation (5), multiply both sides of equation (4) by -5 and add to equation (5). The final equivalent system is

$$x + y + z = 70 \tag{1}$$

$$y + \frac{1}{4}z = \frac{35}{2} \tag{5}$$

$$\frac{55}{4}z = \frac{1045}{2}. \tag{6}$$

Equation (6) gives $z = 38$. Substituting this result into equation (5) gives $y = 8$, and finally, from equation (1), $x = 24$. The teller had 24 fives, 8 tens, and 38 twenties. Check this answer in the words of the original problem. ■

2.1 EXERCISES

Use the elimination method to solve the systems of two equations in two unknowns in Exercises 1–16. Check your answers.

1. $x + y = 9$
$2x - y = 0$

2. $4x + y = 9$
$3x - y = 5$

3. $5x + 3y = 7$
$7x - 3y = -19$

4. $2x + 7y = -8$
$-2x + 3y = -12$

5. $3x + 2y = -6$
$5x - 2y = -10$

6. $-6x + 2y = 8$
$5x - 2y = -8$

7. $2x - 3y = -7$
$5x + 4y = 17$

8. $4m + 3n = -1$
$2m + 5n = 3$

9. $5p + 7q = 6$
$10p - 3q = 46$

10. $12s - 5t = 9$
$3s - 8t = -18$

11. $6x + 7y = -2$
$7x - 6y = 26$

12. $2a + 9b = 3$
$5a + 7b = -8$

13. $3x + 2y = 5$
$6x + 4y = 8$

14. $9x - 5y = 1$
$-18x + 10y = 1$

15. $4x - y = 9$
$-8x + 2y = -18$

16. $3x + 5y + 2 = 0$
$9x + 15y + 6 = 0$

In Exercises 17–20, first multiply both sides of each equation by its common denominator to eliminate the fractions. Then use the elimination method to solve. Check your answers.

17. $\dfrac{x}{2} + \dfrac{y}{3} = 8$
$\dfrac{2x}{3} + \dfrac{3y}{2} = 17$

18. $\dfrac{x}{5} + 3y = 31$
$2x - \dfrac{y}{5} = 8$

19. $\dfrac{x}{2} + y = \dfrac{3}{2}$
$\dfrac{x}{3} + y = \dfrac{1}{3}$

20. $x + \dfrac{y}{3} = -6$
$\dfrac{x}{5} + \dfrac{y}{4} = -\dfrac{7}{4}$

In Exercises 21–34, use the echelon method to solve each of the systems of three equations in three unknowns. Check your answers.

21. $x + y + z = 2$
$2x + y - z = 5$
$x - y + z = -2$

22. $2x + y + z = 9$
$-x - y + z = 1$
$3x - y + z = 9$

23. $x + 3y + 4z = 14$
$2x - 3y + 2z = 10$
$3x - y + z = 9$

24. $4x - y + 3z = -2$
$3x + 5y - z = 15$
$-2x + y + 4z = 14$

25. $x + 2y + 3z = 8$
$3x - y + 2z = 5$
$-2x - 4y - 6z = 5$

26. $3x - 2y - 8z = 1$
$9x - 6y - 24z = -2$
$x - y + z = 1$

27. $2x - 4y + z = -4$
$x + 2y - z = 0$
$-x + y + z = 6$

28. $4x - 3y + z = 9$
$3x + 2y - 2z = 4$
$x - y + 3z = 5$

29. $x + 4y - z = 6$
$2x - y + z = 3$
$3x + 2y + 3z = 16$

30. $3x + y - z = 7$
$2x - 3y + z = -7$
$x - 4y + 3z = -6$

31. $5m + n - 3p = -6$
$2m + 3n + p = 5$
$-3m - 2n + 4p = 3$

32. $2r - 5s + 4t = -35$
$5r + 3s - t = 1$
$r + s + t = 1$

33. $a - 3b - 2c = -3$
$3a + 2b - c = 12$
$-a - b + 4c = 3$

34. $2x + 2y + 2z = 6$
$3x - 3y - 4z = -1$
$x + y + 3z = 11$

Solve the systems of equations in Exercises 35–40. Let x be the parameter.

35. $5x + 3y + 4z = 19$
$3x - y + z = -4$

36. $3x + y - z = 0$
$2x - y + 3z = -7$

37. $x + 2y + 3z = 11$
$2x - y + z = 2$

38. $-x + y - z = -7$
$2x + 3y + z = 7$

39. $x + y - z + 2w = -20$
$2x - y + z + w = 11$
$3x - 2y + z - 2w = 27$

40. $4x + 3y + z + 2w = 1$
$-2x - y + 2z + 3w = 0$
$x + 4y + z - w = 12$

Solve each of the systems of equations in Exercises 41–46.

41. $5x + 2y = 7$
$-2x + y = -10$
$x - 3y = 15$

42. $9x - 2y = -14$
$3x + y = -4$
$-6x - 2y = 8$

43. $x + 7y = 5$
$4x - 3y = 2$
$-x + 2y = 10$

44. $-3x - 2y = 11$
$x + 2y = -14$
$5x + y = -9$

45. $x + y = 2$
$y + z = 4$
$x + z = 3$
$y - z = 8$

46. $2x + y = 7$
$x + 3z = 5$
$y - 2z = 6$
$x + 4y = 10$

Write a system of equations for Exercises 47–52; then solve the system.

47. A working couple earned a total of $4352. The wife earned $64 per day; the husband earned $8 per day less. Find the number of days each worked if the total number of days worked by both was 72.

48. Midtown Manufacturing Company makes two products, plastic plates and plastic cups. Both require time on two machines: a batch of plates—one hour on machine A and two hours on machine B; a batch of cups—three hours on machine A and one hour on machine B. Both machines operate 15 hours a day. How many batches of each product can be produced in a day under these conditions?

49. A company produces two models of bicycles, model 201 and model 301. Model 201 requires 2 hours of assembly time and model 301 requires 3 hours of assembly time. The parts for model 201 cost $25 per bike and the parts for model 301 cost $30 per bike. If the company has a total of 34 hours of assembly time and $365 available per day for these two models, how many of each can be made in a day?

50. Juanita invests $10,000, received from her grandmother, in three ways. With one part, she buys mutual funds which offer a return of 8% per year. The second part, which amounts to twice the first, is used to buy government bonds at 9% per year. She puts the rest in the bank at 5% annual interest. The first year her investments bring a return of $830. How much did she invest in each way?

51. To get the necessary funds for a planned expansion, a small company took out three loans totaling $25,000. The company was able to borrow some of the money at 16%. They borrowed $2000 more than one-half the amount of the 16% loan at 20%, and the rest at 18%. The total annual interest on the loans was $4440. How much did they borrow at each rate?

52. The business analyst for Midtown Manufacturing wants to find an equation which can be used to project sales of a relatively new product. For the years 1982, 1983, and 1984 sales were \$15,000, \$32,000, and \$123,000 respectively.

   (a) Graph the sales for the years 1982, 1983, and 1984 letting the year 1982 equal 0 on the x-axis. Let the values on the vertical axis be in thousands. [For example, the point (1983, 32,000) will be graphed as (1, 32).]

   (b) Find the equation of the straight line $ax + by = c$ through the points for 1982 and 1984.

   (c) Find the equation of the parabola $y = ax^2 + bx + c$ through the three given points.

   (d) Find the projected sales for 1987 first by using the equation from part (b) and second, by using the equation from part (c). If you were to estimate sales of the product in 1987 which result would you choose? Why?

In Exercises 53 and 54, find the value of k for which each system has a single solution, then find the solution of the system.

53.
$$\begin{aligned} 4x \quad\quad + 8z &= 12 \\ 2y - z &= -2 \\ 3x + y + z &= -1 \\ x + y - kz &= -7 \end{aligned}$$

54.
$$\begin{aligned} 2x + y + z &= 4 \\ 3y + z &= -2 \\ x + y - z &= -3 \\ 4x \quad\quad + kz &= 8 \end{aligned}$$

2.2   Solution of Linear Systems by the Gauss-Jordan Method

In the last section the echelon method was used to solve linear systems of equations. Since the variables are always the same, we really need to keep track of just the coefficients and the constants. For example, let's look at the system we solved in Examples 4 and 5 of the previous section,

$$\begin{aligned} 2x + y - z &= 2 \\ x + 3y + 2z &= 1 \\ x + y + z &= 2. \end{aligned}$$

This system can be written in an abbreviated form as

$$\begin{bmatrix} 2 & 1 & -1 & 2 \\ 1 & 3 & 2 & 1 \\ 1 & 1 & 1 & 2 \end{bmatrix}.$$

Such a rectangular array of numbers enclosed by brackets is called a **matrix** (plural: **matrices**). Each number in the array is an **element** or **entry**. To separate the constants in the last column of the matrix from the coefficients of the variables, use a vertical line, producing the following **augmented matrix.**

$$\begin{bmatrix} 2 & 1 & -1 & \bigm| & 2 \\ 1 & 3 & 2 & \bigm| & 1 \\ 1 & 1 & 1 & \bigm| & 2 \end{bmatrix}$$

The rows of the augmented matrix can be transformed in the same way as the equations of the system, since the matrix is just a shortened form of the system. The **row operations** on the augmented matrix which correspond to the transformations of systems of equations are given in the following theorem.

Row Operations

For any augmented matrix of a system of equations, the following operations produce the augmented matrix of an equivalent system:

1. interchanging any two rows;
2. multiplying the elements of a row by any nonzero real number;
3. adding a multiple of the elements of one row to the corresponding elements of some other row.

Row operations, like the transformations of systems of equations, are reversible. If they are used to go from matrix A to matrix B, then it is possible to use row operations to transform B back into A. In addition to their use in solving equations, row operations are very important in the simplex method of Chapter 4.

By the first row operation, the matrix

$$\begin{bmatrix} 1 & 3 & 5 & 6 \\ 0 & 1 & 2 & 3 \\ 2 & 1 & -2 & -5 \end{bmatrix} \quad \text{becomes} \quad \begin{bmatrix} 0 & 1 & 2 & 3 \\ 1 & 3 & 5 & 6 \\ 2 & 1 & -2 & -5 \end{bmatrix}$$

by interchanging the first two rows. Row three is left unchanged.

The second row operation allows us to change

$$\begin{bmatrix} 1 & 3 & 5 & 6 \\ 0 & 1 & 2 & 3 \\ 2 & 1 & -2 & -5 \end{bmatrix} \quad \text{to} \quad \begin{bmatrix} -2 & -6 & -10 & -12 \\ 0 & 1 & 2 & 3 \\ 2 & 1 & -2 & -5 \end{bmatrix}$$

by multiplying the elements of the first row of the original matrix by -2. Note that rows two and three are left unchanged.

Using the third row operation,

$$\begin{bmatrix} 1 & 3 & 5 & 6 \\ 0 & 1 & 2 & 3 \\ 2 & 1 & -2 & -5 \end{bmatrix} \quad \text{becomes} \quad \begin{bmatrix} -1 & 2 & 7 & 11 \\ 0 & 1 & 2 & 3 \\ 2 & 1 & -2 & -5 \end{bmatrix}$$

after first multiplying each element in the third row of the original matrix by -1 and then adding the results to the corresponding elements in the first row of that matrix. Work as follows.

$$\begin{bmatrix} 1 + 2(-1) & 3 + 1(-1) & 5 + (-2)(-1) & 6 + (-5)(-1) \\ 0 & 1 & 2 & 3 \\ 2 & 1 & -2 & -5 \end{bmatrix} = \begin{bmatrix} -1 & 2 & 7 & 11 \\ 0 & 1 & 2 & 3 \\ 2 & 1 & -2 & -5 \end{bmatrix}$$

Again rows two and three are left unchanged, *even though the elements of row three were used to transform row one.*

The Gauss-Jordan Method   The *Gauss-Jordan method* is an extension of the echelon method of solving systems. Before the Gauss-Jordan method can be used, the system must be in proper form: the terms with variables should be on the left and the constants on the right in each equation, with the variables in the same order in each equation. The following example illustrates the use of the Gauss-Jordan method to solve a system of equations.

EXAMPLE 1

Solve the system

$$3x - 4y = 1 \tag{1}$$
$$5x + 2y = 19. \tag{2}$$

The system is already in the proper form. The solution procedure is parallel to the echelon method of Section 2.1, except for the last step. We show the echelon method on the left below and the Gauss-Jordan method on the right. First, write the augmented matrix for the system.

Echelon Method

$$3x - 4y = 1 \tag{1}$$
$$5x + 2y = 19 \tag{2}$$

Multiply both sides of equation (1) by 1/3 so that x has a coefficient of 1.

$$x - \frac{4}{3}y = \frac{1}{3} \tag{3}$$
$$5x + 2y = 19 \tag{2}$$

Eliminate x from equation (2) by adding -5 times equation (3) to equation (2).

$$x - \frac{4}{3}y = \frac{1}{3} \tag{3}$$
$$\frac{26}{3}y = \frac{52}{3} \tag{4}$$

Multiply both sides of equation (4) by 3/26 to get $y = 2$.

$$x - \frac{4}{3}y = \frac{1}{3} \tag{3}$$
$$y = 2 \tag{5}$$

Substitute $y = 2$ into equation (3) and solve for x to get $x = 3$.

$$x = 3 \tag{6}$$
$$y = 2 \tag{5}$$

Gauss-Jordan Method

$$\begin{bmatrix} 3 & -4 & | & 1 \\ 5 & 2 & | & 19 \end{bmatrix}$$

Using row operation (2), multiply each element of row 1 by 1/3.

$$\begin{bmatrix} 1 & -\frac{4}{3} & | & \frac{1}{3} \\ 5 & 2 & | & 19 \end{bmatrix}$$

Using row operation (3), add -5 times the elements of row 1 to the elements of row 2.

$$\begin{bmatrix} 1 & -\frac{4}{3} & | & \frac{1}{3} \\ 0 & \frac{26}{3} & | & \frac{52}{3} \end{bmatrix}$$

Multiply the elements of row 2 by 3/26, using row operation (2).

$$\begin{bmatrix} 1 & -\frac{4}{3} & | & \frac{1}{3} \\ 0 & 1 & | & 2 \end{bmatrix}$$

Multiply the elements of row 2 by 4/3 and add to the elements of row 1 (row operation (3)).

$$\begin{bmatrix} 1 & 0 & | & 3 \\ 0 & 1 & | & 2 \end{bmatrix}$$

The solution of the system, (3, 2), can be read directly from the last column of the final matrix. ∎

In the final matrix above, the columns to the left of the vertical line were transformed into the 2 × 2 identity matrix. When using row operations to transform the matrix, it is best to work column by column from left to right. For each column, the first change should produce a 1 in the proper position. Next, perform the steps that give zeros in the remainder of the column. Then proceed to the next column in the matrix.

EXAMPLE 2

Use the Gauss-Jordan method to solve the system

$$x + 5z = -6 + y$$
$$3x + 3y = 10 + z$$
$$x + 3y + 2z = 5.$$

First, rewrite the system in proper form as follows.

$$x - y + 5z = -6$$
$$3x + 3y - z = 10$$
$$x + 3y + 2z = 5$$

Begin the solution by writing the augmented matrix of the linear system.

$$\begin{bmatrix} 1 & -1 & 5 & -6 \\ 3 & 3 & -1 & 10 \\ 1 & 3 & 2 & 5 \end{bmatrix}$$

Our method of solution will be to use row transformations to rewrite this matrix in the form

$$\begin{bmatrix} 1 & 0 & 0 & m \\ 0 & 1 & 0 & n \\ 0 & 0 & 1 & p \end{bmatrix},$$

where m, n, and p are real numbers. From this final form of the matrix, the solution can be read: $x = m$, $y = n$, and $z = p$.

There is already a 1 for the first element in column one. To get 0 for the second element in column one, multiply each element in the first row by -3 and add the results to the corresponding elements in row two (using row operation (3)).

$$\begin{bmatrix} 1 & -1 & 5 & -6 \\ 0 & 6 & -16 & 28 \\ 1 & 3 & 2 & 5 \end{bmatrix}$$

To change the last element in column one to 0, multiply each element in the first row by -1 and add each result to the corresponding elements of the third row (again using row operation (3)).

$$\begin{bmatrix} 1 & -1 & 5 & -6 \\ 0 & 6 & -16 & 28 \\ 0 & 4 & -3 & 11 \end{bmatrix}$$

This transforms the first column. Transform the second and third columns in a similar manner.

$$\begin{bmatrix} 1 & -1 & 5 & | & -6 \\ 0 & 1 & -\frac{8}{3} & | & \frac{14}{3} \\ 0 & 4 & -3 & | & 11 \end{bmatrix}$$ Second row multiplied by $\frac{1}{6}$ [row operation (2)]

$$\begin{bmatrix} 1 & 0 & \frac{7}{3} & | & -\frac{4}{3} \\ 0 & 1 & -\frac{8}{3} & | & \frac{14}{3} \\ 0 & 4 & -3 & | & 11 \end{bmatrix}$$ Second row added to first row [row operation (3)]

$$\begin{bmatrix} 1 & 0 & \frac{7}{3} & | & -\frac{4}{3} \\ 0 & 1 & -\frac{8}{3} & | & \frac{14}{3} \\ 0 & 0 & \frac{23}{3} & | & -\frac{23}{3} \end{bmatrix}$$ -4 times second row added to third row [row operation (3)]

$$\begin{bmatrix} 1 & 0 & \frac{7}{3} & | & -\frac{4}{3} \\ 0 & 1 & -\frac{8}{3} & | & \frac{14}{3} \\ 0 & 0 & 1 & | & -1 \end{bmatrix}$$ Third row multiplied by $\frac{3}{23}$ [row operation (2)]

$$\begin{bmatrix} 1 & 0 & 0 & | & 1 \\ 0 & 1 & -\frac{8}{3} & | & \frac{14}{3} \\ 0 & 0 & 1 & | & -1 \end{bmatrix}$$ $-\dfrac{7}{3}$ times third row added to first row [row operation (3)]

$$\begin{bmatrix} 1 & 0 & 0 & | & 1 \\ 0 & 1 & 0 & | & 2 \\ 0 & 0 & 1 & | & -1 \end{bmatrix}$$ $\dfrac{8}{3}$ times third row added to second row [row operation (3)]

The linear system associated with the final augmented matrix is

$$\begin{aligned} x &= 1 \\ y &= 2 \\ z &= -1, \end{aligned}$$

and the solution is $(1, 2, -1)$. ▓

In summary, the Gauss-Jordan method of solving a linear system requires the following steps.

The Gauss-Jordan Method of Solving a Linear System

1. Write all equations with variable terms on the left and constants on the right. Be sure the variables are in the same order in all equations.
2. Write the augmented matrix that corresponds to the system.
3. Use row operations to transform the first column so that the first element is 1 and the remaining elements are 0.
4. Use row operations to transform the second column so that the second element is 1 and the remaining elements are 0.
5. Use row operations to transform the third column so that the third element is 1 and the remaining elements are 0.
6. Continue in this way until the last row is in the form $[0 \quad 0 \quad 0 \ldots$ $0 \quad 1 \mid k]$, where k is a constant.

EXAMPLE 3

Use the Gauss-Jordan method to solve the system

$$x + y = 2$$
$$2x + 2y = 5.$$

Begin by writing the augmented matrix.

$$\begin{bmatrix} 1 & 1 & | & 2 \\ 2 & 2 & | & 5 \end{bmatrix}$$

The first element in column one is already 1. To get a 0 for the second element in column one, multiply the numbers in row one by -2 and add the results to the corresponding elements in row two.

$$\begin{bmatrix} 1 & 1 & | & 2 \\ 0 & 0 & | & 1 \end{bmatrix}$$

The next step is to get a 1 for the second element in column two. Since this is impossible, we cannot go further. This matrix leads to the system

$$x + y = 2$$
$$0x + 0y = 1.$$

Since the second equation is $0 = 1$, the system is inconsistent and has no solution. The row $\begin{bmatrix} 0 & 0 & | & 1 \end{bmatrix}$ is a signal that the given system is inconsistent. ▪

EXAMPLE 4

Use the Gauss-Jordan method to solve the system

$$x + 2y - z = 0$$
$$3x - y + z = 6$$
$$-2x - 4y + 2z = 0.$$

The augmented matrix is

$$\begin{bmatrix} 1 & 2 & -1 & | & 0 \\ 3 & -1 & 1 & | & 6 \\ -2 & -4 & 2 & | & 0 \end{bmatrix}.$$

The first element in column one is 1. Use row operations to get zeros in the rest of column one.

$$\begin{bmatrix} 1 & 2 & -1 & | & 0 \\ 0 & -7 & 4 & | & 6 \\ -2 & -4 & 2 & | & 0 \end{bmatrix}$$

$$\begin{bmatrix} 1 & 2 & -1 & | & 0 \\ 0 & -7 & 4 & | & 6 \\ 0 & 0 & 0 & | & 0 \end{bmatrix}$$

The row of all zeros in the last matrix is a signal that two of the equations (the first and last) are dependent. Continuing, multiply row 2 by $-1/7$.

$$\begin{bmatrix} 1 & 2 & -1 & | & 0 \\ 0 & 1 & -\frac{4}{7} & | & -\frac{6}{7} \\ 0 & 0 & 0 & | & 0 \end{bmatrix}$$

Finally, add -2 times row 2 to row 1.

$$\begin{bmatrix} 1 & 0 & \frac{1}{7} & \frac{12}{7} \\ 0 & 1 & -\frac{4}{7} & -\frac{6}{7} \\ 0 & 0 & 0 & 0 \end{bmatrix}$$

This is as far as we can go with the Gauss-Jordan Method. To complete the solution write the equations that correspond to the first two lines of the matrix.

$$x \quad + \frac{1}{7}z = \frac{12}{7}$$

$$y - \frac{4}{7}z = -\frac{6}{7}$$

Solving the first equation for x and the second equation for y gives

$$x = -\frac{1}{7}z + \frac{12}{7} \quad \text{and} \quad y = \frac{4}{7}z - \frac{6}{7}.$$

The solution may be written

$$\left\{ \left(-\frac{1}{7}z + \frac{12}{7}, \frac{4}{7}z - \frac{6}{7}, z \right) \right\}. \quad \blacksquare$$

Although the examples have used only systems with two equations and variables or three equations and variables, the Gauss-Jordan method can be used for any system with n equations and n variables. In fact, it can be used with n equations and m variables, as Example 4 illustrated. The system in Example 4 actually had just two equations with three variables. The method does become tedious even with three equations and three variables. However, it is very suitable for use by computers. A computer can produce the solution to a fairly large system very quickly.*

2.2 EXERCISES

Write the augmented matrix for each of the systems in Exercises 1–10. **Do not solve.**

1. $2x + 3y = 11$
$\quad x + 2y = 8$

2. $3x + 5y = -13$
$\quad 2x + 3y = -9$

3. $x = 6 - 5y$
$\quad\quad y = 1$

4. $7y = 1 - 2x$
$\quad 5x = -15$

5. $2x + y + z = 3$
$\quad 3x - 4y + 2z = -7$
$\quad x + y + z = 2$

6. $4x - 2y + 3z = 4$
$\quad 3x + 5y + z = 7$
$\quad 5x - y + 4z = 7$

---

*See D. R. Coscia, *Computer Applications for Finite Mathematics and Calculus,* Scott, Foresman and Company, 1986.

7. $\begin{aligned} y &= 2 - x \\ 2y &= -4 - z \\ z &= 2 \end{aligned}$

8. $\begin{aligned} x &= 6 \\ y &= 2 - 2z \\ x &= 6 + 3z \end{aligned}$

9. $\begin{aligned} x &= 5 \\ y &= -2 \\ z &= 3 \end{aligned}$

10. $\begin{aligned} x &= 8 \\ y + z &= 6 \\ z &= 2 \end{aligned}$

Write the system of equations associated with each of the augmented matrices in Exercises 11–16. **Do not solve.**

11. $\begin{bmatrix} 1 & 0 & | & 2 \\ 0 & 1 & | & 3 \end{bmatrix}$

12. $\begin{bmatrix} 1 & 0 & | & 5 \\ 0 & 1 & | & -3 \end{bmatrix}$

13. $\begin{bmatrix} 2 & 1 & | & 1 \\ 3 & -2 & | & -9 \end{bmatrix}$

14. $\begin{bmatrix} 1 & -5 & | & -18 \\ 6 & 2 & | & 20 \end{bmatrix}$

15. $\begin{bmatrix} 1 & 0 & 0 & | & 2 \\ 0 & 1 & 0 & | & 3 \\ 0 & 0 & 1 & | & -2 \end{bmatrix}$

16. $\begin{bmatrix} 1 & 0 & 1 & | & 4 \\ 0 & 1 & 0 & | & 2 \\ 0 & 0 & 1 & | & 3 \end{bmatrix}$

Use the Gauss-Jordan method to solve the systems of equations in Exercises 17–42.

17. $\begin{aligned} x + y &= 5 \\ x - y &= -1 \end{aligned}$

18. $\begin{aligned} x + 2y &= 5 \\ 2x + y &= -2 \end{aligned}$

19. $\begin{aligned} x + y &= -3 \\ 2x - 5y &= -6 \end{aligned}$

20. $\begin{aligned} 3x - 2y &= 4 \\ 3x + y &= -2 \end{aligned}$

21. $\begin{aligned} 2x &= 10 + 3y \\ 2y &= 5 - 2x \end{aligned}$

22. $\begin{aligned} y &= 5 - 4x \\ 2x &= 3 - y \end{aligned}$

23. $\begin{aligned} 2x - 5y &= 10 \\ 4x - 5y &= 15 \end{aligned}$

24. $\begin{aligned} 4x - 2y &= 3 \\ -2x + 3y &= 1 \end{aligned}$

25. $\begin{aligned} 2x - 3y &= 2 \\ 4x - 6y &= 1 \end{aligned}$

26. $\begin{aligned} x + 2y &= 1 \\ 2x + 4y &= 3 \end{aligned}$

27. $\begin{aligned} 6x - 3y &= 1 \\ -12x + 6y &= -2 \end{aligned}$

28. $\begin{aligned} x - y &= 1 \\ -x + y &= -1 \end{aligned}$

29. $\begin{aligned} x + y &= -1 \\ y + z &= 4 \\ x + z &= 1 \end{aligned}$

30. $\begin{aligned} x - z &= -3 \\ y + z &= 9 \\ x + z &= 7 \end{aligned}$

31. $\begin{aligned} x + y - z &= 6 \\ 2x - y + z &= -9 \\ x - 2y + 3z &= 1 \end{aligned}$

32. $\begin{aligned} x + 3y - 6z &= 7 \\ 2x - y + 2z &= 0 \\ x + y + 2z &= -1 \end{aligned}$

33. $\begin{aligned} y &= x - 1 \\ y &= 6 + z \\ z &= -1 - x \end{aligned}$

34. $\begin{aligned} x &= 1 - y \\ 2x &= z \\ 2z &= -2 - y \end{aligned}$

35. $\begin{aligned} x - 2y + z &= 5 \\ 2x + y - z &= 2 \\ -2x + 4y - 2z &= 2 \end{aligned}$

36. $\begin{aligned} 3x + 5y - z &= 0 \\ 4x - y + 2z &= 1 \\ -6x - 10y + 2z &= 0 \end{aligned}$

37. $\begin{aligned} 2x + 3y + z &= 9 \\ 4x + y - 3z &= -7 \\ 6x + 2y - 4z &= -8 \end{aligned}$

38. $\begin{aligned} 3x + 2y - z &= -16 \\ 6x - 4y + 3z &= 12 \\ 3x + 3y + z &= -11 \end{aligned}$

39. $\begin{aligned} 5x - 4y + 2z &= 4 \\ 10x + 3y - z &= 27 \\ 15x - 5y + 3z &= 25 \end{aligned}$

40. $\begin{aligned} 4x - 2y - 3z &= -23 \\ -4x + 3y + z &= 11 \\ 8x - 5y + 4z &= 6 \end{aligned}$

41. $\begin{aligned} x + 2y - w &= 3 \\ 2x + 4z + 2w &= -6 \\ x + 2y - z &= 6 \\ 2x - y + z + w &= -3 \end{aligned}$

42. $\begin{aligned} x + 3y - 2z - w &= 9 \\ 2x + 4y + 2w &= 10 \\ -3x - 5y + 2z - w &= -15 \\ x - y - 3z + 2w &= 6 \end{aligned}$

43. At rush hours, substantial traffic congestion is encountered at the traffic intersections shown in the figure. (The streets are all one way.)

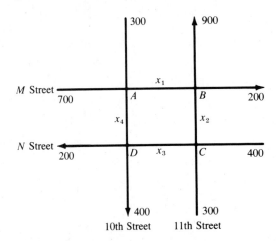

The city wishes to improve the signals at these corners so as to speed the flow of traffic. The traffic engineers first gather data. As the figure shows, 700 cars per hour come down M Street to intersection A; 300 cars per hour come to intersection A on 10th Street. A total of x_1 of these cars leave A on M Street, while x_4 cars leave A on 10th Street. The number of cars entering A must equal the number leaving, so that

$$x_1 + x_4 = 700 + 300$$
or
$$x_1 + x_4 = 1000.$$

For intersection B, x_1 cars enter B on M Street, and x_2 cars enter B on 11th Street. The figure shows that 900 cars leave B on 11th while 200 leave on M. We have

$$x_1 + x_2 = 900 + 200$$
$$x_1 + x_2 = 1100.$$

At intersection C, 400 cars enter on N Street, 300 on 11th Street, while x_2 leave on 11th Street and x_3 leave on N Street. This gives

$$x_2 + x_3 = 400 + 300$$
$$x_2 + x_3 = 700.$$

Finally, intersection D has x_3 cars entering on N and x_4 entering on 10th. There are 400 leaving D on 10th and 200 leaving on N, so that

$$x_3 + x_4 = 400 + 200$$
$$x_3 + x_4 = 600.$$

(a) Use the four equations to set up an augmented matrix, and then use the Gauss-Jordan method to solve it. (Hint: keep going until you get a row of all zeros.)

(b) Since you got a row of all zeros, the system of equations does not have a unique solution. Write three equations, corresponding to the three nonzero rows of the matrix.

(c) Solve each of the equations for x_4.

(d) One of your equations should have been $x_4 = 1000 - x_1$. What is the largest possible value of x_1 so that x_4 is not negative? What is the largest value of x_4 so that x_1 is not negative?

(e) Your second equation should have been $x_4 = x_2 - 100$. Find the smallest possible value of x_2 so that x_4 is not negative.

(f) For the third equation, $x_4 = 600 - x_3$, find the largest possible values of x_3 and x_4 so that neither variable is negative.

(g) Look at your answers for parts (d)–(f). What is the maximum value of x_4 so that all the equations are satisfied and all variables are nonnegative? Of x_3? Of x_2? Of x_1?

44. A manufacturer purchases a part for use at both of its two plants—one at Roseville, California, the other at Akron, Ohio. The part is available in limited quantities from two suppliers. Each supplier has 75 units available. The Roseville plant needs 40 units and the Akron plant requires 75 units. The first supplier charges $70 per unit delivered to Roseville and $90 per unit delivered to Akron. Corresponding costs from the second supplier are $80 and $120. The manufacturer wants to order a total of 75 units from the first, less expensive, supplier, with the remaining 40 units to come from the second supplier. If the company spends $10,750 to purchase the required number of units for the two plants, find the number of units that should be purchased from each supplier for each plant as follows:

(a) Assign variables to the four unknowns.

(b) Write a system of five equations with the four variables. (Not all equations will involve all four variables.)

(c) Use the Gauss-Jordan method to solve the system of equations.

Solve the linear systems in Exercises 45–48.

45.
$$2.1x + 3.5y + 9.4z = 15.6$$
$$6.8x - 1.5y + 7.5z = 26.4$$
$$3.7x + 2.5y - 6.1z = 18.7$$

46.
$$9.03x - 5.91y + 2.68z = 29.5$$
$$3.94x + 6.82y + 1.53z = 35.4$$
$$2.79x + 1.68y - 6.23z = 12.1$$

47.
$$10.47x + 3.52y + 2.58z - 6.42w = 218.65$$
$$8.62x - 4.93y - 1.75z + 2.83w = 157.03$$
$$4.92x + 6.83y - 2.97z + 2.65w = 462.3$$
$$2.86x + 19.1y - 6.24z - 8.73w = 398.4$$

48.
$$28.6x + 94.5y + 16.0z - 2.94w = 198.3$$
$$16.7x + 44.3y - 27.3z + 8.9w = 254.7$$
$$12.5x - 38.7y + 92.5z + 22.4w = 562.7$$
$$40.1x - 28.3y + 17.5z - 10.2w = 375.4$$

In Exercises 49–52, write a system of equations and then solve it.

49. Natural Brand plant food is made from three chemicals. The mix must include 10.8% of the first chemical and the other two chemicals must be in the ratio of 4 to 3 as measured by weight. How much of each chemical is required to make 750 kilograms of the plant food?

50. Three species of bacteria are fed three foods, I, II, and III. A bacterium of the first species consumes 1.3 units each of foods I and II and 2.3 units of food III each day. A bacterium of the second species consumes 1.1 units of food I, 2.4 units of food II, and 3.7 units of food III each day. A bacterium of the third species consumes 8.1 units of I, 2.9 units of II, and 5.1 units of III each day. If 16,000 units of I, 28,000 units of II, and 44,000 units of III are supplied each day, how many of each species can be maintained in this environment?

51. A lake is stocked each spring with three species of fish, A, B, and C. Three foods, I, II, and III, are available in the lake. Each fish of species A requires 1.32 units of food I, 2.9 units of food II, and 1.75 units of food III on the average each day. Species B fish each require 2.1 units of food I, .95 unit of food II, and .6 unit of food III daily. Species C fish require .86, 1.52, and 2.01 units of I, II, and III per day, respectively. If 490 units of food I, 897 units of food II, and 653 units of food III are available daily, how many of each species should be stocked?

52. A company produces three combinations of mixed vegetables which sell in one kilogram packages. Italian style combines .3 kilogram of zucchini, .3 of broccoli, and .4 of carrots. French style combines .6 kilogram of broccoli and .4 of carrots. Oriental style combines .2 kilogram of zucchini, .5 of broccoli, and .3 of carrots. The company has a stock of 16,200 kilograms of zucchini, 41,400 kilograms of broccoli, and 29,400 kilograms of carrots. How many packages of each style should they prepare to use up their supplies?

2.3   Basic Matrix Operations

In the last section we saw how a matrix is used to represent a system of linear equations. The study of matrices has been of interest to mathematicians for some time. Recently, however, the use of matrices has gained greater importance in the fields of management, natural science, and social science because matrices provide such a convenient way to organize data, as Example 1 demonstrates.

EXAMPLE 1

The EZ Life Company manufactures sofas and armchairs in three models, A, B, and C. The company has regional warehouses in New York, Chicago, and San Francisco. In its August shipment, the company sends 10 model A sofas, 12 model B sofas, 5 model C sofas, 15 model A chairs, 20 model B chairs, and 8 model C chairs to each warehouse.

To organize this data, we might first list it as follows.

| sofas | 10 model A | 12 model B | 5 model C |
| chairs | 15 model A | 20 model B | 8 model C |

Alternatively, we might tabulate the data in a chart.

		Model		
		A	B	C
Furniture	Sofas	10	12	5
	Chairs	15	20	8

With the understanding that the numbers in each row refer to the furniture type (sofa, chair) and the numbers in each column refer to the model (A, B, C), the same information can be given by a matrix, as follows.

$$M = \begin{bmatrix} 10 & 12 & 5 \\ 15 & 20 & 8 \end{bmatrix}$$ ▪

Matrices are classified by their **order** (or **dimension**), that is, by the number of rows and columns that they contain. For example, matrix M above has two rows and three columns. This matrix is of **order** 2×3 (read "2 by 3") or **dimension** 2×3. By definition, a matrix with m rows and n columns is of **order** $m \times n$. The number of rows is always given first.

EXAMPLE 2

(a)   The matrix $\begin{bmatrix} 6 & 5 \\ 3 & 4 \\ 5 & -1 \end{bmatrix}$ is of order 3×2.

(b) $\begin{bmatrix} 5 & 8 & 9 \\ 0 & 5 & -3 \\ -4 & 0 & 5 \end{bmatrix}$ is of order 3×3.

(c) $\begin{bmatrix} 1 & 6 & 5 & -2 & 5 \end{bmatrix}$ is of order 1×5.

(d) $\begin{bmatrix} 3 \\ -5 \\ 0 \\ 2 \end{bmatrix}$ is of order 4×1. ▪

A matrix with the same number of rows as columns is called a **square matrix.** The matrix in Example 2(b) above is a square matrix.

A matrix containing only one row is called a **row matrix.** The matrix in Example 2(c) is a row matrix, as are

$$\begin{bmatrix} 5 & 8 \end{bmatrix}, \qquad \begin{bmatrix} 6 & -9 & 2 \end{bmatrix}, \qquad \text{and} \qquad \begin{bmatrix} -4 & 0 & 0 & 0 \end{bmatrix}.$$

A matrix of only one column, as in Example 2(d), is a **column matrix.** Two matrices are **equal** if they are of the same order and if each pair of corresponding elements is equal. By this definition, the matrices

$$\begin{bmatrix} 2 & 1 \\ 3 & -5 \end{bmatrix} \qquad \text{and} \qquad \begin{bmatrix} 1 & 2 \\ -5 & 3 \end{bmatrix}$$

are not equal (even though they contain the same elements and are of the same order) since the corresponding elements differ.

EXAMPLE 3

(a)   From the definition of equality given above, the only way that the statement

$$\begin{bmatrix} 2 & 1 \\ p & q \end{bmatrix} = \begin{bmatrix} x & y \\ -1 & 0 \end{bmatrix}$$

can be true is if $2 = x$, $1 = y$, $p = -1$, and $q = 0$.

(b)   The statement

$$\begin{bmatrix} x \\ y \end{bmatrix} = \begin{bmatrix} 1 \\ 4 \\ 0 \end{bmatrix}$$

can never be true, since the two matrices are of different order. (One is 2×1 and the other is 3×1.)

Addition   The matrix given in Example 1,

$$M = \begin{bmatrix} 10 & 12 & 5 \\ 15 & 20 & 8 \end{bmatrix},$$

shows the August shipment from the EZ Life plant to its New York warehouse. If matrix N below gives the September shipment to the same warehouse, what is the total shipment for each item of furniture for these two months?

$$N = \begin{bmatrix} 45 & 35 & 20 \\ 65 & 40 & 35 \end{bmatrix}$$

If 10 model A sofas were shipped in August and 45 in September, then altogether $10 + 45 = 55$ model A sofas were shipped in the two months. The other corresponding entries can be added in a similar way, to get a new matrix, call it Q, which represents the total shipment for the two months.

$$Q = \begin{bmatrix} 55 & 47 & 25 \\ 80 & 60 & 43 \end{bmatrix}$$

It is convenient to refer to Q as the sum of M and N.

The way these two matrices were added illustrates the following definition of addition of matrices.

Addition of Matrices	**The sum** of two $m \times n$ matrices X and Y is the $m \times n$ matrix $X + Y$ in which each element is the sum of the corresponding elements of X and Y.

It is important to remember that only matrices with the same order or dimension can be added.

EXAMPLE 4

Find each sum when possible.

(a) $\begin{bmatrix} 5 & -6 \\ 8 & 9 \end{bmatrix} + \begin{bmatrix} -4 & 6 \\ 8 & -3 \end{bmatrix} = \begin{bmatrix} 5 + (-4) & -6 + 6 \\ 8 + 8 & 9 + (-3) \end{bmatrix} = \begin{bmatrix} 1 & 0 \\ 16 & 6 \end{bmatrix}$

(b) The matrices

$$A = \begin{bmatrix} 5 & 8 \\ 6 & 2 \end{bmatrix} \quad \text{and} \quad B = \begin{bmatrix} 3 & 9 & 1 \\ 4 & 2 & 5 \end{bmatrix}$$

are of different orders. Therefore, the sum $A + B$ does not exist. ▪

EXAMPLE 5

The September shipments from the EZ Life Company to the New York, San Francisco, and Chicago warehouses are given in matrices N, S, and C below.

$$N = \begin{bmatrix} 45 & 35 & 20 \\ 65 & 40 & 35 \end{bmatrix}, \quad S = \begin{bmatrix} 30 & 32 & 28 \\ 43 & 47 & 30 \end{bmatrix}, \quad C = \begin{bmatrix} 22 & 25 & 38 \\ 31 & 34 & 35 \end{bmatrix}$$

What was the total amount shipped to the three warehouses in September?

The total of the September shipments is represented by the sum of the three matrices N, S, and C.

$$N + S + C = \begin{bmatrix} 45 & 35 & 20 \\ 65 & 40 & 35 \end{bmatrix} + \begin{bmatrix} 30 & 32 & 28 \\ 43 & 47 & 30 \end{bmatrix} + \begin{bmatrix} 22 & 25 & 38 \\ 31 & 34 & 35 \end{bmatrix}$$

$$= \begin{bmatrix} 97 & 92 & 86 \\ 139 & 121 & 100 \end{bmatrix}$$

For example, this sum shows that the total number of model C sofas shipped to the three warehouses in September was 86. ▪

The **additive inverse** (or **negative**) of a matrix X is the matrix $-X$ in which each element is the additive inverse of the corresponding element of X. If

$$A = \begin{bmatrix} 1 & 2 & 3 \\ 0 & -1 & 5 \end{bmatrix} \quad \text{and} \quad B = \begin{bmatrix} -2 & 3 & 0 \\ 1 & -7 & 2 \end{bmatrix},$$

then by the definition of the additive inverse of a matrix,

$$-A = \begin{bmatrix} -1 & -2 & -3 \\ 0 & 1 & -5 \end{bmatrix} \quad \text{and} \quad -B = \begin{bmatrix} 2 & -3 & 0 \\ -1 & 7 & -2 \end{bmatrix}.$$

By the definition of matrix addition, for each matrix X the sum $X + (-X)$ is a **zero matrix**, O, whose elements are all zeros. There is an $m \times n$ zero matrix for each pair of values of m and n. Zero matrices have the following **identity property:** If O is an $m \times n$ zero matrix, and A is any $m \times n$ matrix, then

$$A + O = O + A = A.$$

Subtraction   The **subtraction** of matrices is defined in a manner comparable to subtraction for real numbers.

Subtraction of Matrices	For two $m \times n$ matrices X and Y, the **difference** of X and Y, or $X - Y$, is the matrix defined by $$X - Y = X + (-Y).$$

With A, B, and $-B$ as defined above,

$$A - B = A + (-B) = \begin{bmatrix} 1 & 2 & 3 \\ 0 & -1 & 5 \end{bmatrix} + \begin{bmatrix} 2 & -3 & 0 \\ -1 & 7 & -2 \end{bmatrix}$$

$$= \begin{bmatrix} 3 & -1 & 3 \\ -1 & 6 & 3 \end{bmatrix}.$$

According to this definition, matrix subtraction can be performed by subtracting corresponding elements.

EXAMPLE 6

(a) $[8 \quad 6 \quad -4] - [3 \quad 5 \quad -8] = [5 \quad 1 \quad 4]$

(b)   The matrices

$$\begin{bmatrix} -2 & 5 \\ 0 & 1 \end{bmatrix} \quad \text{and} \quad \begin{bmatrix} 3 \\ 5 \end{bmatrix}$$

have different orders and cannot be subtracted.   ■

EXAMPLE 7

During September the Chicago warehouse of the EZ Life Company shipped out the following numbers of each model.

$$K = \begin{bmatrix} 5 & 10 & 8 \\ 11 & 14 & 15 \end{bmatrix}$$

What was the Chicago warehouse inventory on October 1, taking into account only the number of items received and sent out during the month?

The number of each kind of item received during September is given by matrix C from Example 5; the number of each model sent out during September is given by matrix K. The October 1 inventory will be represented by the matrix $C - K$:

$$\begin{bmatrix} 22 & 25 & 38 \\ 31 & 34 & 35 \end{bmatrix} - \begin{bmatrix} 5 & 10 & 8 \\ 11 & 14 & 15 \end{bmatrix} = \begin{bmatrix} 17 & 15 & 30 \\ 20 & 20 & 20 \end{bmatrix}. \quad ▨$$

2.3 EXERCISES

Mark each of the statements in Exercises 1–6 as *true* or *false*. If false, tell why.

1. $\begin{bmatrix} 1 & 3 \\ 5 & 7 \end{bmatrix} = \begin{bmatrix} 1 & 5 \\ 3 & 7 \end{bmatrix}$

2. $\begin{bmatrix} 1 \\ 2 \\ 3 \end{bmatrix} = [1 \ \ 2 \ \ 3]$

3. $\begin{bmatrix} x \\ y \end{bmatrix} = \begin{bmatrix} 3 \\ 5 \end{bmatrix}$ if $x = 3$ and $y = 5$.

4. $\begin{bmatrix} 3 & 5 & 2 & 8 \\ 1 & -1 & 4 & 0 \end{bmatrix}$ is a 4 × 2 matrix.

5. $\begin{bmatrix} 1 & 9 & -4 \\ 3 & 7 & 2 \\ -1 & 1 & 0 \end{bmatrix}$ is a square matrix.

6. $\begin{bmatrix} 2 & 4 & -1 \\ 3 & 7 & 5 \\ 0 & 0 & 0 \end{bmatrix} = \begin{bmatrix} 2 & 4 & -1 \\ 3 & 7 & 5 \end{bmatrix}$

Find the order of each matrix in Exercises 7–12. Identify any square, column, or row matrices.

7. $\begin{bmatrix} -4 & 8 \\ 2 & 3 \end{bmatrix}$

8. $\begin{bmatrix} -9 & 6 & 2 \\ 4 & 1 & 8 \end{bmatrix}$

9. $\begin{bmatrix} -6 & 8 & 0 & 0 \\ 4 & 1 & 9 & 2 \\ 3 & -5 & 7 & 1 \end{bmatrix}$

10. $[8 \ \ -2 \ \ 4 \ \ 6 \ \ 3]$

11. $\begin{bmatrix} 2 \\ 4 \end{bmatrix}$

12. $[-9]$

Find the values of the variables in Exercises 13–18.

13. $\begin{bmatrix} 2 & 1 \\ 4 & 8 \end{bmatrix} = \begin{bmatrix} x & 1 \\ y & z \end{bmatrix}$

14. $\begin{bmatrix} -5 \\ y \end{bmatrix} = \begin{bmatrix} -5 \\ 8 \end{bmatrix}$

15. $\begin{bmatrix} x + 6 & y + 2 \\ 8 & 3 \end{bmatrix} = \begin{bmatrix} -9 & 7 \\ 8 & k \end{bmatrix}$

16. $\begin{bmatrix} 9 & 7 \\ r & 0 \end{bmatrix} = \begin{bmatrix} m - 3 & n + 5 \\ 8 & 0 \end{bmatrix}$

17. $\begin{bmatrix} -7 + z & 4r & 8s \\ 6p & 2 & 5 \end{bmatrix} + \begin{bmatrix} -9 & 8r & 3 \\ 2 & 5 & 4 \end{bmatrix} = \begin{bmatrix} 2 & 36 & 27 \\ 20 & 7 & 12a \end{bmatrix}$

18. $\begin{bmatrix} a + 2 & 3z + 1 & 5m \\ 4k & 0 & 3 \end{bmatrix} + \begin{bmatrix} 3a & 2z & 5m \\ 2k & 5 & 6 \end{bmatrix} = \begin{bmatrix} 10 & -14 & 80 \\ 10 & 5 & 9 \end{bmatrix}$

In Exercises 19–28 perform the indicated operations where possible.

19. $\begin{bmatrix} 1 & 2 & 5 & -1 \\ 3 & 0 & 2 & -4 \end{bmatrix} + \begin{bmatrix} 8 & 10 & -5 & 3 \\ -2 & -1 & 0 & 0 \end{bmatrix}$

20. $\begin{bmatrix} 1 & 5 \\ 2 & -3 \\ 3 & 7 \end{bmatrix} + \begin{bmatrix} 2 & 3 \\ 8 & 5 \\ -1 & 9 \end{bmatrix}$

21. $\begin{bmatrix} 1 & 5 & 7 \\ 2 & 2 & 3 \end{bmatrix} + \begin{bmatrix} 4 & 8 & -7 \\ 1 & -1 & 5 \end{bmatrix}$

22. $\begin{bmatrix} 2 & 4 \\ -8 & 1 \end{bmatrix} + \begin{bmatrix} 9 & -3 \\ 8 & 5 \end{bmatrix}$

23. $\begin{bmatrix} 1 & 3 & -2 \\ 4 & 7 & 1 \end{bmatrix} + \begin{bmatrix} 3 & 0 \\ 6 & 4 \\ -5 & 2 \end{bmatrix}$

24. $\begin{bmatrix} 1 & 3 & -2 \\ 4 & 7 & 1 \end{bmatrix} - \begin{bmatrix} 3 & 6 & -5 \\ 0 & 4 & 2 \end{bmatrix}$

25. $\begin{bmatrix} 2 & 8 & 12 & 0 \\ 7 & 4 & -1 & 5 \\ 1 & 2 & 0 & 10 \end{bmatrix} - \begin{bmatrix} 1 & 3 & 6 & 9 \\ 2 & -3 & -3 & 4 \\ 8 & 0 & -2 & 17 \end{bmatrix}$

26. $\begin{bmatrix} 2 & 1 \\ 5 & -3 \\ -7 & 2 \\ 9 & 0 \end{bmatrix} + \begin{bmatrix} 1 & -8 & 0 \\ 5 & 3 & 2 \\ -6 & 7 & -5 \\ 2 & -1 & 0 \end{bmatrix}$

27. $\begin{bmatrix} -4x + 2y & -3x + y \\ 6x - 3y & 2x - 5y \end{bmatrix} + \begin{bmatrix} -8x + 6y & 2x \\ 3y - 5x & 6x + 4y \end{bmatrix}$

28. $\begin{bmatrix} 4k & - 8y \\ 6z & - 3x \\ 2k & + 5a \\ -4m & + 2n \end{bmatrix} - \begin{bmatrix} 5k & + 6y \\ 2z & + 5x \\ 4k & + 6a \\ 4m & - 2n \end{bmatrix}$

Using matrices $O = \begin{bmatrix} 0 & 0 \\ 0 & 0 \end{bmatrix}$, $P = \begin{bmatrix} m & n \\ p & q \end{bmatrix}$, $T = \begin{bmatrix} r & s \\ t & u \end{bmatrix}$, and $X = \begin{bmatrix} x & y \\ z & w \end{bmatrix}$, verify the statements in Exercises 29–34.

29. $X + T$ is a 2×2 matrix (Closure property)

30. $X + T = T + X$ (Commutative property of addition of matrices)

31. $X + (T + P) = (X + T) + P$ (Associative property of addition of matrices)

32. $X + (-X) = 0$ (Inverse property of addition of matrices)

33. $P + O = P$ (Identity property of addition of matrices)

34. Which of the above properties are valid for matrices that are not square?

35. When John inventoried his screw collection, he found that he had 7 flathead long screws, 9 flathead medium, 8 flathead short, 2 roundhead long, no roundhead medium, and 6 roundhead short. Write this information first as a 3×2 matrix and then as a 2×3 matrix.

36. At the grocery store, Miguel bought 4 quarts of milk, 2 loaves of bread, 4 chickens, and an apple. Mary bought 2 quarts of milk, a loaf of bread, 5 chickens, and 4 apples. Write this information first as a 2×4 matrix and then as a 4×2 matrix.

37. A dietician prepares a diet specifying the amounts a patient should eat of four basic food groups: group I, meats; group II, fruits and vegetables; group III, breads and starches; group IV, milk products. Amounts are given in "exchanges" which represent 1 ounce (meat), 1/2 cup (fruits and vegetables), 1 slice (bread), 8 ounces (milk), or other suitable measurements.

(a) The number of "exchanges" for breakfast for each of the four food groups respectively are 2, 1, 2, and 1; for lunch, 3, 2, 2, and 1; and for dinner, 4, 3, 2, and 1. Write a 3×4 matrix using this information.

(b) The amounts of fat, carbohydrates, and protein (in appropriate units) in each food group respectively are as follows.

Fat: 5, 0, 0, 10
Carbohydrates: 0, 10, 15, 12
Protein: 7, 1, 2, 8

Use this information to write a 4×3 matrix.

(c) There are 8 calories per exchange of fat, 4 calories per exchange of carbohydrates, and 5 calories per exchange of protein; summarize this data in a 3×1 matrix.

38. At the beginning of a laboratory experiment, five baby rats measured 5.6, 6.4, 6.9, 7.6, and 6.1 centimeters in length, and weighed 144, 138, 149, 152, and 146 grams respectively.

(a) Write a 2×5 matrix using this information.

(b) At the end of two weeks, their lengths were 10.2, 11.4, 11.4, 12.7, and 10.8 centimeters, and they weighed 196, 196, 225, 250, and 230 grams. Write a 2×5 matrix with this information.

(c) Use matrix subtraction and the matrices found in (a) and (b) to write a matrix which gives the amount of change in length and weight for each rat.

(d) The following week the rats gained as shown in the matrix below.

$$\begin{array}{c}\text{Length} \\ \text{Weight}\end{array}\begin{bmatrix} 1.8 & 1.5 & 2.3 & 1.8 & 2.0 \\ 25 & 22 & 29 & 33 & 20 \end{bmatrix}$$

What were their lengths and weights at the end of this week?

2.4 Multiplication of Matrices

In work with matrices, a real number is called a **scalar.**

Product of a Matrix and a Scalar	The **product** of a scalar k and a matrix X is the matrix kX, each of whose elements is k times the corresponding element of X.

For example,

$$(-3)\begin{bmatrix} 2 & -5 \\ 1 & 7 \end{bmatrix} = \begin{bmatrix} -6 & 15 \\ -3 & -21 \end{bmatrix}.$$

Finding the product of two matrices is more involved. However, such multiplication is important in solving practical problems. To understand the reasoning behind matrix multiplication, it may be helpful to consider another example concerning the EZ Life Company discussed in Section 2.3. Suppose sofas and chairs of the same model are often sold as sets with matrix W showing the number of each model set in each warehouse.

$$\begin{array}{c}\text{New York} \\ \text{Chicago} \\ \text{San Francisco}\end{array}\begin{array}{c}\begin{array}{ccc}\text{A} & \text{B} & \text{C}\end{array} \\ \begin{bmatrix} 10 & 7 & 3 \\ 5 & 9 & 6 \\ 4 & 8 & 2 \end{bmatrix}\end{array} = W$$

If the selling price of a model A set is $800, of a model B set $1000, and of a model C set $1200, the total value of the sets in the New York warehouse is found as follows.

Type	Number of sets		Price of set		Total
A	10	×	$800	=	$8000
B	7	×	$1000	=	$7000
C	3	×	$1200	=	$3600
					$18,600
					(Total for New York)

The total value of the three kinds of sets in New York is $18,600.

The work done in the table above is summarized as follows:

$$10(\$800) + 7(\$1000) + 3(\$1200) = \$18,600.$$

In the same way, the Chicago sets have a total value of

$$5(\$800) + 9(\$1000) + 6(\$1200) = \$20,200,$$

and in San Francisco, the total value of the sets is

$$4(\$800) + 8(\$1000) + 2(\$1200) = \$13,600.$$

We can write the selling prices as a column matrix, P, and the total value in each location as a column matrix V.

$$\begin{bmatrix} 800 \\ 1000 \\ 1200 \end{bmatrix} = P \qquad \begin{bmatrix} 18,600 \\ 20,200 \\ 13,600 \end{bmatrix} = V$$

Look at the elements of W and P; multiplying the first, second, and third elements of the first row of W by the first, second, and third elements respectively of the column matrix P and then adding these products gives the first element in V. Doing the same thing with the second row of W gives the second element of V; the third row of W leads to the third element of V, suggesting that it is reasonable to write the product of matrices

$$W = \begin{bmatrix} 10 & 7 & 3 \\ 5 & 9 & 6 \\ 4 & 8 & 2 \end{bmatrix} \qquad \text{and} \qquad P = \begin{bmatrix} 800 \\ 1000 \\ 1200 \end{bmatrix}$$

as

$$WP = \begin{bmatrix} 10 & 7 & 3 \\ 5 & 9 & 6 \\ 4 & 8 & 2 \end{bmatrix} \begin{bmatrix} 800 \\ 1000 \\ 1200 \end{bmatrix} = \begin{bmatrix} 18,600 \\ 20,200 \\ 13,600 \end{bmatrix} = V.$$

The product was found by multiplying the elements of the *rows* of the matrix on the left and the corresponding elements of the *column* of the matrix on the right, and then finding the sum of these separate products. Notice that the product of a 3×3 matrix and a 3×1 matrix is a 3×1 matrix.

The **product** AB of an $m \times n$ matrix A and an $n \times k$ matrix B is found as follows. Multiply each element of the *first row* of A by the corresponding element of the *first column* of B. The sum of these n products is the *first row, first column* element of AB. Similarly, the sum of the products found by multiplying the elements of the *first row* of A times the corresponding elements of the *second column* of B gives the *first row, second column* element of AB, and so on.

Product of

Two Matrices

Let A be an $m \times n$ matrix and let B be an $n \times k$ matrix. To find the ith row, jth column element of the **product matrix** AB, multiply each element in the ith row of A by the corresponding element in the jth column of B. The sum of these products will give the row i, column j element of AB. The product matrix AB is of order $m \times k$.

EXAMPLE 1

Find the product AB given

$$A = \begin{bmatrix} 2 & 3 & -1 \\ 4 & 2 & 2 \end{bmatrix} \quad \text{and} \quad B = \begin{bmatrix} 1 \\ 8 \\ 6 \end{bmatrix}.$$

Step 1. Multiply the elements of the first row of A and the corresponding elements of the column of B.

$$\begin{bmatrix} 2 & 3 & -1 \\ 4 & 2 & 2 \end{bmatrix} \begin{bmatrix} 1 \\ 8 \\ 6 \end{bmatrix} \quad 2 \cdot 1 + 3 \cdot 8 + (-1) \cdot 6 = 20$$

Therefore, 20 is the first row entry of the product matrix AB.

Step 2. Multiply the elements of the second row of A with the corresponding elements of B.

$$\begin{bmatrix} 2 & 3 & -1 \\ 4 & 2 & 2 \end{bmatrix} \begin{bmatrix} 1 \\ 8 \\ 6 \end{bmatrix} \quad 4 \cdot 1 + 2 \cdot 8 + 2 \cdot 6 = 32$$

The second row entry of the product is 32.

Step 3. Write the product as a column matrix using the two entries found above.

$$AB = \begin{bmatrix} 2 & 3 & -1 \\ 4 & 2 & 2 \end{bmatrix} \begin{bmatrix} 1 \\ 8 \\ 6 \end{bmatrix} = \begin{bmatrix} 20 \\ 32 \end{bmatrix} \quad \blacksquare$$

EXAMPLE 2

Find the product CD given

$$C = \begin{bmatrix} -3 & 4 & 2 \\ 5 & 0 & 4 \end{bmatrix} \quad \text{and} \quad D = \begin{bmatrix} -6 & 4 \\ 2 & 3 \\ 3 & -2 \end{bmatrix}.$$

Step 1.

$$\begin{bmatrix} -3 & 4 & 2 \\ 5 & 0 & 4 \end{bmatrix} \begin{bmatrix} -6 & 4 \\ 2 & 3 \\ 3 & -2 \end{bmatrix} \quad (-3) \cdot (-6) + 4 \cdot 2 + 2 \cdot 3 = 32$$

Step 2.

$$\begin{bmatrix} \boxed{-3 \ \ 4 \ \ 2} \\ 5 \ \ 0 \ \ 4 \end{bmatrix} \begin{bmatrix} -6 & 4 \\ 2 & 3 \\ 3 & -2 \end{bmatrix} \quad (-3) \ \cdot \ \boxed{4} \ + \ \boxed{4} \ \cdot \ \boxed{3} \ + \ 2 \ \cdot \ \boxed{(-2)} \ = \ -4$$

Step 3.

$$\begin{bmatrix} -3 \ \ 4 \ \ 2 \\ \boxed{5 \ \ 0 \ \ 4} \end{bmatrix} \begin{bmatrix} -6 & 4 \\ 2 & 3 \\ 3 & -2 \end{bmatrix} \quad \boxed{5} \ \cdot \ \boxed{(-6)} \ + \ \boxed{0} \ \cdot \ 2 \ + \ \boxed{4} \ \cdot \ 3 \ = \ -18$$

Step 4.

$$\begin{bmatrix} -3 \ \ 4 \ \ 2 \\ \boxed{5 \ \ 0 \ \ 4} \end{bmatrix} \begin{bmatrix} -6 & 4 \\ 2 & 3 \\ 3 & -2 \end{bmatrix} \quad \boxed{5} \ \cdot \ \boxed{4} \ + \ \boxed{0} \ \cdot \ 3 \ + \ \boxed{4} \ \cdot \ \boxed{(-2)} \ = \ 12$$

Step 5.   The product is

$$CD = \begin{bmatrix} -3 & 4 & 2 \\ 5 & 0 & 4 \end{bmatrix} \begin{bmatrix} -6 & 4 \\ 2 & 3 \\ 3 & -2 \end{bmatrix} = \begin{bmatrix} 32 & -4 \\ -18 & 12 \end{bmatrix}.$$

Here the product of a 2×3 matrix and a 3×2 matrix is a 2×2 matrix. ▣

As the definition of matrix multiplication shows,

> **the product AB of two matrices A and B can be found only if the number of columns of A is the same as the number of rows of B.**

The final product will have as many rows as A and as many columns as B.

EXAMPLE 3

Suppose matrix A is 2×2 and matrix B is 2×4. Can the product AB be calculated? What is the order of the product?

The following diagram helps decide the answers to these questions.

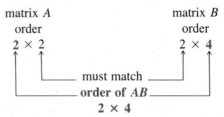

The product of A and B can be found because A has two columns and B has two rows. The order of the product is 2×4. ▣

EXAMPLE 4

Find BA given

$$A = \begin{bmatrix} 1 & -3 \\ 7 & 2 \end{bmatrix} \quad \text{and} \quad B = \begin{bmatrix} 1 & 0 & -1 \\ 3 & 1 & 4 \end{bmatrix}.$$

Since B is a 2×3 matrix and A is a 2×2 matrix, the product BA cannot be found. ▨

EXAMPLE 5

A contractor builds three kinds of houses, models A, B, and C, with a choice of two styles, Spanish or contemporary. Matrix P shows the number of each kind of house planned for a new 100-home subdivision. The amounts for each of the exterior materials depend primarily on the style of the house. These amounts are shown in matrix Q. (Concrete is in cubic yards, lumber in units of 1000 board feet, brick in 1000's, and shingles in units of 100 square feet.) Matrix R gives the cost in dollars for each kind of material.

$$\begin{array}{c} \\ \text{Model A} \\ \text{Model B} \\ \text{Model C} \end{array} \begin{array}{cc} \text{Spanish} & \text{Contemporary} \\ \left[\begin{array}{cc} 0 & 30 \\ 10 & 20 \\ 20 & 20 \end{array}\right] \end{array} = P$$

$$\begin{array}{c} \\ \text{Spanish} \\ \text{Contemporary} \end{array} \begin{array}{cccc} \text{Concrete} & \text{Lumber} & \text{Brick} & \text{Shingles} \\ \left[\begin{array}{cccc} 10 & 2 & 0 & 2 \\ 50 & 1 & 20 & 2 \end{array}\right] \end{array} = Q$$

$$\begin{array}{c} \\ \text{Concrete} \\ \text{Lumber} \\ \text{Brick} \\ \text{Shingles} \end{array} \begin{array}{c} \text{Cost per unit} \\ \left[\begin{array}{c} 20 \\ 180 \\ 60 \\ 25 \end{array}\right] \end{array} = R$$

(a) What is the total cost of these materials for each model house?

To find the cost for each model, first find PQ, which shows the amount of each material needed for each model house.

$$PQ = \begin{bmatrix} 0 & 30 \\ 10 & 20 \\ 20 & 20 \end{bmatrix} \begin{bmatrix} 10 & 2 & 0 & 2 \\ 50 & 1 & 20 & 2 \end{bmatrix}$$

$$= \begin{array}{cccc} \text{Concrete} & \text{Lumber} & \text{Brick} & \text{Shingles} \\ \left[\begin{array}{cccc} 1500 & 30 & 600 & 60 \\ 1100 & 40 & 400 & 60 \\ 1200 & 60 & 400 & 80 \end{array}\right] & \begin{array}{c} \text{Model A} \\ \text{Model B} \\ \text{Model C} \end{array} \end{array}$$

Now multiply PQ and R, the cost matrix, to get the total cost of the exterior materials for each model house.

$$\begin{bmatrix} 1500 & 30 & 600 & 60 \\ 1100 & 40 & 400 & 60 \\ 1200 & 60 & 400 & 80 \end{bmatrix} \begin{bmatrix} 20 \\ 180 \\ 60 \\ 25 \end{bmatrix} = \begin{array}{c} \text{Cost} \\ \left[\begin{array}{c} 72,900 \\ 54,700 \\ 60,800 \end{array}\right] & \begin{array}{c} \text{Model A} \\ \text{Model B} \\ \text{Model C} \end{array} \end{array}$$

(b) How much of each of the four kinds of material must be ordered?

The totals of the columns of matrix PQ will give a matrix whose elements represent the total amounts of each material needed for the subdivision. Let us call this matrix T, and write it as a row matrix.

$$T = [3800 \quad 130 \quad 1400 \quad 200]$$

(c) What is the total cost for exterior material?

For the total cost of all the exterior materials, find the product of matrix T, the matrix showing the total amounts of each material, and matrix R, the cost matrix. (To multiply these and get a 1×1 matrix, representing total cost, we must multiply a 1×4 matrix by a 4×1 matrix. This is why T was written as a row matrix in (b) above.)

$$TR = [3800 \quad 130 \quad 1400 \quad 200] \begin{bmatrix} 20 \\ 180 \\ 60 \\ 25 \end{bmatrix} = [188,400].$$

(d) Suppose the contractor builds the same number of homes in five subdivisions. Calculate the total amount of each exterior material for each model for all five subdivisions.

Multiply PQ by the scalar 5, as follows.

$$5 \begin{bmatrix} 1500 & 30 & 600 & 60 \\ 1100 & 40 & 400 & 60 \\ 1200 & 60 & 400 & 80 \end{bmatrix} = \begin{bmatrix} 7500 & 150 & 3000 & 300 \\ 5500 & 200 & 2000 & 300 \\ 6000 & 300 & 2000 & 400 \end{bmatrix}$$

We can introduce a notation to help us keep track of the quantities a matrix represents. For example, we can say that matrix P, from Example 5, represents models/styles, matrix Q represents styles/materials, and matrix R represents materials/cost. In each case, write the meaning of the rows first and the columns second. In the product PQ of Example 5, the rows of the matrix represented models and the columns represented materials. Therefore, the matrix product PQ represents models/materials. Note that the common quantity, styles, in both P and Q was eliminated in the product PQ. By this method, the product $(PQ)R$ represents models/cost.

In practical problems this notation helps decide in which order to multiply matrices so that the results are meaningful. In Example 5(c) either RT or TR could have been found. However, since T represents subdivisions/materials and R represents materials/cost, the product TR gives subdivisions/cost.

2.4 EXERCISES

In Exercises 1–8, the dimensions of two matrices A and B are given. Find the dimensions of the product AB and the product BA, whenever these products exist.

1. A is 2×2, B is 2×2

2. A is 3×3, B is 3×3

3. A is 4×2, B is 2×4

4. A is 3×1, B is 1×3

5. A is 3×5, B is 5×2

6. A is 4×3, B is 3×6

7. A is 4×2, B is 3×4

8. A is 7×3, B is 2×7

Let
$$A = \begin{bmatrix} -2 & 4 \\ 0 & 3 \end{bmatrix} \quad \text{and} \quad B = \begin{bmatrix} -6 & 2 \\ 4 & 0 \end{bmatrix}.$$

Find each of the following.

9. $2A$

10. $-3B$

11. $-4B$

12. $5A$

13. $-4A + 5B$

14. $3A - 10B$

Find each of the matrix products in Exercises 15–26 where possible.

15. $\begin{bmatrix} 1 & 2 \\ 3 & 4 \end{bmatrix}\begin{bmatrix} -1 \\ 7 \end{bmatrix}$

16. $\begin{bmatrix} -1 & 5 \\ 7 & 0 \end{bmatrix}\begin{bmatrix} 6 \\ 2 \end{bmatrix}$

17. $\begin{bmatrix} 2 & 2 & -1 \\ 3 & 0 & 1 \end{bmatrix}\begin{bmatrix} 0 & 2 \\ -1 & 4 \\ 0 & 2 \end{bmatrix}$

18. $\begin{bmatrix} -9 & 2 & 1 \\ 3 & 0 & 0 \end{bmatrix}\begin{bmatrix} 2 \\ -1 \\ 4 \end{bmatrix}$

19. $\begin{bmatrix} 1 & 2 \\ 3 & 4 \end{bmatrix}\begin{bmatrix} -1 & 5 \\ 7 & 0 \end{bmatrix}$

20. $\begin{bmatrix} -1 & 5 \\ 7 & 0 \end{bmatrix}\begin{bmatrix} 1 & 2 \\ 3 & 4 \end{bmatrix}$

21. $\begin{bmatrix} -2 & -3 & 7 \\ 1 & 5 & 6 \end{bmatrix}\begin{bmatrix} 1 \\ 2 \\ 3 \end{bmatrix}$

22. $\begin{bmatrix} 6 \\ 5 \\ 4 \end{bmatrix}[-1 \quad 1 \quad 1]$

23. $\left(\begin{bmatrix} 4 & 3 \\ 1 & 2 \\ 0 & -5 \end{bmatrix}\begin{bmatrix} 2 & -2 \\ 1 & -1 \end{bmatrix}\right)\begin{bmatrix} 10 \\ 0 \end{bmatrix}$

24. $\begin{bmatrix} 4 & 3 \\ 1 & 2 \\ 0 & -5 \end{bmatrix}\left(\begin{bmatrix} 2 & -2 \\ 1 & -1 \end{bmatrix}\begin{bmatrix} 10 \\ 0 \end{bmatrix}\right)$

25. $\begin{bmatrix} 2 & -2 \\ 1 & -1 \end{bmatrix}\left(\begin{bmatrix} 4 & 3 \\ 1 & 2 \end{bmatrix} + \begin{bmatrix} 7 & 0 \\ -1 & 5 \end{bmatrix}\right)$

26. $\begin{bmatrix} 2 & -2 \\ 1 & -1 \end{bmatrix}\begin{bmatrix} 4 & 3 \\ 1 & 2 \end{bmatrix} + \begin{bmatrix} 2 & -2 \\ 1 & -1 \end{bmatrix}\begin{bmatrix} 7 & 0 \\ -1 & 5 \end{bmatrix}$

27. Let
$$A = \begin{bmatrix} -2 & 4 \\ 1 & 3 \end{bmatrix} \quad \text{and} \quad B = \begin{bmatrix} -2 & 1 \\ 3 & 6 \end{bmatrix}.$$

   (a) Find AB. **(b)** Find BA.

   (c) Did you get the same answer in parts (a) and (b)? Do you think that matrix multiplication is commutative?

   (d) In general, for matrices A and B such that AB and BA both exist, does AB always equal BA?

Given matrices
$$P = \begin{bmatrix} m & n \\ p & q \end{bmatrix}, \quad X = \begin{bmatrix} x & y \\ z & w \end{bmatrix}, \quad T = \begin{bmatrix} r & s \\ t & u \end{bmatrix},$$
verify that the statements in Exercises 28–32 are true. The statements are valid for any matrices whenever matrix multiplication and addition can be carried out. This, of course, depends on the *order* of the matrices.

28. $(PX)T = P(XT)$ (Associative property: see Exercises 23 and 24.)

29. $P(X + T) = PX + PT$ (Distributive property: see Exercises 25 and 26.)

30. PX is a 2×2 matrix (Closure property)

31. $k(X + T) = kX + kT$ for any real number k

32. $(k + h)P = kP + hP$ for any real numbers k and h

33. Let I be the matrix $I = \begin{bmatrix} 1 & 0 \\ 0 & 1 \end{bmatrix}$, and let matrices P, X, and T be defined as above.

(a) Find IP, PI, IX.

(b) Without calculating, guess what the matrix IT might be.

(c) Suggest a reason for naming a matrix such as I an *identity* matrix.

34. The Bread Box, a small neighborhood bakery, sells four main items: sweet rolls, bread, cake, and pie. The amount of eggs or of certain other main ingredients (in cups) required to make these items is given in matrix A.

$$A = \begin{array}{c} \\ \\ \\ \\ \end{array}\begin{array}{ccccc} \text{Eggs} & \text{Flour} & \text{Sugar} & \text{Shortening} & \text{Milk} \\ \begin{bmatrix} 1 & 4 & \frac{1}{4} & \frac{1}{4} & 1 \\ 0 & 3 & 0 & \frac{1}{4} & 0 \\ 4 & 3 & 2 & 1 & 1 \\ 0 & 1 & 0 & \frac{1}{3} & 0 \end{bmatrix} & \begin{array}{l} \text{Sweet rolls (dozen)} \\ \text{Bread (loaves)} \\ \text{Cake (1)} \\ \text{Pie (1)} \end{array} \end{array}$$

The cost (in cents per egg or per cup) for each ingredient when purchased in large lots and in small lots is given by matrix B.

$$\begin{array}{c} \text{Cost} \end{array}$$

$$B = \begin{array}{cc} \text{Large lot} & \text{Small lot} \\ \begin{bmatrix} 5 & 5 \\ 8 & 10 \\ 10 & 12 \\ 12 & 15 \\ 5 & 6 \end{bmatrix} & \begin{array}{l} \text{Eggs} \\ \text{Flour} \\ \text{Sugar} \\ \text{Shortening} \\ \text{Milk} \end{array} \end{array}$$

(a) Use matrix multiplication to find a matrix representing the comparative costs per item under the two purchase options.

Suppose a day's orders consist of 20 dozen sweet rolls, 200 loaves of bread, 50 cakes, and 60 pies.

(b) Represent these orders as a 1×4 matrix and use matrix multiplication to write as a matrix the amount of each ingredient required to fill the day's orders.

(c) Use matrix multiplication to find a matrix representing the costs under the two purchase options to fill the day's orders.

35. In Exercise 37, Section 2.3, label the matrices found in parts (a), (b), and (c) respectively X, Y, and Z.

(a) Find the product matrix XY. What do the entries of this matrix represent?

(b) Find the product matrix YZ. What do the entries represent?

36. Show that the system of linear equations

$$\begin{aligned} 2x_1 + 3x_2 + x_3 &= 5 \\ x_1 - 4x_2 + 5x_3 &= 8 \end{aligned}$$

can be written as the matrix equation

$$\begin{bmatrix} 2 & 3 & 1 \\ 1 & -4 & 5 \end{bmatrix} \begin{bmatrix} x_1 \\ x_2 \\ x_3 \end{bmatrix} = \begin{bmatrix} 5 \\ 8 \end{bmatrix}.$$

Solve the system and substitute into the matrix equation to check the results.

37. Let $A = \begin{bmatrix} 1 & 2 \\ -3 & 5 \end{bmatrix}$, $\quad X = \begin{bmatrix} x_1 \\ x_2 \end{bmatrix}$, and $\quad B = \begin{bmatrix} -4 \\ 12 \end{bmatrix}$.

Show that the equation $AX = B$ represents a linear system of two equations in two unknowns. Solve the system and substitute into the matrix equation to check your results.

Use the following matrices to find the matrix products in Exercises 38–44.

$$A = \begin{bmatrix} 2 & 3 & -1 & 5 & 10 \\ 2 & 8 & 7 & 4 & 3 \\ -1 & -4 & -12 & 6 & 8 \\ 2 & 5 & 7 & 1 & 4 \end{bmatrix} \qquad B = \begin{bmatrix} 9 & 3 & 7 & -6 \\ -1 & 0 & 4 & 2 \\ -10 & -7 & 6 & 9 \\ 8 & 4 & 2 & -1 \\ 2 & -5 & 3 & 7 \end{bmatrix}$$

$$C = \begin{bmatrix} -6 & 8 & 2 & 4 & -3 \\ 1 & 9 & 7 & -12 & 5 \\ 15 & 2 & -8 & 10 & 11 \\ 4 & 7 & 9 & 6 & -2 \\ 1 & 3 & 8 & 23 & 4 \end{bmatrix} \qquad D = \begin{bmatrix} 5 & -3 & 7 & 9 & 2 \\ 6 & 8 & -5 & 2 & 1 \\ 3 & 7 & -4 & 2 & 11 \\ 5 & -3 & 9 & 4 & -1 \\ 0 & 3 & 2 & 5 & 1 \end{bmatrix}$$

38. AC **39.** CD **40.** DC **41.** CA **42.** Is $AC = CA$?

43. Is $CD = DC$?

44. Find $C + D$, $(C + D)B$, CB, DB, and $CB + DB$. Does $(C + D)B = CB + DB$?

EXTENDED APPLICATION   Routing

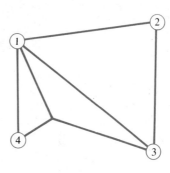

FIGURE 1

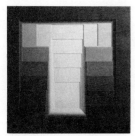

The diagram in Figure 1 shows the roads connecting four cities. Another way of representing this information is shown in matrix A, where the entries represent the number of roads connecting two cities without passing through another city.* For example, from

---

*Taken from Hugh G. Campbell, *Matrices With Applications*, © 1968, p. 50—51. Reprinted by permission of Prentice-Hall, Inc., Englewood Cliffs, N.J.

the diagram we see that there are two roads connecting city 1 to city 4 without passing through either city 2 or 3. This information is entered in row 1, column 4 and again in row 4, column 1 of matrix A.

$$A = \begin{bmatrix} 0 & 1 & 2 & 2 \\ 1 & 0 & 1 & 0 \\ 2 & 1 & 0 & 1 \\ 2 & 0 & 1 & 0 \end{bmatrix}$$

Note that there are 0 roads connecting each city to itself. Also, there is one road connecting cities 3 and 2.

How many ways are there to go from city 1 to city 2, for example, by going through exactly one other city? Since we must go through one other city, we must go through either city 3 or city 4. On the diagram in Figure 1, we see that we can go from city 1 to city 2 through city 3 in 2 ways. We can go from city 1 to city 3 in 2 ways and then from city 3 to city 2 in one way, giving the $2 \cdot 1 = 2$ ways to get from city 1 to city 2 through city 3. It is not possible to go from city 1 to city 2 through city 4, because there is no direct route between cities 4 and 2.

Now multiply matrix A by itself, to get A^2. Let the first row, second column entry of A^2 be b_{12}. (We use a_{ij} to denote the entry in the i-th row and j-th column of matrix A.) The entry b_{12} is found as follows.

$$\begin{aligned} b_{12} &= a_{11}a_{12} + a_{12}a_{22} + a_{13}a_{32} + a_{14}a_{42} \\ &= 0 \cdot 1 + 1 \cdot 0 + 2 \cdot 1 + 2 \cdot 0 \\ &= 2. \end{aligned}$$

The matrix A^2 gives the number of ways to travel between any two cities by passing through exactly one other city. The first product $0 \cdot 1$ in the calculations above represents the number of ways to go from city 1 to city 1 (0) and then from city 1 to city 2 (1). The 0 result indicates that such a trip does not involve a third city. The only non-zero product ($2 \cdot 1$) represents the two routes from city 1 to city 3 and the one route from city 3 to city 2 which result in the $2 \cdot 1$ or 2 routes from city 1 to city 2 by going through city 3.

Similarly, A^3 gives the number of ways to travel between any two cities by passing through exactly two cities. Also, $A + A^2$ represents the total number of ways to travel between two cities with at most one intermediate city.

The diagram can be given many other interpretations. For example, the lines could represent lines of mutual influence between people or nations; they could represent communication lines such as telephone lines.

EXERCISES

1. Use matrix A from the text to find A^2. Then answer the following questions.

   (a) How many ways are there to travel from city 1 to city 3 by passing through exactly one city?

   (b) How many ways are there to travel from city 2 to city 4 by passing through exactly one city?

   (c) How many ways are there to travel from city 1 to city 3 by passing through at most one city?

   (d) How many ways are there to travel from city 2 to city 4 by passing through at most one city?

2. Find A^3. Then answer the following questions.

    (a) How many ways are there to travel between cities 1 and 4 by passing through exactly two cities?

    (b) How many ways are there to travel between cities 1 and 4 by passing through at most two cities?

3. A small telephone system connects three cities. There are four lines between cities 3 and 2, three lines connecting city 3 with city 1 and two lines between cities 1 and 2.

    (a) Write a matrix B to represent this information.

    (b) Find B^2.

    (c) How many lines which connect cities 1 and 2 go through exactly one other city (city 3)?

    (d) How many lines which connect cities 1 and 2 go through at most one other city?

4. The figure shows four southern cities served by Delta Airlines.

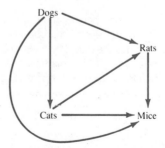

    (a) Write a matrix to represent the number of non-stop routes between cities.

    (b) Find the number of one-stop flights between Houston and Jackson.

    (c) Find the number of flights between Houston and Jackson which require at most one stop.

    (d) Find the number of one-stop flights between New Orleans and Houston.

5. The figure shows a food web. The arrows indicate the food sources of each population. For example, cats feed on rats and on mice.

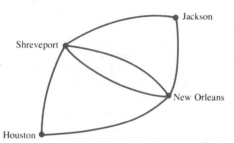

    (a) Write a matrix C in which each row and corresponding column represents a population in the food chain. Enter a one when the population in a given row feeds on the population in the given column and a zero otherwise.

    (b) Calculate and interpret C^2.

 6. Find A^2, B^2, and C^2 for the matrices used in these problems.

EXTENDED   Contagion

APPLICATION

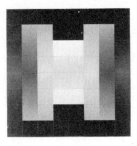

Suppose that three people have contracted a contagious disease.* A second group of five people may have been in contact with the three infected persons. A third group of six people may have been in contact with the second group. We can form a 3×5 matrix P with rows representing the first group of three and columns representing the second group of five. We enter a one in the corresponding position if a person in the first group has contact with a person in the second group. These direct contacts are called *first-order contacts*. Similarly we form a 5×6 matrix Q representing the first-order contacts between the second and third group. For example, suppose

$$P = \begin{bmatrix} 1 & 0 & 0 & 1 & 0 \\ 0 & 0 & 1 & 1 & 0 \\ 1 & 1 & 0 & 0 & 0 \end{bmatrix} \quad \text{and} \quad Q = \begin{bmatrix} 1 & 1 & 0 & 1 & 1 & 1 \\ 0 & 0 & 0 & 0 & 1 & 0 \\ 0 & 0 & 0 & 0 & 0 & 0 \\ 0 & 1 & 0 & 1 & 0 & 0 \\ 1 & 0 & 0 & 0 & 1 & 0 \end{bmatrix}.$$

From matrix P we see that the first person in the first group had contact with the first and fourth persons in the second group. Also, none of the first group had contact with the last person in the second group.

A *second-order contact* is an indirect contact between persons in the first and third group through some person in the second group. The product matrix PQ indicates these contacts. Verify that the second row, fourth column entry of PQ is 1. That is, there is one second-order contact between the second person in group 1 and the fourth person in group 3. Let a_{ij} denote the element in the i-th row and j-th column of the matrix PQ. By looking at the products which form a_{24} below, we see that the common contact was with the fourth individual in group 2. (The p_{ij} are entries in P, and the q_{ij} are entries in Q.)

$$\begin{aligned} a_{24} &= p_{21}q_{14} + p_{22}q_{24} + p_{23}q_{34} + p_{24}q_{44} + p_{25}q_{54} \\ &= 0 \cdot 1 \quad + 0 \cdot 0 \quad + 1 \cdot 0 \quad + 1 \cdot 1 \quad + 0 \cdot 1 \\ &= 1. \end{aligned}$$

The second person in group 1 and the fourth person in group 3 both had contact with the fourth person in group 2.

This idea could be extended to third-, fourth-, and larger order contacts. It indicates a way to use matrices to trace the spread of a contagious disease. It could also pertain to the dispersal of ideas or anything that might pass from one individual to another.

EXERCISES

1. Find the second-order contact matrix PQ mentioned in the text.

2. How many second-order contacts were there between the second contagious person and the third person in the third group?

---

*Reprinted by permission of Stanley I. Grossman and James E. Turner from *Mathematics for the Biological Sciences* (New York: Macmillan Publishing Company, Inc., 1974). See also Stanley I. Grossman, *Finite Mathematics with Applications to Business, Life Sciences, and Social Sciences* (Belmont, CA: Wadsworth Publishing Company, 1983), p. 103.

3. Is there anyone in the third group who has had no contacts at all with the first group?

4. The totals of the columns in *PQ* give the total number of second-order contacts per person, while the column totals in *P* and *Q* give the total number of first-order contacts per person. Which person has the most contacts, counting both first- and second-order contacts?

5. Find the matrix product in Exercise 1.

2.5 Matrix Inverses

In Section 2.3, we defined a zero matrix which has properties similar to those of the real number zero, the identity for addition. The real number 1 is the identity element for multiplication: for any real number a, $a \cdot 1 = 1 \cdot a = a$. In this section, we define an *identity matrix I* which has properties similar to those of the number 1. This identity matrix is then used to find the multiplicative inverse of any square matrix which has an inverse.

If I is to be the identity matrix, the products AI and IA must both equal A. This means that an identity matrix exists only for square matrices. Otherwise, IA and AI could not both be found. The **2 × 2 identity matrix** which satisfies these conditions is

$$I = \begin{bmatrix} 1 & 0 \\ 0 & 1 \end{bmatrix}.$$

To check that I, as defined above, is really the 2 × 2 identity matrix, let

$$A = \begin{bmatrix} a & b \\ c & d \end{bmatrix}.$$

Then AI and IA should both equal A.

$$AI = \begin{bmatrix} a & b \\ c & d \end{bmatrix}\begin{bmatrix} 1 & 0 \\ 0 & 1 \end{bmatrix} = \begin{bmatrix} a(1) + b(0) & a(0) + b(1) \\ c(1) + d(0) & c(0) + d(1) \end{bmatrix} = \begin{bmatrix} a & b \\ c & d \end{bmatrix} = A$$

$$IA = \begin{bmatrix} 1 & 0 \\ 0 & 1 \end{bmatrix}\begin{bmatrix} a & b \\ c & d \end{bmatrix} = \begin{bmatrix} 1(a) + 0(c) & 1(b) + 0(d) \\ 0(a) + 1(c) & 0(b) + 1(d) \end{bmatrix} = \begin{bmatrix} a & b \\ c & d \end{bmatrix} = A$$

This verifies that I has been defined correctly. (It can also be shown that I is the only 2 × 2 identity matrix.)

The identity matrices for 3 × 3 matrices and 4 × 4 matrices, respectively, are

$$I = \begin{bmatrix} 1 & 0 & 0 \\ 0 & 1 & 0 \\ 0 & 0 & 1 \end{bmatrix} \quad \text{and} \quad I = \begin{bmatrix} 1 & 0 & 0 & 0 \\ 0 & 1 & 0 & 0 \\ 0 & 0 & 1 & 0 \\ 0 & 0 & 0 & 1 \end{bmatrix}.$$

By generalizing, an $n \times n$ identity matrix can be determined for any value of n.

Recall that the multiplicative inverse of the nonzero real number a is $1/a$. The product of a and its multiplicative inverse $1/a$ is 1. Now we try to do a similar thing with matrices: given a matrix A, can we find a matrix A^{-1} (read "A-inverse") satisfying both

$$AA^{-1} = I \quad \text{and} \quad A^{-1}A = I?$$

It turns out that we often can find this matrix inverse A^{-1}, using the row operations of Section 2.2. Before doing this, we might mention that the symbol A^{-1} does not mean $1/A$; the symbol A^{-1} is just the notation for the inverse of matrix A. Also, only square matrices can have inverses. If an inverse exists, it is unique. That is, any given square matrix has no more than one inverse. The proof of this is left to Exercise 50 of this section.

As an example, let us find the inverse of

$$A = \begin{bmatrix} 2 & 4 \\ 1 & -1 \end{bmatrix}.$$

Let the unknown inverse matrix be

$$A^{-1} = \begin{bmatrix} x & y \\ z & w \end{bmatrix}.$$

By the definition of matrix inverse, $AA^{-1} = I$, or

$$AA^{-1} = \begin{bmatrix} 2 & 4 \\ 1 & -1 \end{bmatrix}\begin{bmatrix} x & y \\ z & w \end{bmatrix} = \begin{bmatrix} 1 & 0 \\ 0 & 1 \end{bmatrix}.$$

By matrix multiplication,

$$\begin{bmatrix} 2x + 4z & 2y + 4w \\ x - z & y - w \end{bmatrix} = \begin{bmatrix} 1 & 0 \\ 0 & 1 \end{bmatrix}.$$

Setting corresponding elements equal gives the system of equations

$$2x + 4z = 1 \tag{1}$$
$$2y + 4w = 0 \tag{2}$$
$$x - z = 0 \tag{3}$$
$$y - w = 1. \tag{4}$$

Since equations (1) and (3) involve only x and z, while equations (2) and (4) involve only y and w, these four equations lead to two systems of equations,

$$\begin{array}{cc} 2x + 4z = 1 & 2y + 4w = 0 \\ & \text{and} \\ x - z = 0 & y - w = 1. \end{array}$$

Writing the two systems as augmented matrices gives

$$\begin{bmatrix} 2 & 4 & | & 1 \\ 1 & -1 & | & 0 \end{bmatrix} \quad \text{and} \quad \begin{bmatrix} 2 & 4 & | & 0 \\ 1 & -1 & | & 1 \end{bmatrix}.$$

Each of these systems can be solved by the Gauss-Jordan method. However, since the elements to the left of the vertical bar are identical, the two systems can be combined into one matrix

$$\left[\begin{array}{rr|rr} 2 & 4 & 1 & 0 \\ 1 & -1 & 0 & 1 \end{array}\right]$$

and solved simultaneously as follows. Exchange the two rows to get a 1 in the upper left corner.

$$\left[\begin{array}{rr|rr} 1 & -1 & 0 & 1 \\ 2 & 4 & 1 & 0 \end{array}\right]$$

Multiply row one by -2 and add the results to row two to get

$$\left[\begin{array}{rr|rr} 1 & -1 & 0 & 1 \\ 0 & 6 & 1 & -2 \end{array}\right].$$

Now, to get a 1 in the second row, second column position, multiply row two by 1/6.

$$\left[\begin{array}{rr|rr} 1 & -1 & 0 & 1 \\ 0 & 1 & \frac{1}{6} & -\frac{1}{3} \end{array}\right]$$

Finally, add row two to row one to get a 0 in the second column above the 1.

$$\left[\begin{array}{rr|rr} 1 & 0 & \frac{1}{6} & \frac{2}{3} \\ 0 & 1 & \frac{1}{6} & -\frac{1}{3} \end{array}\right]$$

The numbers in the first column to the right of the vertical bar give the values of x and z. The second column gives the values of y and w. That is,

$$\left[\begin{array}{rr|rr} 1 & 0 & x & y \\ 0 & 1 & z & w \end{array}\right] = \left[\begin{array}{rr|rr} 1 & 0 & \frac{1}{6} & \frac{2}{3} \\ 0 & 1 & \frac{1}{6} & -\frac{1}{3} \end{array}\right]$$

so that

$$A^{-1} = \left[\begin{array}{rr} x & y \\ z & w \end{array}\right] = \left[\begin{array}{rr} \frac{1}{6} & \frac{2}{3} \\ \frac{1}{6} & -\frac{1}{3} \end{array}\right].$$

To check, multiply A by A^{-1}. The result should be I.

$$AA^{-1} = \left[\begin{array}{rr} 2 & 4 \\ 1 & -1 \end{array}\right]\left[\begin{array}{rr} \frac{1}{6} & \frac{2}{3} \\ \frac{1}{6} & -\frac{1}{3} \end{array}\right] = \left[\begin{array}{cc} \frac{1}{3} + \frac{2}{3} & \frac{4}{3} - \frac{4}{3} \\ \frac{1}{6} - \frac{1}{6} & \frac{2}{3} + \frac{1}{3} \end{array}\right] = \left[\begin{array}{rr} 1 & 0 \\ 0 & 1 \end{array}\right] = I.$$

Verify that $A^{-1}A = I$, also. Finally,

$$A^{-1} = \left[\begin{array}{rr} \frac{1}{6} & \frac{2}{3} \\ \frac{1}{6} & -\frac{1}{3} \end{array}\right].$$

Finding an Inverse Matrix

To obtain A^{-1} for any $n \times n$ matrix A for which A^{-1} exists, follow these steps.

1. Form the augmented matrix $[A|I]$, where I is the $n \times n$ identity matrix.
2. Perform row operations on $[A|I]$ to get a matrix of the form $[I|B]$.
3. Matrix B is A^{-1}.

EXAMPLE 1

Find A^{-1} if $A = \begin{bmatrix} 1 & 0 & 1 \\ 2 & -2 & -1 \\ 3 & 0 & 0 \end{bmatrix}$.

Write the augmented matrix $[A|I]$.

$$[A|I] = \begin{bmatrix} 1 & 0 & 1 & | & 1 & 0 & 0 \\ 2 & -2 & -1 & | & 0 & 1 & 0 \\ 3 & 0 & 0 & | & 0 & 0 & 1 \end{bmatrix}$$

Since 1 is already in the upper left-hand corner as desired, begin by selecting the row operation which will result in a 0 for the first element in row two. Multiply row one by -2 and add the result to row two. This gives

$$\begin{bmatrix} 1 & 0 & 1 & | & 1 & 0 & 0 \\ 0 & -2 & -3 & | & -2 & 1 & 0 \\ 3 & 0 & 0 & | & 0 & 0 & 1 \end{bmatrix}.$$

To get 0 for the first element in row three, multiply row one by -3 and add to row three. The new matrix is

$$\begin{bmatrix} 1 & 0 & 1 & | & 1 & 0 & 0 \\ 0 & -2 & -3 & | & -2 & 1 & 0 \\ 0 & 0 & -3 & | & -3 & 0 & 1 \end{bmatrix}.$$

To get 1 for the second element in row two, multiply row two by $-1/2$, obtaining the new matrix

$$\begin{bmatrix} 1 & 0 & 1 & | & 1 & 0 & 0 \\ 0 & 1 & \frac{3}{2} & | & 1 & -\frac{1}{2} & 0 \\ 0 & 0 & -3 & | & -3 & 0 & 1 \end{bmatrix}.$$

To get 1 for the third element in row three, multiply row three by $-1/3$, with the result

$$\begin{bmatrix} 1 & 0 & 1 & | & 1 & 0 & 0 \\ 0 & 1 & \frac{3}{2} & | & 1 & -\frac{1}{2} & 0 \\ 0 & 0 & 1 & | & 1 & 0 & -\frac{1}{3} \end{bmatrix}.$$

To get 0 for the third element in row one, multiply row three by -1 and add to row one, which gives

$$\begin{bmatrix} 1 & 0 & 0 & | & 0 & 0 & \frac{1}{3} \\ 0 & 1 & \frac{3}{2} & | & 1 & -\frac{1}{2} & 0 \\ 0 & 0 & 1 & | & 1 & 0 & -\frac{1}{3} \end{bmatrix}.$$

To get 0 for the third element in row two, multiply row three by $-3/2$ and add to row two.

$$\left[\begin{array}{ccc|ccc} 1 & 0 & 0 & 0 & 0 & \frac{1}{3} \\ 0 & 1 & 0 & -\frac{1}{2} & -\frac{1}{2} & \frac{1}{2} \\ 0 & 0 & 1 & 1 & 0 & -\frac{1}{3} \end{array}\right]$$

From the last transformation, the desired inverse is

$$A^{-1} = \begin{bmatrix} 0 & 0 & \frac{1}{3} \\ -\frac{1}{2} & -\frac{1}{2} & \frac{1}{2} \\ 1 & 0 & -\frac{1}{3} \end{bmatrix}.$$

Confirm this by forming the products $A^{-1}A$ and AA^{-1}, both of which should equal I. ▩

EXAMPLE 2 Find A^{-1} if $A = \begin{bmatrix} 2 & -4 \\ 1 & -2 \end{bmatrix}$.

Using row operations to transform the first column of the augmented matrix

$$\left[\begin{array}{cc|cc} 2 & -4 & 1 & 0 \\ 1 & -2 & 0 & 1 \end{array}\right]$$

results in the following matrices.

$$\left[\begin{array}{cc|cc} 1 & -2 & \frac{1}{2} & 0 \\ 1 & -2 & 0 & 1 \end{array}\right]$$

$$\left[\begin{array}{cc|cc} 1 & -2 & \frac{1}{2} & 0 \\ 0 & 0 & -\frac{1}{2} & 1 \end{array}\right]$$

At this point, the matrix should be transformed so that the second element of row two will be 1. Since that element is now 0, there is no way to complete the desired transformation.

What is wrong? Just as the real number 0 has no multiplicative inverse, some matrices do not have inverses. Matrix A is an example of a matrix that has no inverse: there is no matrix A^{-1} such that $AA^{-1} = A^{-1}A = A$. ▩

Solving Systems of Equations with Inverses Matrices were used to solve systems of linear equations by the Gauss-Jordan method in Section 2.2. Another way to use matrices to solve linear systems is to write the system as a matrix equation $AX = B$, where A is the matrix of the coefficients of the variables of the system, X is the matrix of the variables, and B is the matrix of the constants. Matrix A is called the **coefficient matrix.**

To solve the matrix equation $AX = B$, first see if A^{-1} exists. Assuming A^{-1} exists and using the facts that $A^{-1}A = I$ and $IX = X$ gives

$$\begin{aligned} AX &= B \\ A^{-1}(AX) &= A^{-1}B \qquad \text{Multiply both sides by } A^{-1} \\ (A^{-1}A)X &= A^{-1}B \\ IX &= A^{-1}B \\ X &= A^{-1}B. \end{aligned}$$

When multiplying by matrices on both sides of a matrix equation, be careful to multiply in the same order on both sides of the equation, since multiplication of matrices is not commutative (unlike multiplication of real numbers).

Solving a System

$AX = B$ **Using**

Matrix Inverses

To solve a system of equations $AX = B$ where A is the matrix of coefficients, X is the matrix of variables, and B is the matrix of constants, first find A^{-1}. Then $X = A^{-1}B$.

This method is most practical in cases where several systems with the same coefficient matrix, but different constants, are to be solved. Then just one inverse matrix must be found.

EXAMPLE 3

Use the inverse of the coefficient matrix to solve the linear system

$$\begin{aligned} 2x - 3y &= 4 \\ x + 5y &= 2. \end{aligned}$$

To represent the system as a matrix equation, use the coefficient matrix of the system together with the matrix of variables and the matrix of constants.

$$A = \begin{bmatrix} 2 & -3 \\ 1 & 5 \end{bmatrix}, \qquad X = \begin{bmatrix} x \\ y \end{bmatrix}, \qquad \text{and} \qquad B = \begin{bmatrix} 4 \\ 2 \end{bmatrix}.$$

The system can then be written in matrix form as the equation $AX = B$ since

$$AX = \begin{bmatrix} 2 & -3 \\ 1 & 5 \end{bmatrix}\begin{bmatrix} x \\ y \end{bmatrix} = \begin{bmatrix} 2x - 3y \\ x + 5y \end{bmatrix} = \begin{bmatrix} 4 \\ 2 \end{bmatrix} = B.$$

To solve the system, first find A^{-1}. Do this by using row operations on matrix $[A|I]$ to get

$$\begin{bmatrix} 1 & 0 & \frac{5}{13} & \frac{3}{13} \\ 0 & 1 & -\frac{1}{13} & \frac{2}{13} \end{bmatrix}.$$

From this result,

$$A^{-1} = \begin{bmatrix} \frac{5}{13} & \frac{3}{13} \\ -\frac{1}{13} & \frac{2}{13} \end{bmatrix}.$$

Next, find the product $A^{-1}B$.

$$A^{-1}B = \begin{bmatrix} \frac{5}{13} & \frac{3}{13} \\ -\frac{1}{13} & \frac{2}{13} \end{bmatrix}\begin{bmatrix} 4 \\ 2 \end{bmatrix} = \begin{bmatrix} 2 \\ 0 \end{bmatrix}$$

Since $X = A^{-1}B$,

$$X = \begin{bmatrix} x \\ y \end{bmatrix} = \begin{bmatrix} 2 \\ 0 \end{bmatrix}.$$

The solution of the system is $(2, 0)$. ▪

EXAMPLE 4

Use the inverse of the coefficient matrix to solve the system

$$-x - 2y + 2z = 9$$
$$2x + y - z = -3$$
$$3x - 2y + z = -6.$$

The needed matrices are

$$A = \begin{bmatrix} -1 & -2 & 2 \\ 2 & 1 & -1 \\ 3 & -2 & 1 \end{bmatrix}, \quad X = \begin{bmatrix} x \\ y \\ z \end{bmatrix}, \quad \text{and} \quad B = \begin{bmatrix} 9 \\ -3 \\ -6 \end{bmatrix}.$$

To find A^{-1}, start with matrix

$$[A|I] = \begin{bmatrix} -1 & -2 & 2 & | & 1 & 0 & 0 \\ 2 & 1 & -1 & | & 0 & 1 & 0 \\ 3 & -2 & 1 & | & 0 & 0 & 1 \end{bmatrix}$$

and use row operations to get $[I|A^{-1}]$, from which

$$A^{-1} = \begin{bmatrix} \frac{1}{3} & \frac{2}{3} & 0 \\ \frac{5}{3} & \frac{7}{3} & -1 \\ \frac{7}{3} & \frac{8}{3} & -1 \end{bmatrix}.$$

Now find $A^{-1}B$.

$$A^{-1}B = \begin{bmatrix} \frac{1}{3} & \frac{2}{3} & 0 \\ \frac{5}{3} & \frac{7}{3} & -1 \\ \frac{7}{3} & \frac{8}{3} & -1 \end{bmatrix} \begin{bmatrix} 9 \\ -3 \\ -6 \end{bmatrix} = \begin{bmatrix} 1 \\ 14 \\ 19 \end{bmatrix}$$

Since $X = A^{-1}B$,

$$X = \begin{bmatrix} x \\ y \\ z \end{bmatrix} = \begin{bmatrix} 1 \\ 14 \\ 19 \end{bmatrix}.$$

From this result, $x = 1$, $y = 14$, $z = 19$ and the solution is (1, 14, 19.)

2.5 EXERCISES

In Exercises 1–8, decide whether or not the given matrices are inverses of each other.
(Check to see if their product is the identity matrix I.)

1. $\begin{bmatrix} 2 & 3 \\ 1 & 1 \end{bmatrix}$ and $\begin{bmatrix} -1 & 3 \\ 1 & -2 \end{bmatrix}$

2. $\begin{bmatrix} 5 & 7 \\ 2 & 3 \end{bmatrix}$ and $\begin{bmatrix} 3 & -7 \\ -2 & 5 \end{bmatrix}$

3. $\begin{bmatrix} 2 & 1 \\ 3 & 2 \end{bmatrix}$ and $\begin{bmatrix} 2 & 1 \\ -3 & 2 \end{bmatrix}$

4. $\begin{bmatrix} -1 & 2 \\ 3 & -5 \end{bmatrix}$ and $\begin{bmatrix} -5 & -2 \\ -3 & -1 \end{bmatrix}$

5. $\begin{bmatrix} 1 & 2 & 0 \\ 0 & 1 & 0 \\ 0 & 1 & 0 \end{bmatrix}$ and $\begin{bmatrix} 1 & -2 & 0 \\ 0 & 1 & 0 \\ 0 & -1 & 1 \end{bmatrix}$

6. $\begin{bmatrix} 0 & 1 & 0 \\ 0 & 0 & -2 \\ 1 & -1 & 0 \end{bmatrix}$ and $\begin{bmatrix} 1 & 0 & 1 \\ 1 & 0 & 0 \\ 0 & -1 & 0 \end{bmatrix}$

7. $\begin{bmatrix} 1 & 3 & 3 \\ 1 & 4 & 3 \\ 1 & 3 & 4 \end{bmatrix}$ and $\begin{bmatrix} 7 & -3 & -3 \\ -1 & 1 & 0 \\ -1 & 0 & 1 \end{bmatrix}$

8. $\begin{bmatrix} -1 & 0 & 2 \\ 3 & 1 & 0 \\ 0 & 2 & -3 \end{bmatrix}$ and $\begin{bmatrix} -\frac{1}{5} & \frac{4}{15} & -\frac{2}{15} \\ \frac{3}{5} & \frac{1}{5} & \frac{2}{5} \\ \frac{2}{5} & \frac{2}{15} & -\frac{1}{15} \end{bmatrix}$

Find the inverse, if it exists, for each of the matrices in Exercises 9–24.

9. $\begin{bmatrix} 1 & -1 \\ 2 & 0 \end{bmatrix}$

10. $\begin{bmatrix} -1 & 2 \\ -2 & -1 \end{bmatrix}$

11. $\begin{bmatrix} 3 & -1 \\ -5 & 2 \end{bmatrix}$

12. $\begin{bmatrix} -1 & -2 \\ 3 & 4 \end{bmatrix}$

13. $\begin{bmatrix} -6 & 4 \\ -3 & 2 \end{bmatrix}$

14. $\begin{bmatrix} 5 & 10 \\ -3 & -6 \end{bmatrix}$

15. $\begin{bmatrix} 1 & 0 & 0 \\ 0 & -1 & 0 \\ 1 & 0 & 1 \end{bmatrix}$

16. $\begin{bmatrix} 1 & 0 & 1 \\ 0 & -1 & 0 \\ 2 & 1 & 1 \end{bmatrix}$

17. $\begin{bmatrix} -1 & -1 & -1 \\ 4 & 5 & 0 \\ 0 & 1 & -3 \end{bmatrix}$

18. $\begin{bmatrix} 2 & 0 & 4 \\ 3 & 1 & 5 \\ -1 & 1 & -2 \end{bmatrix}$

19. $\begin{bmatrix} 1 & 2 & 3 \\ -3 & -2 & -1 \\ -1 & 0 & 1 \end{bmatrix}$

20. $\begin{bmatrix} 2 & 0 & 4 \\ 1 & 0 & -1 \\ 3 & 0 & -2 \end{bmatrix}$

21. $\begin{bmatrix} 2 & 4 & 6 \\ -1 & -4 & -3 \\ 0 & 1 & -1 \end{bmatrix}$

22. $\begin{bmatrix} 2 & 2 & -4 \\ 2 & 6 & 0 \\ -3 & -3 & 5 \end{bmatrix}$

23. $\begin{bmatrix} 1 & -2 & 3 & 0 \\ 0 & 1 & -1 & 1 \\ -2 & 2 & -2 & 4 \\ 0 & 2 & -3 & 1 \end{bmatrix}$

24. $\begin{bmatrix} 1 & 1 & 0 & 2 \\ 2 & -1 & 1 & -1 \\ 3 & 3 & 2 & -2 \\ 1 & 2 & 1 & 0 \end{bmatrix}$

Solve each of the systems of equations in Exercises 25–32 by using the inverse of the coefficient matrix.

25. $\begin{aligned} 2x + 3y &= 10 \\ x - y &= -5 \end{aligned}$

26. $\begin{aligned} -x + 2y &= 15 \\ -2x - y &= 20 \end{aligned}$

27. $\begin{aligned} 2x + y &= 5 \\ 5x + 3y &= 13 \end{aligned}$

28. $\begin{aligned} -x - 2y &= 8 \\ 3x + 4y &= 24 \end{aligned}$

29. $\begin{aligned} -x + y &= 1 \\ 2x - y &= 1 \end{aligned}$

30. $\begin{aligned} 3x - 6y &= 1 \\ -5x + 9y &= -1 \end{aligned}$

31. $\begin{aligned} -x - 8y &= 12 \\ 3x + 24y &= -36 \end{aligned}$

32. $\begin{aligned} x + 3y &= -14 \\ 2x - y &= 7 \end{aligned}$

Solve each of the systems of equations in Exercises 33–40 by using the inverse of the coefficient matrix. The inverses for the first four problems are found in Exercises 17, 18, 21, and 22 above.

33. $\begin{aligned} -x - y - z &= 1 \\ 4x + 5y \quad &= -2 \\ y - 3z &= 3 \end{aligned}$

34. $\begin{aligned} 2x + \quad 4z &= -8 \\ 3x + y + 5z &= 2 \\ -x + y - 2z &= 4 \end{aligned}$

35. $\begin{aligned} 2x + 4y + 6z &= 4 \\ -x - 4y - 3z &= 8 \\ y - z &= -4 \end{aligned}$

36. $\begin{aligned} 2x + 2y - 4z &= 12 \\ 2x + 6y \quad &= 16 \\ -3x - 3y + 5z &= -20 \end{aligned}$

37. $\begin{aligned} x + 2y + 3z &= 5 \\ 2x + 3y + 2z &= 2 \\ -x - 2y - 4z &= -1 \end{aligned}$

38. $\begin{aligned} x + y - 3z &= 4 \\ 2x + 4y - 4z &= 8 \\ -x + y + 4z &= -3 \end{aligned}$

39. $\begin{aligned} 2x - 2y \quad &= 5 \\ 4y + 8z &= 7 \\ x \quad + 2z &= 1 \end{aligned}$

40. $\begin{aligned} x \quad + z &= 3 \\ y + 2z &= 8 \\ -x + y \quad &= 4 \end{aligned}$

Solve the systems of equations in Exercises 41–42 by using the inverse of the coefficient matrix. The inverses were found in Exercises 23 and 24.

41.
$$\begin{aligned} x - 2y + 3z &= 4 \\ y - z + w &= -8 \\ -2x + 2y - 2z + 4w &= 12 \\ 2y - 3z + w &= -4 \end{aligned}$$

42.
$$\begin{aligned} x + y + 2w &= 3 \\ 2x - y + z - w &= 3 \\ 3x + 3y + 2z - 2w &= 5 \\ x + 2y + z &= 3 \end{aligned}$$

Let $A = \begin{bmatrix} a & b \\ c & d \end{bmatrix}$. Show that statements 43–45 are true.

43. $IA = A$

44. $AI = A$

45. $A \cdot O = O$

46. Find A^{-1}. (Assume $ad - bc \neq 0$.) Show that $AA^{-1} = I$.

47. Show that $A^{-1}A = I$.

48. Using the definitions and properties listed in this section, show that for square matrices A and B of the same order, if $AB = O$ and if A^{-1} exists, then $B = O$.

49. The Bread Box Bakery sells three types of cakes, each requiring the amounts of the basic ingredients shown in the following matrix.

$$\begin{array}{cc} & \begin{array}{c} \text{Types of cake} \\ \text{I} \quad \text{II} \quad \text{III} \end{array} \\ \begin{array}{l} \text{Flour (cups)} \\ \text{Sugar (cups)} \\ \text{Eggs} \end{array} & \begin{bmatrix} 2 & 4 & 2 \\ 2 & 1 & 2 \\ 2 & 1 & 3 \end{bmatrix} \end{array}$$

To fill its daily orders for these three kinds of cake, the bakery uses 72 cups of flour, 48 cups of sugar, and 60 eggs.

(a) Write a 3×1 matrix for the amounts used daily.

(b) Let the number of daily orders for cakes be a 3×1 matrix X with entries x_1, x_2, and x_3. Write a matrix equation which you can solve for X, using the given matrix and the matrix from part (a).

(c) Solve the equation you wrote in part (b) to find the number of daily orders for each type of cake.

50. Prove that, if it exists, the inverse of a matrix is unique. Hint: Assume there are two inverses B and C for some matrix A, so that $AB = BA = I$ and $AC = CA = I$. Multiply the first equation by C and the second by B.

Use matrices C and D to find the inverses in Exercises 51–54.

$$C = \begin{bmatrix} -6 & 8 & 2 & 4 & -3 \\ 1 & 9 & 7 & -12 & 5 \\ 15 & 2 & -8 & 10 & 11 \\ 4 & 7 & 9 & 6 & -2 \\ 1 & 3 & 8 & 23 & 4 \end{bmatrix} \qquad D = \begin{bmatrix} 5 & -3 & 7 & 9 & 2 \\ 6 & 8 & -5 & 2 & 1 \\ 3 & 7 & -4 & 2 & 11 \\ 5 & -3 & 9 & 4 & -1 \\ 0 & 3 & 2 & 5 & 1 \end{bmatrix}$$

51. C^{-1}

52. $(CD)^{-1}$

53. D^{-1}

54. Is $C^{-1}D^{-1} = (CD)^{-1}$?

Solve the matrix equation $AX = B$ for X, given A and B as follows.

55.
$$A = \begin{bmatrix} 2 & 3 & 5 \\ 1 & 7 & 9 \\ -3 & 2 & 10 \end{bmatrix} \qquad B = \begin{bmatrix} 3 \\ 4 \\ 1 \end{bmatrix}$$

56.
$$A = \begin{bmatrix} 2 & 5 & 7 & 9 \\ 1 & 3 & -4 & 6 \\ -1 & 0 & 5 & 8 \\ 2 & -2 & 4 & 10 \end{bmatrix} \qquad B = \begin{bmatrix} 3 \\ 7 \\ -1 \\ 5 \end{bmatrix}$$

57.
$$A = \begin{bmatrix} 3 & 2 & -1 & -2 & 6 \\ -5 & 17 & 4 & 3 & 15 \\ 7 & 9 & -3 & -7 & 12 \\ 9 & -2 & 1 & 4 & 8 \\ 1 & 21 & 9 & -7 & 25 \end{bmatrix} \qquad B = \begin{bmatrix} -2 \\ 5 \\ 3 \\ -8 \\ 25 \end{bmatrix}$$

EXTENDED APPLICATION

Code Theory

Governments need sophisticated methods of coding and decoding messages. One example of such an advanced code uses matrix theory. Such a code takes the letters in the words and divides them into groups. (Each space between words is treated as a letter; punctuation is disregarded.) Then, numbers are assigned to the letters of the alphabet. For our purposes, let the letter *a* correspond to 1, *b* to 2, and so on. We let the number 27 correspond to a space between words.

For example, the message

mathematics is for the birds

can be divided into groups of three letters each.

mat   hem   ati   cs-   is-   for   -th   e-b   ird   s--

Note that we used "-" to represent a space between words. We now write a column matrix for each group of three symbols using the corresponding numbers, as determined above, instead of letters. For example, the letters *mat* can be encoded as

$$\begin{bmatrix} 13 \\ 1 \\ 20 \end{bmatrix}.$$

The coded message then is the set of 3×1 column matrices.

$$\begin{bmatrix} 13 \\ 1 \\ 20 \end{bmatrix} \begin{bmatrix} 8 \\ 5 \\ 13 \end{bmatrix} \begin{bmatrix} 1 \\ 20 \\ 9 \end{bmatrix} \begin{bmatrix} 3 \\ 19 \\ 27 \end{bmatrix} \begin{bmatrix} 9 \\ 19 \\ 27 \end{bmatrix} \begin{bmatrix} 6 \\ 15 \\ 18 \end{bmatrix} \begin{bmatrix} 27 \\ 20 \\ 8 \end{bmatrix} \begin{bmatrix} 5 \\ 27 \\ 2 \end{bmatrix} \begin{bmatrix} 9 \\ 18 \\ 4 \end{bmatrix} \begin{bmatrix} 19 \\ 27 \\ 27 \end{bmatrix}$$

We can further complicate the code by choosing a matrix which has an inverse, in this case a 3×3 matrix, call it *M*, and find the products of this matrix and each of the above column matrices. (Note that the size of each group, the assignment of numbers to letters, and the choice of matrix M must all be predetermined.)

Suppose

$$M = \begin{bmatrix} 1 & 3 & 3 \\ 1 & 4 & 3 \\ 1 & 3 & 4 \end{bmatrix}.$$

If we find the products of M and the column matrices above, we have a new set of column matrices,

$$\begin{bmatrix} 76 \\ 77 \\ 96 \end{bmatrix} \begin{bmatrix} 62 \\ 67 \\ 75 \end{bmatrix} \quad \text{and so on.}$$

The entries of these matrices can then be transmitted to an agent as the message *76, 77, 96, 62, 67, 75,* and so on.

The agent receiving the message divides it into groups of numbers and forms each group into a column matrix. After multiplying each column matrix by the matrix M^{-1}, the message can be read.

Although this type of code is relatively simple, it is actually difficult to break. Many ramifications are possible. For example, a long message might be placed in groups of 20, thus requiring a 20×20 matrix for coding and decoding. Finding the inverse of such a matrix would require an impractical amount of time if calculated by hand. For this reason some of the largest computers are used by government agencies involved in coding.

EXERCISES

1. Let $M = \begin{bmatrix} 4 & -1 \\ 2 & 6 \end{bmatrix}$

   (a) Use M to encode the message: *Meet at the cave.* Use 2×1 matrices.

   (b) What matrix should be used to decode the message?

2. Let $M = \begin{bmatrix} -1 & 2 \\ 2 & -5 \end{bmatrix}.$

   Encode the message: *Attack at dawn unless too cold.*

3. Matrix M from Exercise 2 was used to encode the following message. Decode it.

$$\begin{bmatrix} -17 \\ 33 \end{bmatrix} \begin{bmatrix} 26 \\ -72 \end{bmatrix} \begin{bmatrix} 53 \\ -133 \end{bmatrix} \begin{bmatrix} 21 \\ -54 \end{bmatrix} \begin{bmatrix} 41 \\ -103 \end{bmatrix} \begin{bmatrix} 35 \\ -97 \end{bmatrix} \begin{bmatrix} 29 \\ -77 \end{bmatrix} \begin{bmatrix} -15 \\ 24 \end{bmatrix} \begin{bmatrix} 39 \\ -98 \end{bmatrix}$$

4. Finish encoding the message given in the text.

2.6   Input-Output Models

Nobel prize winner Wassily Leontief developed an interesting application of matrix theory to economics. His matrix models for studying the interdependencies in an economy are called *input-output* models. In practice these models are very complicated with many variables. We discuss only simple examples with few variables.

Input-output models are concerned with the production and flow of goods (and perhaps services). In an economy with n basic commodities, or sectors, the production of each commodity uses some (perhaps all) of the commodities in the economy as inputs. The amounts of each commodity used in the production of one unit of each commodity can be written as an $n \times n$ matrix A, called the **technological** or **input-output matrix** of the economy.

EXAMPLE 1

Suppose a simplified economy involves just three commodity categories: agriculture, manufacturing, and transportation, all in appropriate units. Production of 1 unit of agriculture requires 1/2 unit of manufacturing and 1/4 unit of transportation. Production of 1 unit of manufacturing requires 1/4 unit of agriculture and 1/4 unit of transportation; while production of 1 unit of transportation requires 1/3 unit of agriculture and 1/4 unit of manufacturing. Give the input-output matrix of this economy.

The matrix is shown below.

$$\begin{array}{c} \\ \text{Agriculture} \\ \text{Manufacturing} \\ \text{Transportation} \end{array} \begin{array}{ccc} \text{Agric.} & \text{Manuf.} & \text{Trans.} \end{array} \\ \begin{bmatrix} 0 & \frac{1}{4} & \frac{1}{3} \\ \frac{1}{2} & 0 & \frac{1}{4} \\ \frac{1}{4} & \frac{1}{4} & 0 \end{bmatrix} = A$$

The first column of the input-output matrix represents the amount of each of the three commodities consumed in the production of 1 unit of agriculture. The second column gives the corresponding amounts required to produce 1 unit of manufacturing, and the last column gives the amounts needed to produce one unit of transportation. (Although it is perhaps unrealistic that production of a unit of each commodity requires none of that commodity, the simpler matrix involved is useful for our purposes.) ▨

Another matrix used with the input-output matrix is the matrix giving the amount of each commodity produced, called the **production matrix,** or the matrix of gross output. In an economy producing n commodities, the production matrix can be represented by a column matrix X with entries $x_1, x_2, x_3, \ldots, x_n$.

EXAMPLE 2

In Example 1, suppose the production matrix is

$$X = \begin{bmatrix} 60 \\ 52 \\ 48 \end{bmatrix}.$$

Then 60 units of agriculture, 52 units of manufacturing and 48 units of transportation are produced. As 1/4 unit of agriculture is used for each unit of manufacturing produced, $1/4 \times 52 = 13$ units of agriculture must be used up in the "production" of manufacturing. Similarly, $1/3 \times 48 = 16$ units of agriculture will be used up in the "production" of transportation. Thus $13 + 16 = 29$ units of agriculture are used for production in the economy. Look again at the matrices A and X. Since X gives the number of units of each commodity produced and A gives the amount (in units) of each commodity used to produce one unit of the various commodities, the matrix product AX gives the amount of each commodity used up in the production process.

$$AX = \begin{bmatrix} 0 & \frac{1}{4} & \frac{1}{3} \\ \frac{1}{2} & 0 & \frac{1}{4} \\ \frac{1}{4} & \frac{1}{4} & 0 \end{bmatrix} \begin{bmatrix} 60 \\ 52 \\ 48 \end{bmatrix} = \begin{bmatrix} 29 \\ 42 \\ 28 \end{bmatrix}$$

From this result 29 units of agriculture, 42 units of manufacturing, and 28 units of transportation are used up to produce 60 units of agriculture, 52 units of manufacturing, and 48 units of transportation. ▩

We have seen that the matrix product AX represents the amount of each commodity used up in the production process. The remainder (if any) must be enough to satisfy the demand for the various commodities from outside the production system. In an n-commodity economy, this demand can be represented by a **demand matrix** D with entries $d_1, d_2, \ldots, d_n$. The difference between the production matrix, X, and the amount, AX, used up in the production process must equal the demand, D, or

$$D = X - AX.$$

In Example 2,

$$D = \begin{bmatrix} 60 \\ 52 \\ 48 \end{bmatrix} - \begin{bmatrix} 29 \\ 42 \\ 28 \end{bmatrix} = \begin{bmatrix} 31 \\ 10 \\ 20 \end{bmatrix},$$

so that production of 60 units of agriculture, 52 units of manufacturing, and 48 units of transportation would satisfy a demand of 31, 10, and 20 units of each, respectively.

Another way to state the relationship between production, X, and demand, D, is to express X as $X = D + AX$. In practice, A and D usually are known and X must be found. That is, we need to decide on the amounts of production necessary to satisfy the required demands. Matrix algebra can be used to solve the equation $D = X - AX$ for X.

$$D = X - AX$$
$$D = IX - AX$$
$$D = (I - A)X$$

If the matrix $I - A$ has an inverse, then

$$X = (I - A)^{-1}D.$$

EXAMPLE 3

Suppose, in the 3-commodity economy of Examples 1 and 2, there is a demand for 516 units of agriculture, 258 units of manufacturing, and 129 units of transportation. What should production of each commodity be?

The demand matrix is

$$D = \begin{bmatrix} 516 \\ 258 \\ 129 \end{bmatrix}.$$

To find the production matrix X, first calculate $I - A$.

$$I - A = \begin{bmatrix} 1 & 0 & 0 \\ 0 & 1 & 0 \\ 0 & 0 & 1 \end{bmatrix} - \begin{bmatrix} 0 & \frac{1}{4} & \frac{1}{3} \\ \frac{1}{2} & 0 & \frac{1}{4} \\ \frac{1}{4} & \frac{1}{4} & 0 \end{bmatrix} = \begin{bmatrix} 1 & -\frac{1}{4} & -\frac{1}{3} \\ -\frac{1}{2} & 1 & -\frac{1}{4} \\ -\frac{1}{4} & -\frac{1}{4} & 1 \end{bmatrix}$$

Use row operations to find the inverse of $I - A$ (the entries are rounded to two decimal places).

$$(I - A)^{-1} = \begin{bmatrix} 1.40 & .50 & .59 \\ .84 & 1.36 & .62 \\ .56 & .47 & 1.30 \end{bmatrix}$$

Since $X = (I - A)^{-1}D$,

$$X = \begin{bmatrix} 1.40 & .50 & .59 \\ .84 & 1.36 & .62 \\ .56 & .47 & 1.30 \end{bmatrix} \begin{bmatrix} 516 \\ 258 \\ 129 \end{bmatrix} = \begin{bmatrix} 928 \\ 864 \\ 578 \end{bmatrix}.$$

(Entries have been rounded to the nearest whole numbers).

The last result shows that production of 928 units of agriculture, 864 units of manufacturing, and 578 units of transportation is required to satisfy demands of 516, 258, and 129 units respectively. ▪

EXAMPLE 4

An economy depends on two basic products, wheat and oil. To produce 1 metric ton of wheat requires .25 metric tons of wheat and .33 metric tons of oil. Production of 1 metric ton of oil consumes .08 metric tons of wheat and .11 metric tons of oil. Find the production which will satisfy a demand of 500 metric tons of wheat and 1000 metric tons of oil.

The input-output matrix, A, and $I - A$ are

$$A = \begin{bmatrix} .25 & .08 \\ .33 & .11 \end{bmatrix} \quad \text{and} \quad I - A = \begin{bmatrix} .75 & -.08 \\ -.33 & .89 \end{bmatrix}.$$

Next, calculate $(I - A)^{-1}$.

$$(I - A)^{-1} = \begin{bmatrix} 1.39 & .13 \\ .51 & 1.17 \end{bmatrix} \quad \text{(rounded)}$$

To find the production matrix X, use the equation $X = (I - A)^{-1}D$, with

$$D = \begin{bmatrix} 500 \\ 1000 \end{bmatrix}.$$

The production matrix is

$$X = \begin{bmatrix} 1.39 & .13 \\ .51 & 1.17 \end{bmatrix} \begin{bmatrix} 500 \\ 1000 \end{bmatrix} = \begin{bmatrix} 815 \\ 1425 \end{bmatrix}.$$

Production of 815 metric tons of wheat and 1425 metric tons of oil are required to satisfy the indicated demand. ▪

The model we have discussed is referred to as an **open model,** since it allows for a surplus from the production equal to D. In the **closed model,** all the production is consumed internally in the production process so that $X = AX$. There is nothing left over to satisfy any outside demands from other parts of the economy, or from other economies. In this case, the sum of each column in the input-output matrix equals one.

To solve the equation $X = AX$ for X, first let O represent an n-row column matrix with each element equal to 0. Write $X = AX$ or $X - AX = O$: then

$$IX - AX = O,$$

$$(I - A)X = O.$$

The system of equations which corresponds to $(I - A)X = O$ does not have a single unique solution. However, it can be solved in terms of a parameter. As we saw in Section 2.1, this means there are infinitely many solutions.

EXAMPLE 5

Use matrix A below to find the production of each commodity in a closed model.

$$A = \begin{bmatrix} \frac{1}{2} & \frac{1}{4} & \frac{1}{3} \\ 0 & \frac{1}{4} & \frac{1}{3} \\ \frac{1}{2} & \frac{1}{2} & \frac{1}{3} \end{bmatrix}$$

Find the value of $I - A$, then set $(I - A)X = O$ to find X.

$$I - A = \begin{bmatrix} \frac{1}{2} & -\frac{1}{4} & -\frac{1}{3} \\ 0 & \frac{3}{4} & -\frac{1}{3} \\ -\frac{1}{2} & -\frac{1}{2} & \frac{2}{3} \end{bmatrix}$$

$$(I - A)X = \begin{bmatrix} \frac{1}{2} & -\frac{1}{4} & -\frac{1}{3} \\ 0 & \frac{3}{4} & -\frac{1}{3} \\ -\frac{1}{2} & -\frac{1}{2} & \frac{2}{3} \end{bmatrix} \begin{bmatrix} x_1 \\ x_2 \\ x_3 \end{bmatrix} = \begin{bmatrix} 0 \\ 0 \\ 0 \end{bmatrix}$$

Multiply to get

$$\begin{bmatrix} \frac{1}{2} x_1 - \frac{1}{4} x_2 - \frac{1}{3} x_3 \\ 0 x_1 + \frac{3}{4} x_2 - \frac{1}{3} x_3 \\ -\frac{1}{2} x_1 - \frac{1}{2} x_2 + \frac{2}{3} x_3 \end{bmatrix} = \begin{bmatrix} 0 \\ 0 \\ 0 \end{bmatrix}.$$

From the last matrix equation, we get the following system.

$$\frac{1}{2} x_1 - \frac{1}{4} x_2 - \frac{1}{3} x_3 = 0$$

$$\frac{3}{4} x_2 - \frac{1}{3} x_3 = 0$$

$$-\frac{1}{2} x_1 - \frac{1}{2} x_2 + \frac{2}{3} x_3 = 0$$

Solving the system with x_3 as the parameter gives the solution of the system which can be written as

$$x_1 = \tfrac{8}{9} x_3$$

$$x_2 = \tfrac{4}{9} x_3$$

$$x_3 \quad \text{arbitrary.}$$

If $x_3 = 9$, then $x_1 = 8$ and $x_2 = 4$, with the production of the three commodities in the ratio $8:4:9$. ▨

2.6 EXERCISES

Find the production matrix for the following input-output and demand matrices using the open model.

1. $A = \begin{bmatrix} .5 & .4 \\ .25 & .2 \end{bmatrix}$ $D = \begin{bmatrix} 2 \\ 4 \end{bmatrix}$

2. $A = \begin{bmatrix} .2 & .04 \\ .6 & .05 \end{bmatrix}$ $D = \begin{bmatrix} 3 \\ 10 \end{bmatrix}$

3. $A = \begin{bmatrix} .1 & .03 \\ .07 & .6 \end{bmatrix}$ $D = \begin{bmatrix} 5 \\ 10 \end{bmatrix}$

4. $A = \begin{bmatrix} .01 & .03 \\ .05 & .05 \end{bmatrix}$ $D = \begin{bmatrix} 100 \\ 200 \end{bmatrix}$

5. $A = \begin{bmatrix} .4 & 0 & .3 \\ 0 & .8 & .1 \\ 0 & .2 & .4 \end{bmatrix}$ $D = \begin{bmatrix} 1 \\ 3 \\ 2 \end{bmatrix}$

6. $A = \begin{bmatrix} .1 & .5 & 0 \\ 0 & .3 & .4 \\ .1 & .2 & .1 \end{bmatrix}$ $D = \begin{bmatrix} 10 \\ 4 \\ 2 \end{bmatrix}$

In Exercises 7 and 8, refer to Example 4.

7. If the demand is changed to 690 metric tons of wheat and 920 metric tons of oil, how many units of each commodity should be produced?

8. Change the technological matrix so that production of 1 ton of wheat requires 1/5 metric ton of oil (and no wheat), and the production of 1 metric ton of oil requires 1/3 metric ton of wheat (and no oil). To satisfy the same demand matrix, how many units of each commodity should be produced?

In Exercises 9–12, refer to Example 3.

9. If the demand is changed to 516 units of each commodity, how many units of each commodity should be produced?

10. Suppose 1/3 unit of manufacturing (no agriculture or transportation) is required to produce 1 unit of agriculture, 1/4 unit of transportation is required to produce 1 unit of manufacturing, and 1/2 unit of agriculture is required to produce 1 unit of transportation. How many units of each commodity should be produced to satisfy a demand of 1000 units for each commodity?

11. Suppose 1/4 unit of manufacturing and 1/2 unit of transportation are required to produce 1 unit of agriculture, 1/2 unit of agriculture and 1/4 unit of transportation to produce 1 unit of manufacturing, and 1/4 unit of agriculture and 1/4 unit of manufacturing to produce one unit of transportation. How many units of each commodity should be produced to satisfy a demand of 1000 units for each commodity?

12. If the technological matrix is changed so that 1/4 unit of manufacturing and 1/2 unit of transportation are required to produce 1 unit of agriculture, 1/2 unit of agriculture and 1/4 unit of transportation are required to produce 1 unit of manufacturing, and 1/4 unit each of agriculture and manufacturing are required to produce 1 unit of transportation, find the number of units of each commodity which should be produced to satisfy a demand for 500 units of each commodity.

13. A primitive economy depends on two basic goods, yams and pork. Production of 1 bushel of yams requires 1/4 bushel of yams and 1/2 of a pig. To produce 1 pig requires 1/6 bushel of yams. Find the amount of each commodity which should be produced to get

   (a) 1 bushel of yams and 1 pig;

   (b) 100 bushels of yams and 70 pigs.

14. Use the input-output matrix

$$
\begin{array}{cc}
 & \text{yams} \quad \text{pigs} \\
\begin{array}{c} \text{yams} \\ \text{pigs} \end{array} &
\left[\begin{array}{cc} \frac{1}{4} & \frac{1}{2} \\ \frac{3}{4} & \frac{1}{2} \end{array} \right]
\end{array}
$$

and the closed model to find the ratios of yams and pigs produced.

Find the ratios of products A, B, and C, using a closed model.

15.
$$
\begin{array}{cccc}
 & A & B & C \\
\begin{array}{c} A \\ B \\ C \end{array} &
\left[\begin{array}{ccc} .3 & .1 & .8 \\ .5 & .6 & .1 \\ .2 & .3 & .1 \end{array} \right]
\end{array}
$$

16.
$$
\begin{array}{cccc}
 & A & B & C \\
\begin{array}{c} A \\ B \\ C \end{array} &
\left[\begin{array}{ccc} .2 & .1 & .5 \\ .4 & .3 & .4 \\ .4 & .6 & .1 \end{array} \right]
\end{array}
$$

Solve the following input-output problems.

17.
$$
A = \left[\begin{array}{cccc} .25 & .25 & .25 & .05 \\ .01 & .02 & .01 & .1 \\ .3 & .3 & .01 & .1 \\ .2 & .01 & .3 & .01 \end{array} \right] \qquad D = \left[\begin{array}{c} 2930 \\ 3570 \\ 2300 \\ 580 \end{array} \right]
$$

18.
$$
A = \left[\begin{array}{cccc} .2 & .1 & .2 & .2 \\ .3 & .05 & .07 & .02 \\ .1 & .03 & .02 & .01 \\ .05 & .3 & .05 & .03 \end{array} \right] \qquad D = \left[\begin{array}{c} 5000 \\ 1000 \\ 8000 \\ 500 \end{array} \right]
$$

19. A simple economy depends on three commodities: oil, corn, and coffee. Production of one unit of oil requires .1 unit of oil, .2 unit of corn, and no units of coffee. To produce one unit of corn requires .2 unit of oil, .1 unit of corn, and .05 unit of coffee. To produce one unit of coffee requires .1 unit of oil, .05 unit of corn, and .1 unit of coffee. Find the gross production required to give a net production of 1000 units each of oil, corn, and coffee.

EXTENDED

APPLICATION

Leontief's Model of the American Economy

In the April 1965 issue of *Scientific American,* Leontief explained his input-output system, using the 1958 American economy as an example.* He divided the economy into 81 sectors, grouped into six families of related sectors. In order to keep the discussion reasonably simple, we will treat each family of sectors as a single sector and so, in effect, work with a six sector model. The sectors are listed in Table 1.

The workings of the American economy in 1958 are described in the input-output table (Table 2) based on Leontief's figures. We will demonstrate the meaning of Table 2 by considering the first left-hand column of numbers. The numbers in this column mean that 1 unit of final nonmetal production requires the consumption of 0.170 unit of (other) final nonmetal production, 0.003 unit of final metal output, 0.025 unit of basic metal products, and so on down the column. Since the unit of measurement that Leontief used for this table is millions of dollars, we conclude that the production of $1 million worth of final nonmetal production consumes $0.170 million, or $170,000, worth of other final nonmetal products, $3000 of final metal production, $25,000 of basic metal products, and so on. Similarly, the entry in the column headed FM and opposite S of 0.074 means that $74,000 worth of output from the service industries goes into the production of $1 million worth of final metal products, and the number 0.358 in the column headed E and opposite E means that $358,000 worth of energy must be consumed to produce $1 million worth of energy.

Table 1	Sector	Examples
	Final nonmetal (FN)	Furniture, processed food
	Final metal (FM)	Household appliances, motor vehicles
	Basic metal (BM)	Machine-shop products, mining
	Basic nonmetal (BN)	Agriculture, printing
	Energy (E)	Petroleum, coal
	Services (S)	Amusements, real estate

Table 2		FN	FM	BM	BN	E	S
	FN	0.170	0.004	0	0.029	0	0.008
	FM	0.003	0.295	0.018	0.002	0.004	0.016
	BM	0.025	0.173	0.460	0.007	0.011	0.007
	BN	0.348	0.037	0.021	0.403	0.011	0.048
	E	0.007	0.001	0.039	0.025	0.358	0.025
	S	0.120	0.074	0.104	0.123	0.173	0.234

*From *Applied Finite Mathematics* by Robert F. Brown and Brenda W. Brown. © 1977 by Wadsworth Publishing Company, Inc. Reprinted by permission of Wadsworth Publishing Company, Belmont, California 94002.

By the underlying assumption of Leontief's model, the production of n units (n = any number) of final nonmetal production consumes $0.170n$ unit of final nonmetal output, $0.003n$ unit of final metal output, $0.025n$ unit of basic metal production, and so on. Thus, production of $50 million worth of products from the final nonmetal section of the 1958 American economy required $(0.170)(50) = 8.5$ units ($8.5 million) worth of final nonmetal output, $(0.003)(50) = 0.15$ unit of final metal output, $(0.025)(50) = 1.25$ units of basic metal production, and so on.

Example 1

According to the simplified input-output table for the 1958 American economy, how many dollars worth of final metal products, basic nonmetal products, and services are required to produce $120 million worth of basic metal products?

Each unit ($1 million worth) of basic metal products requires 0.018 unit of final metal products because the number in the BM column opposite FM is 0.018. Thus, $120 million, or 120 units, requires $(0.018)(120) = 2.16$ units, or $2.16 million of final metal products. Similarly, 120 units of basic metal production uses $(0.021)(120) = 2.52$ units of basic nonmetal production and $(0.104)(120) = 12.48$ units of services, or $2.52 million and $12.48 million of basic nonmetal output and services, respectively.

The Leontief model also involves a *bill of demands,* that is, a list of requirements for units of output beyond that required for its inner workings as described in the input-output table. These demands represent exports, surpluses, government and individual consumption, and the like. The bill of demands for the simplified version of the 1958 American economy we have been using was (in millions)

FN	$99,640
FM	$75,548
BM	$14,444
BN	$33,501
E	$23,527
S	$263,985

We can now use the methods developed above to answer the question: how many units of output from each sector are needed in order to run the economy and fill the bill of demands? The units of output from each sector required to run the economy and fill the bill of demands is unknown, so we denote them by variables. In our example, there are six quantities which are, at the moment, unknown. The number of units of final nonmetal production required to solve the problem will be our first unknown, because this sector is represented by the first row of the input-output matrix. The unknown quantity of final nonmetal units will be represented by the symbol x_1. Following the same pattern, we represent the unknown quantities in the following manner:

x_1 = units of final nonmetal production required,

x_2 = units of final metal production required,

x_3 = units of basic metal production required,

x_4 = units of basic nonmetal production required,

x_5 = units of energy required,

x_6 = units of services required.

These six numbers are the quantities we are attempting to calculate.

To find these numbers, first let A be the 6 × 6 matrix corresponding to the input-output table.

$$A = \begin{bmatrix} 0.170 & 0.004 & 0 & 0.029 & 0 & 0.008 \\ 0.003 & 0.295 & 0.018 & 0.002 & 0.004 & 0.016 \\ 0.025 & 0.173 & 0.460 & 0.007 & 0.011 & 0.007 \\ 0.348 & 0.037 & 0.021 & 0.403 & 0.011 & 0.048 \\ 0.007 & 0.001 & 0.039 & 0.025 & 0.358 & 0.025 \\ 0.120 & 0.074 & 0.104 & 0.123 & 0.173 & 0.234 \end{bmatrix}$$

A is the input-output matrix. The bill of demands leads to a 6 × 1 demand matrix D, and X is the matrix of unknowns.

$$D = \begin{bmatrix} 99,640 \\ 75,548 \\ 14,444 \\ 33,501 \\ 23,527 \\ 263,985 \end{bmatrix} \quad \text{and} \quad X = \begin{bmatrix} x_1 \\ x_2 \\ x_3 \\ x_4 \\ x_5 \\ x_6 \end{bmatrix}$$

Now we need to find $I - A$.

$$I - A = \begin{bmatrix} 1 & 0 & 0 & 0 & 0 & 0 \\ 0 & 1 & 0 & 0 & 0 & 0 \\ 0 & 0 & 1 & 0 & 0 & 0 \\ 0 & 0 & 0 & 1 & 0 & 0 \\ 0 & 0 & 0 & 0 & 1 & 0 \\ 0 & 0 & 0 & 0 & 0 & 1 \end{bmatrix} - \begin{bmatrix} 0.170 & 0.004 & 0 & 0.029 & 0 & 0.008 \\ 0.003 & 0.295 & 0.018 & 0.002 & 0.004 & 0.016 \\ 0.025 & 0.173 & 0.460 & 0.007 & 0.011 & 0.007 \\ 0.348 & 0.037 & 0.021 & 0.403 & 0.011 & 0.048 \\ 0.007 & 0.001 & 0.039 & 0.025 & 0.358 & 0.025 \\ 0.120 & 0.074 & 0.104 & 0.123 & 0.173 & 0.234 \end{bmatrix}$$

$$= \begin{bmatrix} 0.830 & -0.004 & 0 & -0.029 & 0 & -0.008 \\ -0.003 & 0.705 & -0.018 & -0.002 & -0.004 & -0.016 \\ -0.025 & -0.173 & 0.540 & -0.007 & -0.011 & -0.007 \\ -0.348 & -0.037 & -0.021 & 0.597 & -0.011 & -0.048 \\ -0.007 & -0.001 & -0.039 & -0.025 & 0.642 & -0.025 \\ -0.120 & -0.074 & -0.104 & -0.123 & -0.173 & 0.766 \end{bmatrix}$$

Find the inverse (actually an approximation) by the methods of this chapter.

$$(I - A)^{-1} = \begin{bmatrix} 1.234 & 0.014 & 0.006 & 0.064 & 0.007 & 0.018 \\ 0.017 & 1.436 & 0.057 & 0.012 & 0.020 & 0.032 \\ 0.071 & 0.465 & 1.877 & 0.019 & 0.045 & 0.031 \\ 0.751 & 0.134 & 0.100 & 1.740 & 0.066 & 0.124 \\ 0.060 & 0.045 & 0.130 & 0.082 & 1.578 & 0.059 \\ 0.339 & 0.236 & 0.307 & 0.312 & 0.376 & 1.349 \end{bmatrix}.$$

Therefore, $X = (I - A)^{-1}D =$

$$\begin{bmatrix} 1.234 & 0.014 & 0.006 & 0.064 & 0.007 & 0.018 \\ 0.017 & 1.436 & 0.057 & 0.012 & 0.020 & 0.032 \\ 0.071 & 0.465 & 1.877 & 0.019 & 0.045 & 0.031 \\ 0.751 & 0.134 & 0.100 & 1.740 & 0.066 & 0.124 \\ 0.060 & 0.045 & 0.130 & 0.082 & 1.578 & 0.059 \\ 0.339 & 0.236 & 0.307 & 0.312 & 0.376 & 1.349 \end{bmatrix} \begin{bmatrix} 99,640 \\ 75,548 \\ 14,444 \\ 33,501 \\ 23,527 \\ 263,985 \end{bmatrix} = \begin{bmatrix} 131,161 \\ 120,324 \\ 79,194 \\ 178,936 \\ 66,703 \\ 426,542 \end{bmatrix}.$$

From this result,

$$x_1 = 131,161$$
$$x_2 = 120,324$$
$$x_3 = 79,194$$
$$x_4 = 178,936$$
$$x_5 = 66,703$$
$$x_6 = 426,542$$

In other words, by this model 131,161 units ($131,161 million worth) of final non-metal production, 120,324 units of final metal output, 79,194 units of basic metal products, and so on are required to run the 1958 American economy and completely fill the stated bill of demands.

EXERCISES

1. A much simplified version of Leontief's 42 sector analysis of the 1947 American economy divides the economy into just three sectors: agriculture, manufacturing, and the household (i.e., the sector of the economy which produces labor). It consists of the following input-output table:

	Agriculture	Manufacturing	Household
Agriculture	0.245	0.102	0.051
Manufacturing	0.099	0.291	0.279
Household	0.433	0.372	0.011

The bill of demands (in billions of dollars) is

Agriculture	2.88
Manufacturing	31.45
Household	30.91.

(a) Write the input-output matrix A, the demand matrix D, and the matrix X.
(b) Compute $I - A$. (c) Check that

$$(I - A)^{-1} = \begin{bmatrix} 1.454 & 0.291 & 0.157 \\ 0.533 & 1.763 & 0.525 \\ 0.837 & 0.791 & 1.278 \end{bmatrix}$$

is an approximation to the inverse of $I - A$ by calculating $(I - A)^{-1}(I - A)$.
(d) Use the matrix of part (c) to compute X. (e) Explain the meaning of the numbers in X in dollars.

2. An analysis of the 1958 Israeli economy* is here simplified by grouping the economy into three sectors: agriculture, manufacturing, and energy. The input-output table is the following.

	Agriculture	Manufacturing	Energy
Agriculture	0.293	0	0
Manufacturing	0.014	0.207	0.017
Energy	0.044	0.010	0.216

Exports (in thousands of Israeli pounds) were

Agriculture	138,213
Manufacturing	17,597
Energy	1,786

(a) Write the input-output matrix A and the demand (export) matrix D. (b) Compute I − A. (c) Check that

$$(I - A)^{-1} = \begin{bmatrix} 1.414 & 0 & 0 \\ 0.027 & 1.261 & 0.027 \\ 0.080 & 0.016 & 1.276 \end{bmatrix}$$

is an approximation to the inverse of I − A by calculating $(I - A)^{-1}(I - A)$. (d) Use the matrix of part (c) to determine the number of Israeli pounds worth of agricultural products, manufactured goods, and energy required to run this model of the Israeli economy and export the stated value of products.

KEY WORDS

system of equations
first degree equation in *n* unknowns
inconsistent system
dependent equations
equivalent system
elimination method
echelon method
parameter
matrix
element (entry)
augmented matrix
row operations
Gauss-Jordan method

dimension (order)
square matrix
row matrix
column matrix
zero matrix
scalar
identity matrix
multiplicative inverse of a matrix
input-output matrix
production matrix
demand matrix

---

*Wassily Leontief, *Input-Output Economics* (New York: Oxford University Press, 1966), pp. 54—57.

Chapter 2   REVIEW EXERCISES

Solve each of the systems in Exercises 1–4 by the echelon method.

1. $2x + 3y = 10$
   $-3x + y = 18$

2. $\dfrac{x}{2} + \dfrac{y}{4} = 3$

   $\dfrac{x}{4} - \dfrac{y}{2} = 4$

3. $2x - 3y + z = -5$
   $x + 4y + 2z = 13$
   $5x + 5y + 3z = 14$

4. $x - y \quad\;\; = 3$
   $2x + 3y + z = 13$
   $3x \quad\quad - 2z = 21$

Write each of Exercises 5–8 as a system of equations and solve.

5. An office supply manufacturer makes two kinds of paper clips, standard, and extra large. To make 1000 standard paper clips requires 1/4 hour on a cutting machine and 1/2 hour on a machine which shapes the clips. One thousand extra large paper clips require 1/3 hour on each machine. The manager of paper clip production has four hours per day available on the cutting machine and six hours per day on the shaping machine. How many of each kind of clip can he make?

6. Jane Schmidt plans to buy shares of two stocks. One costs $32 per share and pays dividends of $1.20 per share. The other costs $23 per share and pays dividends of $1.40 per share. She has $10,100 to spend and wants to earn dividends of $540. How many shares of each stock should she buy?

7. The Waputi Indians make woven blankets, rugs, and skirts. Each blanket requires 24 hours for spinning the yarn, 4 hours for dying the yarn, and 15 hours for weaving. Rugs require 30, 5, and 18 hours, and skirts 12, 3, and 9 hours respectively. If there are 306, 59, and 201 hours available for spinning, dying, and weaving respectively, how many of each item can be made? (Hint: Simplify the equations you write, if possible, before solving the system.)

8. An oil refinery in Tulsa sells 50% of its production to a Chicago distributor, 20% to a Dallas distributor, and 30% to an Atlanta distributor. Another refinery in New Orleans sells 40% of its production to the Chicago distributor, 40% to the Dallas distributor, and 20% to the Atlanta distributor. A third refinery in Ardmore sells the same distributors 30%, 40%, and 30% of its production. The three distributors received 219,000, 192,000, and 144,000 gallons of oil respectively. How many gallons of oil were produced at each of the three plants?

Solve the systems in Exercises 9–13 by the Gauss-Jordan method.

9. $2x + 4y = -6$
   $-3x - 5y = 12$

10. $x + 2y = -9$
   $4x + 9y = 41$

11. $x - y + 3z = 13$
   $4x + y + 2z = 17$
   $3x + 2y + 2z = 1$

12. $x + \quad\;\; - 2z = 5$
   $3x + 2y \quad\quad = 8$
   $-x \quad\quad + 2z = 10$

13. $3x - 6y + 9z = 12$
   $-x + 2y - 3z = -4$
   $x + y + 2z = 7$

In Exercises 14–17, find the order of the matrices, find the values of any variables, and identify any square, row, or column matrices.

14. $\begin{bmatrix} 2 & 3 \\ 5 & q \end{bmatrix} = \begin{bmatrix} a & b \\ c & 9 \end{bmatrix}$

15. $\begin{bmatrix} 2 & x \\ y & 6 \\ 5 & z \end{bmatrix} = \begin{bmatrix} a & -1 \\ 4 & 6 \\ p & 7 \end{bmatrix}$

16. $\begin{bmatrix} m & 4 & z & -1 \end{bmatrix} = \begin{bmatrix} 12 & k & -8 & r \end{bmatrix}$

17. $\begin{bmatrix} a+5 & 3b & 6 \\ 4c & 2+d & -3 \\ -1 & 4p & q-1 \end{bmatrix} = \begin{bmatrix} -7 & b+2 & 2k-3 \\ 3 & 2d-1 & 4l \\ m & 12 & 8 \end{bmatrix}$

18. The activities of a grazing animal can be classified roughly into three categories: grazing, moving, and resting. Suppose horses spend 8 hours grazing, 8 moving, and 8 resting; cattle spend 10 grazing, 5 moving and 9 resting; sheep spend 7 grazing, 10 moving, and 7 resting; and goats spend 8 grazing, 9 moving, and 7 resting. Write this information as a 4 × 3 matrix.

19. The New York Stock Exchange reports in the daily newspapers give the dividend, price to earnings ratio, sales (in hundreds of shares), last price, and change in price for each company. Write the following stock reports as a 4 × 5 matrix. American Telephone & Telegraph: 5, 7, 2532, 52 3/8, −1/4. General Electric: 3, 9, 1464, 56, +1/8. Mobil Oil: 2.50, 5, 4974, 41, −1 1/2. Sears: 1.36, 10, 1754, 18 7/8, +1/2.

Given the matrices

$$A = \begin{bmatrix} 4 & 10 \\ -2 & -3 \\ 6 & 9 \end{bmatrix}, \qquad B = \begin{bmatrix} 2 & 3 & -2 \\ 2 & 4 & 0 \\ 0 & 1 & 2 \end{bmatrix}, \qquad C = \begin{bmatrix} 5 & 0 \\ -1 & 3 \\ 4 & 7 \end{bmatrix},$$

$$D = \begin{bmatrix} 6 \\ 1 \\ 0 \end{bmatrix}, \qquad E = \begin{bmatrix} 1 & 3 & -4 \end{bmatrix}, \qquad F = \begin{bmatrix} -1 & 4 \\ 3 & 7 \end{bmatrix}, \qquad G = \begin{bmatrix} 2 & 5 \\ 1 & 6 \end{bmatrix},$$

find each of the following which exists.

20. $A + C$ **21.** $2G - 4F$ **22.** $3C + 2A$ **23.** $B - A$

24. $2A - 5C$ **25.** AF **26.** AC **27.** DE

28. ED **29.** BD **30.** EA **31.** F^{-1}

32. B^{-1} **33.** $(A + C)^{-1}$

Find the inverse of each of the following matrices that has an inverse.

34. $\begin{bmatrix} 2 & 1 \\ 5 & 3 \end{bmatrix}$ **35.** $\begin{bmatrix} -4 & 2 \\ 0 & 3 \end{bmatrix}$ **36.** $\begin{bmatrix} 2 & 0 \\ -1 & 5 \end{bmatrix}$ **37.** $\begin{bmatrix} 6 & 4 \\ 3 & 2 \end{bmatrix}$

38. $\begin{bmatrix} 2 & -1 & 0 \\ 1 & 0 & 1 \\ 1 & -2 & 0 \end{bmatrix}$ **39.** $\begin{bmatrix} 2 & 0 & 4 \\ 1 & -1 & 0 \\ 0 & 1 & -2 \end{bmatrix}$

40. $\begin{bmatrix} 1 & 3 & 6 \\ 4 & 0 & 9 \\ 5 & 15 & 30 \end{bmatrix}$ **41.** $\begin{bmatrix} 2 & 3 & 5 \\ -2 & -3 & -5 \\ 1 & 4 & 2 \end{bmatrix}$

Solve the matrix equation $AX = B$ for X using the matrices in Exercises 42–45.

42. $A = \begin{bmatrix} 2 & 4 \\ -1 & -3 \end{bmatrix}, \quad B = \begin{bmatrix} 8 \\ 3 \end{bmatrix}$

43. $A = \begin{bmatrix} 1 & 3 \\ -2 & 4 \end{bmatrix}, \quad B = \begin{bmatrix} 15 \\ 10 \end{bmatrix}$

44. $A = \begin{bmatrix} 1 & 0 & 2 \\ -1 & 1 & 0 \\ 3 & 0 & 4 \end{bmatrix}, \quad B = \begin{bmatrix} 8 \\ 4 \\ -6 \end{bmatrix}$

45. $A = \begin{bmatrix} 2 & 4 & 0 \\ 1 & -2 & 0 \\ 0 & 0 & 3 \end{bmatrix}, \quad B = \begin{bmatrix} 72 \\ -24 \\ 48 \end{bmatrix}$

46. A printer has three orders for pamphlets which require three kinds of paper as shown in the following matrix.

Orders

		I	II	III
	High-grade	10	5	8
Paper	Medium-grade	12	0	4
	Coated	0	10	5

The printer has on hand 3170 sheets of high-grade paper, 2360 sheets of medium-grade paper, and 1800 sheets of coated paper. All the paper must be used in preparing the order.

(a) Write a 3×1 matrix for the amounts of paper on hand.

(b) Write a matrix of variables to represent the number of pamphlets that must be printed in each of the three orders.

(c) Write a matrix equation using the given matrix and your matrices from parts (a) and (b).

(d) Solve the equation from part (c).

Solve each of the following systems of equations by inverses.

47. $2x + y = 5$
$3x - 2y = 4$

48. $5x + 10y = 80$
$3x - 2y = 120$

49. $x + y + z = 1$
$2x + y \quad\quad = -2$
$3y + z = 2$

Find the production matrix given the following input-output and demand matrices.

50. $A = \begin{bmatrix} .01 & .05 \\ .04 & .03 \end{bmatrix} \quad D = \begin{bmatrix} 200 \\ 300 \end{bmatrix}$

51. $A = \begin{bmatrix} .2 & .1 & .3 \\ .1 & 0 & .2 \\ 0 & 0 & .4 \end{bmatrix} \quad D = \begin{bmatrix} 500 \\ 200 \\ 100 \end{bmatrix}$

52. An economy depends on two commodities, goats and cheese. It takes 2/3 of a unit of goats to produce 1 unit of cheese and 1/2 unit of cheese to produce 1 unit of goats.

(a) Write the input-output matrix for this economy.

(b) Find the production required to satisfy a demand of 400 units of cheese and 800 units of goats.

LINEAR PROGRAMMING: THE GRAPHICAL METHOD

Karl Gerstner. From the series *Aperspective 3* (The Large Sliding Mirror Picture), 1953/55.

Many realistic problems involve inequalities—a factory can manufacture *no more than* 12 items on a shift, or a medical researcher must interview *at least* a hundred patients to be sure that a new treatment for a disease is better than the old treatment. *Linear inequalities* of the form $ax + by \leq c$ (or with $\geq$, $<$, or $>$ instead of $\leq$) can be used in a process called *linear programming* to *optimize* (find the maximum or minimum for) a given situation.

In this chapter we look at some linear programming problems that can be solved by graphical methods. Then, in Chapter 4, we discuss the *simplex method,* a general method for solving linear programming problems with many variables.

3.1   Graphing Linear Inequalities

As mentioned above,

Linear Inequality

> A **linear inequality** in two variables has the form
> $$ax + by \leq c$$
> for real numbers a, b, and c, with a and b not both 0.

While our definitions and theorems are usually given for $\leq$, keep in mind that $\leq$ may be replaced with $\geq$, $<$, or $>$.

EXAMPLE 1

Graph the linear inequality $3x - 2y \leq 6$.

Because of the "$=$" portion of $\leq$, the points of the line $3x - 2y = 6$ satisfy the linear inequality $3x - 2y \leq 6$ and are part of its graph. As in Chapter 1, find the intercepts by first letting $x = 0$ and then letting $y = 0$; use these points to get the graph of $3x - 2y = 6$ shown in Figure 1.

The points on the line satisfy "$3x - 2y$ *equals* 6." To locate the points satisfying "$3x - 2y$ *is less than* or equal to 6," first solve $3x - 2y \leq 6$ for y.

$$3x - 2y \leq 6$$
$$-2y \leq -3x + 6$$
$$y \geq \frac{3}{2}x - 3$$

(Recall that multiplying both sides of an inequality by a negative number reverses the direction of the inequality symbol.)

As shown in Figure 2, the points *above* the line $3x - 2y = 6$ satisfy

$$y > \frac{3}{2}x - 3,$$

while those below the line satisfy

$$y < \frac{3}{2}x - 3.$$

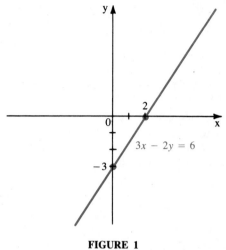

FIGURE 1

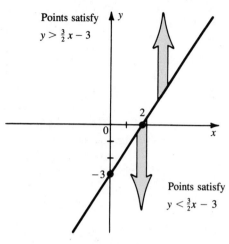

FIGURE 2

The line itself is the **boundary.** In summary, the inequality $3x - 2y \leq 6$ is satisfied by all points *on or above* the line $3x - 2y = 6$. Indicate the points above the line by shading, as in Figure 3. The line and shaded region of Figure 3 make up the graph of the linear inequality $3x - 2y \leq 6$. ▪

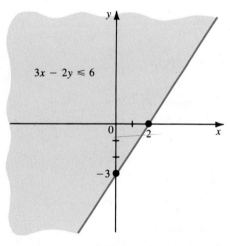

FIGURE 3

EXAMPLE 2

Graph $x + 4y < 4$.

The boundary here is the line $x + 4y = 4$. Since the points on this line do not satisfy $x + 4y < 4$, the line is drawn dashed, as in Figure 4. To decide whether to shade the region above the line or the region below the line, solve for y.

$$x + 4y < 4$$

$$4y < -x + 4$$

$$y < -\frac{1}{4}x + 1$$

Since y is less than $(-1/4)x + 1$, the solution is the region below the boundary, as shown by the shaded portion of Figure 4. ■

There is an alternate way to find the correct region to shade, or to check the method shown above. Choose as a test point any point not on the boundary line. For example, in Example 2 we could choose the point $(1, 0)$, which is not on the line $x + 4y = 4$. Substitute 1 for x and 0 for y in the given inequality.

$$x + 4y < 4$$

$$1 + 4(0) < 4 \qquad \text{Let } x = 1, y = 0$$

$$1 < 4 \qquad \text{True}$$

Since the result $1 < 4$ is true, the test point $(1, 0)$ belongs on the side of the line where all the points satisfy $x + 4y < 4$. For this reason, shade the side containing $(1, 0)$, as in Figure 4. Choosing a different test point, such as $(1, 5)$, would produce a false result when substituted into the given inequality. In this case, shade the side of the line *not including* the test point.

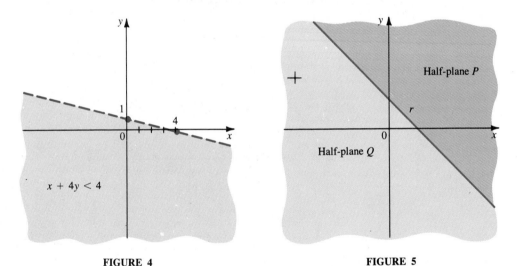

FIGURE 4   FIGURE 5

As the examples above suggest, the graph of a linear inequality is a region in the plane, perhaps including the line which is the boundary of the region. Each of the shaded regions is an example of a **half-plane,** a region on one side of a line. For example, in Figure 5 line r divides the plane into half-planes P and Q. The points of r belong to neither P nor Q. Line r is the boundary of each half-plane.

EXAMPLE 3

Graph $x \leq -1$.

   Recall that the graph of $x = -1$ is the vertical line through $(-1, 0)$. To decide which half-plane belongs to the solution, choose a test point. If we choose $(2, 0)$, and replace x with 2, we get a false statement:

$$x < -1$$

$$2 < -1. \quad \textbf{False}$$

The correct half-plane is the one that does *not* contain $(2, 0)$; it is shaded in Figure 6.   ▧

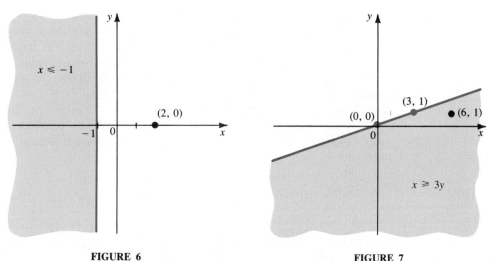

FIGURE 6   **FIGURE 7**

EXAMPLE 4

Graph $x \geq 3y$.

   Start by graphing the boundary, $x = 3y$. If $x = 0$, then $y = 0$, giving the point $(0, 0)$. Setting $y = 0$ would produce $(0, 0)$ again. To get a second point on the line, choose another number for x. Choosing $x = 3$ gives $y = 1$, with $(3, 1)$ a point on the line $x = 3y$. The points $(0, 0)$ and $(3, 1)$ lead to the line graphed in Figure 7. To decide on which half-plane to shade, let us choose $(6, 1)$ as a test point. (Any point that is not on the line $x = 3y$ may be used.) Replacing x with 6 and y with 1 in the original inequality gives a true statement, so the half-plane containing $(6, 1)$ is shaded, as shown in Figure 7.   ▧

Let us now summarize the steps in graphing a linear inequality.

Graphing a Linear
Inequality

1. Draw the graph of the boundary line. Make the line solid if the inequality involves $\leq$ or $\geq$; make the line dashed if the inequality involves $<$ or $>$.

2. Decide which half-plane to shade: either
   (a) solve the inequality for y; shade the region above the line if $\geq$, below if $\leq$, or
   (b) choose any point not on the line as a test point; shade the half-plane that includes the test point if the test point satisfies the original inequality; otherwise, shade the half-plane on the other side of the boundary line.

Systems of Inequalities   Realistic problems often involve many inequalities. For example, a manufacturing problem might produce inequalities resulting from production requirements, as well as inequalities about cost requirements. A collection of at least two inequalities is called a **system of inequalities.** The **solution** of a system of inequalities is made up of all those points that satisfy all the inequalities of the system at the same time. To graph the solution of a system of inequalities, graph all the inequalities on the same axes and identify, by heavy shading, the region common to all graphs. The next example shows how this is done.

EXAMPLE 5

Graph the system

$$y < -3x + 12$$
$$x < 2y.$$

The heavily shaded region in Figure 8 shows all the points that satisfy both inequalities of the system. Since the points on the boundary lines are not in the solution, the boundary lines are dashed.

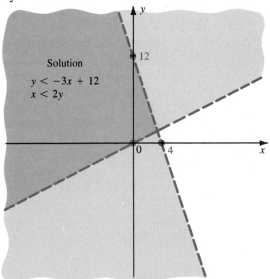

FIGURE 8

The heavily shaded region of Figure 8 is sometimes called the **region of feasible solutions,** or just the **feasible region,** since it is made up of all the points that satisfy (are feasible for) each inequality of the system.   ▧

EXAMPLE 6

Graph the feasible region for the system

$$2x - 5y \leq 10$$
$$x + 2y \leq 8$$
$$x \geq 0$$
$$y \geq 0.$$

On the same axes, graph each inequality by graphing the boundary and choosing the appropriate half-plane. Then find the feasible region by locating the overlap of all the half-planes. This feasible region is shaded in Figure 9. The inequalities $x \geq 0$ and $y \geq 0$ restrict the feasible region to the first quadrant.   ▧

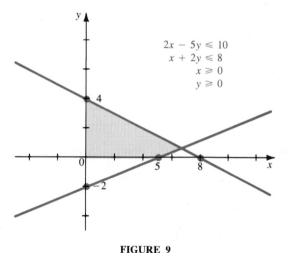

FIGURE 9

Applications   As we shall see in the rest of this chapter, many realistic problems lead to systems of linear inequalities. The next example is typical of such problems.

EXAMPLE 7

Midtown Manufacturing Company makes plastic plates and cups, both of which require time on two machines. A unit of plates requires one hour on machine A and two on machine B, while a unit of cups requires three hours on machine A and one on machine B. Each machine is operated for at most 15 hours per day. The profit on each unit of plates is $250 and on each unit of cups is $400. How many units of plates and cups should be manufactured to maximize the total profit?

Start by making a chart which summarizes the given information.

	Number Made	Time on Machine A	B	Profit Per Unit
Plates	x	1	2	$250
Cups	y	3	1	$400
Maximum Time Available		15	15	

Here x represents the number of units of plates to be made, and y represents the number of units of cups.

On machine A, x units of plates require a total of $1 \cdot x = x$ hours while y units of cups require $3 \cdot y = 3y$ hours. Since machine A is available no more than 15 hours a day,

$$x + 3y \leq 15.$$

The requirement that machine B be used no more than 15 hours a day gives

$$2x + y \leq 15.$$

It is not possible to produce a negative number of cups or plates, so that

$$x \geq 0 \quad \text{and} \quad y \geq 0.$$

The feasible region for our system of inequalities is shown in Figure 10.

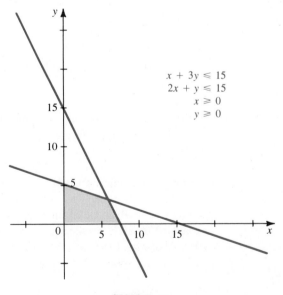

$$x + 3y \leq 15$$
$$2x + y \leq 15$$
$$x \geq 0$$
$$y \geq 0$$

FIGURE 10

3.1 EXERCISES

Graph the linear inequalities in Exercises 1–26.

1. $x + y \leq 2$

2. $y \leq x + 1$

3. $x \geq 3 + y$

4. $y \geq x - 3$

5. $4x - y < 6$

6. $3y + x > 4$

7. $3x + y < 6$

8. $2x - y > 2$

9. $x + 3y \geq -2$

10. $2x + 3y \leq 6$

11. $4x + 3y > -3$

12. $5x + 3y > 15$

13. $2x - 4y < 3$

14. $4x - 3y < 12$

15. $x \leq 5y$

16. $2x \geq y$

17. $-3x < y$

18. $-x > 6y$

19. $x + y \leq 0$

20. $3x + 2y \geq 0$

21. $y < x$

22. $y > -2x$

23. $x < 4$

24. $y > 5$

25. $y \leq -2$

26. $x \geq 3$

Graph the feasible region for the systems of inequalities in Exercises 27–40.

27. $x + y \leq 1$
$x - y \geq 2$

28. $3x - 4y < 6$
$2x + 5y > 15$

29. $2x - y < 1$
$3x + y < 6$

30. $x + 3y \leq 6$
$2x + 4y \geq 7$

31. $-x - y < 5$
$2x - y < 4$

32. $6x - 4y > 8$
$3x + 2y > 4$

33. $x + y \leq 4$
$x - y \leq 5$
$4x + y \leq -4$

34. $3x - 2y \geq 6$
$x + y \leq -5$
$y \leq 4$

35. $-2 < x < 3$
$-1 \leq y \leq 5$
$2x + y < 6$

36. $-2 < x < 2$
$y > 1$
$x - y > 0$

37. $2y + x \geq -5$
$y \leq 3 + x$
$x \geq 0$
$y \geq 0$

38. $2x + 3y \leq 12$
$2x + 3y > -6$
$3x + y < 4$
$x \geq 0$
$y \geq 0$

39. $3x + 4y > 12$
$2x - 3y < 6$
$0 \leq y \leq 2$
$x \geq 0$

40. $0 \leq x \leq 9$
$x - 2y \geq 4$
$3x + 5y \leq 30$
$y \geq 0$

41. A small pottery shop makes two kinds of planters, glazed and unglazed. The glazed type requires 1/2 hour to throw on the wheel and 1 hour in the kiln. The unglazed type takes 1 hour to throw on the wheel and 6 hours in the kiln. The wheel is available for at most 8 hours a day and the kiln is available for at most 20 hours per day. The profit on each glazed pot is $1.50 and on each unglazed pot $1.00. How many of each kind of pot should be produced in order to maximize profit?

(a) Complete this chart.

	Number	Wheel	Kiln	Profit on each
Glazed	x			$1.50
Unglazed	y			$1.00
Maximum Hours Available				

(b) Set up a system of inequalities and graph the feasible region.

42. Carmella and Walt produce handmade shawls and afghans. They spin the yarn, dye it, and then weave it. A shawl requires 1 hour of spinning, 1 hour of dyeing, and 1 hour of weaving. An afghan needs 2 hours of spinning, 1 of dyeing, and 4 of weaving. They make a $16 profit per shawl and a $20 profit per afghan. Together, they spend at most 8 hours spinning, 6 hours dyeing, and 14 hours weaving. How many of each item should they make to maximize profit?

(a) Complete this chart.

	Number	Hours for: Spinning	Weaving	Dyeing	Profit on each
Shawls	x				$16
Afghans	y				$20
Maximum Hours Available		8	6	14	

(b) Set up a system of inequalities and graph the feasible region.

43. The California Almond Growers have 2400 boxes of almonds to be shipped from their plant in Sacramento to Des Moines and San Antonio. The Des Moines market needs at least 1000 boxes, while the San Antonio market must have at least 800 boxes. Let x = the number of boxes to be shipped to Des Moines and y = the number of boxes to be shipped to San Antonio.

(a) Write a system of inequalities to express the conditions of the problem.

(b) Graph the feasible region of the system.

44. A cement manufacturer produces at least 3.2 million barrels of cement annually. He is told by the Environmental Protection Agency that his operation emits 2.5 pounds of dust for each barrel produced. The EPA has ruled that annual emissions must be reduced to 1.8 million pounds. To do this the manufacturer plans to replace the present dust collectors with two types of electronic precipitators. One type would reduce emissions to .5 pounds per barrel and would cost 16¢ per barrel. The other would reduce the dust to .3 pounds per barrel and would cost 20¢ per barrel. The manufacturer does not want to spend more than .8 million dollars on the precipitators. He needs to know how many barrels he should produce with each type.

(a) Let x = the number of barrels in millions produced with the first type and y = the number of barrels in millions produced with the second type. Write inequalities to express the manufacturer's restrictions.

(b) Graph the feasible region of the system.

3.2   Mathematical Models for Linear Programming

Many mathematical models designed to solve problems in business, biology, and economics involve finding the optimum value (either the maximum or the minimum) of a function, subject to certain restrictions. In a **linear programming** problem, we must find the maximum or minimum value of a function, called the **objec-**

tive function, while satisfying a set of restrictions, or **constraints,** given by linear inequalities.

In this section we see how to set up linear programming problems in two variables. In the next section we will solve such problems.

EXAMPLE 1

A farmer raises only geese and pigs. She wants to raise no more than 16 animals including no more than 10 geese. She spends $5 to raise a goose and $15 to raise a pig, and has $180 available for this project. Find the maximum profit she can make if each goose produces a profit of $6 and each pig a profit of $20.

Let x represent the number of geese to be produced, and let y represent the number of pigs. Start by summarizing the information of the problem in a table.

	Number	Cost to Raise	Profit Each
Geese	x	$5	$6
Pigs	y	$15	$20
Maximum Funds Available		$180	

Use this table to write the necessary constraints. Since the total number of animals cannot exceed 16, the first constraint is

$$x + y \leq 16.$$

"No more than 10 geese" leads to

$$x \leq 10.$$

The cost to raise x geese at $5 per goose is $5x$ dollars, while the cost for y pigs at $15 each is $15y$ dollars. Since only $180 is available,

$$5x + 15y \leq 180.$$

The number of geese and pigs cannot be negative:

$$x \geq 0, \qquad y \geq 0.$$

The farmer wants to know the number of geese and the number of pigs that should be raised for maximum profit. Each goose produces a profit of $6, and each pig, $20. If z represents total profit, then

$$z = 6x + 20y.$$

In summary, the mathematical model for the given linear programming problem is as follows:

maximize $\quad z = 6x + 20y$ (1)

subject to: $\quad x + y \leq 16$ (2)

$$x \leq 10 \quad (3)$$

$$5x + 15y \leq 180 \quad (4)$$

$$x \geq 0, \, y \geq 0 \quad (5)$$

Here $z = 6x + 20y$ is the objective function, while inequalities (2)–(4) are the constraints.

Using the methods of the previous section, graph, as in Figure 11, the feasible region for the system of inequalities (2)–(5).

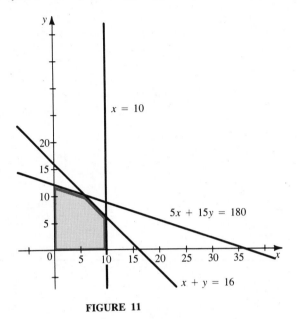

FIGURE 11

Any value in the feasible region of Figure 11 will satisfy all the constraints of the problem. However, in most problems only one point in the feasible region will lead to maximum profit. In the next section, we will see that maximum profit is found by looking at all the *corner points* in the feasible region; a **corner point** is a point in the feasible region where the boundary lines of two constraints cross. The feasible region of Figure 11 has been redrawn in Figure 12, with all the corner points identified.

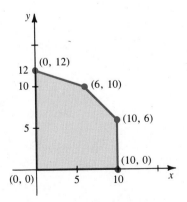

FIGURE 12

Since corner points occur where two straight lines cross, the coordinates of the corner point are the solution of a system of linear equations. For example, the corner point (6, 10) of Figure 12 is found by solving the system

$$x + y = 16$$
$$5x + 15y = 180.$$

By the methods of Chapter 2, the solution of this system is (6, 10). ▩

EXAMPLE 2

An office manager needs to purchase new filing cabinets. He knows that Ace cabinets cost $40 each, require 6 square feet of floor space, and hold 8 cubic feet of files. On the other hand, each Excello cabinet costs $80, requires 8 square feet of floor space, and holds 12 cubic feet. His budget permits him to spend no more than $560 on files, while the office has room for no more than 72 square feet of cabinets. The manager desires the greatest storage capacity within the limitations imposed by funds and space. How many of each type cabinet should he buy?

Let x represent the number of Ace cabinets to be bought and let y represent the number of Excello cabinets. Summarize the information of the problem in a table.

	Number	Cost of each	Space required	Storage capacity
Ace	x	$40	6 sq ft	8 cu ft
Excello	y	$80	8 sq ft	12 cu ft
Maximum Available		$560	72 sq ft	

The constraints imposed by cost and space are as follows.

$$40x + 80y \leq 560 \qquad \text{cost}$$
$$6x + 8y \leq 72 \qquad \text{floor space}$$

Since the number of cabinets cannot be negative, $x \geq 0$ and $y \geq 0$. The objective function to be maximized gives the amount of storage capacity provided by some combination of Ace and Excello cabinets. From the information in the table, the objective function is

$$\text{storage space} = z = 8x + 12y.$$

In summary, the given problem has produced the mathematical model

$$\text{maximize} \qquad z = 8x + 12y$$
$$\text{subject to:} \qquad 40x + 80y \leq 560$$
$$6x + 8y \leq 72$$
$$x \geq 0, \qquad y \geq 0.$$

A graph of the feasible region is shown in Figure 13. Three of the corner points can be identified from the graph as (0, 0), (0, 7), and (12, 0). The fourth corner point, labeled Q in the figure, can be found by solving the system of equations

$$40x + 80y = 560$$
$$6x + 8y = 72.$$

Solve this system to find that Q is the point (8, 3). ▪

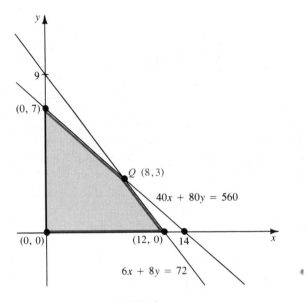

FIGURE 13

EXAMPLE 3

Certain laboratory animals must have at least 30 grams of protein and at least 20 grams of fat per feeding period. These nutrients come from food A, which costs 18¢ per unit and supplies 2 grams of protein and 4 of fat, and food B, with 6 grams of protein and 2 of fat, costing 12¢ per unit. Food B is bought under a long term contract requiring that at least 2 units of B be used per serving. How much of each food must be bought to produce minimum cost per serving?

Let x represent the amount of food A needed, and y the amount of food B. Use the given information to produce the following table.

Food	Number of units	Grams of protein	Grams of fat	Cost
A	x	2	4	18¢
B	y	6	2	12¢
Minimum Required		30	20	

The mathematical model is

$$\text{minimize} \quad z = .18x + .12y$$

$$\text{subject to:} \quad 2x + 6y \geq 30$$

$$4x + 2y \geq 20$$

$$y \geq 2$$

$$x \geq 0, \; y \geq 0.$$

(The constraint $y \geq 0$ is redundant because of the constraint $y \geq 2$.) A graph of the feasible region is shown in Figure 14.

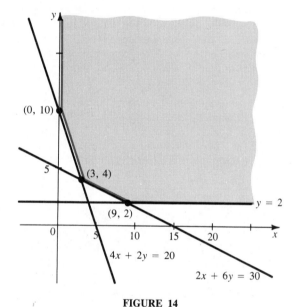

FIGURE 14

The feasible region in Figure 14 is an **unbounded** feasible region—the region extends indefinitely to the upper right. With this region it would not be possible to *maximize* the objective function, because the total cost of the food could always be increased by encouraging the animals to eat more. ▪

3.2 EXERCISES

Write Exercises 1–6 as linear inequalities. Identify all variables used. (Not all the information is used in Exercises 5 and 6.)

1. Product A requires 2 hours on machine I, while product B needs 3 hours on the same machine. The machine is available at most 45 hours per week.

2. A cow requires a third of an acre of pasture and a sheep needs a quarter acre. A rancher wants to use at least 120 acres of pasture.

3. John needs at least 25 units of vitamin A per day. Green pills provide 4 units and red pills provide 1.

4. Sandra spends 3 hours selling a small computer and 5 hours selling a larger model. She works no more than 45 hours per week.

5. Coffee costing $6 a pound is to be mixed with coffee costing $5 a pound to get at least 50 pounds of a mixture.

6. A tank in an oil refinery holds 120 gallons. The tank contains a mixture of light oil worth $1.25 per gallon and heavy oil worth $.80 per gallon.

In Exercises 7–16, set up a mathematical model, graph the feasible region, and identify all corner points. Do not try to solve the problem.

7. A manufacturer of refrigerators must ship at least 100 refrigerators to its two West coast warehouses. Each warehouse holds a maximum of 100 refrigerators. Warehouse A holds 25 refrigerators already, while warehouse B has 20 on hand. It costs $12 to ship a refrigerator to warehouse A and $10 to ship one to warehouse B. How many refrigerators should be shipped to each warehouse to minimize cost? What is the minimum cost?

8. Mark, who is ill, takes vitamin pills. Each day he must have at least 16 units of vitamin A, 5 units of vitamin B_1, and 20 units of vitamin C. He can choose between pill #1 which contains 8 units of A, 1 of B_1, and 2 of C, and pill #2 which contains 2 units of A, 1 of B_1, and 7 of C. Pill #1 costs 15¢ and pill #2 costs 30¢. How many of each pill should he buy in order to minimize his cost? What is the minimum cost?

9. A machine shop manufactures two types of bolts. Each can be made on any of three groups of machines, but the time required on each group differs, as shown in the table below.

		Machine groups		
		I	II	III
Bolts	Type 1	.1 minute	.1 minute	.1 minute
	Type 2	.1 minute	.4 minute	.15 minute

Production schedules are made up one day at a time. In a day, there are 1240, 720, and 300 minutes available, respectively, on these machines. Type 1 bolts sell for 10¢ and type 2 bolts for 12¢. How many of each type of bolt should be manufactured per week to maximize revenue? What is the maximum revenue?

10. Seall Manufacturing Company makes color television sets. It produces a bargain set that sells for $100 profit and a deluxe set that sells for $150 profit. On the assembly line the bargain set requires 3 hours, while the deluxe set takes 5 hours. The cabinet shop spends one hour on the cabinet for the bargain set and 3 hours on the cabinet for the deluxe set. Both sets require 2 hours of time for testing and packing. On a particular production run the Seall Company has available 3900 work hours on the assembly line, 2100 work hours in the cabinet shop, and 2200 work hours in the testing and packing department. How many sets of each type should it produce to make maximum profit? What is the maximum profit?

11. The manufacturing process requires that oil refineries must manufacture at least two gallons of gasoline for every one of fuel oil. To meet the winter demand for fuel oil, at least 3 million gallons a day must be produced. The demand for gasoline is no more than 6.4 million gallons per day. If the refinery sells gasoline for $1.25 per gallon, and fuel oil for $1 per gallon, how much of each should be produced to maximize revenue? Find the maximum revenue.

12. In a small town in South Carolina, zoning rules require that the window space (in square feet) in a house be at least one-sixth of the space used up by solid walls. The cost to heat the house is 2¢ for each square foot of solid walls and 8¢ for each square foot of windows. Find the maximum total area (windows plus walls) if $16 is available to pay for heat.

13. A candy company has 100 kilograms of chocolate-covered nuts and 125 kilograms of chocolate-covered raisins to be sold as two different mixes. One mix will contain half nuts and half raisins and will sell for $6 per kilogram. The other mix will contain 1/3 nuts and 2/3 raisins and will sell for $4.80 per kilogram. How many kilograms of each mix should the company prepare for maximum revenue?

14. Ms. Oliveras was given the following advice. She should supplement her daily diet with at least 6000 USP units of vitamin A, at least 195 milligrams of vitamin C, and at least 600 USP units of vitamin D. Ms. Oliveras finds that Mason's Pharmacy carries Brand X vitamin pills at 5¢ each and Brand Y vitamins at 4¢ each. Each Brand X pill contains 3000 USP units of A, 45 milligrams of C, and 75 USP units of D, while the Brand Y pills contain 1000 USP units of A, 50 milligrams of C, and 200 USP units of D. What combination of vitamin pills should she buy to obtain the least possible cost? What is the least possible cost per day?

15. Sam, who is dieting, requires two food supplements, I and II. He can get these supplements from two different products, A and B, as shown in the following table.

		Supplement (grams per serving)	
		I	II
Product	A	3	2
	B	2	4

Sam's physician has recommended that he include at least 15 grams of each supplement in his daily diet. If product A costs 25¢ per serving and product B costs 40¢ per serving, how can he satisfy his requirements most economically? Find the minimum cost.

16. A small country can grow only two crops for export, coffee and cocoa. The country has 500,000 hectares of land available for the crops. Long-term contracts require that at least 100,000 hectares be devoted to coffee and at least 200,000 hectares to cocoa. Cocoa must be processed locally, and production bottlenecks limit cocoa to 270,000 hectares. Coffee requires two workers per hectare, with cocoa requiring five. No more than 1,750,000 people are available for these crops. Coffee produces a profit of $220 per hectare, and cocoa a profit of $310 per hectare. How many hectares should the country devote to each crop in order to maximize the profit? Find the maximum profit.

3.3   Solving Linear Programming Problems Graphically

In the last section we saw how to set up a linear programming problem by writing an objective function and the necessary constraints. We then graphed the feasible region and identified all corner points. In this section we complete this process and go on to solve the linear programming problems. The method of solving these problems from the graph of the feasible region is explained in the next example.

EXAMPLE 1

Solve the following linear programming problem:

$$\text{maximize} \quad z = 2x + 5y$$
$$\text{subject to:} \quad 3x + 2y \leq 6$$
$$-2x + 4y \leq 8$$
$$x \geq 0, \; y \geq 0.$$

The feasible region is graphed in Figure 15. The coordinates of point A, (1/2, 9/4), can be found by solving the system

$$3x + 2y = 6$$
$$-2x + 4y = 8.$$

Every point in the feasible region satisfies all the constraints. However, we want to find those points that produce the maximum possible value of the objective function. To see how to find this maximum value, let us add to the graph of Figure 15 lines which represent the objective function $z = 2x + 5y$ for various sample values of z. If we choose the values 0, 5, 10, and 15 for z, the objective function becomes (in turn)

$$0 = 2x + 5y, \quad 5 = 2x + 5y, \quad 10 = 2x + 5y, \quad 15 = 2x + 5y.$$

These four lines are graphed in Figure 16. (Why are all the lines parallel?) The figure shows that z cannot take on the value 15 because the graph for $z = 15$ is entirely outside the feasible region. The maximum possible value of z will be obtained from a line parallel to the others and between the lines representing the objective function when $z = 10$ and $z = 15$. The value of z will be as large as possible and all constraints will be satisfied, if this line just touches the feasible region. This occurs at point A. We found above that A has coordinates (1/2, 9/4). The value of z at this point is

$$z = 2x + 5y = 2\left(\frac{1}{2}\right) + 5\left(\frac{9}{4}\right) = 12\frac{1}{4}.$$

The maximum possible value of z is 12 1/4. Of all the points in the feasible region, A leads to the largest possible value of z. ∎

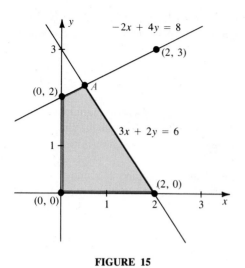

FIGURE 15

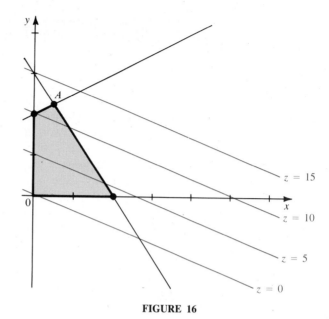

FIGURE 16

EXAMPLE 2

Solve the linear programming problem

$$\text{minimize} \quad z = 2x + 4y$$
$$\text{subject to:} \quad x + 2y \geq 10$$
$$3x + \ y \geq 10$$
$$x \geq 0, \ y \geq \ 0.$$

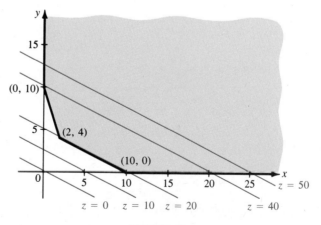

FIGURE 17

Figure 17 shows the feasible region and the lines that result when z in the objective function is replaced by 0, 10, 20, 40, and 50. The line representing the objective function touches the region of feasible solutions when $z = 20$. Two corner points, $(2, 4)$ and $(10, 0)$, lie on this line. In this case, both $(2, 4)$ and $(10, 0)$ as well as all the points on the boundary line between them give the same optimum value of z. There is an infinite number of equally "good" values of x and y which give the same minimum value of the objective function $z = 2x + 4y$. This minimum value is 20.   ■

The feasible region in Example 1 above is *bounded*, since the region is enclosed by boundary lines on all sides. As we shall see, linear programming problems with bounded regions always have solutions. On the other hand, the feasible region in Example 2 is *unbounded* and there would be no solution if we had tried to *maximize* the value of the objective function.

We can draw some general conclusions from the method of solution used in Examples 1 and 2. Figure 18 shows various feasible regions and the lines that result from various values of z. (We assume the lines are in order from left to right as z increases.) In part (a) of the figure, the objective function takes on its minimum value at corner point Q and its maximum value at P. The minimum is again at Q in part (b), but the maximum occurs at P_1 or P_2, or any point on the line segment connecting them. Finally, in part (c), the minimum value occurs at Q, but the objective function has no maximum value because the feasible region is unbounded.

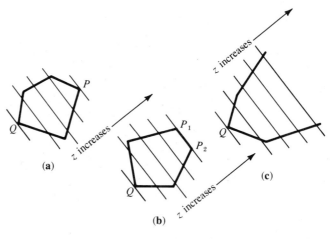

(a)

(b)

(c)

FIGURE 18

The preceding discussion suggests the truth of the **corner point theorem.**

Corner Point **Theorem**	If an optimum value (either a maximum or a minimum) of the objective function exists, it will occur at one or more of the corner points of the feasible region.

This theorem simplifies the job of finding an optimum value: First, graph the feasible region and find all corner points. Then test each corner point in the objective function. Finally, identify the corner point producing the optimum solution. For unbounded regions, you must decide whether or not the required optimum can be found; see Example 2.

With the theorem, we could have solved the problem in Example 1 by identifying the four corner points of Figure 15: (0, 0), (0, 2), (1/2, 9/4), and (2, 0). We would then substitute each of the four points into the objective function, $z = 2x + 5y$ to identify the corner point that produces the maximum value of z.

Corner Point	Value of $z = 2x + 5y$
(0, 0)	$2(0) + 5(0) = 0$
(0, 2)	$2(0) + 5(2) = 10$
$(\frac{1}{2}, \frac{9}{4})$	$2(\frac{1}{2}) + 5(\frac{9}{4}) = 12\frac{1}{4}$ (maximum)
(2, 0)	$2(2) + 5(0) = 4$

From these results, the corner point (1/2, 9/4) yields the maximum value of 12 1/4. This is the same result found earlier.

EXAMPLE 3

Sketch the feasible region for the following set of constraints.

$$3y - 2x \geq 0$$
$$y + 8x \leq 52$$
$$y - 2x \leq 2$$
$$x \geq 3$$

Then find the maximum and minimum values of the objective function

$$z = 5x + 2y.$$

The graph in Figure 19 shows that the feasible region is bounded. Use the corner points from the graph to find the maximum and minimum values of the objective function.

Corner point	Value of $z = 5x + 2y$
(3, 2)	$5(3) + 2(2) = 19$ (minimum)
(6, 4)	$5(6) + 2(4) = 38$
(5, 12)	$5(5) + 2(12) = 49$ (maximum)
(3, 8)	$5(3) + 2(8) = 31$

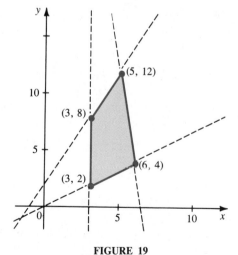

FIGURE 19

The minimum value of $z = 5x + 2y$ is 19 at the corner point (3, 2). The maximum value is 49 at (5, 12).

We shall end this section by completing the solution of Example 2 from the last section.

EXAMPLE 4

An office manager needs to purchase new filing cabinets. He knows that Ace cabinets cost $40 each, require 6 square feet of floor space, and hold 8 cubic feet of files. On the other hand, each Excello cabinet costs $80, requires 8 square feet of floor space, and holds 12 cubic feet. His budget permits him to spend no more than $560 on files, while the office has room for no more than 72 square feet of cabinets. The manager desires the greatest storage capacity within the limitations imposed by funds and space. How many of each type of cabinet should he buy?

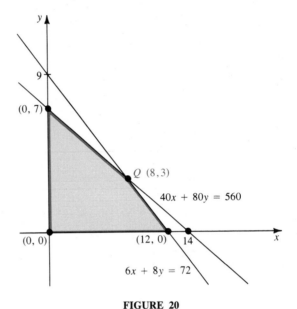

FIGURE 20

Figure 20 repeats the feasible region and corner points found in Example 2 of the previous section. Now test these four points in the objective function to determine the maximum value of z. The results are shown in the table.

Corner point	Value of $z = 8x + 12y$
$(0, 0)$	0
$(0, 7)$	84
$(12, 0)$	96
$(8, 3)$	100 (maximum)

The objective function, which represents storage space, is maximized when $x = 8$ and $y = 3$. The manager should buy 8 Ace cabinets and 3 Excello cabinets. ▪

Let us now summarize the steps in solving a linear programming problem by the graphical method.

<table>
<tr><td>Solving a Linear
Programming
Problem</td><td>

1. Write the objective function and all necessary constraints.

2. Graph the feasible region.

3. Identify all corner points.

4. Find the value of the objective function at each corner point.

5. For a bounded region, the solution is given by the corner point producing the optimum value of the objective function.

6. For an unbounded region, check that a solution actually exists. If it does, it will occur at a corner point.
</td></tr>
</table>

3.3 EXERCISES

Exercises 1–6 show regions of feasible solutions. Use these regions to find maximum and minimum values of each given objective function.

1. $z = 3x + 5y$

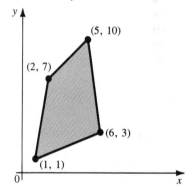

2. $z = 6x + y$

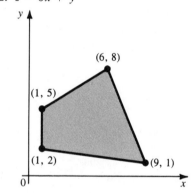

3. $z = .40x + .75y$

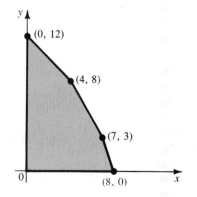

4. $z = .35x + 1.25y$

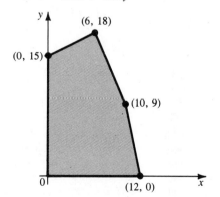

5. $z = 2x + 3y$

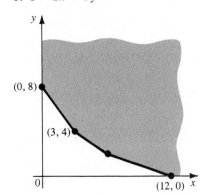

6. $z = 5x + 6y$

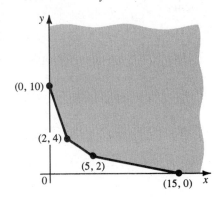

Use graphical methods to solve problems 7–14.

7. Maximize $z = 5x + 2y$
subject to: $2x + 3y \leq 6$
           $4x + y \leq 6$
           $x \geq 0, y \geq 0$

8. Minimize $z = x + 3y$
subject to: $x + y \leq 10$
           $5x + 2y \geq 20$
           $-x + 2y \geq 0$
           $x \geq 0, y \geq 0$

9. Maximize $z = 2x + y$
subject to: $3x - y \geq 12$
           $x + y \leq 15$
           $x \geq 2, y \geq 5$

10. Maximize $z = x + 3y$
subject to: $2x + 3y \leq 100$
           $5x + 4y \leq 200$
           $x \geq 10, y \geq 20$

11. Maximize $z = 4x + 2y$
subject to: $x - y \leq 10$
           $5x + 3y \leq 75$
           $x \geq 0, y \geq 0$

12. Maximize $z = 4x + 5y$
subject to: $10x - 5y \leq 100$
           $20x + 10y \geq 150$
           $x \geq 0, y \geq 0$

13. Find values of $x \geq 0$ and $y \geq 0$ which maximize $z = 10x + 12y$ subject to each of the following sets of constraints.

(a) $x + y \leq 20$
     $x + 3y \leq 24$

(b) $3x + y \leq 15$
     $x + 2y \leq 18$

(c) $2x + 5y \geq 22$
     $4x + 3y \leq 28$
     $2x + 2y \leq 17$

14. Find values of $x \geq 0$ and $y \geq 0$ which minimize $z = 3x + 2y$ subject to each of the following sets of constraints.

(a) $10x + 7y \leq 42$
     $4x + 10y \geq 35$

(b) $6x + 5y \geq 25$
     $2x + 6y \geq 15$

(c) $x + 2y \geq 10$
     $2x + y \geq 12$
     $x - y \leq 8$

In Exercises 15–24, complete the solution of the problems that were set up in Exercises 7–16 of the previous section.

15. A manufacturer of refrigerators must ship at least 100 refrigerators to its two West coast warehouses. Each warehouse holds a maximum of 100 refrigerators. Warehouse A holds 25 refrigerators already, while warehouse B has 20 on hand. It costs $12 to ship a refrigerator to warehouse A and $10 to ship one to warehouse B. How many refrigerators should be shipped to each warehouse to minimize cost? What is the minimum cost?

16. Mark, who is ill, takes vitamin pills. Each day he must have at least 16 units of vitamin A, 5 units of vitamin B_1, and 20 units of vitamin C. He can choose between pill #1 which contains 8 units of A, 1 of B_1, and 2 of C, and pill #2 which contains 2 units of A, 1 of B_1, and 7 of C. Pill #1 costs 15¢ and pill #2 costs 30¢. How many of each pill should he buy in order to minimize his cost? What is the minimum cost?

17. A machine shop manufactures two types of bolts. Each can be made on any of three groups of machines, but the time required on each group differs, as shown in the table below.

		Machine groups		
		I	II	III
Bolts	Type 1	.1 minute	.1 minute	.1 minute
	Type 2	.1 minute	.4 minute	.5 minute

Production schedules are made up one day at a time. In a day there are 240, 720, and 160 minutes available, respectively, on these machines. Type 1 bolts sell for 10¢ and type 2 bolts for 12¢. How many of each type of bolt should be manufactured per week to maximize revenue? What is the maximum revenue?

18. Seall Manufacturing Company makes color television sets. It produces a bargain set that sells for $100 profit and a deluxe set that sells for $150 profit. On the assembly line the bargain set requires 3 hours, while the deluxe set takes 5 hours. The cabinet shop spends one hour on the cabinet for the bargain set and 3 hours on the cabinet for the deluxe set. Both sets require 2 hours of time for testing and packing. On a particular production run the Seall Company has available 3900 work hours on the assembly line, 2100 work hours in the cabinet shop, and 2200 work hours in the testing and packing department. How many sets of each type should it produce to make maximum profit? What is the maximum profit?

19. The manufacturing process requires that oil refineries must manufacture at least two gallons of gasoline for every one of fuel oil. To meet the winter demand for fuel oil, at least 3 million gallons a day must be produced. The demand for gasoline is no more than 6.4 million gallons per day. If the refinery sells gasoline for $1.25 per gallon, and fuel oil for $1 per gallon, how much of each should be produced to maximize revenue? Find the maximum revenue.

20. In a small town in South Carolina, zoning rules require that the window space (in square feet) in a house be at least one-sixth of the space used up by solid walls. The cost to heat the house is 2¢ for each square foot of solid walls and 8¢ for each square foot of windows. Find the maximum total area (windows plus walls) if $16 is available to pay for heat.

21. A candy company has 100 kilograms of chocolate-covered nuts and 125 kilograms of chocolate-covered raisins to be sold as two different mixes. One mix will contain half nuts and half raisins and will sell for $6 per kilogram. The other mix will contain 1/3 nuts and 2/3 raisins and will sell for $4.80 per kilogram. How many kilograms of each mix should the company prepare for maximum revenue? Find the maximum revenue.

22. Ms. Oliveras was given the following advice. She should supplement her daily diet with at least 6000 USP units of vitamin A, at least 195 milligrams of vitamin C, and at least 600 USP units of vitamin D. Ms. Oliveras finds that Mason's Pharmacy carries Brand X vitamin pills at 5¢ each and Brand Y vitamins at 4¢ each. Each Brand X pill contains 3000 USP units of A, 45 milligrams of C, and 75 USP units of D, while

Brand Y pills contain 1000 USP units of A, 50 milligrams of C, and 200 USP units of D. What combination of vitamin pills should she buy to obtain the least possible cost? What is the least possible cost per day?

23. Sam, who is dieting, requires two food supplements, I and II. He can get these supplements from two different products, A and B, as shown in the following table.

		Supplement	
		(grams per serving)	
		I	II
Product	A	3	2
	B	2	4

Sam's physician has recommended that he include at least 15 grams of each supplement in his daily diet. If product A costs 25¢ per serving and product B costs 40¢ per serving, how can he satisfy his requirements most economically? Find the minimum cost.

24. A small country can grow only two crops for export, coffee and cocoa. The country has 500,000 hectares of land available for the crops. Long-term contracts require that at least 100,000 hectares be devoted to coffee and at least 200,000 hectares to cocoa. Cocoa must be processed locally, and production bottlenecks limit cocoa to 270,000 hectares. Coffee requires two workers per hectare, with cocoa requiring five. No more than 1,750,000 people are available for these crops. Coffee produces a profit of $220 per hectare, and cocoa a profit of $310 per hectare. How many hectares should the country devote to each crop in order to maximize the profit? Find the maximum profit.

The importance of linear programming is shown by the inclusion of linear programming problems on most examinations for Certified Public Accountant. Answer the following questions from one such examination.*

The Random Company manufactures two products, Zeta and Beta. Each product must pass through two processing operations. All materials are introduced at the start of Process No. 1. There are no work in process inventories. Random may produce either one product exclusively or various combinations of both products subject to the following constraints:

	Process No. 1	*Process No. 2*	*Contribution Margin Per Unit*
Hours required to produce one unit of:			
Zeta	1 hour	1 hour	$4.00
Beta	2 hours	3 hours	5.25
Total capacity in hours per day	1,000 hours	1,275 hours	

A shortage of technical labor has limited Beta production to 400 units per day. There are no constraints on the production of Zeta other than the hour constraints in the above schedule. Assume that all relationships between capacity and production are linear.

---

25. Given the objective to maximize total contribution margin, what is the production constraint for Process No. 1?

    a. Zeta + Beta $\leq$ 1,000.

    b. Zeta + 2 Beta $\leq$ 1,000.

    c. Zeta + Beta $\geq$ 1,000.

    d. Zeta + 2 Beta $\geq$ 1,000.

26. Given the objective to maximize total contribution margin, what is the labor constraint for production of Beta?

    a. Beta $\leq$ 400.   **c.** Beta $\leq$ 425.

    b. Beta $\geq$ 400.   **d.** Beta $\geq$ 425.

27. What is the objective function of the data presented?

    a. Zeta + 2 Beta = \$9.25.

    b. \$4.00 Zeta + 3(\$5.25) Beta = Total Contribution Margin.

    c. \$4.00 Zeta + \$5.25 Beta = Total Contribution Margin.

    d. 2(\$4.00) Zeta + 3(\$5.25) Beta = Total Contribution Margin.

KEY WORDS

system of inequalities	constraints
half-plane	region of feasible solutions
boundary	corner point
linear inequality	bounded
objective function	unbounded

Chapter 3   REVIEW EXERCISES

Graph each of the linear inequalities in Exercises 1–6.

1. $y \geq 2x + 3$ **2.** $3x - y \leq 5$ **3.** $3x + 4y \leq 12$

4. $2x - 6y \geq 18$ **5.** $y \geq x$ **6.** $y \leq 3$

Graph the solution of each of the systems of inequalities in Exercises 7–12. Find all corner points.

7. $x + y \leq 6$
    $2x - y \geq 3$

8. $4x + y \geq 8$
    $2x - 3y \leq 6$

9. $-4 \leq x \leq 2$
    $-1 \leq y \leq 3$
    $x + y \leq 4$

10. $2 \leq x \leq 5$
    $1 \leq y \leq 7$
    $x - y \leq 3$

11. $x + 3y \geq 6$
    $4x - 3y \leq 12$
    $x \geq 0$
    $y \geq 0$

12. $x + 2y \leq 4$
    $2x \quad 3y \leq 6$
    $x \geq 0$
    $y \geq 0$

Set up a system of inequalities for problems 13 and 14; then graph the solution of the system.

13. A bakery makes both cakes and cookies. Each batch of cakes requires two hours in the oven and three hours in the decorating room. Each batch of cookies needs one and a half hours in the oven and two thirds of an hour in the decorating room. The oven is available no more than 15 hours a day, while the decorating room can be used no more than 13 hours a day.

14. A company makes two kinds of pizza, basic and plain. Basic contains cheese and beef, while plain contains onions and beef. The company sells at least three units a day of basic, and at least two units of plain. The beef costs $5 per unit for basic, and $4 per unit for plain. They can spend no more than $50 per day on beef. Dough for basic is $2 per unit, while dough for plain is $1 per unit. The company can spend no more than $16 per day on dough.

Use the given regions to find the maximum and minimum values of the objective function $z = 2x + 4y$.

15.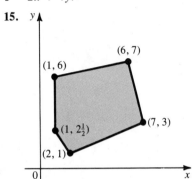

16.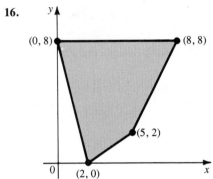

Use the graphical method to solve Exercises 17–22.

17. Maximize $z = 2x + 4y$
    subject to: $3x + 2y \leq 12$
                   $5x + y \geq 5$
                   $x \geq 0,\ y \geq 0$

18. Minimize $z = 3x + 2y$
    subject to: $8x + 9y \geq 72$
                   $6x + 8y \geq 72$
                   $x \geq 0,\ y \geq 0$

19. Minimize $z = 4x + 2y$
    subject to: $x + y \leq 50$
                   $2x + y \geq 20$
                   $x + 2y \geq 30$
                   $x \geq 0,\ y \geq 0$

20. Maximize $z = 4x + 3y$
    subject to: $2x + 7y \leq 14$
                   $2x + 3y \leq 10$
                   $x \geq 0,\ y \geq 0$

21. How many batches of cakes and cookies should the bakery of Exercise 13 make in order to maximize profits if cookies produce a profit of $20 per batch and cakes produce a profit of $30 per batch?

22. How many units of each kind of pizza should the company of Exercise 14 make in order to maximize profits if basic sells for $20 per unit and plain for $15 per unit?

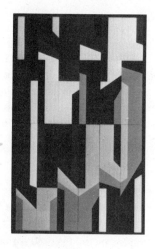
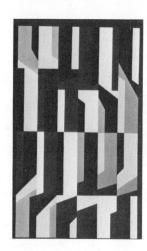

LINEAR PROGRAMMING: THE SIMPLEX METHOD

Karl Gerstner. From the series *Aperspective I* (The Endless Spiral at a Right Angle), 1952–1956.

In the previous chapter, we solved linear programming problems by the graphical method. This method illustrates the basic ideas of linear programming, but it is practical only for problems with two variables. For problems with more than two variables, or with two variables and many constraints, the simplex method is used.

The simplex method starts with the selection of one corner point (often the origin) from the feasible region. Then, in a systematic way, another corner point is found which improves the value of the objective function. Finally, an optimum solution is reached or it can be seen that none exists.

The simplex method requires a number of steps. We have divided the presentation of these steps into two parts. First, in Section 4.1, we set up the problem and begin the method, and then, in Section 4.2, we complete the method.

4.1   Slack Variables and the Pivot

Because the simplex method is used for problems with many variables, it is usually not convenient to use letters such as x, y, z, or w as variable names. Instead, the symbols x_1 (read "x-sub-one"), x_2, x_3, and so on, are used. These variable names lend themselves easily to use on the computer. In the simplex method, all constraints must be expressed in the linear form

$$a_1 x_1 + a_2 x_2 + a_3 x_3 + \ldots \leq b$$

where x_1, x_2, x_3, . . . are variables and a_1, a_2, . . . , b are constants.

We shall first discuss the simplex method for linear programming problems in *standard maximum form*.

Standard **Maximum Form**	A linear programming problem is in **standard maximum form** if **1.** the objective function is to be maximized; **2.** all variables are nonnegative ($x_i \geq 0$); **3.** all constraints involve $\leq$; **4.** the constants in the constraints are all nonnegative ($b \geq 0$).

(In Sections 4.3 and 4.4 we discuss problems which do not meet all of these conditions.)

Begin the simplex method by converting the constraints, which are linear inequalities, into linear equations. Do this by adding a nonnegative variable, called a **slack variable**, to each constraint. For example, convert the inequality $x_1 + x_2 \leq 10$ into an equation by adding the slack variable x_3, to get

$$x_1 + x_2 + x_3 = 10, \qquad \text{where } x_3 \geq 0.$$

The inequality $x_1 + x_2 \leq 10$ says that the sum $x_1 + x_2$ is less than or perhaps equal to 10. The variable x_3 "takes up any slack" and represents the amount by which $x_1 + x_2$ fails to equal 10. For example, if $x_1 + x_2$ equals 8, then x_3 is 2. If $x_1 + x_2 = 10$, the value of x_3 is 0.

EXAMPLE 1   Restate the following linear programming problem by introducing slack variables.

$$\text{maximize} \quad z = 3x_1 + 2x_2 + x_3$$
$$\text{subject to:} \quad 2x_1 + x_2 + x_3 \leq 150$$
$$2x_1 + 2x_2 + 8x_3 \leq 200$$
$$2x_1 + 3x_2 + x_3 \leq 320$$

with $x_1 \geq 0$, $x_2 \geq 0$, $x_3 \geq 0$.

Rewrite the three constraints as equations by adding slack variables x_4, x_5, and x_6, one for each constraint. By this process, the problem is restated as

$$\text{maximize} \quad z = 3x_1 + 2x_2 + x_3$$
$$\text{subject to:} \quad 2x_1 + x_2 + x_3 + x_4 \qquad\qquad = 150$$
$$2x_1 + 2x_2 + 8x_3 \qquad + x_5 \qquad = 200$$
$$2x_1 + 3x_2 + x_3 \qquad\qquad + x_6 = 320$$

with $x_1 \geq 0$, $x_2 \geq 0$, $x_3 \geq 0$, $x_4 \geq 0$, $x_5 \geq 0$, $x_6 \geq 0$. ■

Adding slack variables to the constraints converts a linear programming problem into a system of linear equations. These equations should have all variables on the left of the equals sign and all constants on the right. All the equations of Example 1 satisfy this condition except for the objective function, $z = 3x_1 + 2x_2 + x_3$, which may be written with all variables on the left as

$$-3x_1 - 2x_2 - x_3 + z = 0.$$

Now the equations of Example 1 can be written as the augmented matrix

$$
\begin{array}{ccccccc}
x_1 & x_2 & x_3 & x_4 & x_5 & x_6 & z
\end{array}
$$

$$
\left[
\begin{array}{ccccccc|c}
2 & 1 & 1 & 1 & 0 & 0 & 0 & 150 \\
2 & 2 & 8 & 0 & 1 & 0 & 0 & 200 \\
2 & 3 & 1 & 0 & 0 & 1 & 0 & 320 \\
\hline
-3 & -2 & -1 & 0 & 0 & 0 & 1 & 0
\end{array}
\right]
$$

indicators

This matrix is called the **initial simplex tableau.** The numbers in the bottom row, which are from the objective function, are called **indicators** (except for the 0 at the far right). The column headed z will never change in all our future work, and will be omitted from now on.

EXAMPLE 2

Set up the initial simplex tableau for the following problem:

A farmer has 100 acres of available land which he wishes to plant with a mixture of potatoes, corn, and cabbage. It costs him \$400 to produce an acre of potatoes, \$160 to produce an acre of corn, and \$280 to produce an acre of cabbage. He has a maximum of \$20,000 to spend. He makes a profit of \$120 per acre of potatoes, \$40 per acre of corn, and \$60 per acre of cabbage. How many acres of each crop should he plant to maximize his profit?

Summarize the given information as follows.

Crop	Number of acres	Cost per acre	Profit per acre
Potatoes	x_1	\$400	\$120
Corn	x_2	160	40
Cabbage	x_3	280	60
Maximum available	100	\$20,000	

If the number of acres allotted to each of the three crops is represented by x_1, x_2, and x_3, respectively, then the constraints of the example can be expressed as

$$x_1 + x_2 + x_3 \le 100 \quad \text{(number of acres)},$$
$$400x_1 + 160x_2 + 280x_3 \le 20{,}000 \quad \text{(production costs)},$$

where x_1, x_2, and x_3 are all nonnegative. The first of these constraints says that $x_1 + x_2 + x_3$ is less than or perhaps equal to 100. Use x_4 as the slack variable, giving the equation

$$x_1 + x_2 + x_3 + x_4 = 100.$$

Here x_4 represents the amount of the farmer's 100 acres that will not be used. (x_4 may be 0 or any value up to 100.)

In the same way, the constraint $400x_1 + 160x_2 + 280x_3 \le 20{,}000$ can be converted into an equation by adding a slack variable, x_5:

$$400x_1 + 160x_2 + 280x_3 + x_5 = 20{,}000.$$

The slack variable x_5 represents any unused portion of the farmer's \$20,000 capital. (Again, x_5 may be any value from 0 to 20,000.)

The objective function represents the profit. The farmer wants to maximize

$$z = 120x_1 + 40x_2 + 60x_3.$$

We have now set up the following linear programming problem:

$$\text{maximize} \quad z = 120x_1 + 40x_2 + 60x_3$$
$$\text{subject to:} \quad x_1 + x_2 + x_3 + x_4 = 100$$
$$400x_1 + 160x_2 + 280x_3 + x_5 = 20{,}000.$$

with $x_1 \ge 0$, $x_2 \ge 0$, $x_3 \ge 0$, $x_4 \ge 0$, $x_5 \ge 0$. Rewrite the objective function as $-120x_1 - 40x_2 - 60x_3 + z = 0$, with the initial simplex tableau as follows.

$$
\begin{array}{ccccc}
x_1 & x_2 & x_3 & x_4 & x_5 \\
\end{array}
$$

$$
\left[
\begin{array}{ccccc|c}
1 & 1 & 1 & 1 & 0 & 100 \\
400 & 160 & 280 & 0 & 1 & 20{,}000 \\
\hline
-120 & -40 & -60 & 0 & 0 & 0
\end{array}
\right]
$$

Since the x_4 and x_5 columns in this tableau make up the identity matrix, these variables are called **basic variables.** If we let $x_4 = 100$ (the entry to the far right in the row where the x_4 column has a 1), and let $x_5 = 20{,}000$, the system of equations

$$
\begin{aligned}
x_1 + x_2 + x_3 + x_4 &= 100 \\
400x_1 + 160x_2 + 280x_3 \quad + x_5 &= 20{,}000
\end{aligned}
$$

becomes

$$
\begin{aligned}
x_1 + x_2 + x_3 + 100 &= 100 \\
400x_1 + 160x_2 + 280x_3 \quad + 20{,}000 &= 20{,}000
\end{aligned}
$$

or

$$
\begin{aligned}
x_1 + x_2 + x_3 &= 0 \\
400x_1 + 160x_2 + 280x_3 &= 0.
\end{aligned}
$$

Since $x_1 \geq 0$, $x_2 \geq 0$, and $x_3 \geq 0$, the only possible solution for this last system of equations is $x_1 = 0$, $x_2 = 0$, and $x_3 = 0$. This solution, which corresponds to the origin of the region of feasible solutions, is hardly optimal—it produces a profit of \$0 for the farmer. In the next section we use the simplex method to start with this solution and improve it to find the maximum possible profit. ▪

EXAMPLE 3

Read a solution from the matrix below.

$$
\begin{array}{ccccc}
x_1 & x_2 & x_3 & x_4 & x_5 \\
\end{array}
$$

$$
\left[
\begin{array}{ccccc|c}
2 & 1 & 8 & 5 & 0 & 27 \\
9 & 0 & 3 & 12 & 1 & 45 \\
\hline
-2 & 0 & -4 & 0 & 0 & 0
\end{array}
\right]
$$

The variables x_2 and x_5 are basic variables. The 1 in the x_2 column is in the first row. This means that $x_2 = 27$ (the far right number in the first row). Also, $x_5 = 45$. Letting $x_2 = 27$ and $x_5 = 45$ forces x_1, x_3, and x_4 to be zero. The solution is thus $x_1 = 0$, $x_2 = 27$, $x_3 = 0$, $x_4 = 0$, and $x_5 = 45$. ▪

Pivots   Solutions read directly from the initial simplex tableau are seldom, if ever, optimal. It is necessary to proceed to other solutions (corresponding to other corner points of the feasible region) until an optimum solution is found. To get these other solutions, use the row transformations of Chapter 2 to change the tableau by "pivoting" about one of the nonzero entries of the tableau. Pivoting, explained in the next example, produces a new tableau leading to another solution of the system of equations obtained from the original problem.

EXAMPLE 4

Pivot about the indicated 2 of the initial simplex tableau

$$
\begin{array}{cccccc}
x_1 & x_2 & x_3 & x_4 & x_5 & x_6 \\
\end{array}
$$

$$
\left[
\begin{array}{cccccc|c}
2 & 1 & 1 & 1 & 0 & 0 & 150 \\
2 & 2 & 8 & 0 & 1 & 0 & 200 \\
2 & 3 & 1 & 0 & 0 & 1 & 320 \\
\hline
-3 & -2 & -1 & 0 & 0 & 0 & 0
\end{array}
\right].
$$

To pivot about the indicated 2, change x_1 into a basic variable by getting a 1 where the 2 is now and changing all other entries in the x_1 column to 0. Start by multiplying each entry of row 1 by 1/2.

$$
\begin{array}{cccccc}
x_1 & x_2 & x_3 & x_4 & x_5 & x_6 \\
\end{array}
$$

$$
\left[
\begin{array}{cccccc|c}
1 & \frac{1}{2} & \frac{1}{2} & \frac{1}{2} & 0 & 0 & 75 \\
2 & 2 & 8 & 0 & 1 & 0 & 200 \\
2 & 3 & 1 & 0 & 0 & 1 & 320 \\
\hline
-3 & -2 & -1 & 0 & 0 & 0 & 0
\end{array}
\right]
$$

Now get 0 in row 2, column 1 by multiplying each entry in row 1 by -2 and adding the result to the corresponding entry in row 2.

$$
\begin{array}{cccccc}
x_1 & x_2 & x_3 & x_4 & x_5 & x_6 \\
\end{array}
$$

$$
\left[
\begin{array}{cccccc|c}
1 & \frac{1}{2} & \frac{1}{2} & \frac{1}{2} & 0 & 0 & 75 \\
0 & 1 & 7 & -1 & 1 & 0 & 50 \\
2 & 3 & 1 & 0 & 0 & 1 & 320 \\
\hline
-3 & -2 & -1 & 0 & 0 & 0 & 0
\end{array}
\right]
$$

Change the 2 in row 3, column 1 to a 0 by a similar process.

$$
\begin{array}{cccccc}
x_1 & x_2 & x_3 & x_4 & x_5 & x_6 \\
\end{array}
$$

$$
\left[
\begin{array}{cccccc|c}
1 & \frac{1}{2} & \frac{1}{2} & \frac{1}{2} & 0 & 0 & 75 \\
0 & 1 & 7 & -1 & 1 & 0 & 50 \\
0 & 2 & 0 & -1 & 0 & 1 & 170 \\
\hline
-3 & -2 & -1 & 0 & 0 & 0 & 0
\end{array}
\right]
$$

Finally, change the indicator -3 to 0 by multiplying each entry in row 1 by 3 and adding the result to the corresponding entry in row 4.

$$
\begin{array}{cccccc}
x_1 & x_2 & x_3 & x_4 & x_5 & x_6 \\
\end{array}
$$

$$
\left[
\begin{array}{cccccc|c}
1 & \frac{1}{2} & \frac{1}{2} & \frac{1}{2} & 0 & 0 & 75 \\
0 & 1 & 7 & -1 & 1 & 0 & 50 \\
0 & 2 & 0 & -1 & 0 & 1 & 170 \\
\hline
0 & -\frac{1}{2} & \frac{1}{2} & \frac{3}{2} & 0 & 0 & 225
\end{array}
\right]
$$

This simplex tableau gives the solution $x_1 = 75$, $x_2 = 0$, $x_3 = 0$, $x_4 = 0$, $x_5 = 50$, and $x_6 = 170$. Substituting these results into the objective function gives $z = 225$. (The value of z is always the number in the lower right-hand corner.) ■

In the simplex method, this process is repeated until an optimum solution is found, if one exists. In the next section, we discuss how to decide where to pivot to improve the value of the objective function. We also show how to tell when an optimum solution has been reached or does not exist.

4.1 EXERCISES

Convert each of the inequalities in Exercises 1–4 into equations by adding a slack variable.

1. $x_1 + 2x_2 \leq 6$

2. $3x_1 + 5x_2 \leq 100$

3. $2x_1 + 4x_2 + 3x_3 \leq 100$

4. $8x_1 + 6x_2 + 5x_3 \leq 250$

For Exercises 5–8, **(a)** determine the number of slack variables needed; **(b)** name them; **(c)** use slack variables to convert each constraint into a linear equation.

5. Maximize $z = 10x_1 + 12x_2$

subject to: $4x_1 + 2x_2 \leq 20$
$5x_1 + x_2 \leq 50$
$2x_1 + 3x_2 \leq 25$

and $x_1 \geq 0,\ x_2 \geq 0.$

6. Maximize $z = 1.2x_1 + 3.5x_2$

subject to: $2.4x_1 + 1.5x_2 \leq 10$
$1.7x_1 + 1.9x_2 \leq 15$

and $x_1 \geq 0,\ x_2 \geq 0.$

7. Maximize $z = 8x_1 + 3x_2 + x_3$

subject to: $7x_1 + 6x_2 + 8x_3 \leq 118$
$4x_1 + 5x_2 + 10x_3 \leq 220$

and $x_1 \geq 0,\ x_2 \geq 0,\ x_3 \geq 0.$

8. Maximize $z = 12x_1 + 15x_2 + 10x_3$

subject to: $2x_1 + 2x_2 + x_3 \leq 8$
$x_1 + 4x_2 + 3x_3 \leq 12$

and $x_1 \geq 0,\ x_2 \geq 0,\ x_3 \geq 0.$

Write the solution that can be read from Exercises 9–12.

9.

x_1	x_2	x_3	x_4	x_5	
2	2	0	3	1	15
3	4	1	6	0	20
-2	-1	0	1	0	10

10.

x_1	x_2	x_3	x_4	x_5	
0	2	1	1	3	5
1	5	0	1	2	8
0	-2	0	1	1	10

11.

x_1	x_2	x_3	x_4	x_5	x_6	
6	2	1	3	0	0	8
2	2	0	1	0	1	7
2	1	0	3	1	0	6
-3	-2	0	2	0	0	12

12.

x_1	x_2	x_3	x_4	x_5	x_6	
0	2	0	1	2	2	3
0	3	1	0	1	2	2
1	4	0	0	3	5	5
0	-4	0	0	4	3	20

Pivot as indicated in the simplex tableau in Exercises 13–18. Read the solution from the final result.

13.

x_1	x_2	x_3	x_4	x_5	
1	2	4	1	0	56
2	2	1	0	1	40
-1	-3	-2	0	0	0

14.

x_1	x_2	x_3	x_4	x_5	
5	4	1	1	0	50
3	3	2	0	1	40
-1	-2	-4	0	0	0

15.

x_1	x_2	x_3	x_4	x_5	x_6	
2	2	1	1	0	0	12
1	2	3	0	1	0	45
3	1	1	0	0	1	20
-2	-1	-3	0	0	0	0

16.

x_1	x_2	x_3	x_4	x_5	x_6	
4	2	3	1	0	0	22
2	2	5	0	1	0	28
1	3	2	0	0	1	45
-3	-2	-4	0	0	0	0

17.

x_1	x_2	x_3	x_4	x_5	x_6	
1	1	1	1	0	0	60
3	1	2	0	1	0	100
1	2	3	0	0	1	200
-1	-1	-2	0	0	0	0

18.

x_1	x_2	x_3	x_4	x_5	x_6	x_7	
1	2	3	1	1	0	0	115
2	1	8	5	0	1	0	200
1	0	1	0	0	0	1	50
-2	-1	-1	-1	0	0	0	0

Introduce slack variables as necessary and then write the initial simplex tableau for the linear programming problems in Exercises 19–24.

19. Find $x_1 \geq 0$ and $x_2 \geq 0$ such that

$$2x_1 + 3x_2 \leq 6$$
$$4x_1 + x_2 \leq 6$$

and $z = 5x_1 + x_2$ is maximized.

20. Find $x_1 \geq 50$ and $x_2 \geq 50$ such that

$$2x_1 + 3x_2 \leq 100$$
$$5x_1 + 4x_2 \leq 200$$

and $z = x_1 + 3x_2$ is maximized.

21. Find $x_1 \geq 0$ and $x_2 \geq 0$ such that

$$x_1 + x_2 \leq 10$$
$$5x_1 + 2x_2 \leq 20$$
$$x_1 + 2x_2 \leq 36$$

and $z = x_1 + 3x_2$ is maximized.

22. Find $x_1 \geq 0$ and $x_2 \geq 0$ such that

$$x_1 + x_2 \leq 10$$
$$5x_1 + 3x_2 \leq 75$$

and $z = 4x_1 + 2x_2$ is maximized.

23. Find $x_1 \geq 0$ and $x_2 \geq 0$ such that

$$3x_1 + x_2 \leq 12$$
$$x_1 + x_2 \leq 15$$

and $z = 2x_1 + x_2$ is maximized.

24. Find $x_1 \geq 0$ and $x_2 \geq 0$ such that

$$10x_1 + 4x_2 \leq 100$$
$$20x_1 + 10x_2 \leq 150$$

and $z = 4x_1 + 5x_2$ is maximized.

Set up Exercises 25–30 for solution by the simplex method; that is, express the linear constraints and objective function, add slack variables, and set up the initial simplex tableau.

25. A candy company has 100 kilograms of chocolate-covered nuts and 125 kilograms of chocolate-covered raisins to be sold as two different mixtures. One mix will contain half nuts and half raisins and will sell for $6 per kilogram. The other mix will contain 1/3 nuts and 2/3 raisins, and will sell for $4.80 per kilogram. How many kilograms of each mix should the company prepare for maximum revenue? (This is Exercise 13, Section 3.2.)

26. Seall Manufacturing Company makes color television sets. It produces a bargain set that sells for $100 profit and a deluxe set that sells for $150 profit. On the assembly line the bargain set requires 3 hours' work, while the deluxe set takes 5 hours. The cabinet shop spends one hour on the cabinet for the bargain set and 3 hours on the cabinet for the deluxe set. Both sets require 2 hours of time for testing and packing. On a particular production run the Seall Company has available 3900 work hours on the assembly line, 2100 work hours in the cabinet shop, and 2200 work hours in the testing and packing department. How many sets of each type should it produce to make maximum profit? What is the maximum profit? (See Exercise 10, Section 3.2.)

27. A small boat manufacturer builds three types of fiberglass boats: prams, runabouts, and trimarans. The pram sells at a profit of $75, the runabout at a profit of $90, and the trimaran at a profit of $100. The factory is divided into two sections. Section A does the molding and construction work, while section B does the painting, finishing and equipping. The pram takes 1 hour in section A and 2 hours in section B. The runabout takes 2 hours in A and 5 hours in B. The trimaran takes 3 hours in A and 4 hours in B. Section A has a total of 6240 hours available and section B has 10,800 hours available for the year. The manufacturer has ordered a supply of fiberglass that will build at most 3000 boats, figuring the average amount used per boat. How many of each type of boat should be made to produce maximum profit? What is the maximum profit?

28. Caroline's Quality Candy Confectionery is famous for fudge, chocolate cremes, and pralines. Its candy-making equipment is set up to make 100-pound batches at a time. Currently there is a chocolate shortage and the company can get only 120 pounds of chocolate in the next shipment. On a week's run, the confectionery's cooking and processing equipment is available for a total of 42 machine hours. During the same period the employees have a total of 56 work hours available for packaging. A batch of fudge requires 20 pounds of chocolate while a batch of cremes uses 25 pounds of chocolate. The cooking and processing take 120 minutes for fudge, 150 minutes for chocolate cremes, and 200 minutes for pralines. The packaging times measured in minutes per one pound box are 1, 2, and 3 respectively, for fudge, cremes, and pralines. Determine how many batches of each type of candy the confectionery should make, assuming that the profit per pound box is 50¢ on fudge, 40¢ on chocolate cremes, and 45¢ on pralines. What is the maximum profit?

29. A cat breeder has the following amounts of cat food: 90 units of tuna, 80 units of liver, and 50 units of chicken. To raise a Siamese cat, the breeder must use 2 units of tuna, 1 of liver, and 1 of chicken per day, while raising a Persian cat requires 1, 2, and 1 units respectively per day. If a Siamese cat sells for $12, while a Persian cat sells for $10, how many of each should be raised in order to obtain maximum gross income? What is the maximum gross income?

30. Banal, Inc. produces art for motel rooms. Its painters can turn out mountain scenes, seascapes, and pictures of clowns. Each painting is worked on by three different artists, T, D, and H. Artist T works only 25 hours per week, while D and H work 45 and 40 hours per week, respectively. Artist T spends 1 hour on a mountain scene, 2 hours on a seascape, and 1 hour on a clown. Corresponding times for D and H are 3, 2, and 2 hours, and 2, 1, and 4 hours, respectively. Banal makes $20 on a mountain scene, $18 on a seascape, and $22 from a clown. The head painting packer can't stand clowns, so that no more than 4 clown paintings may be done in a week. Find the number of each type of painting that should be made weekly in order to maximize profit. Find the maximum possible profit.

4.2 Solving Maximization Problems

We have learned how to prepare a linear programming problem for solution by first converting the constraints to linear equations with slack variables. We then wrote the coefficients of the variables from the linear equations as an augmented matrix. Finally, we used the pivot to go from one vertex of the region of feasible solutions to another.

Now we are ready to put all this together and produce an optimum value for the objective function. To see how this is done, let us complete the example about the farmer. (Recall Example 2 from Section 4.1.)

In the previous section we set up the following simplex tableau.

$$
\begin{array}{ccccc}
x_1 & x_2 & x_3 & x_4 & x_5 \\
\end{array}
$$

$$
\left[
\begin{array}{ccccc|c}
1 & 1 & 1 & 1 & 0 & 100 \\
400 & 160 & 280 & 0 & 1 & 20{,}000 \\
\hline
-120 & -40 & -60 & 0 & 0 & 0
\end{array}
\right]
$$

This tableau leads to the solution $x_1 = 0$, $x_2 = 0$, $x_3 = 0$, $x_4 = 100$, and $x_5 = 20{,}000$. These values produce a value of 0 for z. Since a value of 0 for the farmer's profit is not an optimum, we try to improve this value.

The coefficients of x_1, x_2, and x_3 in the objective function are nonzero, so the profit could be improved by making any one of these variables take on a non-zero value in a solution. To decide which variable to use, look at the indicators in the initial simplex tableau above. The coefficient of x_1, -120, is the "most negative" of the indicators. This means that x_1 has the largest coefficient in the objective function, so that profit is increased the most by increasing x_1.

If x_1 is nonzero in the solution, then x_1 will be a basic variable. This means that either x_4 or x_5 no longer will be a basic variable. To decide which variable will no longer be basic, start with the equations of the system,

$$
\begin{aligned}
x_1 + \quad x_2 + \quad x_3 + x_4 \qquad &= \quad 100 \\
400x_1 + 160x_2 + 280x_3 \qquad + x_5 &= 20{,}000.
\end{aligned}
$$

and solve for x_4 and x_5 respectively.

$$
\begin{aligned}
x_4 &= 100 - x_1 - x_2 - x_3 \\
x_5 &= 20{,}000 - 400x_1 - 160x_2 - 280x_3
\end{aligned}
$$

Only x_1 is being changed to a nonzero value; both x_2 and x_3 keep the value 0. Replacing x_2 and x_3 with 0 gives

$$
\begin{aligned}
x_4 &= 100 - x_1 \\
x_5 &= 20{,}000 - 400x_1.
\end{aligned}
$$

Since both x_4 and x_5 must remain nonnegative, there is a limit to how much the value of x_1 can be increased. The equation $x_4 = 100 - x_1$ (or $x_4 = 100 - 1x_1$) shows that x_1 cannot exceed 100/1, or 100. The second equation, $x_5 = 20{,}000 - 400x_1$, shows that x_1 cannot exceed 20,000/400, or 50. To satisfy both these conditions, x_1 cannot exceed 50, the smaller of 50 and 100. If we let x_1 take the value 50, then $x_1 = 50$, $x_2 = 0$, $x_3 = 0$, and $x_5 = 0$. Since $x_4 = 100 - x_1$, then

$$
x_4 = 100 - 50 = 50.
$$

This solution gives a profit of

$$
\begin{aligned}
z &= 120x_1 + 40x_2 + 60x_3 + 0x_4 + 0x_5 \\
&= 120(50) + 40(0) + 60(0) + 0(50) + 0(0) = 6000.
\end{aligned}
$$

The same result could have been found from the initial simplex tableau given above. To use the tableau, select the most negative indicator. (If no indicator is negative, then the value of the objective function cannot be improved.)

$$
\begin{array}{c}
\begin{array}{ccccc}
x_1 & x_2 & x_3 & x_4 & x_5
\end{array} \\
\left[
\begin{array}{ccccc|c}
1 & 1 & 1 & 1 & 0 & 100 \\
400 & 160 & 280 & 0 & 1 & 20{,}000 \\
\hline
-120 & -40 & -60 & 0 & 0 & 0
\end{array}
\right]
\end{array}
$$

↑—most negative indicator

The most negative indicator identifies the variable whose value is to be made nonzero. To find the variable which is now basic and which will become nonbasic, calculate the quotients that were found above. Do this by dividing each number from the right side of the tableau by the corresponding number from the column with the most negative indicator.

Quotients

$$100/1 = 100$$

smaller → $20{,}000/400 = 50$

$$
\begin{array}{c}
\begin{array}{ccccc}
x_1 & x_2 & x_3 & x_4 & x_5
\end{array} \\
\left[
\begin{array}{ccccc|c}
1 & 1 & 1 & 1 & 0 & 100 \\
400 & 160 & 280 & 0 & 1 & 20{,}000 \\
\hline
-120 & -40 & -60 & 0 & 0 & 0
\end{array}
\right]
\end{array}
$$

The smaller quotient is 50, from the second row. This identifies 400 as the pivot. Use 400 as pivot, and the appropriate row transformations, to get the second simplex tableau as follows: get 1 in the pivot position by multiplying each element of the second row by 1/400. Then multiply each of the entries in the second row by -1 and add the results to the corresponding entries in the first row, to get a 0 above the pivot. Get a 0 below the pivot, as the first indicator, in a similar way. The new tableau is

$$
\begin{array}{c}
\begin{array}{ccccc}
x_1 & x_2 & x_3 & x_4 & x_5
\end{array} \\
\left[
\begin{array}{ccccc|c}
0 & .6 & .3 & 1 & -.0025 & 50 \\
1 & .4 & .7 & 0 & .0025 & 50 \\
\hline
0 & 8 & 24 & 0 & .3 & 6000
\end{array}
\right]
\end{array}
$$

and the solution read from this tableau is

$$x_1 = 50, \quad x_2 = 0, \quad x_3 = 0, \quad x_4 = 50, \quad x_5 = 0,$$

the same result found above. The entry 6000 (in color) in the lower right corner of the tableau gives the value of the objective function for this solution:

$$z = \$6000.$$

None of the indicators in the final simplex tableau is negative, which means that the value of z cannot be improved beyond $6000. To see why, recall that the last row gives the coefficients of the objective function. Including the coefficient of 1 for the z column which was dropped gives

$$0x_1 + 8x_2 + 24x_3 + 0x_4 + .3x_5 + z = 6000,$$

or
$$z = 6000 - 0x_1 - 8x_2 - 24x_3 - 0x_4 - .3x_5.$$

Since x_2, x_3, and x_5 are zero, $z = 6000$, but if any of these three variables were to increase, z would decrease.

This result suggests that the optimal solution has been found as soon as no indicators are negative. As long as an indicator is negative, the value of the objective function can be improved. Just find a new pivot and repeat the process until no negative indicators remain.

We can finally state the solution to the problem about the farmer: the optimum value of z is 6000, where $x_1 = 50$, $x_2 = 0$, $x_3 = 0$, $x_4 = 50$, and $x_5 = 0$. That is, the farmer will make a maximum profit of \$6000 by planting 50 acres of potatoes. Another 50 acres should be left unplanted. It may seem strange that leaving assets unused can produce a maximum profit, but such results actually occur often.

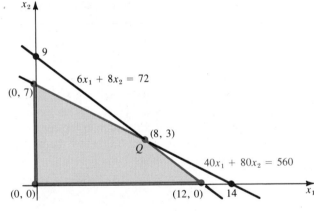

FIGURE 1

EXAMPLE 1

To compare the simplex method with the geometric method, use the simplex method to solve the problem of Example 4, Section 3.2. The graph is shown again in Figure 1. The objective function to be maximized was

$$z = 8x_1 + 12x_2. \qquad \text{(storage space)}$$

(Since we are using the simplex method, we use x_1 and x_2 as variables instead of x and y.) The constraints were as follows:

$$40x_1 + 80x_2 \le 560 \qquad \text{(cost)}$$

$$6x_1 + 8x_2 \le 72 \qquad \text{(floor space)}$$

$$x_1 \ge 0, \ x_2 \ge 0.$$

Add a slack variable to each constraint.

$$40x_1 + 80x_2 + x_3 \qquad = 560$$
$$6x_1 + 8x_2 \qquad + x_4 = 72.$$

Write the initial simplex tableau.

$$
\begin{array}{cccc}
x_1 & x_2 & x_3 & x_4 \\
\end{array}
$$

$$
\left[
\begin{array}{cccc|c}
40 & 80 & 1 & 0 & 560 \\
6 & 8 & 0 & 1 & 72 \\
\hline
-8 & -12 & 0 & 0 & 0
\end{array}
\right]
$$

This tableau leads to the solution $x_1 = 0$, $x_2 = 0$, $x_3 = 560$, and $x_4 = 72$, with $z = 0$, which corresponds to the origin in Figure 1. The most negative indicator is -12. The necessary quotients are

$$\frac{560}{80} = 7 \qquad \text{and} \qquad \frac{72}{8} = 9.$$

The smaller quotient is 7, giving 80 as the pivot. Use row transformations to get the new tableau.

$$
\left[
\begin{array}{cccc|c}
\frac{1}{2} & 1 & \frac{1}{80} & 0 & 7 \\
2 & 0 & -\frac{1}{10} & 1 & 16 \\
\hline
-2 & 0 & \frac{3}{20} & 0 & 84
\end{array}
\right]
$$

The solution from this tableau is $x_1 = 0$, $x_2 = 7$, $x_3 = 0$, and $x_4 = 16$, with $z = 84$, which corresponds to the corner point $(0, 7)$ in Figure 1. Because of the indicator -2, the value of z can be improved. Use the 2 in row 2, column 1 as pivot to get the final tableau.

$$
\left[
\begin{array}{cccc|c}
0 & 1 & \frac{3}{80} & -\frac{1}{4} & 3 \\
1 & 0 & -\frac{1}{20} & \frac{1}{2} & 8 \\
\hline
0 & 0 & \frac{1}{20} & 1 & 100
\end{array}
\right]
$$

Here the solution is $x_1 = 8$, $x_2 = 3$, $x_3 = 0$, and $x_4 = 0$, with $z = 100$. This solution, which corresponds to the corner point $(8, 3)$ in Figure 1, is the same as the solution found earlier.

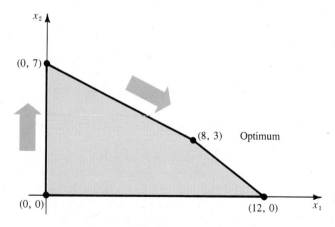

FIGURE 2

As we have seen, each simplex tableau above gave a solution corresponding to one of the corner points of the feasible region. As shown in Figure 2, the first solution corresponded to the origin, with $z = 0$. By choosing the appropriate pivot, we moved systematically to a new corner point, $(0, 7)$, which improved the value of z to 84. The next tableau took us to $(8, 3)$, producing the optimum value of $z = 100$. There was no reason to test the last corner point, $(12, 0)$, since the optimum value of z was found before that point was reached. ▪

The next example shows how to handle zero or a negative number in the column containing the pivot.

EXAMPLE 2

Find the pivot for the following initial simplex tableau.

$$
\begin{array}{ccccc}
x_1 & x_2 & x_3 & x_4 & x_5 \\
\end{array}
$$

$$
\left[
\begin{array}{ccccc|c}
1 & -2 & 1 & 0 & 0 & 100 \\
3 & 4 & 0 & 1 & 0 & 200 \\
5 & 0 & 0 & 0 & 1 & 150 \\
\hline
-10 & -25 & 0 & 0 & 0 & 0
\end{array}
\right]
$$

The most negative indicator is -25. To find the pivot, find the quotients formed by the entries in the right-most column and in the x_2 column: $100/(-2)$, $200/4$, and $150/0$. Since division by 0 is meaningless, disregard the quotient $150/0$, which comes from the equation

$$5x_1 + 0x_2 + 0x_3 + 0x_4 + x_5 = 150.$$

If $x_1 = 0$, the equation reduces to

$$0x_2 + x_5 = 150 \qquad \text{or} \qquad x_5 = 150 - 0x_2.$$

Since the pivot is in the x_2 column, x_5 cannot be 0. In general, disregard quotients with a 0 denominator.

The quotients predict the value of a variable in the solution, and thus cannot be negative. In this example, the quotient $100/(-2) = -50$ comes from the equation

$$x_1 - 2x_2 + x_3 + 0x_4 + 0x_5 = 100.$$

For $x_1 = 0$, this becomes

$$x_3 = 100 + 2x_2.$$

If x_3 is to be nonnegative, then

$$100 + 2x_2 \geq 0$$

$$x_2 \geq -50.$$

Since x_2 must be nonnegative anyway, this equation tells us nothing new. For this reason, disregard negative quotients also.

The only usable quotient is $200/4 = 50$, making 4 the pivot. If all the quotients are either negative or have zero denominators, no optimum solution will be found. The quotients, then, determine whether or not an optimum solution exists. ▪

Let us now summarize the steps involved in solving a standard maximum linear programming problem by the simplex method.

Simplex Method

1. Determine the objective function.

2. Write all necessary constraints.

3. Convert each constraint into an equation by adding slack variables.

4. Set up the initial simplex tableau.

5. Locate the most negative indicator. If there are two such indicators, choose either.

6. Form the necessary quotients to find the pivot. Disregard any negative quotients or quotients with a 0 denominator. The smallest nonnegative quotient gives the location of the pivot. If all quotients must be disregarded, no maximum solution exists.* If two quotients are equally the smallest, let either determine the pivot.†

7. Transform the tableau so that the pivot becomes 1 and all other numbers in that column become 0.

8. If the indicators are all positive or 0, this is the final tableau. If not, go back to Step 5 above and repeat the process until a tableau with no negative indicators is obtained.

9. Read the solution from this final tableau. The maximum value of the objective function is the number in the lower right corner of the final tableau.

Although linear programming problems with more than a few variables would seem to be very complex, in practical applications many entries in the simplex tableau are zeros.

4.2 EXERCISES

In Exercises 1–6, the initial tableau of a linear programming problem is given. Use the simplex method to solve each problem.

1.

$$
\begin{array}{ccccc}
x_1 & x_2 & x_3 & x_4 & x_5 \\
\end{array}
$$

$$
\left[
\begin{array}{ccccc|c}
1 & 2 & 4 & 1 & 0 & 8 \\
2 & 2 & 1 & 0 & 1 & 10 \\
\hline
-2 & -5 & -1 & 0 & 0 & 0
\end{array}
\right]
$$

2.

$$
\begin{array}{ccccc}
x_1 & x_2 & x_3 & x_4 & x_5 \\
\end{array}
$$

$$
\left[
\begin{array}{ccccc|c}
2 & 2 & 1 & 1 & 0 & 10 \\
1 & 2 & 3 & 0 & 1 & 15 \\
\hline
-3 & -2 & -1 & 0 & 0 & 0
\end{array}
\right]
$$

---

*Some special circumstances are noted at the end of Section 4.3.

†It may be that the first choice of a pivot does not produce a solution. In that case, try the other choice.

3.

$$\begin{array}{ccccc} x_1 & x_2 & x_3 & x_4 & x_5 \end{array}$$

$$\begin{bmatrix} 1 & 3 & 1 & 0 & 0 & | & 12 \\ 2 & 1 & 0 & 1 & 0 & | & 10 \\ 1 & 1 & 0 & 0 & 1 & | & 4 \\ \hline -2 & -1 & 0 & 0 & 0 & | & 0 \end{bmatrix}$$

4.

$$\begin{array}{cccccc} x_1 & x_2 & x_3 & x_4 & x_5 & x_6 \end{array}$$

$$\begin{bmatrix} 2 & 2 & 1 & 1 & 0 & 0 & | & 50 \\ 1 & 1 & 3 & 0 & 1 & 0 & | & 40 \\ 4 & 2 & 5 & 0 & 0 & 1 & | & 80 \\ \hline -2 & -3 & -5 & 0 & 0 & 0 & | & 0 \end{bmatrix}$$

5.

$$\begin{array}{cccccc} x_1 & x_2 & x_3 & x_4 & x_5 & x_6 \end{array}$$

$$\begin{bmatrix} 2 & 2 & 8 & 1 & 0 & 0 & | & 40 \\ 4 & -5 & 6 & 0 & 1 & 0 & | & 60 \\ 2 & -2 & 6 & 0 & 0 & 1 & | & 24 \\ \hline -14 & -10 & -12 & 0 & 0 & 0 & | & 0 \end{bmatrix}$$

6.

$$\begin{array}{ccccc} x_1 & x_2 & x_3 & x_4 & x_5 \end{array}$$

$$\begin{bmatrix} 3 & 2 & 4 & 1 & 0 & | & 18 \\ 2 & 1 & 5 & 0 & 1 & | & 8 \\ \hline -1 & -4 & -2 & 0 & 0 & | & 0 \end{bmatrix}$$

Use the simplex method to solve Exercises 7–14.

7. Maximize $z = 4x_1 + 3x_2$

subject to: $2x_1 + 3x_2 \le 11$
$x_1 + 2x_2 \le 6,$

and $x_1 \ge 0,\ x_2 \ge 0$

8. Maximize $z = 2x_1 + 3x_2$

subject to: $3x_1 + 5x_2 \le 29$
$2x_1 + x_2 \le 10,$

and $x_1 \ge 0,\ x_2 \ge 0$

9. Maximize $z = 10x_1 + 12x_2$

subject to: $4x_1 + 2x_2 \le 20$
$5x_1 + x_2 \le 50$
$2x_1 + 2x_2 \le 24$

and $x_1 \ge 0,\ x_2 \ge 0.$

10. Maximize $z = 1.2x_1 + 3.5x_2$

subject to: $2.4x_1 + 1.5x_2 \le 10$
$1.7x_1 + 1.9x_2 \le 15$

and $x_1 \ge 0,\ x_2 \ge 0.$

11. Maximize $z = 8x_1 + 3x_2 + x_3$

subject to: $x_1 + 6x_2 + 8x_3 \le 118$
$x_1 + 5x_2 + 10x_3 \le 220$

and $x_1 \ge 0,\ x_2 \ge 0,\ x_3 \ge 0.$

12. Maximize $z = 12x_1 + 15x_2 + 5x_3$

subject to: $2x_1 + 2x_2 + x_3 \le 8$
$x_1 + 4x_2 + 3x_3 \le 12$

and $x_1 \ge 0,\ x_2 \ge 0,\ x_3 \ge 0.$

13. Maximize $z = x_1 + 2x_2 + x_3 + 5x_4$

subject to: $x_1 + 2x_2 + x_3 + x_4 \le 50$
$3x_1 + x_2 + 2x_3 + x_4 \le 100$

and $x_1 \ge 0,\ x_2 \ge 0,\ x_3 \ge 0,\ x_4 \ge 0.$

14. Maximize $z = x_1 + x_2 + 4x_3 + 5x_4$

subject to: $x_1 + 2x_2 + 3x_3 + x_4 \le 115$
$2x_1 + x_2 + 8x_3 + 5x_4 \le 200$
$x_1 + x_3 \le 50$

and $x_1 \ge 0,\ x_2 \ge 0,\ x_3 \ge 0,\ x_4 \ge 0.$

Set up and solve Exercises 15–20 by the simplex method.

15. A biologist has 500 kilograms of nutrient A, 600 kilograms of nutrient B, and 300 kilograms of nutrient C. These nutrients will be used to make 4 types of food, whose contents (in percent of nutrient per kilogram of food) and whose "growth values" are as shown below.

	Nutrient (%)			
Food	A	B	C	Growth value
P	0	0	100	90
Q	0	75	25	70
R	37.5	50	12.5	60
S	62.5	37.5	0	50

How many kilograms of each food should be produced in order to maximize total growth value? Find the maximum growth value.

16. A baker has 150 units of flour, 90 units of sugar, and 150 of raisins. A loaf of raisin bread requires 1 unit of flour, 1 of sugar and 2 of raisins, while a raisin cake needs 5, 2, and 1 units, respectively. If raisin bread sells for 35¢ a loaf and raisin cake for 80¢ each, how many of each should be baked so that gross income is maximized? What is the maximum gross income?

17. A candy company has 100 kilograms of chocolate-covered nuts and 125 kilograms of chocolate-covered raisins to be sold as two different mixtures. One mix will contain half nuts and half raisins and will sell for $6 per kilogram. The other mix will contain 1/3 nuts and 2/3 raisins, and will sell for $4.80 per kilogram. How many kilograms of each mix should the company prepare for maximum revenue? (See Exercise 25, Section 4.1.) Find the maximum revenue.

18. Caroline's Quality Candy Confectionery is famous for fudge, chocolate cremes, and pralines. Its candy-making equipment is set up to make 100-pound batches at a time. Currently there is a chocolate shortage and the company can get only 120 pounds of chocolate in the next shipment. On a week's run, the confectionery's cooking and processing equipment is available for a total of 42 machine hours. During the same period the employees have a total of 56 work hours available for packaging. A batch of fudge requires 20 pounds of chocolate while a batch of cremes uses 25 pounds of chocolate. The cooking and processing take 120 minutes for fudge, 150 minutes for chocolate cremes, and 200 minutes for pralines. The packaging times measured in minutes per one pound box are 1, 2, and 3, respectively for fudge, cremes and pralines. Determine how many batches of each type of candy the confectionery should make, assuming that the profit per pound box is 50¢ on fudge, 40¢ on chocolate cremes, and 45¢ on pralines. Also, find the maximum profit for the week. (See Exercise 28, Section 4.1.)

19. A manufacturer of bicycles builds one-, three-, and ten-speed models. The bicycles need both aluminum and steel. The company has available 91,800 units of steel and 42,000 units of aluminum. The one-, three-, and ten-speed models need respectively 17, 27, and 34 units of steel, and 12, 21, and 15 units of aluminum. How many of each type of bicycle should be made in order to maximize profit if the company makes $8 per one-speed bike, $12 per three-speed, and $22 per ten-speed? What is the maximum possible profit?

20. A political party is planning a half-hour television show. The show will have 3 minutes of direct requests for money from viewers. Three of the party's politicians will be on the show—a senator, a congresswoman, and a governor. The senator, a party "elder statesman," demands that he be on at least twice as long as the governor. The total time taken by the senator and the governor must be at least twice the time taken by the congresswoman. Based on a pre-show survey, it is believed that 40, 60, and 50 (in thousands) viewers will watch the program for each minute the senator, congresswoman, and governor, respectively are on the air. Find the time that should be alloted to each politician in order to get the maximum number of viewers. Find the maximum number of viewers.

The next two problems come from past CPA examinations.* Select the appropriate answer for each question.

---

*Material from *Uniform CPA Examination Questions and Unofficial Answers*, copyright © 1973, 1974, 1975 by the American Institute of Certified Public Accountants, Inc., is reprinted with permission.

21. The Ball Company manufactures three types of lamps, labeled A, B, and C. Each lamp is processed in two departments, I and II. Total available man-hours per day for departments I and II are 400 and 600, respectively. No additional labor is available. Time requirements and profit per unit for each lamp type is as follows:

	A	B	C
Man-hours in I	2	3	1
Man-hours in II	4	2	3
Profit per unit	$5	$4	$3

The company has assigned you as the accounting member of its profit planning committee to determine the numbers of types of A, B, and C lamps that it should produce in order to maximize its total profit from the sale of lamps. The following questions relate to a linear programming model that your group has developed.

(a) The coefficients of the objective function would be
   (1) 4, 2, 3.   (2) 2, 3, 1.
   (3) 5, 4, 3.   (4) 400, 600.

(b) The constraints in the model would be
   (1) 2, 3, 1.   (2) 5, 4, 3.
   (3) 4, 2, 3.   (4) 400, 600.

(c) The constraint imposed by the available man-hours in department 1 could be expressed as
   (1) $4X_1 + 2X_2 + 3X_3 \leq 400$.   (2) $4X_1 + 2X_2 + 3X_3 \geq 400$.
   (3) $2X_1 + 3X_2 + 1X_3 \leq 400$.   (4) $2X_1 + 3X_2 + 1X_3 \geq 400$.

22. The Golden Hawk Manufacturing Company wants to maximize the profits on products A, B, and C. The contribution margin for each product follows:

Product	Contribution margin
A	$2
B	$5
C	$4

The production requirements and departmental capacities, by departments, are as follows:

Department	Production requirements by product (hours)			Departmental capacity (total hours)
	A	B	C	
Assembling	2	3	2	30,000
Painting	1	2	2	38,000
Finishing	2	3	1	28,000

(a) What is the profit-maximization formula for the Golden Hawk Company?
   (1) $2A + $5B + $4C = X$ (where X = profit)   (2) $5A + 8B + 5C \leq 96,000$
   (3) $2A + $5B + $4C \leq X$ (4) $2A + $5B + $4C = 96,000$

(b) What is the constraint for the Painting Department of the Golden Hawk Company?
   (1) $1A + 2B + 2C \geq 38{,}000$
   (2) $\$2A + \$5B + \$4C \geq 38{,}000$
   (3) $1A + 2B + 2C \leq 38{,}000$
   (4) $2A + 3B + 2C \leq 30{,}000$

Determine the constraints and the objective function for Exercises 23 and 24, then solve each problem.

23. A manufacturer makes two products, toy trucks and toy fire engines. Both are processed in four different departments, each of which has a limited capacity. The sheet metal department can handle at least $1\frac{1}{2}$ times as many trucks as fire engines. The truck assembly department can handle at most 6700 trucks per week, while the fire engine assembly department assembles at most 5500 fire engines weekly. The painting department, which finishes both toys, has a maximum capacity of 12,000 per week. If the profit is $8.50 for a toy truck and $12.10 for a toy fire engine, how many of each item should the company produce to maximize profit?

24. The average weights of the three species stocked in the lake referred to in Section 2.2, Exercise 51 are 1.62, 2.14, and 3.01 kilograms for species A, B, and C, respectively. If the largest amounts of food that can be supplied each day are given as in Exercise 51, how should the lake be stocked to maximize the weight of the fish supported by the lake?

4.3   Mixed Constraints

So far we have used the simplex method only to solve standard maximum linear programming problems. In this section we extend this work to include linear programming problems with mixed $\leq$ and $\geq$ constraints. Then we see how solving these problems gives a method of solving minimum problems. (An alternate approach to minimum problems is given in the next section.)

Problems with $\leq$ ***and*** $\geq$ ***Constraints***   Suppose a new constraint is added to the farmer problem from Example 2 of Section 4.1: to satisfy orders from regular buyers, the farmer must plant a total of at least 60 acres of the three crops. This constraint introduces the new inequality

$$x_1 + x_2 + x_3 \geq 60.$$

As before, this inequality must be rewritten as an equation in which the variables all represent nonnegative numbers. The inequality $x_1 + x_2 + x_3 \geq 60$ means that

$$x_1 + x_2 + x_3 - x_6 = 60$$

for some nonnegative variable x_6. (Remember that x_4 and x_5 are the slack variables in the problem.)

The new variable, x_6, is called a **surplus variable.** The value of this variable represents the excess number of acres (over 60) which may be planted. Since the total number of acres planted is to be no more than 100 but at least 60, the value of x_6 can vary from 0 to 40.

We must now solve the system of equations

$$
\begin{aligned}
x_1 + x_2 + x_3 + x_4 & = 100 \\
400x_1 + 160x_2 + 280x_3 + x_5 & = 20{,}000 \\
x_1 + x_2 + x_3 - x_6 &= 60 \\
-120x_1 - 40x_2 - 60x_3 + z &= 0
\end{aligned}
$$

with x_1, x_2, x_3, x_4, x_5, and x_6 all nonnegative.

Set up the initial simplex tableau. (The z column is omitted as before.)

$$
\begin{array}{cccccc}
x_1 & x_2 & x_3 & x_4 & x_5 & x_6 \\
\end{array}
$$
$$
\left[
\begin{array}{cccccc|c}
1 & 1 & 1 & 1 & 0 & 0 & 100 \\
400 & 160 & 280 & 0 & 1 & 0 & 20{,}000 \\
1 & 1 & 1 & 0 & 0 & -1 & 60 \\
\hline
-120 & -40 & -60 & 0 & 0 & 0 & 0
\end{array}
\right]
$$

This tableau gives the solution

$$x_1 = 0, \quad x_2 = 0, \quad x_3 = 0, \quad x_4 = 100, \quad x_5 = 20{,}000, \quad x_6 = -60.$$

But this is not a feasible solution, since x_6 is negative. All the variables in any feasible solution must be nonnegative.

When a negative value of a variable appears, use row operations to transform the matrix until a solution is found in which all variables are nonnegative. The difficulty is caused by the -1 in row three of the matrix. We do not have the third column of the usual 3×3 identity matrix. To get around this, use row transformations to change a column that has nonzero entries (such as the x_1, x_2, or x_3 columns) to one in which the third row entry is 1 and the other entries are 0. The choice of a column is arbitrary. Let's choose the x_2 column and if this choice does not lead to a feasible solution, try one of the other columns.

The third row entry in the x_2 column is already 1. Using row transformations to get 0's in the rest of the column gives the following tableau.

$$
\begin{array}{cccccc}
x_1 & x_2 & x_3 & x_4 & x_5 & x_6 \\
\end{array}
$$
$$
\left[
\begin{array}{cccccc|c}
0 & 0 & 0 & 1 & 0 & 1 & 40 \\
240 & 0 & 120 & 0 & 1 & 160 & 10{,}400 \\
1 & 1 & 1 & 0 & 0 & -1 & 60 \\
\hline
-80 & 0 & -20 & 0 & 0 & -40 & 2400
\end{array}
\right]
$$

This tableau gives the solution

$$x_1 = 0, \quad x_2 = 60, \quad x_3 = 0, \quad x_4 = 40, \quad x_5 = 10{,}400, \quad \text{and} \quad x_6 = 0,$$

which is feasible. The process of applying row transformations to get a feasible solution is called *phase I* of the solution. In *phase II*, the simplex method is applied as usual. The pivot is 240:

$$\begin{array}{c} \begin{matrix} x_1 & x_2 & & x_3 & x_4 & x_5 & & x_6 \end{matrix} \\ \left[\begin{array}{cccccc|c} 0 & 0 & 0 & 1 & 0 & 1 & 40 \\ 240 & 0 & 120 & 0 & 1 & 160 & 10{,}400 \\ \hline 1 & 1 & 1 & 0 & 0 & -1 & 60 \\ \hline -80 & 0 & -20 & 0 & 0 & -40 & 2400 \end{array} \right] \end{array}$$

$$\begin{array}{c} \begin{matrix} x_1 & x_2 & x_3 & x_4 & & x_5 & & x_6 \end{matrix} \\ \left[\begin{array}{cccc|c|c|c} 0 & 0 & 0 & 1 & 0 & 1 & 40 \\ 1 & 0 & .5 & 0 & .004 & .667 & 43.3 \\ 0 & 1 & .5 & 0 & -.004 & -1.667 & 16.7 \\ 0 & 0 & 20 & 0 & .32 & 13.4 & 5864 \end{array} \right] \ \text{(rounded)} \end{array}$$

The second matrix above has been obtained from the first by standard row operations; some numbers in it have been rounded.

This final tableau gives

$$x_1 = 43.3, \quad x_2 = 16.7, \quad x_3 = 0, \quad x_4 = 40, \quad x_5 = 0, \quad \text{and} \quad x_6 = 0.$$

For maximum profit with this new constraint, the farmer should plant 43.3 acres of potatoes, 16.7 acres of corn, and no cabbage. Forty acres of the 100 available should not be planted. The profit will be $5864, less than the $6000 profit if he planted only 50 acres of potatoes. Because of the additional constraint that at least 60 acres must be planted, the profit is reduced.

EXAMPLE 1

Maximize $\quad z = 10x_1 + 8x_2$

subject to: $\quad 4x_1 + 4x_2 \geq 60$
$\qquad\qquad\ \ 2x_1 + 5x_2 \leq 120$

and $x_1 \geq 0$, $x_2 \geq 0$.

Add slack or surplus variables to the contraints as needed to get the system

$$\begin{aligned} 4x_1 + 4x_2 - x_3 \qquad\qquad\quad &= 60 \\ 2x_1 + 5x_2 \qquad\quad + x_4 \qquad\ &= 120 \\ -10x_1 - 8x_2 \qquad\qquad\quad + z &= 0. \end{aligned}$$

Now write the first simplex tableau.

$$\begin{array}{c} \begin{matrix} x_1 & x_2 & x_3 & x_4 \end{matrix} \\ \left[\begin{array}{cccc|c} 4 & 4 & -1 & 0 & 60 \\ 2 & 5 & 0 & 1 & 120 \\ \hline -10 & -8 & 0 & 0 & 0 \end{array} \right] \end{array}$$

The solution here,

$$x_1 = 0, \quad x_2 = 0, \quad x_3 = -60, \quad \text{and} \quad x_4 = 120,$$

is not feasible, because of the -60. In phase I, use row transformations to modify the tableau to produce a feasible solution. We need a column with 1 in the first row and 0's in the rest of the rows. Let us choose the x_1 column. Multiply the entries in the first row by 1/4 to get 1 in the top row of the column. Then use row transformations to get 0's in the other rows of that column.

$$
\begin{array}{cccc}
x_1 & x_2 & x_3 & x_4 \\
\end{array}
$$
$$
\left[
\begin{array}{cccc|c}
1 & 1 & -\frac{1}{4} & 0 & 15 \\
0 & 3 & \frac{1}{2} & 1 & 90 \\
0 & 2 & -\frac{5}{2} & 0 & 150
\end{array}
\right]
$$

This solution,

$$x_1 = 15, \quad x_2 = 0, \quad x_3 = 0, \quad \text{and} \quad x_4 = 90,$$

is feasible, so phase I is complete. Perform phase II by completing the solution in the usual way. The pivot is 1/2. The next tableau is

$$
\begin{array}{cccc}
x_1 & x_2 & x_3 & x_4 \\
\end{array}
$$
$$
\left[
\begin{array}{cccc|c}
1 & \frac{5}{2} & 0 & \frac{1}{2} & 60 \\
0 & 6 & 1 & 2 & 180 \\
0 & 17 & 0 & 5 & 600
\end{array}
\right].
$$

No indicators are negative, so we have found the optimum value of the objective function:

$$z = 600 \qquad \text{when } x_1 = 60 \qquad \text{and} \qquad x_2 = 0. \quad \blacksquare$$

The approach discussed above is used to solve problems where the constraints are mixed $\leq$ and $\geq$ inequalities. The method also can be used to solve a problem where the constant term is negative. (This is not likely to happen in an application, however.)

Minimization Problems   We defined a standard maximum linear programming problem earlier in this chapter. Now we can define a **standard minimum linear programming problem**:

Standard	A linear programming problem is in **standard minimum form** if
Minimum Form	**1.** the objective function is to be minimized;
	2. all variables are nonnegative;
	3. all constraints involve $\geq$;
	4. the constants in the constraints are all nonnegative.

The difference between maximum and minimum problems is in conditions 1 and 3: in standard minimum problems the objective function is to be *minimized*, and all constraints must have $\geq$ instead of $\leq$.

Standard minimum problems can be solved with the method of surplus variables presented above. To solve a minimum problem, first observe that the minimum of an objective function is the same as the *maximum* of the *negative* of the function, as suggested by Figure 3.

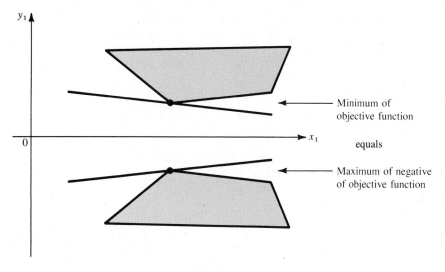

FIGURE 3

The next example illustrates this process. We use y_1 and y_2 as variables, and w for the objective function as a reminder that this is a minimum problem.

EXAMPLE 2

Minimize $\quad w = 3y_1 + 2y_2$

subject to: $\qquad y_1 + 3y_2 \geq 6$

$\qquad\qquad 2y_1 + y_2 \geq 3$

and $y_1 \geq 0, \quad y_2 \geq 0$.

Change this to a maximization problem by letting z equal the *negative* of the objective function: $z = -w$. Then find the *maximum* value of z.

$$z = -w = -3y_1 - 2y_2$$

The problem can now be stated as follows.

maximize $\quad z = -3y_1 - 2y_2$

subject to: $\qquad y_1 + 3y_2 \geq 6$

$\qquad\qquad 2y_1 + y_2 \geq 3$

and $y_1 \geq 0, \ y_2 \geq 0$.

For phase I of the solution, add surplus variables and set up the first tableau.

$$
\begin{array}{cccc}
y_1 & y_2 & y_3 & y_4 \\
\end{array}
$$
$$
\left[
\begin{array}{cccc|c}
1 & 3 & -1 & 0 & 6 \\
2 & 1 & 0 & -1 & 3 \\
\hline
3 & 2 & 0 & 0 & 0 \\
\end{array}
\right]
$$

The solution, $y_1 = 0$, $y_2 = 0$, $y_3 = -6$, and $y_4 = -3$, contains negative numbers. Row transformations must be used to get a tableau with a feasible solution.

Let's use the y_1 column since it already has a 1 in the first row. First, get a 0 in the second row, and then a 0 in the third row.

$$
\begin{array}{cccc}
y_1 & y_2 & y_3 & y_4 \\
\end{array}
$$
$$
\left[
\begin{array}{cccc|c}
1 & 3 & -1 & 0 & 6 \\
0 & -5 & 2 & -1 & -9 \\
0 & -7 & 3 & 0 & -18
\end{array}
\right]
$$

This tableau has a feasible solution. Now, in phase II, complete the solution as usual by the simplex method. The pivot is -5.

$$
\begin{array}{cccc}
y_1 & y_2 & y_3 & y_4 \\
\end{array}
$$
$$
\left[
\begin{array}{cccc|c}
1 & 0 & \frac{1}{5} & -\frac{3}{5} & \frac{3}{5} \\
0 & 1 & -\frac{2}{5} & \frac{1}{5} & \frac{9}{5} \\
0 & 0 & \frac{1}{5} & \frac{7}{5} & -\frac{27}{5}
\end{array}
\right]
$$

Here the solution is

$$
y_1 = \frac{3}{5}, \quad y_2 = \frac{9}{5}, \quad y_3 = 0, \quad \text{and } y_4 = 0.
$$

This solution is feasible, and the tableau has no negative indicators. Since $z = -27/5$ and $z = -w$, then $w = 27/5$ is the minimum value, which is obtained when $y_1 = 3/5$ and $y_2 = 9/5$. ■

Let us summarize the steps involved in the phase I and phase II method used to solve nonstandard problems in this section.

Solving

Nonstandard

Problems

1. If necessary, convert the problem to a maximum problem.
2. Add slack variables and subtract surplus variables as needed.
3. Write the initial simplex tableau.
4. If the solution from this tableau is not feasible, use row transformations to get a feasible solution (phase I).
5. After a feasible solution is reached, solve by the simplex method (phase II).

We certainly have not covered all the possible complications that can arise in using the simplex method. Some of the difficulties include the following:

1. Some of the constraints may be *equations* instead of inequalities. In this case, *artificial variables* must be used.
2. Occasionally, a transformation will cycle—that is, produce a "new" solution which was an earlier solution in the process. These situations are known as *degeneracies* and special methods are available for handling them.
3. It may not be possible to convert a nonfeasible basic solution to a feasible basic solution. In that case, no solution can satisfy all the constraints. Graphically, this means there is no region of feasible solutions.

(These difficulties are covered in more detail in advanced texts. One example of a text that you might find helpful is *An Introduction to Management Science*, Third Edition, by David R. Anderson, Dennis J. Sweeney, and Thomas A. Williams, 1982, West Publishing Company.)

Two linear programming models in actual use, one on making ice cream, the other on merit pay, are presented at the end of this chapter. These models illustrate the usefulness of linear programming. In most real applications, the number of variables is so large that these problems could not be solved without the use of a method, like the simplex method, which can be adapted to a computer.

4.3 EXERCISES

Rewrite each system of inequalities, adding slack variables or subtracting surplus variables as necessary.

1. $2x_1 + 3x_2 \leq 8$
$x_1 + 4x_2 \geq 7$

2. $5x_1 + 8x_2 \leq 10$
$6x_1 + 2x_2 \geq 7$

3. $x_1 + x_2 + x_3 \leq 100$
$x_1 + x_2 + x_3 \geq 75$
$x_1 + x_2 \qquad \geq 27$

4. $2x_1 \qquad + x_3 \leq 40$
$x_1 + x_2 \qquad \geq 18$
$x_1 \qquad + x_3 \geq 20$

Convert Exercises 5–8 into maximization problems.

5. Minimize $w = 4x_1 + 3x_2 + 2x_3$

subject to: $x_1 + x_2 + x_3 \geq 5$
$x_1 + x_2 \qquad \geq 4$
$2x_1 + x_2 + 3x_3 \geq 15$

and $x_1 \geq 0$, $x_2 \geq 0$, $x_3 \geq 0$.

6. Minimize $w = 8x_1 + 3x_2 + x_3$

subject to: $7x_1 + 6x_2 + 8x_3 \geq 18$
$4x_1 + 5x_2 + 10x_3 \geq 20$

and $x_1 \geq 0$, $x_2 \geq 0$, $x_3 \geq 0$.

7. Minimize $w = x_1 + 2x_2 + x_3 + 5x_4$

subject to: $x_1 + x_2 + x_3 + x_4 \geq 50$
$3x_1 + x_2 + 2x_3 + x_4 \geq 100$

and $x_1 \geq 0$, $x_2 \geq 0$, $x_3 \geq 0$, $x_4 \geq 0$.

8. Minimize $w = x_1 + x_2 + 4x_3$

subject to: $x_1 + 2x_2 + 3x_3 \geq 115$
$2x_1 + x_2 + x_3 \leq 200$
$x_1 \qquad + x_3 \geq 50$

and $x_1 \geq 0$, $x_2 \geq 0$, $x_3 \geq 0$.

Use the simplex method to solve Exercises 9–14.

9. Find $x_1 \geq 0$ and $x_2 \geq 0$ such that

$x_1 + 2x_2 \geq 24$
$x_1 + x_2 \leq 40$

and $z = 12x_1 + 10x_2$ is maximized.

10. Find $x_1 \geq 0$ and $x_2 \geq 0$ such that

$3x_1 + 4x_2 \geq 48$
$2x_1 + 4x_2 \leq 60$

and $z = 6x_1 + 8x_2$ is maximized.

11. Find $x_1 \geq 0$, $x_2 \geq 0$, and $x_3 \geq 0$ such that

$x_1 + x_2 + x_3 \leq 150$
$x_1 + x_2 + x_3 \geq 100$

and $z = 2x_1 + 5x_2 + 3x_3$ is maximized.

12. Find $x_1 \geq 0$, $x_2 \geq 0$, and $x_3 \geq 0$ such that

$x_1 + x_2 + 2x_3 \leq 38$
$2x_1 + x_2 + x_3 \geq 24$

and $z = 3x_1 + 2x_2 + 2x_3$ is maximized.

13. Find $x_1 \geq 0$ and $x_2 \geq 0$ such that

$$x_1 + x_2 \leq 100$$
$$x_1 + x_2 \geq 50$$
$$2x_1 + x_2 \leq 110$$

and $z = 2x_1 + 3x_2$ is maximized.

14. Find $x_1 \geq 0$ and $x_2 \geq 0$ such that

$$x_1 + 2x_2 \leq 18$$
$$x_1 + 3x_2 \geq 12$$
$$2x_1 + 2x_2 \leq 24$$

and $z = 5x_1 + 10x_2$ is maximized.

Solve each of the following by the two-phase method.

15. Find $y_1 \geq 0$, $y_2 \geq 0$ such that

$$10y_1 + 5y_2 \geq 100$$
$$20y_1 + 10y_2 \geq 150$$

and $w = 4y_1 + 5y_2$ is minimized.

16. Minimize $w = 3y_1 + 2y_2$ subject to

$$2y_1 + 3y_2 \geq 60$$
$$y_1 + 4y_2 \geq 40$$

and $y_1 \geq 0$, $y_2 \geq 0$.

17. Minimize $w = 2y_1 + y_2 + 3y_3$ subject to

$$y_1 + y_2 + y_3 \geq 100$$
$$2y_1 + y_2 \geq 50$$

and $y_1 \geq 0$, $y_2 \geq 0$, $y_3 \geq 0$.

18. Minimize $w = 3y_1 + 2y_2$ subject to

$$y_1 + 2y_2 \geq 10$$
$$y_1 + y_2 \geq 8$$
$$2y_1 + y_2 \geq 12$$

and $y_1 \geq 0$, $y_2 \geq 0$.

Use the simplex method to solve Exercises 19–25.

19. Brand X Canners produce canned whole tomatoes and tomato sauce. This season, they have available 3,000,000 kilograms of tomatoes for these two products. To meet the demands of regular customers, they must produce at least 80,000 kilograms of sauce and 800,000 kilograms of whole tomatoes. The cost per kilogram is $4 to produce canned whole tomatoes and $3.25 to produce tomato sauce. How many kilograms of tomatoes should they use for each product to minimize cost?

20. Sam, who is dieting, requires two food supplements, I and II. He can get these supplements from two different products, A and B, as shown in the table.

Supplement
(grams per serving)

	I	II
Product A	3	2
B	2	4

Sam's physician has recommended that he include at least 15 grams of each supplement in his daily diet. If product A costs 25¢ per serving and product B costs 40¢ per serving, how can he satisfy his requirements most economically? Find the minimum cost. (See Exercise 15, Section 3.2.)

21. Mark, who is ill, takes vitamin pills. Each day he must have at least 16 units of vitamin A, 5 units of vitamin B_1, and 20 units of vitamin C. He can choose between pill #1 which costs 10 cents and contains 8 units of A, 1 of B_1, and 2 of C, and pill #2 which costs 20 cents and contains 2 units of A, 1 of B_1, and 7 of C. How many of each pill should he buy in order to minimize his cost? (See Exercise 8, Section 3.2.)

22. A brewery produces regular beer and a lower-carbohydrate "light" beer. Steady customers of the brewery buy 12 units of regular beer and 10 units of light beer. While setting up the brewery to produce the beers, the management decides to produce extra beer, beyond that needed to satisfy the steady customers. The cost per unit of regular beer is $36,000 and the cost per unit of light beer is $48,000. The number of units of light beer should not exceed twice the number of units of regular beer. At least twenty additional units of beer can be sold. How much of each type beer should be made so as to minimize total production costs?

23. The chemistry department at a local college decides to stock at least 800 small test tubes and 500 large test tubes. It wants to buy at least 1500 test tubes to take advantage of a special price. Since the small tubes are broken twice as often as the larger, the department will order at least twice as many small tubes as large. If the small test tubes cost 15¢ each and the large ones, made of a cheaper glass, cost 12¢ each, how many of each size should they order to minimize cost?

24. Topgrade Turf lawn seed mixtures contain three types of seeds: bluegrass, rye, and bermuda. The costs per pound of the three types of seed are 20¢, 15¢, and 5¢. In each mixture there must be at least 20% bluegrass seed and the amount of bermuda must be no more than the amount of rye. To fill current orders, the company must make at least 5000 pounds of the mixture. How much of each kind of seed should be used to minimize cost?

25. A biologist must make a nutrient for her algae. The nutrient must contain the three basic elements D, E, and F, and must contain at least 10 kilograms of D, 12 kilograms of E, and 20 kilograms of F. The nutrient is made from three ingredients, I, II, and III. The quantity of D, E, and F in one unit of each of the ingredients is as given in the following chart.

One unit of ingredient	Contains the following elements in kilograms			Cost of one unit of ingredient
	D	E	F	
I	4	3	0	4
II	1	2	4	7
III	10	1	5	5

How many units of each ingredient are required to meet her needs at minimum cost?

Determine the constraints and the objective function for Exercises 26 and 27, then solve each problem.

26. Natural Brand plant food is made from three chemicals. (See Section 2.2, Exercise 49.) In a batch of the plant food there must be at least 81 kilograms of the first chemical and the other two chemicals must be in the ratio of 4 to 3. If the three chemicals cost $1.09, $.87, and $.65 per kilogram, respectively, how much of each should be used to minimize the cost of producing at least 750 kilograms of the plant food?

27. A company is developing a new additive for gasoline. The additive is a mixture of three liquid ingredients, I, II, and III. For proper performance, the total amount of additive must be at least 10 ounces per gallon of gasoline. However, for safety reasons, the amount of additive should not exceed 15 ounces per gallon of gasoline. At least 1/4 ounce of ingredient I must be used for every ounce of ingredient II and at least 1 ounce of ingredient III must be used for every ounce of ingredient I. If the cost of I, II, and III is $.30, $.09, and $.27 per ounce, respectively, find the mixture of the three ingredients which produces the minimum cost of the additive. How much of the additive should be used per gallon of gasoline?

Solve the following linear programming problem, which has both "greater than" and "less than" constraints.

28. A popular soft drink called Sugarlo, which is advertised as having a sugar content of no more than 10%, is blended from five ingredients, each of which has some sugar content. Water may also be added to dilute the mixture. The sugar content of the ingredients and their costs per gallon are given below.

	Ingredient					
	1	2	3	4	5	Water
Sugar content (%)	.28	.19	.43	.57	.22	0
Cost ($/gal.)	.48	.32	.53	.28	.43	.04

At least .01 of the content of Sugarlo must come from ingredients 3 or 4, .01 must come from ingredients 2 or 5, and .01 from ingredients 1 or 4. How much of each ingredient should be used in preparing 15,000 gallons of Sugarlo to minimize the cost?

4.4   Duality (Optional)

An interesting connection exists between standard maximum and standard minimum problems. It turns out that any solution of a standard maximum problem produces the solution of an associated standard minimum problem, and vice-versa. Each of these associated problems is called the **dual** of the other. One advantage of duals is that standard minimum problems can be solved by the simplex methods already discussed. Let us explain the idea of a dual with an example. (This is similar to Example 2 of the previous section; compare this method of solution with the one given there.)

EXAMPLE 1

Minimize $w = 8y_1 + 16y_2$
subject to: $y_1 + 5y_2 \geq 9$
$$2y_1 + 2y_2 \geq 10$$
and $y_1 \geq 0, \quad y_2 \geq 0.$

(As mentioned earlier, we use y_1 and y_2 as variables and w as the objective function as a reminder that this is a minimum problem.) Without considering slack variables just yet, write the augmented matrix of the system of inequalities, and include the coefficients of the objective function (not their negatives) as the last row in the matrix.

$$\begin{bmatrix} 1 & 5 & | & 9 \\ 2 & 2 & | & 10 \\ 8 & 16 & | & 0 \end{bmatrix}$$

Look now at the following new matrix, obtained from the one above by interchanging rows and columns.

$$\begin{bmatrix} 1 & 2 & | & 8 \\ 5 & 2 & | & 16 \\ 9 & 10 & | & 0 \end{bmatrix}$$

The *rows* of the first matrix (for the minimizing problem) are the *columns* of the second matrix.

The entries in this second matrix could be used to write the following standard maximum linear programming problem (again ignoring the fact that the numbers in the last row are not negative):

$$\text{maximize} \quad z = 9x_1 + 10x_2$$
$$\text{subject to:} \quad x_1 + 2x_2 \le 8$$
$$5x_1 + 2x_2 \le 16$$

with all variables nonnegative.

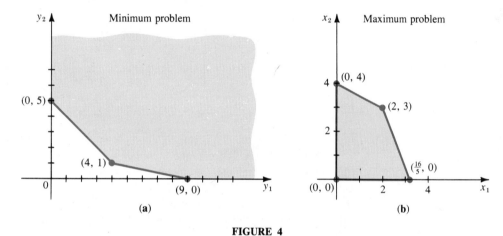

(a)   (b)

FIGURE 4

Figure 4(a) shows the graphical solution to the minimum problem given above, while Figure 4(b) shows the solution of the maximum problem produced by exchanging rows and columns.

Corner point	$w = 8y_1 + 16y_2$		Corner point	$z = 9x_1 + 10x_2$	
(0, 5)	80		(0, 0)	0	
(4, 1)	**48**	minimum	(0, 4)	40	
(9, 0)	72		**(2, 3)**	**48**	maximum
			$(\frac{16}{5}, 0)$	28.8	

The minimum is 48 when   The maximum is 48 when
$y_1 = 4, y_2 = 1$. $x_1 = 2, x_2 = 3$.

The two feasible regions in Figure 4 are different and the corner points are different, but the values of the objective functions are equal—both are 48. An even closer connection between the two problems is shown by using the simplex method to solve the maximum problem given above.

Maximum Problem

$$
\begin{array}{cccc}
x_1 & x_2 & x_3 & x_4 \\
\end{array}
$$

$$
\left[
\begin{array}{cccc|c}
1 & 2 & 1 & 0 & 8 \\
5 & 2 & 0 & 1 & 16 \\
\hline
-9 & -10 & 0 & 0 & 0 \\
\end{array}
\right]
$$

$$
\begin{array}{cccc}
x_1 & x_2 & x_3 & x_4 \\
\end{array}
$$

$$
\left[
\begin{array}{cccc|c}
\frac{1}{2} & 1 & \frac{1}{2} & 0 & 4 \\
4 & 0 & -1 & 1 & 8 \\
\hline
-4 & 0 & 5 & 0 & 40 \\
\end{array}
\right]
$$

$$
\begin{array}{cccc}
x_1 & x_2 & x_3 & x_4 \\
\end{array}
$$

$$
\left[
\begin{array}{cccc|c}
0 & 1 & \frac{5}{8} & -\frac{1}{8} & 3 \\
1 & 0 & -\frac{1}{4} & \frac{1}{4} & 2 \\
\hline
0 & 0 & 4 & 1 & 48 \\
\end{array}
\right]
$$

The maximum is 48 when

$$x_1 = 2, \quad x_2 = 3.$$

Notice that the solution to the *minimum problem* is found in the bottom row of the final simplex tableau for the maximum problem. This result suggests that standard minimum problems can be solved by forming the dual standard maximum problem, solving it by the simplex method, and then reading the solution for the minimum problem from the bottom row of the final simplex tableau. ▧

Before using this method to actually solve a minimum problem, let us find the duals of some typical linear programming problems. The process of exchanging the rows and columns of a matrix, which is used to find the dual, is called **transposing** the matrix, and each of the two matrices is the **transpose** of the other.

EXAMPLE 2

Find the transpose of each matrix.

(a)
$$
A = \begin{bmatrix}
2 & -1 & 5 \\
6 & 8 & 0 \\
-3 & 7 & -1
\end{bmatrix}.
$$

Write the rows of matrix A as the columns of the transpose.

$$
\text{transpose of } A = \begin{bmatrix}
2 & 6 & -3 \\
-1 & 8 & 7 \\
5 & 0 & -1
\end{bmatrix}
$$

(b)   the transpose of
$$
\begin{bmatrix}
1 & 2 & 4 & 0 \\
2 & 1 & 7 & 6
\end{bmatrix}
$$
is
$$
\begin{bmatrix}
1 & 2 \\
2 & 1 \\
4 & 7 \\
0 & 6
\end{bmatrix}. \quad ▧
$$

EXAMPLE 3

Write the dual of the following standard maximum linear programming problems.

(a) Maximize $z = 2x_1 + 5x_2$

subject to: $x_1 + x_2 \leq 10$
$2x_1 + x_2 \leq 8$

and $x_1 \geq 0, \quad x_2 \geq 0.$

Begin by writing the augmented matrix for the given problem.

$$\begin{bmatrix} 1 & 1 & 10 \\ 2 & 1 & 8 \\ 2 & 5 & 0 \end{bmatrix}$$

Form the transpose of this matrix, to get

$$\begin{bmatrix} 1 & 2 & 2 \\ 1 & 1 & 5 \\ 10 & 8 & 0 \end{bmatrix}.$$

The dual problem is stated from this second matrix as follows (using y instead of x):

Minimize $w = 10y_1 + 8y_2$

subject to: $y_1 + 2y_2 \geq 2$

$y_1 + y_2 \geq 5$

and $y_1 \geq 0, \quad y_2 \geq 0.$

(b)   *Given problem*   *Dual*

Given problem	*Dual*
Minimize $w = 7y_1 + 5y_2 + 8y_3$	Maximize $z = 10x_1 + 8x_2 + 25x_3$
subject to:	subject to:
$3y_1 + 2y_2 + y_3 \geq 10$	$3x_1 + x_2 + 4x_3 \leq 7$
$y_1 + y_2 + y_3 \geq 8$	$2x_1 + x_2 + 5x_3 \leq 5$
$4y_1 + 5y_2 \geq 25$	$x_1 + x_2 \leq 8$
and $y_1 \geq 0, \quad y_2 \geq 0, \quad y_3 \geq 0.$	and $x_1 \geq 0, x_2 \geq 0, x_3 \geq 0.$ ∎

In Example 3, all the constraints of the given standard maximum problems were $\leq$ inequalities, while all those in the dual minimum problems were $\geq$ inequalities. This is generally the case; inequalities are reversed when the dual problem is stated.

The following table shows the close connection between a problem and its dual.

Given Problem	Dual Problem
m variables	*n* variables
n constraints	*m* constraints
coefficients from objective function	constants
constants	coefficients from objective function

The next theorem, whose proof requires advanced methods, guarantees that a standard minimum problem can be solved by forming a dual standard maximum problem.

Theorem of Duality

The objective function w of a minimizing linear programming problem takes on a minimum value if and only if the objective function z of the corresponding dual maximizing problem takes on a maximum value. The maximum value of z equals the minimum value of w.

This method is illustrated in the following example. (This is Example 2 of the previous section; compare this solution with the one given there.)

EXAMPLE 4

Minimize $w = 3y_1 + 2y_2$

subject to: $y_1 + 3y_2 \geq 6$
$$2y_1 + y_2 \geq 3$$

and $y_1 \geq 0, \quad y_2 \geq 0.$

Use the given information to write the matrix

$$\begin{bmatrix} 1 & 3 & | & 6 \\ 2 & 1 & | & 3 \\ 3 & 2 & | & 0 \end{bmatrix}.$$

Transpose to get the following matrix for the dual problem.

$$\begin{bmatrix} 1 & 2 & | & 3 \\ 3 & 1 & | & 2 \\ 6 & 3 & | & 0 \end{bmatrix}$$

Write the dual problem from this matrix, as follows:

maximize $z = 6x_1 + 3x_2$

subject to: $x_1 + 2x_2 \leq 3$
$$3x_1 + x_2 \leq 2$$

and $x_1 \geq 0, \quad x_2 \geq 0.$

Solve this standard maximum problem using the simplex method. Start by introducing slack variables to give the system

$$x_1 + 2x_2 + x_3 \qquad\qquad = 3$$
$$3x_1 + x_2 \qquad + x_4 \qquad = 2$$
$$-6x_1 - 3x_2 - 0x_3 - 0x_4 + z = 0$$

with $x_1 \geq 0, \quad x_2 \geq 0, \quad x_3 \geq 0, \quad x_4 \geq 0.$

The first tableau for this system is given below, with the pivot as indicated.

$$
\begin{array}{c}
\text{Quotients} \\
3/1 = 3 \\
2/3
\end{array}
\quad
\begin{array}{cccc}
x_1 & x_2 & x_3 & x_4 \\
\end{array}
\left[
\begin{array}{cccc|c}
1 & 2 & 1 & 0 & 3 \\
3 & 1 & 0 & 1 & 2 \\
-6 & -3 & 0 & 0 & 0
\end{array}
\right]
$$

The simplex method gives the following final tableau.

$$
\begin{array}{cccc}
x_1 & x_2 & x_3 & x_4 \\
\end{array}
\left[
\begin{array}{cccc|c}
0 & 1 & \frac{3}{5} & -\frac{1}{5} & \frac{7}{5} \\
1 & 0 & -\frac{1}{5} & \frac{2}{5} & \frac{1}{5} \\
0 & 0 & \frac{3}{5} & \frac{9}{5} & \frac{27}{5}
\end{array}
\right]
$$

The last row of this final tableau shows that the solution of the given *standard minimum problem* is as follows:

The minimum value of $w = 3y_1 + 2y_2$, subject to the given constraints, is 27/5 and occurs when $y_1 = 3/5$ and $y_2 = 9/5$.

The minimum value of w, 27/5, is the same as the maximum value of z. ■

Let us summarize the steps in solving a standard minimum linear programming problem by the method of duals.

Solving Minimum Problems With Duals
1. Find the dual standard maximum problem.
2. Solve the maximum problem using the simplex method.
3. The minimum value of the objective function w is the maximum value of the objective function z.
4. The optimum solution is given by the entries in the bottom row of the columns corresponding to the slack variables.

Further Uses of the Dual The dual is useful not only in solving minimum problems, but also in seeing how small changes in one variable will affect the value of the objective function. For example, suppose an animal breeder needs at least 6 units per day of nutrient A and at least 3 units of nutrient B and that the breeder can choose between two different feeds, feed 1 and feed 2. Find the minimum cost for the breeder if each bag of feed 1 costs $3 and provides 1 unit of nutrient A and 2 units of B, while each bag of feed 2 costs $2 and provides 3 units of nutrient A and 1 of B.

If y_1 represents the number of bags of feed 1 and y_2 represents the number of bags of feed 2, the given information leads to

$$\text{minimize} \quad w = 3y_1 + 2y_2$$
$$\text{subject to:} \quad y_1 + 3y_2 \geq 6$$
$$2y_1 + y_2 \geq 3$$

and $y_1 \geq 0, \quad y_2 \geq 0.$

This standard minimum linear programming problem is the one we solved in Example 4 of this section. In that example, we formed the dual and reached the following final tableau:

$$
\begin{array}{cccc}
x_1 & x_2 & x_3 & x_4 \\
\end{array}
$$
$$
\left[
\begin{array}{cccc|c}
0 & 1 & \frac{3}{5} & -\frac{1}{5} & \frac{7}{5} \\
1 & 0 & -\frac{1}{5} & \frac{2}{5} & \frac{1}{5} \\
\hline
0 & 0 & \frac{3}{5} & \frac{9}{5} & \frac{27}{5}
\end{array}
\right].
$$

This final tableau shows that the breeder will obtain minimum feed costs by using 3/5 bag of feed 1 and 9/5 bag of feed 2 per day, for a daily cost of 27/5 = 5.40 dollars.

The top two numbers in the right-most column give the **imputed costs** in terms of the necessary nutrients. From the final tableau, $x_2 = 7/5$ and $x_1 = 1/5$, which means that a unit of nutrient A costs 1/5 = .20 dollars, while a unit of nutrient B costs 7/5 = 1.40 dollars. The minimum daily cost, $5.40, is found by the following procedure.

$$(\$.20 \text{ per unit of A}) \times (6 \text{ units of A}) = \$1.20$$
$$+ (\$1.40 \text{ per unit of B}) \times (3 \text{ units of B}) = \underline{\$4.20}$$
$$\$5.40 \text{ total}$$

These two numbers from the dual, $.20 and $1.40, also allow the breeder to estimate feed costs for "small" changes in nutrient requirements. For example, an increase of one unit in the requirement for each nutrient would produce a total cost of

$5.40	(6 units of A, 3 of B)
.20	(an extra unit of A)
1.40	(extra of B)
$7.00	total per day.

The numbers .20 and 1.40 are called the **shadow values** of the nutrients.

4.4 EXERCISES

Find the transpose of each matrix in Exercises 1–4.

1. $\begin{bmatrix} 1 & 2 & 3 \\ 3 & 2 & 1 \\ 1 & 10 & 0 \end{bmatrix}$

2. $\begin{bmatrix} 2 & 5 & 8 & 6 & 0 \\ 1 & -1 & 0 & 12 & 14 \end{bmatrix}$

3. $\begin{bmatrix} -1 & 4 & 6 & 12 \\ 13 & 25 & 0 & 4 \\ -2 & -1 & 11 & 3 \end{bmatrix}$

4. $\begin{bmatrix} 1 & 11 & 15 \\ 0 & 10 & -6 \\ 4 & 12 & -2 \\ 1 & -1 & 13 \\ 2 & 25 & -1 \end{bmatrix}$

State the dual problem for Exercises 5–8.

5. Maximize $z = 4x_1 + 3x_2 + 2x_3$

   subject to:
   $$x_1 + x_2 + x_3 \leq 5$$
   $$x_1 + x_2 \qquad \leq 4$$
   $$2x_1 + x_2 + 3x_3 \leq 15$$

   and $x_1 \geq 0, \quad x_2 \geq 0, \quad x_3 \geq 0.$

6. Maximize $z = 8x_1 + 3x_2 + x_3$

   subject to:
   $$7x_1 + 6x_2 + 8x_3 \leq 18$$
   $$4x_1 + 5x_2 + 10x_3 \leq 20$$

   and $x_1 \geq 0, \quad x_2 \geq 0, \quad x_3 \geq 0.$

7. Minimize $w = y_1 + 2y_2 + y_3 + 5y_4$

   subject to:
   $$y_1 + y_2 + y_3 + y_4 \geq 50$$
   $$3y_1 + y_2 + 2y_3 + y_4 \geq 100$$

   and $y_1 \geq 0, \quad y_2 \geq 0, \quad y_3 \geq 0, \quad y_4 \geq 0.$

8. Minimize $w = y_1 + y_2 + 4y_3$

   subject to:
   $$y_1 + 2y_2 + 3y_3 \geq 115$$
   $$2y_1 + y_2 + 8y_3 \geq 200$$
   $$y_1 \qquad + y_3 \geq 50$$

   and $y_1 \geq 0, \quad y_2 \geq 0, \quad y_3 \geq 0.$

Use the simplex method to solve Exercises 9–14.

9. Find $y_1 \geq 0$ and $y_2 \geq 0$ such that
   $$2y_1 + 3y_2 \geq 6$$
   $$2y_1 + y_2 \geq 7$$
   and $w = 5y_1 + 2y_2$ is minimized.

10. Find $y_1 \geq 0$ and $y_2 \geq 0$ such that
    $$3y_1 + y_2 \geq 12$$
    $$y_1 + 4y_2 \geq 16$$
    and $w = 2y_1 + y_2$ is minimized.

11. Find $y_1 \geq 0$ and $y_2 \geq 0$ such that
    $$10y_1 + 5y_2 \geq 100$$
    $$20y_1 + 10y_2 \geq 150$$
    and $w = 4y_1 + 5y_2$ is minimized.

12. Minimize $w = 3y_1 + 2y_2$

    subject to:
    $$2y_1 + 3y_2 \geq 60$$
    $$y_1 + 4y_2 \geq 40$$

    and $y_1 \geq 0, \quad y_2 \geq 0.$

13. Minimize $w = 2y_1 + y_2 + 3y_3$

    subject to:
    $$y_1 + y_2 + y_3 \geq 100$$
    $$2y_1 + y_2 \qquad \geq 50$$

    and $y_1 \geq 0, \quad y_2 \geq 0, \quad y_3 \geq 0.$

14. Minimize $w = 3y_1 + 2y_2$

    subject to:
    $$y_1 + 2y_2 \geq 10$$
    $$y_1 + y_2 \geq 8$$
    $$2y_1 + y_2 \geq 12$$

    and $y_1 \geq 0, \quad y_2 \geq 0.$

Exercises 15 and 17 are repeated from the previous section. Solve them with the method of duals and compare the solutions with Exercises 19 and 21 in Section 4.3.

15. Brand X Canners produce canned whole tomatoes and tomato sauce. This season, they have available 3,000,000 kilograms of tomatoes for these two products. To meet the demands of regular customers, they must produce at least 80,000 kilograms of sauce

and 800,000 kilograms of whole tomatoes. The cost per kilogram is $4 to produce canned whole tomatoes and $3.25 to produce tomato sauce. How many kilograms of tomatoes should they use for each product to minimize cost?

16. Sam, who is dieting, requires two food supplements, I and II. He can get these supplements from two different products, A and B, as shown in the following table.

Supplement
(grams per serving)

$$\text{Product} \quad \begin{matrix} & \text{I} & \text{II} \\ \text{A} & 3 & 2 \\ \text{B} & 2 & 4 \end{matrix}$$

Sam's physician has recommended that he include at least 15 grams of each supplement in his daily diet. If product A costs 25¢ per serving and product B costs 40¢ per serving, how can he satisfy his requirements most economically?

17. Mark, who is ill, takes vitamin pills. Each day he must have at least 16 units of vitamin A, 5 units of vitamin B_1, and 20 units of vitamin C. He can choose between pill #1 which costs 10 cents and contains 8 units of A, 1 of B_1, and 2 of C, and pill #2 which costs 20 cents and contains 2 units of A, 1 of B_1, and 7 of C. How many of each pill should he buy in order to minimize his cost?

18. Refer to the example at the end of the section on minimizing the daily cost of feeds.

   (a) Find a combination of feeds that will cost $7.00 and give 7 units of A and 4 units of B.

   (b) Use the dual variables to predict the daily cost of feed if the requirements change to 5 units of A and 4 units of B. Find a combination of feeds to meet these requirements at the predicted price.

19. A small toy manufacturing firm has 200 squares of felt, 600 ounces of stuffing, and 90 feet of trim available to make two types of toys, a small bear and a monkey. The bear requires 1 square of felt and 4 ounces of stuffing. The monkey requires 2 squares of felt, 3 ounces of stuffing, and 1 foot of trim. The firm makes $1 profit on each bear and $1.50 profit on each monkey. The linear program to maximize profit is

$$\begin{aligned} \text{maximize} \quad & x_1 + 1.5x_2 = z \\ \text{subject to:} \quad & x_1 + 2x_2 \le 200 \\ & 4x_1 + 3x_2 \le 600 \\ & x_2 \le 90 \end{aligned}$$

The final simplex tableau is

$$\begin{bmatrix} 0 & 1 & .8 & -.2 & 0 & | & 40 \\ 1 & 0 & -.6 & .4 & 0 & | & 120 \\ 0 & 0 & -.8 & .2 & 1 & | & 50 \\ 0 & 0 & .6 & .1 & 0 & | & 180 \end{bmatrix}$$

   (a) What is the corresponding dual problem?

   (b) What is the optimal solution to the dual problem?

   (c) Use the shadow values to estimate the profit the firm will make if their supply of felt increases to 210 squares.

   (d) How much profit will the firm make if their supply of stuffing is cut to 590 ounces and their supply of trim is cut to 80 feet?

20. Refer to the problem about the farmer solved at the beginning of Section 4.2.

   (a) Give the dual problem.

   (b) Use the shadow values to estimate the farmer's profit if land is cut to 90 acres but capital increases to $21,000.

   (c) Suppose the farmer has 110 acres but only $19,000. Find the optimum profit and the planting strategy that will produce this profit.

Determine the constraints and the objective function for Exercises 21 and 22, then solve each problem by the simplex method.

21. Natural Brand plant food is made from three chemicals. In a batch of the plant food there must be at least 81 kilograms of the first chemical and the other two chemicals must be in the ratio of 4 to 3. If the three chemicals cost $1.09, $.87, and $.65 per kilogram, respectively, how much of each should be used to minimize the cost of producing at least 750 kilograms of the plant food?

22. A company is developing a new additive for gasoline. The additive is a mixture of three liquid ingredients, I, II, and III. For proper performance, the total amount of additive must be at least 10 ounces per gallon of gasoline. However, for safety reasons, the amount of additive should not exceed 15 ounces per gallon of gasoline. At least 1/4 ounce of ingredient I must be used for every ounce of ingredient II and at least 1 ounce of ingredient III must be used for every ounce of ingredient I. If the cost of I, II, and III is $.30, $.09, and $.27 per ounce, respectively, find the mixture of the three ingredients which produces the minimum cost of the additive. How much of the additive should be used per gallon of gasoline?

EXTENDED

APPLICATION

Making Ice Cream*

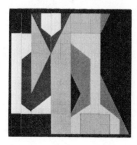

The first step in the commercial manufacture of ice cream is to blend several ingredients (such as dairy products, eggs, and sugar) to obtain a mix which meets the necessary minimum quality restrictions regarding butterfat content, serum solids, and so on.

   Usually, many different combinations of ingredients may be blended to obtain a mix of the necessary quality. Within this range of possible substitutes, the firm desires the combination that produces minimum total cost. This problem is quite suitable for solution by linear programming methods.

   A "mid-quality" line of ice cream requires the following minimum percentages of constituents by weight:

fat	16%
serum solids	8%
sugar solids	16%
egg solids	.35%
stabilizer	.25%
emulsifier	.15%
Total	40.75%

*From *Linear Programming in Industry: Theory and Application, An Introduction* by Sven Danø, Fourth revised and enlarged edition. Copyright © 1974 by Springer-Verlag/Wien. Reprinted by permission of Springer-Verlag New York, Inc.

Ingredients	1	2	3	4	5	6	7	8	9
	40% cream	23% cream	Butter	Plastic cream	Butter oil	4% milk	Skim condensed milk	Skim milk powder	Liquid sugar
Cost ($/lb)	.298	.174	.580	.576	.718	.045	.052	.165	.061
Constituents									
(1) Fat	.400	.230	.805	.800	.998	.040			
(2) Serum solids	.054	.069		.025		.078	.280	.970	
(3) Sugar solids									.707
(4) Egg solids									
(5) Stabilizer									
(6) Emulsifier									

The balance of the mix is water. A batch of mix is made by blending a number of ingredients, each of which contains one or more of the necessary constituents, and nothing else. The chart above shows the possible ingredients and their costs.

In setting up the mathematical model, use $c_1, c_2, \ldots, c_{14}$ as the cost per unit of the ingredients, and $x_1, x_2, \ldots, x_{14}$ for the quantities of ingredients. The table shows the composition of each ingredient. For example, one pound of ingredient 1 (the 40% cream) contains .400 pounds of fat and .054 pounds of serum solids, with the balance being water.

The ice cream mix is made up in batches of 100 pounds at a time. For a batch to contain 16% fat, at least $100(.16) = 16$ pounds of fat is necessary. Fat is contained in ingredients 1, 2, 3, 4, 5, 6, 10, and 11. The requirement of at least 16 pounds of fat produces the constraint

$$.400x_1 + .230x_2 + .805x_3 + .800x_4 + .998x_5 + .040x_6 + .500x_{10}$$
$$+ .625x_{11} \geq 16.$$

Similar constraints can be obtained for the other constituents. Because of the minimum requirements, the total of the ingredients will be at least 40.75 pounds, or

$$x_1 + x_2 + \ldots + x_{13} \geq 40.75.$$

The balance of the 100 pounds is water, making $x_{14} \leq 59.25$.

The table shows that ingredients 12 and 13 must be used—there is no alternate way of getting these constituents into the final mix. For a 100 pound batch of ice cream, $x_{12} = .25$ pound and $x_{13} = .15$ pound. Removing x_{12} and x_{13} as variables permits a substantial simplification of the model: the problem is now reduced to the following system of four constraints:

$$.400x_1 + .230x_2 + .805x_3 + .800x_4 + .998x_5 + .040x_6 + .500x_{10}$$
$$+ .625x_{11} \geq 16$$

$$.054x_1 + .069x_2 + .025x_4 + .078x_6 + .280x_7 + .970x_8 \geq 8$$

$$.707x_9 + .100x_{10} \geq 16$$

$$.350x_{10} + .315x_{11} \geq .35$$

Ingredients	10	11	12	13	14	Requirements
	Sugared egg yolk	Powdered egg yolk	Stabilizer	Emulsifier	Water	
Cost ($/lb)	.425	1.090	.600	.420	0	
Constituents						
(1) Fat	.500	.625				16
(2) Serum solids						8
(3) Sugar solids	.100					16
(4) Egg solids	.350	.315				.35
(5) Stabilizer			1			.25
(6) Emulsifier				1		.15

The objective function, which is to be minimized, is

$$c = .298x_1 + .174x_2 + \ldots + 1.090x_{11}.$$

As usual, $x_1 \geq 0$, $x_2 \geq 0, \ldots, x_{14} \geq 0$.

Solving this linear programming problem with the simplex method gives

$$x_2 = 67.394, \qquad x_8 = 3.459, \qquad x_9 = 22.483, \qquad x_{10} = 1.000.$$

The total cost of these ingredients is $14.094. To this, we must add the cost of ingredients 12 and 13, producing total cost of

$$14.094 + (.600)(.250) + (.420)(.150) = 14.307,$$

or $14.307.

EXERCISES

1. Find the mix of ingredients needed for a 100-pound batch of the following grades of ice cream.
   a. "generic," sold in a white box, with at least 14% fat and at least 6% serum solids (all other ingredients the same);
   b. "premium," sold with a funny foreign name, with at least 17% fat and at least 16.5% sugar solids (all other ingredients the same).

2. Solve the example in the text by using a computer.

EXTENDED

APPLICATION

Merit Pay—The Upjohn Company

Individuals doing the same job within the management of a company often receive different salaries. These salaries may differ because of length of service, productivity of an individual worker, and so on. However, for each job there is usually an established minimum and maximum salary.

Many companies make annual reviews of the salary of each of their management employees. At these reviews, an employee may receive a general cost of living increase, an increase based on merit, both, or neither.

In this case, we look at a mathematical model for distributing merit increases in an optimum way.* An individual who is due for salary review may be described as shown in the figure below. Here i represents the number of the employee whose salary is being reviewed.

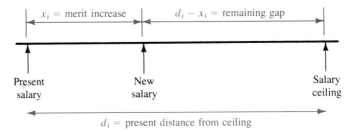

Here the salary ceiling is the maximum salary for the job classification, x_i is the merit increase to be awarded to the individual ($x_i \geq 0$), d_i is the present distance of the current salary from the salary ceiling, and the difference, $d_i - x_i$, is the remaining gap.

We let w_i be a measure of the relative worth of the individual to the company. This is the most difficult variable of the model to actually calculate. One way to evaluate w_i is to give a rating sheet to a number of co-workers and supervisors of employee i. An average rating can be obtained and then divided by the highest rating received by an employee with that same job. This number then gives the worth of employee i relative to all other employees with that job.

The best way to allocate money available for merit pay increases is to minimize

$$\sum_{i=1}^{n} w_i(d_i - x_i).$$

This sum is found by multiplying the relative worth of employee i and the distance of employee i from the salary gap, after any merit increase. Here n represents the total number of employees who have this job. The one constraint here is that the total of all merit increases cannot exceed P, the total amount available for merit increases. That is,

$$\sum_{i=1}^{n} x_i \leq P.$$

*Based on part of a paper by Jack Northam, Head, Mathematical Services Department, The Upjohn Company, Kalamazoo, Michigan.

Also, the increases for an employee must not put that employee over the maximum salary. That is, for employee i,

$$x_i \le d_i.$$

We can simplify the objective function, using rules from algebra.

$$\sum_{i=1}^{n} w_i(d_i - x_i) = \sum_{i=1}^{n} (w_i d_i - w_i x_i)$$

$$= \sum_{i=1}^{n} w_i d_i - \sum_{i=1}^{n} w_i x_i$$

For a given individual, w_i and d_i are constant. Therefore, $w_i d_i$ is some constant, say Z, and

$$\sum_{i=1}^{n} w(d_i - x_i) = Z - \sum_{i=1}^{n} w_i x_i.$$

We want to minimize the sum on the left; we can do so by *maximizing* the sum on the right. (Why?) Thus, the original model simplifies to maximizing

$$\sum_{i=1}^{n} w_i x_i,$$

subject to

$$\sum_{i=1}^{n} x_i \le p \quad \text{and} \quad x_i \le d_i$$

for each i.

EXERCISES

Here are the current salary information and job evaluation averages for six employees who have the same job. The salary ceiling is $1700 per month.

Employee number	Evaluation average	Current salary
1	570	$1600
2	500	$1550
3	450	$1500
4	600	$1610
5	520	$1530
6	565	$1420

1. Find w_i for each employee by dividing that employee's evaluation average by the highest evaluation average.

2. Use the simplex method to find the merit increase for each employee. Assume that p is 400.

KEY WORDS

simplex method	dual
slack variable	surplus variable
basic feasible solution	phase I
pivot	phase II
simplex tableau	transpose

Chapter 4   REVIEW EXERCISES

For Exercises 1–4, (a) select appropriate variables, (b) write the objective function, (c) write the constraints as inequalities.

1. Roberta Hernandez sells three items, A, B, and C, in her gift shop. Each unit of A costs her $5 to buy, $1 to sell and $2 to deliver. For each unit of B, the costs are $3, $2 and $1 respectively, and for each unit of C the costs are $6, $2, and $5 respectively. The profit on A is $4, on B it is $3, and on C, $3. How many of each should she get to maximize her profit if she can spend $1200 to buy, $800 on selling costs, and $500 on delivery costs?

2. An investor is considering three types of investment: a high risk venture into oil leases with a potential return of 15%, a medium risk investment in bonds with a 9% return, and a relatively safe stock investment with a 5% return. He has $50,000 to invest. Because of the risk, he will limit his investment in oil leases and bonds to 30% and his investment in oil leases and stock to 50%. How much should he invest in each to maximize his return assuming investment returns are as expected?

3. The Aged Wood Winery makes two white wines, Fruity and Crystal, from two kinds of grapes and sugar. The wines require the following amounts of each ingredient per gallon and produce a profit per gallon as shown below.

	Grape A (bushels)	Grape B (bushels)	Sugar (pounds)	Profit (dollars)
Fruity	2	2	2	12
Crystal	1	3	1	15

The winery has available 110 bushels of grape A, 125 bushels of grape B, and 90 pounds of sugar. How much of each wine should be made to maximize profit?

4. A company makes three sizes of plastic bags: 5 gallon, 10 gallon and 20 gallon. The production time in hours for cutting, sealing, and packaging a unit of each size is shown below.

size	cutting	sealing	packaging
5 gallon	1	1	2
10 gallon	1.1	1.2	3
20 gallon	1.5	1.3	4

There are at most 8 hours available each day for each of the three operations. If the profit on a unit of 5-gallon bags is $1, 10-gallon bags is $.90, and 20-gallon bags is $.95, how many of each size should be made per day?

For Exercises 5–8, **(a)** add slack variables or subtract surplus variables, and **(b)** set up the initial simplex tableau.

5. Maximize $z = 5x_1 + 3x_2$

subject to: $2x_1 + 5x_2 \leq 50$
$x_1 + 3x_2 \leq 25$
$4x_1 + x_2 \leq 18$
$x_1 + x_2 \leq 12$

and $x_1 \geq 0, x_2 \geq 0.$

6. Maximize $z = 25x_1 + 30x_2$

subject to: $3x_1 + 5x_2 \leq 47$
$x_1 + x_2 \leq 25$
$5x_1 + 2x_2 \leq 35$
$2x_1 + x_2 \leq 30$

and $x_1 \geq 0, x_2 \geq 0.$

7. Maximize $z = 5x_1 + 8x_2 + 6x_3$

subject to: $x_1 + x_2 + x_3 \leq 90$
$2x_1 + 5x_2 + x_3 \leq 120$
$x_1 + 3x_2 \geq 80$

and $x_1 \geq 0, x_2 \geq 0, x_3 \geq 0.$

8. Maximize $z = 2x_1 + 3x_2 + 4x_3$

subject to: $x_1 + x_2 + x_3 \geq 100$
$2x_1 + 3x_2 \leq 500$
$x_1 + 2x_3 \leq 350$

and $x_1 \geq 0, x_2 \geq 0, x_3 \geq 0.$

Use the simplex method to solve the maximizing linear programming problems with initial tableaus as given in Exercises 9–12.

9.

$$\begin{array}{ccccc} x_1 & x_2 & x_3 & x_4 & x_5 \\ \end{array}$$
$$\left[\begin{array}{ccccc|c} 1 & 2 & 3 & 1 & 0 & 28 \\ 2 & 4 & 1 & 0 & 1 & 32 \\ \hline -5 & -2 & -3 & 0 & 0 & 0 \end{array}\right]$$

10.

$$\begin{array}{cccc} x_1 & x_2 & x_3 & x_4 \\ \end{array}$$
$$\left[\begin{array}{cccc|c} 2 & 1 & 1 & 0 & 10 \\ 1 & 3 & 0 & 1 & 16 \\ \hline -2 & -3 & 0 & 0 & 0 \end{array}\right]$$

11.

$$\begin{array}{cccccc} x_1 & x_2 & x_3 & x_4 & x_5 & x_6 \\ \end{array}$$
$$\left[\begin{array}{cccccc|c} 1 & 2 & 2 & 1 & 0 & 0 & 50 \\ 3 & 1 & 0 & 0 & 1 & 0 & 20 \\ 1 & 0 & 2 & 0 & 0 & -1 & 15 \\ \hline -5 & -3 & -2 & 0 & 0 & 0 & 0 \end{array}\right]$$

12.

$$\begin{array}{ccccc} x_1 & x_2 & x_3 & x_4 & x_5 \\ \end{array}$$
$$\left[\begin{array}{ccccc|c} 3 & 6 & -1 & 0 & 0 & 28 \\ 1 & 1 & 0 & 1 & 0 & 12 \\ 2 & 1 & 0 & 0 & 1 & 16 \\ \hline -1 & -2 & 0 & 0 & 0 & 0 \end{array}\right]$$

Convert the problems of Exercises 13–15 into maximization problems.

13. Minimize $w = 10x_1 + 15x_2$

subject to: $x_1 + x_2 \geq 17$
$5x_1 + 8x_2 \geq 42$

and $x_1 \geq 0, x_2 \geq 0.$

14. Minimize $w = 20x_1 + 15x_2 + 18x_3$

subject to: $2x_1 + x_2 + x_3 \geq 112$
$x_1 + x_2 + x_3 \geq 80$
$x_1 + x_2 \geq 45$

and $x_1 \geq 0, x_2 \geq 0, x_3 \geq 0.$

15. Minimize $w = 7x_1 + 2x_2 + 3x_3$

subject to: $x_1 + x_2 + 2x_3 \geq 48$
$x_1 + x_2 \geq 12$
$x_3 \geq 10$
$3x_1 + x_3 \geq 30$

and $x_1 \geq 0, x_2 \geq 0, x_3 \geq 0.$

The tableaus in Exercises 16–20 are the final tableaus of minimizing problems. State the solution and the minimum value of the objective function for each problem.

16.

$$
\begin{array}{cccccc}
x_1 & x_2 & x_3 & x_4 & x_5 & x_6 \\
\end{array}
$$

$$
\left[
\begin{array}{cccccc|c}
1 & 0 & 0 & 3 & 1 & 2 & 12 \\
0 & 0 & 1 & 4 & 5 & 3 & 5 \\
0 & 1 & 0 & -2 & 7 & -6 & 8 \\
\hline
0 & 0 & 0 & 5 & 7 & 3 & -172 \\
\end{array}
\right]
$$

17.

$$
\begin{array}{cccccc}
x_1 & x_2 & x_3 & x_4 & x_5 & x_6 \\
\end{array}
$$

$$
\left[
\begin{array}{cccccc|c}
0 & 0 & 3 & 0 & 1 & 1 & 2 \\
1 & 0 & -2 & 0 & 2 & 0 & 8 \\
0 & 1 & 7 & 0 & 0 & 0 & 12 \\
0 & 0 & 1 & 1 & -4 & 0 & 1 \\
\hline
0 & 0 & 5 & 0 & 8 & 0 & -62 \\
\end{array}
\right]
$$

18.

$$
\begin{array}{ccccc}
x_1 & x_2 & x_3 & x_4 & x_5 \\
\end{array}
$$

$$
\left[
\begin{array}{ccccc|c}
5 & 1 & 0 & 7 & -1 & 100 \\
-2 & 0 & 1 & 1 & 3 & 27 \\
\hline
12 & 0 & 0 & 7 & 2 & -640 \\
\end{array}
\right]
$$

19. Solve Exercise 1.

20. Solve Exercise 2.

21. Solve Exercise 3.

22. Solve Exercise 4.

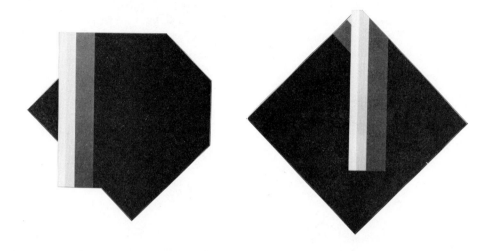

SETS AND COUNTING

Karl Gerstner. From the series *Progressive Penetration* (Finite-Infinite Series), 1960. Pierburg Collection, Neuss, West Germany.

We have used sets from time to time throughout this book. Now in this chapter we present a more detailed discussion of sets. The terminology and concepts of sets have proved to be very useful. Sets, which are collections of objects, help to clarify and classify many mathematical ideas, making them easier to understand. Sets are particularly useful in presenting the topics of probability. The principles of counting, discussed later in this chapter, will also be needed to find probabilities.

5.1   Sets

Think of a **set** as a collection of objects. We could form a set containing one of each type of coin now put out by the government. Another set might be made up of all the students in your class. In mathematics, sets are often made up of numbers. The set consisting of the numbers 3, 4, and 5 is written

$$\{3, 4, 5\},$$

with set braces, { }, enclosing the numbers belonging to the set. The numbers 3, 4, and 5 are called the **elements** or **members** of this set. To show that 4 is an element of the set $\{3, 4, 5\}$ use the symbol $\in$ and write

$$4 \in \{3, 4, 5\}.$$

Also, $5 \in \{3, 4, 5\}$. To show that 8 is *not* an element of this set, place a slash through the symbol.

$$8 \notin \{3, 4, 5\}$$

Sets are often named with capital letters, so that if

$$B = \{5, 6, 7\},$$

then, for example, $6 \in B$ and $10 \notin B$.

Two sets are **equal** if they contain the same elements. The sets $\{5, 6, 7\}$, $\{7, 6, 5\}$, and $\{6, 5, 7\}$ all contain exactly the same elements and are equal. In symbols,

$$\{5, 6, 7\} = \{7, 6, 5\} = \{6, 5, 7\}.$$

Sets which do not contain exactly the same elements are *not equal*. For example, the sets $\{5, 6, 7\}$ and $\{7, 8, 9\}$ do not contain exactly the same elements and are not equal. This is written as follows:

$$\{5, 6, 7\} \neq \{7, 8, 9\}.$$

Sometimes we are more interested in a common property of the elements in a set, rather than a list of the elements. This common property can be expressed by using **set-builder notation:** the set

$$\{x \mid x \text{ has property } P\}$$

(read "the set of all elements x such that x has property P") represents the set of all elements x having some stated property P.

EXAMPLE 1

Write the elements belonging to each of the following sets.

(a) {$x | x$ is a counting number less than 5}

The counting numbers less than 5 make up the set {1, 2, 3, 4}.

(b) {$x | x$ is a state that touches Florida} = {Alabama, Georgia} ▪

When discussing a particular situation or problem, we can identify a **universal set** that contains all the elements appearing in any set used in that particular problem. The letter U is used to represent the universal set.

For example, when discussing the set of company employees who favor a certain pension proposal, the universal set might be the set of all company employees. In discussing the types of species found by Charles Darwin on the Galápagos Islands, the universal set might be the set of all species on all Pacific islands.

Sometimes every element of one set also belongs to another set. For example, if

$$A = \{3, 4, 5, 6\}$$

and

$$B = \{2, 3, 4, 5, 6, 7, 8\},$$

then every element of A is also an element of B. This means that A is a **subset** of B, written $A \subset B$. For example, the set of all presidents of corporations is a subset of the set of all executives of corporations.

EXAMPLE 2

Decide whether the following statements are true or false.

(a) {3, 4, 5, 6} = {4, 6, 3, 5}

Both sets contain exactly the same elements; the sets are equal. The given statement is true. (The fact that the elements are in a different order doesn't matter.)

(b) {5, 6, 9, 10} $\subset$ {5, 6, 7, 8, 9, 10, 11}

Every element of the first set is also an element of the second, making the given statement true. ▪

Figure 1 shows a set A which is a subset of a set B. The rectangle represents the universal set, U. Such diagrams, called **Venn diagrams,** are used to help clarify relationships among sets.

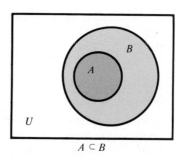

$A \subset B$

FIGURE 1

By the definition of subset, the **empty set** (which contains no elements) is a subset of every set. That is, if A is any set, and the symbol $\varnothing$ represents the empty set, then $\varnothing \subset A$. Also, the definition of subset can be used to show that every set is a subset of itself: that is, if A is any set, then $A \subset A$. In summary,

For any set A,

$$\varnothing \subset A \quad \text{and} \quad A \subset A.$$

EXAMPLE 3

List all possible subsets for each of the following sets.

(a) $\{7, 8\}$

There are four subsets of $\{7, 8\}$:

$$\varnothing, \quad \{7\}, \quad \{8\}, \quad \{7, 8\}.$$

(b) $\{a, b, c\}$

There are eight subsets of $\{a, b, c\}$:

$$\varnothing, \quad \{a\}, \quad \{b\}, \quad \{c\}, \quad \{a, b\}, \quad \{a, c\}, \quad \{b, c\}, \quad \{a, b, c\}. \quad \blacksquare$$

The **cardinal number** of a set is the number of distinct elements in the set. The cardinal number of the set A is written $n(A)$. For example, the set

$$A = \{a, b, c, d, e\}$$

has cardinal number 5, written

$$n(A) = 5.$$

Since the empty set has no elements, its cardinal number is 0, by definition. Thus, $n(\varnothing) = 0$.

EXAMPLE 4

Give the cardinal number of each of the following sets.

(a) $B = \{2, 5, 7, 9, 10, 12, 15\}$.

This set has seven elements, so $n(B) = 7$.

(b) $C = \{x, y, z\}$.

Since set C has three elements, $n(C) = 3$. $\quad \blacksquare$

In Example 3, we found all the subsets of $\{7, 8\}$ and all the subsets of $\{a, b, c\}$ by trial and error. An alternate method uses a **tree diagram,** a systematic way of listing all the subsets of a given set. Figures 2(a) and (b) show tree diagrams for finding the subsets of $\{7, 8\}$ and $\{a, b, c\}$.

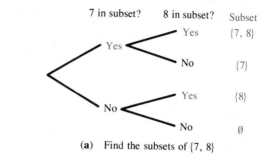

(a) Find the subsets of {7, 8}

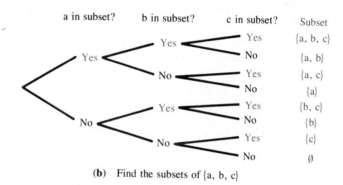

(b) Find the subsets of {a, b, c}

FIGURE 2

Examples and tree diagrams similar to the ones above suggest the following rule, which we prove in Section 5.5.

> **A set of n distinct elements has 2^n subsets.**

EXAMPLE 5

Find the number of subsets for each of the following sets.

(a) {3, 4, 5, 6, 7}

This set has five elements; thus it has 2^5 or 32 subsets.

(b) {−1, 2, 3, 4, 5, 6, 12, 14}

This set has 8 elements and therefore has 2^8 or 256 subsets.

(c) ∅

The empty set has 0 elements, and $2^0 = 1$ subset. (Compare this result with Exercise 39 below.) ▪

5.1 EXERCISES

Write *true* or *false* for Exercises 1–18.

1. $3 \in \{2, 5, 7, 9, 10\}$

2. $6 \in \{-2, 6, 9, 5\}$

3. $1 \in \{3, 4, 5, 1, 11\}$

4. $12 \in \{19, 17, 14, 13, 12\}$

5. $9 \notin \{2, 1, 5, 8\}$

6. $3 \notin \{7, 6, 5, 4\}$

7. $\{2, 5, 8, 9\} = \{2, 5, 9, 8\}$

8. $\{3, 0, 9, 6, 2\} = \{2, 9, 0, 3, 6\}$

9. $\{5, 8, 9\} = \{5, 8, 9, 0\}$

10. $\{3, 7, 12, 14\} = \{3, 7, 12, 14, 0\}$

11. {all counting numbers less than 6} = $\{1, 2, 3, 4, 5, 6\}$

12. {all whole numbers greater than 7 and less than 10} = $\{8, 9\}$

13. {all whole numbers not greater than 4} = $\{0, 1, 2, 3\}$

14. {all counting numbers not greater than 3} = $\{0, 1, 2\}$

15. $\{x \mid x$ is a whole number, $x \le 5\} = \{0, 1, 2, 3, 4, 5\}$

16. $\{x \mid x$ is an integer, $-3 \le x < 4\} = \{-3, -2, -1, 0, 1, 2, 3, 4\}$

17. $\{x \mid x$ is an odd integer, $6 \le x \le 18\} = \{7, 9, 11, 15, 17\}$

18. $\{x \mid x$ is an even counting number, $x \le 9\} = \{0, 2, 4, 6, 8\}$

Let

$A = \{2, 4, 6, 8, 10, 12\}$ $D = \{2, 10\}$

$B = \{2, 4, 8, 10\}$ $U = \{2, 4, 6, 8, 10, 12, 14\}$

$C = \{4, 10, 12\}$

Write *true* or *false* for Exercises 19–34.

19. $A \subset U$

20. $C \subset U$

21. $D \subset B$

22. $D \subset A$

23. $A \subset B$

24. $B \subset C$

25. $\varnothing \subset A$

26. $\varnothing \subset \varnothing$

27. $\{4, 8, 10\} \subset B$

28. $\{0, 2\} \subset D$

29. $D \not\subset B$

30. $A \not\subset C$

31. There are exactly 32 subsets of A.

32. There are exactly 16 subsets of B.

33. There are exactly 6 subsets of C.

34. There are exactly 4 subsets of D.

Find the number of subsets for each of the sets in Exercises 35–42.

35. $\{4, 5, 6\}$

36. $\{3, 7, 9, 10\}$

37. $\{5, 9, 10, 15, 17\}$

38. $\{6, 9, 1, 4, 3, 2\}$

39. $\{\varnothing\}$

40. $\{0\}$

41. $\{x \mid x$ is a counting number between 6 and 12}

42. $\{x \mid x$ is a whole number between 8 and 12}

Give the cardinal number of each of the sets in Exercises 43–48.

43. $\{m, p, q, n\}$

44. $\{a, b, c, d, e, f\}$

45. $\{1, 2, 3\}$

46. $\{0\}$

47. $\varnothing$

48. $\{0, \varnothing\}$

49. A candy bar of a certain size contains 220 calories. Suppose you eat two of these candy bars and then decide to exercise and get rid of the calories. A list of possible exercises shows the following information.

Exercise	Abbreviation	Calories per hour
Sitting around	s	100
Light exercise	l	170
Moderate exercise	m	300
Severe exercise	e	450
Very severe exercise	u	600

The universal set here is $U = \{s, l, m, e, u\}$. Find all subsets of U (with no element listed twice) that will burn off the calories from the candy bars in **(a)** one hour; **(b)** two hours.

50. The list below includes the producers of most (93%) of the hazardous wastes in the United States.

Let x be the number associated with an industry in the table opposite. The universal set is $U = \{1, 2, 3, 4, 5, 6\}$. List the elements of the following subsets of U.

(a) $\{x|$the industry produces more than 15% of the wastes$\}$.

(b) $\{x|$the industry produces less than 5% of the wastes$\}$.

(c) Find all subsets of U containing industries which produce a total of at least 50% of the waste.

Industry	%
Inorganic Chemicals (1)	11
Organic Chemicals (2)	34
Electroplating (3)	12
Petroleum Refining (4)	5
Smelting and Refining (5)	26
Textiles Dyeing and Finishing (6)	5

5.2   Set Operations

Given a set A and a universal set U, the set of all elements of U which do *not* belong to A is called the **complement** of set A. For example, if set A is the set of all the female students in a class, and U is the set of all students in the class, then the complement of A would be the set of all male students in the class. The complement of set A is written A'. (Read: "*A*-prime.") The Venn diagram of Figure 3 shows a set B. Its complement, B', is shown in color.

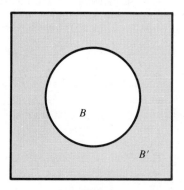

FIGURE 3

EXAMPLE 1

Let $U = \{1, 2, 3, 4, 5, 6, 7\}$, $A = \{1, 3, 5, 7\}$, and $B = \{3, 4, 6\}$. Find each of of the following sets.

(a) A'

Set A' contains the elements of U that are not in A.

$$A' = \{2, 4, 6\}$$

(b) $B' = \{1, 2, 5, 7\}$

(c) $\varnothing' = U$ and $U' = \varnothing$ ▪

Given two sets A and B, the set of all elements belonging to both set A and set B is called the **intersection** of the two sets, written $A \cap B$. For example, the elements that belong to both $A = \{1, 2, 4, 5, 7\}$ and $B = \{2, 4, 5, 7, 9, 11\}$ are 2, 4, 5, and 7, so that

$$A \cap B = \{1, 2, 4, 5, 7\} \cap \{2, 4, 5, 7, 9, 11\} = \{2, 4, 5, 7\}.$$

The Venn diagram of Figure 4 shows two sets A and B; their intersection, $A \cap B$, is shown in color.

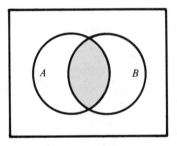

FIGURE 4

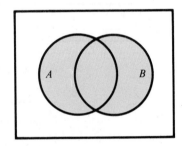

FIGURE 5

EXAMPLE 2

(a) $\{9, 15, 25, 36\} \cap \{15, 20, 25, 30, 35\} = \{15, 25\}$

The elements 15 and 25 are the only ones belonging to both sets.

(b) $\{-2, -3, -4, -5, -6\} \cap \{-4, -3, -2, -1, 0, 1, 2\} = \{-4, -3, -2\}$ ▪

Two sets that have no elements in common are called **disjoint sets.** For example, there are no elements common to both $\{50, 51, 54\}$ and $\{52, 53, 55, 56\}$, so that these two sets are disjoint, and

$$\{50, 51, 54\} \cap \{52, 53, 55, 56\} = \varnothing.$$

The result of this example can be generalized: for any sets A and B, if A and B are disjoint sets then $A \cap B = \varnothing$.

The set of all elements belonging to either set A or set B or both is called the **union** of the two sets, written $A \cup B$. For example,

$$\{1, 3, 5\} \cup \{3, 5, 7, 9\} = \{1, 3, 5, 7, 9\}.$$

The Venn diagram of Figure 5 shows two sets A and B, with their union, $A \cup B$, shown in color.

EXAMPLE 3

(a) Find the union of $\{1, 2, 5, 9, 14\}$ and $\{1, 3, 4, 8\}$.

Begin by listing the elements of the first set, $\{1, 2, 5, 9, 14\}$. Then include any elements from the second set that are not already listed. Doing this gives

$$\{1, 2, 5, 9, 14\} \cup \{1, 3, 4, 8\} = \{1, 2, 3, 4, 5, 8, 9, 14\}.$$

(b) $\{1, 3, 5, 7\} \cup \{2, 4, 6\} = \{1, 2, 3, 4, 5, 6, 7\}.$ ▪

Finding the complement of a set, the intersection of two sets, or the union of two sets are examples of **set operations.** These are similar to operations on numbers, such as addition, subtraction, multiplication, and division.

The next box summarizes the various operations on sets.

Operations on Sets

Let A and B be any sets with U the universal set.

Then

the **complement** of A, written A', is

$$A' = \{x \mid x \notin A \text{ and } x \in U\};$$

the **intersection** of A and B is

$$A \cap B = \{x \mid x \in A \text{ and } x \in B\};$$

the **union** of A and B is

$$A \cup B = \{x \mid x \in A \text{ or } x \in B\}.$$

EXAMPLE 4

The table below gives the current dividend, price-to-earnings ratio (the quotient of the price per share and the annual earnings per share), and price change at the end of a day for six companies, as listed on the New York Stock Exchange.

Stock	Dividend	Price to earnings ratio	Price change
ATT	5	6	$+\frac{1}{8}$
GE	3	9	0
Hershey	1.4	6	$+\frac{3}{8}$
IBM	3.44	12	$-\frac{3}{8}$
Mobil	3.40	6	$-1\frac{5}{8}$
RCA	1.80	7	$-\frac{1}{4}$

Let set A include all stocks with a dividend greater than \$3, B all stocks with a price to earnings ratio of at least 10, and C all stocks with a positive price change. Find the following.

(a) A'

Set A' contains all the listed stocks outside set A, those with a dividend less than or equal to \$3, so $A' = \{$GE, Hershey, RCA$\}$.

(b) $A \cap B$

The intersection of A and B will contain those stocks that offer a dividend greater than \$3 *and* have a price to earnings ratio of at least 10.

$$A \cap B = \{\text{IBM}\}$$

(c) $A \cup C$

We want the set of all stocks with a dividend greater than \$3 *or* a positive price change (or both).

$$A \cup C = \{\text{ATT, Hershey, IBM, Mobil}\} \quad \blacksquare$$

5.2 EXERCISES

Write *true* or *false* for Exercises 1–12.

1. $\{5, 7, 9, 19\} \cap \{7, 9, 11, 15\} = \{7, 9\}$

2. $\{8, 11, 15\} \cap \{8, 11, 19, 20\} = \{8, 11\}$

3. $\{2, 1, 7\} \cup \{1, 5, 9\} = \{1\}$

4. $\{6, 12, 14, 16\} \cup \{6, 14, 19\} = \{6, 14\}$

5. $\{3, 2, 5, 9\} \cap \{2, 7, 8, 10\} = \{2\}$

6. $\{8, 9, 6\} \cup \{9, 8, 6\} = \{8, 9\}$

7. $\{3, 5, 9, 10\} \cap \varnothing = \{3, 5, 9, 10\}$

8. $\{3, 5, 9, 10\} \cup \varnothing = \{3, 5, 9, 10\}$

9. $\{1, 2, 4\} \cup \{1, 2, 4\} = \{1, 2, 4\}$

10. $\{1, 2, 4\} \cap \{1, 2, 4\} = \varnothing$

11. $\varnothing \cup \varnothing = \varnothing$

12. $\varnothing \cap \varnothing = \varnothing$

Let $U = \{2, 3, 4, 5, 7, 9\}$, $X = \{2, 3, 4, 5\}$, $Y = \{3, 5, 7, 9\}$, and $Z = \{2, 4, 5, 7, 9\}$.
Find each of the sets in Exercises 13–26.

13. $X \cap Y$

14. $X \cup Y$

15. $Y \cup Z$

16. $Y \cap Z$

17. $X \cup U$

18. $Y \cap U$

19. X'

20. Y'

21. $X' \cap Y'$

22. $X' \cap Z$

23. $Z' \cap \varnothing$

24. $Y' \cup \varnothing$

25. $X \cup (Y \cap Z)$

26. $Y \cap (X \cup Z)$

Let $U = \{$all students in this school$\}$
   $M = \{$all students taking this course$\}$
   $N = \{$all students taking accounting$\}$
   $P = \{$all students taking zoology$\}$
Describe each of the following sets in words.

27. M'

28. $M \cup N$

29. $N \cap P$

30. $N' \cap P'$

31. $M \cup P$

32. $P' \cup M'$

Given $U = \{1, 2, 3, 4, 5, 6, 7, 8, 9, 10\}$, $P = \{2, 4, 6, 8, 10\}$, $Q = \{4, 5, 6\}$, and $R = \{4\}$, find the cardinal number of the sets in Exercises 33–40.

33. $P \cup Q$ **34.** $P \cap Q$ **35.** P' **36.** Q'

37. $P' \cap Q$ **38.** $P \cup R'$ **39.** $P \cup (R \cap Q)$ **40.** $P \cap (R \cup Q)$

Refer to Example 4 in the text. Describe each of the sets in Exercises 41–46 in words. Then list the elements of each set.

41. B' **42.** C' **43.** $B \cap C$ **44.** $A \cup B$

45. $(A \cap B)'$ **46.** $(A \cup C)'$

47. The lists below show some symptoms of an overactive thyroid and an underactive thyroid.

Underactive thyroid	Overactive thyroid
Sleepiness, s	Insomnia, i
Dry hands, d	Moist hands, m
Intolerance of cold, c	Intolerance of heat, h
Goiter, g	Goiter, g

(a) Find the smallest possible universal set U that includes all the symptoms listed.

Let N be the set of symptoms for an underactive thyroid, and let O be the set of symptoms for an overactive thyroid. Find each of the following sets.

(b) O' **(c)** N' **(d)** $N \cap O$ **(e)** $N \cup O$ **(f)** $N \cap O'$

48. Let A and B be sets with cardinal numbers $n(A) = a$ and $n(B) = b$, respectively. Answer *true* or *false* for the following statements:

(a) $n(A \cup B) = n(A) + n(B)$;   **(b)** $n(A \cup B) = n(A) + n(B) - n(A \cap B)$.

5.3   Venn Diagrams

Venn diagrams were used in the last section to help in understanding set union and intersection. The rectangular region of a Venn diagram represents the universal set U. Including only a single set A inside the universal set, as in Figure 6, divides U into two regions. Region 1 represents those elements of U outside set A, while region 2 represents those elements belonging to set A. (Our numbering of these regions is arbitrary.)

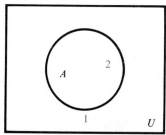

One set leads to 2 regions
(numbering is arbitrary)

FIGURE 6

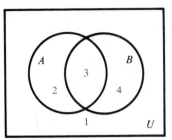

Two sets lead to 4 regions
(numbering is arbitrary)

FIGURE 7

The Venn diagram of Figure 7 shows two sets inside U. These two sets divide the universal set into four regions. As labeled in Figure 7, region 1 includes those elements outside of both set A and set B. Region 2 includes those elements belonging to A and not to B. Region 3 includes those elements belonging to both A and B. Which elements belong to region 4? (Again, the labeling is arbitrary.)

EXAMPLE 1

Draw Venn diagrams similar to Figure 7 and shade the regions representing the following sets.

(a) $A' \cap B$

Set A' contains all the elements outside of set A. As labeled in Figure 7, A' is made up of regions 1 and 4. Set B is made up of the elements in regions 3 and 4. The intersection of sets A' and B, the set $A' \cap B$, is made up of the elements in the region common to regions 1 and 4 and regions 3 and 4. The result, region 4, is shaded in Figure 8.

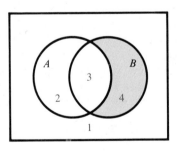

FIGURE 8

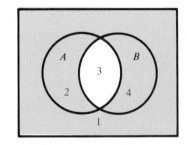

FIGURE 9

(b) $A' \cup B'$

Again, set A' is represented by regions 1 and 4, while B' is made up of regions 1 and 2. To find $A' \cup B'$, identify the elements belonging to either regions 1 and 4 or to regions 1 and 2. The result, regions 1, 2, and 4, is shaded in Figure 9. ▪

Venn diagrams can also be drawn with three sets inside U. These three sets divide the universal set into eight regions, which can be numbered (arbitrarily) as in Figure 10.

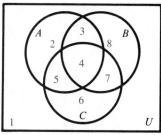

Three sets lead to 8 regions

FIGURE 10   **FIGURE 11**

EXAMPLE 2

Shade $A' \cup (B \cap C')$ on a Venn diagram.

First find $B \cap C'$. Set B is made up of regions 3, 4, 7, and 8, while C' is made up of regions 1, 2, 3, and 8. The overlap of these regions, the set $B \cap C'$, is made up of regions 3 and 8. Set A' is made up of regions 1, 6, 7, and 8. The union of regions 3 and 8 and regions 1, 6, 7, 8 is regions 1, 3, 6, 7 and 8, which are shaded in Figure 11. ▨

Applications   Venn diagrams and the cardinal number of a set can be used to solve problems that result from surveying groups of people. As an example, suppose a group of 60 freshman business students at a large university was surveyed, with the following results.

19 of the students read *Business Week;*
18 read *The Wall Street Journal;*
50 read *Fortune;*
13 read *Business Week* and *The Journal;*
11 read *The Journal* and *Fortune;*
13 read *Business Week* and *Fortune;*
 9 read all three.

Let us use this data to help answer the following questions.
(a) How many students read none of the publications?
(b) How many read only *Fortune?*
(c) How many read *Business Week* and *The Journal,* but not *Fortune?*

Many of the students are listed more than once in the data above. For example, some of the 50 students who read *Fortune* also read *Business Week*. The 9 students who read all three are counted in the 13 who read *Business Week* and *Fortune*, and so on.

We can use a Venn diagram, as shown in Figure 12 on the next page, to better illustrate this data. Since 9 students read all three publications, begin by placing 9 in the area that belongs to all three regions, as shown in Figure 13. Of the 13 students who read *Business Week* and *Fortune* 9 also read *The Journal*. Therefore,

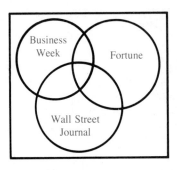

FIGURE 12

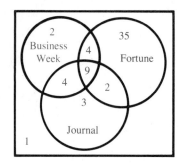

FIGURE 13

only $13 - 9 = 4$ read just *Business Week* and *Fortune*. Place the number 4 in the area of Figure 13 common to *Business Week* and *Fortune* readers. In the same way, place 4 in the region common only to *Business Week* and *The Journal*, and 2 in the region common only to *Fortune* and *The Journal*.

We know 19 students read *Business Week*. However, we have already placed $4 + 9 + 4 = 17$ readers in the region representing *Business Week*. The balance of this region will contain only $19 - 17 = 2$ students. These 2 students read *Business Week* only—not *Fortune* and not *The Journal*. In the same way, 3 students read only *The Journal* and 35 read only *Fortune*.

A total of $2 + 4 + 3 + 4 + 9 + 2 + 35 = 59$ students are placed in the three circles of Figure 13. Since 60 students were surveyed, $60 - 59 = 1$ student reads none of the three publications, and 1 is placed outside all three regions.

We can now use Figure 13 to answer the questions asked above.

(a) Only 1 student reads none of the three publications.

(b) From Figure 13, there are 35 students who read only *Fortune*.

(c) The overlap of the regions representing *Business Week* and *The Journal* shows that 4 students read *Business Week* and *The Journal* but not *Fortune*.

EXAMPLE 3

Jeff Friedman is a section chief for an electric utility company. The employees in his section cut down tall trees, climb poles, and splice wire. Friedman reported the following information to the management of the utility.

Of the 100 employees in my section,
45 can cut tall trees;
50 can climb poles;
57 can splice wire;
28 can cut trees and climb poles;
20 can climb poles and splice wire;
25 can cut trees and splice wire;
11 can do all three;
 9 can't do any of the three (management trainees).

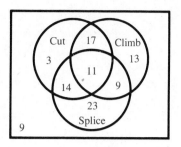

FIGURE 14

The data supplied by Friedman lead to the numbers shown in Figure 14. Add all the numbers from the regions to get the total number of employees:

$$9 + 3 + 14 + 23 + 11 + 9 + 17 + 13 = 99.$$

Friedman claimed to have 100 employees, but his data indicates only 99. The management decided that Friedman didn't qualify as a section chief, and reassigned him as a nightshift meter reader in Guam. (Moral: he should have taken this course.) ▪

Note that in both examples above, we started in the innermost region, the intersection of the three categories. This is usually the best way to begin solving these problems.

5.3 EXERCISES

Use a Venn diagram similar to Figure 7 to show each of the sets in Exercises 1–8.

1. $B \cap A'$ **2.** $A \cup B'$ **3.** $A' \cup B$ **4.** $A' \cap B'$

5. $B' \cup (A' \cap B')$ **6.** $(A \cap B) \cup B'$ **7.** U' **8.** $\varnothing'$

Use a Venn diagram similar to Figure 10 to show each of the sets in Exercises 9–16.

9. $(A \cap B) \cap C$ **10.** $(A \cap C') \cup B$

11. $A \cap (B \cup C')$ **12.** $A' \cap (B \cap C)$

13. $(A' \cap B') \cap C$ **14.** $(A \cap B') \cup C$

15. $(A \cap B') \cap C$ **16.** $A' \cap (B' \cup C)$

17. If $n(A) = 5$, $n(B) = 8$, and $n(A \cap B) = 4$, what is $n(A \cup B)$?

18. If $n(A) = 12$, $n(B) = 27$, and $n(A \cup B) = 30$, what is $n(A \cap B)$?

19. Suppose $n(B) = 7$, $n(A \cap B) = 3$, and $n(A \cup B) = 20$. What is $n(A)$?

20. Suppose $n(A \cap B) = 5$, $n(A \cup B) = 35$, and $n(A) = 13$. What is $n(B)$?

Draw a Venn diagram and use the given information to fill in the number of elements for each region.

21. $n(U) = 38$, $n(A) = 16$, $n(A \cap B) = 12$, $n(B') = 20$

22. $n(A) = 26$, $n(B) = 10$, $n(A \cup B) = 30$, $n(A') = 17$

23. $n(A \cup B) = 17$, $n(A \cap B) = 3$, $n(A) = 8$, $n(A' \cup B') = 21$

24. $n(A') = 28$, $n(B) = 25$, $n(A' \cup B') = 45$, $n(A \cap B) = 12$

25. $n(A) = 28$, $n(B) = 34$, $n(C) = 25$, $n(A \cap B) = 14$, $n(B \cap C) = 15$, $n(A \cap C) = 11$, $n(A \cap B \cap C) = 9$, $n(U) = 59$

26. $n(A) = 54$, $n(A \cap B) = 22$, $n(A \cup B) \doteq 85$, $n(A \cap B \cap C) = 4$, $n(A \cap C) = 15$, $n(B \cap C) = 16$, $n(C) = 44$, $n(B') = 63$

27. $n(A \cap B) = 6$, $n(A \cap B \cap C) = 4$, $n(A \cap C) = 7$, $n(B \cap C) = 4$, $n(A \cap C') = 11$, $n(B \cap C') = 8$, $n(C) = 15$, $n(A' \cap B' \cap C') = 5$

28. $n(A) = 13$, $n(A \cap B \cap C) = 4$, $n(A \cap C) = 6$, $n(A \cap B') = 6$, $n(B \cap C) = 6$, $n(B \cap C') = 11$, $n(B \cup C) = 22$, $n(A' \cap B' \cap C') = 5$

Use Venn diagrams to answer the following questions.

29. Jeff Friedman, of Example 3 in the text, was again reassigned, this time to the home economics department of the electric utility. He interviewed 140 people in a suburban shopping center to find out some of their cooking habits. He obtained the following results. Should he be reassigned yet one more time?

　　58 use microwave ovens;
　　63 use electric ranges;
　　58 use gas ranges;
　　19 use microwave ovens and electric ranges;
　　17 use microwave ovens and gas ranges;
　　 4 use both gas and electric ranges;
　　 1 uses all three;
　　 2 cook only with solar energy.

30. Toward the middle of the harvesting season, peaches for canning come in three types: earlies, lates, and extra lates, depending on the expected date of ripening. During a certain week, the following data was recorded at a fruit delivery station.

　　34 trucks went out carrying early peaches;
　　61 had late peaches;
　　50 had extra lates;
　　25 had earlies and lates;
　　30 had lates and extra lates;
　　 8 had earlies and extra lates;
　　 6 had all three;
　　 9 had only figs (no peaches at all).

　(a) How many trucks had only late variety peaches?

　(b) How many had only extra lates?

　(c) How many had only one type of peaches?

　(d) How many trucks in all went out during the week?

31. A chicken farmer surveyed his flock with the following results. The farmer had

　　 9 fat red roosters;
　　 2 fat red hens;
　　37 fat chickens;
　　26 fat roosters;
　　 7 thin brown hens;
　　18 thin brown roosters;
　　 6 thin red roosters;
　　 5 thin red hens.

Answer the following questions about the flock. Hint: you need a Venn diagram with regions for fat, for male (a rooster is a male, a hen is a female), and for red (assume that brown and red are opposites in the chicken world). How many chickens were

(a) fat?   **(b)** red?   **(c)** male?   **(d)** fat, but not male?

(e) brown, but not fat?   **(f)** red and fat?

32. Country-western songs emphasize three basic themes: love, prison, and trucks. A survey of the local country-western radio station produced the following data.

> 12 songs were about a truck driver who was in love while in prison;
> 13 about a prisoner in love;
> 28 about a person in love;
> 18 about a truck driver in love;
> 3 about a truck driver in prison who was not in love;
> 2 about a prisoner who was not in love and did not drive a truck;
> 8 about a person out of jail who was not in love, and did not drive a truck;
> 16 about truck drivers who were not in prison.

(a) How many songs were surveyed?

Find the number of songs about

(b) truck drivers;   **(c)** prisoners;   **(d)** truck drivers in prison;

(e) people not in prison;   **(f)** people not in love.

33. After a genetics experiment, the number of pea plants having certain characteristics was tallied, with the results as follows.

> 22 were tall;
> 25 had green peas;
> 39 had smooth peas;
> 9 were tall and had green peas;
> 17 were tall and had smooth peas;
> 20 had green peas and smooth peas;
> 6 had all three characteristics;
> 4 had none of the characteristics.

(a) Find the total number of plants counted.

(b) How many plants were tall and had peas which were neither smooth nor green?

(c) How many plants were not tall but had peas which were smooth and green?

34. Human blood can contain either no antigens, the A antigen, the B antigen, or both the A and B antigens. A third antigen, called the Rh antigen, is important in human reproduction, and again may or may not be present in an individual. Blood is called type A-positive if the individual has the A and Rh, but not the B antigen. A person having only the A and B antigens is said to have type AB-negative blood. A person having only the Rh antigen has type O-positive blood. Other blood types are defined in a similar manner. Identify the blood type of the individuals in regions (a)–(g) below.

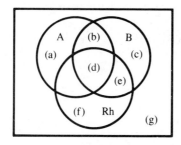

35. (Use the diagram from Exercise 34.) In a certain hospital, the following data were recorded.

> 25 patients had the A antigen;
> 17 had the A and B antigens;
> 27 had the B antigen;
> 22 had the B and Rh antigens;
> 30 had the Rh antigen;
> 12 had none of the antigens;
> 16 had the A and Rh antigens;
> 15 had all three antigens.

How many patients

(a) were represented?

(b) had exactly one antigen?

(c) had exactly two antigens?

(d) had O-positive blood?

(e) had AB-positive blood?

(f) had B-negative blood?

(g) had O-negative blood?

(h) had A-positive blood?

36. A survey of 80 sophomores at a western college showed that

> 36 take English;
> 32 take history;
> 32 take political science;
> 16 take political science and history;
> 16 take history and English;
> 14 take political science and English;
> 6 take all three.

How many students:

(a) take English and neither of the other two?

(b) take none of the three courses?

(c) take history, but neither of the other two?

(d) take political science and history, but not English?

(e) do not take political science?

37. The following table shows the number of people in a certain small town in Georgia who fit in the given categories.

Age	Drink vodka (V)	Drink bourbon (B)	Drink gin (G)	Totals
21–25 (Y)	40	15	15	70
26–35 (M)	30	30	20	80
over 35 (O)	10	50	10	70
Totals	80	95	45	220

Using the letters given in the table, find the number of people in each of the following sets.

(a) $Y \cap V$

(b) $M \cap B$

(c) $M \cup (B \cap Y)$

(d) $Y' \cap (B \cup G)$

(e) $O' \cup G$

(f) $M' \cap (V' \cap G')$

38. The following table shows the results of a survey in a medium-sized town in Tennessee. The survey asked questions about the investment habits of local citizens.

Age	Stocks (S)	Bonds (B)	Savings accounts (A)	Totals
18–29 (Y)	6	2	15	23
30–49 (M)	14	5	14	33
50 or over (O)	32	20	12	64
Totals	52	27	41	120

Using the letters given in the table, find the number of people in each of the following sets.

(a) $Y \cap B$ **(b)** $M \cup A$ **(c)** $Y \cap (S \cup B)$

(d) $O' \cup (S \cup A)$ **(e)** $(M' \cup O') \cap B$

For the statements of Exercises 39–42 draw Venn diagrams for the sets on each side of the equals sign. Show that the Venn diagrams are the same.*

39. $(A \cup B)' = A' \cap B'$

40. $(A \cap B)' = A' \cup B'$

41. $A \cap (B \cup C) = (A \cap B) \cup (A \cap C)$

42. $A \cup (B \cap C) = (A \cup B) \cap (A \cup C)$

43. Let $n(A)$ represent the number of elements in set A. Verify that $n(A \cup B) = n(A) + n(B) - n(A \cap B)$ for sets $A = \{1, 2, 3, 4, 5\}$ and $B = \{3, 5, 7\}$.

44. Do you think the statement in Exercise 43 is true for all sets A and B?

5.4 Permutations and Combinations

After making do with your old automobile for several years, you finally decide to replace it with a new small super-economy model. You drive over to Ned's New Car Emporium to choose the car that's just right for you. Once there, you find that you can select from 5 models, each with 4 power options, a choice of 8 exterior color combinations and 3 interior colors. How many different new cars are available to you? Problems of this sort are best solved by the counting principles discussed in this section. These counting methods are very useful in probability.

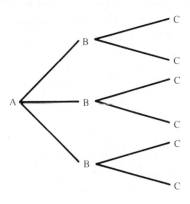

FIGURE 15

---

*The statements in Exercises 39 and 40 are known as De Morgan's Laws. They are named for the English mathematician Augustus De Morgan (1806–71).

Let us begin with a simpler example. If there are three roads from town A to town B and two roads from town B to town C, in how many ways can we travel from A to C by way of B? For each of the three roads from A there are two different routes leading from B to C, making $3 \cdot 2 = 6$ different ways for the trip, as shown in Figure 15. This example illustrates a general principle of counting, called the **multiplication principle.**

Multiplication Principle

Suppose n choices must be made, with

m_1 ways to make choice 1,

m_2 ways to make choice 2,

and so on, with

m_n ways to make choice n.

Then there are

$$m_1 \cdot m_2 \cdot \cdot \cdot m_n$$

different ways to make the entire sequence of choices.

Using this multiplication principle, there are

$$5 \cdot 4 \cdot 8 \cdot 3 = 480$$

ways of selecting a new car at Ned's.

EXAMPLE 1

A teacher has 5 different books that he wishes to arrange side by side. How many different arrangements are possible?

Five choices will be made, one for each space which will hold a book. Any of the five possible books could be chosen for the first space. There are four possible choices for the second space, since one book has already been placed in the first space, three possible choices for the third space, and so on. By the multiplication principle, the number of different possible arrangements is $5 \cdot 4 \cdot 3 \cdot 2 \cdot 1 = 120$. ▨

The use of the multiplication principle often leads to products such as $5 \cdot 4 \cdot 3 \cdot 2 \cdot 1$. For convenience, the symbol $n!$ (read "n *factorial*") is used for such products. By definition,

***n*-factorial**

For any natural number n,

$$n! = n(n - 1)(n - 2) \cdot \cdot \cdot (3)(2)(1).$$

With this symbol, the product $5 \cdot 4 \cdot 3 \cdot 2 \cdot 1$ can be written as $5!$. Also, $3! = 3 \cdot 2 \cdot 1 = 6$. The definition of $n!$ could be used to show that

$n[(n - 1)!] = n!$ for all natural numbers $n \geq 2$. It is helpful if this result also holds for $n = 1$. This can only happen if 0! is defined to equal 1:

$$0! = 1.$$

EXAMPLE 2

Suppose the teacher in Example 1 wishes to place only 3 of the 5 books on his desk. How many arrangements of 3 books are possible?

The teacher again has 5 ways to fill the first space, 4 ways to fill the second space, and 3 ways to fill the third. Since he wants to use only 3 books, only 3 spaces can be filled (3 events) instead of 5, for $5 \cdot 4 \cdot 3 = 60$ arrangements. ▪

Permutations   The answer 60 in Example 2 is called the number of permutations of 5 things taken 3 at a time. A **permutation** of r (where $r \geq 1$) elements from a set of n elements is any arrangement, *without repetition*, of the r elements. The number of permutations of n things taken r at a time (with $r \leq n$) is written $P(n, r)$. Based on the work in Example 2 above, $P(5, 3) = 5 \cdot 4 \cdot 3 = 60$. Factorial notation can be used to express this product as follows.

$$5 \cdot 4 \cdot 3 = 5 \cdot 4 \cdot 3 \cdot \frac{2 \cdot 1}{2 \cdot 1} = \frac{5 \cdot 4 \cdot 3 \cdot 2 \cdot 1}{2 \cdot 1} = \frac{5!}{2!} = \frac{5!}{(5 - 3)!}$$

This example illustrates the general rule of permutations which is stated in the following box.

Permutations

> If $P(n, r)$ (where $r \leq n$) is the number of permutations of n elements taken r at a time, then
>
> $$P(n, r) = \frac{n!}{(n - r)!}.$$

The proof of this rule follows the discussion of Example 2 above. There are n ways to choose the first of the r elements, $n - 1$ ways to choose the second, and $n - r + 1$ ways to choose the rth element. This makes

$$P(n, r) = n(n - 1)(n - 2) \cdots (n - r + 1).$$

Now multiply on the right by $(n - r)!/(n - r)!$.

$$P(n, r) = n(n - 1)(n - 2) \cdots (n - r + 1) \cdot \frac{(n - r)!}{(n - r)!}$$

$$= \frac{n(n - 1)(n - 2) \cdots (n - r + 1)(n - r)!}{(n - r)!}$$

$$= \frac{n!}{(n - r)!}.$$

To find $P(n, r)$, either the result in the box or direct application of the multiplication principle may be used, as the following example shows.

EXAMPLE 3

Find the number of permutations of 8 elements taken 3 at a time.

Since 3 choices are to be made, the multiplication principle gives $P(8, 3) = 8 \cdot 7 \cdot 6 = 336$. Alternatively, use the formula above to get

$$P(8, 3) = \frac{8!}{(8 - 3)!} = \frac{8!}{5!} = \frac{8 \cdot 7 \cdot 6 \cdot 5!}{5!} = 8 \cdot 7 \cdot 6 = 336 \quad \blacksquare$$

Combinations   In Example 2 above, we found that there are 60 ways that a teacher can arrange 3 of 5 different books on his desk. That is, there are 60 permutations of 5 things taken 3 at a time. Suppose now that the teacher does not wish to arrange the books on his desk, but rather wishes to choose, without regard to order, any 3 of the 5 books for a book sale to raise money for his school. In how many ways can he do this?

At first glance, we might say 60 again, but this is incorrect. The number 60 counts all possible *arrangements* of 3 books chosen from 5. However, the following arrangements would all lead to the same set of three books being given to the book sale.

mystery-biography-textbook	biography-textbook-mystery
mystery-textbook-biography	textbook-biography-mystery
biography-mystery-textbook	textbook-mystery-biography

The list shows 6 different *arrangements* of 3 books, but only one *set* of 3 books. A subset of items selected *without regard to order* is called a **combination.** The number of combinations of 5 things taken 3 at a time is written $\binom{5}{3}$.

To evaluate $\binom{5}{3}$, start with the $5 \cdot 4 \cdot 3$ *permutations* of 5 things taken 3 at a time. Since order doesn't matter, and each subset of 3 items from the set of 5 items can have its elements rearranged in $3 \cdot 2 \cdot 1 = 3!$ ways, $\binom{5}{3}$ can be found by dividing the number of permutations by 3!, or

$$\binom{5}{3} = \frac{5 \cdot 4 \cdot 3}{3!} = \frac{5 \cdot 4 \cdot 3}{3 \cdot 2 \cdot 1} = 10.$$

There are 10 ways that the teacher can choose 3 books for the book sale. Generalizing this discussion gives the following formula for the number of combinations of n elements taken r at a time:

$$\binom{n}{r} = \frac{P(n, r)}{r!}.$$

A more useful version of this formula can be found as follows.

$$\binom{n}{r} = \frac{P(n, r)}{r!}$$

$$= \frac{n!}{(n - r)!} \cdot \frac{1}{r!}$$

$$= \frac{n!}{(n - r)!\,r!}$$

This last form is the most useful for calculation. The steps above lead to the following result.

Combinations

If $\binom{n}{r}$ **is the number of combinations of** n **elements taken** r **at a time, then**

$$\binom{n}{r} = \frac{n!}{(n-r)!\, r!}.$$

The table of combinations in the Appendix gives the values of $\binom{n}{r}$ for $n \le 20$.

EXAMPLE 4

How many committees of 3 people can be formed from a group of 8 people?

A committee is an unordered set, so we want $\binom{8}{3}$, which can be found with the formula in the box.

$$\binom{8}{3} = \frac{8!}{5!3!} = \frac{8 \cdot 7 \cdot 6 \cdot 5 \cdot 4 \cdot 3 \cdot 2 \cdot 1}{5 \cdot 4 \cdot 3 \cdot 2 \cdot 1 \cdot 3 \cdot 2 \cdot 1} = \frac{8 \cdot 7 \cdot 6}{3 \cdot 2 \cdot 1} = 56. \quad \blacksquare$$

EXAMPLE 5

From a group of 30 employees, 3 are to be selected to work on a special project.

(a) In how many different ways can the employees be selected?

Here we wish to know the number of 3-element combinations that can be formed from a set of 30 elements. (We want combinations, not permutations, since order within the group of 3 doesn't matter.)

$$\binom{30}{3} = \frac{30!}{27!3!} = \frac{30 \cdot 29 \cdot 28 \cdot 27!}{27! \cdot 3 \cdot 2 \cdot 1}$$

$$= \frac{30 \cdot 29 \cdot 28}{3 \cdot 2 \cdot 1}$$

$$= 4060$$

There are 4060 ways to select the project group.

(b) In how many ways can the group of 3 be selected if one particular person must work on the project?

Since one person has already been selected for the project, the problem is reduced to selecting 2 more people from the remaining 29 employees.

$$\binom{29}{2} = \frac{29!}{27!2!} = \frac{29 \cdot 28 \cdot 27!}{27! \cdot 2 \cdot 1} = \frac{29 \cdot 28}{2 \cdot 1} = 29 \cdot 14 = 406$$

In this case, the project group can be selected in 406 ways. $\blacksquare$

The formulas for permutations and combinations given in this section will be very useful in solving probability problems in the next chapter. Difficulty in using these formulas often comes from being unable to select between them. In the next examples, we concentrate on recognizing which formulas to use.

EXAMPLE 6	A manager must select 4 employees for promotion: 12 employees are eligible.

(a)   In how many ways can the four be chosen?

Since there is no reason to differentiate among the 4 who are selected, use combinations.

$$\binom{12}{4} = \frac{12!}{4!8!} = 495$$

(b)   In how many ways can 4 employees be chosen (from 12) to be placed in 4 different jobs?

In this case, once a group of 4 is selected, they can be assigned in many different ways (or arrangements) to the 4 jobs. Therefore, this problem requires permutations.

$$P(12, 4) = \frac{12!}{8!} = 11,880 \quad \blacksquare$$

EXAMPLE 7	In how many ways can a full house of aces and eights (3 aces and 2 eights) be dealt in five card poker?

Here, we are not interested in the arrangement of the three aces or the two eights. Use combinations and the multiplication principle. There are $\binom{4}{3}$ ways to get 3 aces from the 4 aces in the deck, and $\binom{4}{2}$ ways to get 2 eights. The number of ways to get 3 aces and 2 eights is

$$\binom{4}{3} \cdot \binom{4}{2} = 4 \cdot 6 = 24. \quad \blacksquare$$

EXAMPLE 8	In how many ways can a flush be dealt in five-card poker? (A flush is a five-card hand of the same suit.)

The total number of ways that 5 cards of a particular suit of 13 cards can be dealt is $\binom{13}{5}$. Since the arrangement of the five cards is not important, use combinations. There are four different suits, so the multiplication principle gives

$$4 \cdot \binom{13}{5} = 4 \cdot 1287 = 5148$$

ways to deal a 5-card flush.   ▨

The following table outlines the similarities of permutations and combinations as well as their differences.

Permutations	**Combinations**
Number of ways of selecting r items out of n items	
Repetitions are not allowed	
Order is important	Order is not important
Arrangements of r items from a set of n items	Subsets of r items from a set of n items
$P(n, r) = \dfrac{n!}{(n - r)!}$	$\dbinom{n}{r} = \dfrac{n!}{(n - r)!r!}$

It should be stressed that not all counting problems lend themselves to either of these techniques. Whenever a tree diagram or the multiplication principle can be used directly, then use it.

5.4 EXERCISES

Evaluate the factorials, permutations, and combinations in Exercises 1–12.

1. $P(4, 2)$

2. $3!$

3. $\binom{8}{3}$

4. $7!$

5. $P(8, 1)$

6. $\binom{8}{1}$

7. $4!$

8. $P(4, 4)$

9. $\binom{12}{5}$

10. $\binom{10}{8}$

11. $P(13, 2)$

12. $P(12, 3)$

You can use a computer to find values for Exercises 13–20.

13. $P(25,12)$

14. $P(38,17)$

15. $P(14,5)$

16. $P(17,12)$

17. $\binom{21}{10}$

18. $\binom{34}{25}$

19. $\binom{25}{16}$

20. $\binom{30}{15}$

21. How many different two-card hands can be dealt from an ordinary deck (52 cards)?

22. How many different four-card hands can be dealt from an ordinary deck?

23. Five cards are marked with the numbers 1, 2, 3, 4, and 5, then shuffled, and two cards are drawn. How many different two-card combinations are possible?

24. Marbles are drawn without replacement from a bag containing 15 marbles.
  (a) How many samples of 2 marbles can be drawn?
  (b) How many samples of 4 marbles can be drawn?
  (c) If the bag contains 3 yellow, 4 white, and 8 blue marbles, how many samples of 2 marbles can be drawn in which both marbles are blue?

25. Use the multiplication principle to decide how many 7-digit telephone numbers are possible if the first digit cannot be zero and
  (a) only odd digits may be used;
  (b) the telephone number must be a multiple of 10 (that is, it must end in zero);
  (c) the telephone number must be a multiple of 100;
  (d) the first three digits are 481;
  (e) no repetitions are allowed?

26. How many different license numbers consisting of 3 letters followed by 3 digits are possible?

27. In a club with 8 men and 11 women members, how many 5-member committees can be chosen that have **(a)** all men; **(b)** all women; **(c)** 3 men and 2 women.

28. Five cards are drawn from an ordinary deck. In how many ways is it possible to draw
  (a) all red cards;
  (b) all face cards (face cards are the Jack, Queen, and King);
  (c) no face card;
  (d) exactly 2 face cards;
  (e) 1 heart, 2 diamonds, and 2 clubs.

29. If a baseball coach has 5 good hitters and 4 poor hitters on the bench and chooses 3 players at random, in how many ways can he choose at least 2 good hitters?

30. A technical institute gives 12 different introductory courses, with each course given for a week. Of these courses, 5 do not require a knowledge of mathematics. If you take a course a week for three weeks, and don't repeat a course, how many arrangements are possible that do not require a knowledge of mathematics?

31. A bag contains 5 black, 1 red, and 3 yellow jelly beans; you reach in and select 3. How many samples are possible in which the jelly beans are

(a) all black;   (b) all red;

(c) all yellow;   (d) 2 black, 1 red;

(e) 2 black, 1 yellow;   (f) 2 yellow, 1 black;

(g) 2 red, 1 yellow.

32. A crate of 25 apples has 5 rotten ones. How many samples of 3 apples might be drawn

(a) from the crate?

(b) in which all three are rotten?

(c) with two good apples and one rotten apple?

33. How many different types of homes are available if a builder offers a choice of 5 basic plans, 3 roof styles, and 2 exterior finishes?

34. An auto manufacturer produces 7 models, each available in 6 different colors, with 4 different upholstery fabrics, and 5 interior colors. How many varieties of the auto are available?

35. How many different 4-letter radio station call letters can be made

(a) if the first letter must be K or W and no letter may be repeated?

(b) if repeats are allowed (but the first letter is K or W)?

(c) How many 4-letter call letters (starting with K or W) with no repeats end in R?

36. A business school gives one section each of typing, shorthand, transcription, business English, technical writing, and accounting. In how many ways can a student arrange a schedule if 3 courses are taken and none of the sections overlap?

37. In how many ways can an employer select 2 new employees from a group of 4 applicants?

38. Hal's Hamburger Hamlet sells hamburgers with cheese, relish, lettuce, tomato, mustard, or catsup. How many different kinds of hamburgers can be made using any three of the extras?

39. A group of 7 workers decides to send a delegation of 2 to their supervisor to discuss their grievances.

(a) How many delegations are possible?

(b) If it is decided that a particular employee must be in the delegation, how many different delegations are possible?

(c) If there are 2 women and 5 men in the group, how many delegations would include at least 1 woman?

40. In how many ways can 7 of 10 monkeys be arranged in a row for a genetics experiment?

41. A group of 3 students is to be selected from a group of 12 students to take part in a special class in cell biology.

(a) In how many ways can this be done?

(b) In how many ways can the group which will *not* take part be chosen?

42. In an experiment on plant hardiness, a researcher gathers 6 wheat plants, 3 barley plants, and 2 rye plants. She wishes to select 4 plants to test.

(a) In how many ways can this be done?

(b) In how many ways can this be done if exactly 2 wheat plants must be included?

43. In an experiment on social interaction, 6 people will sit in 6 seats in a row. In how many ways can this be done?

44. A couple has narrowed down the choice of a name for their new baby to 3 first names and 5 middle names. How many different first and middle name arrangements are possible?

45. A session at a management meeting is to be made up of 5 presentations, 2 on motivation, 2 on stress, and 1 on the foreign threat. In how many ways may the presentations be arranged?

46. How many different license plate numbers can be formed using 3 letters followed by 3 digits if no repeats are allowed?

47. How many license plate numbers (see Exercise 46) are possible if there are no repeats and either numbers or letters can come first?

48. An economics club has 30 members. If a committee of 4 is to be selected, in how many ways can it be done?

49. A city council is composed of 5 liberals and 4 conservatives. A delegation of 3 is to be selected to attend a convention.

(a) How many delegations are possible?

(b) How many delegations could have all liberals?

(c) How many delegations could have 2 liberals and 1 conservative?

(d) If one member of the council serves as mayor, how many delegations which include the mayor are possible?

50. The coach of the Morton Valley Softball Team has 6 good hitters and 8 poor hitters. He chooses 3 hitters at random.

(a) In how many ways can he choose 2 good hitters and 1 poor hitter?

(b) In how many ways can he choose all good hitters?

51. How many 5-card poker hands are possible with a regular deck of 52 cards?

52. How many 5-card poker hands with all cards from the same suit are possible?

53. How many 13-card bridge hands are possible with a regular deck of 52 cards?

54. How many 13-card bridge hands with 4 aces are possible?

55. Eleven drugs have been found to be effective in the treatment of a disease. It is believed that the sequence in which the drugs are administered is important in the effectiveness of the treatment. In how many orders can 5 of the 11 drugs be administered?

56. A biologist is attempting to classify 52,000 species of insects by assigning 3 initials to each species. Is it possible to classify all the species in this way? If not, how many initials should be used?

5.5 The Binomial Theorem (Optional)

Evaluating the expression $(x + y)^n$ for various values of n gives a family of expressions, called **expansions,** which are important in the study of mathematics generally, and in particular in the study of probability (in the next chapter). For example,

$$(x + y)^1 = x + y$$
$$(x + y)^2 = x^2 + 2xy + y^2$$
$$(x + y)^3 = x^3 + 3x^2y + 3xy^2 + y^3$$
$$(x + y)^4 = x^4 + 4x^3y + 6x^2y^2 + 4xy^3 + y^4$$
$$(x + y)^5 = x^5 + 5x^4y + 10x^3y^2 + 10x^2y^3 + 5xy^4 + y^5.$$

Inspection of these expansions shows a pattern. Let us try to identify the pattern so that we can write a general expression for $(x + y)^n$.

First, each expansion begins with x raised to the same power as the binomial itself. That is, the expansion of $(x + y)^1$ has first term x^1, that of $(x + y)^2$ starts with x^2, while $(x + y)^3$ has first term x^3, and so on. The last term in each expansion is y raised to the same power as the binomial. Based on this, the expansion of $(x + y)^n$ should begin with x^n and end with the term y^n.

Also, the exponents on x decrease by 1 in each term after the first, while the exponents on y, beginning with y in the second term, increase by 1 in each succeeding term, with the *variables* in the expansion of $(x + y)^n$ having the following pattern:

$$x^n, \quad x^{n-1}y, \quad x^{n-2}y^2, \quad x^{n-3}y^3, \quad \ldots, \quad x^2y^{n-2}, \quad xy^{n-1}, \quad y^n.$$

This pattern shows that the sum of the exponents on x and y in each term is n. For example, in the third term above, the variable is $x^{n-2}y^2$, and the sum of the exponents, $n - 2 + 2$, is n.

Now let us try to find a pattern for the *coefficients* in the terms of the expansions shown above. In the product

$$(x + y)^5 = (x + y)(x + y)(x + y)(x + y)(x + y), \qquad (*)$$

the variable x occurs 5 times, once in each factor. To get the first term of the expansion, form the product of these 5 x's to get x^5. The product x^5 can occur in just one way, by taking an x from each factor in (*), so that the coefficient of x^5 is 1. We can get the term with x^4y in more than one way. For example, the x's could come from the first 4 factors and the y from the last factor, or the x's might be taken from the last 4 factors and the y from the first, and so on. Since there are 5 factors of $x + y$ in (*), from which exactly 4 x's must be selected for the term x^4y, there are

$\binom{5}{4} = 5$ of the x^4y terms. Therefore, the term x^4y has coefficient 5. In this manner, combinations can be used to find the coefficients for each term of the expansion:

$$(x + y)^5 = x^5 + \binom{5}{4}x^4y + \binom{5}{3}x^3y^2 + \binom{5}{2}x^2y^3 + \binom{5}{1}xy^4 + y^5.$$

The coefficient 1 of the first and last terms could be written $\binom{5}{5}$ or $\binom{5}{0}$ to complete the pattern.

Generalizing from this special case, the coefficient for any term of $(x + y)^n$ in which the variable is $x^{n-r}y^r$ is $\binom{n}{n-r}$. The **binomial theorem** gives the general binomial expansion.

Binomial Theorem

For any positive integer n,

$$(x + y)^n = \binom{n}{n}x^n + \binom{n}{n-1}x^{n-1}y + \binom{n}{n-2}x^{n-2}y^2$$
$$+ \binom{n}{n-3}x^{n-3}y^3 + \cdots + \binom{n}{1}xy^{n-1} + \binom{n}{0}y^n.$$

A proof of the binomial theorem requires the method of mathematical induction. Details are given in most college algebra texts.

EXAMPLE 1

Write out the binomial expansion of $(a + b)^7$.

Use the binomial theorem.

$$(a + b)^7 = a^7 + \binom{7}{6}a^6b + \binom{7}{5}a^5b^2 + \binom{7}{4}a^4b^3 + \binom{7}{3}a^3b^4$$
$$+ \binom{7}{2}a^2b^5 + \binom{7}{1}ab^6 + b^7$$
$$= a^7 + 7a^6b + 21a^5b^2 + 35a^4b^3 + 35a^3b^4$$
$$+ 21a^2b^5 + 7ab^6 + b^7 \quad \blacksquare$$

EXAMPLE 2

Expand $\left(a - \dfrac{b}{2} \right)^4$

Use the binomial theorem to write

$$\left(a - \frac{b}{2} \right)^4 = \left[a + \left(-\frac{b}{2} \right) \right]^4$$
$$= a^4 + \binom{4}{3}a^3\left(-\frac{b}{2} \right) + \binom{4}{2}a^2\left(-\frac{b}{2} \right)^2 + \binom{4}{1}a\left(-\frac{b}{2} \right)^3 + \left(-\frac{b}{2} \right)^4$$
$$= a^4 + 4a^3\left(-\frac{b}{2} \right) + 6a^2\left(\frac{b^2}{4} \right) + 4a\left(-\frac{b^3}{8} \right) + \frac{b^4}{16}$$
$$= a^4 - 2a^3b + \frac{3}{2}a^2b^2 - \frac{1}{2}ab^3 + \frac{1}{16}b^4. \quad \blacksquare$$

Pascal's Triangle   Another method for finding the coefficients of the terms in a binomial expansion is by ***Pascal's triangle,*** in Figure 16. The nth row in the triangle gives the coefficients for the expansion of $(x + y)^n$. To see this, compare the numbers in the rows shown below with the coefficients of the expansions given at the beginning of this section. Each number in the triangle is found by adding the two numbers directly above it. Two illustrations of this are shown in color on the triangle below. A disadvantage of this method of finding coefficients is that the entire triangle must be produced down to the row which gives the desired coefficients.

$$
\begin{array}{ccccccccccc}
 & & & & & 1 & & & & & \\
 & & & & 1 & & 1 & & & & \\
 & & & 1 & & 2 & & 1 & & & \\
 & & 1 & & 3 & & 3 & & 1 & & \\
 & 1 & & 4 & & 6 & & 4 & & 1 & \\
1 & & 5 & & 10 & & 10 & & 5 & & 1 \\
\end{array}
$$

FIGURE 16

The binomial theorem can be used to prove the following result, used in Section 5.1.

A set of n distinct elements has 2^n subsets.

We will illustrate the proof for $n = 6$. Subsets of a set of 6 elements can be chosen as follows: there are $\binom{6}{6}$ subsets with 6 elements, $\binom{6}{5}$ subsets with 5 elements, $\binom{6}{4}$ subsets with 4 elements and so on. Altogether there are

$$\binom{6}{6} + \binom{6}{5} + \binom{6}{4} + \binom{6}{3} + \binom{6}{2} + \binom{6}{1} + \binom{6}{0}$$

subsets. By the binomial theorem,

$$(x + y)^6 = \binom{6}{6}x^6 + \binom{6}{5}x^5y + \binom{6}{4}x^4y^2 + \binom{6}{3}x^3y^3 + \binom{6}{2}x^2y^4$$
$$+ \binom{6}{1}xy^5 + \binom{6}{0}y^6.$$

If $x = 1$ and $y = 1$,

$$(1 + 1)^6 = \binom{6}{6} \cdot 1^6 + \binom{6}{5} \cdot 1^5 \cdot 1 + \binom{6}{4} \cdot 1^4 \cdot 1^2 + \binom{6}{3} \cdot 1^3 \cdot 1^3$$
$$+ \binom{6}{2} \cdot 1^2 \cdot 1^4 + \binom{6}{1} \cdot 1 \cdot 1^5 + \binom{6}{0} \cdot 1^6$$

or $$2^6 = \binom{6}{6} + \binom{6}{5} + \binom{6}{4} + \binom{6}{3} + \binom{6}{2} + \binom{6}{1} + \binom{6}{0}.$$

Thus the total number of subsets of a set of 6 elements is $2^6 = 64$. In the general case, using the binomial theorem in the same way,

$$2^n = \binom{n}{n} + \binom{n}{n-1} + \binom{n}{n-2} + \cdots + \binom{n}{0},$$

so the total number of subsets is 2^n.

EXAMPLE 3	The Yummy Yogurt Shoppe offers either chocolate or vanilla yogurt with a choice of 3 fruit toppings, chocolate topping, and chopped nuts. How many different servings are possible with one flavor of yogurt and any combination of toppings?

Use the multiplication principle first. There are really 2 basic choices—a flavor of yogurt and a combination of toppings. A flavor can be selected in 2 ways. The 4 toppings plus nuts form a set of 5 elements. The number of different subsets which can be selected from a set of 5 elements is 2^5, making the number of different servings

$$2 \cdot 2^5 = 2^6 = 64. \quad \blacksquare$$

5.5 EXERCISES

Write out the binomial expansion and simplify the terms in Exercises 1–6.

1. $(m + n)^4$

2. $(p - q)^5$

3. $(3x - 2y)^6$

4. $(2x + t^3)^4$

5. $\left(\dfrac{m}{2} - 3n\right)^5$

6. $\left(2p + \dfrac{q}{3}\right)^3$

In Exercises 7–10, write out the first four terms of the binomial expansion and simplify.

7. $(p + q)^{10}$

8. $(r + 5)^9$

9. $(a + 2b)^{15}$

10. $(3c + d)^{12}$

11. How many different subsets can be chosen from a set of ten elements?

12. How many different subsets can be chosen from a set of eight elements?

13. How many different pizzas can be chosen if you can have cheese, beef, sausage, pepper, tomatoes, and onion?

14. How many different vanilla sundaes can be chosen if the available trimmings are chocolate, strawberry, apricot, pineapple, peanuts, walnuts, and pecan crunch?

15. How many different school programs can be selected from 20 course offerings if at least two courses and no more than six courses can be selected? (Assume no courses overlap.)

16. How many different committees can be selected from a group of 16 people if the committee must have between 2 and 5 people (inclusive)?

17. A buffet offers 4 kinds of salad to any of which can be added sliced beets, bean sprouts, chopped egg, and sliced mushrooms. How many different salads are possible?

18. The buffet in Exercise 17 offers 3 meat and 2 fish entrees. How many different entree combinations are possible?

KEY WORDS

set
element (member)
set-builder notation
universal set
subset
Venn diagram
empty set
tree diagram
complement
intersection

disjoint sets
union
set operations
multiplication principle
factorial
permutations
combinations
expansion
binomial theorem

Chapter 5   REVIEW EXERCISES

Write *true* or *false* for Exercises 1–10.

1. $9 \in \{8, 4, -3, -9, 6\}$

2. $4 \notin \{3, 9, 7\}$

3. $2 \notin \{0, 1, 2, 3, 4\}$

4. $0 \in \{0, 1, 2, 3, 4\}$

5. $\{3, 4, 5\} \subset \{2, 3, 4, 5, 6\}$

6. $\{1, 2, 5, 8\} \subset \{1, 2, 5, 10, 11\}$

7. $\{3, 6, 9, 10\} \subset \{3, 9, 11, 13\}$

8. $\varnothing \subset \{1\}$

9. $\{2, 8\} \not\subset \{2, 4, 6, 8\}$

10. $0 \subset \varnothing$

List the elements in the sets in Exercises 11–14. Give the cardinal number of each set.

11. $\{x \mid x$ is a counting number more than 5 and less than 8$\}$

12. $\{x \mid x$ is an integer, $-3 \le x < 1\}$

13. {all counting numbers less than five}

14. {all whole numbers not greater than 2}

Let $U = \{a, b, c, d, e, f, g\}$, $K = \{c, d, f, g\}$, and $R = \{a, c, d, e, g\}$. Find the following.

15. the number of subsets of K

16. the number of subsets of R

17. K'

18. R'

19. $K \cap R$

20. $K \cup R$

21. $(K \cap R)'$

22. $(K \cup R)'$

23. $\varnothing'$

24. U'

Let $U = $ {all employees of the K.O. Brown Company}
$A = $ {employees in the accounting department}
$B = $ {employees in the sales department}
$C = $ {employees with at least 10 years in the company}
$D = $ {employees with an MBA degree}

Describe the sets of Exercises 25–30 in words.

25. $A \cap C$

26. $B \cap D$

27. $A \cup D$

28. $A' \cap D$

29. $B' \cap C'$

30. $(B \cup C)'$

Draw Venn diagrams for Exercises 31–34.

31. $A \cup B'$

32. $A' \cap B$

33. $(A \cap B) \cup C$

34. $(A \cup B)' \cap C$

A telephone survey of television viewers revealed the following information. Use this information for Exercises 35–38.

20 watch situation comedies
19 watch game shows
27 watch movies
5 watch both situation comedies and game shows
8 watch both game shows and movies
10 watch both situation comedies and movies
3 watch all three
6 watch none of these

35. How many viewers were interviewed?

36. How many viewers watch comedies and movies but not game shows?

37. How many viewers watch only movies?

38. How many viewers watch comedies and game shows but not movies?

39. In how many ways can 6 business tycoons line up their golf carts at the country club?

40. In how many ways can a sample of 3 oranges be taken from a bag of a dozen oranges?

41. In how many ways can a selection of 2 pictures from a group of 5 different pictures be arranged in a row on a wall?

42. In how many ways can the pictures of Exercise 41 be arranged if a certain one must be first?

43. In a Chinese restaurant the menu lists 8 items in column A and 6 items in column B. To order a dinner, the diner is told to select 3 items from column A and 2 from column B. How many dinners are possible?

44. A spokesperson is to be selected from each of 3 departments in a small college. If there are 7 people in the first department, 5 in the second department, and 4 in the third department, how many different groups of 3 representatives are possible?

45. Write out the binomial expansion of $(2m + n)^5$.

46. Write out the first 3 terms of the binomial expansion of $(a + b)^{16}$.

47. Write out the first 4 terms of the binomial expansion of $(x - y/2)^{20}$.

48. How many different sums can be formed from combinations of two or more of the numbers 2, 5, 10, and 13?

49. How many different collections can be formed from a set of 8 old coins, if each collection must contain at least 2 coins?

50. How many sets of three or more books can be formed from a collection of six books?

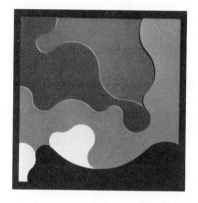

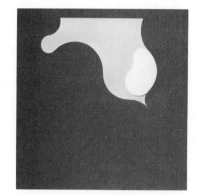

PROBABILITY

Karl Gerstner. From the series *AlgoRhythm 3*, 1973. Roche AG, Basel.

If you go to a supermarket and buy five pounds of peaches at 54¢ per pound, you can easily find the *exact* price of your purchase: $2.70. Such a purchase is **deterministic:** the result can be found *exactly*.

On the other hand, the produce manager of the market is faced with the problem of ordering peaches. The manager may have a good estimate of the number of pounds of peaches that will be sold during the day, but there is no way to know exactly. The number of items that customers will purchase during a day is **random:** the number needed cannot be predicted exactly.

A great many problems that come up in applications of mathematics are random phenomena—those for which exact prediction is impossible. The best that can be done is to construct a mathematical model that gives the *probability* of certain events. The basics of probability are discussed in this chapter, with applications of probability discussed in succeeding chapters.

6.1   Sample Spaces

In probability, each repetition of an experiment is called a **trial.** The possible results of each trial are **outcomes.** An example of a probability experiment is the tossing of a coin. Each trial of the experiment (each toss) has two possible outcomes, heads and tails, abbreviated h and t, respectively. If the two outcomes, h and t, are equally likely to occur, then the coin is not "loaded" to favor one side over the other. Such a coin is called **fair.** For a coin that is not loaded, this "equally likely" assumption is made for each trial.

Since *two* equally likely outcomes are possible, h and t, and just *one* of them is heads, we would expect that a coin tossed many, many times would come up heads approximately 1/2 of the time. We also would expect that the more times the coin was tossed, the closer the occurrence of heads should be to 1/2.

Suppose an experiment could be repeated again and again under unchanging conditions. Suppose the experiment is repeated n times, and that a certain outcome happens m times. The ratio m/n is called the **relative frequency** of the outcome after n trials.

If this ratio m/n approaches closer and closer to some fixed number p as n gets larger and larger, then p is called the **probability** of the outcome. If p exists, then

$$p \approx \frac{m}{n}$$

as n gets larger and larger.

This approach to probability is consistent with most people's intuitive feeling as to the meaning of probability—a way of measuring the likelihood of occurrence of a certain outcome. For example, since 1/4 of the cards in an ordinary deck are diamonds, we would assume that if we drew a card from a well-shuffled deck, kept track of whether it was a diamond or not, and then replaced the card in the deck, after a large number of repetitions of the experiment about 1/4 of the cards drawn would be diamonds.

This definition of probability, on the other hand, has the disadvantage of not being precise, since it uses phrases such as "approaches closer and closer" and "gets larger and larger." In the first few sections of this chapter a more precise meaning is given to the terms associated with probability.

The probability of heads on a single toss of a fair coin is 1/2. This is written

$$P(h) = \frac{1}{2}.$$

Also, $P(t) = 1/2$.

EXAMPLE 1

Suppose we spin the spinner of Figure 1.

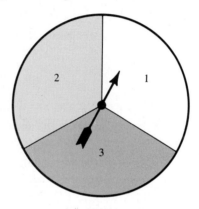

FIGURE 1

(a) Find the probability that it will point to 1.

A natural assumption is that if this spinner were spun many, many times, it would point to 1 about 1/3 of the time, so that

$$P(1) = \frac{1}{3}.$$

(b) Find the probability that it will point to 2.

Since 2 is one of three possible outcomes, $P(2) = 1/3$. ▪

An ordinary die is a cube whose six faces show the numbers 1, 2, 3, 4, 5, and 6. If the die is not "loaded" to favor certain faces over others, then any one of the six faces is equally likely to come up when the die is rolled.

EXAMPLE 2

(a) If a single fair die is rolled, find the probability of rolling the number 4.

Since one out of six faces shows a 4, $P(4) = 1/6$.

(b) Using the same die, find the probability of rolling the number 6.

Since one out of six faces shows a 6, $P(6) = 1/6$. ▪

Sample Space   Sometimes we are interested in a result that is satisfied by more than one of the possible outcomes. To find the probability that the spinner in Example 1 will point to an odd number, notice that two of the three possible outcomes are odd numbers, 1 and 3, with

$$P(\text{odd}) = \frac{2}{3}.$$

The set of all possible outcomes for an experiment is the **sample space** for the experiment. A sample space for the experiment of tossing a coin is made up of the two outcomes, heads (h) and tails (t). If S represents this sample space, then

$$S = \{h, t\}.$$

In the same way, the sample space for tossing a single fair die is

$$\{1, 2, 3, 4, 5, 6\}.$$

EXAMPLE 3

(a) For the purposes of a certain public opinion poll, people are classified as young, middle-aged, or older, and as male or female. The sample space for this poll would be a set of ordered pairs:

{(young, male), (young, female), (middle-aged, male), (middle-aged, female), (older, male), (older, female)}.

(b) A firm can run its assembly line at a low, medium, or high rate. With each speed, the firm may find 1%, 2%, or 3% of the items from the line defective. Placing the line speed first in an ordered pair, and the rate of defectives second, gives the sample space

{(low, 1%), (low, 2%), (low, 3%), (medium, 1%), (medium, 2%), (medium, 3%), (high, 1%), (high, 2%), (high, 3%)}.

(c) A manufacturer tests automobile tires by running a tire until it fails or until tread depth reaches a certain unsafe level. The number of miles that the tire lasts, m, is recorded. At least in theory, m can be any nonnegative real number, so that the sample space is

$$\{m \mid m \geq 0\}.$$

However, for a particular type of tire, there would be practical limits on m, so that the sample space might then be

$$\{m \mid 0 \leq m \leq 50{,}000\}. \quad \blacksquare$$

An **event** is a subset of a sample space. If the sample space for tossing a coin is $S = \{h, t\}$, then one event is $E = \{h\}$, which represents the outcome "heads." For the sample space of tossing a single fair die, $\{1, 2, 3, 4, 5, 6\}$, one event is $\{2, 4, 6\}$, or "the number showing on top is even."

EXAMPLE 4

An experiment consists of studying all possible families having exactly three children. Let *b* represent "boy" and *g* represent "girl."

(a)   Write a sample space for the experiment.

A family can have three boys, written *bbb*, three girls, *ggg*, or various combinations, such as *bgg*. The sample space is made up of all such outcomes (there are eight).

$$S = \{bbb,\ bbg,\ bgb,\ gbb,\ bgg,\ gbg,\ ggb,\ ggg\}.$$

(b)   Write event *H*, "the family has exactly two girls."

Families can have exactly two girls with either *bgg*, *gbg*, or *ggb*, so that event *H* is

$$H = \{bgg,\ gbg,\ ggb\}.$$

(c)   Write the event *J*, "the family has three girls."

Only *ggg* satisfies this condition, so

$$J = \{ggg\}. \quad \blacksquare$$

In Example 4(c), event *J* had only one possible outcome, *ggg*. Such an event, with only one possible outcome, is a **simple event.** If event *E* equals the sample space *S*, then *E* is a **certain event.** If event $E = \varnothing$, then *E* is an **impossible event.**

EXAMPLE 5

Suppose a die is rolled. As we have seen, the sample space is $\{1, 2, 3, 4, 5, 6\}$.

(a)   The event "the die has a four showing" is a simple event, $\{4\}$. The event has only one possible outcome.

(b)   The event "the number showing is less than ten" equals the sample space, $S = \{1, 2, 3, 4, 5, 6\}$. This event is a certain event; if a die is rolled the number showing (either 1, 2, 3, 4, 5, or 6), must be less than ten.

(c)   The event "the die has 7 showing" is the empty set, $\varnothing$; this event is impossible.   ▪

Events are sets, so the union, intersection, and complement of events can be formed.

EXAMPLE 6

A die is tossed; let *E* be the event "the number showing is more than 3", and let *F* be the event "the number showing is even." Then

$$E = \{4, 5, 6\} \quad \text{and} \quad F = \{2, 4, 6\}.$$

(a) $E \cap F$ is the event "the number showing is more than 3 *and* is even", the outcomes common to *both E* and *F*.

$$E \cap F = \{4, 6\}.$$

(b) $E \cup F$ is the event "the number showing is more than 3 *or* is even", the outcomes of E or F, or both.

$$E \cup F = \{2, 4, 5, 6\}.$$

(c) Event E' is the event "the number showing is *not* more than 3"; the elements
of the sample space that are *not* in E. (Event E' is the *complement* of
event E.)

$$E' = \{1, 2, 3\}.$$

The sketches of Figure 2 show the events $E \cap F$, $E \cup F$, and E'. ▪

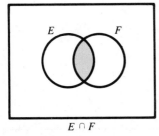
$E \cap F$

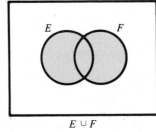
$E \cup F$

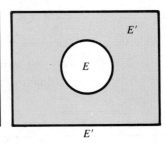
E'

FIGURE 2

Two events that cannot both occur at the same time, such as both a head and a
tail on the same toss of a coin, are **mutually exclusive events.** The events A and B
are mutually exclusive events if $A \cap B = \emptyset$.

EXAMPLE 7

Let $S = \{1, 2, 3, 4, 5, 6\}$, the sample space for tossing a die. Let $E = \{4, 5, 6\}$,
and let $G = \{1, 2\}$. Then E and G are mutually exclusive events since they have
no outcomes in common: $E \cap G = \emptyset$. See Figure 3. ▪

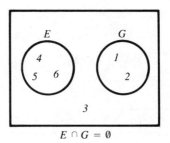
$E \cap G = \emptyset$

FIGURE 3

In summary:

Events

> Let E and F be events for a sample space S. Then
>
> $E \cap F$ occurs when both E and F occur;
> $E \cup F$ occurs when either E or F or both occur;
> E' occurs when E does not occur;
> E and F are mutually exclusive if $E \cap F = \varnothing$.

Remember that a simple event has only one possible outcome.

6.1 EXERCISES

Write sample spaces for the experiments in Exercises 1–12. (The sample spaces in Exercises 11–12 are infinite.)

1. Choose a month of the year.

2. Pick a day in April.

3. Ask a student how many points she earned on a recent 80-point test.

4. Ask a person how many hours (to the nearest hour) he watched television yesterday.

5. The management of an oil company must decide whether to go ahead with a new oil shale plant, or cancel it.

6. A record is kept for three days about whether a particular stock goes up or down.

7. The length of life of a light bulb is measured to the nearest hour; the bulbs never last more than 5000 hours.

8. Toss a coin and roll a die.

9. Toss a coin four times.

10. A box contains five balls, numbered 1, 2, 3, 4, and 5. A ball is drawn at random, the number on it recorded, and the ball replaced. After shaking the box, a second ball is drawn, and its number is recorded.

11. A coin is tossed until a head appears.

12. A die is rolled, but only "odd" (1, 3, 5) or "even" (2, 4, 6) is recorded. Roll the die until odd appears.

13. A die is tossed twice, with the tosses recorded as ordered pairs. Write the
    (a) sample space;
    (b) event F, the first die is 3;
    (c) event G, the sum of the dice is 8;
    (d) event H, the sum of the dice is 13.

14. One urn contains four balls, labeled 1, 2, 3, and 4. A second urn contains five balls, labeled 1, 2, 3, 4, and 5. An experiment consists of taking one ball from the first urn, and then taking a ball from the second urn. Find the

(a) sample space;

(b) event E, the first ball is even;

(c) event F, the second ball is even;

(d) event G, the sum of the numbers on the two balls is 5;

(e) event H, the sum of the numbers on the two balls is 1.

15. A coin is tossed until two heads appear, or until the coin is tossed five times, whichever comes first. Write the

(a) sample space;

(b) event E, the coin is tossed exactly two times;

(c) event F, the coin is tossed exactly three times;

(d) event G, the coin is tossed exactly five times, without getting two heads.

16. A committee of two people is selected from five executives, Abbot, Babbit, Coats, Dickson, and Ellsberg. Write the

(a) sample space;

(b) event E, Coats is on the committee;

(c) event F, Dickson and Ellsberg are not both on the committee;

(d) event G, both Abbot and Coats are on the committee.

17. The management of a firm wishes to check on the opinions of its assembly line workers. To do this, the workers are first divided into various categories. Define events E, F, and G as follows.

E: worker is female

F: worker has worked less than five years

G: worker contributes to a voluntary retirement plan

Describe each of the following events in words.

(a) E' (b) F' (c) $E \cap F$

(d) $F \cup G$ (e) $E \cup G'$ (f) $F' \cap G'$

18. For a medical experiment, people are classified as to whether they smoke, have a family history of heart disease, and are overweight. Define events E, F, and G as follows.

E: person smokes

F: person has a family history of heart disease

G: person is overweight

Describe each of the following events in words.

(a) G' (b) $E \cup F$ (c) $F \cap G$

(d) $E' \cap F$ (e) $E \cup G'$ (f) $F' \cup G'$

Decide if the events in Exercises 19–24 are mutually exclusive.

19. Owning a car and owning a truck.

20. Wearing glasses and wearing sandals.

21. Being married and being over 30 years old.

22. Being a teen-ager and being over 30 years old.

23. Rolling a die once and getting a 4 and an odd number.

24. A person being both male and a postal worker.

25. If E is an event, must E and E' be mutually exclusive?

26. Let E and F be mutually exclusive events. Let F and G be mutually exclusive events. Must E and G be mutually exclusive events?

27. Suppose E and F are mutually exclusive events. Must E' and F' be mutually exclusive events?

28. Suppose E and F are mutually exclusive events. Must E and $(E \cup F)'$ be mutually exclusive events?

29. A person is taking accounting and business law. Let E be the event that the student passes accounting, and let F be the event that the student passes business law. Write each of the following using E, F, $\cup$, $\cap$, and $'$, as needed. The student

(a) fails accounting; (b) passes both;

(c) fails both; (d) passes accounting but not business law;

(e) passes exactly one course; (f) passes at least one course.

30. Let E and F be events. Write the following, using $\cap$, $\cup$, or $'$, as needed.

(a) E does not happen (b) neither happens (c) both happen

(d) E happens, but not F (e) one or the other happens, but not both

31. Let $S = \{r, s, t\}$. Write all events associated with S.

32. Let $S = \{1, 2, 3, 4, \ldots, n\}$, where n is a positive integer. How many different events could be obtained from S?

6.2 Basics of Probability

Given a sample space S, we now need to assign to each event that can be obtained from S a number, called the **probability of the event.** This number will indicate the relative likelihood of the various events. In the remainder of this chapter, attention is restricted to sample spaces with a *finite* number of elements.

For events that are *equally likely*, the probability of the event can be found from the following **basic probability principle:**

Basic Probability Principle

Let a sample space S have n possible equally likely outcomes. Let event E contain m of these outcomes, all distinct. Then the **probability** that event E occurs, written $P(E)$, is

$$P(E) = \frac{m}{n}.$$

This same result can also be given in terms of the cardinal number of a set. (Recall from Chapter 5 that $n(E)$ represents the number of elements in a finite set E.) With the same assumptions given above,

$$P(E) = \frac{n(E)}{n(S)}.$$

EXAMPLE 1

Suppose a single fair die is rolled. The sample space is $S = \{1, 2, 3, 4, 5, 6\}$. Set S contains 6 outcomes, all of which are equally likely. (This makes $n = 6$ in the box above.) Find the probability of the following outcomes.

(a) $E = \{1, 2\}$.

Event E contains two elements, so

$$P(E) = \frac{2}{6} = \frac{1}{3}.$$

By this result, a 1 or 2 will show up on a single die about 1/3 of the time.

(b) An even number is rolled.

Let event $F = \{2, 4, 6\}$ be the event "an even number is rolled." Event F contains three elements, so

$$P(F) = \frac{3}{6} = \frac{1}{2}.$$

(c) The die shows a 7.

A die can never show 7. If G is this event, then $G = \varnothing$, and

$$P(G) = \frac{0}{6} = 0.$$

This event is impossible. ▪

EXAMPLE 2

If a single playing card is drawn at random from an ordinary 52-card bridge deck, find the probability of each of the following events.

(a) An ace is drawn.

There are four aces in the deck, out of 52 cards, so

$$P(\text{ace}) = \frac{4}{52} = \frac{1}{13}.$$

(b) A face card is drawn.

Since there are 12 face cards,

$$P(\text{face card}) = \frac{12}{52} = \frac{3}{13}.$$

(c) A spade is drawn.

The deck contains 13 spades, so

$$P(\text{spade}) = \frac{13}{52} = \frac{1}{4}.$$

(d) A spade or a heart is drawn.

Besides the 13 spades, the deck contains 13 hearts, so

$$P(\text{spade or heart}) = \frac{26}{52} = \frac{1}{2}. \quad ▪$$

EXAMPLE 3

The manager of a department store has decided to make a study on the size of purchases made by people coming into the store. To begin, he chooses a day that seems fairly typical and gathers the following data. (Purchases have been rounded to the nearest dollar, with sales tax ignored.)

Amount of Purchase	Number of Customers
$0	158
$1–$5	94
$6–$9	203
$10–$19	126
$20–$49	47
$50–$99	38
$100 and over	53

[handwritten: $ 10–19 = 126/179]

[handwritten total: 719]

First, the manager might add the numbers of customers to find that 719 people came into the store that day. Of these 719 people, $126/179 \approx .175$ made a purchase of at least $10 but no more than $19. Also, $53/719 \approx .074$ of the customers spent $100 or more. Thus, the probability (on this given day) that a customer entering the store will spend from $10 to $19 is .175, and the probability that the customer will spend $100 or more is .074. Probabilities for the various purchase amounts can be assigned in the same way, giving the results of the following table.

Size of Purchase	Probability
$0	.220
$1–$5	.131
$6–$9	.282
$10–$19	.175
$20–$49	.065
$50–$99	.053
$100 and over	.074
Total	1.000

From the table, .282 of the customers spend from $6 to $9, inclusive—over a quarter of the customers. Since this price range attracts so many customers, perhaps the store's advertising should emphasize items in, or near, this price range.

The manager should use this table of probabilities to help in predicting the results on other days only if the manager is reasonably sure that the day when the measurements were made is fairly typical of the other days the store is open—for example, on the last few days before Christmas the probabilities might be quite different. ▨

Probability Distributions In Example 3 the outcomes were various purchase amounts, and a probability was assigned to each outcome. By this process, a **probability distribution** can be set up; that is, to each possible outcome of an experiment, a number, called the *probability* of that outcome, is assigned.

As we have seen, one way to think of these probabilities is as relative frequencies; that is, for a large number of sales days of the type measured in the table, approximately 13% of all purchases would be in the $1–$5 range, approximately 28% in the $6–$9 range, and so on.

EXAMPLE 4

Set up a probability distribution for the number of girls in a family with three children.

Start by writing the sample space, which shows the possible number of boys and girls in a family of three children, $S = \{bbb, bbg, bgb, gbb, bgg, gbg, ggb, ggg\}$. Let event E_0 be "the family has no girls;" from the sample space, $E_0 = \{bbb\}$.

In a similar way, let $E_1 = \{bbg, bgb, gbb\}$, $E_2 = \{bgg, gbg, ggb\}$, and $E_3 = \{ggg\}$. Sample space S has eight possible outcomes, and event E_1, for example, has three elements, giving $P(E_1) = 3/8$. Doing the same thing for the other events gives the following probability distribution.

Number of Girls	Probability
0	1/8
1	3/8
2	3/8
3	1/8
Total	1

(Here we assume that the probability of having a girl baby and a boy baby is equal. This assumption is not quite exact in actual fact, but the correct fraction is not far from 1/2.) ▪

The probability distributions that were set up above suggest the following properties of probability. (Recall that a simple event contains only one possible outcome.)

Properties of Probability

Let $S = \{s_1, s_2, s_3, \ldots, s_n\}$ be the sample space obtained from the union of the n distinct simple events $\{s_1\}, \{s_2\}, \{s_3\}, \ldots, \{s_n\}$ with associated probabilities $p_1, p_2, p_3, \ldots, p_n$. Then

1. $0 \le p_1 \le 1, 0 \le p_2 \le 1, \cdots, 0 \le p_n \le 1$
   (All probabilities are between 0 and 1, inclusive.);
2. $p_1 + p_2 + p_3 + \cdots + p_n = 1$;
   (The sum of all probabilities for a sample space is 1.);
3. $P(S) = 1$;
4. $P(\emptyset) = 0$.

The Addition Principle   Suppose event E is the union of several simple events, say

$$E = \{s_1,\ s_2,\ s_3\} = \{s_1\} \cup \{s_2\} \cup \{s_3\}.$$

To find $P(E)$, the probability of event E, add the probabilities for each of the simple events making up E. For $E = \{s_1,\ s_2,\ s_3\}$,

$$P(E) = P(\{s_1\}) + P(\{s_2\}) + P(\{s_3\}).$$

The generalization of this result is called the *addition principle:*

Addition Principle

Suppose $E = \{s_1,\ s_2,\ s_3,\ \cdots,\ s_m\}$, where $\{s_1\},\ \{s_2\},\ \{s_3\},\ \cdots,\ \{s_m\}$ are distinct simple events. Then

$$P(E) = P(\{s_1\}) + P(\{s_2\}) + P(\{s_3\}) + \cdots + P(\{s_m\}).$$

The addition rule *does not necessarily apply* to the addition of probabilities of events that are not simple. For example, the sum of the probability of getting at least 4 on a single roll of a die, and the probability of getting an even number on a single roll is *not* equal to the probability of getting at least 4 or an even number on a single roll. That is, $P(\text{at least } 4) = P(4, 5,\text{ or } 6) = 1/2$, $P(\text{even number}) = P(2, 4,\text{ or } 6) = 1/2$, and $P(\text{at least } 4\text{ or even}) = P(2, 4, 5,\text{ or } 6) = 2/3$, with $P(\text{at least } 4) + P(\text{even number}) \neq P(\text{at least } 4\text{ or even})$.

EXAMPLE 5

Refer to Example 3 and find the probability that a customer spends at least \$6 but less than \$50.

This event is the union of three simple events, spending from \$6 to \$9, spending from \$10 to \$19, or spending from \$20-\$49. The probability of spending at least \$6 but less than \$50 can thus be found by the addition principle.

$P(\text{spending at least \$6 but less than \$50})$

$$= P(\text{spending \$6-\$9}) + P(\text{spending \$10-\$19}) + P(\text{spending \$20-\$49})$$

$$= .282 + .175 + .065 = .522. \quad \blacksquare$$

Let us now extend the addition rule to events that are not necessarily simple events, but that are mutually exclusive events. Suppose that E and F are mutually exclusive events, with $E = \{s_1,\ s_2,\ \cdots,\ s_n\}$, and $F = \{t_1,\ t_2,\ \cdots,\ t_m\}$, where $\{s_1\},\ \{s_2\},\ \cdots,\ \{s_n\}$ and $\{t_1\},\ \{t_2\},\ \cdots,\ \{t_m\}$ are simple events. Then

$$P(E) + P(F) = P(\{s_1,\ s_2,\ \cdots,\ s_n\}) + P(\{t_1,\ t_2,\ \cdots,\ t_m\})$$

$$= P(\{s_1\}) + P(\{s_2\}) + \cdots + P(\{s_n\})$$
$$+ P(\{t_1\}) + P(\{t_2\}) + \cdots + P(\{t_m\})$$

$$= P(\{s_1,\ s_2,\ \cdots,\ s_n,\ t_1,\ t_2,\ \cdots,\ t_m\})$$

$$= P(E \cup F).$$

Addition for Mutually Exclusive Events

> For *mutually exclusive* events E and F,
> $$P(E \cup F) = P(E) + P(F).$$

EXAMPLE 6

Use the probability distribution of Example 4 to find the probability that a family with three children has at least two girls.

Event E, "the family has at least two girls," is the union of two mutually exclusive events, "the family has two girls," and "the family has three girls." By the result in the box,

$$P(E) = P(\text{at least two girls}) = P(2 \text{ girls}) + P(3 \text{ girls})$$

$$= \frac{3}{8} + \frac{1}{8} = \frac{1}{2}. \quad \blacksquare$$

Recall that the set of all outcomes in a sample space that do not belong to an event E is called the *complement* of E, written E'. For example, in the experiment of drawing a single card from a well-shuffled deck of 52 cards, let E be the event "the card is an ace." Then E' is the event "the card is not an ace." Using this definition of E', for any event E from a sample space S,

$$E \cup E' = S \quad \text{and} \quad E \cap E' = \varnothing.$$

Since $E \cap E' = \varnothing$, events E and E' are mutually exclusive, so that

$$P(E \cup E') = P(E) + P(E').$$

However, $E \cup E' = S$, the sample space, and $P(S) = 1$. Thus

$$P(E \cup E') = P(E) + P(E') = 1,$$

giving two alternate and useful results:

Complements

> $$P(E) = 1 - P(E') \quad \text{and} \quad P(E') = 1 - P(E).$$

EXAMPLE 7

In a particular experiment, $P(E) = 2/7$. Find $P(E')$.

$$P(E') = 1 - P(E) = 1 - \frac{2}{7} = \frac{5}{7} \quad \blacksquare$$

The next example shows that it is sometimes easier to find $P(E)$ by first finding $P(E')$, and then finding $P(E) = 1 - P(E')$.

EXAMPLE 8

In Example 3 above, find the probability that a customer spends less than $100.

Let E be the event "a customer spends less than $100". From the table of Example 3,

$$P(E) = .220 + .131 + .282 + .175 + .065 + .053 = .926.$$

We can also find $P(E)$ by noting that if E is the event "a customer spends less than $100," then E' is the event "a customer spends $100 and over." From the table, $P(E') = .074$, and

$$P(E) = 1 - P(E') = 1 - .074 = .926.$$

Here $P(E)$ is easier to calculate as $1 - P(E')$. ◾

Odds Sometimes probability statements are given in terms of *odds*, a comparison of $P(E)$ with $P(E')$:

Odds

> The **odds in favor** of an event E is defined as the ratio of $P(E)$ to $P(E')$, or
>
> $$\frac{P(E)}{P(E')}.$$

EXAMPLE 9

Suppose the weather forecaster says that the probability of rain tomorrow is 1/3. Find the odds in favor of rain tomorrow.

Let E be the event "rain tomorrow." Then E' is the event "no rain tomorrow." Since $P(E) = 1/3$, we have $P(E') = 2/3$. By the definition of odds,

$$\text{odds in favor of rain} = \frac{1/3}{2/3} = \frac{1}{2}, \qquad \text{written} \quad 1 \text{ to } 2, \quad \text{or} \quad 1:2.$$

On the other hand, the odds that it will *not* rain are

$$\frac{2/3}{1/3} = \frac{2}{1}, \qquad \text{written} \quad 2 \text{ to } 1, \quad \text{or} \quad 2:1. \quad ◾$$

If we know that the odds in favor of an event are, say, 3 to 5, then the probability of the event is 3/8, while the probability of the complement of the event is 5/8. (Odds of 3 to 5 indicate 3 outcomes in favor of the event out of a total of 8 outcomes.) In general, if the odds favoring event E are m to n, then

$$P(E) = \frac{m}{m + n} \qquad \text{and} \qquad P(E') = \frac{n}{m + n}.$$

EXAMPLE 10

The odds that a particular bid will be the low bid are 4 to 5. Find the probability that the bid will be the low bid.

Odds of 4 to 5 show 4 favorable chances out of $4 + 5 = 9$ chances altogether:

$$P(\text{bid will be low bid}) = \frac{4}{4 + 5} = \frac{4}{9}. \qquad \begin{array}{c} \text{odds for bid} \\ 4\ m \qquad 5\ n \end{array}$$

There is a 5/9 chance that the bid will *not* be the low bid. ◾

Subjective Probabilities   The formulas above let us find the probability of an event that can be repeated exactly, again and again. However, we also would like to be able to assign probabilities to many occurrences that cannot be exactly repeated. For example, we might want to give the probability of rain on the day planned for the company picnic, or the probability that the earnings of a firm will increase by 30%, or the probability that a given number of pounds of peaches will be sold on a given day (as mentioned in the introduction to this chapter). The probabilities for these events are known as **subjective probabilities,** and must be assigned, if at all, on the basis of personal judgment. A sales manager may use past experience to assign a probability to the success of the current July sale, but since this year's sale can never be exactly like that of past or future Julys, it is still a subjective assignment of probability.

In many cases, no information is available and probability must be assigned on the basis of hunches or expectations. In fact, sometimes it is necessary to assign probabilities to events that will happen only once.

One difficulty with subjective probability is that different people may assign different probabilities to the same event. Nevertheless, subjective probabilities can be assigned to many occurrences where the objective approach to probability cannot be used. In a later chapter, we illustrate the use of subjective probability in more detail.

6.2 EXERCISES

A single fair die is rolled. Find the probability of the events in Exercises 1–4.

1. a 2   **2.** an odd number   **3.** a number less than 5   **4.** a number greater than 2

A card is drawn from a well-shuffled deck of 52 cards. Find the probability of drawing

5. a 9;   **6.** a black card;   **7.** a black 9;

8. a heart;   **9.** the 9 of hearts;   **10.** a face card.

A single fair die is rolled. Find the odds in favor of rolling

11. the number 5;   **12.** 3, 4, or 5;   **13.** 1, 2, 3, or 4;   **14.** some number less than 2.

List the simple events whose union forms each of the events in Exercises 15–18.

15. getting an even number on a roll of a die

16. drawing a card that is both a heart and a face card from an ordinary deck

17. a record is made of whether a company's annual profit goes up, down, or stays the same

18. a batch of 7 items was checked, and the number of defectives recorded

An experiment is conducted for which the sample space is $S = \{s_1, s_2, s_3, s_4, s_5\}$. Which of the probability distributions in Exercises 19–24 is possible for this experiment? If a distribution is not possible, tell why.

19.

Outcomes	s_1	s_2	s_3	s_4	s_5
Probability	.09	.32	.21	.25	.13

$S = 1$

20.

Outcomes	s_1	s_2	s_3	s_4	s_5
Probability	.92	.03	0	.02	.03

21.

Outcomes	s_1	s_2	s_3	s_4	s_5
Probability	$\frac{1}{3}$	$\frac{1}{4}$	$\frac{1}{6}$	$\frac{1}{8}$	$\frac{1}{10}$

$S = 0.1152777$ $\emptyset = 0$

22.

Outcomes	s_1	s_2	s_3	s_4	s_5
Probability	$\frac{1}{5}$	$\frac{1}{3}$	$\frac{1}{4}$	$\frac{1}{5}$	$\frac{1}{10}$

23.

Outcomes	s_1	s_2	s_3	s_4	s_5
Probability	.64	$-.08$	.30	.12	.02

$S = 1$

24.

Outcomes	s_1	s_2	s_3	s_4	s_5
Probability	.05	.35	.5	.2	$-.3$

The table below gives a certain golfer's probabilities of scoring in various ranges on a par-70 course.

Range	Probability
below 60	.01
60–64	.08
65–69	.15
70–74	.28
75–79	.22
80–84	.08
85–89	.06
90–94	.04
95–99	.02
100 or more	.06

$1 - .23 = .77$

$= .24$

$27.\ .28 + .22$

In a given round, find the probability that the golfer's score will be

25. 90 or higher;

26. below par of 70;

27. in the 70's;

28. in the 90's;

29. not in the 60's;

30. not in the 60's or 70's.

31. Find the odds in favor of the golfer shooting below par.

32. Find the odds against the golfer shooting in the 70s.

Fransisco has set up the following probability distribution for the number of hours it will take him to finish his homework.

Hours	1	2	3	4	5	6
Probability	.05	.10	.20	.40	.10	.15

Find the probability that his homework will take

33. fewer than 3 hours;

34. 3 hours or less;

35. more than 2 hours;

36. at least 2 hours;

37. more than 1 hour and less than 5 hours;

38. 8 hours.

A marble is drawn from a box containing 3 yellow, 4 white, and 8 blue marbles. Find the probability of drawing

39. a yellow marble;

40. a blue marble;

41. a white marble.

For this same marble experiment, find the odds in favor of drawing a

42. yellow marble;   **43.** blue marble;   **44.** white marble.

45. Find the odds of not drawing a white marble.

46. The probability that a company will make a profit this year is .74. Find the odds against the company making a profit.

47. If the odds that it will rain are 4 to 7, what is the probability of rain?

48. If the odds that a given candidate will win an election are 3 to 2, what is the probability that the candidate will lose?

The probability distribution for a given experiment having sample space $S = \{s_1, s_2, s_3, s_4, s_5, s_6\}$ is shown here.

Outcomes	s_1	s_2	s_3	s_4	s_5	s_6
Probability	.17	.03	.09	.46	.21	.04

Let $E = \{s_1, s_2, s_5\}$, and let $F = \{s_4, s_5\}$. Find each of the following probabilities.

49. $P(E)$ **50.** $P(F)$ **51.** $P(E \cap F)$ **52.** $P(E \cup F)$ **53.** $P(E' \cup F')$ **54.** $P(E' \cap F)$

Which of the following are examples of subjective probability?

55. the probability of heads on five consecutive tosses of a coin

56. the probability that a freshman entering college will graduate with a degree

57. the probability that a person is allergic to penicillin

58. the probability of drawing an ace from a standard deck of 52 cards

59. the probability that a person will get lung cancer from smoking cigarettes

60. a weather forecaster predicts a 70% chance of rain tomorrow

61. a gambler claims that on a roll of a fair die, $P(\text{even}) = 1/2$

62. a surgeon gives a patient a 90% chance of a full recovery

63. a bridge player has a 1/4 chance of being dealt a diamond

64. a forest ranger states that the probability of a short fire season this year is only 3 in 10

65. On page 134 of Roger Staubach's autobiography, *First Down, Lifetime to Go,* Staubach makes the following statement regarding his experience in Vietnam: "Odds against a direct hit are very low but when your life is in danger, you don't worry too much about the odds." Is this wording consistent with our definition of odds, for and against? How could it have been said so as to be technically correct?

One way to solve a probability problem is to repeat the experiment (or a simulation of the experiment) many times, keeping track of the results. Then the probability can be approximated using the basic definition of the probability of an event E: $P(E) = m/n$, where m favorable outcomes occur in n trials of an experiment. This is called the *Monte Carlo* method of finding probabilities. Suppose a coin is tossed five times. Use the Monte Carlo method to approximate the probabilities in Exercises 66 and 67. Then calculate the theoretical probabilities using the methods of the text and compare the results.

66. $P(4 \text{ heads})$ **67.** $P(2 \text{ heads}, 1 \text{ tail}, 2 \text{ heads})$ (in the order given)

Use the Monte Carlo method to approximate the following probabilities if four cards are drawn from 52.

68. $P(\text{any two cards and then two kings})$ **69.** $P(\text{two kings})$

EXTENDED

APPLICATION

Making a First Down

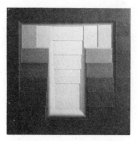

A first down is desirable in football—it guarantees four more plays by the team making it, assuming no score or turnover occurs in the plays. After getting a first down, a team can get another by advancing the ball at least ten yards. During the four plays given by a first down, a team's position will be indicated by a phrase such as "third and 4," which means that the team has already had two of its four plays, and that 4 more yards are needed to get the 10 yards necessary for another first down. An article in a management journal* offers the following results for 189 games of a recent National Football League season. "Trials" represents the number of times a team tried to make a first down, given that it was currently playing either a third or a fourth down. Here n represents the number of yards still needed for a first down.

n	Trials	Successes	Probability of making first down with n yards to go
1	543	388	
2	327	186	
3	356	146	
4	302	97	
5	336	91	

EXERCISES

1. Complete the table.

2. Why is the sum of the answers in Exercise 1 not equal to 1?

6.3 Extending the Addition Rule

We saw in the previous section that for mutually exclusive events E and F,

$$P(E \cup F) = P(E) + P(F). \tag{1}$$

This result can now be extended to *any* two events E and F.

*Reprinted by permission of Virgil Carter and Robert Machols, "Optimal Strategies on Fourth Down," *Management Science,* Vol. 24, No. 16, December 1978, copyright © 1978 The Institute of Management Sciences.

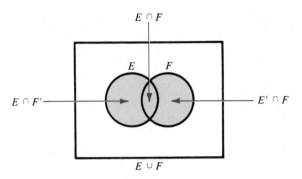

FIGURE 4

To obtain this more general result, take the region $E \cup F$ of Figure 4 and break it into three disjoint regions: that part of E not including F, $E \cap F'$; the intersection, $E \cap F$; and that part of F not including E, $E' \cap F$. By this process, $E \cup F$ becomes

$$E \cup F = (E \cap F') \cup (E \cap F) \cup (E' \cap F).$$

Since all three of the sets on the right are disjoint, use an extension of property (1) above to get

$$P(E \cup F) = P(E \cap F') + P(E \cap F) + P(E' \cap F). \tag{2}$$

As illustrated by Figure 4,

$$E = (E \cap F') \cup (E \cap F) \qquad \text{and} \qquad F = (E' \cap F) \cup (E \cap F)$$

so that, by (1) above,

$$P(E) = P(E \cap F') + P(E \cap F) \tag{3}$$

and

$$P(F) = P(E' \cap F) + P(E \cap F). \tag{4}$$

From (3),

$$P(E \cap F') = P(E) - P(E \cap F) \tag{5}$$

and from (4),

$$P(E' \cap F) = P(F) - P(E \cap F). \tag{6}$$

Substituting from equations (5) and (6) into equation (2) gives

$$P(E \cup F) = P(E) + P(F) - P(E \cap F). \tag{7}$$

This result is called the *extended addition principle*.

Extended Addition

Principle

For any two events E and F from a sample space S,
$$P(E \cup F) = P(E) + P(F) - P(E \cap F).$$

Notice the similarity of this result to the formula for the number of elements in the union of two sets, given in Chapter 5.

EXAMPLE 1

If a single card is drawn from an ordinary deck, find the probability that it will be red or a face card.

Let R and F represent the events "red" and "face card" respectively. Then

$$P(R) = \frac{26}{52}, \qquad P(F) = \frac{12}{52}, \qquad \text{and} \qquad P(R \cap F) = \frac{6}{52}.$$

(There are six red face cards in a deck.) By the extended addition principle,

$$P(R \cup F) = P(R) + P(F) - P(R \cap F)$$

$$= \frac{26}{52} + \frac{12}{52} - \frac{6}{52}$$

$$= \frac{32}{52} = \frac{8}{13}. \quad \blacksquare$$

EXAMPLE 2

Suppose two fair dice are rolled. Find each of the following probabilities.

(a) The first die shows a 2 or the sum is 6 or 7

The sample space for the throw of two dice is shown in Figure 5. The two events are labeled A and B. From the diagram,

$$P(A) = \frac{6}{36}, \qquad P(B) = \frac{11}{36}, \qquad \text{and} \qquad P(A \cap B) = \frac{2}{36}.$$

By the extended addition principle,

$$P(A \cup B) = P(A) + P(B) - P(A \cap B),$$

$$P(A \cup B) = \frac{6}{36} + \frac{11}{36} - \frac{2}{36} = \frac{15}{36} = \frac{5}{12}.$$

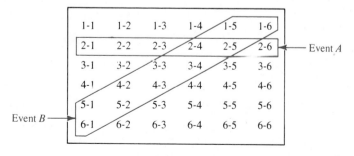

FIGURE 5

(b)   the sum is 11 or the second die is 5

P(sum is 11) $= 2/36$, P(second die is 5) $= 6/36$, and P(sum is 11 and second die is 5) $= 1/36$, so

$$P(\text{sum is 11 or second die is 5}) = \frac{2}{36} + \frac{6}{36} - \frac{1}{36} = \frac{7}{36}. \quad \blacksquare$$

EXAMPLE 3

The personnel director at a medium sized manufacturing company has received 20 applications from people applying for a job as plant manager. Of these 20 people, 8 have MBA degrees, 9 have previous related experience, and 5 have both MBA degrees and experience. Find the probability that a given candidate has an MBA degree or previous related experience.

Use M for "has degree" and E for "has experience." As stated, $P(M) = 8/20$, $P(E) = 9/20$, and $P(M \cap E) = 5/20$, with

$$P(M \cup E) = \frac{8}{20} + \frac{9}{20} - \frac{5}{20} = \frac{12}{20} = \frac{3}{5}. \quad \blacksquare$$

EXAMPLE 4

Exam

Susan is a college student who receives heavy sweaters from her aunt at the first sign of cold weather. The probability that a sweater is the wrong size is .47, the probability that it is a loud color is .59, and the probability that it is both the wrong size and a loud color is .31. Let W represent the event "wrong size," while L represents "loud color." Place the given information on a Venn diagram by starting with .31 in the intersection of the regions for W and L. Event W has probability .47. Since .31 has already been placed inside the intersection of W and L,

$$.47 - .31 = .16$$

goes inside region W, but outside the intersection of W and L. In the same way,

$$.59 - .31 = .28$$

goes inside the region for L, and outside the overlap.

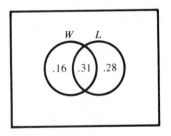

FIGURE 6

(a)   Find the probability that the sweater is the correct size and not a loud color.

Using regions W and L, this event becomes $W' \cap L'$. From the Venn diagram of Figure 6, the labeled regions have probability

$$.16 + .31 + .28 = .75.$$

Since the entire region of the Venn diagram is assumed to have probability 1, the region outside W and L, or $W' \cap L'$, has probability

$$1 - .75 = .25.$$

The probability is .25 that the sweater is the correct size and not a loud color.

(b) Find the probability that the sweater is the correct size or is not loud.

The region $W' \cup L'$ has probability

$$.25 + .16 + .28 = .69. \quad \blacksquare$$

6.3 EXERCISES

Two dice are rolled. Find the probability of rolling the sums in Exercises 1–14.

1. 2	**2.** 4	**3.** 5	**4.** 6
5. 8	**6.** 9	**7.** 10	**8.** 13

9. 9 or more   **10.** less than 7   **11.** between 5 and 8

12. not more than 5   **13.** not less than 8   **14.** between 3 and 7

One card is drawn from an ordinary deck of 52 cards. Find the probability of drawing

15. a 9 or a 10;   **16.** red or a 3;

17. a 9 or black 10;   **18.** a heart or black;

19. less than 4 (count aces as 1s);   **20.** a diamond or a 7;

21. a black card or an ace;   **22.** a heart or a jack.

Ms. Elliott invites ten relatives to a party: her mother, two aunts, three uncles, two brothers, one male cousin, and one female cousin. If the chances of any one guest arriving first are equally likely, find the probability that the first guest to arrive is

23. a brother or uncle;   **24.** a brother or cousin;

25. a brother or her mother;   **26.** an uncle or a cousin;

27. a male or a cousin;   **28.** a female or a cousin.

The numbers 1, 2, 3, 4, and 5 are written on slips of paper and two slips are drawn at random without replacement. Find each of the following probabilities.

29. the sum of the numbers is 9   **30.** both numbers are even

31. the sum of the numbers is 5 or less   **32.** one of the numbers is even or greater than 3

33. the first number is 2 or the sum is 6   **34.** the sum is 5 or the second number is 2

35. A student feels that her probability of passing accounting is .74, of passing mathematics is .39, and that her probability of passing both courses is .25. Find the probability that the student passes at least one course.

36. Suppose that 8% of a certain batch of calculators have a defective case, and that 11% have defective batteries. Also, 3% have both a defective case and defective batteries. A calculator is selected from the batch at random. Find the probability that the calculator has a good case and good batteries.

The table below shows the probability that a customer of a department store will make a purchase in the indicated range.

Cost	Probability
below $2	.07
$2–$4.99	.18
$5–$9.99	.21
$10–$19.99	.16
$20–$39.99	.11
$40–$69.99	.09
$70–$99.99	.07
$100–$149.99	.08
$150 or over	.03

Find the probability that a customer makes a purchase which is

37. less than $5;

38. $10 to $69.99;

39. $20 or more;

40. more than $4.99;

41. less than $100;

42. $100 or more.

Suppose $P(E) = .26$, $P(F) = .41$, and $P(E \cap F) = .17$. Use a Venn diagram to help find each of the following.

43. $P(E \cup F)$

44. $P(E' \cap F)$

45. $P(E \cap F')$

46. $P(E' \cup F')$

Let $P(Z) = .42$, $P(Y) = .38$, and $P(Z \cup Y) = .61$. Find each of the following probabilities.

47. $P(Z' \cap Y')$

48. $P(Z' \cup Y')$

49. $P(Z' \cup Y)$

50. $P(Z \cap Y')$

Color blindness is an inherited characteristic which is sex-linked, so that it is more common in males than in females. If M represents male and C represents red-green color blindness, we use the relative frequencies of the incidence of males and of red-green color blindness as probabilities to get $P(C) = .049$, $P(M \cap C) = .042$, $P(M \cup C) = .534$. Find the following.

51. $P(C')$

52. $P(M)$

53. $P(M')$

54. $P(M' \cap C')$

55. $P(C \cap M')$

56. $P(C \cup M')$

Gregor Mendel, an Austrian monk, was the first to use probability in the study of genetics. In an effort to understand the mechanism of character transmittal from one generation to the next in plants, he counted the number of occurrences of various characteristics. Mendel found that the flower color in certain pea plants obeyed this scheme:

Pure red crossed with pure white produces red.

The red offspring received from its parents genes for both red (R) and white (W) but in this case red is *dominant* and white *recessive,* so the offspring exhibits the color red. However, the offspring still carries both genes, and when two such offspring are crossed, several things can happen in the third generation. The table below, which is called a *Punnet square,* shows the possibilities.

		2nd parent	
		R	W
1st parent	R	RR	RW
	W	WR	WW

Use the fact that red is dominant over white to find

57. P(red);   3/4   **58.** P(white).

Mendel found no dominance in snapdragons, with one red gene and one white gene producing pink-flowered offspring. These second generation pinks, however, still carry one red and one white gene, and when they are crossed, the next generation still yields the Punnet square above. Find

59. P(red);   **60.** P(pink);   **61.** P(white).

(Mendel verified these probability ratios experimentally and did the same for many character units other than flower color. His work, published in 1866, was not recognized until 1890.)

In most animals and plants, it is very unusual for the number of main parts of the organism (arms, legs, toes, flower petals, etc.) to vary from generation to generation. Some species, however, have *meristic variability,* in which the number of certain body parts varies from generation to generation. One researcher studied the front feet of certain guinea pigs and produced the following probabilities.*

$$P\text{(only four toes, all perfect)} = .77$$
$$P\text{(one imperfect toe and four good ones)} = .13$$
$$P\text{(exactly five good toes)} = .10$$

Find the probability of each of the following events.

62. no more than four good toes

63. five toes, whether perfect or not

64. Let E, F, and G be events from a sample space S. Show that

$$P(E \cup F \cup G) = P(E) + P(F) + P(G) - P(E \cap F) - P(E \cap G) - P(F \cap G)$$
$$+ P(E \cap F \cap G).$$

(Hint: let $H = E \cup F$ and use equation (7).)

65. A group of three people, each with a different type of hat, decides to exchange hats. To do so, they toss their hats into a pile. Each person then takes a hat at random. Find the probability that at least one person gets his own hat.

66. Prove equation (2) in this section.

Approximate the following probabilities, using the Monte Carlo method.

67. A jeweler received 8 identical watches each in a box marked with the serial number of the watch. An assistant, who does not know that the boxes are marked, is told to polish the watches and then put them back in the boxes. She puts them in the boxes at random. What is the probability that she gets at least one watch in the right box?

68. A check room attendant has 10 hats but has lost the numbers identifying them. If he gives them back randomly, what is the probability that at least 2 of the hats are given back correctly?

---

*From "An Analysis of Variability in Guinea Pigs" by J. R. Wright in *Genetics* 19, pp. 506–536. Reprinted by permission.

6.4   Applications of Counting

In Chapter 5 we studied permutations and combinations—ways of counting the number of outcomes for various kinds of experiments. In this section we use these methods of counting to help solve problems in probability. The solution to many of these problems depends on the basic probability principle of Section 6.2:

> Let a sample space S have n possible equally likely outcomes, and let event E contain m of these outcomes, all distinct elements. The probability that event E occurs is
>
> $$P(E) = \frac{m}{n}.$$

EXAMPLE 1

From a group of 22 employees, 4 are to be selected to present a list of grievances to management.

(a)   In how many ways can this be done?

We must select 4 employees from a group of 22; this can be done in $\binom{22}{4}$ ways. From Section 5.4,

$$\binom{22}{4} = \frac{22!}{4!18!} = \frac{22(21)(20)(19)}{4(3)(2)(1)} = 7315.$$

There are 7315 ways to choose 4 people from 22.

(b)   One of the employees is Jill Streitsel; the group agrees that she must be one of the 4 people chosen. Find the probability that Streitsel will be among the 4 chosen.

If Streitsel must be one of the 4 people, the problem reduces to finding the number of ways that the additional 3 employees can be chosen. The 3 are chosen from 21 employees; this can be done in

$$\binom{21}{3} = \frac{21!}{3!18!} = \frac{21(20)(19)}{3(2)(1)} = 1330$$

ways. The probability that Streitsel will be one of the 4 employees chosen is

$$P(\text{Streitsel is chosen}) = \frac{1330}{7315} \approx .182.$$

The probability that she will *not* be chosen is $1 - .182 = .818$. ▪

EXAMPLE 2

When shipping diesel engines abroad, it is common to pack 12 engines in one container which is then loaded on a rail car and sent to a port. Suppose that a company has received complaints from its customers that many of the engines arrive in nonworking condition. To help solve this problem, the company decides to make a spot check of containers after loading—the company will test 3 engines from a container at random; if any of the 3 are nonworking, the container will not be shipped until each engine in it is checked. Suppose a given container has 2 nonworking engines, and find the probability that the container will not be shipped.

The container will not be shipped if the sample of 3 engines contains 1 or 2 defective engines. If $P(1 \text{ defective})$ represents the probability of exactly 1 defective engine in the sample, then

$$P(\text{not shipping}) = P(1 \text{ defective}) + P(2 \text{ defectives}).$$

There are $\binom{12}{3}$ ways to choose the 3 engines for testing:

$$\binom{12}{3} = \frac{12!}{3!9!} = \frac{12(11)(10)}{3(2)(1)} = 220.$$

There are $\binom{2}{1}$ ways of choosing 1 defective engine from the 2 in the container, and for each of these ways, there are $\binom{10}{2}$ ways of choosing 2 good engines from among the 10 in the container. This makes

$$\binom{2}{1}\binom{10}{2} = \frac{2!}{1!1!} \cdot \frac{10!}{2!8!} = 2(45) = 90$$

ways of choosing a sample of 3 engines containing one defective, with

$$P(1 \text{ defective}) = \frac{90}{220}.$$

There are $\binom{2}{2}$ ways of choosing 2 defective engines from the 2 defective engines in the container, and $\binom{10}{1}$ ways of choosing 1 good engine from among the 10 good engines, for

$$\binom{2}{2}\binom{10}{1} = \frac{2!}{2!0!} \cdot \frac{10!}{1!9!} = 1(10) = 10$$

ways of choosing a sample of 3 engines containing 2 defectives. Finally,

$$P(2 \text{ defectives}) = \frac{10}{220}$$

and

$$P(\text{not shipping}) = P(1 \text{ defective}) + P(2 \text{ defectives})$$

$$= \frac{90}{220} + \frac{10}{220} = \frac{100}{220} \approx .455.$$

The probability is $1 - .455 = .545$ that the container *will* be shipped, even though it has 2 defective engines. The management must decide if this probability is acceptable; if not, it may be necessary to test more than three engines from a container. ∎

Instead of finding the sum $P(1 \text{ defective}) + P(2 \text{ defectives})$, the result in Example 2 could be found as $1 - P(\text{no defectives})$.

$$P(\text{not shipping}) = 1 - P(\text{no defectives in sample})$$

$$= 1 - \frac{\binom{2}{0}\binom{10}{3}}{\binom{12}{3}}$$

$$= 1 - \frac{1(120)}{220}$$

$$= 1 - \frac{120}{220} = \frac{100}{220} \approx .455$$

EXAMPLE 3

In a common form of the card game *poker*, a hand of 5 cards is dealt to each player from a deck of 52 cards. There are a total of

$$\binom{52}{5} = \frac{52!}{5!47!} = 2,598,960$$

such hands possible. Find each of the following probabilities.

(a) a hand containing only hearts, called a *heart flush*

There are 13 hearts in a deck, with

$$\binom{13}{5} = \frac{13!}{5!8!} = \frac{13(12)(11)(10)(9)}{5(4)(3)(2)(1)} = 1287$$

different hands containing only hearts. The probability of a heart flush is

$$P(\text{heart flush}) = \frac{1287}{2,598,960} = \frac{33}{66,640} \approx .000495.$$

(b) a flush of any suit

There are 4 suits in a deck, so

$$P(\text{flush}) = 4 \cdot P(\text{heart flush}) = 4 \cdot \frac{33}{66,640} \approx .00198.$$

(c) a full house of aces and eights (3 aces and 2 eights)

There are $\binom{4}{3}$ ways to choose 3 aces from among the 4 in the deck, and $\binom{4}{2}$ ways to choose 2 eights.

$$P(3 \text{ aces}, 2 \text{ eights}) = \frac{\binom{4}{3} \cdot \binom{4}{2}}{2,598,960} = \frac{1}{108,290} \approx .00000923.$$

(d) any full house (3 cards of one value, 2 of another)

The 13 values in a deck give 13 choices for the first value, leaving 12 choices for the second value (order *is* important here, since a full house of aces and eights is not the same as a full house of eights and aces). From part (c), the probability for any *particular* full house is $1/108,290$; the probability of *any* full house is

$$P(\text{full house}) = 13 \cdot 12 \cdot \left(\frac{1}{108,290}\right) = \frac{156}{108,290} \approx .00144. \quad \blacksquare$$

EXAMPLE 4

Suppose a group of n people is in a room. Find the probability that at least 2 of the people have the same birthday.

Here we refer to the month and the day, not necessarily the same year. Also, ignore leap years, and assume that each day in the year is equally likely as a birthday. Let us first find the probability that *no 2 people* among 5 people have the same birthday. There are 365 different birthdays possible for the first of the 5 people, 364 for the second (so that the people have different birthdays), 363 for the third, and so on. The number of ways the 5 people can have different birthdays is the number of permutations of 365 things (days) taken 5 at a time, or

$$P(365, 5) = 365 \cdot 364 \cdot 363 \cdot 362 \cdot 361.$$

The number of ways that the 5 people can have the same or different birthdays is

$$365 \cdot 365 \cdot 365 \cdot 365 \cdot 365 = (365)^5.$$

Finally, the *probability* that none of the 5 people have the same birthday is

$$\frac{P(365, 5)}{(365)^5} = \frac{365 \cdot 364 \cdot 363 \cdot 362 \cdot 361}{365 \cdot 365 \cdot 365 \cdot 365 \cdot 365} \approx .973.$$

The probability that at least 2 of the 5 people *do* have the same birthday is $1 - .973 = .027$.

We can extend this same result for more than 5 people. Generalizing, the probability that no 2 people among n people have the same birthday is

$$\frac{P(365, n)}{(365)^n}.$$

The probability that at least 2 of the n people *do* have the same birthday is

$$1 - \frac{P(365, n)}{(365)^n}.$$

The following table shows this probability for various values of n.

Number of People, n	Probability that Two Have the Same Birthday
5	.027
10	.117
15	.253
20	.411
22	.476
23	.507
25	.569
30	.706
35	.814
40	.891
50	.970
365	1

The probability that 2 people among 23 have the same birthday is .507, a little more than half. Many people are surprised at this result—somehow it seems that a larger number of people should be required. ▓

6.4 EXERCISES

A shipment of 9 typewriters contains 2 defectives. Find the probability that a sample of the following size, drawn from the 9, will not contain a defective.

1. 1   **2.** 2   **3.** 3   **4.** 4

Refer to Example 2. The management feels that the probability of .545 that a container will be shipped even though it contains 2 defectives is too high. They decide to increase the sample size chosen. Find the probability that a container will be shipped even though it contains 2 defectives if the sample size is increased to

5. 4;   **6.** 5.

A basket contains 6 red apples and 4 yellow apples. A sample of 3 apples is drawn. Find the probability that the sample contains

7. all red apples;   **8.** all yellow apples;

9. 2 yellow and 1 red apple;   **10.** more red than yellow apples.

Two cards are drawn at random from an ordinary deck of 52 cards.

11. How many two card hands are possible?

Find the probability that the two card hand contains

12. two aces;   **13.** at least one ace;

14. all spades;   **15.** two cards of the same suit;

16. only face cards;   **17.** no face cards;

18. no card higher than 8 (count ace as 1).

Twenty-six slips of paper are each marked with a different letter of the alphabet, and placed in a basket. A slip is pulled out, its letter recorded (in the order in which the slip was drawn), and the slip replaced. This is done 5 times. Find the probabilities that the "word" formed

19. is "chuck";   **20.** starts with p;

21. has all different letters;   **22.** contains no x, y, or z.

Find the probability of the following hands at poker. Assume aces are either high or low.

23. royal flush (5 highest cards of a single suit)

24. straight flush (5 in a row in a single suit, but not a royal flush)

25. four of a kind (4 cards of the same value)

26. straight (5 cards in a row, not all of the same suit) with ace either high or low

A bridge hand is made up of 13 cards from a deck of 52. Set up the probability that a hand chosen at random

27. contains only hearts;   **28.** has 4 aces;

29. contains exactly 3 aces and exactly 3 kings;

30. has 6 of one suit, 5 of another, and 2 of another.

31. Set up the probability that at least 2 of the 39 Presidents of the United States have had the same birthday.

32. Estimate the probability that at least 2 of the 100 U.S. Senators have the same birthday.

33. Give the probability that 2 of the 435 members of the House of Representatives have the same birthday.

34. Show that the probability that in a group of n people *exactly one* pair have the same birthday is

$$\binom{n}{2} \cdot \frac{P(365, n-1)}{(365)^n}.$$

35. To win a contest, a player must match 4 movie stars with his or her baby picture. Suppose this is done at random. Find the probability of getting no matches correct; of getting exactly 2 correct.

36. A contractor has hired a decorator to send 3 different sofas out to the contractor's model homes each week for a year. The contractor does not want exactly the same 3 sofas sent out twice. Find the minimum number of sofas that the decorator will need.

37. An elevator has 4 passengers and stops at 7 floors. It is equally likely that a person will get off at any one of the 7 floors. Find the probability that no 2 passengers leave at the same floor.

Exercises 38–44 involve the idea of a *circular permutation:* the number of ways of arranging distinct objects in a circle. The number of ways of arranging n distinct objects in a line is $n!$, but there are fewer ways for arranging the n items in a circle since the first item could be placed in any of n locations.

38. Show that the number of ways of arranging n distinct items in a circle is $(n-1)!$.

Find the number of ways of arranging the following number of distinct items in a circle.

39. 4
40. 7
41. 10

Use the idea of a circular permutation for Exercises 42–44.

42. Suppose that 8 people sit at a circular table. Find the probability that 2 particular people are sitting next to each other.

43. A keyring contains 7 keys; one black, one gold, and 5 silver. If the keys are arranged at random on the ring, find the probability that the black key is next to the gold key.

44. A circular table for a board of directors has 10 seats for the 10 attending members of the board. The chairman of the board always sits closest to the window. The vice president for sales, who is currently out of favor, will sit 3 positions to the chairman's left, since the chairman doesn't see so well out of his left eye. The chairman's daughter-in-law will sit opposite him. All other members take seats at random. Find the probability that a particular other member will sit next to the chairman.

45. Rework Exercises 23–26 using the Monte Carlo method to approximate the answers with $n = 25$. Since each hand has 5 cards, you will need $25 \cdot 5 = 125$ random numbers to "look at" 25 hands. Compare these experimental results with the theoretical results.

46. Rework Exercises 27–30 using the Monte Carlo method to approximate the answers with $n = 20$. Since each hand has 13 cards, you will need $20 \cdot 13 = 260$ random numbers to "look at" 20 hands.

6.5 Conditional Probability

The training manager for a large stockbrokerage firm has noticed that some of the firm's brokers use the firm's research advice, while other brokers tend to go with their own feelings of which stocks will go up. To see if the research department is better than just the feelings of the brokers, the manager conducted a survey of 100 brokers, with results as shown in the following table.

	A. Picked Stocks that Went Up	Didn't Pick Stocks that Went Up	Totals
B. Used research	30	15	45
Didn't use research	30	25	55
Totals	60	40	100

Letting A represent the event "picked stocks that went up," and letting B represent the event "used research," we can find the following probabilities.

$$P(A) = \frac{60}{100} = .6 \qquad P(A') = \frac{40}{100} = .4$$

$$P(B) = \frac{45}{100} = .45 \qquad P(B') = \frac{55}{100} = .55$$

Suppose we want to find the probability that a broker using research will pick stocks that go up. From the table above, of the 45 brokers who use research, 30 picked stocks that went up, with

$$P(\text{broker who uses research picks stocks that go up}) = \frac{30}{45} = .667.$$

This is a different number than the probability that a broker picks stocks that go up, .6, since we have additional information (the broker uses research) which reduced the sample space. In other words, we found the probability that a broker picks stocks that go up, A, given the additional information that the broker uses research, B. This is called the *conditional probability* of event A, given that event B has occurred, written $P(A|B)$. In the example above,

$$P(A|B) = \frac{30}{45},$$

which can be written as

$$P(A|B) = \frac{30/100}{45/100} = \frac{P(A \cap B)}{P(B)}.$$

where $P(A \cap B)$ represents, as usual, the probability that both A and B will occur.

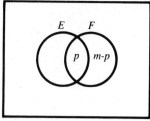

Event F has a total of m elements

FIGURE 7

Let us generalize this result. Assume that E and F are two events for a particular experiment. Assume that the sample space S for this experiment has n possible equally likely outcomes. Suppose event F has m elements, while $E \cap F$ has p elements ($p \leq m$). Using the fundamental principle of probability,

$$P(F) = \frac{m}{n} \quad \text{and} \quad P(E \cap F) = \frac{p}{n}.$$

We now want $P(E|F)$, the probability that E occurs given that F has occurred. Since we assume F has occurred, look only at the m elements inside F. (See Figure 7). Of these m elements, there are p elements where E also occurs, since $E \cap F$ has p elements. This makes

$$P(E|F) = \frac{p}{m}.$$

Divide numerator and denominator by n to get

$$P(E|F) = \frac{\dfrac{p}{n}}{\dfrac{m}{n}} = \frac{P(E \cap F)}{P(F)}.$$

This result is actually chosen as the definition of conditional probability.

Definition of Conditional Probability

The **conditional probability** of event E given event F, written $P(E|F)$, is

$$P(E|F) = \frac{P(E \cap F)}{P(F)}, \qquad P(F) \neq 0.$$

EXAMPLE 1

Use the information given in the chart at the beginning of this section to find the following probabilities.

(a) $P(B|A)$

By the definition of conditional probability,

$$P(B|A) = \frac{P(B \cap A)}{P(A)}.$$

In the example, $P(B \cap A) = 30/100$, and $P(A) = 60/100$, with

$$P(B|A) = \frac{30/100}{60/100} = \frac{1}{2}.$$

If a broker picked stocks that went up, then the probability is 1/2 that the broker used research.

(b) $P(A'|B)$

$$P(A'|B) = \frac{P(A' \cap B)}{P(B)} = \frac{15/100}{45/100} = \frac{1}{3}.$$

(c) $P(B'|A')$

$$P(B'|A') = \frac{P(B' \cap A')}{P(A')} = \frac{25/100}{40/100} = \frac{5}{8}.$$ ▮

Venn diagrams can be used to illustrate problems in conditional probability. A Venn diagram for Example 1, in which the probabilities are used to indicate the number in the set defined by each region, is shown in Figure 8. In the diagram, $P(B|A)$ is found by reducing the sample space to just set A. Then $P(B|A)$ is the ratio of the number in that part of set B which is also in A to the number in set A, or $.3/.6 = .5$.

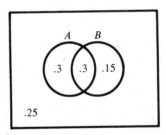

FIGURE 8

Two fair coins were tossed, and it is known that at least one was heads. Find the probability that both were heads.

The sample space has four equally likely outcomes, $S = \{hh, ht, th, tt\}$. Define two events:

$$E_1 = \text{at least one head},   \text{or } E_1 = \{hh, ht, th\}.$$
$$E_2 = \text{two heads},   \text{or } E_2 = \{hh\}.$$

Since there are four equally likely outcomes, $P(E_1) = 3/4$. Also, $P(E_1 \cap E_2) = 1/4$. We want the probability that both were heads, given that at least one was a head; that is, we want to find $P(E_2|E_1)$. Use the definition above.

$$P(E_2|E_1) = \frac{P(E_2 \cap E_1)}{P(E_1)} = \frac{1/4}{3/4} = \frac{1}{3}$$ ▮

In the definition of conditional probability given earlier, we can multiply both sides of the equation for $P(E|F)$ by $P(F)$ to get the following ***product rule*** for probability:

Product Rule

> **For any events E and F,**
> $$P(E \cap F) = P(F) \cdot P(E|F).$$

The product rule gives us a method for finding the probability that events E and F both occur, as illustrated by the next few examples.

EXAMPLE 3

A class is 2/5 women and 3/5 men. Of the women, 25% are business majors. Find the probability that a student chosen at random is a woman business major.

Let B and W represent the events "business major" and "woman," respectively. We want to find $P(B \cap W)$. By the product rule,

$$P(B \cap W) = P(W) \cdot P(B|W).$$

Using the given information, $P(W) = 2/5 = .4$ and $P(B|W) = .25$. Thus

$$P(B \cap W) = .4(.25) = .10. \quad \blacksquare$$

EXAMPLE 4

A company needs to hire a new director of advertising. It has decided to try to hire either person A or person B, who are assistant advertising directors for its major competitor. In trying to decide between A and B, the company does research on the campaigns managed by either A or B (no campaign is managed by both), and finds that A is in charge of twice as many advertising campaigns as B. Also, A's campaigns have satisfactory results three out of four times, while B's campaigns have satisfactory results only two out of five times. Suppose one of the competitor's advertising campaigns (managed by A or B) is selected. Find the probabilities of the following events.

(a)   A is in charge of an advertising campaign that produces satisfactory results.

First construct a *tree diagram* showing the various possible outcomes for this experiment, as in Figure 9. (Recall the discussion of tree diagrams in Section 5.1.) Since A does twice as many jobs as B, the probabilities of A and B having done the job are 2/3 and 1/3 respectively, as shown on the first stage of the tree. The second stage shows four different conditional probabilities. The ratings for the advertising campaigns are S (satisfactory) and U (unsatisfactory). For example, along the branch from B to S,

$$P(S|B) = \frac{2}{5}$$

since B has satisfactory results in 2 out of 5 campaigns.

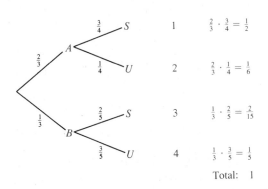

Executive   Campaign   Branch   Probability

FIGURE 9

Each of the four composite branches in the tree is numbered, with its probability given on the right. At each point where the tree branches, the sum of the probabilities is 1. The event that A has a campaign with a satisfactory result (event $A \cap S$) is associated with branch 1, so

$$P(A \cap S) = \frac{1}{2}.$$

(b)   B runs the campaign and produces satisfactory results.

This event, $B \cap S$, is shown on branch 3:

$$P(B \cap S) = \frac{2}{15}.$$

(c)   The campaign is satisfactory.

The result S combines branches 1 and 3, so

$$P(S) = \frac{1}{2} + \frac{2}{15} = \frac{19}{30}.$$

(d)   The campaign is unsatisfactory.

Event U combines branches 2 and 4, so

$$P(U) = \frac{1}{6} + \frac{1}{5} = \frac{11}{30}.$$

Alternatively, $P(U) = 1 - P(S) = 1 - 19/30 = 11/30$.

(e)   Either A runs the campaign or the results are satisfactory (or both).

Event A combines branches 1 and 2, while event S combines branches 1 and 3. Thus, we use branches 1, 2, and 3.

$$P(A \cup S) = \frac{1}{2} + \frac{1}{6} + \frac{2}{15} = \frac{4}{5}$$

The next three examples could be worked with combinations, as explained in the previous section. In this section we show an alternate approach, using tree diagrams and conditional probability.

EXAMPLE 5

[handwritten: 2W 1G]

From a box containing 3 white, 2 green, and 1 red marble, two marbles are drawn one at a time without replacing the first before the second is drawn. Find the probability that one white and one green marble are drawn.

A tree diagram showing the various possible outcomes is given in Figure 10. In this diagram, W represents the event "drawing a white marble" and G represents "drawing a green marble." On the first draw, $P(W$ on the 1st$) = 3/6 = 1/2$ because 3 of the 6 marbles in the box are white. On the second draw, $P(G$ on the 2nd$|W$ on the 1st$) = 2/5$. One white marble has been removed, leaving 5, of which 2 are green.

[handwritten notes:]
A. 3/6 marbles = 1/2
B. how do you achieve:
W = 2/5
G = 3/5 } 2nd choice
R = 3/5

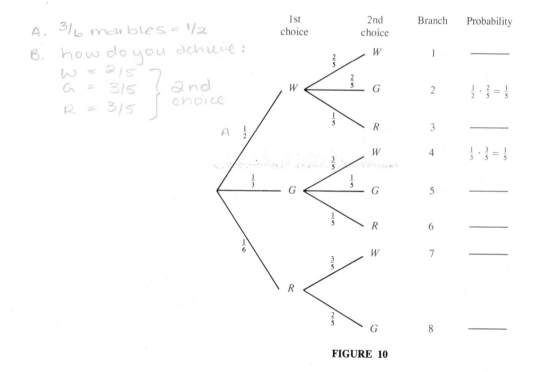

FIGURE 10

Now we want to find the probability of drawing one white marble and one green marble. This event can occur in two ways: drawing a white marble first and then a green one (branch 2 of the tree diagram), or drawing a green marble first and then a white one (branch 4). For branch 2,

$$P(W \text{ on 1st}) \cdot P(G \text{ on 2nd}|W \text{ on 1st}) = \frac{1}{2} \cdot \frac{2}{5} = \frac{1}{5}.$$

For branch 4, where the green marble is drawn first,

$$P(G \text{ on 1st}) \cdot P(W \text{ on 2nd}|G \text{ on 1st}) = \frac{1}{3} \cdot \frac{3}{5} = \frac{1}{5}.$$

Since the two events are mutually exclusive, the final probability is the sum of these two probabilities, or

$$P(\text{one } W, \text{ one } G) = P(W \text{ on 1st}) \cdot P(G \text{ on 2nd}|W \text{ on 1st})$$
$$+ P(G \text{ on 1st}) \cdot P(W \text{ on 2nd}|G \text{ on 1st}) = \frac{2}{5}. \quad \blacksquare$$

The product rule is often helpful with *stochastic processes,* where the outcome of an experiment depends on the outcomes of previous experiments. For example, the outcome of a draw of a card from a deck depends on any cards previously drawn. (Stochastic processes are studied in more detail in a later chapter.)

Two cards are drawn without replacement from an ordinary deck. Find the probability that the first card is a heart and the second card is red.

EXAMPLE 6

Start with the tree diagram of Figure 11.

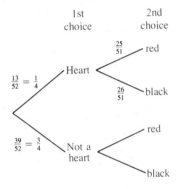

On the first draw, since there are 13 hearts in the 52 cards, the probability of drawing a heart is $13/52 = 1/4$. On the second draw, since a heart has been drawn already, there are 25 red cards in the remaining 51 cards. Thus, the probability of drawing a red card on the second draw, given that the first is a heart, is 25/51. Therefore,

$$P(\text{heart on first and red on second})$$
$$= P(\text{heart on first}) \cdot P(\text{red on second}|\text{heart on first})$$
$$= \frac{1}{4} \cdot \frac{25}{51} = \frac{25}{204} \approx .1225. \quad \blacksquare$$

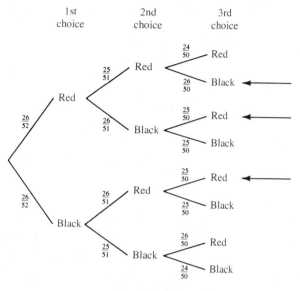

FIGURE 12

EXAMPLE 7

Three cards are drawn without replacement from an ordinary deck. Find the probability that exactly two of the cards are red.

Here we need a tree diagram with three stages, as shown in Figure 12. The three branches indicated with arrows produce exactly two red cards from the three draws. Multiply the probabilities along each of these branches and then add.

$$P(\text{exactly two red cards}) = \frac{26}{52} \cdot \frac{25}{51} \cdot \frac{26}{50} + \frac{26}{52} \cdot \frac{26}{51} \cdot \frac{25}{50} + \frac{26}{52} \cdot \frac{26}{51} \cdot \frac{25}{50}$$

$$= \frac{50,700}{132,600} = \frac{13}{34} \approx .382. \quad \blacksquare$$

Independent Events   Suppose a fair coin is tossed and gives heads. The probability of heads on the next toss is still 1/2; the fact that heads was obtained on a given toss has no effect on the outcome of the next toss. Coin tosses are *independent events,* since knowledge of the outcome of one toss does not help decide on the outcome of the next toss. Rolls of a fair die are independent events; the fact that a 2 came up on one roll does not help increase our knowledge of the outcome of the next roll. On the other hand, the events "today is cloudy" and "today is rainy" are *dependent events;* if we know that it is cloudy, we know that there is an increased chance of rain.

If events E and F are independent, then the knowledge that E has occurred gives us no (probability) information about the occurrence or nonoccurrence of event F. That is, $P(F)$ is exactly the same as $P(F|E)$, or

$$P(F|E) = P(F).$$

This, in fact, is the formal definition of independent events:

Definition of Independent Events	E and F are **independent events** if $$P(F|E) = P(F).$$

Using this definition, the product rule can be simplified for independent events.

Product Rule	If E and F are independent events, then $$P(E \cap F) = P(E) \cdot P(F).$$

EXAMPLE 8

A calculator requires a key-stroke assembly and a logic circuit. Assume that 99% of the key-stroke assemblies are satisfactory and 97% of the logic circuits are satisfactory. Find the probability that a finished calculator will be satisfactory.

If the failure of a key stroke assembly and the failure of a logic circuit are independent events, then

P(satisfactory calculator)

$\quad = P$(satisfactory key-stroke assembly) $\cdot$ P(satisfactory logic circuit)

$\quad = (.99)(.97) \approx .96$.

The probability of a defective calculator is $1 - .96 = .04$. ▪

EXAMPLE 9

When black-coated mice are crossed with brown-coated mice, a pair of genes, one from each parent, determines the coat color of the offspring. Let b represent the gene for brown and B the gene for black. If a mouse carries either one B gene and one b gene (Bb or bB) or two B genes (BB), the coat will be black. If the mouse carries two b genes (bb), the coat will be brown. Find the probability that a mouse born to a brown-coated female and a black-coated male who is known to carry the Bb combination will be brown.

To be brown-coated, the offspring must receive one b gene from each parent. The brown-coated parent carries two b genes, so that the probability of getting one b gene from the mother is 1. The probability of getting one b gene from the black-coated father is $1/2$. Therefore, since these are independent events, the probability of a brown-coated offspring from these parents is $1 \cdot 1/2 = 1/2$. ▪

It is common for students to confuse the ideas of *mutually exclusive* events and *independent* events. Events E and F are mutually exclusive if $E \cap F = \varnothing$. For example, if a family has exactly one child, the only possible outcomes are $B = \{boy\}$ and $G = \{girl\}$. These two events are mutually exclusive. However, the events are *not* independent, since $P(G|B) = 0$ (if a family with only one child has a boy, the probability it has a girl is then 0). Since $P(G|B) \neq P(G)$, the events are not independent.

Of all the families with exactly *two* children, the events $G_1 = \{$first child is a girl$\}$ and $G_2 = \{$second child is a girl$\}$ are independent, since $P(G_2|G_1)$ equals $P(G_2)$. However, G_1 and G_2 are not mutually exclusive, since $G_1 \cap G_2 = \{$both children are girls$\} \neq \varnothing$.

The only way to show that two events E and F are independent is to show that $P(F|E) = P(F)$.

6.5 EXERCISES

If a single fair die is rolled, find the probability of rolling

1. a 2, given that the number rolled was odd;

2. a 4, given that the number rolled was even;

3. an even number, given that the number rolled was 6.

If two fair dice are rolled, find the probability of rolling

4. a sum of 8, given the sum was greater than 7;

5. a sum of 6, given the roll was a "double" (two identical numbers);

6. a double, given that the sum was 9.

If 2 cards are drawn without replacement from an ordinary deck, find the probability that

7. the second is a heart, given that the first is a heart;

8. they are both hearts;

9. the second is black, given that the first is a spade;

10. the second is a face card, given that the first is a jack.

If 5 cards are drawn without replacement from an ordinary deck, find the probability that all the cards are

11. diamonds;

12. diamonds, given that the first and second were diamonds;

13. diamonds, given that the first four were diamonds;

14. clubs, given that the third was a spade;

15. the same suit.

A smooth-talking young man has a 1/3 probability of talking a policeman out of giving him a speeding ticket. The probability that he is stopped for speeding during a given weekend is 1/2. Find the probability that

16. he will receive no speeding tickets on a given weekend;

17. he will receive no speeding tickets on 3 consecutive weekends.

Slips of paper marked with the digits 1, 2, 3, 4, and 5 are placed in a box and mixed well. If two slips are drawn (without replacement), find the probability that

18. the first is even and the second is odd;

19. the first is a 3 and the second a number greater than 3;

20. both are even;

21. both are marked 3.

Two marbles are drawn without replacement from a jar with 4 black and 3 white marbles. Find the probability that

22. both are white;

23. both are black;

24. the second is white given that the first is black;

25. the first is black and the second is white;

26. one is black and the other is white.

The Midtown Bank has found that most customers at the tellers' windows either cash a check or make a deposit. The chart below indicates the transactions for one teller for one day.

	Cash Check	No Check	Totals
Make deposit	50	20	70
No deposit	30	10	40
Totals	80	30	110

Letting C represent "cashing a check" and D represent "making a deposit," express each of the following probabilities in words and find its value.

27. $P(C|D)$

28. $P(D'|C)$

29. $P(C'|D')$

30. $P(C'|D)$

31. $P[(C \cap D)']$

A pet shop has 10 puppies, 6 of them males. There are 3 beagles (1 male), 1 cocker spaniel (male), and 6 poodles. Construct a table similar to the one above and find the probability that one of these puppies, chosen at random, is

32. a beagle;

33. a beagle, given that it is a male;

34. a male, given that it is a beagle;

35. a cocker spaniel, given that it is a female;

36. a poodle, given that it is a male;

37. a female, given that it is a beagle.

A bicycle factory runs two assembly lines, A and B. If 95% of line A's products pass inspection, while only 90% of line B's products pass inspection, and 60% of the factory's bikes come off assembly line B (the rest off A), find the probability that one of the factory's bikes did not pass inspection and came off

38. assembly line A;

39. assembly line B.

40. Both of a certain pea plant's parents had a gene for red and a gene for white flowers. (See the exercises for Section 6.3.) If the offspring has red flowers, find the probability that it combined a gene for red and a gene for white (rather than two for red).

Assuming that boy and girl babies are equally likely, fill in the remaining probabilities on the tree diagram and use the information to find the probability that a family with three children has all girls, given that

41. the first is a girl;

42. the third is a girl;

43. the second is a girl;

44. at least two are girls;

45. at least one is a girl.

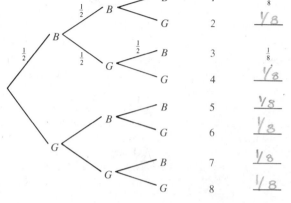

| 1st child | 2d | 3d | Branch | Probability |

41. ¼

43. ¼

45. ⅐

The following table shows frequencies for red-green color blindness, where M represents male and C represents color-blind. Use this table to find the following probabilities.

46. $P(M)$ **47.** $P(C)$

48. $P(M \cap C)$ **49.** $P(M \cup C)$

50. $P(M|C)$ **51.** $P(C|M)$

52. $P(M'|C)$

	M	M'	Totals
C	.042	.007	.049
C'	.485	.466	.951
Totals	.527	.473	1.000

53. Are the events C and M described above dependent?

54. A scientist wishes to determine if there is any dependence between color blindness (C) and deafness (D). Given the probabilities listed in the table below, what should his findings be? (See Exercises 46–53.)

	D	D'	Totals
C	.0004	.0796	.0800
C'	.0046	.9154	.9200
Totals	.0050	.9950	1.0000

The Motor Vehicle Department has found that the probability of a person passing the test for a driver's license on the first try is .75. The probability that an individual who fails on the first test will pass on the second try is .80, and the probability that an individual who fails the first and second tests will pass the third time is .70. Find the probability that an individual

55. fails both the first and second tests;

56. will fail three times in a row;

57. will require at least two tries to pass the test.

According to a booklet put out by Frontier Airlines, 98% of all scheduled Frontier flights actually take place. (The other flights are cancelled due to weather, equipment problems, and so on.) Assume that the event that a given flight takes place is independent of the event that another flight takes place.

58. Elizabeth Thornton plans to visit her company's branch offices; her journey requires three separate flights on Frontier. What is the probability that all these flights will take place?

59. Based on the reasons we gave for a flight to be cancelled, how realistic is the assumption of independence that we made?

60. In one area, 4% of the population drives a luxury car. However, 17% of the CPAs drive a luxury car. Are the events "drive a luxury car" and "person is a CPA" independent?

61. Corporations where a computer is essential to day-to-day operations, such as banks, often have a second backup computer in case of failure by the main computer. Suppose there is a .003 chance that the main computer will fail in a given time period, and a .005 chance that the backup computer will fail while the main computer is being repaired. Assume these failures represent independent events, and find the fraction of the time that the corporation can assume it will have computer service. How realistic is our assumption of independence?

62. A key component of a space rocket will fail with a probability of .03. How many such components must be used as backups to ensure the probability that at least one of the components will work is .999999?

In searching for a new drug with commercial possibilities, drug company researchers use the ratio

$$N_S : N_A : N_p : 1.$$

That is, if the company gives preliminary screening to N_S substances, it may find that N_A of them are worthy of further study, with N_P of these surviving into full scale development. Finally, 1 of the substances will result in a marketable drug. Typical numbers used by Smith, Kline, and French Laboratories in planning research budgets might be $2000 : 30 : 8 : 1.$* Use this ratio in the following exercises.

63. Suppose a compound has been chosen for preliminary screening. Find the probability that the compound will survive and become a marketable drug.

64. Find the probability that the compound will not lead to a marketable drug.

65. Suppose the number of such compounds receiving preliminary screening is a. Set up the probability that none of them produces a marketable drug. (Assume independence throughout these exercises.)

66. Use your results from Exercise 65 to set up the probability that at least one of the drugs will prove marketable.

67. Suppose now that N scientists are employed in the preliminary screening, and that each scientist can screen c compounds per year. Set up the probability that no marketable drugs will be discovered in a year.

68. Set up the probability that at least one marketable drug will be discovered.

---

*Reprinted by permission of E. B. Pyle, III, B. Douglas, G. W. Ebright, W. J. Westlake, A. B. Bender, "Scientific Manpower Allocation to New Drug Screening Programs," *Management Science*, Vol. 19, No. 12, August 1973, copyright © 1973 The Institute of Management Sciences.

For the following exercises, evaluate your answer in Exercise 68 for the following values of N and c. Use a calculator with a y^x key, or a computer.

69. $N = 100$, $c = 6$

70. $N = 25$, $c = 10$

Let E and F be events which are neither the empty set nor the sample space S. Identify the following as true or false.

71. $P(E|E) = 1$

72. $P(E|E') = 1$

73. $P(\emptyset|F) = 0$

74. $P(S|E) = P(E)$

75. $P(F|S) = P(F)$

76. $P(E|F) = P(F|E)$

77. $P(E|E \cap F) = 0$

78. If $P(E|F) = P(E \cap F)$, then $P(F) = 1$

79. Let E and F be mutually exclusive events such that $P(F) > 0$. Find $P(E|F)$.

80. If $E \subset F$, where $E \neq \emptyset$, find $P(F|E)$ and $P(E|F)$.

81. Let F_1, F_2, and F_3 be a set of pairwise mutually exclusive events (that is, $F_1 \cap F_2 = \emptyset$, $F_1 \cap F_3 = \emptyset$, and $F_2 \cap F_3 = \emptyset$), with sample space $S = F_1 \cup F_2 \cup F_3$. Let E be any event. Show that

$$P(E) = P(F_1) \cdot P(E|F_1) + P(F_2) \cdot P(E|F_2) + P(F_3) \cdot P(E|F_3).$$

82. Show that for three events E, F, and G,

$$P(E \cap F \cap G) = P(E) \cdot P(F|E) \cdot P(G|E \cap F).$$

6.6 Bayes' Formula

Suppose the probability that a person gets lung cancer, given that the person smokes a pack or more of cigarettes daily, is known. For a research project, it might be necessary to know the probability that a person smokes a pack or more of cigarettes daily, given that the person has lung cancer. More generally, if $P(E|F)$ is known for two events E and F, can $P(F|E)$ be found? It turns out that it can, using the formula to be developed in this section. To find this formula, let us start with the product rule:

$$P(E \cap F) = P(E) \cdot P(F|E),$$

which can also be written as $P(F \cap E) = P(F) \cdot P(E|F)$. From the fact that $P(E \cap F) = P(F \cap E)$,

$$P(E) \cdot P(F|E) = P(F) \cdot P(E|F),$$

or

$$P(F|E) = \frac{P(F) \cdot P(E|F)}{P(E)}. \tag{1}$$

Given the two events E and F, if E occurs, then either F also occurs or F' also occurs. The probabilities of $E \cap F$ and $E \cap F'$ can be expressed as follows.

$$P(E \cap F) = P(F) \cdot P(E|F)$$
$$P(E \cap F') = P(F') \cdot P(E|F')$$

Since $(E \cap F) \cup (E \cap F') = E$ (because F and F' form the sample space),

$$P(E) = P(E \cap F) + P(E \cap F')$$

or $$P(E) = P(F) \cdot P(E|F) + P(F') \cdot P(E|F').$$

From this, equation (1) produces the following result, a special case of Bayes' Formula, which is discussed in more generality later in this section.

Bayes' Formula	
(Special Case)	$$P(F|E) = \frac{P(F) \cdot P(E|F)}{P(F) \cdot P(E|F) + P(F') \cdot P(E|F')}. \qquad (2)$$

EXAMPLE 1

For a fixed length of time, the probability of worker error on the production line is .1, the probability that an accident will occur when there is a worker error is .3, and the probability that an accident will occur when there is no worker error is .2. Find the probability of a worker error if there is an accident.

Let A represent the event of an accident, and let E represent the event of worker error. From the information above,

$$P(E) = .1, \qquad P(A|E) = .3, \qquad \text{and} \quad P(A|E') = .2.$$

These probabilities are shown on the tree diagram of Figure 13.

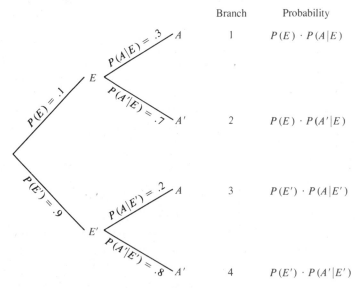

	Branch	Probability
	1	$P(E) \cdot P(A|E)$
	2	$P(E) \cdot P(A'|E)$
	3	$P(E') \cdot P(A|E')$
	4	$P(E') \cdot P(A'|E')$

FIGURE 13

Find $P(E|A)$ using equation (2) above:

$$P(E|A) = \frac{P(E) \cdot P(A|E)}{P(E) \cdot P(A|E) + P(E') \cdot P(A|E')}$$

$$= \frac{(.1)(.3)}{(.1)(.3) + (.9)(.2)} = \frac{1}{7}.$$

In a similar manner, the probability that an accident is not due to worker error is $P(E'|A)$, or

$$P(E'|A) = \frac{P(E') \cdot P(A|E')}{P(E') \cdot P(A|E') + P(E) \cdot P(A|E)}$$

$$= \frac{(.9)(.2)}{(.9)(.2) + (.1)(.3)} = \frac{6}{7}. \quad \blacksquare$$

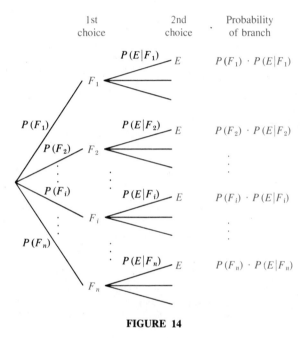

FIGURE 14

Equation (2) above can be generalized to more than two possibilities. To do so, use the tree diagram of Figure 14. This diagram shows the paths that can produce some event E. We assume that the events F_1, F_2, $\cdots$, F_n are pairwise mutually exclusive events (that is, events which, taken two at a time, are disjoint) whose union is the sample space, and that E is an event that has occurred.

To find the probability $P(F_i|E)$, where $1 \le i \le n$, divide the probability for the branch containing $P(E|F_i)$ by the sum of the probabilities of all the branches producing event E. That is,

Bayes' Formula

$$P(F_i|E) = \frac{P(F_i) \cdot P(E|F_i)}{P(F_1) \cdot P(E|F_1) + P(F_2) \cdot P(E|F_2) + \cdots + P(F_n) \cdot P(E|F_n)}.$$

This result is known as **Bayes' Formula,** after the Reverend Thomas Bayes, whose paper on probability was published a little over two hundred years ago.

The basic statement of Bayes' Formula can be daunting. Actually, it is easier to remember the formula by thinking of the tree diagram that produced it. Go through the following steps.

Using Bayes'

Formula

1. Start a tree diagram with branches representing events F_1, F_2, $\cdots$, F_n. Label each branch with its corresponding probability.
2. From the end of each of these branches, draw a branch for event E. Label this branch with the probability of getting to it, $P(E|F_i)$.
3. You now have n different paths that result in event E. Next to each path, put its probability—the product of the probabilities that the first branch occurs, $P(F_i)$, and that the second branch occurs, $P(E|F_i)$; that is, the product $P(F_i) \cdot P(E|F_i)$.
4. The desired probability is given by the probability of the branch you want, divided by the sum of the probabilities of all the branches producing event E.

EXAMPLE 2

Based on past experience, a company knows that an experienced machine operator (one or more years of experience) will produce a defective item 1% of the time. People with some experience (up to one year) have a 2.5% defect rate, while new people have a 6% defect rate. At any one time, the company has 60% experienced employees, 30% with some experience, and 10% new employees. Find the probability that a particular defective item was produced by a new operator.

Let E represent the event "an item is defective," with F_1 representing "item was made by an experienced operator," F_2 "item was made by a person with some experience," and F_3 "item was made by a new employee." Then

$$P(F_1) = .60 \qquad P(E|F_1) = .01$$
$$P(F_2) = .30 \qquad P(E|F_2) = .025$$
$$P(F_3) = .10 \qquad P(E|F_3) = .06.$$

We need to find $P(F_3|E)$, the probability that an item was produced by a new operator, given that it is defective. First, draw a tree diagram using the given information, as in Figure 15. The steps leading to event E are shown in heavy type.

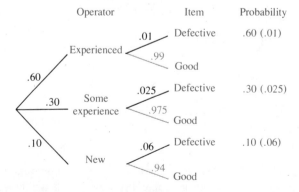

FIGURE 15

Find $P(F_3|E)$ with the bottom branch of the tree in Figure 15; divide the probability for this branch by the sum of the probabilities of all the branches leading to E, or

$$P(F_3|E) = \frac{.10(.06)}{.60(.01) + .30(.025) + .10(.06)} = \frac{.006}{.0195} = \frac{4}{13}.$$

In a similar way

$$P(F_2|E) = \frac{.30(.025)}{.60(.01) + .30(.025) + .10(.06)} = \frac{.0075}{.0195} = \frac{5}{13}.$$

Finally, $P(F_1|E) = 4/13$. Check that $P(F_1|E) + P(F_2|E) + P(F_3|E) = 1$. (That is, the defective item was made by *someone*.) ▨

EXAMPLE 3

A manufacturer buys items from six different suppliers. The fraction of the total number of items obtained from each supplier, along with the probability that an item purchased from that supplier is defective, is shown in the following chart.

Supplier	Fraction of Total Supplied	Probability of Defective
1	.05	.04
2	.12	.02
3	.16	.07
4	.23	.01
5	.35	.03
6	.09	.05

Find the probability that a defective item came from supplier 5.
Let F_1 be the event that an item came from supplier 1, with F_2, F_3, F_4, F_5, and F_6 defined in a similar manner. Let E be the event that an item is defective. We want to find $P(F_5|E)$. By Bayes' Formula (draw a tree),

$$P(F_5|E) = \frac{(.35)(.03)}{(.05)(.04) + (.12)(.02) + (.16)(.07) + (.23)(.01) + (.35)(.03) + (.09)(.05)}$$

$$= \frac{.0105}{.0329} \approx .319.$$

There is about a 32% chance that a defective item came from supplier 5. ▨

6.6 EXERCISES

For two events M and N, $P(M) = .4$, $P(N|M) = .3$, and $P(N|M') = .4$. Find each of the following.

1. $P(M|N)$

2. $P(M'|N)$

For mutually exclusive events R_1, R_2, R_3, we have $P(R_1) = .05$, $P(R_2) = .6$, and $P(R_3) = .35$. Also, $P(Q|R_1) = .40$, $P(Q|R_2) = .30$, and $P(Q|R_3) = .60$. Find each of the following.

3. $P(R_1|Q)$ **4.** $P(R_2|Q)$ **5.** $P(R_3|Q)$ **6.** $P(R_1'|Q)$

Suppose you have three jars with the following contents: 2 black balls and 1 white ball in the first; 1 black ball and 2 white balls in the second; and 1 black ball and 1 white ball in the third. One jar is to be selected, and then one ball is to be drawn from the selected jar. If the probabilities of selecting the first, second, or third jar are 1/2, 1/3, and 1/6 respectively, find the probability that if a white ball is drawn, it came from

7. the second jar   **8.** the third jar.

The following table shows the fraction of the population in various income levels, as well as the probability that a person from that income level will take an airline flight within the next year.

Income Level	Proportion of Population	Probability of a Flight During the Next Year
$0–$5999	12.8%	.04
$6000–$9999	14.6%	.06
$10,000–$14,999	18.5%	.07
$15,000–$19,999	17.8%	.09
$20,000–$24,999	13.9%	.12
$25,000 and over	22.4%	.13

If a person is selected at random from an airline flight, find the probability that the person has an income level of

9. $10,000–$14,999;   **10.** $25,000 and over.

The following table shows the proportion of people over 18 who are in various age categories, along with the probability that a person in a given age category will vote in a general election.

Age	Proportion of Voting Age Population	Probability of a Person of This Age Voting
18–21	11.0%	.48
22–24	7.6%	.53
25–44	37.6%	.68
45–64	28.3%	.64
65 or over	15.5%	.74

Suppose a voter is picked at random. Find the probability that the voter is in the following age categories.

11. 18–21   **12.** 65 or over

Of all the people applying for a certain job, 70% are qualified, and 30% are not. The personnel manager claims that she approves qualified people 85% of the time; she approves an unqualified person 20% of the time. Find each of the following probabilities.

13. A person is qualified if he or she was approved by the manager.

14. A person is unqualified if he or she was approved by the manager.

A building contractor buys 70% of his cement from supplier A, and 30% from supplier B. A total of 90% of the bags from A arrive undamaged, while 95% of the bags from B come undamaged. Give the probability that a damaged bag is from supplier

15. A; **16.** B.

The probability that a customer of a local department store will be a "slow pay" is .02. The probability that a "slow pay" will make a large down payment when buying a refrigerator is .14. The probability that a person who is not a "slow pay" will make a large down payment when buying a refrigerator is .50. Suppose a customer makes a large down payment on a refrigerator. Find the probability that the customer is

17. a "slow pay;" **18.** not a "slow pay."

Companies A, B, and C produce 15%, 40%, and 45% respectively of the major appliances sold in a certain area. In that area, 1% of the Company A appliances, 1 1/2% of the Company B appliances, and 2% of the Company C appliances need service within the first year. Suppose a defective appliance is chosen at random; find the probability that it was manufactured by Company

19. A; **20.** B.

On a given weekend in the fall, a tire company can buy television advertising time for a college football game, a baseball game, or a professional football game. If the company sponsors the college game, there is a 70% chance of a high rating, a 50% chance if they sponsor a baseball game, and a 60% chance if they sponsor a professional football game. The probability of the company sponsoring these various games is .5, .2, and .3, respectively. Suppose the company does get a high rating; find the probability that it sponsored

21. a college game; **22.** a professional football game.

According to readings in business publications, there is a 50% chance of a booming economy next summer, a 20% chance of a mediocre economy, and a 30% chance of a recession. The probabilities that a particular investment strategy will produce a huge profit under each of these possibilities are .1, .6, and .3 respectively. Suppose it turns out that the strategy does produce huge profits; find the probability that the economy was

23. booming; **24.** in recession.

25. The probability that a person with certain symptoms has hepatitis is .8. The blood test used to confirm this diagnosis gives positive results for 90% of those who have the disease and 5% of those without the disease. What is the probability that an individual with the symptoms who reacts positively to the test has hepatitis?

A recent issue of *Newsweek* described a new test for toxemia, a disease that affects pregnant women. To perform the test, the woman lies on her left side and then rolls over on her back. The test is considered positive if there is a 20 mm rise in her blood pressure within one minute. The article gives the following probabilities, where T represents having toxemia at some time during the pregnancy, and N represents a negative test.

$$P(T'|N) = .90, \quad \text{and} \quad P(T|N') = .75.$$

Assume that $P(N') = .11$, and find each of the following.

26. $P(N|T)$ **27.** $P(N'|T)$

28. In a certain county, the Democrats have 53% of the registered voters, 12% of whom are under 21. The Republicans have 47% of all registered voters, of whom 10% are under 21. If Kay is a registered voter who is under 21, what is the probability that she is a Democrat?

Let F, G, and H be nonempty events with $F \cap G = \varnothing$, $F \cap H = \varnothing$, and $G \cap H = \varnothing$.
Let $S = F \cup G \cup H$. Let E be any event. Prove each of the following.

29. $P(E) = P(E \cap F) + P(E \cap G) + P(E \cap H)$

30. $P(E) = P(E|F) \cdot P(F) + P(E|G) \cdot P(G) + P(E|H) \cdot P(H)$

EXTENDED

APPLICATION

Medical Diagnosis

When a patient is examined, information, typically incomplete, is obtained about his state of health. Probability theory provides a mathematical model appropriate for this situation, as well as a procedure for quantitatively interpreting such partial information to arrive at a reasonable diagnosis.*

To do this, we list the states of health that can be distinguished in such a way that the patient can be in one and only one state at the time of the examination. For each state of health H, we associate a number $P(H)$ between 0 and 1 such that the sum of all these numbers is 1. This number $P(H)$ represents the probability, before examination, that a patient is in the state of health H, and $P(H)$ may be chosen subjectively from medical experience, using any information available prior to the examination. The probability may be most conveniently established from clinical records, that is, a mean probability is established for patients in general, although the number would vary from patient to patient. Of course, the more information that is brought to bear in establishing $P(H)$, the better the diagnosis.

For example, limiting the discussion to the condition of a patient's heart, suppose there are exactly 3 states of health, with probabilities as follows:

	State of health H	$P(H)$
H_1	patient has a normal heart	.8
H_2	patient has minor heart irregularities	.15
H_3	patient has a severe heart condition	.05

Having selected $P(H)$, the information of the examination is processed. First, the results of the examination must be classified. The examination itself consists of observing the state of a number of characteristics of the patient. Let us assume that the examination for a heart condition consists of a stethoscope examination and a cardiogram. The outcome of such an examination, C, might be one of the following:

C_1— stethoscope shows normal heart
        and cardiogram shows normal heart;

C_2— stethoscope shows normal heart
        and cardiogram shows minor irregularities,

and so on.

---

*This example is based on "Probabilistic Medical Diagnosis," Roger Wright, from *Some Mathematical Models in Biology*, Robert M. Thrall, ed., rev. ed., (The University of Michigan, 1967), by permission of Robert M. Thrall.

It remains to assess for each state of health H the conditional probability $P(C|H)$ of each examination outcome C using only the knowledge that a patient is in a given state of health. (This may be based on the medical knowledge and clinical experience of the doctor.) The conditional probabilities $P(C|H)$ will not vary from patient to patient, so that they may be built into a diagnostic system, although they should be reviewed periodically.

Suppose the result of the examination is C_1. Let us assume the following probabilities:

$$P(C_1|H_1) = .9$$
$$P(C_1|H_2) = .4$$
$$P(C_1|H_3) = .1.$$

Now, for a given patient, the appropriate probability associated with each state of health H, after examination, is $P(H|C)$ where C is the outcome of the examination. This can be calculated by using Bayes' Formula. For example, to find $P(H_1|C_1)$ — that is, the probability that the patient has a normal heart given that the examination showed a normal stethoscope examination and a normal cardiogram — we use Bayes' Formula as follows:

$$P(H_1|C_1) = \frac{P(C_1|H_1)P(H_1)}{P(C_1|H_1)P(H_1) + P(C_1|H_2)P(H_2) + P(C_1|H_3)P(H_3)}$$

$$= \frac{(.9)(.8)}{(.9)(.8) + (.4)(.15) + (.1)(.05)} \approx .92.$$

Hence, the probability is about .92 that the patient has a normal heart on the basis of the examination results. This means that in 8 out of 100 patients, some abnormality will be present and not be detected by the stethoscope or the cardiogram.

EXERCISES

1. Find $P(H_2|C_1)$.

2. Assuming the following probabilities, find $P(H_1|C_2)$:
   $$P(C_2|H_1) = .2, \qquad P(C_2|H_2) = .8, \qquad P(C_2|H_3) = .3.$$

3. Assuming the probabilities of Exercise 2, find $P(H_3|C_2)$.

6.7 Bernoulli Trials

Many probability problems are concerned with experiments in which an event is repeated many times. For example, we might want to find the probability of getting 7 heads in 8 tosses of a coin, or hitting a target 6 times out of 6, or finding 1 defective item in a sample of 15 items. Probability problems of this kind are called **repeated trials** problems, or **Bernoulli processes.** In each case, some outcome is designated a success, and any other outcome is considered a failure. Thus, if the probability of a success in a single trial is p, the probability of failure will be $1 - p$. Repeated trials problems, or *binomial problems*, must satisfy the following conditions.

Bernoulli Trials

> 1. The same experiment is repeated several times.
> 2. There are only two possible outcomes, success and failure.
> 3. The repeated trials are independent.
> 4. The probability of each outcome remains the same for each trial.

Let us consider the solution of a problem of this type. Suppose we want to find the probability of getting 5 ones on 5 rolls of a die. The probability of getting a one on 1 roll is 1/6, while the probability of any other result is 5/6.

$$P(5 \text{ ones on 5 rolls}) = P(1) \cdot P(1) \cdot P(1) \cdot P(1) \cdot P(1) = \left(\frac{1}{6}\right)^5$$

$$\approx .00013$$

Now, let us find the probability of getting a one exactly 4 times in 5 rolls of the die. The desired outcome for this experiment can occur in more than one way, as shown below, where s represents getting a success (a one), and f represents getting a failure (any other result).

$$
\begin{array}{ccccc}
s & s & s & s & f \\
s & s & s & f & s \\
s & s & f & s & s \\
s & f & s & s & s \\
f & s & s & s & s \\
\end{array}
$$

The probability of each of these five outcomes is

$$\left(\frac{1}{6}\right)^4 \left(\frac{5}{6}\right).$$

Since the five outcomes represent mutually exclusive alternative events, add the five probabilities.

$$P(4 \text{ ones in 5 rolls}) = 5\left(\frac{1}{6}\right)^4 \left(\frac{5}{6}\right) = \frac{5^2}{6^5} \approx .0032$$

In the same way, we can compute the probability of rolling a one exactly 3 times in 5 rolls of a die. The probability of any one way of achieving 3 successes and 2 failures will be

$$\left(\frac{1}{6}\right)^3 \left(\frac{5}{6}\right)^2.$$

Again the desired outcome can occur in more than one way. Let the set {1, 2, 3, 4, 5} represent the first, second, third, fourth, and fifth tosses. The number of 3-element subsets of this set will correspond to the number of ways in which 3 successes and 2 failures can occur. Using combinations, there are $\binom{5}{3}$ such subsets.

Since $\binom{5}{3} = 5!/(3!2!) = 10$,

$$P(3 \text{ ones in } 5 \text{ rolls}) = 10\left(\frac{1}{6}\right)^3\left(\frac{5}{6}\right)^2 = \frac{250}{6^5} \approx .032.$$

Suppose now that the probability of a success on one trial of a Bernoulli experiment is p, and the probability of exactly x successes in n repeated trials is needed. It is possible that the x successes could come first, followed by $n - x$ failures:

$$\underbrace{s \quad s \quad s \cdots s}_{x \text{ successes, then}} \quad \underbrace{f \quad f \cdots f.}_{n - x \text{ failures}} \tag{1}$$

The probability of this result is

$$P(s \quad s \quad s \cdots s \quad s \quad f \quad f \cdots f)$$

$$= \underbrace{P(s) \cdot P(s) \cdot P(s) \cdots P(s)}_{x \text{ factors}} \cdot \underbrace{P(f) \cdot P(f) \cdots P(f)}_{n - x \text{ factors}}$$

$$= \underbrace{p \cdot p \cdot p \cdots p}_{x \text{ factors}} \cdot \underbrace{(1 - p) \cdot (1 - p) \cdots (1 - p)}_{n - x \text{ factors}}$$

$$= p^x(1 - p)^{n-x}.$$

The x successes could also be obtained by rearranging the letters in (1) above. There are $\binom{n}{x}$ ways of choosing the x places where the s's occur and the $n - x$ places where the f's occur, so the probability of exactly x successes is

$$\binom{n}{x} p^x(1 - p)^{n-x}.$$

A summary follows.

Probability In a Bernoulli Experiment	If p is the probability of success in a single trial of a Bernoulli experiment, the probability of x successes and $n - x$ failures in n independent repeated trials of the experiment is $$\binom{n}{x} \cdot p^x \cdot (1 - p)^{n-x}.$$

EXAMPLE 1

The advertising agency which handles the Diet Supercola account thinks that 40% of all consumers prefer this product over its competitors. Suppose a sample of 6 people is chosen. Assume that all responses are independent of each other. Find the probability of the following.

(a)   Exactly 3 of the 6 people prefer Diet Supercola.

In this example, $P(\text{success}) = P(\text{prefer Diet Supercola}) = .4$. The sample is made up of 6 people, so $n = 6$. To find the probability that exactly 3 people prefer this drink, let $x = 3$.

$$P(\text{exactly 3}) = \binom{6}{3}(.4)^3(1 - .4)^{6-3}$$
$$= 20(.4)^3(.6)^3$$
$$= 20(.064)(.216)$$
$$= .27648$$

(b)   None of the 6 people prefer Diet Supercola.

Let $x = 0$.

$$P(\text{exactly 0}) = \binom{6}{0}(.4)^0(1 - .4)^6 = 1(1)(.6)^6 \approx .0467 \quad \blacksquare$$

EXAMPLE 2

At a certain school in northern Michigan, 80% of the students ski. If 5 students at this school are selected, and their responses are independent, then the probability that exactly 1 of the 5 students skis is

$$P(\text{exactly 1}) = \binom{5}{1}(.8)^1(.2)^4 = .0064,$$

while the probability that exactly four of the five students ski is

$$P(\text{exactly 4}) = \binom{5}{4}(.8)^4(.2)^1 = .4096. \quad \blacksquare$$

EXAMPLE 3

Find each of the following probabilities.

(a)   the probability of getting exactly seven heads in eight tosses of a fair coin

The probability of success, getting a head in a single toss, is 1/2. The probability of a failure, getting a tail, is $1 - 1/2 = 1/2$. Thus,

$$P(\text{7 heads in 8 tosses}) = \binom{8}{7}\left(\frac{1}{2}\right)^7\left(\frac{1}{2}\right)^1 = 8\left(\frac{1}{2}\right)^8 = .03125.$$

(b)   the probability of 2 fours in 8 rolls of a die

The probability of success, a 4, is 1/6, while the probability of failure (a number other than 4), is 5/6.

$$P(\text{2 fours in 8 rolls}) = \binom{8}{2}\left(\frac{1}{6}\right)^2\left(\frac{5}{6}\right)^6 \approx .2605 \quad \blacksquare$$

EXAMPLE 4

Assuming that selection of items for a sample can be treated as independent trials, find the probability of the occurrence of one defective item in a random sample of 15 items from a production line, if the probability that any one item is defective is .01.

The probability of success (a defective item), is .01, while the probability of failure (an acceptable item) is .99. This makes

$$P(1 \text{ defective in 15 items}) = \binom{15}{1}(.01)^1(.99)^{14}$$

$$= 15(.01)(.99)^{14}$$

$$\approx .130. \quad \blacksquare$$

EXAMPLE 5

A new style of shoe is sweeping the country. In one area, 30% of all the shoes are of this type. Assume that these sales are independent events, and find the following probabilities.

(a) Of 10 people who buy shoes, at least 8 buy the new shoe style.

Let success be "buy the new style", so that $P(\text{success}) = .3$. For at least 8 people out of 10 to buy the shoe, it must be sold to 8, 9, or 10 people, with

$$P(\text{at least } 8) = P(8) + P(9) + P(10)$$

$$= \binom{10}{8}(.3)^8(.7)^2 + \binom{10}{9}(.3)^9(.7)^1 + \binom{10}{10}(.3)^{10}(.7)^0$$

$$\approx .0014467 + .0001378 + .0000059$$

$$= .0015904.$$

(b) Of 10 people who buy shoes, no more than 7 buy the new shoe style.

"No more than 7" means 0, 1, 2, 3, 4, 5, 6, or 7 people buy the shoe. We could add $P(0)$, $P(1)$, and so on, but it is easier to use the formula $P(E) = 1 - P(E')$. The complement of "no more than 7" is "8 or more." Finally,

$$P(\text{no more than } 7) = 1 - P(8 \text{ or more})$$

$$= 1 - .0015904 \quad \text{(answer from part (a))}$$

$$= .9984096. \quad \blacksquare$$

The Probability of k Trials for m Successes In the rest of this section, we will find the probability that k trials will be needed to guarantee m successes in a Bernoulli experiment. As an example, suppose that a salesperson in a very competitive business makes a sale in one client visit out of five, so $P(\text{sale}) = .2$. The probability of a sale on the first call is .2. The probability that the *first* sale will be on the *second* call is

$$P(\text{no sale on first}) \cdot P(\text{sale on second}) = .8(.2) = .16.$$

The probability that the *first* sale will be on the *third* call is

$$(.8)^2(.2) = .128.$$

Generalizing, the probability that the first sale will be on the kth call is

$$(.8)^{k-1}(.2).$$

EXAMPLE 6

How many calls must this salesperson make to have an 80% chance of making a sale?

There is a .2 chance of making a sale on the first call, a .16 chance of making the first sale on the second call, a .128 chance of making the first sale on the third call, and so on. The probability of a sale by the kth call is the sum of all the probabilities of sales on calls 1, 2, 3, $\cdots$, k. A calculator gives the results of the following table.

Call Number	Probability That First Sale is on That Call	Total of all Probabilities up to and Including This Call
1	$(.8)^0(.2) = .2$	.2
2	$(.8)^1(.2) = .16$	.36
3	$(.8)^2(.2) = .128$	.488
4	$(.8)^3(.2) = .1024$	.5904
5	$(.8)^4(.2) \approx .082$	$\approx .672$
6	$(.8)^5(.2) \approx .066$	$\approx .738$
7	$(.8)^6(.2) \approx .052$	$\approx .790$
8	$(.8)^7(.2) \approx .042$	$\approx .832$

The salesperson must make 8 calls to have an 80% chance of making one sale. ■

This result can be generalized: let p be the probability of success on one trial in a Bernoulli experiment. Then to find the probability that k trials will be needed to guarantee m successes, we must assume the kth trial was a success, and that $m - 1$ successes were distributed in some order among the other $k - 1$ trials. The desired probability is thus

$$\left[\binom{k-1}{m-1}p^{(m-1)} \cdot (1-p)^{(k-1)-(m-1)}\right] \cdot p$$

or

$$\binom{k-1}{m-1}p^m \cdot (1-p)^{k-m}.$$

EXAMPLE 7

Find the probability that the salesperson of Example 6 will require 9 calls to make 3 sales.

Let $k = 9$ and $m = 3$. We know that $p = .2$. The desired probability is

$$\binom{9-1}{3-1}(.2)^3(1-.2)^{9-3} = \binom{8}{2}(.2)^3(.8)^6 \approx .0587. \quad ■$$

6.7 EXERCISES

Suppose that a family has 5 children. Also, suppose that the probability of having a girl is 1/2. Find the probability that the family will have

1. exactly 2 girls;

2. exactly 3 girls;

3. no girls;

4. no boys;

5. at least 4 girls;

7. no more than 3 boys;

6. at least 3 boys;

8. no more than 4 girls.

A die is rolled 12 times. Find the probability of rolling

9. exactly 12 ones;

11. exactly 1 one;

13. no more than 3 ones;

10. exactly 6 ones;

12. exactly 2 ones;

14. no more than 1 one.

A coin is tossed 5 times. Find the probability of getting

15. all heads;

17. no more than 3 heads;

16. exactly 3 heads;

18. at least 3 heads.

A factory tests a random sample of 20 transistors for defectives. The probability that a particular transistor will be defective has been established by past experience to be .05.

19. What is the probability that there are no defectives in the sample?

20. What is the probability that the number of defectives in the sample is at most 2?

A company gives prospective employees a 6-question multiple-choice test. Each question has 5 possible answers, so that there is a 1/5 or 20% chance of answering a question correctly just by guessing. Find the probability of answering, by chance,

21. exactly 2 questions correctly;

23. at least 4 correctly;

22. no questions correctly;

24. no more than 3 correctly.

25. Over the last decade, 10% of all clients of J. K. Loss & Company have lost their life savings. Suppose a sample of 3 of the current clients of the firm is chosen. Assuming independence, find the probability that exactly one of the 3 clients will lose everything.

According to a recent article in a business publication, only 20% of the population of the United States has never had a Big Burg hamburger at a major fast-food chain. Assume independence and find the probability that in a random sample of 10 people

26. exactly 2 never had a Big Burg;

28. 3 or fewer never had a Big Burg;

27. exactly 5 never had a Big Burg;

29. 4 or more *have* had a Big Burg.

A new drug cures 70% of the people taking it. Suppose 20 people take the drug; find the probability that

30. exactly 18 are cured;

32. at least 17 are cured;

31. exactly 17 are cured;

33. at least 18 are cured.

In a 10-question multiple-choice biology test with 5 choices for each question, a student who did not prepare guesses on each item. Find the probability that he answers

34. exactly 6 questions correctly;

36. at least 8 correctly;

35. exactly 7 correctly;

37. less than 8 correctly.

Assume that the probability that a person will die within a month after a certain operation is 20%. Find the probability that in 3 such operations

38. all 3 people survive;

40. at least 2 people survive;

39. exactly 1 person survives;

41. no more than 1 person survives.

Six mice from the same litter, all suffering from a vitamin A deficiency, are fed a certain dose of carrots. If the probability of recovery under such treatment is .70, find the probability that

42. none recover;

43. exactly 3 of the 6 recover;

44. all recover;

45. no more than 3 recover.

46. In an experiment on the effects of a radiation dose on cells, a beam of radioactive particles is aimed at a group of 10 cells. Find the probability that 8 of the cells will be hit by the beam, if the probability that any single cell will be hit is .6. (Assume independence.)

47. The probability of a mutation of a given gene under a dose of 1 roentgen of radiation is approximately 2.5×10^{-7}. What is the probability that in 10,000 genes, at least 1 mutation occurs?

48. A new drug being tested causes a serious side effect in 5 out of 100 patients. What is the probability that no side effects occur in a sample of 10 patients taking the drug?

An economist feels that the probability that a person at a certain income level will buy a new car this year is .2. Find the probability that among 12 such people,

49. exactly 4 buy a new car;

50. exactly 6 buy a new car;

51. no more than 3 buy a new car;

52. at least 3 buy a new car.

Find the probability that the following numbers of tosses of a fair coin will be required to obtain three heads.

53. 5   **54.** 6   **55.** 8   **56.** 10

Find the probability that the following numbers of rolls of a fair die will be required to get 4 fives.

57. 6   **58.** 10   **59.** 12   **60.** 16

The probability that a given exploration team sent out by a mining company will find commercial quantities of iron ore is .15. How many such teams must the company send out to have the following probabilities of finding ore? *not handled by either of formulas*

61. 60%   **62.** 75%   **63.** 80%

64. Suppose we find the probability of r successes out of n trials for a Bernoulli experiment having probability p. Show that the result is the same as for the probability of $n - r$ successes out of n trials for a Bernoulli experiment having probability $1 - p$.

Calculate each of the probabilities in Exercises 65–68.

65. A flu vaccine has a probability of 80% of preventing a person who is inoculated from getting flu. A county health office inoculates 134 people. What is the probability that

    (a) exactly 10 of them get the flu?

    (b) no more than 10 get the flu?

    (c) none of them get the flu?

66. The probability that a male will be color-blind is .042. What is the probability that in a group of 53 men

    (a) exactly five are color-blind?

    (b) no more than five are color-blind?

    (c) at least 1 is color-blind?

67. The probability that a certain machine turns out a defective item is .05. What is the probability that in a run of 75 items

  (a) exactly 5 defectives are produced?

  (b) no defectives are produced?

  (c) at least 1 defective is produced?

68. A company is taking a survey to find out if people like their product. Their last survey indicated that 70% of the population like their product. Based on that, of a sample of 58 people, what is the probability that

  (a) all 58 like the product?

  (b) from 28 to 30 (inclusive) like the product?

KEY WORDS

experiment	**simple event**
trial	**certain event**
outcome	**impossible event**
sample space	**mutually exclusive events**
probability distribution	**probability of an event**
addition principle	**stochastic processes**
complement of an event	**independent events**
odds	**dependent events**
subjective probability	**Bayes' formula**
conditional probability	**repeated trials**
tree diagram	**Bernoulli experiments**
product rule	**binomial problems**
event	

Chapter 6   REVIEW EXERCISES

Write sample spaces for the following.

  1. a die is rolled

  2. a card is drawn from a deck containing only the thirteen spades

  3. the weight of a person is measured to the nearest half pound; the scale will not measure more than 300 pounds

  4. a coin is tossed four times

An urn contains five balls labeled 3, 5, 7, 9, and 11, respectively, while a second urn contains four red and two green balls. An experiment consists of pulling one ball from each urn, in turn. Write each of the following.

  5. the sample space

  6. event E, the first ball is greater than 5

  7. event F, the second ball is green

  8. Are the outcomes in the sample space equally likely?

A company sells typewriters and copiers. Let E be the event "a customer buys a typewriter," and let F be the event "a customer buys a copier." Write each of the following using $\cap$, $\cup$, or $'$ as necessary.

9. A customer buys neither

10. A customer buys at least one

When a single card is drawn from an ordinary deck, find the probability that it will be

11. a heart;

12. a red queen;

13. a face card;

14. black or a face card;

15. red, given it is a queen;

16. a jack, given it is a face card;

17. a face card, given it is a king.

Find the odds in favor of a card drawn from an ordinary deck being

18. a club

19. a black jack

20. a red face card or a queen

A sample shipment of five swimming pool filters is chosen at random. The probability of exactly 0, 1, 2, 3, 4, or 5 filters being defective is given in the following table.

Number Defective	0	1	2	3	4	5
Probability	.31	.25	.18	.12	.08	.06

Find the probability that the following number of filters is defective.

21. no more than 3

22. at least 3

The square shows the four possible (equally likely) combinations when both parents are carriers of the sickle cell anemia trait. Each carrier parent has normal cells (N) and trait cells (T).

	2nd Parent	
	N_2	T_2
1st Parent N_1		$N_1 T_2$
T_1		

23. Complete the table.

24. If the disease occurs only when two trait cells combine, find the probability that a child born to these parents will have sickle cell anemia.

25. The child will carry the trait but not have the disease if a normal cell combines with a trait cell. Find this probability.

26. Find the probability that the child is neither a carrier nor has the disease.

Find the probability for the following sums when two fair dice are rolled.

27. 8

28. 0

29. at least 10

30. no more than 5

31. odd and greater than 8

32. 12, given it is greater than 10

33. 7, given that at least one die is 4

34. at least 9, given that at least one die is 5

Suppose $P(E) = .51$, $P(F) = .37$, and $P(E \cap F) = .22$. Find each of the following probabilities.

35. $P(E \cup F)$

36. $P(E \cap F')$

37. $P(E' \cup F)$

38. $P(E' \cap F')$

A basket contains 4 black, 2 blue, and 5 green balls. A sample of 3 balls is drawn. Find the probability that the sample contains

39. all black balls;

40. all blue balls;

41. 2 black balls and 1 green ball;

42. exactly 2 black balls;

43. 2 green and 1 blue ball;

44. exactly 1 blue ball.

Suppose two cards are drawn without replacement from an ordinary deck of 52. Find the probability that

45. both cards are red;

46. both cards are spades;

47. at least one card is a spade;

48. the second card is red given that the first card was a diamond;

49. the second card is a face card, given that the first card was not;

50. the second card is a five, given that the first card was the five of diamonds.

The table below shows the results of a survey of 1000 new or used car buyers of a certain model car.

	Satisfied	Not Satisfied	Totals
New	300	100	400
Used	450	150	600
Totals	750	250	1000

Let S represent the event "satisfied", and N the event "bought a new car." Find each of the following.

51. $P(N \cap S)$

52. $P(N \cup S')$

53. $P(N|S)$

54. $P(N'|S)$

55. $P(S|N')$

56. $P(S'|N')$

Of the appliance repair shops listed in the phone book, 80% are competent and 20% are not. A competent shop can repair an appliance correctly 95% of the time; an incompetent shop can repair an appliance correctly 60% of the time. Suppose an appliance was repaired correctly. Find the probability that it was repaired by

57. a competent shop;

58. an incompetent shop.

Suppose an appliance was repaired incorrectly. Find the probability that it was repaired by

59. a competent shop;

60. an incompetent shop.

61. Box A contains 5 red balls and 1 black ball; box B contains 2 red and 3 black balls. A box is chosen, and a ball is selected from it. The probability of choosing box A is 3/8. If the selected ball is black, what is the probability that it came from box A?

62. Find the probability that the ball in Exercise 61 came from box B, given that it is red.

Suppose a family plans six children, and the probability that a particular child is a girl is 1/2. Find the probability that the family will have

63. exactly 3 girls;

64. all girls;

65. at least 4 girls;

66. no more than 2 boys.

A certain machine used to manufacture screws produces a defective rate of .01. A random sample of 20 screws is selected. Find the probability that the sample contains

67. exactly 4 defective screws;   **68.** exactly 3 defective screws;

69. no more than 4 defective screws.

70. *Set up* the probability that the sample has 12 or more defective screws. (Do not evaluate.)

71. An oil company finds oil with 14% of the wells that it drills. How many wells must the company drill to have the following probabilities of finding oil?

   (a) 2/3   **(b)** 3/4

72. *Randomized Response Method for Getting Honest Answers to Sensitive Questions.** * Basically, this is a method to guarantee an individual that answers to sensitive questions will be anonymous, thus encouraging a truthful response. This method is, in effect, an application of the formula for finding the probability of an intersection and operates as follows. Two questions A and B are posed, one of which is sensitive and the other not. The probability of receiving a ''yes'' to the nonsensitive question must be known. For example, one could ask

   A: Does your Social Security number end in an odd digit? (Nonsensitive)
   B: Have you ever intentionally cheated on your income taxes? (Sensitive)

We know that $P(\text{answer yes}|\text{answer } A) = 1/2$. We wish to approximate $P(\text{answer yes}|\text{answer } B)$. The subject is asked to flip a coin and answer A if the coin comes up heads and otherwise to answer B. In this way, the interviewer does not know which question the subject is answering. Thus, a ''yes'' answer is not incriminating. There is no way for the interviewer to know whether the subject is saying ''Yes, my Social Security number ends in an odd digit'' or ''Yes, I have intentionally cheated on my income taxes.'' The percentage of subjects in the group answering ''yes'' is used to approximate $P(\text{answer yes})$.

   (a) Use the fact that the event ''answer yes'' is the union of the event ''answer yes and answer A'' with the event ''answer yes and answer B'' to prove that

$$P(\text{answer yes}|\text{answer B})$$
$$= \frac{P(\text{answer yes}) - P(\text{answer yes}|\text{answer A}) \cdot P(\text{answer A})}{P(\text{answer B})}$$

   (b) If this technique is tried on 100 subjects and 60 answered ''yes,'' what is the approximate probability that a person randomly selected from the group has intentionally cheated on income taxes?

*From *Applied Statistics With Probability* by J. S. Milton and J. J. Corbet. Copyright © 1979 by Litton Educational Publishing, Inc. Reprinted by permission of Brooks/Cole Publishing Company, Monterey, California.

STATISTICS AND PROBABILITY DISTRIBUTIONS

Karl Gerstner. From the series *Color Form*, Archetypal Conversion Cycle, 1970–1975, 1977. Paul Gredinger Collection, Düsseldorf.

Statistics deals with the collection and summarization of data, and methods of drawing conclusions about a population based on data from a sample of the population. Statistical models have become increasingly useful in a variety of fields—for example, manufacturing, government, agriculture, medicine, the social sciences, and in all types of research. In this chapter we give a brief introduction to some of the key topics from statistical theory.

7.1   Basic Properties of Probability Distributions

Random Variables   A bank is interested in improving its services to the public. The manager decides to begin by finding the amount of time tellers spend on each transaction. She decides to time the transactions to the nearest minute. To each transaction, then, will be assigned one of the numbers 0, 1, 2, 3, 4, · · ·. That is, if T represents the experiment of timing a transaction, then T may take on any of the values from the list 0, 1, 2, 3, 4, · · ·. Since the value that T takes on for a particular transaction is random, T is called a *random variable*.

Random Variable

> A **random variable** is a function that assigns a real number to each outcome of an experiment.

It is common to use upper case letters, such as X or Y, for random variables. Lower case letters, such as x or y, are then used for a particular value of the random variable.

Probability Distributions   Suppose that the bank manager finds the times for 75 different transactions, with results as shown in Table 1. As the table shows, the shortest transaction time was 1 minute, with 3 transactions of 1-minute duration. The longest time was 10 minutes. Only one transaction took that long.

In Table 1, the ten values assumed by the random variable T are listed in the first column and the number of occurrences corresponding to each of these values, the **frequency** of that value, is given in the second column. Table 1 is an example of a **frequency distribution,** a table listing the frequencies for each value a random variable may assume.

Now suppose that several weeks after starting new procedures to speed up transactions, the manager takes another survey. This time she includes 57 transactions, and she records their times as shown in the frequency distribution of Table 2.

Table 1

Time	Frequency
1	3
2	5
3	9
4	12
5	15
6	11
7	10
8	6
9	3
10	1
	Total: 75

Table 2

Time	Frequency
1	4
2	5
3	8
4	10
5	12
6	17
7	0
8	1
9	0
10	0
	Total: 57

Do the results in Table 2 indicate an improvement? It is hard to compare the two tables, since one is based on 75 transactions and the other on 57. To make them comparable, we can add a column to each table which will give the relative frequency of each transaction time. These results are shown in Tables 3 and 4. Where necessary, decimals are rounded to the nearest hundredth. To find a **relative frequency,** divide each frequency by the total of the frequencies. Here the individual frequencies are divided by 75 or 57 respectively.

Table 3

Time	Frequency	Relative Frequency
1	3	$\frac{3}{75} = .04$
2	5	$\frac{5}{75} \approx .07$
3	9	$\frac{9}{75} = .12$
4	12	$\frac{12}{75} = .16$
5	15	$\frac{15}{75} = .20$
6	11	$\frac{11}{75} \approx .15$
7	10	$\frac{10}{75} \approx .13$
8	6	$\frac{6}{75} = .08$
9	3	$\frac{3}{75} = .04$
10	1	$\frac{1}{75} \approx .01$

Table 4

Time	Frequency	Relative Frequency
1	4	$\frac{4}{57} \approx .07$
2	5	$\frac{5}{57} \approx .09$
3	8	$\frac{8}{57} \approx .14$
4	10	$\frac{10}{57} \approx .18$
5	12	$\frac{12}{57} \approx .21$
6	17	$\frac{17}{57} \approx .30$
7	0	$\frac{0}{57} = 0$
8	1	$\frac{1}{57} \approx .02$
9	0	$\frac{0}{57} = 0$
10	0	$\frac{0}{57} = 0$

Whether the differences in relative frequency between the distributions in Tables 3 and 4 are interpreted as desirable or undesirable depends on management goals. If the manager wanted to eliminate the most time-consuming transactions, the results appear to be desirable. However, before the new procedures were followed, the largest relative frequency of transactions, .20 of all transactions, was for a transaction of 5 minutes. After the new procedures, the largest relative frequency, .30, corresponds to a transaction of 6 minutes. At any rate, the results shown in the two tables are easier to compare using relative frequencies.

The relative frequencies of Tables 3 and 4 can be considered as probabilities. A table, such as Table 3 or Table 4, which gives the set of possible values of a random variable, along with the corresponding probabilities, is called a **probability distribution.** The sum of the probabilities shown in a probability distribution must always be 1. (The sum in an actual distribution may vary slightly from 1 due to rounding.)

EXAMPLE 1

Many plants have seed pods with a variable number of seeds. One variety of green beans has no more than 6 seeds per pod. Suppose that examination of 30 such bean pods gave the results shown in Table 5. Here the random variable X tells the number of seeds per pod. Give a probability distribution for these results.

The probabilities are found by computing the relative frequencies. A total of 30 bean pods were examined, so each frequency should be divided by 30 to get the probabilities shown in the distribution of Table 6. Some of the results have been rounded to the nearest hundredth.

Table 5

X	Frequency
0	3
1	4
2	6
3	8
4	5
5	3
6	1
	Total: 30

Table 6

X	Frequency	Probability
0	3	$\frac{3}{30} = .10$
1	4	$\frac{4}{30} \approx .13$
2	6	$\frac{6}{30} = .20$
3	8	$\frac{8}{30} \approx .27$
4	5	$\frac{5}{30} \approx .17$
5	3	$\frac{3}{30} = .10$
6	1	$\frac{1}{30} \approx .03$
	Total: 30	

As shown in Table 6, the probability that the random variable X takes on the value 2 is 6/30, or .20. This is often written as

$$P(X = 2) = .20.$$

Also, $P(X = 5) = .10$, and $P(X = 6) \approx .03$. ▨

Instead of writing the probability distribution of the number of seeds as a table, we could write the same information as a set of ordered pairs:

{(0, .10), (1, .13), (2, .20), (3, .27), (4, .17), (5, .10), (6, .03)}.

There is just one probability for each value of the random variable. Thus, a probability distribution defines a function, called a **probability distribution function,** or, simply, a **probability function.** We shall use the terms "probability distribution" and "probability function" interchangeably. The function described in

Example 1 is a **discrete function,** since it has a finite number of ordered pairs. A **continuous** probability distribution function has an infinite number of values of the random variable, corresponding to an interval on the number line. Continuous probability distribution functions are discussed in Section 7.4.

The information in a probability distribution is often displayed graphically in a special kind of bar graph called a **histogram.** The bars all have the same width. The heights of the bars are determined by the frequencies. A histogram for the data of Table 3 is given in Figure 1. A histogram shows important characteristics of a distribution which may not be evident in tabular form, such as the relative sizes of the probabilities and any symmetry in the distribution.

The area of the bar above $T = 1$ in Figure 1 is the product of 1 and .04, or $.04 \times 1 = .04$. Since each bar has a width of 1, its area is equal to the probability which corresponds to that value of T. The probability that a particular value will occur is thus given by the area of the appropriate bar of the graph. For example, the probability of a transaction time less than four minutes is the sum of the areas for $T = 1$, $T = 2$, and $T = 3$. This area, shown in color in Figure 2, corresponds to 23% of the total area, since

$$P(T < 4) = P(T = 1) + P(T = 2) + P(T = 3)$$
$$= .04 + .07 + .12 = .23.$$

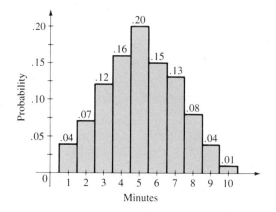

FIGURE 1

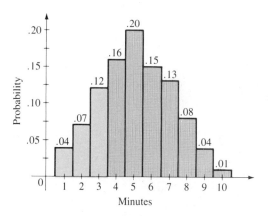

FIGURE 2

<table>
<tr><td>**EXAMPLE 2**</td></tr>
</table>

Construct a histogram for the probability distribution of Example 1. Then find the area which gives the probability that the number of seeds will be more than 4.

A histogram for this distribution is shown in Figure 3. The portion of the histogram in color represents

$$P(X > 4) = P(X = 5) + P(X = 6)$$
$$= .10 + .03 = .13,$$

or 13% of the total area.   ■

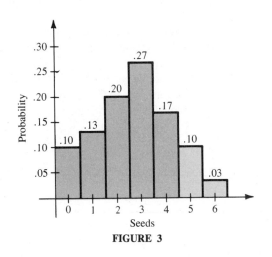

FIGURE 3

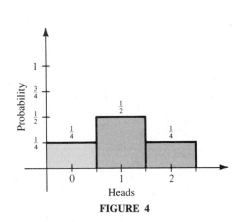

FIGURE 4

EXAMPLE 3

(a)   Give the probability distribution for the number of heads showing when two coins are tossed.

Let X represent the random variable, number of heads. Then X can take on the values 0, 1, or 2. Now find the probability of each outcome. The results are shown in Table 7.

Table 7

x	$P(X = x)$
0	$\frac{1}{4}$
1	$\frac{1}{2}$
2	$\frac{1}{4}$

(b)   Draw a histogram for the distribution of Table 7. Which bars represent the probability that at least one coin comes up heads?

The histogram is shown in Figure 4. The portion in color represents

$$P(X \geq 1) = P(X = 1) + P(X = 2) = \frac{3}{4}.$$ ■

7.1 EXERCISES

In Exercises 1–6, (a) give the probability distribution, and (b) sketch its histogram.

1. In a seed-viability test 50 seeds were placed in 10 rows of five seeds each. After a period of time, the number which germinated in each row were counted with the following results.

Number Germinated	Frequency
0	0
1	0
2	1
3	3
4	4
5	2
Total:	10

2. At a large supermarket during the 5-o'clock rush, the number of customers waiting in each of 10 check-out lines was counted. The results are shown below.

Number Waiting	Frequency
2	1
3	2
4	4
5	2
6	0
7	1
Total:	10

3. At a training program for police officers, each member of a class of 25 took 6 shots at a target. The total number of bullseyes are shown in the table below.

Number of Bullseyes	Frequency
0	0
1	1
2	0
3	4
4	10
5	8
6	2
Total:	25

4. A class of 42 students took a 10-point quiz. The frequency of scores is given below.

Number of Points	Frequency
5	2
6	5
7	10
8	15
9	7
10	3
Total:	42

5. Five mice are inoculated against a disease. After an incubation period, the number who contract the disease is noted. The experiment is repeated 20 times, with the results shown at the side.

Number With the Disease	Frequency
0	3
1	5
2	6
3	3
4	2
5	1
Total:	20

6. The telephone company kept track of the calls for the correct time during a 24-hour period for two weeks. The results are shown at right.

Number of Calls	Frequency
28	1
29	1
30	2
31	3
32	2
33	2
34	2
35	1
Total:	14

For each of the experiments in Exercises 7–12, let X determine a random variable, and use your knowledge of probability to prepare a probability distribution.

7. Four coins are tossed and the number of heads is observed each time.

8. Two dice are rolled and the total number of points is noted.

9. Three cards are drawn from a deck. The number of aces is counted.

10. Two balls are drawn from a bag in which there are 4 white balls and 2 black balls. The number of black balls is counted.

11. A ballplayer with a batting average of .290 comes to bat 4 times in a game. The number of hits is counted.

12. Five cards are drawn from a deck. The number of black threes is counted.

For Exercises 13–18, draw a histogram and shade the region which gives the indicated probability.

13. Exercise 7; $P(X \le 2)$

14. Exercise 8; $P(X \ge 11)$

15. Exercise 9; P(at least one ace)

16. Exercise 10; P(at least one black ball)

17. Exercise 11; $P(X = 2 \text{ or } X = 3)$

18. Exercise 12; $P(1 \le X \le 2)$

19. The frequency with which letters occur in a large sample of any written language does not vary much. Therefore, determining the frequency of each letter in a coded message

is usually the first step in deciphering it. The percent frequencies of the letters in the English language are as follows.

Letter	%	Letter	%	Letters	%
E	13	S, H	6	W, G, B	1.5
T	9	D	4	V	1
A, O	8	L	3.5	K, X, J	0.5
N	7	C, U, M	3	Q, Z	0.2
I, R	6.5	F, P, Y	2		

Use the introductory paragraph of this exercise as a sample of the English language. Find the percent frequency for each letter in the sample. Compare your results with the frequencies given above.

20. The following message is written in a code in which the frequency of the symbols is the main key to the solution.

)? − −8)) y * + 8506 * 3 × 6 ; 4 ?* 7* & × * −6.48 ( ) 985)?

(8 + 2: ;48) 81 & ?(;46 *3)y *;48 & (+8(* 509 + & 8 () 8 = 8

(5* − 8 − 5(81 ? 098 ;4 & +)& 15 * 50:)6)6 *; ? 6;6 & * 0? − 7

(a) Find the frequency of each symbol.

(b) By comparing the high-frequency symbols with the high-frequency letters in English, and the low-frequency symbols with the low-frequency letters, try to decipher the message. (Hint: Look for repeated two-symbol combinations and double letters for added clues. Try to identify vowels first.)

7.2 Expected Value

In working with experimental data, it is often useful to have a typical or "average" number that represents the entire set of data. For example, we compare our heights and weights to those of the typical or "average" person on weight charts. Students are familiar with the "class average" and their own "average" at any time in a given course.

In a recent year, a citizen of the United States could expect to complete about 12 years of school, to be a member of a household earning $20,091 per year, and to live in a household of 2.7 people. What do we mean here by "expect"? Many people have completed less than 12 years of school; many others have completed more. Many households have less income than $20,091 per year; many others have more. The idea of a household of 2.7 people is a little hard to swallow. The numbers all refer to *averages*. When the term "expect" is used in this way, it refers to *mathematical expectation*, which we shall see is a kind of average.

The **arithmetic mean,** or **average,** of a set of numbers is the sum of the numbers in the set, divided by the total number of numbers. To write the sum of the n numbers $x_1, x_2, x_3, \cdots, x_n$ in a compact way, use **summation notation:** using the Greek letter Σ (sigma), the sum $x_1 + x_2 + x_3 + \cdots + x_n$ is written

$$x_1 + x_2 + x_3 + \cdots + x_n = \sum_{i=1}^{n} x_i.$$

The symbol $\bar{x}$ (read x-bar) is used to represent the mean, so that the mean of the n numbers x_1, x_2, x_3, $\cdots$, x_n is

$$\bar{x} = \frac{\sum_{i=1}^{n} x_i}{n}.$$

For example, the mean of the set of numbers 2, 3, 5, 6, 8 is

$$\frac{2 + 3 + 5 + 6 + 8}{5} = \frac{24}{5} = 4.8.$$

What about an average value for a random variable? Can we use the mean to find it? As an example, let us find the average number of offspring for a certain species of pheasant, given the probability distribution in Table 8.

Table 8

Number of Offspring	Frequency	Probability
0	8	.08
1	14	.14
2	29	.29
3	32	.32
4	17	.17
Total:	100	

We might be tempted to find the typical number of offspring by averaging the numbers 0, 1, 2, 3, and 4, which represent the numbers of offspring possible. This won't work, however, since the various numbers of offspring do not occur with equal probability: for example, 3 offspring are much more common than 0 or 1 offspring. The differing probabilities of occurrence can be taken into account with a **weighted average,** found by multiplying each of the possible numbers of offspring by its corresponding probability, as follows:

typical number of offspring $= 0(.08) + 1(.14) + 2(.29) + 3(.32) + 4(.17)$

$$= 0 + .14 + .58 + .96 + .68$$

$$= 2.36.$$

Based on the data above, the typical family of pheasants has 2.36 offspring.

It is certainly not possible for a pair of pheasants to produce 2.36 offspring. However, if the number of offspring produced by many different pairs of pheasants are found, then the average, or the mean, of these numbers will be about 2.36.

We can use the idea of this example to define the mean, or expected value, of a probability distribution. This is done as follows.

Expected Value

Suppose the random variable X can take on the n values $x_1, x_2, x_3, \cdots,$ x_n. Also, suppose the probabilities that each of these values occurs are respectively $p_1, p_2, p_3, \cdots, p_n$. Then the **expected value** of the random variable is

$$E(X) = x_1 p_1 + x_2 p_2 + x_3 p_3 + \cdots + x_n p_n.$$

The symbol μ (the Greek letter mu) is used for the expected value of the random variable X. As in the example above, the expected value of a random variable may be a number which can never occur on any one trial of the experiment.

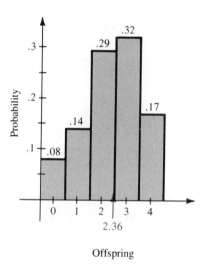

FIGURE 5

Physically, the expected value of a probability distribution represents a balance point. Figure 5 shows a histogram for the distribution of the pheasant offspring. If the histogram is thought of as a series of weights with magnitudes represented by the heights of the bars, then the system would balance if supported at the point corresponding to the expected value.

EXAMPLE 1

The local church decides to raise money by raffling a microwave oven worth $400. A total of 2000 tickets are sold at $1 each. Find the expected value of winning for a person who buys one ticket in the raffle.

Here the random variable represents the possible amounts of net winnings, where net winnings = amount of winning − cost of ticket. The net winnings of the person winning the oven are $400 (amount of winning) − $1 (cost of ticket) = $399. The net winnings for each losing ticket are $0 − $1 = −$1.

The probability of winning is 1 in 2000, or 1/2000, while the probability of losing is 1999/2000. See Table 9.

Table 9

Outcome (net winning)	Probability
$399	$\dfrac{1}{2000}$
$-$1	$\dfrac{1999}{2000}$

The expected winnings for a person buying one ticket are

$$399\left(\frac{1}{2000}\right) + (-1)\left(\frac{1999}{2000}\right) = \frac{399}{2000} - \frac{1999}{2000} = -\frac{1600}{2000} = -.80.$$

On the average, a person buying one ticket in the raffle will lose $.80, or 80¢.

It is not possible to lose 80¢ in this raffle—you either lose $1, or you win a $400 prize. However, if you bought tickets in many such raffles over a long period of time, you would lose 80¢ per ticket, on the average. ▨

EXAMPLE 2

What is the expected number of girls in a family having exactly three children?

Some families with three children will have 0 girls, others will have 1 girl, and so on. We need to find the probabilities associated with 0, 1, 2, or 3 girls in a family of three children. To find these probabilities, first write the sample space S of all possible three-child families: $S = \{ggg, ggb, bgg, gbb, bgb, bbg, bbb, gbg\}$. This sample space gives the probabilities shown in Table 10, assuming that the probability of a girl at each birth is 1/2.

Table 10

Outcome (number of girls)	Probability
0	$\frac{1}{8}$
1	$\frac{3}{8}$
2	$\frac{3}{8}$
3	$\frac{1}{8}$

The expected number of girls can now be found by multiplying each outcome (number of girls) by its corresponding probability and finding the sum of these values.

$$\text{expected number of girls} = 0 \cdot \frac{1}{8} + 1 \cdot \frac{3}{8} + 2 \cdot \frac{3}{8} + 3 \cdot \frac{1}{8}$$

$$= \frac{3}{8} + \frac{6}{8} + \frac{3}{8}$$

$$= \frac{12}{8} = \frac{3}{2} = 1.5$$

On the average, a three-child family will have 1.5 girls. ▨

EXAMPLE 3

Each day Donna and Mary toss a coin to see who buys the coffee (40¢ a cup). One tosses and the other calls the outcome. If the person who calls the outcome is correct, the other buys the coffee; otherwise the caller pays. Find Donna's expected winnings.

Assume that an honest coin is used, that Mary tosses the coin, and that Donna calls the outcome. The possible results and corresponding probabilities are shown below.

	Possible Results			
Result of toss	H	H	T	T
Call	H	T	H	T
Caller wins?	Yes	No	No	Yes
Probability	$\frac{1}{4}$	$\frac{1}{4}$	$\frac{1}{4}$	$\frac{1}{4}$

Donna wins a 40¢ cup of coffee whenever the results and calls match, and loses a 40¢ cup when there is no match. Her expected winnings are

$$(.40)\left(\frac{1}{4}\right) + (-.40)\left(\frac{1}{4}\right) + (-.40)\left(\frac{1}{4}\right) + (.40)\left(\frac{1}{4}\right) = 0.$$

On the average, over the long run, Donna neither wins nor loses. ▪

A game with an expected value of 0 (such as the one of Example 3) is called a **fair game.** Casinos do not offer fair games. If they did, they would win (on the average) $0, and have a hard time paying the help! Casino games have expected winnings for the house that vary from 1.5 cents per dollar to 60 cents per dollar. Exercises 18–21 at the end of the section ask you to find the expected winnings for certain games of chance.

The idea of expected value can be very useful in decision making, as shown by the next example.

EXAMPLE 4

At age 50, you receive a letter from the Mutual of Mauritania Insurance Company. According to the letter, you must tell the company immediately which of the following two options you will choose: take $20,000 at age 60 (if you are alive, $0 otherwise) or $30,000 at age 70 (again, if you are alive, $0 otherwise). Based only on the idea of expected value, which should you choose?

Life insurance companies have constructed elaborate tables showing the probability of a person living a given number of years into the future. From a recent such table, the probability of living from age 50 to age 60 is .88, while the probability of living from age 50 to 70 is .64. The expected values of the two options are given below.

$$\text{First option: } (20,000)(.88) + (0)(.12) = 17,600$$

$$\text{Second option: } (30,000)(.64) + (0)(.36) = 19,200$$

Based strictly on expected values, choose the second option. ▪

Handwritten top: 9. 1st prize = $100 Second = $40 & 2 prizes.

w1 99 $\frac{(100-1)}{cost\ ticket}$ $\frac{1}{500}$

w2 39 $\frac{2}{500}$

Loser −1 $\frac{497}{500}$

E(x) = 99/500 + $\frac{39 \times 2}{500}$ − $\frac{497}{500}$ = −.64

7.2 EXERCISES

Find the expected value for each of the random variables in Exercises 1–4.

1.

x	2	3	4	5
$P(X = x)$	.1	.4	.3	.2

Handwritten: E(x) = 2(.1) + 3(.4) + 4(.3) + 5(.2) = 3.6

2.

y	4	6	8	10
$P(Y = y)$	.4	.4	.05	.15

3.

z	9	12	15	18	21
$P(Z = z)$	.14	.22	.36	.18	.10

Handwritten: E(x) 9(.14) + 12(.22) + 15(.36) + 18(.18) + 21(.10) = 14.64

4.

x	30	32	36	38	44
$P(X = x)$	.31	.30	.29	.06	.04

Find the expected value for the random variable X having probability functions graphed as in Exercises 5–8.

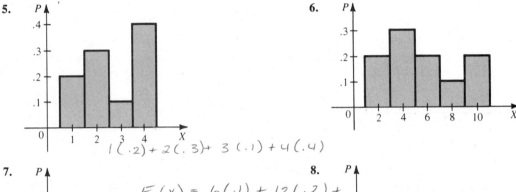

5.

Handwritten: 1(.2) + 2(.3) + 3(.1) + 4(.4)

6.

7.

Handwritten: E(x) = 6(.1) + 12(.2) + 18(.4) + 24(.2) + 30(.1) = 18

8.

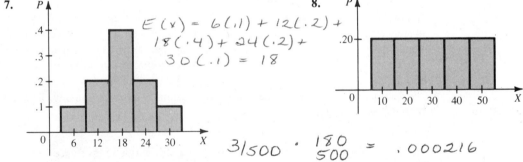

Handwritten: 3/500 · $\frac{180}{500}$ = .000216

9. A raffle offers a first prize of $100, and two second prizes of $40 each. One ticket costs $1, and 500 tickets are sold. Find the expected winnings for a person who buys one ticket. Is this a fair game?   *top of page.*   *not a fair game.*

10. A raffle offers a first prize of $1000, two second prizes of $300 each, and twenty prizes of $10 each. If 10,000 tickets are sold at 50¢ each, find the expected winnings for a person buying one ticket. Is this a fair game?

Many of the following exercises use the ideas of combinations, which were discussed in Chapter 5.

11. If 3 marbles are drawn from a bag containing 3 yellow and 4 white marbles, what is the expected number of yellow marbles in the sample?

Handwritten:
1 — 3/7
1 − 4/7
2 − 3/7
3 4/7
3 − 3/7
4/7

3/7 + 3/7 + 3/7 = 9/7

12. If 5 apples in a barrel of 25 apples are known to be rotten, what is the expected number of rotten apples in a sample of 2 apples?

13. A delegation of 3 is selected from a city council made up of 5 liberals and 4 conservatives.
    (a) What is the expected number of liberals on the committee? *5/3 = 1.67*
    (b) What is the expected number of conservatives? *4/3 = 1.33*

14. From a group of 2 women and 5 men, a delegation of 2 is selected. Find the expected number of women in the delegation.

15. In a club with 20 senior and 10 junior members, what is the expected number of junior members on a 3-member committee? *10/30 + 10/30 + 10/30 = 1*

16. If 2 cards are drawn at one time from a deck of 52 cards, what is the expected number of diamonds?

17. Suppose someone offers to pay you $5 if you draw 2 diamonds in the game of Exercise 16. He says that you should pay 50¢ for the chance to play. Is this a fair game?

Find the expected winnings for the games of chance described in Exercises 18–21.

18. In one form of roulette, you bet $1 on "even." If one of the 18 even numbers comes up, you get your dollar back, plus another one. If one of the 20 noneven (18 odd, 0, and 00) numbers comes up, you lose.

19. In another form of roulette, there are only 19 noneven numbers (no 00).

20. Numbers is an illegal game where you bet $1 on any three-digit number from 000 to 999. If your number comes up, you get $500.

21. In one form of the game Keno, the house has a pot containing 80 balls, each marked with a different number from 1 to 80. You buy a ticket for $1 and mark one of the 80 numbers on it. The house then selects 20 numbers at random. If your number is among the 20, you get $3.20 (for a net winning of $2.20).

22. Use the assumptions of Example 3 to find Mary's expected winnings. If Mary tosses and Donna calls, is it still a fair game?

23. Suppose one day Mary brings a two-headed coin and uses it to toss for the coffee. Since Mary tosses, Donna calls.
    (a) Is this still a fair game? *1/2*
    (b) What is Donna's expected gain if she calls heads? *40¢*
    (c) If she calls tails? *-40¢*

24. Find the expected number of girls in a family of four children.

25. Find the expected number of boys in a family of five children.

26. Jack must choose at age 40 to inherit either $25,000 at age 50 (if he is still alive) or $30,000 at age 55 (if he is still alive). If the probabilities for a person of age 40 to live to be 50 and 55 are .90 and .85, respectively, which choice gives him the larger expected inheritance?

27. An insurance company has written 100 policies of $10,000, 500 of $5000, and 1000 policies of $1000 on people of age 20. If experience shows that the probability of dying during the twentieth year of life is .001, how much can the company expect to pay out during the year the policies were written?

28. A builder is considering a job which promises a profit of $30,000 with a probability of .7 or a loss (due to bad weather, strikes, and such) of $10,000 with a probability of .3. What is the expected profit?

x **29.** Experience has shown that a ski lodge will be full (160 guests) during the Christmas holidays if there is a heavy snow pack in December, while a light snowfall in December means that they will have only 90 guests. What is the expected number of guests if the probability for a heavy snow in December is .40? (Assume that there must either be a light snowfall or a heavy snowfall.)

30. A magazine distributor offers a first prize of $100,000, two second prizes of $40,000 each, and two third prizes of $10,000 each. A total of 2,000,000 entries are received in the contest. Find the expected winnings if you submit one entry to the contest. If it would cost you 25¢ in time, paper, and stamps to enter, would it be worth it?

31. A local used-car dealer gets complaints about his cars, as shown in the following table.

Number of complaints per day	0	1	2	3	4	5	6
Probability	.01	.05	.15	.26	.33	.14	.06

$$0(.01) + 1(.05) + 2(.15) + 3(.26) + 4(.33)$$

Find the expected number of complaints per day. $$+ 5(.14) + 6(.06) = 3.51$$

32. I can take one of two jobs. With job A, there is a 50% chance that I will make $60,000 per year after 5 years, and a 50% chance of making $30,000. With job B, there is a 30% chance that I will make $90,000 per year after 5 years and a 70% chance that I will make $20,000. Based strictly on expected value, which job should I take?

33. Levi Strauss and Company* uses expected value to help its salespeople rate their accounts. For each account, a salesperson estimates potential additional volume and the probability of getting it. The product of these gives the expected value of the potential, which is added to the existing volume. The totals are then classified as A, B, or C as follows: below $40,000, class C; between $40,000 and $55,000, class B; above $55,000, class A. Complete the following chart for one of its salespeople.

Account Number	Existing Volume	Potential Additional Volume	Probability of Getting It	Expected Value of Potential	Existing Volume + Expected Value of Potential	Class
1	$15,000	$10,000	.25	$2,500	$17,500	C
2	40,000	0	—	—	40,000	C
3	20,000	(10,000 ×	.20) =	2000	22,000	C
4	50,000	10,000	.10	1000	57,000	B
5	5,000	50,000	.50	25000	30000	C
6	0	100,000	.60	60000	60,000	A
7	30,000	20,000	.80	16000	46,000	B

34. At the end of play in a major golf tournament, two players, an "old pro" and a "new kid," are tied. Suppose first prize is $80,000 and second prize is $20,000. Find the expected winnings for the old pro if

$$22\,000 = 20,000 + 2000$$

(a) both players are of equal ability,

(b) the new kid will freeze up, giving the old pro a 3/4 chance of winning.

35. In a certain animal species, the probability that a healthy adult female will have no offspring in a given year is .31, while the probability of 1, 2, 3, or 4 offspring are respectively .21, .19, .17, and .12. Find the expected number of offspring.

$$1(.21) + 2(.19) + 3(.17) + 4(.12)$$

*This example was supplied by James McDonald, Levi Strauss and Company, San Francisco.

$$= 1.58$$

36. According to an article in a magazine not known for its accuracy, a male decreases his life expectancy by one year, on the average, for every point that his blood pressure is above 120. The average life expectancy for a male is 76 years. Find the life expectancy for a male whose blood pressure is

(a) 135;   (b) 150;   (c) 115;   (d) 100.

(e) Suppose a certain male has a blood pressure of 145. Find his life expectancy. How would you interpret the result to him?

✗ **37.** One of the few methods that can be used in an attempt to cut the severity of a hurricane is to *seed* the storm. In this process, silver iodide crystals are dropped into the storm. Unfortunately, silver iodide crystals sometimes cause the storm to *increase* its speed. Wind speeds may also increase or decrease even with no seeding. The probabilities and amounts of property damage in the following tree diagram are from an article by R. A. Howard, J. E. Matheson, and D. W. North, "The Decision to Seed Hurricanes."*

(a) Find the expected amount of damage under each option, "seed" and "do not seed."   *94.0 seed*
   116.0 do not seed.

(b) To minimize total expected damage, what option should be chosen?   *Seed*

	Change in wind speed	Property damage (millions of dollars)
0.038	+32%	335.8
0.143	+16%	191.1
Seed 0.392	0	100.0
0.255	−16%	46.7
0.172	−34%	16.3
0.054	+32%	335.8
0.206	+16%	191.1
Do not seed 0.480	0	100.0
0.206	−16%	46.7
0.054	−34%	16.3

*"The Decision to Seed Hurricanes," Howard, R. A. et al., *Science,* Vol. 176, pp. 1191–1202, Fig. 7, 16 June 1972. Copyright © 1972 by the American Association for the Advancement of Science. Reprinted by permission of the American Association for the Advancement of Science and SRI International, Menlo Park, California.

38. A contest at a fast-food restaurant offered the following cash prizes and probabilities of winning on one visit.

Prize	Probability
$100,000	$\dfrac{1}{176,402,500}$
$25,000	$\dfrac{1}{39,200,556}$
$5000	$\dfrac{1}{17,640,250}$
$1000	$\dfrac{1}{1,568,022}$
$100	$\dfrac{1}{282,244}$
$5	$\dfrac{1}{7056}$
$1	$\dfrac{1}{588}$

Suppose you spend $1 to buy a bus pass that lets you go to 25 different restaurants in the chain and pick up entry forms. Find your expected value.

EXTENDED

APPLICATION

Optimal Inventory for a Service Truck

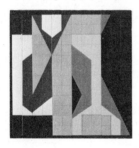

For many different items it is difficult or impossible to take the item to a central repair facility when service for the item is required. Washing machines, large television sets, office copiers, and computers are only a few examples of such items. Service for items of this type is commonly performed by sending a repair person to the item, with the person driving to the item in a truck containing various parts that might be required in repairing the item. Ideally, the truck should contain all the parts that might be required in repairing the item. However, most parts would be needed only infrequently, so that inventory costs for the parts would be high.

An optimum policy for deciding on the parts to stock on a truck would require that the probability of not being able to repair an item without a trip back to the warehouse for needed parts be as low as possible, consistent with minimum inventory costs. An analysis similar to the one below was developed at the Xerox Corporation.*

To set up a mathematical model for deciding on the optimum truck stocking policy, let us assume that a broken machine might require one of 5 different parts (we could assume any number of different parts—we use 5 to simplify the notation). Suppose also that the probability that a particular machine requires part 1 is p_1, that it requires part 2 is p_2, and so on. Assume also that the failure of different part types are independent, and that at most one part of each type is used on a given job.

Suppose that, on the average, a repair person makes N service calls per time period.

*Reprinted by permission of Stephen Smith, John Chambers, and Eli Shlifer, "Optimal Inventories Based on Job Completion Rate for Repairs Requiring Multiple Items," *Management Science*, Vol. 26, No. 8, August 1980, copyright © 1980 The Institute of Management Sciences.

If the repair person is unable to make a repair because at least one of the parts is unavailable, there is a penalty cost, L, corresponding to wasted time for the repair person, an extra trip to the parts depot, customer unhappiness, and so on. For each of the parts carried on the truck, an average inventory cost is incurred. Let H_i be the average inventory cost for part i, where $1 \le i \le 5$.

Let M_1 represent a policy of carrying only part 1 on the repair truck, M_{24} represent a policy of carrying only parts 2 and 4, with M_{12345} and M_0 representing policies of carrying all parts and no parts, respectively.

For policy M_{35}, carrying parts 3 and 5 only, the expected cost per time period per repair person, written $C(M_{35})$, is

$$C(M_{35}) = (H_3 + H_5) + NL[1 - (1 - p_1)(1 - p_2)(1 - p_4)].$$

(The expression in brackets represents the probability of needing at least one of the parts not carried, 1, 2, or 4 here.) As further examples, $C(M_{125})$ is

$$C(M_{125}) = (H_1 + H_2 + H_5) + NL[1 - (1 - p_3)(1 - p_4)],$$

while
$$C(M_{12345}) = (H_1 + H_2 + H_3 + H_4 + H_5) + NL[1 - 1]$$
$$= H_1 + H_2 + H_3 + H_4 + H_5,$$

and
$$C(M_0) = NL[1 - (1 - p_1)(1 - p_2)(1 - p_3)(1 - p_4)(1 - p_5)].$$

To find the best policy, evaluate $C(M_0)$, $C(M_1)$, $\cdots$, $C(M_{12345})$ and choose the smallest result. (A general solution method is in the *Management Science* paper.)

Example

Suppose that for a particular item, only 3 possible parts might need to be replaced. By studying past records of failures of the item, and finding necessary inventory costs, suppose that the following values have been found.

p_1	p_2	p_3	H_1	H_2	H_3
.09	.24	.17	$15	$40	$9

Suppose $N = 3$ and L is $54. Then, as an example,

$$C(M_1) = H_1 + NL[1 - (1 - p_2)(1 - p_3)]$$
$$= 15 + 3(54)[1 - (1 - .24)(1 - .17)]$$
$$= 15 + 3(54)[1 - (.76)(.83)]$$
$$\approx 15 + 59.81$$
$$= 74.81.$$

Thus, if policy M_1 is followed (carrying only part 1 on the truck), the expected cost per repair person per time period is $74.81. Also,

$$C(M_{23}) = H_2 + H_3 + NL[1 - (1 - p_1)]$$
$$= 40 + 9 + 3(54)[.09]$$
$$= 63.58,$$

so that M_{23} is a better policy than M_1. By finding the expected values for all other possible policies (see the exercises below), the optimum policy may be chosen. ∎

EXERCISES

1. Refer to the example above and find each of the following.
   (a) $C(M_0)$ **(b)** $C(M_2)$ **(c)** $C(M_3)$ **(d)** $C(M_{12})$
   (e) $C(M_{13})$ **(f)** $C(M_{123})$.

2. Which policy leads to lowest expected cost?

3. In the example above, $p_1 + p_2 + p_3 = .09 + .24 + .17 = .50$. Why is it not necessary that the probabilities add to 1?

4. Suppose an item to be repaired might need one of n different parts. How many different policies would then need to be evaluated?

EXTENDED

APPLICATION

Bidding on a Potential Oil Field—Signal Oil

Signal Oil, with headquarters in Los Angeles, is a major petroleum company. In this example we use probability and expected values to help determine the best bid price for a new off-shore oil field. The company has used all the modern methods of oil exploration to help interpret the economic potential of each tract.*

Two uncontrollable (and therefore uncertain) variables dominate a problem of this type: (a) the amount of commercial oil reserves that might be found in a tract, and (b) the length of time that would be required to develop and begin commercial production using these reserves. Another important variable is the amount to be bid for the right to develop the tract. Although the bid is a variable, it is not subject to uncertainty, but is under the control of the company. The company must analyze the effects of bids of various sizes along with the variables involving uncertainty so that the proper bid can be made.

The following chart shows the probabilities of various events. Commercial production includes events B_2, B_3, and B_4. Note that commercial production is given a 20% chance of occurring, with an 80% chance of the occurrence of less than a commercially profitable level of oil reserves.

	Oil Reserves	
Event B_j	Millions of Barrels	Chance of Occurrence
B_1	0.0	.80
B_2	19.0	.06
B_3	25.5	.10
B_4	30.6	.04

*This example was supplied by Kenneth P. King, Senior Planning Analyst, Signal Oil Company.

Any delay in beginning the commercial development of the field adversely affects the overall profitability of the project. This delay can be caused by seasonal weather variation in the offshore area, together with its relative isolation and the uncertainty of drilling rig availability. Beginning development in a shorter-than-normal time would require a concerted speedup effort that would incur cost increases over the normal period of development. This additional cost, however, is somewhat offset by the fact that the income from the field would be received sooner. The chart below shows the probabilities of various lengths of time required for commercial development to begin.

Years From Bid to Start of Drilling

Event A_i	Years	Chance of Occurrence
A_1	2	.75
A_2	1	.13
A_3	3	.12

The time required for drilling to begin is independent of the quantity of reserves in the field. Hence, for each possible value of i and j, we have

$$P(A_i \text{ and } B_j) = P(A_i) \cdot P(B_j).$$

For example, $P(2 \text{ years' delay and } 25.5 \text{ million barrels}) = P(A_1 \text{ and } B_3) = P(A_1) \cdot P(B_3) = (.75)(.10) = .075$. The chart below shows the probabilities for all possible cases, along with the payoffs to the company for different bid levels.

Payoff (in millions of dollars)

Case	Event	Probability	$0 Bid	$2	$5	$10
1	A_1 and B_1	.600	−1.1	−2.3	−4.0	−6.9
2	A_1 and B_2	.045	10.4	8.4	5.4	0.4
3	A_1 and B_3	.075	17.0	15.0	12.0	7.0
4	A_1 and B_4	.030	22.2	20.2	17.2	12.2
5	A_2 and B_1	.104	−1.1	−2.3	−4.0	−6.9
6	A_2 and B_2	.008	13.2	11.2	8.2	3.2
7	A_2 and B_3	.013	21.5	19.5	16.5	11.5
8	A_2 and B_4	.005	27.7	25.7	22.7	17.7
9	A_3 and B_1	.096	−1.1	−2.3	−4.0	−6.9
10	A_3 and B_2	.007	7.5	5.5	2.5	−2.5
11	A_3 and B_3	.012	13.0	11.0	8.0	3.0
12	A_3 and B_4	.005	17.5	15.5	12.5	7.5
	Total:	1.000				

Now the company must calculate the expected value for each different bid level. For example, the expected value at a bid level of $2 million is given by

$E(\text{bid of \$2 million}) = (-2.3)(.600) + (8.4)(.045)$

$+ (15.0)(.075) + \cdots + (15.5)(.005).$

If the expected values for various possible bid levels are found in the same way and plotted, we get the graph in the following figure. Using techniques from mathematics of finance (the payoffs above are actually present values), the company knows that the expected value of a profitable bid must be $0 or more. As shown in the figure, this means that $3.5 million is the most the company can bid for this particular tract.

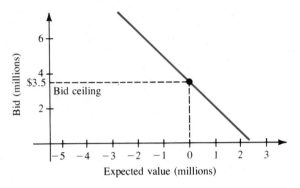

---

1. Calculate E(bid of $2 million).

2. Calculate E(bid of $5 million).

7.3   Variance and Standard Deviation

The mean of a distribution gives us an average value of the distribution, but the mean tells us nothing about the *spread* of the numbers in the distribution. For example, suppose seven measurements of the thickness (in cm) of a copper wire produced by one machine were

$$.010, \quad .010, \quad .009, \quad .008, \quad .007, \quad .009, \quad .010,$$

and seven measurements of the same type of wire produced by another machine were

$$.014, \quad .004, \quad .013, \quad .005, \quad .009, \quad .004, \quad .014.$$

The mean of both samples is .009, yet the two samples are quite dissimilar; the amount of dispersion or variation within the samples is different. In addition to the mean, we need another kind of measure, which describes the variation of the numbers in a distribution.

Since the mean represents the center of the distribution, one way to measure the variation within a set of numbers might be to find the average of their distances from the mean. That is, if the numbers are $x_1, x_2, \cdots, x_n$ and the mean is $\bar{x}$, we might first find the differences $x_1 - \bar{x}, x_2 - \bar{x}, \cdots, x_n - \bar{x}$, and then find the mean of the differences. However, it turns out that the sum of these differences is always 0, so that their mean would also be 0. To see why, look at the four numbers x_1, x_2, x_3, x_4 having mean $\bar{x}$. The sum of the four differences is

$$\sum_{i=1}^{4} (x_i - \bar{x}) = (x_1 - \bar{x}) + (x_2 - \bar{x}) + (x_3 - \bar{x}) + (x_4 - \bar{x})$$
$$= x_1 + x_2 + x_3 + x_4 - 4(\bar{x})$$

By definition, $\bar{x} = (x_1 + x_2 + x_3 + x_4)/4$, giving

$$\bar{x} = x_1 + x_2 + x_3 + x_4 - 4\left(\frac{x_1 + x_2 + x_3 + x_4}{4}\right)$$
$$= 0.$$

While we proved this result only for four values, the proof could be extended to any finite number of values.

Since the sum of the differences from the mean is always 0, the mean of these differences also would be 0—not a good measure of the variability of a distribution. It turns out that a very useful measure of variability is found by *squaring* the differences from the mean.

For example, let us use the seven measurements given above,

.010, .010, .009, .008, .007, .009, .010.

The mean of these numbers is .009. Subtracting the mean from each of the seven values gives the differences

.001, .001, 0, −.001, −.002, 0, .001. = 0

(Check that the sum of these differences is 0.) Now square each difference, getting

.000001, .000001, 0, .000001, .000004, 0, .000001. add & divide by 7

Next, find the mean of these squares, which is .00000114 (rounded).

This number, the mean of the squares of the differences, is called the **variance** of the distribution. If X is the random variable for the distribution, then the variance is written Var(X). The variance gives a measure of the variation of the numbers in the distribution, but, since we used the squared differences to get it, the size of the variance does not reflect the actual amount of variation. To correct this problem, another measure of variation is used, the **standard deviation,** which is the square root of the variance. The symbol σ (the Greek lower case sigma) is used for standard deviation. The standard deviation of the distribution discussed above is

$$\sigma = \sqrt{.00000114} \approx .001.$$

EXAMPLE 1

Find the standard deviation of the seven measurements of copper wire produced by the second machine in the example above.

It is best to arrange the work in columns as in Table 11.

[handwritten annotations in left margin:]

Ex.

mean = .014 + .004 + .013 +
.005 + .009 + .004 +
.014 = .009 mean

(e) x − x̄ = .014/.009 = .005

.005² = .000025

do for all.

* .014 − .009 = .005

[handwritten above table: divide this by 7 = .009]

Table 11

x	$x - \bar{x}$	$(x - \bar{x})^2$
.014	.005	.000025
.004	−.005	.000025
.013	.004	.000016
.005	−.004	.000016
.009	0	0
.004	−.005	.000025
.014	.005	.000025
	Total:	.000132

As we have seen, the column $x - \bar{x}$ always should have a sum of 0. This is a good way to check your work at that point. To get the variance, divide the sum of the $(x - \bar{x})^2$ column by the number of values in the set, seven in this case. Then take the square root to get the standard deviation.

$$\text{variance} = \frac{.000132}{7} \approx .0000189$$

$$\sigma = \sqrt{.0000189} \approx .004$$

Both measures of variation, the variance and the standard deviation, are larger for this sample than for the first sample, showing that the first machine produces copper wire with less variation than the second. ■

Variance is defined as follows:*

Variance; Standard Deviation

The **variance** of a set of n numbers $x_1, x_2, x_3, \cdots x_n$, with mean $\bar{x}$, is

$$\text{Var}(x) = \frac{\Sigma(x - \bar{x})^2}{n}.$$

The **standard deviation** of the set is

$$\sigma = \sqrt{\frac{\Sigma(x - \bar{x})^2}{n}}.$$

Variation for a probability distribution is measured in a similar way.

---

*These formulas sometimes have $n - 1$ instead of n in the denominator. Some calculators which compute variance and standard deviation use n, and others use $n - 1$. Be sure to check how your calculator works before using it for the exercises.

Variance for a Probability Distribution	If a random variable X takes on the n values $x_1, x_2, x_3, \cdots, x_n$ with respective probabilities $p_1, p_2, p_3, \cdots, p_n$, and if its expected value is $E(X) = \mu$, then the **variance** of X is $$\text{Var}(X) = p_1(x_1 - \mu)^2 + p_2(x_2 - \mu)^2 + \cdots + p_n(x_n - \mu)^2.$$ The **standard deviation** of X is $$\sigma = \sqrt{\text{Var}(X)}.$$

EXAMPLE 2

Find the variance and the standard deviation of the number of pheasant offspring given the following probability distribution.

Table 12

X	p_i
0	.08
1	.14
2	.29
3	.32
4	.17

Exam!

In Section 7.2, we found the mean of this distribution, $\mu = 2.36$. To use the formula in the box it is easiest to work in columns as in Example 1.

Note!
 $X \cdot p_i = $ *mean*
Then add them up.

$|e| = -2.36^2 = 5.57$

Table 13

X	p_i	$x_i - \mu$	$(x_i - \mu)^2$	$p_i(x_i - \mu)^2$
0	.08	-2.36	5.57	.45
1	.14	-1.36	1.85	.26
2	.29	$-.36$	.13	.04
3	.32	.64	.41	.13
4	.17	1.64	2.69	.46
			Total:	1.34

$= .08(5.57)$
$= .45$

The total of the last column gives the variance, 1.34. To find the standard deviation, take the square root of the variance.

$$\sigma = \sqrt{1.34} \approx 1.16 \quad \blacksquare$$

Chebyshev's Theorem Suppose we know only the mean, or expected value, μ of a distribution, along with the standard deviation σ. What then can be said about the values of the distribution? For example, if σ is very small, we would expect most of the values of the distribution to be close to μ, while a larger value of σ would suggest more spread in the values. One estimate of the fraction of values that lie within a specified distance of the mean is given by **Chebyshev's Theorem,** named after the Russian mathematician P. L. Chebyshev, 1821–94.

Chebyshev's Theorem

For any distribution of numbers with mean μ and standard deviation σ, the probability that a number will lie within k standard deviations of the mean is at least

$$1 - \frac{1}{k^2}.$$

That is,

$$P(\mu - k\sigma \le X \le \mu + k\sigma) \ge 1 - \frac{1}{k^2}.$$

EXAMPLE 3

By Chebyshev's Theorem, at least

$$1 - \frac{1}{3^2} = 1 - \frac{1}{9} = \frac{8}{9},$$

or about 89%, of the numbers in any distribution lie within 3 standard deviations of the mean. Figure 6 shows a geometric interpretation of this result. ▨

At least 89% of the distribution falls
in this interval

$$\mu - 3\sigma \quad \mu - 2\sigma \quad \mu - \sigma \quad \mu \quad \mu + \sigma \quad \mu + 2\sigma \quad \mu + 3\sigma$$

FIGURE 6

Suppose a distribution has mean 52 and standard deviation 3.5. Then "3 standard deviations" is $3 \times 3.5 = 10.5$, and "three standard deviations from the mean" is

$$52 - 10.5 \quad \text{to} \quad 52 + 10.5,$$

or

$$41.5 \quad \text{to} \quad 62.5.$$

By Example 3, at least 89% of the values in this distribution will lie between 41.5 and 62.5.

Chebyshev's Theorem gets much of its importance from the fact that it applies to *any* distribution—only the mean and the standard deviation must be known. Other results given later produce more accurate estimates, but only with additional information about the distribution.

EXAMPLE 4

The Forever Power Company claims that their batteries have a mean life of 26.2 hours with a standard deviation of 4.1 hours. In a shipment of 100 batteries, about how many will have a life within 2 standard deviations of the mean—that is, between $26.2 - (4.1 \times 2) = 18$ and $26.2 + (4.1 \times 2) = 34.4$ hours?

Use Chebyshev's Theorem with $k = 2$. At least

$$1 - \frac{1}{2^2} = 1 - \frac{1}{4} = \frac{3}{4},$$

or 75%, of the batteries should have a life within 2 standard deviations of the mean. At least $75\% \times 100 = 75$ of the batteries can be expected to last between 18 and 34.4 hours. ▪

7.3 EXERCISES

(handwritten: $-11, -15, -24, 21, 29, 18, -18. = 121, 225, 576$ $441, 841, 324$ 324 $= 2852$ over 7 $= 407.43$ $= \sqrt{407.43}$)

Find the standard deviation for each of the sets of numbers in Exercises 1–6. *(handwritten: exam.)*

1. 42; 38; 29; 74; 82; 71; 35 *(handwritten: mean = 53)*

2. 122; 132; 141; 158; 162; 169; 180

3. 241; 248; 251; 257; 252; 287

4. 51; 58; 62; 64; 67; 71; 74; 78; 82; 93

5. 3; 7; 4; 12; 15; 18; 19; 27; 24; 11

6. 15; 42; 53; 7; 9; 12; 28; 47; 63; 14

Find the variance and standard deviation for each of the following probability distributions. *(handwritten: exam)*

7.

x_i	2	3	4	5
p_i	.1	.3	.4	.2

(handwritten: use ex. 2.)

8.

x_i	10	20	30	40
p_i	.1	.5	.3	.1

9.

x_i	.01	.02	.03	.04	.05
p_i	.1	.5	.2	.1	.1

10.

x_i	100	105	110	115	120
p_i	.01	.08	.20	.50	.21

Find the standard deviation of the random variable in each of the following problems. (See Exercises 11–14 in Section 7.2.) *(handwritten: omit   9.)*

11. The number of yellow marbles, if 3 marbles are drawn from a bag containing 3 yellow and 4 white marbles.

12. The number of rotten apples, if 2 apples are drawn from a barrel of 25 apples, 5 of which are known to be rotten.

13. The number of liberals on a committee of 3 selected from a city council made up of 5 liberals and 4 conservatives.

14. The number of women in a delegation of 2 selected from a group of 2 women and 5 men.

Exercises 15 and 16 give histograms of two probability distributions. Decide from the graphs without any calculations which distribution has the greatest variance. *(handwritten: ⤳ = 15)*

15.

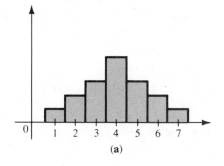

(a)

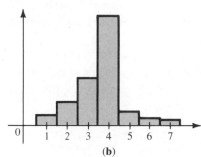

(b)

16.

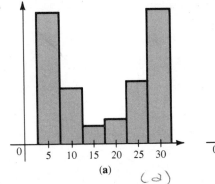

(a)   (ɔ)

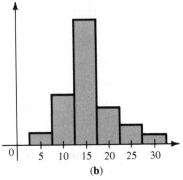

(b)

For Exercises 17 and 18, the histogram of a probability distribution is given. Calculate the variance.

17.   **18.**

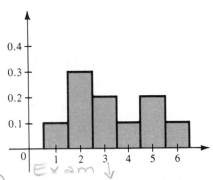

Exam ↓

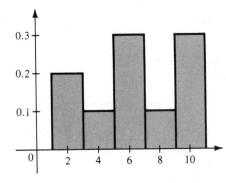

19. Use Chebyshev's Theorem to find the fraction of a distribution that lies within the following numbers of standard deviations from the mean.

   (a) 2   (b) 4   (c) 5 $d = 1 - 1/k^2$ $1 - \frac{1}{2^2} = 1 - 1/4 = .75$ $\sigma = 6$

20. A probability distribution has an expected value of 50 and a standard deviation of 6. Use Chebyshev's Theorem to tell what percent of the numbers lie between each of the following values. $d = 1 - 1/2^2 = 1 - 1/4 = .75$

   mean = 50

   (a) 38 and 62   (b) 32 and 68   (c) 26 and 74   (d) 20 and 80

   (e) less than 38 or more than 62   (f) less than 32 or more than 68

21. The weekly wages of the seven employees of Harold's Hardware Store are $180, $190, $240, $256, $300, $360, and $714.   ★ like ex. 1

   (a) Find the mean and standard deviation of this distribution.

   (b) How many of the seven employees earn within one standard deviation of the   6 mean?

   (c) How many earn within two standard deviations of the mean?   6

   (d) What does Chebyshev's Theorem give as the number earning within two standard deviations of the mean? $1 - \frac{1}{2^2} = .75$

22. The Forever Power Company conducted tests on the life of its batteries and those of a competitor (Brand X). They found that their batteries had a mean life in hours of 26.2 with a standard deviation of 4.1 (see Example 4). Their results for a sample of 10 Brand X batteries were as follows: 15, 18, 19, 23, 25, 25, 28, 30, 34, 38.

   (a) Find the mean and standard deviation for Brand X batteries.

(b) Which batteries have a more uniform life in hours?

(c) Which batteries have the highest average life in hours?

23. The Quaker Oats Company conducted a survey to determine if a proposed premium, to be included in their cereal, was appealing enough to generate new sales.* Four cities were used as test markets, where the cereal was distributed with the premium, and four cities as control markets, where the cereal was distributed without the premium. The eight cities were chosen on the basis of their similarity in terms of population, per capita income, and total cereal purchase volume. The results were as follows.

<table>
<tr><td></td><td colspan="2">Percent Change in Average
Market Shares Per Month</td></tr>
<tr><td rowspan="4">Test cities</td><td>1</td><td>+18</td></tr>
<tr><td>2</td><td>+15</td></tr>
<tr><td>3</td><td>+7</td></tr>
<tr><td>4</td><td>+10</td></tr>
<tr><td rowspan="4">Control cities</td><td>1</td><td>+1</td></tr>
<tr><td>2</td><td>−8</td></tr>
<tr><td>3</td><td>−5</td></tr>
<tr><td>4</td><td>0</td></tr>
</table>

(a) Find the mean of the change in market share for the four test cities.

(b) Find the mean of the change in market share for the four control cities.

(c) Find the standard deviation of the change in market share for the test cities.

(d) Find the standard deviation of the change in market share for the control cities.

(e) Find the difference between the means of (a) and (b). This difference represents the estimate of the percent change in sales due to the premium.

(f) The two standard deviations from (c) and (d) were used to calculate an "error" of ±7.95 for the estimate in (e). With this amount of error, what is the smallest and largest estimate of the increase in sales?

On the basis of the interval estimate of part (f) the company decided to mass produce the premium and distribute it nationally.

24. Show that the formula for variance given in the text can be rewritten as

$$\frac{1}{n^2}[n \cdot \Sigma(x^2) - (\Sigma x)^2].$$

Use a computer to solve the problems in Exercises 25–28.

25. Twenty-five laboratory rats used in an experiment to test the food value of a new product made the following weight gains in grams:

5.25	5.03	4.90	4.97	5.03
5.12	5.08	5.15	5.20	4.95
4.90	5.00	5.13	5.18	5.18
5.22	5.04	5.09	5.10	5.11
5.23	5.22	5.19	4.99	4.93

Find the mean gain and the standard deviation of the gains.

---

*This example was supplied by Jeffery S. Berman, Senior Analyst, Marketing Information, Quaker Oats Company.

26. An assembly-line machine turns out washers with the following thicknesses in mm.

1.20	1.01	1.25	2.20	2.58	2.19
1.29	1.15	2.05	1.46	1.90	2.03
2.13	1.86	1.65	2.27	1.64	2.19
2.25	2.08	1.96	1.83	1.17	2.24

Find the mean and standard deviation of these thicknesses.

27. The prices of pork bellies futures on the Chicago Mercantile Exchange over a period of several weeks were as follows:

48.25	48.50	47.75	48.45	46.85
47.10	46.50	46.90	46.60	47.00
46.35	46.65	46.85	47.20	46.60
47.00	45.00	45.15	44.65	45.15
46.25	45.90	46.10	45.82	45.70
47.05	46.95	46.90	47.15	47.10

Find the mean and standard deviation.

28. A medical laboratory tested 21 samples of human blood for acidity on the pH scale with the following results.

7.1	7.5	7.3	7.4	7.6	7.2	7.3
7.4	7.5	7.3	7.2	7.4	7.3	7.5
7.5	7.4	7.4	7.1	7.3	7.4	7.4

Find the mean and standard deviation.

7.4   The Normal Distribution

The bank transaction times in the example of Section 7.1 were timed to the nearest minute. Theoretically at least, they could have been timed to the nearest tenth of a minute, or hundredth of a minute, or even more accurately. Actually it is possible for the transaction times to take on any real number value greater than 0. As mentioned earlier, a distribution in which the random variable can take any real number value within some interval is a **continuous distribution.**

The distribution of heights (in inches) of college freshmen women is another example of a continuous distribution, since these heights include infinitely many possible measurements, such as 53, 58.5, 66.3, 72.666 . . . , and so on. Figure 7 shows the continuous distribution of heights of college freshmen women. Here the most frequent heights occur near the center of the interval shown.

Another continuous curve, which approximates the distribution of yearly incomes in the United States, is shown in Figure 8. From the graph, it can be seen that the most frequent incomes are grouped near the low end of the interval. This kind of distribution, where the peak is not at the center, is called **skewed.**

Many different experiments produce probability distributions which come from a very important class of continuous distributions called **normal probability distributions.** The distribution shown in Figure 7 is approximately a normal distribution,

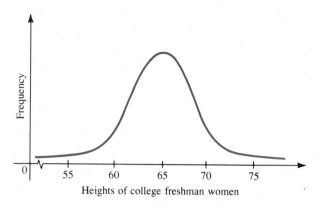

FIGURE 7

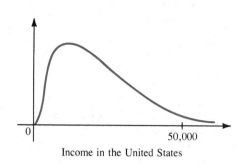

FIGURE 8

while the one of Figure 8 is not. The distribution of the lengths of the leaves of a certain tree would approximate a normal distribution, as should the distribution of the actual weights of cereal boxes that have an average weight of 16 ounces.

Each normal probability distribution has associated with it a bell-shaped curve, such as the one in Figure 9. This curve, called a **normal curve,** is symmetric about a vertical line drawn through the mean, μ. Vertical lines drawn at points $+1\sigma$ and -1σ from the mean show where the direction of "curvature" of the graph changes. (For those who have studied calculus, these points are the inflection points of the graph.)

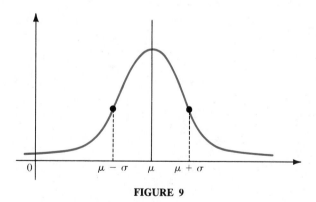

FIGURE 9

A normal curve never touches the x-axis—it extends indefinitely in both directions. The area under a normal curve is always the same: 1. If the value of the mean μ is fixed, changing the value of σ will change the shape of the normal curve. A larger value of σ produces a "flatter" normal curve, while smaller values of σ produce more values near the mean, which results in a "taller" normal curve. See Figure 10.

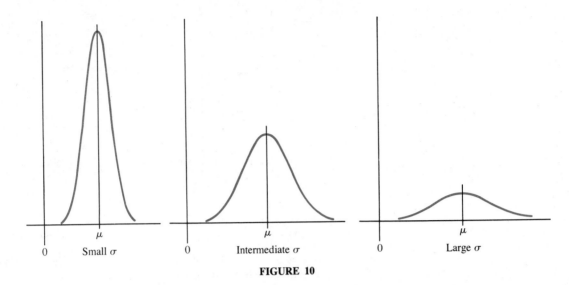

FIGURE 10

An experiment which has normally distributed outcomes and its associated normal curve are connected by the fact that the probability that an experiment produces a result between a and b is equal to the area under the normal curve from a to b. That is, the shaded area in Figure 11 gives the probability that the experimental outcome is between a and b. (Notice how the work under discussion in this section is related to the work with histograms in Section 7.1. Refer to pages 302 to 304.)

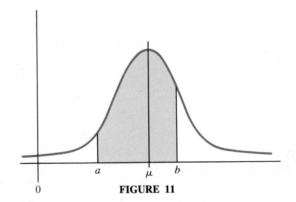

FIGURE 11

Since a normal curve is symmetric about the mean, and since the total area under a normal curve is 1, the probability that a particular outcome is below the mean is 1/2. A normal curve comes from a continuous distribution, with an infinite number of possible values, so that the probability of the occurrence of any particular value is 0.

Probabilities for a

Normal Probability

Distribution

Let X be a random variable with a normal probability distribution. Then

1. $P(a \leq X \leq b)$ is the area under the associated normal curve between a and b;

2. $P(X < \mu) = 1/2$;

3. $P(X > \mu) = 1/2$;

4. $P(X = x) = 0$ for any real number x;

5. $P(X < x) = P(X \leq x)$ for any real number x.

Part (5) follows from part (4).

The equation of the normal curve having mean μ and standard deviation σ is given by

$$y = \frac{1}{\sigma \sqrt{2\pi}} \, e^{-[(x-\mu)/\sigma]^2/2},$$

where $e \approx 2.7182818$. To find probabilities from normal curves, we would need to use this equation, along with calculus. Doing so would produce an infinite number of different tables, one for each pair of values of μ and σ. We get around this problem by using just one table, the table for the normal curve where $\mu = 0$ and $\sigma = 1$, to find values for any normal curve.

The normal curve having $\mu = 0$ and $\sigma = 1$ is called the **standard normal curve.** The normal curve table in the Appendix gives the areas under the standard normal curve, along with a sketch of the curve. The values in this table include the total area under the standard normal curve to the left of the number z.

EXAMPLE 1

Find the following areas from the table for the standard normal curve.

(a)   to the left of $z = 1.25$.

Look up 1.25 in the normal curve table. The corresponding area is .8944, so the shaded area shown in Figure 12 is .8944. This area represents 89.44% of the total area under the normal curve.

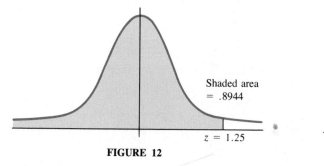

Shaded area
= .8944

$z = 1.25$

FIGURE 12

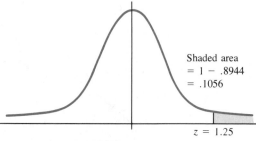

Shaded area
= 1 − .8944
= .1056

$z = 1.25$

FIGURE 13

(b)   to the right of $z = 1.25$.

In part (a) we found that the area to the left of $z = 1.25$ is .8944. The total area under the normal curve is 1, so that the area to the right of $z = 1.25$ is

$$1 - .8944 = 1.0000 - .8944 = .1056.$$

See Figure 13 on page 331, where the shaded area represents 10.56% of the total area under the normal curve.

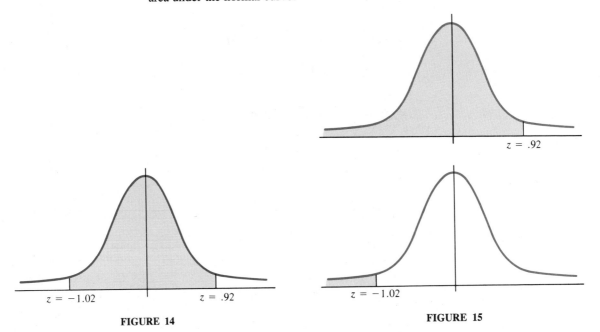

FIGURE 14

FIGURE 15

(c)   between $z = -1.02$ and $z = .92$

To find this area, shaded in Figure 14, start with the area to the left of $z = .92$ and subtract the area to the left of $z = -1.02$. See Figure 15. The result is .8212 − .1539 = .6673.   ▧

If a normal distribution does not have $\mu = 0$ and $\sigma = 1$, use the following theorem, which is stated without proof.

Area Under a

Normal Curve

Suppose a normal distribution has mean μ and standard deviation σ. The area under the associated normal curve that is to the left of the value x is exactly the same as the area to the left of

$$z = \frac{x - \mu}{\sigma}$$

for the standard normal curve.

Using this result, the normal curve table can be used for *any* normal curve with any values of μ and σ. The number z in the theorem is called a **z-score.**

EXAMPLE 2

A normal distribution has mean 46 and standard deviation 7.2. Find the following areas under the associated normal curve.

(a)   to the left of 50

Find the appropriate z-score using $x = 50$, $\mu = 46$, and $\sigma = 7.2$. Round to the nearest hundredth.

$$z = \frac{50 - 46}{7.2} = \frac{4}{7.2} \approx .56$$

From the table, the desired area is .7123.

(b)   to the right of 39

$$z = \frac{39 - 46}{7.2} = \frac{-7}{7.2} \approx -.97$$

The area to the *left* of $z = -.97$ is .1660, so that the area to the *right* is

$$1 - .1660 = .8340.$$

(c)   between 32 and 43

Find z-scores for both values.

$$z = \frac{32 - 46}{7.2} = \frac{-14}{7.2} \approx -1.94 \qquad \text{and} \qquad z = \frac{43 - 46}{7.2} = \frac{-3}{7.2} \approx -.42$$

Start with the area to the left of $z = -.42$ and subtract the area to the left of $z = -1.94$, which gives

$$.3372 - .0262 = .3110. \quad \blacksquare$$

The z-scores are actually standard deviation multiples—that is, a z-score of 2.5 corresponds to a value 2.5 standard deviations above the mean. Looking up $z = 1.00$ and $z = -1.00$ in the table shows that

$$.8413 - .1587 = .6826,$$

or 68.26%, of the area under a normal curve lies within one standard deviation of the mean. Also,

$$.9772 - .0228 = .9544,$$

or 95.44% of the area lies within two standard deviations of the mean. These results, summarized in Figure 16 (page 334), can be used to get a quick estimate of results when working with normal curves.

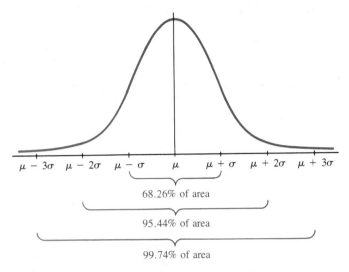

FIGURE 16

EXAMPLE 3

Suppose that the average salesperson for Dixie Office Supplies drives $\mu = 1200$ miles per month in a company car, with standard deviation $\sigma = 150$ miles. Assume that the number of miles driven is closely approximated by a normal curve. Find the percent of all drivers traveling

(a) between 1200 and 1600 miles per month.

First find the number of standard deviations above the mean that corresponds to 1600 miles. This is done by finding the z-score for 1600.

$$z = \frac{x - \mu}{\sigma}$$

$$= \frac{1600 - 1200}{150} \qquad \text{Let } x = 1600, \quad \mu = 1200, \quad \sigma = 150$$

$$= \frac{400}{150}$$

$$z \approx 2.67$$

From the table, the area to the left of $z = 2.67$ is .9962. Since $\mu = 1200$, the value 1200 corresponds to $z = 0$, the area to the left of $z = 0$ is .5000, and

$$.9962 - .5000 = .4962,$$

or 49.62% of the drivers travel between 1200 and 1600 miles per month. See Figure 17.

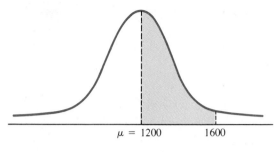

$\mu = 1200$ 1600

FIGURE 17

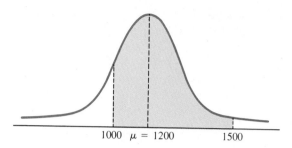

1000 $\mu = 1200$ 1500

FIGURE 18

(b) between 1000 and 1500 miles per month.

As shown in Figure 18, z-scores for both $x = 1000$ and $x = 1500$ are needed.

For $x = 1000$,   For $x = 1500$,

$$z = \frac{1000 - 1200}{150} \qquad z = \frac{1500 - 1200}{150}$$

$$= \frac{-200}{150} \qquad\qquad = \frac{300}{150}$$

$$z \approx -1.33 \qquad\qquad z = 2.00$$

From the table, $z = -1.33$ leads to an area of .0918, while $z = 2.00$ corresponds to .9772. A total of $.9772 - .0918 = .8854$, or 88.54%, of all drivers travel between 1000 and 1500 miles per month. ▧

Suppose a normal distribution has $\mu = 1000$ and $\sigma = 150$. Then the method of this section can be used to show that 95.44% of all values lie within 2 standard deviations of the mean; that is, between

$$1000 - (2 \times 150) = 700 \qquad \text{and} \qquad 1000 + (2 \times 150) = 1300.$$

Chebyshev's Theorem (Section 7.3) says that *at least*

$$1 - \frac{1}{2^2} = 1 - \frac{1}{4} = \frac{3}{4},$$

or 75% of the values lie between 7000 and 1300. The difference between 95.44% and at least 75%, from Chebyshev's Theorem, comes from the fact that Chebyshev's Theorem applies to *any* distribution, while the methods of this section apply only to *normal* distributions. Thus it should not be surprising that having more information (a normal distribution) should produce more accurate results (95.44% instead of "at least 75%.")

mean = 0 = .5

-3σ -2σ -1σ   μ 1σ 2σ 3σ   *2.50*

.5 = μ -1.71 = .0436

7.4 EXERCISES

5. .5 - (.0436) = 45.64
★ when -minus you do mean - r

Find the percent of the area under a normal curve between the mean and the number of standard deviations from the mean in Exercises 1–8.

1 btw mean & 2.50

1. 2.50   *0 = .5*   **2.** 1.68   **3.** 0.45   **4.** 0.81

5. −1.71 *.50 = .9950*   **6.** −2.04   **7.** 3.11   **8.** 2.80

.9938 - .5 = .4938

Find the percent of the total area under the normal curve between the z-scores in Exercises 9–16.

1.41   2.83

9. $z = 1.41$ and $z = 2.83$ *.9207   .9977*   **10.** $z = 0.64$ and $z = 2.11$

11. $z = -2.48$ and $z = -0.05$ *.9977 - .9207*   **12.** $z = -1.74$ and $z = -1.02$
.0066   .4801   = 7.7%
13. $z = -3.11$ and $z = 1.44$ **14.** $z = -2.94$ and $z = -0.43$
.0009   .9251 11. .4801 - .0066
15. $z = -0.42$ and $z = 0.42$ *= 47.35*   **16.** $z = -1.98$ and $z = 1.98$
13. .9251 - .0009 = 92.42%

Find a z-score satisfying the following conditions. (Hint: use the table backwards.)

17. look up .05 in the

17. 5% of the total area is to the left of z   **18.** 1% of the total area is to the left of z

other column
19. 15% of the total area is to the right of z *.05 = -1.64* **20.** 25% of the total area is to the right of z

19. 1.04 when it says right use .85 instead of .15

z = \frac{x - μ}{r}

A certain type of light bulb has an average life of 500 hours, with a standard deviation of 100 hours. The length of life of the bulb can be closely approximated by a normal curve. An amusement park buys and installs 10,000 such bulbs. Find the total number that can be expected to last   *z = \frac{500 - 500}{100} = 0; 0 intable*   *23. 500 = u r = 100 = stand dev. x = 500*

21. at least 500 hours;   *10,000(.5) = 5000*   **22.** less than 500 hours;

23. between 500 and 650 hours; *\frac{650 - 500}{100} = 1.5*   **24.** between 300 and 500 hours;

25. between 650 and 780 hours;   *(.9332)*   **26.** between 290 and 540 hours;

27. less than 740 hours; *10,000(.9332)*   **28.** more than 300 hours;
= 9332
29. more than 790 hours;   *9332 - 5000 = 4332 light bulbs last*   **30.** less than 410 hours.

A box of oatmeal must contain 16 ounces. The machine that fills the oatmeal boxes is set so that, on the average, a box contains 16.5 ounces. The boxes filled by the machine have weights that can be closely approximated by a normal curve. What fraction of the boxes filled by the machine are underweight if the standard deviation is

u = 16.5
31. x = 16   z = \frac{x-u}{r}
r = .5
z = \frac{16 - 16.5}{.5} = -1

31. .5 ounce;   **32.** .3 ounce;   **33.** .2 ounce;   **34.** .1 ounce? *15.87%*

The chickens at Colonel Thompson's Ranch have a mean weight of 1850 grams with a standard deviation of 150 grams. The weights of the chickens are closely approximated by a normal curve. Find the percent of all chickens having weights

on pg. 337

35. more than 1700 grams;   **36.** less than 1800 grams;

37. between 1750 grams and 1900 grams;   **38.** between 1600 grams and 2000 grams;

39. less than 1550 grams;   **40.** more than 2100 grams.

In nutrition, the Recommended Daily Allowance of vitamins is a number set by the government as a guide to an individual's daily vitamin intake. Actually, vitamin needs vary drastically from person to person, but the needs are very closely approximated by a normal curve. To calculate the Recommended Daily Allowance, the government first finds the average need for vitamins among people in the population, and the standard deviation. The Recommended Daily Allowance is then defined as the mean plus 2.5 times the standard deviation.

41. What percentage of the population will receive adequate amounts of vitamins under this plan?

27. $\dfrac{740-500}{100} = 2.4 \; (.9918)$ $\dfrac{10,000 \,(.9918)}{= \; 9918}$

29. more than 790 hrs.
$\dfrac{790-500}{100} = 2.9 \quad (.9981)$
$1 - .9981 = .0019$
$10,000 \,(.0019) = 19$

$Z = \dfrac{x-u}{r}$

Find the recommended daily allowance for the vitamins in Exercises 42–44.

42. mean = 1800 units, standard deviation = 140 units

43. mean = 159 units, standard deviation = 12 units

44. mean = 1200 units, standard deviation = 92 units

35. u = 1850
r = 150
x = 1700
$= \dfrac{1700 - 1850}{150} = -1 \quad (.1587)$
$1 - .1587 = .8413$
✻ *more than*

Assume the distributions in Exercises 45–52 are all normal, and use the areas under the normal curve given in the table to answer the questions.

45. A machine produces bolts with an average diameter of .25 inches and a standard deviation of .02 inches. What is the probability that a bolt will be produced with a diameter greater than .3 inches?

46. The mean monthly income of the trainees of an engineering firm is $1200 with a standard deviation of $200. Find the probability that an individual trainee earns less than $1000 per month.

47. A machine that fills quart milk cartons is set up to average 32.2 ounces per carton, with a standard deviation of 1.2 ounces. What is the probability that a filled carton will contain less than 32 ounces of milk?

37. $\dfrac{1750 - 1850}{150}$
$= -.66 \text{ or } .67$
$.2514$
$\dfrac{1900 - 1850}{150}$
$= .33$
$= .6293$
$.6293 - .2514 = .3779$

48. The average contribution to the campaign of Polly Potter, a candidate for city council, was $50 with a standard deviation of $15. How many of the 200 people who contributed to Polly's campaign gave between $30 and $100?

49. At the Discount Market, the average weekly grocery bill is $32.25 with a standard deviation of $9.50. What are the largest and smallest amounts spent by the middle 50% of this market's customers?

50. The mean clotting time of blood is 7.45 seconds with a standard deviation of 3.6 seconds. What is the probability that an individual's blood clotting time will be less than 7 seconds or greater than 8 seconds?

51. The average size of the fish in Lake Amotan is 12.3 inches with a standard deviation of 4.1 inches. Find the probability of catching a fish there longer than 18 inches.

★ IF IT says more than do 1 − no#

52. To be graded extra large, an egg must weigh at least 2.2 ounces. If the average weight for an egg is 1.5 ounces with a standard deviation of .4 ounces, how many of five dozen eggs would you expect to grade extra large?

One professor uses the following grading system for assigning letter grades in a course.

Grade	Score in Class
A	greater than $\mu + \frac{3}{2}\sigma$
B	$\mu + \frac{1}{2}\sigma$ to $\mu + \frac{3}{2}\sigma$
C	$\mu - \frac{1}{2}\sigma$ to $\mu + \frac{1}{2}\sigma$
D	$\mu - \frac{3}{2}\sigma$ to $\mu - \frac{1}{2}\sigma$
F	below $\mu - \frac{3}{2}\sigma$

What percent of the students receive the following grades?

53. A

54. B

55. C

56. Do you think this system would be more likely to be fair in a large freshman class in psychology or in a graduate seminar of five students? Why?

A teacher gives a test to a large group of students. The results are closely approximated by a normal curve. The mean is 74, with a standard deviation of 6. The teacher wishes to give A's to the top 8% of the students and F's to the bottom 8%. A grade of B is given to the next 15%, with D's given similarly. All other students get C's. Find the bottom cutoff (rounded to the nearest whole number) for the following grades. (Hint: use the table in the Appendix backwards.)

57. A   **58.** B   **59.** C   **60.** D

Use a computer to find the following probabilities by finding the comparable area under a standard normal curve.

61. $P(1.372 \leq X \leq 2.548)$ **62.** $P(-2.751 \leq X \leq 1.693)$ **63.** $P(X > -2.476)$

64. $P(X < 1.692)$ **65.** $P(X < -.4753)$ **66.** $P(X > .2509)$

Use a computer to find the following probabilities for a distribution with a mean of 35.693 and a standard deviation of 7.104.

67. $P(12.275 < X < 28.432)$ **68.** $P(X > 38.913)$

69. $P(X < 17.462)$ **70.** $P(17.462 \leq X \leq 53.106)$

EXTENDED   **Inventory Control**

APPLICATION

A department store must control its inventory carefully.* It should not reorder too often, because it then builds up a large warehouse full of merchandise, which is expensive to hold. On the other hand, it must reorder sufficiently often to be sure of having sufficient stock to meet customer demand. The company desires a simple chart that can be used by its employees to determine the best possible time to reorder merchandise. The merchandise level on hand will be checked periodically. At the end of each period, if the level on hand is less than some predetermined level given in the chart, which considers sales rate and waiting time for orders, the item will be reordered. The example uses the following variables.

F = frequency of stock review (in weeks)
r = acceptable risk of being out of stock (in percent)
P = level of inventory at which reordering should occur
L = waiting time for order to arrive (in weeks)
S = sales rate in units per week
M = minimum level of merchandise to guarantee that the probability of being out of stock is no higher than r
z = z-score (from table of cumulative distribution) corresponding to r

Goods should not be reordered until inventory on hand has declined to a level less than the rate of sales per week, S, times the sum of the number of weeks until the next stock review, F, and the expected waiting time in weeks, L, plus a minimum level of merchandise, M, necessary to guarantee that the probability of being out of stock is no higher than r. That is, $P = S(F + L) + M$.

---

*Example supplied by Leonard W. Cooper, Operations Research Project Director, Federated Department Stores.

To find M, which depends on S, F, and L, we shall assume that both sales and waiting time are normally distributed. With this assumption, a formula from more advanced statistics courses permits us to write $M = z\sqrt{2S(F + L)}$, where z is the z-score (from the table) corresponding to r, and $\sqrt{2S(F + L)}$ is the standard deviation of normally distributed deviations in sales rate and waiting time.

Combining these two formulas, we have

$$P = S(F + L) + z\sqrt{2S(F + L)}.$$

Suppose the firm wishes to be 95% sure of having goods to sell, so that $r = 5\%$. From the table, we find $z = 1.64$. Hence, for $r = 5\%$,

$$P = S(F + L) + 1.64\sqrt{2S(F + L)}.$$

Based on this formula, the chart below was prepared.

REORDER LEVELS (P) Reorder merchandise when inventory on hand falls below the levels given in the chart. $r = 5\%$, $F = 1$ week						
Rate of Sales (S) (Units/Week)	Waiting Time in Weeks for Order (L)					
	1	**2**	**3**	**4**	**5**	**6**
9	28	39	50	61	71	81
10	30	43	55	66	78	89
11	33	46	59	72	85	97
12	35	50	64	78	92	105
13	38	54	69	84	99	113
14	40	57	83	89	105	121
15	43	61	78	95	112	129
$r = 5\%$, $F = 4$ weeks						
Rate of Sales (S) (Units/Week)	Waiting Time in Weeks for Order (L)					
	1	**2**	**3**	**4**	**5**	**6**
1	10	12	13	15	16	17
2	17	20	23	25	28	30
3	24	28	32	35	39	43
4	30	35	40	45	50	55

By using the chart, if an item is reviewed every 4 weeks ($F = 4$), the waiting time for a reorder is 3 weeks ($L = 3$), and the rate of sales is 2 per week ($S = 2$), then the item should be reordered when the number on hand falls at or below 23.

EXERCISES

1. Suppose an item is reviewed weekly, and the waiting time for a reorder is 4 weeks. If the average sales per week of the item is 12 units, and the current inventory level is 85 units, should it be reordered? What if the inventory level is 50 units?

2. Suppose an item is reviewed every four weeks. If orders require a 5-week waiting time, and if sales average 3 units per week, should the item be reordered if current inventory is 50 units? What if current inventory is 30?

7.5   The Normal Curve Approximation to the
Binomial Distribution

In many practical situations, experiments have only two possible outcomes: *success* or *failure*. Examples of such experiments, called *binomial trials,* or *Bernoulli trials,* include tossing a coin (perhaps *h* would be called a success, with *t* a failure); rolling a die with the two outcomes being, for instance, 5, a success, and a number other than 5, a failure; or choosing a radio from a large batch and deciding if the radio is defective or not. (Bernoulli trials were first discussed in Section 6.7)

A *binomial distribution* must satisfy the following properties. The experiment is a series of independent trials with only two outcomes possible, success and failure. The probability of each outcome must be constant from trial to trial.

As an example, suppose a die is tossed 5 times. Identify a result of 1 or 2 as a success, with any other result a failure. Since each trial (each toss) can result in a success or a failure, the result of the 5 tosses can be any number of successes from 0 through 5. Not all of these six possible outcomes are equally likely. The various probabilities can be found with the result from Section 6.7:

$$P(X = x) = \binom{n}{x}p^x(1 - p)^{n - x},$$

where n is the number of trials, x is the number of successes, p is the probability of success on a single trial, and $P(X = x)$ gives the probability that x of the n trials result in successes. In this example, $n = 5$ and $p = 1/3$, since either a 1 or a 2 results in a success. The results for this experiment are tabulated in Table 14.

Table 14

x	$P(X = x)$
0	$\binom{5}{0}\left(\frac{1}{3}\right)^0\left(\frac{2}{3}\right)^5 = \frac{32}{243}$
1	$\binom{5}{1}\left(\frac{1}{3}\right)^1\left(\frac{2}{3}\right)^4 = \frac{80}{243}$
2	$\binom{5}{2}\left(\frac{1}{3}\right)^2\left(\frac{2}{3}\right)^3 = \frac{80}{243}$
3	$\binom{5}{3}\left(\frac{1}{3}\right)^3\left(\frac{2}{3}\right)^2 = \frac{40}{243}$
4	$\binom{5}{4}\left(\frac{1}{3}\right)^4\left(\frac{2}{3}\right)^1 = \frac{10}{243}$
5	$\binom{5}{5}\left(\frac{1}{3}\right)^5\left(\frac{2}{3}\right)^0 = \frac{1}{243}$

By definition, the mean μ of a probability distribution is given by the expected value of X. Expected value is found by finding the products of outcomes and probabilities. For the distribution of Table 14,

$$\mu = 0\left(\frac{32}{243}\right) + 1\left(\frac{80}{243}\right) + 2\left(\frac{80}{243}\right) + 3\left(\frac{40}{243}\right) + 4\left(\frac{10}{243}\right) + 5\left(\frac{1}{243}\right)$$

$$= \frac{405}{243} = 1\frac{2}{3}.$$

For a binomial distribution, which is a special kind of probability distribution, it can be shown that the method for finding the mean reduces to the formula

$$\mu = np,$$

where n is the number of trials and p is the probability of success on a single trial. Using this simplified formula, the computation of the mean in the example above is

$$\mu = np = 5\left(\frac{1}{3}\right) = 1\frac{2}{3},$$

which agrees with the result obtained using the expected value.

Like the mean, the variance, $\text{Var}(X)$, of a probability distribution is an expected value—the expected value of the squared deviations from the mean, $(x - \mu)^2$. To find the variance for the example given above, first use the mean $\mu = 5/3$ and find the quantities $(x - \mu)^2$. (See Table 15.)

Table 15

x	$P(X = x)$	$x - \mu$	$(x - \mu)^2$
0	$\frac{32}{243}$	$\frac{-5}{3}$	$\frac{25}{9}$
1	$\frac{80}{243}$	$\frac{-2}{3}$	$\frac{4}{9}$
2	$\frac{80}{243}$	$\frac{1}{3}$	$\frac{1}{9}$
3	$\frac{40}{243}$	$\frac{4}{3}$	$\frac{16}{9}$
4	$\frac{10}{243}$	$\frac{7}{3}$	$\frac{49}{9}$
5	$\frac{1}{243}$	$\frac{10}{3}$	$\frac{100}{9}$

Find $\text{Var}(X)$ by finding the sum of the products $[(x - \mu)^2][P(X = x)]$.

$$\text{Var}(X) = \frac{25}{9}\left(\frac{32}{243}\right) + \frac{4}{9}\left(\frac{80}{243}\right) + \frac{1}{9}\left(\frac{80}{243}\right) + \frac{16}{9}\left(\frac{40}{243}\right) + \frac{49}{9}\left(\frac{10}{243}\right) + \frac{100}{9}\left(\frac{1}{243}\right)$$

$$= \frac{10}{9} = 1\frac{1}{9}$$

To find the standard deviation σ, find $\sqrt{10/9}$ or $\sqrt{10}/3$, or approximately 1.05.

Just as with the mean, the variance of a binomial distribution can be found with a relatively simple formula. Again, it can be shown that

$$\text{Var}(X) = np(1 - p) \quad \text{and} \quad \sigma = \sqrt{np(1 - p)}.$$

By substituting the appropriate values for n and p from the example into this new formula,

$$\text{Var}(X) = 5\left(\frac{1}{3}\right)\left(\frac{2}{3}\right) = 10/9 = 1\frac{1}{9},$$

which agrees with our previous result.

A summary of these results is given below.

Binomial

Distribution

Suppose an experiment is a series of n independent repeated trials, where the probability of a success in a single trial is always p. Let x be the number of successes in the n trials. Then the probability that exactly x successes will occur in n trials is given by

$$\binom{n}{x}p^x(1 - p)^{n-x}.$$

The mean μ and variance $\text{Var}(X)$ of this binomial distribution are respectively

$$\mu = np \quad \text{and} \quad \text{Var}(X) = np(1 - p).$$

The standard deviation σ is

$$\sigma = \sqrt{np(1 - p)}.$$

EXAMPLE 1

The probability that a plate selected at random from the assembly line in a china factory will be defective is .01. A sample of three is to be selected. Write the distribution for the number of defective plates in the sample, and give its mean and standard deviation.

Since three plates will be selected, the possible number of defective plates ranges from 0 to 3. Here, n (the number of trials) is 3, and p (the probability of selecting a defective on a single trial) is .01. The distribution and the probability of each outcome are shown in Table 16.

The mean of the distribution is

$$\mu = np = 3(.01) = .03.$$

The standard deviation is

$$\sigma = \sqrt{np(1 - p)} = \sqrt{3(.01)(.99)} = \sqrt{.0297} = .17. \quad \blacksquare$$

The binomial distribution is extremely useful, but its use can lead to complicated calculations if n is large. However, the normal curve of the previous section

Table 16

x	$P(X = x)$
0	$\binom{3}{0}(.01)^0(.99)^3 = .970$
1	$\binom{3}{1}(.01)(.99)^2 = .029$
2	$\binom{3}{2}(.01)^2(.99) = .0003$
3	$\binom{3}{3}(.01)^3(.99)^0 = .000001$

can be used to get a good approximation to the binomial distribution. This approximation was first discovered by Abraham DeMoivre in 1718 for the case $p = 1/2$. The result was generalized by the French mathematician Laplace in a book published in 1812.

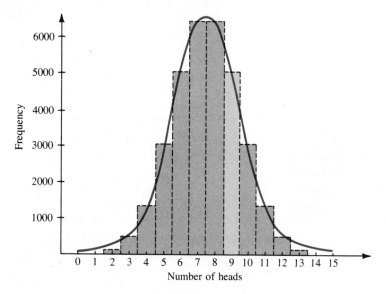

FIGURE 19

To see how the normal curve is used, look at the bar graph and normal curve in Figure 19. This histogram shows the expected number of heads if one coin is tossed 15 times, with the experiment repeated 32,768 times. Since the probability of heads on one toss is 1/2 and $n = 15$, the mean of this distribution is

$$\mu = np = 15\left(\frac{1}{2}\right) = 7.5.$$

The standard deviation is

$$\sigma = \sqrt{15\left(\frac{1}{2}\right)\left(1 - \frac{1}{2}\right)}$$

$$= \sqrt{15\left(\frac{1}{2}\right)\left(\frac{1}{2}\right)}$$

$$= \sqrt{3.75} \approx 1.94.$$

In Figure 19 we have superimposed the normal curve with $\mu = 7.5$ and $\sigma = 1.94$ over the bar graph of the distribution.

Suppose we need to know the fraction of the time that exactly 9 heads would be obtained in the 15 tosses. We could work this out using the methods above. After extensive calculations, we would get .153. This answer is about the same fraction that would be found by dividing the area of the bar in color in Figure 19 by the total area of all 16 bars in the graph. (Some of the bars at the extreme left and right ends of the graph are too short to show up.)

As the graph suggests, the area in color is approximately equal to the area under the normal curve from $x = 8.5$ to $x = 9.5$. The normal curve is higher than the top of the bar in the left half but lower in the right half.

To find the area under the normal curve from $x = 8.5$ to $x = 9.5$, first find z-scores, as in the last section. Do this with the mean and the standard deviation for the distribution, which we have already calculated, to get z-scores for $x = 8.5$ and $x = 9.5$.

For $x = 8.5$ 　　　　　 For $x = 9.5$

$$z = \frac{8.5 - 7.5}{1.94} \qquad z = \frac{9.5 - 7.5}{1.94}$$

$$= \frac{1.00}{1.94} \qquad\quad = \frac{2.00}{1.94}$$

$$z \approx .52 \qquad\qquad z \approx 1.03$$

From the table of normal curves, $z = .52$ gives an area of .6985, while $z = 1.03$ gives .8485. To find the desired result, subtract these two numbers.

$$.8485 - .6985 = .1500$$

This answer (.1500) is not far from the exact answer, .153, found above.

EXAMPLE 2

About 6% of the bolts produced by a certain machine are defective.

(a)　Find the probability that in a sample of 100 bolts, 3 or fewer are defective.

This problem satisfies the conditions of the definition of a binomial distribution, so the normal curve approximation can be used. First find the mean and the standard deviation using $n = 100$ and $p = 6\% = .06$.

$$\mu = 100(.06) \qquad \sigma = \sqrt{100(.06)(1 - .06)}$$
$$= 6 \qquad\qquad = \sqrt{100(.06)(.94)}$$
$$\qquad\qquad = \sqrt{5.64} \approx 2.37$$

As the graph of Figure 20 shows, we need to find the area to the left of $x = 3.5$ (since we want 3 or fewer defective bolts). The z-score corresponding to $x = 3.5$ is

$$z = \frac{3.5 - 6}{2.37} = \frac{-2.5}{2.37} \approx -1.05.$$

From the table, $z = -1.05$ leads to an area of .1469, so that the probability of getting 3 or fewer defective bolts in a set of 100 bolts is .1469, or 14.69%.

(b) Find the probability of getting exactly 11 defective bolts in a sample of 100 bolts.

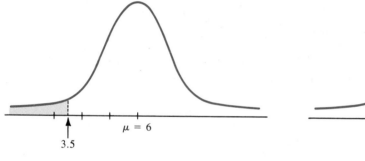

FIGURE 20	**FIGURE 21**

As Figure 21 shows, we need the area between $x = 10.5$ and $x = 11.5$.

$$\text{If } x = 10.5, \text{ then } z = \frac{10.5 - 6}{2.37} \approx 1.90.$$

$$\text{If } x = 11.5, \text{ then } z = \frac{11.5 - 6}{2.37} \approx 2.32.$$

Look in the table; $z = 1.90$ gives an area of .9713, while $z = 2.32$ yields .9898. The final answer is the difference of these numbers, or

$$.9898 - .9713 = .0185.$$

There is about a 1.85% chance of having exactly 11 defective bolts. ▨

The normal curve approximation to the binomial distribution is usually quite accurate, especially for practical problems. For n up to say, 15 or 20, it is usually not too difficult to actually calculate the binomial probabilities directly. For larger values of n, a rule of thumb is that the normal curve approximation can be used as long as both np and $n(1 - p)$ are at least 5.

7.5   EXERCISES

In Exercises 1–6, several binomial experiments are described. For each one, give (a) the distribution; (b) the mean; (c) the standard deviation.

1. A die is rolled six times and the number of 1's that come up is tallied. Write the distribution of 1's that can be expected to occur.

2. A 6-item multiple choice test has 4 possible answers for each item. A student selects all his answers randomly. Give the distribution of correct answers.

3. To maintain quality control on the production line, the Bright Lite Company randomly selects 3 light bulbs each day for testing. Experience has shown a defective rate of .02. Write the distribution for the number of defectives in the daily samples.

4. In a taste test, each member of a panel of 4 is given 2 glasses of Supercola, one made using the old formula and one with the new formula, and asked to identify the new formula. Assuming the panelists operate independently, write the distribution of the number of successful identifications, if each judge actually guesses.

5. The probability that a radish seed will germinate is .7. Joe's mother gives him 4 seeds to plant. Write the distribution for the number of seeds which germinate.

6. Five patients in Ward 8 of Memorial Hospital have a disease with a known mortality rate of .1. Write the distribution of the number who survive.

Work the following problems involving binomial experiments.

7. The probability that an infant will die in the first year of life is about .025. In a group of 500 babies, what are the mean and standard deviation of the number of babies who can be expected to die in their first year of life?

8. The probability that a particular kind of mouse will have a brown coat is 1/4. In a litter of 8, assuming independence, how many could be expected to have a brown coat? With what standard deviation?

9. A certain drug is effective 80% of the time. Give the mean and standard deviation of the number of patients using the drug who recover, out of a group of 64 patients.

10. The probability that a newborn infant will be a girl is .49. If 50 infants are born on Susan B. Anthony's birthday, how many can be expected to be girls? With what standard deviation?

For the remaining exercises, use the normal curve approximation to the binomial distribution.

Suppose 16 coins are tossed. Find the probability of getting exactly

11. 8 heads;   12. 7 heads;   13. 10 tails;   14. 12 tails.

Suppose 1000 coins are tossed. Find the probability of getting each of the following. (Hint: $\sqrt{250} = 15.8$)

15. exactly 500 heads   16. exactly 510 heads   17. 480 heads or more
18. less than 470 tails   19. less than 518 heads   20. more than 550 tails

A die is tossed 120 times. Find the probability of getting each of the following. (Hint: $\sigma = 4.08$)

21. exactly 20 fives   22. exactly 24 sixes   23. exactly 17 threes
24. exactly 22 twos   25. more than 18 threes   26. fewer than 22 sixes

Two percent of the quartz heaters produced in a certain plant are defective. Suppose the plant produced 10,000 such heaters last month. Find the probability that among these heaters

27. fewer than 170 were defective;

28. more than 222 were defective.

A new drug cures 80% of the patients to whom it is administered. It is given to 25 patients. Find the probability that among these patients

29. exactly 20 are cured;

30. exactly 23 are cured;

31. all are cured;

32. no one is cured;

33. 12 or fewer are cured;

34. between 17 and 23 are cured.

35. An experimental drug causes a rash in 15% of all people taking it. If the drug is given to 12,000 people, find the probability that more than 1700 people will get the rash.

36. In one state, 55% of the voters expect to vote for Jones. Suppose 1400 people are asked for the name of the person they expect to vote for. Find the probability that at least 700 people will say that they expect to vote for Jones.

37. Rework Exercises 30–33 of Section 6.7 using the normal curve to approximate the binomial probabilities. Compare your answers with the results found in Section 6.7 for the binomial distribution.

38. A coin is tossed 100 times. Find the probability of

(a) exactly 50 heads;   (b) at least 55 heads;   (c) no more than 40 heads.

KEY WORDS

random variable	fair game
frequency distribution	variance
probability distribution	standard deviation
probability distribution function	Chebyshev's Theorem
discrete distribution function	skewed distribution
continuous distribution function	normal distribution
histogram	normal curve
mathematical expectation	standard normal distribution
average	z-score
arithmetic mean	binomial distribution
expected value	

Chapter 7   REVIEW EXERCISES

In Exercises 1–5, (a) give a probability distribution and (b) sketch its histogram.

1.

X	1	2	3	4	5
Frequency	3	7	9	3	2

2.

X	8	9	10	11	12	13	14
Frequency	1	0	2	5	8	4	3

3. A coin is tossed three times and the number of heads is recorded.

4. A pair of dice are rolled and the number of points showing is recorded.

5. Patients in groups of five were given a new treatment for a fatal disease. The experiment was repeated ten times with the following results.

Number Who Survived	Frequency
0	1
1	1
2	2
3	3
4	3
5	0
Total:	10

In Exercises 6 and 7, give the probability which corresponds to the shaded region of the figure.

6.

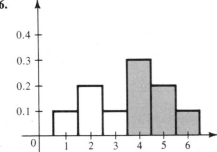

7.

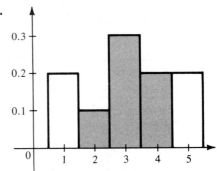

Solve the following problems.

8. You pay $6 to play in a game where you will roll a die, with payoffs as follows: $8 for a 6, $7 for a 5, $4 otherwise. What is your mathematical expectation? Is the game fair?

9. A lottery has a first prize of $5000, two second prizes of $1000 each, and two $100 third prizes. A total of ten thousand tickets is sold, at $1 each. Find the expected winnings of a person buying one ticket.

10. Find the expected number of girls in a family of 5 children.

11. A developer can buy a piece of property that will produce a profit of $16,000 with probability .7, or a loss of $9000 with probability .3. What is the expected profit?

12. Game boards for a recent United Airlines contest could be obtained by sending a self addressed stamped envelope to a certain address. The prize was a ticket for any city to which United flies. Assume that the value of the ticket was $1000 (we might as well go first class), and that the probability that a particular game board would win was 1/4000. If the stamps to enter the contest cost 30¢, and envelopes are 1¢ each, find the expected winnings for a person ordering one game board.

Find the expected value of the random variable in each of the following.

13. the data in Exercise 2

14. the experiment of Exercise 3

15. the experiment of Exercise 5

16. 3 cards are drawn from a standard deck of 52 cards.

   (a) What is the expected number of aces?

   (b) What is the expected number of clubs?

17. Suppose someone offers to pay you $100 if you draw three cards from a standard deck of 52 cards and all the cards are clubs. What should you pay for the chance to win if it is a fair game?

Find the variance and standard deviation of the random variable in the following.

18. the data in Exercise 3

19. the experiment of Exercise 5

20. The annual returns of two stocks for three years are given below.

	1980	1981	1982
Stock I	11%	−1%	14%
Stock II	9%	5%	10%

   (a) Find the mean and standard deviation for each stock over the three-year period.

   (b) If you are looking for security with an 8% return, which of these two stocks would you choose?

21. The weight gains of 2 groups of 10 rats fed on two different experimental diets were as follows:

	Weight Gains									
Diet A	1	0	3	7	1	1	5	4	1	4
Diet B	2	1	1	2	3	2	1	0	1	0

Compute the mean and standard deviation for each group.

   (a) Which diet produced the greatest mean gain?

   (b) Which diet produced the most consistent gain?

22. A probability distribution has an expected value of 28 and a standard deviation of 4. Use Chebyshev's Theorem to decide what percent of the distribution is

   (a) between 20 and 36;   **(b)** less than 23.2 or greater than 32.8.

23. **(a)** Find the percent of the area under a normal curve within 2.5 standard deviations of the mean.

   (b) Compare your answer to part **(a)** with the result using Chebyshev's Theorem.

24. Find the percent of the total area under the normal curve which corresponds to

   (a) $z \geq 2.2$,   **(b)** between $z = -1.3$ and $z = .2$.

25. Find a z-score such that 8% of the area under the curve is to the right of z.

26. A machine which fills quart milk cartons is set to fill them with 32.1 oz. If the actual contents of the cartons vary normally with a standard deviation of .1 oz., what percent of the cartons contain less than a quart (32 oz.)?

27. The probability that a can of beer from a certain brewery is defective is .005. A sample of 4 cans is selected at random. Write a distribution for the number of defective cans in the sample, and give its mean and standard deviation.

28. Find the probability of getting the following number of heads in 15 tosses of a coin.
    (a) exactly 7
    (b) between 7 and 10
    (c) at least 10

29. The probability that a small business will go bankrupt in its first year is .21. For 50 such small businesses, find the following probabilities.
    (a) exactly 8 go bankrupt.
    (b) no more than 2 go bankrupt.

30. On standard IQ tests, the mean is 100, with a standard deviation of 15. The results are very close to fitting a normal curve. Suppose an IQ test is given to a very large group of people. Find the percentage of those people whose IQ score is
    (a) more than 130;
    (b) less than 85;
    (c) between 85 and 115.

31. The residents of a certain Eastern suburb average 42 minutes a day commuting to work, with a standard deviation of 12 minutes. Assume that commuting times are closely approximated by a normal curve and find the percent of the residents of this suburb who commute
    (a) at least 50 minutes per day;   (b) no more than 35 minutes per day;
    (c) between 32 and 40 minutes per day;   (d) between 38 and 60 minutes per day.

32. About 6% of the frankfurters produced by a certain machine are overstuffed, and thus defective. Find the probability that in a sample of 500 frankfurters,
    (a) 25 or fewer are overstuffed (Hint: $\sigma = 5.3$);
    (b) exactly 30 are overstuffed;
    (c) more than 40 are overstuffed.

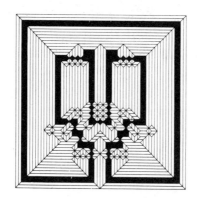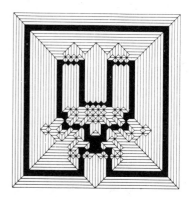

MARKOV CHAINS

Karl Gerstner. Drawings from *Color Lines C1/L9*, Intro Version, 1957, 1976–77.

In Chapter 6 we briefly studied *stochastic processes,* mathematical models in which the outcome of an experiment depends on the outcome of previous experiments. In this chapter we study a special type of stochastic process called a **Markov chain;** here the outcome of an experiment depends only on the outcome of the previous experiment. That is, given the present state of the system, future states are independent of past states. Such experiments are common enough in applications to make their study worthwhile. Markov chains are named after the Russian mathematician A. A. Markov, 1856–1922, who started the theory of stochastic processes.

8.1   Basic Properties of Markov Chains

Transition Matrix   In sociology, it is convenient to classify people by income as *lower class, middle class,* and *upper class.* The strongest determinant of the income class of an individual turns out to be the income class of the individual's parents. For example, if we say that an individual in the lower income class is in *state 1,* an individual in the middle income class is in *state 2,* and an individual in the upper income class is in *state 3,* then we might have the following probabilities of change in income class from one generation to the next.

		Next Generation		
	State	*1*	*2*	*3*
Current	1	.65	.28	.07
Generation	2	.15	.67	.18
	3	.12	.36	.52

This chart shows that if an individual is in state 1 (lower income class) then there is a probability of .65 that any offspring will be in the lower class, a probability of .28 that offspring will be in the middle class, and a probability of .07 that offspring will be in the upper class.

The symbol p_{ij} will be used for the probability of transition from state i to state j, in one generation. For example, p_{23} represents the probability that a person in state 2 will have offspring in state 3; from the table above,

$$p_{23} = .18.$$

Also from the table, $p_{31} = .12$, $p_{22} = .67$, and so on.

The table above can be written as a matrix, with the states indicated at the side and top; this matrix is called a **transition matrix.** If P represents the transition matrix for the table above, then

$$
\begin{array}{c}
\begin{array}{ccc} 1 & 2 & 3 \end{array} \\
\begin{array}{c} 1 \\ 2 \\ 3 \end{array}
\begin{bmatrix}
.65 & .28 & .07 \\
.15 & .67 & .18 \\
.12 & .36 & .52
\end{bmatrix} = P.
\end{array}
$$

A transition matrix has several features:

1. It is square, since all possible states must be used both as rows and as columns.
2. All entries are between 0 and 1, inclusive; this is because all entries represent probabilities.
3. The sum of the entries in any row must be 1, since the numbers in the row give the probability of changing from the state at the left to one of the states indicated across the top.

Markov Chains   A transition matrix, such as matrix P above, also shows two of the key features of a Markov chain.

Markov Chain

A sequence of trials of an experiment is a *Markov chain* if

1. the outcome of each experiment is one of a set of discrete states,
2. the outcome of an experiment depends only on the present state, and not on any past states.

For example, in the transition matrix above, a person is assumed to be in one of three discrete states (lower, middle, or upper class) with any offspring in one of these same three discrete states.

EXAMPLE 1

A small town has only two drycleaners, Johnson and NorthClean. Johnson's manager desires to increase the firm's market share by an extensive advertising campaign. After the campaign, a market research firm finds that there is a probability of .8 that a customer of Johnson's will bring their next batch of dirty items to Johnson, and a .35 chance that a NorthClean customer will switch to Johnson for their next batch. Write a transition matrix showing this information.

Here we must assume that the probability that a customer comes to a given cleaners depends only on where the last load of clothes was taken. If there is an .8 chance that a Johnson customer will return to Johnson, then there must be a $1 - .8 = .2$ chance that the customer will switch to NorthClean. In the same way, there is a $1 - .35 = .65$ chance that a NorthClean customer will return to NorthClean. These probabilities give the following transition matrix.

$$
\begin{array}{c}
\text{\textit{Second load}} \\
\begin{array}{cc}
\text{Johnson} & \text{NorthClean}
\end{array}
\end{array}
$$

$$
\textit{First load} \quad
\begin{array}{c}
\text{Johnson} \\
\text{NorthClean}
\end{array}
\begin{bmatrix}
.8 & .2 \\
.35 & .65
\end{bmatrix}
$$

We shall come back to this transition matrix later in this section (See Example 4). ■

Look again at transition matrix P for social class changes.

$$
\begin{array}{c c}
 & \begin{array}{c c c} 1 & 2 & 3 \end{array} \\
\begin{array}{c} 1 \\ 2 \\ 3 \end{array} &
\left[\begin{array}{c c c}
.65 & .28 & .07 \\
.15 & .67 & .18 \\
.12 & .36 & .52
\end{array} \right] = P
\end{array}
$$

This matrix shows the probability of change in social class from one generation to the next. Now let us investigate the probabilities for changes in social class over *two* generations. For example, if a parent is upper class (state 3), what is the probability that a grandchild will be in state 2?

To find out, start with a tree diagram as shown in Figure 1; the various probabilities come from transition matrix P.

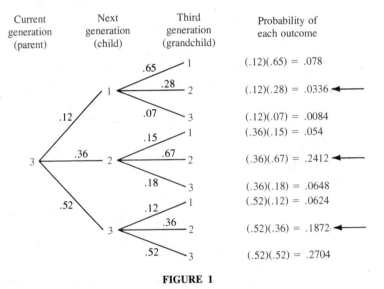

FIGURE 1

The arrows point to the outcomes "grandchild in state 2"; the grandchild can get to state 2 after having had parents in either state 1, state 2, or state 3. The probability that a parent in state 3 will have a grandchild in state 2 is given by the sum of the probabilities indicated with arrows, or

$$.0336 + .2412 + .1872 = .4620.$$

We used p_{ij} to represent the probability of changing from state i to state j in one generation. This notation can be used to write the probability that a parent in state 3 will have a grandchild in state 2:

$$p_{31} \cdot p_{12} + p_{32} \cdot p_{22} + p_{33} \cdot p_{32}.$$

This sum of products of probabilities should remind you of matrix multiplication— it is nothing more than one step in the process of multiplying matrix P by itself.

In particular, it is row 3 of P times column 2 of P. If P^2 represents the matrix product $P \cdot P$, then P^2 gives the probabilities of a transition from one state to another in *two* repetitions of an experiment. Generalizing,

P^k gives the probabilities of a transition from one state to another in k repetitions of an experiment.

EXAMPLE 2

For transition matrix P (social class changes),

$$P^2 = \begin{bmatrix} .65 & .28 & .07 \\ .15 & .67 & .18 \\ .12 & .36 & .52 \end{bmatrix} \begin{bmatrix} .65 & .28 & .07 \\ .15 & .67 & .18 \\ .12 & .36 & .52 \end{bmatrix} \approx \begin{bmatrix} .47 & .39 & .13 \\ .22 & .56 & .22 \\ .19 & .46 & .34 \end{bmatrix}.$$

(The numbers in the product have been rounded to the same number of decimal places as in matrix P.) The entry in row 3, column 2 of P^2 gives the probability that a person in state 3 will have an offspring in state 2 two generations later. This number, .46, is the result (rounded to 2 decimal places) found through use of the tree diagram.

Row 1, column 3 of P^2 gives the number .13, the probability that a person in state 1 will have an offspring in state 3, but two generations later. How would the entry .47 be interpreted? ■

EXAMPLE 3

In the same way that matrix P^2 gives the probability of transitions after *two* generations, the matrix $P^3 = P \cdot P^2$ gives the probabilities of change after *three* generations.

For matrix P,

$$P^3 = P \cdot P^2 = \begin{bmatrix} .65 & .28 & .07 \\ .15 & .67 & .18 \\ .12 & .36 & .52 \end{bmatrix} \begin{bmatrix} .47 & .39 & .13 \\ .22 & .56 & .22 \\ .19 & .46 & .34 \end{bmatrix} \approx \begin{bmatrix} .38 & .44 & .17 \\ .25 & .52 & .23 \\ .23 & .49 & .27 \end{bmatrix}.$$

(The rows of P^3 don't necessarily total 1 exactly because of rounding errors.) Matrix P^3 gives a probability of .25 that a person in state 2 will have an offspring in state 1 *three generations* later. The probability is .52 that a person in state 2 will have, three generations later, an offspring in state 2. ■

EXAMPLE 4

Let us return to the transition matrix for the cleaners.

Second load

		Johnson	NorthClean
First load	Johnson	.8	.2
	NorthClean	.35	.65

As this matrix shows, there is a .8 chance that persons bringing their first load to Johnson will also bring their second load to Johnson, and so on. To find the probabilities for the third load, the second stage of this Markov chain, find the square of the transition matrix. If C represents the transition matrix, then

$$C^2 = C \cdot C = \begin{bmatrix} .8 & .2 \\ .35 & .65 \end{bmatrix} \begin{bmatrix} .8 & .2 \\ .35 & .65 \end{bmatrix} = \begin{bmatrix} .71 & .29 \\ .51 & .49 \end{bmatrix}.$$

From C^2, the probability that a person bringing their first load of clothes to Johnson will also bring their third load to Johnson is .71; the probability that a person bringing their first load to NorthClean will bring their third load to NorthClean is .49.

The cube of matrix C gives the probabilities for the fourth load, the third step in our experiment.

$$C^3 = C \cdot C^2 = \begin{bmatrix} .67 & .33 \\ .58 & .42 \end{bmatrix}$$

The probability is .58, for example, that persons bringing their first load to North-Clean will bring their fourth load to Johnson. ■

Distribution of States   Look again at the transition matrix for social class changes:

$$P = \begin{bmatrix} .65 & .28 & .07 \\ .15 & .67 & .18 \\ .12 & .36 & .52 \end{bmatrix}.$$

Suppose the following table gives the initial distribution of people in the three social classes.

Class	State	Proportion
lower	1	21%
middle	2	68%
upper	3	11%

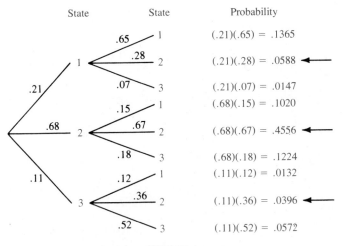

FIGURE 2

To find how these proportions would change after one generation, we use the tree diagram of Figure 2. For example, to find the proportion of people in state 2 after one generation, add the numbers indicated with arrows.

$$.0588 + .4556 + .0396 = .5540$$

In a similar way, the proportion of people in state 1 after one generation is

$$.1365 + .1020 + .0132 = .2517.$$

For state 3, the proportion is

$$.0147 + .1224 + .0572 = .1943.$$

The initial distribution of states, 21%, 68%, and 11%, becomes, after one generation, 25.17% in state 1, 55.4% in state 2, and 19.43% in state 3. These distributions can be written as *probability vectors* (where the percents have been changed to decimals rounded to the nearest hundredth):

$$[.21 \quad .68 \quad .11] \quad \text{and} \quad [.25 \quad .55 \quad .19]$$

respectively. A **probability vector** is a matrix of only one row, having nonnegative entries, with the sum of the entries 1.

The work with the tree diagram to find the distribution of states after one generation is exactly the work required to multiply the initial probability vector, $[.21 \quad .68 \quad .11]$, and the transition matrix P:

$$[.21 \quad .68 \quad .11] \begin{bmatrix} .65 & .28 & .07 \\ .15 & .67 & .18 \\ .12 & .36 & .52 \end{bmatrix} \approx [.25 \quad .55 \quad .19].$$

In a similar way, the distribution of social classes after two generations can be found by multiplying the initial probability vector and the square of P, the matrix P^2. Using P^2 from above,

$$[.21 \quad .68 \quad .11] \begin{bmatrix} .47 & .39 & .13 \\ .22 & .56 & .22 \\ .19 & .46 & .34 \end{bmatrix} \approx [.27 \quad .51 \quad .21]$$

In the next section we shall find a long-range prediction for the proportions of the population in each social class. Our work in this section is summarized below.

Suppose a Markov chain has initial probability vector $I = [i_1 \quad i_2 \quad i_3 \quad \cdots \quad i_n]$, and transition matrix P. The probability vector after n repetitions of the experiment is

$$I \cdot P^n.$$

8.1 EXERCISES

Which of the matrices in Exercises 1–9 could be a probability vector?

1. $\begin{bmatrix} \frac{2}{3} & \frac{1}{2} \end{bmatrix}$

2. $\begin{bmatrix} \frac{1}{2} & 1 \end{bmatrix}$

3. $\begin{bmatrix} 0 & 1 \end{bmatrix}$

4. $\begin{bmatrix} .1 & .1 \end{bmatrix}$

5. $\begin{bmatrix} .4 & .2 & 0 \end{bmatrix}$

6. $\begin{bmatrix} \frac{1}{4} & \frac{1}{8} & \frac{5}{8} \end{bmatrix}$

7. $\begin{bmatrix} .07 & .04 & .37 & .52 \end{bmatrix}$

8. $\begin{bmatrix} .3 & -.1 & .8 \end{bmatrix}$

9. $\begin{bmatrix} 0 & -.2 & .6 & .6 \end{bmatrix}$

Which of the matrices in Exercises 10–18 could be transition matrices, by definition?

10. $\begin{bmatrix} .5 & 0 \\ 0 & .5 \end{bmatrix}$

11. $\begin{bmatrix} \frac{2}{3} & \frac{1}{3} \\ 1 & 0 \end{bmatrix}$

12. $\begin{bmatrix} \frac{1}{4} & \frac{3}{4} \\ \frac{1}{2} & \frac{1}{2} \end{bmatrix}$

13. $\begin{bmatrix} \frac{1}{4} & \frac{3}{4} & 0 \\ 2 & 0 & 1 \\ 1 & \frac{2}{3} & 3 \end{bmatrix}$

14. $\begin{bmatrix} \frac{1}{3} & \frac{1}{3} & \frac{1}{3} \\ 0 & 1 & 0 \\ \frac{1}{2} & 0 & \frac{1}{2} \end{bmatrix}$

15. $\begin{bmatrix} \frac{1}{3} & \frac{1}{2} & 1 \\ 0 & 1 & 0 \\ \frac{1}{2} & \frac{1}{2} & 1 \end{bmatrix}$

16. $\begin{bmatrix} \frac{1}{3} & \frac{1}{2} & 1 \\ \frac{1}{3} & 0 & 0 \\ \frac{1}{3} & \frac{1}{2} & 0 \end{bmatrix}$

17. $\begin{bmatrix} .9 & .1 & 0 \\ .1 & .6 & .3 \\ 0 & .3 & .7 \end{bmatrix}$

18. $\begin{bmatrix} .6 & .2 & .2 \\ .9 & .02 & .08 \\ 0 & 0 & .6 \end{bmatrix}$

Find the first three powers of each of the transition matrices in Exercises 19–24, for example, A, A^2 and A^3. For each transition matrix, find the probability that state 1 changes to state 2 after three repetitions of the experiment.

19. $A = \begin{bmatrix} 1 & 0 \\ .8 & .2 \end{bmatrix}$

20. $B = \begin{bmatrix} .7 & .3 \\ 0 & 1 \end{bmatrix}$

21. $C = \begin{bmatrix} .5 & .5 \\ .72 & .28 \end{bmatrix}$

22. $D = \begin{bmatrix} .3 & .2 & .5 \\ 0 & 0 & 1 \\ .6 & .1 & .3 \end{bmatrix}$

23. $E = \begin{bmatrix} .8 & .1 & .1 \\ .3 & .6 & .1 \\ 0 & 1 & 0 \end{bmatrix}$

24. $F = \begin{bmatrix} .01 & .9 & .09 \\ .72 & .1 & .18 \\ .34 & 0 & .66 \end{bmatrix}$

25. Years ago, about 10% of all cars sold were small, while 90% were large. This has changed drastically; now of the people buying a car in a given year, 20% of small car owners will switch to a large car, while 60% of large car owners will switch to a small car.

  (a) Write a transition matrix using this information.

  (b) Write a probability vector for the initial distribution of cars.

  (c) Square the transition matrix and find the distribution of cars after 2 years.

  Find the distribution of cars after

  (d) 3 years   **(e)** 4 years   **(f)** 5 years.

26. In the example in the text, we used the transition matrix

$$\begin{array}{c} \\ \text{Johnson} \\ \text{NorthClean} \end{array} \begin{array}{cc} \text{Johnson} & \text{NorthClean} \\ \begin{bmatrix} .8 & .2 \\ .35 & .65 \end{bmatrix} \end{array}$$

  Suppose now that we assume that each customer brings in one load of clothes each week. Use various powers of the transition matrix to find the probability that a customer bringing a load of clothes to Johnson initially also brings a load to Johnson after

  (a) 1 week   **(b)** 2 weeks   **(c)** 3 weeks   **(d)** 4 weeks.

27. Suppose Johnson has a 40% market share initially, with NorthClean having a 60% share. Use this information to write a probability vector; use this vector along with the transition matrix above to find the share of the market for each firm after

  (a) 1 week   **(b)** 2 weeks   **(c)** 3 weeks   **(d)** 4 weeks.

28. An insurance company classifies its drivers into three groups: G_0 (no accidents), G_1 (one accident), and G_2 (more than one accident). The probability that a driver in G_0 will stay in G_0 after one year is .85, that the driver will become a G_1 is .10, and that the driver will become a G_2 is .05. A driver in G_1 cannot move to G_0 (this company has a long memory). There is a .8 probability that a G_1 driver will stay in G_1. A G_2 driver must stay in G_2. Write a transition matrix using this information.

29. Suppose that the company of Exercise 28 accepts 50,000 new policyholders, all of whom are in G_0. Find the number in each group after
    (**a**) 1 year   (**b**) 2 years   (**c**) 3 years   (**d**) 4 years.

30. The difficulty with the mathematical model of Exercises 28 and 29 is that no "grace period" is provided; there should be a certain positive probability of moving from G_1 or G_2 back to G_0 (say, after four years with no accidents). A new system with this feature might produce the following transition matrix.

$$\begin{bmatrix} .85 & .10 & .05 \\ .15 & .75 & .10 \\ .10 & .30 & .60 \end{bmatrix}$$

Suppose that when this new policy is adopted, the company has 50,000 policyholders, all in G_0. Find the number in each group after
    (**a**) 1 year   (**b**) 2 years   (**c**) 3 years.

31. Research done by the Gulf Oil Corporation* produced the following transition matrix for the probability that during a given year a person with one form of home heating would switch to another.

		Will switch to		
		Oil	Gas	Electric
	Oil	.825	.175	0
Now has	Gas	.060	.919	.021
	Electric	.049	0	.951

The current share of the market held by these three types of heat is given by the vector $[.26 \quad .60 \quad .14]$. Find the share of the market held by each type of heat after
    (**a**) 1 year   (**b**) 2 years   (**c**) 3 years.

32. In one state, a land use survey showed that 35% of all land was used for agricultural purposes, while 10% was urban. Ten years later, of the agricultural land, 15% had become urban and 80% had remained agricultural. (The remainder lay idle.) Of the idle land, 20% had become urbanized and 10% had been converted for agricultural use. Of the urban land, 90% remained urban and 10% was idle. Assume that these trends continue.
    (**a**) Write a transition matrix using this information.
    (**b**) Write a probability vector for the initial distribution of land.
    Find the land use pattern after
    (**c**) ten years   (**d**) twenty years.

---

*Reprinted by permission of Ali Ezzati, "Forecasting Market Shares of Alternative Home Heating Units," *Management Science,* Vol. 21, No. 4, December 1974, copyright © 1974 The Institute of Management Sciences.

33. In a survey investigating change in housing patterns in one urban area, it was found that 75% of the population lived in single-family dwellings and 25% in multiple housing of some kind. Five years later, in a follow-up survey, of those who had been living in single family dwellings, 90% still did so, but 10% had moved to multiple family dwellings. Of those in multiple family housing, 95% were still living in that type of housing, while 5% had moved to single-family dwellings. Assume that these trends continue.

(a) Write a transition matrix for this information.

(b) Write a probability vector for the initial distribution of housing.

What percent of the population can be expected in each category

(c) five years later   (d) ten years later?

34. At the end of June in a Presidential election year, 40% of the voters were registered as liberal, 45% as conservative, and 15% as independent. Over a one month period, the liberals retained 80% of their constituency, while 15% switched to conservative and 5% to independent. The conservatives retained 70%, and lost 20% to the liberals. The independents retained 60% and lost 20% each to the conservatives and liberals. Assume that these trends continue.

(a) Write a transition matrix using this information.

(b) Write a probability vector for the initial distribution.

Find the percent of each type of voter at the end of

(c) July   (d) August   (e) September   (f) October.

For each of the following transition matrices, find the first five powers of the matrix. Then find the probability that state 2 changes to state 4 after 5 repetitions of the experiment.

35. $\begin{bmatrix} .1 & .2 & .2 & .3 & .2 \\ .2 & .1 & .1 & .2 & .4 \\ .2 & .1 & .4 & .2 & .1 \\ .3 & .1 & .1 & .2 & .3 \\ .1 & .3 & .1 & .1 & .4 \end{bmatrix}$

36. $\begin{bmatrix} .3 & .2 & .3 & .1 & .1 \\ .4 & .2 & .1 & .2 & .1 \\ .1 & .3 & .2 & .2 & .2 \\ .2 & .1 & .3 & .2 & .2 \\ .1 & .1 & .4 & .2 & .2 \end{bmatrix}$

37. A company with a new training program classified each employee in one of the four states: s_1, never in the program; s_2, currently in the program; s_3, discharged; s_4, completed the program. The transition matrix for this company is given below.

$$\begin{array}{c} \\ s_1 \\ s_2 \\ s_3 \\ s_4 \end{array} \begin{array}{cccc} s_1 & s_2 & s_3 & s_4 \\ \begin{bmatrix} .4 & .2 & .05 & .35 \\ 0 & .45 & .05 & .5 \\ 0 & 0 & 1.0 & 0 \\ 0 & 0 & 0 & 1.0 \end{bmatrix} \end{array}$$

(a) What percent of employees who had never been in the program (state s_1) completed the program (state s_4) after the program had been offered five times?

(b) If the initial percent of employees in each state was $[.5 \quad .5 \quad 0 \quad 0]$, find the corresponding percents after the program had been offered four times.

8.2 Regular Markov Chains

By starting with a transition matrix P and an initial probability vector, the nth power of P makes it possible to find the probability vector for n repetitions of an experiment. In this section we try to decide what happens to an initial probability vector "in the long run," that is, as n gets larger and larger.

For example, let us use the transition matrix associated with the dry cleaners example of the previous section,

$$\begin{bmatrix} .8 & .2 \\ .35 & .65 \end{bmatrix}.$$

The initial probability vector, which gives the market share for each firm at the beginning of the experiment, is $[.4 \quad .6]$. The market shares shown in the following table were found by using powers of the transition matrix. (See Exercise 27 of Section 8.1.)

Week	Johnson	NorthClean
Start	.4	.6
1	.53	.47
2	.59	.41
3	.62	.38
4	.63	.37
5	.63	.37
12	.64	.36

The results seem to approach the numbers in the probability vector $[.64 \quad .36]$.

What happens if the initial probability vector is different from $[.4 \quad .6]$? Suppose $[.75 \quad .25]$ is used; the same powers of the transition matrix as above give the following results.

Week	Johnson	NorthClean
Start	.75	.25
1	.69	.31
2	.66	.34
3	.65	.35
4	.64	.36
5	.64	.36
6	.64	.36

Here the results also seem to be approaching the numbers in the probability vector $[.64 \quad .36]$, the same numbers approached with the initial probability vector $[.4 \quad .6]$. In either case, the long-range trend is for a market share of about 64% for Johnson and 36% for NorthClean. Based on the example above, this long-range trend does not depend on the initial distribution of market shares.

Regular Transition Matrices   One of the many applications of Markov chains is in finding these long-range predictions. It is not possible to make long-range predictions with all transition matrices, but for a large set of transition matrices, long-range predictions *are* possible. Such predictions are always possible with **regular transition matrices.** A transition matrix is **regular** if some power of the matrix contains all positive entries. A Markov chain is a **regular Markov chain** if its transition matrix is regular.

EXAMPLE 1

Decide if the following transition matrices are regular.

(a) $A = \begin{bmatrix} .75 & .25 & 0 \\ 0 & .5 & .5 \\ .6 & .4 & 0 \end{bmatrix}$

Square A.

$$A^2 = \begin{bmatrix} .5625 & .3125 & .125 \\ .3 & .45 & .25 \\ .45 & .35 & .2 \end{bmatrix}$$

All entries in A^2 are positive, so that matrix A is regular.

(b) $B = \begin{bmatrix} .5 & 0 & .5 \\ 0 & 1 & 0 \\ 0 & 0 & 1 \end{bmatrix}$

Find various powers of B.

$$B^2 = \begin{bmatrix} .25 & 0 & .75 \\ 0 & 1 & 0 \\ 0 & 0 & 1 \end{bmatrix}; B^3 = \begin{bmatrix} .125 & 0 & .875 \\ 0 & 1 & 0 \\ 0 & 0 & 1 \end{bmatrix}; B^4 = \begin{bmatrix} .0625 & 0 & .9375 \\ 0 & 1 & 0 \\ 0 & 0 & 1 \end{bmatrix}$$

Further powers of B will still give the same zero entries, so that no power of matrix B contains all positive entries. For this reason, B is not regular.   ■

Suppose that v is a probability vector. It turns out that for a regular Markov chain with a transition matrix P, there exists a single vector V such that $v \cdot P^n$ approaches closer and closer to V as n gets larger and larger.

Equilibrium Vector of a Markov Chain

If a Markov chain with transition matrix P is regular, then for any probability vector v, there is a unique vector V such that for large values of n,

$$v \cdot P^n \approx V.$$

Vector V is called the **equilibrium vector** or the **fixed vector** of the Markov chain.

In the example with Johnson Cleaners, we found that the equilibrium vector V is approximately $[.64 \quad .36]$. Vector V can be determined by finding P^n for larger and larger values of n, and then looking for a vector that the product $v \cdot P^n$ approaches. However, such an approach can be very tedious and prone to error. To find a better way, start with the fact that for a large value of n,

$$v \cdot P^n \approx V,$$

as mentioned above. From this result, $v \cdot P^n \cdot P \approx V \cdot P$, so that

$$v \cdot P^n \cdot P = v \cdot P^{n+1} \approx VP.$$

Since $v \cdot P^n \approx V$ for large values of n, it is also true that $v \cdot P^{n+1} \approx V$ for large values of n (the product $v \cdot P^n$ approaches V, so that $v \cdot P^{n+1}$ must also approach V.) Thus, $v \cdot P^{n+1} \approx V$ and $v \cdot P^{n+1} \approx VP$, which suggests that

$$VP = V.$$

If a Markov chain with transition matrix P is regular, then there exists a probability vector V such that

$$VP = V.$$

This vector V gives the long-range trend of the Markov chain. Vector V is found by solving a system of linear equations, as shown in the next examples.

EXAMPLE 2

Find the long-range trend for the Markov chain in the dry cleaning example with transition matrix

$$\begin{bmatrix} .8 & .2 \\ .35 & .65 \end{bmatrix}.$$

This matrix is regular since all entries are positive. Let P represent this transition matrix, and let V be the probability vector $[v_1 \quad v_2]$. We want to find V such that

$$VP = V,$$

or

$$[v_1 \quad v_2]\begin{bmatrix} .8 & .2 \\ .35 & .65 \end{bmatrix} = [v_1 \quad v_2].$$

Use matrix multiplication on the left.

$$[.8v_1 + .35v_2 \quad .2v_1 + .65v_2] = [v_1 \quad v_2]$$

Set corresponding entries from the two matrices equal to get

$$.8v_1 + .35v_2 = v_1 \quad \text{and} \quad .2v_1 + .65v_2 = v_2.$$

Simplify each of these equations.

$$-.2v_1 + .35v_2 = 0 \qquad .2v_1 - .35v_2 = 0$$

These last two equations are really the same. (The equations in the system obtained from $VP = V$ are always dependent.) To find the values of v_1 and v_2, recall that $V = [v_1 \quad v_2]$ is a probability vector, so that

$$v_1 + v_2 = 1.$$

To find v_1 and v_2 solve the system

$$-.2v_1 + .35v_2 = 0$$
$$v_1 + v_2 = 1.$$

From the second equation, $v_1 = 1 - v_2$. Substitute $1 - v_2$ for v_1 in the first equation.

$$-.2(1 - v_2) + .35v_2 = 0$$
$$-.2 + .2v_2 + .35v_2 = 0$$
$$.55v_2 = .2$$
$$v_2 = \frac{4}{11} \approx .364$$

Since $v_1 = 1 - v_2$, $v_1 = 7/11 \approx .636$, and the equilibrium vector is $V = [7/11 \quad 4/11] \approx [.636 \quad .364]$. ∎

Some powers of the transition matrix P of Example 1 (with entries rounded to two decimal places) are shown here.

$$P^2 = \begin{bmatrix} .71 & .29 \\ .51 & .49 \end{bmatrix} \qquad P^3 = \begin{bmatrix} .67 & .33 \\ .58 & .42 \end{bmatrix} \qquad P^4 = \begin{bmatrix} .65 & .35 \\ .62 & .38 \end{bmatrix}$$

$$P^5 = \begin{bmatrix} .65 & .35 \\ .63 & .37 \end{bmatrix} \qquad P^6 = \begin{bmatrix} .64 & .36 \\ .63 & .37 \end{bmatrix} \qquad P^{10} = \begin{bmatrix} .64 & .36 \\ .64 & .36 \end{bmatrix}$$

As these results suggest, higher and higher powers of the transition matrix P approach a matrix having all rows identical; these identical rows have as entries the entries of the equilibrium vector V. This agrees with the statement above: the initial state doesn't matter. Regardless of the initial probability vector, the system will approach a fixed vector V.

Let us summarize the results of this section.

| **Properties of Regular Markov Chains** | Suppose a regular Markov chain has a transition matrix P.

1. For any initial probability vector v, the product $v \cdot P^n$ approaches a unique vector V as n gets larger and larger. Vector V is called the *equilibrium* or *fixed vector*.
2. Vector V has the property that $VP = V$.
3. To find V, solve a system of equations obtained from the matrix equation $VP = V$, and from the fact that the sum of the entries of V is 1.
4. The powers P^n approach closer and closer to a matrix whose rows are made up of the entries of the equilibrium vector V. |

EXAMPLE 3   Find the equilibrium vector for the transition matrix

$$K = \begin{bmatrix} .2 & .6 & .2 \\ .1 & .1 & .8 \\ .3 & .3 & .4 \end{bmatrix}.$$

Matrix K has all positive entries and thus is regular. For this reason, an equilibrium vector V must exist such that $VK = V$. Let $V = [v_1 \quad v_2 \quad v_3]$. Then

$$[v_1 \quad v_2 \quad v_3] \begin{bmatrix} .2 & .6 & .2 \\ .1 & .1 & .8 \\ .3 & .3 & .4 \end{bmatrix} = [v_1 \quad v_2 \quad v_3].$$

Use matrix multiplication on the left.

$$[.2v_1 + .1v_2 + .3v_3 \quad .6v_1 + .1v_2 + .3v_3 \quad .2v_1 + .8v_2 + .4v_3]$$
$$= [v_1 \quad v_2 \quad v_3]$$

Setting corresponding entries equal gives three equations.

$$.2v_1 + .1v_2 + .3v_3 = v_1$$
$$.6v_1 + .1v_2 + .3v_3 = v_2$$
$$.2v_1 + .8v_2 + .4v_3 = v_3$$

Simplifying these equations gives

$$-.8v_1 + .1v_2 + .3v_3 = 0$$
$$.6v_1 - .9v_2 + .3v_3 = 0$$
$$.2v_1 + .8v_2 - .6v_3 = 0.$$

Since V is a probability vector,

$$v_1 + v_2 + v_3 = 1.$$

This gives a system of four equations in three unknowns.

$$-.8v_1 + .1v_2 + .3v_3 = 0$$
$$.6v_1 - .9v_2 + .3v_3 = 0$$
$$.2v_1 + .8v_2 - .6v_3 = 0$$
$$v_1 + v_2 + v_3 = 1$$

This system can be solved with the Gauss-Jordan method presented earlier. Start with the augmented matrix

$$\begin{bmatrix} -.8 & .1 & .3 & | & 0 \\ .6 & -.9 & .3 & | & 0 \\ .2 & .8 & -.6 & | & 0 \\ 1 & 1 & 1 & | & 1 \end{bmatrix}.$$

The solution of this system is $v_1 = 5/23$, $v_2 = 7/23$, $v_3 = 11/23$, and

$$V = \begin{bmatrix} \dfrac{5}{23} & \dfrac{7}{23} & \dfrac{11}{23} \end{bmatrix} \approx [.22 \quad .30 \quad .48]. \quad \blacksquare$$

8.2 EXERCISES

Which of the matrices in Exercises 1–6 are regular?

1. $\begin{bmatrix} .2 & .8 \\ .9 & .1 \end{bmatrix}$

2. $\begin{bmatrix} .22 & .78 \\ .43 & .57 \end{bmatrix}$

3. $\begin{bmatrix} 1 & 0 \\ .6 & .4 \end{bmatrix}$

4. $\begin{bmatrix} .55 & .45 \\ 0 & 1 \end{bmatrix}$

5. $\begin{bmatrix} 0 & 1 & 0 \\ .4 & .2 & .4 \\ 1 & 0 & 0 \end{bmatrix}$

6. $\begin{bmatrix} .3 & .5 & .2 \\ 1 & 0 & 0 \\ .5 & .1 & .4 \end{bmatrix}$

Find the equilibrium vector for each transition matrix in Exercises 7–14.

7. $\begin{bmatrix} \frac{1}{4} & \frac{3}{4} \\ \frac{1}{2} & \frac{1}{2} \end{bmatrix}$

8. $\begin{bmatrix} \frac{2}{3} & \frac{1}{3} \\ \frac{1}{8} & \frac{7}{8} \end{bmatrix}$

9. $\begin{bmatrix} .3 & .7 \\ .4 & .6 \end{bmatrix}$

10. $\begin{bmatrix} .8 & .2 \\ .1 & .9 \end{bmatrix}$

11. $\begin{bmatrix} .1 & .1 & .8 \\ .4 & .4 & .2 \\ .1 & .2 & .7 \end{bmatrix}$

12. $\begin{bmatrix} .5 & .2 & .3 \\ .1 & .4 & .5 \\ .2 & .2 & .6 \end{bmatrix}$

13. $\begin{bmatrix} .25 & .35 & .4 \\ .1 & .3 & .6 \\ .55 & .4 & .05 \end{bmatrix}$

14. $\begin{bmatrix} .16 & .28 & .56 \\ .43 & .12 & .45 \\ .86 & .05 & .09 \end{bmatrix}$

Find the equilibrium vector for each transition matrix in Exercises 15–21. These matrices were first used in the Exercises of Section 8.1. (*Note:* Not all of these transition matrices are regular, but equilibrium vectors still exist. Why doesn't this contradict the work of this section?)

15. car sizes, Exercise 25,

$\begin{bmatrix} .8 & .2 \\ .6 & .4 \end{bmatrix}$

16. housing patterns, Exercise 33,

$\begin{bmatrix} .90 & .10 \\ .05 & .95 \end{bmatrix}$

17. insurance categories, Exercise 28,

$\begin{bmatrix} .85 & .10 & .05 \\ 0 & .80 & .20 \\ 0 & 0 & 1 \end{bmatrix}$

18. ''modified'' insurance categories, Exercise 30,

$\begin{bmatrix} .85 & .10 & .05 \\ .15 & .75 & .10 \\ .10 & .30 & .60 \end{bmatrix}$

19. land use, Exercise 32,

$\begin{bmatrix} .80 & .15 & .05 \\ 0 & .90 & .10 \\ .10 & .20 & .70 \end{bmatrix}$

20. voting registration, Exercise 34,

$\begin{bmatrix} .80 & .15 & .05 \\ .20 & .70 & .10 \\ .20 & .20 & .60 \end{bmatrix}$

21. home heating systems, Exercise 31,

$\begin{bmatrix} .825 & .175 & 0 \\ .060 & .919 & .021 \\ .049 & 0 & .951 \end{bmatrix}$

22. The probability that a complex assembly line works correctly depends on whether or not the line worked correctly the last time it was used. There is a .9 chance that the line will work correctly if it worked correctly the time before, and a .7 chance that it will work correctly if it did *not* work correctly the time before. Set up a transition matrix with this information and find the long-run probability that the line will work correctly.

23. Suppose improvements are made in the assembly line of Exercise 22, so that the transition matrix becomes

$$\begin{array}{c} \\ \text{Works} \\ \text{Doesn't} \end{array} \begin{array}{cc} \text{Works} & \text{Doesn't} \\ \begin{bmatrix} .95 & .05 \\ .80 & .20 \end{bmatrix} \end{array}$$

Find the long-run probability now that the line will work properly.

24. A certain genetic defect is carried only by males. Suppose the probability is .95 that a male offspring will have the defect if his father did, with the probability .10 that a male offspring will have the defect if his father did not have it. Find the long-range prediction for the fraction of the males in the population who will have the defect.

25. Each month, a sales manager classifies her salespeople as low, medium, or high producers. There is a .4 chance that a low producer one month will become a medium producer the following month, and a .1 chance that a low producer will become a high producer. A medium producer will become a low or high producer, respectively, with probabilities .25 and .3. A high producer will become a low or medium producer, respectively, with probabilities .05 and .4. Find the long-range trend for the proportion of low, medium, and high producers.

26. The weather in a certain spot is classified as fair, cloudy without rain, or rainy. A fair day is followed by a fair day 60% of the time, and by a cloudy day 25% of the time. A cloudy day is followed by a cloudy day 35% of the time, and by a rainy day 25% of the time. A rainy day is followed by a cloudy day 40% of the time, and by another rainy day 25% of the time. Find the long-range prediction for the proportion of fair, cloudy, and rainy days.

27. At one liberal arts college, students are classified as humanities majors, science majors, or undecideds. There is a 20% chance that a humanities major will change to a science major from one year to the next, and a 45% chance that a humanities major will change to undecided. A science major will change to humanities with probability .15, and to undecided with probability .35. An undecided will switch to humanities or science with probabilities of .5 and .3 respectively. Find the long-range prediction for the fraction of students in each of these three majors.

28. A large group of mice is kept in a cage having connected compartments A, B, and C. Mice in compartment A move to B with probability .3 and to C with probability .4. Mice in B move to A or C with probabilities of .15 and .55, respectively. Mice in C move to A and B with probabilities of .3 and .6 respectively. Find the long-range prediction for the fraction of mice in each of the compartments.

29. The manager of the slot machines at a major casino makes a decision about whether or not to "loosen up" the slots so that the customers get a larger playback. The manager tells only one other person, a person whose word cannot be trusted. In fact, there is only a probability p, where $0 < p < 1$, that this person will tell the truth. Suppose this person tells several other people, each of whom tell several people, what the manager's decision is. Suppose there is always a probability p that the decision is passed on as heard. Find the long-range prediction for the fraction of the people who will hear the decision correctly. (Hint: use a transition matrix; let the first row be $[p \quad 1 - p]$, with second row $[1 - p \quad p]$.)

30. Find the equilibrium vector for the transition matrix

$$\begin{bmatrix} p & 1 - p \\ 1 - q & q \end{bmatrix}$$

where $0 < p < 1$ and $0 < q < 1$. Under what conditions is this matrix regular?

31. Show that the transition matrix

$$K = \begin{bmatrix} \frac{1}{4} & 0 & \frac{3}{4} \\ 0 & 1 & 0 \\ 0 & 0 & 1 \end{bmatrix}$$

has more than one vector V such that $VK = V$. Why does this not violate the statements of this section?

32. Let

$$P = \begin{bmatrix} a_{11} & a_{12} \\ a_{21} & a_{22} \end{bmatrix}$$

be a regular transition matrix having *column* sums of 1. Show that the equilibrium vector for P is $[1/2 \quad 1/2]$.

Find the equilibrium vector for transition matrices 33 and 34 by taking powers of the matrix.

33.
$$\begin{bmatrix} .1 & .2 & .2 & .3 & .2 \\ .2 & .1 & .1 & .2 & .4 \\ .2 & .1 & .4 & .2 & .1 \\ .3 & .1 & .1 & .2 & .3 \\ .1 & .3 & .1 & .1 & .4 \end{bmatrix}$$

34.
$$\begin{bmatrix} .3 & .2 & .3 & .1 & .1 \\ .4 & .2 & .1 & .2 & .1 \\ .1 & .3 & .2 & .2 & .2 \\ .2 & .1 & .3 & .2 & .2 \\ .1 & .1 & .4 & .2 & .2 \end{bmatrix}$$

35. Find the long range prediction for the percent of employees in each state for the company training program from Exercise 37, Section 8.1. The transition matrix is repeated here.

$$\begin{array}{c} \\ s_1 \\ s_2 \\ s_3 \\ s_4 \end{array} \begin{array}{c} s_1 \quad s_2 \quad s_3 \quad s_4 \\ \begin{bmatrix} .4 & .2 & .05 & .35 \\ 0 & .45 & .05 & .5 \\ 0 & 0 & 1.0 & 0 \\ 0 & 0 & 0 & 1.0 \end{bmatrix} \end{array}$$

8.3 Absorbing Markov Chains

Suppose a Markov chain has transition matrix

$$\begin{array}{c} \\ 1 \\ 2 \\ 3 \end{array} \begin{array}{c} 1 \quad 2 \quad 3 \\ \begin{bmatrix} .3 & .6 & .1 \\ 0 & 1 & 0 \\ .6 & .2 & .2 \end{bmatrix} = P. \end{array}$$

The matrix shows that p_{12}, the probability of going from state 1 to state 2, is .6, while p_{22}, the probability of staying in state 2, is 1. Thus, once state 2 is entered, it is impossible to leave. For this reason, state 2 is called an *absorbing state*.

Generalizing from this example,

Absorbing State

State i of a Markov chain is an **absorbing state** if $p_{ii} = 1$.

Using the idea of an absorbing state, we can define an absorbing Markov chain.

Absorbing Markov Chains

A Markov chain is an **absorbing chain** if and only if the following two conditions are satisfied:

1. The chain has at least one absorbing state.

2. It is possible to go from any nonabsorbing state to an absorbing state (perhaps in more than one step).

EXAMPLE 1

Identify all absorbing states in the Markov chains having the following matrices. Decide if the Markov chain is absorbing.

(a)

$$
\begin{array}{c}
 \\
1 \\
2 \\
3
\end{array}
\begin{array}{ccc}
1 & 2 & 3 \\
\end{array}
\left[
\begin{array}{ccc}
1 & 0 & 0 \\
.3 & .5 & .2 \\
0 & 0 & 1
\end{array}
\right]
$$

Since $p_{11} = 1$ and $p_{33} = 1$, both state 1 and state 3 are absorbing states. (Once these states are reached, they cannot be left.) The only nonabsorbing state is state 2. There is a .3 probability of going from state 2 to the absorbing state 1, so that it is possible to go from the nonabsorbing state to an absorbing state. This Markov chain is absorbing.

(b)

$$
\left[
\begin{array}{cccc}
.6 & 0 & .4 & 0 \\
0 & 1 & 0 & 0 \\
.9 & 0 & .1 & 0 \\
0 & 0 & 0 & 1
\end{array}
\right]
$$

States 2 and 4 are absorbing, with states 1 and 3 nonabsorbing. From state 1, it is possible to go only to states 1 or 3; from state 3 it is possible to go only to states 1 or 3. Thus, neither nonabsorbing state leads to an absorbing state, so that this Markov chain is nonabsorbing. ▪

EXAMPLE 2

(*Gambler's Ruin*) Suppose players A and B have a coin tossing game going on—a fair coin is tossed and the player predicting the toss correctly wins $1 from the other player. Suppose the players have a total of $6 between them, and that the game goes on until one player has no money (is ruined).

Let us agree that the states of this system are the amounts of money held by player A. There are seven possible states: A can have 0, 1, 2, 3, 4, 5, or 6 dollars. When either state 0 or state 6 is reached, the game is over. In any other state, the amount of money held by player A will increase by $1, or decrease by $1, with each of these events having probability 1/2 (since we assume a fair coin). For example, in state 3 (A has $3), there is 1/2 chance of changing to state 2, and a 1/2 chance of changing to state 4. Thus, $p_{32} = 1/2$ and $p_{34} = 1/2$. The probability of changing from state 3 to any other state is 0. Using this information gives the following 7×7 transition matrix.

$$
\begin{array}{c}
 \\
0 \\
1 \\
2 \\
3 \\
4 \\
5 \\
6
\end{array}
\begin{array}{ccccccc}
0 & 1 & 2 & 3 & 4 & 5 & 6 \\
\end{array}
\left[
\begin{array}{ccccccc}
1 & 0 & 0 & 0 & 0 & 0 & 0 \\
\frac{1}{2} & 0 & \frac{1}{2} & 0 & 0 & 0 & 0 \\
0 & \frac{1}{2} & 0 & \frac{1}{2} & 0 & 0 & 0 \\
0 & 0 & \frac{1}{2} & 0 & \frac{1}{2} & 0 & 0 \\
0 & 0 & 0 & \frac{1}{2} & 0 & \frac{1}{2} & 0 \\
0 & 0 & 0 & 0 & \frac{1}{2} & 0 & \frac{1}{2} \\
0 & 0 & 0 & 0 & 0 & 0 & 1
\end{array}
\right] = G
$$

Based on our definition, states 0 and 6 are absorbing—once these states are reached, they can never be left, and the game is over. It is possible to get from one of the nonabsorbing states, 1, 2, 3, 4, or 5, to one of the absorbing states, so the Markov chain is absorbing.

For the long-term trend of the game, find various powers of the transition matrix. A computer or a programmable calculator can be used to verify these results.

$$
G^6 = \begin{bmatrix}
1.0000 & .0000 & .0000 & .0000 & .0000 & .0000 & .0000 \\
.6875 & .0781 & .0000 & .1406 & .0000 & .0625 & .0313 \\
.4531 & .0000 & .2188 & .0000 & .2031 & .0000 & .1250 \\
.2188 & .1406 & .0000 & .2813 & .0000 & .1406 & .2188 \\
.1250 & .0000 & .2031 & .0000 & .2188 & .0000 & .4531 \\
.0313 & .0625 & .0000 & .1406 & .0000 & .0781 & .6875 \\
.0000 & .0000 & .0000 & .0000 & .0000 & .0000 & 1.0000
\end{bmatrix}
$$

$$
G^{10} = \begin{bmatrix}
1.0000 & .0000 & .0000 & .0000 & .0000 & .0000 & .0000 \\
.7539 & .0400 & .0000 & .0791 & .0000 & .0391 & .0879 \\
.5479 & .0000 & .1191 & .0000 & .1182 & .0000 & .2148 \\
.3418 & .0791 & .0000 & .1582 & .0000 & .0791 & .3418 \\
.2148 & .0000 & .1182 & .0000 & .1191 & .0000 & .5479 \\
.0879 & .0391 & .0000 & .0791 & .0000 & .0400 & .7539 \\
.0000 & .0000 & .0000 & .0000 & .0000 & 0000 & 1.0000
\end{bmatrix}
$$

As these results suggest, the system tends to one of the absorbing states, so that the probability is 1 that one of the two gamblers will eventually be wiped out. ▧

In fact, the following can be shown.

> Regardless of the original state of an absorbing Markov chain, in a finite number of steps the chain will enter an absorbing state and then stay in that state.

EXAMPLE 3

Estimate the long-term trend for the transition matrix

$$
P = \begin{bmatrix}
.3 & .2 & .5 \\
0 & 1 & 0 \\
0 & 0 & 1
\end{bmatrix}.
$$

Both states 2 and 3 are absorbing, and since it is possible to go from nonabsorbing state 1 to an absorbing state, the chain will eventually enter either state 2 or state 3. To find the long-term trend, let us find various powers of P.

$$
P^2 = \begin{bmatrix}
.09 & .26 & .65 \\
0 & 1 & 0 \\
0 & 0 & 1
\end{bmatrix}
\qquad
P^4 = \begin{bmatrix}
.0081 & .2834 & .7085 \\
0 & 1 & 0 \\
0 & 0 & 1
\end{bmatrix}
$$

$$
P^8 = \begin{bmatrix}
.0001 & .2857 & .7142 \\
0 & 1 & 0 \\
0 & 0 & 1
\end{bmatrix}
\qquad
P^{16} = \begin{bmatrix}
.0000 & .2857 & .7142 \\
0 & 1 & 0 \\
0 & 0 & 1
\end{bmatrix}
$$

Based on these powers, it appears that the transition matrix is approaching closer and closer to the matrix

$$\begin{bmatrix} 0 & .29 & .71 \\ 0 & 1 & 0 \\ 0 & 0 & 1 \end{bmatrix}.$$

If the system is originally in state 1, there is no chance it will end up in state 1, but a .29 chance that it will end up in state 2 and a .71 chance it will end up in state 3. If the system was originally in state 2 it will end up in state 2; a similar statement can be made for state 3. ∎

This example suggests two further properties of absorbing chains.

Properties of

Absorbing Chains

1. The powers of the transition matrix get closer and closer to some particular matrix.
2. The long-term trend depends on the initial state—changing the initial state can change the final result.

This second fact is different from regular Markov chains, where the final result is independent of the initial state.

We would prefer a method for finding the final probabilities of entering an absorbing state without finding all the powers of the transition matrix, as we did in Example 3. We don't really need to worry about the absorbing states (to enter an absorbing state is to stay there). So, it is necessary only to work with the nonabsorbing states. To see how this is done, let us use as an example the transition matrix from the gambler's ruin problem of Example 2. Rewrite the matrix so that the rows and columns corresponding to the absorbing states come first.

$$
\begin{array}{c}
\overset{\textit{absorbing}}{\overbrace{}}\ \overset{\textit{nonabsorbing}}{\overbrace{}} \\
\begin{array}{c}0\\6\\1\\2\\3\\4\\5\end{array}
\begin{bmatrix}
1 & 0 & 0 & 0 & 0 & 0 & 0 \\
0 & 1 & 0 & 0 & 0 & 0 & 0 \\
\frac{1}{2} & 0 & 0 & \frac{1}{2} & 0 & 0 & 0 \\
0 & 0 & \frac{1}{2} & 0 & \frac{1}{2} & 0 & 0 \\
0 & 0 & 0 & \frac{1}{2} & 0 & \frac{1}{2} & 0 \\
0 & 0 & 0 & 0 & \frac{1}{2} & 0 & \frac{1}{2} \\
0 & \frac{1}{2} & 0 & 0 & 0 & \frac{1}{2} & 0
\end{bmatrix} = G
\end{array}
$$

Let I_2 represent the 2×2 identity matrix in the upper left hand corner, let θ (the Greek letter *theta*) represent the matrix of zeros in the upper right, let R represent the matrix in the lower left, and let Q represent the matrix in the lower right. Using these symbols, G can be written as

$$G = \left[\begin{array}{c|c} I_2 & \theta \\ \hline R & Q \end{array}\right].$$

The **fundamental matrix** for an absorbing Markov chain is defined as matrix F, where

$$F = [I_5 - Q]^{-1}.$$

Here I_5 is the 5×5 identity matrix corresponding in size to matrix Q, so that the difference $I_5 - Q$ exists.

For the gambler's ruin problem,

$$F = \left[\begin{bmatrix} 1 & 0 & 0 & 0 & 0 \\ 0 & 1 & 0 & 0 & 0 \\ 0 & 0 & 1 & 0 & 0 \\ 0 & 0 & 0 & 1 & 0 \\ 0 & 0 & 0 & 0 & 1 \end{bmatrix} - \begin{bmatrix} 0 & \frac{1}{2} & 0 & 0 & 0 \\ \frac{1}{2} & 0 & \frac{1}{2} & 0 & 0 \\ 0 & \frac{1}{2} & 0 & \frac{1}{2} & 0 \\ 0 & 0 & \frac{1}{2} & 0 & \frac{1}{2} \\ 0 & 0 & 0 & \frac{1}{2} & 0 \end{bmatrix} \right]^{-1}$$

$$= \begin{bmatrix} 1 & -\frac{1}{2} & 0 & 0 & 0 \\ -\frac{1}{2} & 1 & -\frac{1}{2} & 0 & 0 \\ 0 & -\frac{1}{2} & 1 & -\frac{1}{2} & 0 \\ 0 & 0 & -\frac{1}{2} & 1 & -\frac{1}{2} \\ 0 & 0 & 0 & -\frac{1}{2} & 1 \end{bmatrix}^{-1}$$

$$\begin{array}{c} \\ 1 \\ 2 \\ = 3 \\ 4 \\ 5 \end{array} \begin{array}{ccccc} 1 & 2 & 3 & 4 & 5 \\ \begin{bmatrix} \frac{5}{3} & \frac{4}{3} & 1 & \frac{2}{3} & \frac{1}{3} \\ \frac{4}{3} & \frac{8}{3} & 2 & \frac{4}{3} & \frac{2}{3} \\ 1 & 2 & 3 & 2 & 1 \\ \frac{2}{3} & \frac{4}{3} & 2 & \frac{8}{3} & \frac{4}{3} \\ \frac{1}{3} & \frac{2}{3} & 1 & \frac{4}{3} & \frac{5}{3} \end{bmatrix} \end{array}.$$

The inverse was found using techniques of Chapter 2.

Finally, use the fundamental matrix F along with matrix R found above to get the product FR.

$$FR = \begin{bmatrix} \frac{5}{3} & \frac{4}{3} & 1 & \frac{2}{3} & \frac{1}{3} \\ \frac{4}{3} & \frac{8}{3} & 2 & \frac{4}{3} & \frac{2}{3} \\ 1 & 2 & 3 & 2 & 1 \\ \frac{2}{3} & \frac{4}{3} & 2 & \frac{8}{3} & \frac{4}{3} \\ \frac{1}{3} & \frac{2}{3} & 1 & \frac{4}{3} & \frac{5}{3} \end{bmatrix} \begin{bmatrix} \frac{1}{2} & 0 \\ 0 & 0 \\ 0 & 0 \\ 0 & 0 \\ 0 & \frac{1}{2} \end{bmatrix} = \begin{array}{c} \\ 1 \\ 2 \\ 3 \\ 4 \\ 5 \end{array} \begin{array}{cc} 0 & 6 \\ \begin{bmatrix} \frac{5}{6} & \frac{1}{6} \\ \frac{2}{3} & \frac{1}{3} \\ \frac{1}{2} & \frac{1}{2} \\ \frac{1}{3} & \frac{2}{3} \\ \frac{1}{6} & \frac{5}{6} \end{bmatrix} \end{array}$$

The product matrix FR gives the probability that if the system was originally in a nonabsorbing state, it ended up in either of the two absorbing states. For example, the probability is 2/3 that if the system was originally in state 2, it ended up in state 0; the probability is 5/6 that if the system was originally in state 5 it ended up in state 6, and so on.

Based on our original statement of the gambler's ruin problem, if player A starts with \$2 (state 2), there is a 2/3 chance of ending in state 0 (player A is ruined); if player A starts with \$5 (state 5) there is a 1/6 chance of player A being ruined, and so on.

Let us summarize what we have learned about absorbing Markov chains.

Properties of
Absorbing Markov
Chains

1. Regardless of the initial state, in a finite number of steps the chain will enter an absorbing state and then stay in that state.

2. The powers of the transition matrix get closer and closer to some particular matrix.

3. The long term trend depends on the initial state.

4. Let G be the transition matrix for an absorbing Markov chain. Rearrange the rows and columns of G so that the absorbing states come first. Matrix G will have the form

$$G = \left[\begin{array}{c|c} I_n & \theta \\ \hline R & Q \end{array}\right]$$

where I_n is an identity matrix, and θ is a matrix of all zeros. The fundamental matrix is defined as

$$F = [I_m - Q]^{-1}$$

where I_m has the same order as Q.

5. The product FR gives the matrix of probabilities that a particular initial nonabsorbing state will lead to a particular absorbing state.

EXAMPLE 4

Find the long term trend for the transition matrix

$$\begin{array}{c} \\ 1 \\ 2 \\ 3 \end{array} \begin{array}{ccc} 1 & 2 & 3 \\ \left[\begin{array}{ccc} .3 & .2 & .5 \\ 0 & 1 & 0 \\ 0 & 0 & 1 \end{array}\right] \end{array} = P$$

of Example 3.

Rewrite the matrix so that absorbing states 2 and 3 come first.

$$\begin{array}{c} \\ 2 \\ 3 \\ 1 \end{array} \begin{array}{ccc} 2 & 3 & 1 \\ \left[\begin{array}{cc|c} 1 & 0 & 0 \\ 0 & 1 & 0 \\ \hline .2 & .5 & .3 \end{array}\right] \end{array}$$

Here $R - [.2 \quad .5]$ and $Q - [.3]$. Find the fundamental matrix F.

$$F = [I_1 - Q]^{-1} = [1 - .3]^{-1} = [.7]^{-1} = [1/.7]$$

The product FR is

$$FR = [1/.7][.2 \quad .5] = [2/7 \quad 5/7] \approx [.286 \quad .714].$$

If the system starts in the nonabsorbing state 1, there is a 2/7 chance of ending up in the absorbing state 2, and a 5/7 chance of ending in the absorbing state 3. ∎

8.3 EXERCISES

Find all absorbing states for the transition matrices in Exercises 1–8. Which are transition matrices for an absorbing Markov chain?

1. $\begin{bmatrix} .15 & .05 & .8 \\ 0 & 1 & 0 \\ .4 & .6 & 0 \end{bmatrix}$ **2.** $\begin{bmatrix} .1 & .5 & .4 \\ .2 & .2 & .6 \\ 0 & 0 & 1 \end{bmatrix}$ **3.** $\begin{bmatrix} .4 & 0 & .6 \\ 0 & 1 & 0 \\ .9 & 0 & .1 \end{bmatrix}$ **4.** $\begin{bmatrix} .5 & .5 & 0 \\ .8 & .2 & 0 \\ 0 & 0 & 1 \end{bmatrix}$

5. $\begin{bmatrix} .2 & .5 & .1 & .2 \\ 0 & 1 & 0 & 0 \\ .9 & .02 & .04 & .04 \\ 0 & 0 & 0 & 1 \end{bmatrix}$ **6.** $\begin{bmatrix} 1 & 0 & 0 & 0 \\ .9 & .1 & 0 & 0 \\ 0 & 0 & 1 & 0 \\ .6 & 0 & .4 & 0 \end{bmatrix}$ **7.** $\begin{bmatrix} .1 & .8 & 0 & .1 \\ 0 & 1 & 0 & 0 \\ 1 & 0 & 0 & 0 \\ 0 & 0 & 0 & 1 \end{bmatrix}$ **8.** $\begin{bmatrix} .32 & .41 & .16 & .11 \\ .42 & .30 & 0 & .28 \\ 0 & 0 & 0 & 1 \\ 1 & 0 & 0 & 0 \end{bmatrix}$

Find the fundamental matrix F for the absorbing matrices in Exercises 9–18. Also find the product matrix FR.

9. $\begin{bmatrix} 1 & 0 & 0 \\ 0 & 1 & 0 \\ .2 & .3 & .5 \end{bmatrix}$ **10.** $\begin{bmatrix} 1 & 0 & 0 \\ .6 & .1 & .3 \\ 0 & 0 & 1 \end{bmatrix}$ **11.** $\begin{bmatrix} .8 & .15 & .05 \\ 0 & 1 & 0 \\ 0 & 0 & 1 \end{bmatrix}$ **12.** $\begin{bmatrix} .42 & .37 & .21 \\ 0 & 1 & 0 \\ 0 & 0 & 1 \end{bmatrix}$

13. $\begin{bmatrix} 1 & 0 & 0 \\ 0 & 1 & 0 \\ \frac{1}{3} & \frac{1}{3} & \frac{1}{3} \end{bmatrix}$ **14.** $\begin{bmatrix} 1 & 0 & 0 \\ \frac{3}{8} & \frac{1}{8} & \frac{1}{2} \\ 0 & 0 & 1 \end{bmatrix}$ **15.** $\begin{bmatrix} 1 & 0 & 0 & 0 \\ \frac{1}{3} & 0 & \frac{2}{3} & 0 \\ 0 & 0 & 1 & 0 \\ \frac{1}{4} & \frac{1}{4} & \frac{1}{4} & \frac{1}{4} \end{bmatrix}$ **16.** $\begin{bmatrix} \frac{1}{4} & \frac{1}{2} & 0 & \frac{1}{4} \\ 0 & 1 & 0 & 0 \\ 0 & 0 & 1 & 0 \\ \frac{1}{2} & 0 & 0 & \frac{1}{2} \end{bmatrix}$

17. $\begin{bmatrix} 1 & 0 & 0 & 0 & 0 \\ 0 & 1 & 0 & 0 & 0 \\ .1 & .2 & .3 & .2 & .2 \\ .3 & .5 & .1 & 0 & .1 \\ 0 & 0 & 0 & 0 & 1 \end{bmatrix}$ **18.** $\begin{bmatrix} .4 & .2 & .3 & 0 & .1 \\ 0 & 1 & 0 & 0 & 0 \\ 0 & 0 & 1 & 0 & 0 \\ .1 & .5 & .1 & .1 & .2 \\ 0 & 0 & 0 & 0 & 1 \end{bmatrix}$

19. Write a transition matrix for a gambler's ruin problem when player A and player B start with a total of $4.

    (a) Find matrix F for this transition matrix, and find the product matrix FR.

    (b) Suppose player A starts with $1. What is the probability of ruin for A?

    (c) Suppose player A starts with $3. What is the probability of ruin for A?

20. Suppose player B (Exercise 19) slips in a coin that is slightly "loaded" — such that the probability that B wins a particular toss changes from 1/2 to 3/5. Suppose that A and B start the game with a total of $5.

    (a) If B starts with $3, find the probabiilty that A will be ruined.

    (b) If B starts with $1, find the probability that A will be ruined.

21. At a particular two-year college, a student has a probability of .25 of flunking out during a given year, a .15 probability of having to repeat the year, and a .6 probability of finishing the year. Use the states at the side.

    (a) Write a transition matrix. Find F and FR.

    (b) Find the probability that a freshman will graduate.

State	Meaning
1	freshman
2	sophomore
3	has flunked out
4	has graduated

22. A rat is placed at random in one of the compartments of the maze pictured below. The probability that a rat in compartment 1 will move to compartment 2 is .3; to compartment 3 is .2; and to compartment 4 is .1. A rat in compartment 2 will move to compartments 1, 4, or 5 with probabilities .2, .6, and .1 respectively. A rat in compartment 3 cannot leave that compartment. A rat in compartment 4 will move to 1, 2, 3, or 5 with probabilities of .1, .1, .4, and .3, respectively. A rat in compartment 5 cannot leave that compartment.

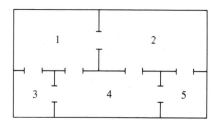

(a) Set up a transition matrix using this information. Find matrices F and FR. Find the probability that a rat ends up in compartment 5 if it was originally in compartment

(b) 1   (c) 2   (d) 3   (e) 4.

It can be shown that the probability of ruin for player A in a game such as the one described in this section is

$$x_a = \frac{b}{a + b} \quad \text{if } r = 1, \quad \text{and} \quad x_a = \frac{r^a - r^{a+b}}{1 - r^{a+b}} \quad \text{if } r \neq 1,$$

where a is the initial amount of money that player A has, b is the initial amount that player B has, $r = (1 - p)/p$, and p is the probability that player A will win on a given play.

23. Find the probability that A will be ruined if $a = 10$, $b = 30$, and $p = .49$.

24. Find the probability in Exercise 23 if p changes to .50.

25. Complete the following chart, assuming $a = 10$ and $b = 10$.

p	.1	.2	.3	.4	.5	.6	.7	.8	.9
x_a									

26. (a) Find F and FR for the transition matrix from Section 8.1 for the company training program

$$\begin{array}{c} \\ s_1 \\ s_2 \\ s_3 \\ s_4 \end{array} \begin{array}{cccc} s_1 & s_2 & s_3 & s_4 \\ \left[\begin{array}{cccc} .4 & .2 & .05 & .35 \\ 0 & .45 & .05 & .5 \\ 0 & 0 & 1 & 0 \\ 0 & 0 & 0 & 1 \end{array}\right]. \end{array}$$

(b) Find the probability that an employee originally in the program is discharged.

(c) Find the probability that an employee who had never been in the program to start, completes the program.

27. Write a transition matrix for a gambler's ruin problem where players A and B start with a total of $10.

(a) Find the probability of ruin for A if A starts with $4.

(b) Find the probability of ruin for A if A starts with $5.

KEY WORDS	state	regular Markov chain
	transition matrix	equilibrium (or fixed) vector
	Markov chain	absorbing state
	probability vector	absorbing chain
	regular transition matrix	fundamental matrix

Chapter 8 REVIEW EXERCISES

Which of the matrices in Exercises 1–4 could be transition matrices?

1. $\begin{bmatrix} .4 & .6 \\ 1 & 0 \end{bmatrix}$
2. $\begin{bmatrix} -.2 & 1.2 \\ .8 & .2 \end{bmatrix}$
3. $\begin{bmatrix} .8 & .2 & 0 \\ 0 & 1 & 0 \\ .1 & .4 & .5 \end{bmatrix}$
4. $\begin{bmatrix} .6 & .2 & .3 \\ .1 & .5 & .4 \\ .3 & .3 & .4 \end{bmatrix}$

For each of the transition matrices in Exercises 5–8, (a) find the first three powers; (b) find the probability that state 2 changes to state 1 after three repetitions of the experiment.

5. $C = \begin{bmatrix} .6 & .4 \\ 1 & 0 \end{bmatrix}$
6. $D = \begin{bmatrix} .3 & .7 \\ .5 & .5 \end{bmatrix}$
7. $E = \begin{bmatrix} .2 & .5 & .3 \\ .1 & .8 & .1 \\ 0 & 1 & 0 \end{bmatrix}$
8. $F = \begin{bmatrix} .14 & .12 & .74 \\ .35 & .28 & .37 \\ .71 & .24 & .05 \end{bmatrix}$

In Exercises 9–12, use the transition matrices T, along with the given initial distribution D, to find the distribution after two repetitions of the experiment. Also predict the long-range distribution.

9. $D = [.3 \quad .7]; \ T = \begin{bmatrix} .4 & .6 \\ .5 & .5 \end{bmatrix}$

10. $D = [.8 \quad .2]; \ T = \begin{bmatrix} .7 & .3 \\ .2 & .8 \end{bmatrix}$

11. $D = [.2 \quad .4 \quad .4]; \ T = \begin{bmatrix} .6 & .2 & .2 \\ .3 & .3 & .4 \\ .5 & .4 & .1 \end{bmatrix}$

12. $D = [.1 \quad .1 \quad .8]; \ T = \begin{bmatrix} .2 & .3 & .5 \\ .1 & .1 & .8 \\ .7 & .1 & .2 \end{bmatrix}$

Currently, 35% of all hot dogs sold in one area are made by Dogkins, while 65% are made by Long Dog. Suppose that Dogkins starts a heavy advertising campaign, with the campaign producing the following transition matrix.

$$
\begin{array}{cc}
 & \begin{array}{cc} \textit{After campaign} \\ \text{Dogkins} \quad \text{Long Dog} \end{array} \\
\begin{array}{c} \textit{Before} \\ \textit{campaign} \end{array} \begin{array}{c} \text{Dogkins} \\ \text{Long Dog} \end{array} & \begin{bmatrix} .8 & .2 \\ .4 & .6 \end{bmatrix}
\end{array}
$$

13. Find the share of the market for each company after

   (a) the campaign   **(b)** three such campaigns.

14. Predict the long-range market share for Dogkins.

A credit card company classifies its customers in three groups, nonusers in a given month, light users, and heavy users. The transition matrix for these states is

$$
\begin{array}{c}
\begin{array}{c} \text{nonuser} \\ \text{light} \\ \text{heavy} \end{array}
\begin{array}{ccc} \text{nonuser} & \text{light} & \text{heavy} \end{array} \\
\begin{array}{c} \text{nonuser} \\ \text{light} \\ \text{heavy} \end{array}
\begin{bmatrix} .8 & .15 & .05 \\ .25 & .55 & .2 \\ .04 & .21 & .75 \end{bmatrix}.
\end{array}
$$

Suppose the initial distribution for the three states is $[.4 \quad .4 \quad .2]$. Find the distribution after

15. 1 month; **16.** 2 months; **17.** 3 months.

18. What is the long-range prediction for the distribution of users?

A medical researcher is studying the risk of heart attack in men. She first divides men into three weight categories, thin, normal, and overweight. By studying the ancestors, children, and grandchildren of these men, the researcher comes up with the transition matrix.

$$
\begin{array}{c}
\text{thin} \\
\text{normal} \\
\text{overweight}
\end{array}
\begin{array}{ccc}
\text{thin} & \text{normal} & \text{overweight} \\
\end{array}
\left[
\begin{array}{ccc}
.3 & .5 & .2 \\
.2 & .6 & .2 \\
.1 & .5 & .4
\end{array}
\right].
$$

Find the probability that a person of normal weight has a thin

19. child **20.** grandchild **21.** great-grandchild.

Find the probability that an overweight man will have an overweight

22. child **23.** grandchild **24.** great-grandchild.

Suppose that the distribution of men by weight is initially given by $[.2 \quad .55 \quad .25]$. Find the distribution after

25. 1 generation **26.** 2 generations **27.** 3 generations

28. Find the long-range prediction for the distribution of weights.

Which of the transition matrices in Exercises 29–31 are regular?

29. $\begin{bmatrix} 0 & 1 \\ .2 & .8 \end{bmatrix}$

30. $\begin{bmatrix} .4 & .2 & .4 \\ 0 & 1 & 0 \\ .6 & .3 & .1 \end{bmatrix}$

31. $\begin{bmatrix} 1 & 0 & 0 \\ 0 & 1 & 0 \\ .3 & .5 & .2 \end{bmatrix}$

Which matrices in Exercises 32–34 are transition matrices for an absorbing Markov chain?

32. $\begin{bmatrix} 1 & 0 & 0 \\ .5 & .1 & .4 \\ 0 & 1 & 0 \end{bmatrix}$

33. $\begin{bmatrix} .2 & 0 & .8 \\ 0 & 1 & 0 \\ .7 & 0 & .3 \end{bmatrix}$

34. $\begin{bmatrix} .5 & .1 & .1 & .3 \\ 0 & 0 & 1 & 0 \\ 1 & 0 & 0 & 0 \\ .1 & .8 & .05 & .05 \end{bmatrix}$

In Exercises 35–38, find the fundamental matrix F for each of the absorbing matrices. Also find the matrix FR.

35. $\begin{bmatrix} .2 & .5 & .3 \\ 0 & 1 & 0 \\ 0 & 0 & 1 \end{bmatrix}$

36. $\begin{bmatrix} 1 & 0 & 0 \\ 0 & 1 & 0 \\ .3 & .1 & .6 \end{bmatrix}$

37. $\begin{bmatrix} \frac{1}{5} & \frac{1}{5} & \frac{2}{5} & \frac{1}{5} \\ 0 & 1 & 0 & 0 \\ \frac{1}{2} & \frac{1}{4} & \frac{1}{8} & \frac{1}{8} \\ 0 & 0 & 0 & 1 \end{bmatrix}$

38. $\begin{bmatrix} .3 & .5 & .1 & .1 \\ .4 & .1 & .3 & .2 \\ 0 & 0 & 1 & 0 \\ 0 & 0 & 0 & 1 \end{bmatrix}$

People in genetics sometimes study the problem of mating offspring from the same two parents; two of these offspring are then mated, and so on. Let A be a dominant gene for some trait, and a the recessive gene. The original offspring can carry genes AA, Aa, or aa. There are six possible ways that these offspring can mate.

State	Mating
1	AA and AA
2	AA and Aa
3	AA and aa
4	Aa and Aa
5	Aa and aa
6	aa and aa

Using these states gives the following transition matrix.

$$
\begin{array}{c}
\quad \\
\begin{matrix} & 1 & 2 & 3 & 4 & 5 & 6 \end{matrix} \\
\begin{matrix} 1 \\ 2 \\ 3 \\ 4 \\ 5 \\ 6 \end{matrix}
\begin{bmatrix}
1 & 0 & 0 & 0 & 0 & 0 \\
\frac{1}{4} & \frac{1}{2} & 0 & \frac{1}{4} & 0 & 0 \\
0 & 0 & 1 & 0 & 0 & 0 \\
\frac{1}{16} & \frac{1}{4} & \frac{1}{8} & \frac{1}{4} & \frac{1}{4} & \frac{1}{16} \\
0 & 0 & 0 & \frac{1}{4} & \frac{1}{2} & \frac{1}{4} \\
0 & 0 & 0 & 0 & 0 & 1
\end{bmatrix}
\end{array}
$$

39. Identify the absorbing states.

40. Find matrix Q.

41. Find F, and the product FR.

42. If the system starts in state 4, find the probability it will end in state 3.

DECISION THEORY

Karl Gerstner. From the series *AlgoRhythm 3*, 1973. Roche AG, Basel.

John F. Kennedy once remarked that he had assumed that as President it would be difficult to choose between distinct, opposite alternatives when a decision needed to be made. Actually, however, he said that he found such decisions easy to make; the hard decisions came when he was faced with choices that were not as clear-cut. Most decisions that we are faced with fall in this last category—decisions that must be made under conditions of uncertainty. *Decision theory* is a mathematical model that provides a systematic way to attack problems of decision making when not all alternatives are clear and unambiguous.

9.1   Decision Making

The idea of expected value, introduced earlier, is used in decision theory. The concepts are explained in the following example.

Freezing temperatures are endangering the orange crop in central California. A farmer can protect his crop by burning smudge pots—the heat from the pots keeps the oranges from freezing. However, burning the pots is expensive; the cost is $2000. The farmer knows that if he burns smudge pots he will be able to sell his crop for a net profit (after smudge pot costs are deducted) of $5000, provided that the freeze does develop and wipes out many of the other orange growers in California. If he does nothing he will either lose $1000 in planting costs if it does freeze, or make a profit of $4800 if it does not freeze. (If it does not freeze, there will be a large supply of oranges, and thus his profit will be lower than if there was a small supply.)

What should the farmer do? He should begin by carefully defining the problem. First he must decide on the **states of nature,** the possible alternatives over which he has no control. Here there are two: freezing temperatures, or no freezing temperatures. Next, the farmer should list the things he can control—his actions or **strategies.** The farmer has two possible strategies: use smudge pots or not use smudge pots. The consequences of each action under each state of nature, called **payoffs,** can be summarized in a **payoff matrix,** as shown below. The payoffs in this case represent the profit for each possible combination of events.

$$
\begin{array}{cc}
 & \begin{array}{cc} \textit{States of nature} \\ \text{Freeze} \quad\quad \text{No freeze} \end{array} \\
\textit{Strategies of farmer} \begin{array}{l} \text{Use smudge pots} \\ \text{Do not use pots} \end{array} & \left[\begin{array}{cc} \$5000 & \$2800 \\ -\$1000 & \$4800 \end{array} \right]
\end{array}
$$

To get the $2800 entry in the payoff matrix, we took the profit if there is no freeze, $4800, and subtracted the $2000 cost of using the smudge pots.

Once the farmer makes the payoff matrix, what then? The farmer might be an optimist (some might call him a gambler); in this case he might assume that the best will happen and go for the biggest number on the matrix ($5000). To get this profit, he must adopt the strategy "use smudge pots."

On the other hand, if the farmer is a pessimist, he would want to minimize the worst thing that could happen. If he uses smudge pots, the worst that could happen to him would be a profit of $2800, which will result if there is no freeze. If he does not use smudge pots, he might face a loss of $1000. To minimize the worst, he once again should adopt the strategy "use smudge pots."

Suppose the farmer decides that he is neither an optimist nor a pessimist, but would like further information before choosing a strategy. For example, he might call the weather forecaster and ask for the probability of a freeze. Further, suppose the forecaster says that this probability is only .1. What should the farmer do? He should recall our earlier discussion of expected value and calculate the expected profit for each of his two possible strategies. If the probability of a freeze is .1, then the probability that there will be no freeze is .9. This information gives the following expected values:

If smudge pots are used: $5000(.1) + 2800(.9) = 3020$

If no smudge pots are used: $-1000(.1) + 4800(.9) = 4220$

Here the maximum expected profit, $4220, is obtained if smudge pots are *not* used. If the probability of a freeze is .6, the expected profit from the strategy "use pots" would be $4120 and from "use no pots," $1320. As the example shows, the farmer's beliefs about the probabilities of a freeze affect his choice of strategy.

EXAMPLE 1

A small Christmas card manufacturer must decide in February about the type of cards she should emphasize in her fall line of cards. She has three possible strategies: emphasize modern cards, emphasize old-fashioned cards, or emphasize a mixture of the two. Her success is dependent on the state of the economy in December. If the economy is strong, she will do well with her modern cards, while in a weak economy people long for the old days and buy old-fashioned cards. In an in-between economy, her mixture of lines would do the best. She first prepares a payoff matrix for all three possibilities. The numbers in the matrix represent her profits in thousands of dollars.

States of nature

		Weak economy	In-between	Strong economy
	Modern	40	85	120
Strategies	Old-fashioned	106	46	83
	Mixture	72	90	68

(a) If the manufacturer is an optimist, she should aim for the biggest number on the matrix, 120 (representing $120,000 in profit). Her strategy in this case would be to produce modern cards.

(b) A pessimistic manufacturer wants to avoid the worst of all bad things that can happen. If she produces modern cards, the worst that can happen is a profit of $40,000. For old-fashioned cards, the worst is a profit of $46,000, while the worst that can happen from a mixture is a profit of $68,000. Her strategy here is to use a mixture.

(c) Suppose the manufacturer reads in a business magazine that leading experts feel there is a 50% chance of a weak economy at Christmas, a 20% chance of an in-between economy, and a 30% chance of a strong economy. The manufacturer can now find her expected profit for each possible strategy.

Modern:	$40(.50) + 85(.20) + 120(.30) = 73$
Old-fashioned:	$106(.50) + 46(.20) + 83(.30) = 87.1$
Mixture:	$72(.50) + 90(.20) + 68(.30) = 74.4$

Here the best strategy is old-fashioned cards; the expected profit is 87.1, or $87,100. ∎

9.1 EXERCISES

1. An investor has $20,000 to invest in stocks. She has two possible strategies: buy conservative blue-chip stocks or buy highly speculative stocks. There are two states of nature: the market goes up or the market goes down. The following payoff matrix shows the net amounts she will have under the various circumstances.

	Market up	Market down
Buy blue-chip	$25,000	$18,000
Buy speculative	$30,000	$11,000

What should the investor do if she is

(a) an optimist;   (b) a pessimist?

(c) Suppose there is a .7 probability of the market going up. What is the best strategy? What is the expected profit?

(d) What is the best strategy if the probability of a market rise is .2?

2. A developer has $100,000 to invest in land. He has a choice of two parcels (at the same price), one on the highway and one on the coast. With both parcels, his ultimate profit depends on whether he faces light opposition from environmental groups or heavy opposition. He estimates that the payoff matrix is as follows (the numbers represent his profit).

		Opposition	
		Light	Heavy
Parcels	Highway	$70,000	$30,000
	Coast	$150,000	− $40,000

What should the developer do if he is

(a) an optimist;   (b) a pessimist?

(c) Suppose the probability of heavy opposition is .8. What is his best strategy? What is the expected profit?

(d) What is the best strategy if the probability of heavy opposition is only .4?

3. Hillsdale College has sold out all tickets for a jazz concert to be held in the stadium. If it rains, the show will have to be moved to the gym, which has a much smaller capacity. The dean must decide in advance whether to set up the seats and the stage in the gym or in the stadium, or both, just in case. The payoff matrix below shows the net profit in each case.

		States of nature	
		Rain	No rain
	Set up in stadium	− $1550	$1500
Strategies	Set up in gym	$1000	$1000
	Set up both	$750	$1400

What strategy should the dean choose if she is

(a) an optimist; (b) a pessimist?

(c) If the weather forecaster predicts rain with a probability of .6, what strategy should she choose to maximize expected profit? What is the maximum expected profit?

4. An analyst must decide what fraction of the items produced by a certain machine are defective. He has already decided that there are three possibilities for the fraction of defective items: .01, .10, and .20. He may recommend two courses of action: repair the machine or make no repairs. The payoff matrix below represents the *costs* to the company in each case.

States of nature

		.01	.10	.20
Strategies	Repair	$130	$130	$130
	No repair	$25	$200	$500

What strategy should the analyst recommend if he is

(a) an optimist; (b) a pessimist?

(c) Suppose the analyst is able to estimate probabilities for the three states of nature as follows.

Fraction of defectives	Probability
.01	.70
.10	.20
.20	.10

Which strategy should he recommend? Find the expected cost to the company if this strategy is chosen.

5. The research department of the Allied Manufacturing Company has developed a new process which it believes will result in an improved product. Management must decide whether or not to go ahead and market the new product. The new product may be better than the old or it may not be better. If the new product is better, and the company decides to market it, sales should increase by $50,000. If it is not better and they replace the old product with the new product on the market, they will lose $25,000 to competitors. If they decide not to market the new product they will lose $40,000 if it is better, and research costs of $10,000 if it is not.

(a) Prepare a payoff matrix.

(b) If management believes the probability that the new product is better to be .4, find the expected profits under each strategy and determine the best action.

6. A businessman is planning to ship a used machine to his plant in Nigeria. He would like to use it there for the next four years. He must decide whether or not to overhaul the machine before sending it. The cost of overhaul is $2600. If the machine fails when in operation in Nigeria, it will cost him $6000 in lost production and repairs. He estimates the probability that it will fail at .3 if he does not overhaul it, and .1 if he does overhaul it. Neglect the possibility that the machine might fail more than once in the four years.

(a) Prepare a payoff matrix.

(b) What should the businessman do to minimize his expected costs?

7. A contractor prepares to bid on a job. If all goes well, his bid should be $30,000, which will cover his costs plus his usual profit margin of $4500. However, if a threatened labor strike actually occurs, his bid should be $40,000 to give him the same

profit. If there is a strike and he bids $30,000, he will lose $5500. If his bid is too high, he may lose the job entirely, while if it is too low, he may lose money.

(a) Prepare a payoff matrix.

(b) If the contractor believes that the probability of a strike is .6, how much should he bid?

8. A community is considering an anti-smoking campaign.* The city council will choose one of three possible strategies: a campaign for everyone over age 10 in the community, a campaign for youths only, or no campaign at all. The two states of nature are a true cause-effect relationship between smoking and cancer and no cause-effect relationship. The costs to the community (including loss of life and productivity) in each case are as shown below.

		States of nature	
		Cause-effect relationship	No cause-effect relationship
	Campaign for all	$100,000	$800,000
Strategies	Campaign for youth	$2,820,000	$20,000
	No campaign	$3,100,100	$0

What action should the city council choose if it is

(a) optimistic;   (b) pessimistic?

(c) If the Director of Public Health estimates that the probability of a true cause-effect relationship is .8, which strategy should the city council choose?

Sometimes the numbers (or payoffs) in a payoff matrix do not represent money (profits or costs, for example), but *utility*. A **utility** is a number which measures the satisfaction (or lack of it) that results from a certain action. The numbers must be assigned by each individual, depending on how he or she feels about a situation. For example, one person might assign a utility of $+20$ for a week's vacation in San Francisco, with -6 being assigned if the vacation were moved to Sacramento. Work Exercises 9 and 10 in the same way as those above.

9. A politician must plan her reelection strategy. She can emphasize jobs or she can emphasize the environment. The voters can be concerned about jobs or about the environment. A payoff matrix showing the utility of each possible outcome is shown below.

		Voters	
		Jobs	Environment
	Jobs	$+25$	-10
Candidate	Environment	-15	$+30$

The political analysts feel that there is a .35 chance that the voters will emphasize jobs. What strategy should the candidate adopt? What is its expected utility?

10. In an accounting class, the instructor permits the students to bring a calculator or a reference book (but not both) to an examination. The examination itself can emphasize either numerical problems or definitions. In trying to decide which aid to take to an examination, a student first decides on the utilities shown in the following payoff matrix.

		Exam emphasizes	
		Numbers	Definitions
	Calculator	$+50$	0
Student chooses	Book	$+10$	$+40$

---

*This problem is based on an article by B. G. Greenberg in the September 1969 issue of the *Journal of the American Statistical Association*.

(a) What strategy should the student choose if the probability that the examination will emphasize numbers is .6? What is the expected utility in this case?

(b) Suppose the probability that the examination emphasizes numbers is .4. What strategy should be chosen by the student?

EXTENDED	Decision Making in Life Insurance
APPLICATION	

When a life insurance company receives an application from an agent requesting insurance on the life of an individual, it knows from experience that the applicant will be in one of three possible states of risk, with proportions as shown.*

States of Risk	Proportions
s_1 = Standard risk	.90
s_2 = Substandard risk (greater risk)	.07
s_3 = Sub-substandard risk (greatest risk)	.03

A particular applicant could be correctly placed if all possible information about the applicant were known. This is not realistic in a practical situation; the company's problem is to obtain the maximum information at the lowest possible cost.

The company can take any of three possible strategies when it receives the application.

Strategies
a_1 = Offer a standard policy
a_2 = Offer a substandard policy (higher rates)
a_3 = Offer a sub-substandard policy (highest rates)

The payoff matrix in Table 1 below shows the payoffs associated with the possible strategies of the company and the states of the applicant. Here M represents the face value of the policy in thousands of dollars (for a $30,000 policy we have $M = 30$). For example, if the applicant is substandard (s_2) and the company offers him or her a standard policy (a_1), the company makes a profit of $13M$ (13 times the face value of the policy in thousands). Strategy a_2 would result in a larger profit of $20M$. However, if the prospective customer is a standard risk (s_1) but the company offers a substandard policy (a_2), the company loses $50 (the cost of preparing a policy) since the customer would reject the policy because it has higher rates than he or she could obtain elsewhere.

---

*This example was supplied by Donald J. vanKeuren, actuary of Metropolitan Life Insurance Company, and Dave Halmstad, senior actuarial assistant. It is based on a paper by Donald Jones.

Table 1

		States of Nature		
		s_1	s_2	s_3
Strategies of company	a_1	$20M$	$13M$	$3M$
	a_2	-50	$20M$	$10M$
	a_3	-50	-50	$20M$

Before deciding on the policy to be offered, the company can perform any of three experiments to help it decide.

$$e_0 = \text{No inspection report (no cost)}$$

$$e_1 = \text{Regular inspection report (cost: \$5)}$$

$$e_2 = \text{Special life report (cost: \$20)}$$

On the basis of this report, the company can classify the applicant as follows.

$$T_1 = \text{Applicant seems to be a standard risk}$$

$$T_2 = \text{Applicant seems to be a substandard risk}$$

$$T_3 = \text{Applicant seems to be a sub-substandard risk}$$

Let $P(s|T)$ represent the probability that an applicant is in state s when the report indicates that he or she is in state T. For example, $P(s_1|T_2)$ represents the probability that an applicant is a standard risk (s_1) when the report indicates that he or she is a substandard risk (T_2). These probabilities, shown in Table 2, are based on Bayes' formula.

Table 2

True State	Regular Report			Special Report		
	$P(s_i|T_1)$	$P(s_i|T_2)$	$P(s_i|T_3)$	$P(s_i|T_1)$	$P(s_i|T_2)$	$P(s_i|T_3)$
s_1	.9695	.8411	.7377	.9984	.2081	.2299
s_2	.0251	.1309	.1148	.0012	.7850	.0268
s_3	.0054	.0280	.1475	.0004	.0069	.7433

Table 2 shows that $P(s_2|T_2)$, the probability that an applicant actually is substandard (s_2) if the regular report indicates substandard (T_2) is only .1309, while $P(s_2|T_2)$, using the special report, is .7850.

We now have probabilities and payoffs that can be used to find expected values for each possible strategy the company might adopt. There are many possibilities here: the company can use one of three experiments, the experiments can indicate one of three states, the company can offer one of three policies, and the applicant can be in one of three states. The figure shows some of these possibilities in a *decision tree*.

In order to find an optimum strategy for the company, consider an example. Suppose the company decides to perform experiment e_2 (special life report) with the report indicating a substandard risk, T_2. Then the expected values E_1, E_2, E_3 for the three possible actions a_1, a_2, a_3, respectively, are as shown below. (Recall: M is a variable, representing the face amount of the policy in thousands.)

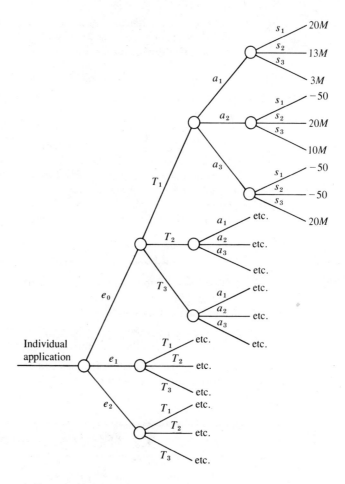

For action a_1 (offer standard policy):

$$E_1 = [P(s_1|T_2)](20M) + [P(s_2|T_2)](13M) + [P(s_3|T_2)](3M)$$
$$= (.2081)(20M) + (.7850)(13M) + (.0069)(3M)$$
$$= 4.162M + 10.205M + .0207M$$
$$\approx 14.388M.$$

For action a_2 (offer a substandard policy):

$$E_2 = [P(s_1|T_2)](-50) + [P(s_2|T_2)](20M) + [P(s_3|T_2)](10M)$$
$$= (.2081)(-50) + (.7850)(20M) + (.0069)(10M)$$
$$= 15.769M - 10.405.$$

For action a_3 (offer a sub-substandard policy):

$$E_3 = [P(s_1|T_2)](-50) + [P(s_2|T_2)](-50) + [P(s_3|T_2)](20M)$$
$$= .138M - 49.655.$$

Strategy a_2 is better than a_3 (for any positive M, $15.769M - 10.405 > .138M - 49.655$). The only choice is between strategies a_1 and a_2. Strategy a_2 is superior if it leads to a higher expected value than a_1. This happens for all values of M such that

$$15.769M - 10.405 > 14.388M$$

$$1.381M > 10.405$$

$$M > 7.535.$$

If the applicant applies for more than $7535 of insurance, the company should use strategy a_2; otherwise it should use a_1.

Similar analyses can be performed for all possible strategies from the decision tree above to find the best strategy. It turns out that the company will maximize its expected profits if it offers a standard policy to all people applying for less than $50,000 in life insurance, with a special report form required for all others.

EXERCISES

1. Find the expected values for each strategy a_1, a_2, and a_3 if the insurance company performs experiment e_1 (a regular report) with the report indicating that the applicant is a substandard risk.

2. Find the expected values for each action if the company performs e_1 with the report indicating that the applicant is a standard risk.

3. Find the expected values for each strategy if e_0 (no report) is selected. (Hint: use the proportions given for the three states s_1, s_2, and s_3 as the probabilities.)

9.2 Strictly Determined Games

The word *game* in the title of this section may have led you to think of checkers or perhaps some card game. While **game theory** does have some application to these recreational games, it was developed in the 1940's to analyze competitive situations in business, warfare, and social situations. Game theory deals with how to make decisions when in competition with an aggressive opponent.

A game can be set up with a payoff matrix, such as the one shown below. This game involves the two players A and B, and is called a **two-person game.** Player A can choose either of the two rows, 1 or 2, while player B can choose either column 1 or column 2. A player's choice is called a **strategy,** just as before. The payoff is at the intersection of the row and column selected. As a general agreement, a positive number represents a payoff from B to A; a negative number represents a payoff from A to B. For example, if A chooses row 2 and B chooses column 2, then B pays $4 to A.

$$
\begin{array}{cc}
 & \text{B} \\
 & \begin{array}{cc} 1 & 2 \end{array} \\
\text{A} \begin{array}{c} 1 \\ 2 \end{array} & \left[\begin{array}{cc} 2 & -1 \\ -3 & 4 \end{array} \right]
\end{array}
$$

EXAMPLE 1

In the payoff matrix shown above, suppose A chooses row 1 and B chooses column 2. Who gets what?

Row 1 and column 2 lead to the number -1. This number represents a payoff of \$1 from A to B.   ▪

While the numbers in the payoff matrix above represent money, they could just as well represent goods or other property.

In the game above, no money enters the game from the outside; whenever one player wins, the other loses. Such a game model is called a **zero-sum game.** The stock market is not a zero-sum game. Stocks can go up or down according to outside forces. Therefore, it is possible that all investors can make or lose money.

Only two-person zero-sum games are discussed in the rest of this chapter. Each player can have many different options. In particular, an $m \times n$ matrix game is one in which player A has m strategies (rows) and player B has n strategies (columns).

Dominant Strategies   In the rest of this section, the best possible strategy for each player is determined. Let us begin with the 3×3 game defined by the following matrix.

$$\begin{array}{c} \\ 1 \\ 2 \\ 3 \end{array} \begin{array}{ccc} 1 & 2 & 3 \\ \left[\begin{array}{ccc} -3 & -6 & 10 \\ 3 & 0 & -9 \\ 5 & -4 & -8 \end{array} \right] \end{array}$$

From B's viewpoint, strategy 2 is better than strategy 1 no matter which strategy A selects. This can be seen by comparing the two columns. If A chooses row 1, receiving \$6 from A is better than receiving \$3; in row 2 breaking even is better than paying \$3, and in row 3, getting \$4 from A is better than paying \$5. Therefore, B should never select strategy 1. Strategy 2 is said to *dominate* strategy 1, and strategy 1 (the dominated strategy) can be removed from consideration, producing the following reduced matrix.

$$\begin{array}{c} \\ 1 \\ 2 \\ 3 \end{array} \begin{array}{cc} 2 & 3 \\ \left[\begin{array}{cc} -6 & 10 \\ 0 & -9 \\ -4 & -8 \end{array} \right] \end{array}$$

Either player may have dominated strategies. In fact, after a dominated strategy for one player is removed, the other player may then have a dominated strategy where there was none before.

Dominant

Strategies

A row for A **dominates** another row if every entry in the first row is *larger* than the corresponding entry in the second row. For a column for B to dominate another, each entry must be *smaller*.

In the 3 × 2 matrix above, neither player now has a dominated strategy. From A's viewpoint strategy 1 is best if B chooses strategy 3, while strategy 2 is best if B chooses strategy 1. Verify that there are no dominated strategies for either player.

EXAMPLE 2

Find any dominated strategies in the games having the following payoff matrices.

(a)

$$\begin{array}{cccc} 1 & 2 & 3 & 4 \end{array}$$

$$\begin{array}{c} 1 \\ 2 \end{array} \begin{bmatrix} -8 & -4 & -6 & -9 \\ -3 & 0 & -9 & 12 \end{bmatrix}$$

Here every entry in column 3 is smaller than the corresponding entry in column 2. Thus, column 3 dominates column 2. By removing the dominated column 2, the final game is as follows.

$$\begin{array}{ccc} 1 & 3 & 4 \end{array}$$

$$\begin{array}{c} 1 \\ 2 \end{array} \begin{bmatrix} -8 & -6 & -9 \\ -3 & -9 & 12 \end{bmatrix}$$

(b)

$$\begin{array}{cc} 1 & 2 \end{array}$$

$$\begin{array}{c} 1 \\ 2 \\ 3 \end{array} \begin{bmatrix} 3 & -2 \\ 0 & 8 \\ 6 & 4 \end{bmatrix}$$

Each entry in row 3 is greater than the corresponding entry in row 1, so that row 3 dominates row 1. Removing row 1 gives the following game.

$$\begin{array}{cc} 1 & 2 \end{array}$$

$$\begin{array}{c} 2 \\ 3 \end{array} \begin{bmatrix} 0 & 8 \\ 6 & 4 \end{bmatrix}$$

Strictly Determined Games Which strategies should the players choose in the following game?

$$\begin{array}{c} & & B \\ & 1 & 2 & 3 \\ A \begin{array}{c} 1 \\ 2 \\ 3 \end{array} & \begin{bmatrix} -9 & 11 & -4 \\ 2 & 3 & 5 \\ -1 & -9 & 6 \end{bmatrix} \end{array}$$

The goal of game theory is to find **optimum strategies,** those which are the most profitable to the respective players. The payoff which results from each player's choosing the optimum strategy is called the **value** of the game.

The simplest strategy for a player is to consistently choose a certain row (or column). Such a strategy is called a **pure strategy,** in contrast to strategies requiring the random choice of a row (or column); these alternate strategies are discussed in the next section.*

To choose a pure strategy in the game above, player A could choose row 1, in hopes of getting the payoff of $11. However, B would quickly discover this, and start playing column 1. By playing column 1, B would receive $9 from A. If

---

*In this section we solve (find the optimum strategies for) only games which have optimum *pure* strategies.

A chooses row 2 consistently, then B would again minimize outgo by choosing column 1 (a payoff of $2 by B to A is better than paying $3 or $5, respectively, to A). By choosing row 3 consistently, A would cause B to choose column 2. The table shows what B will do when A chooses a given row consistently.

A Chooses Pure Strategy	Then B Would Choose	With Payoff
row 1	column 1	$9 to B
row 2	column 1	$2 to A
row 3	column 2	$9 to B

Based on these results, A's optimum strategy is to choose row 2; in this way A will guarantee a minimum payoff of $2 per play of the game, no matter what B does.

The optimum pure strategy in this game for A (the *row* player), is found by identifying the *smallest* number in each row of the payoff matrix; the row giving the *largest* such number gives the optimum strategy.

By going through a similar analysis for player B, we find that B should choose that column which will minimize the amount that A can win. In the game above, B will pay $2 to A if B consistently chooses column 1. By choosing column 2 consistently, B will pay $11 to A, and by choosing column 3 player B will pay $6 to A. The optimum strategy for B is thus to choose column 1—with each play of the game B will pay $2 to A.

The optimum pure strategy in this game for B (the column player) is to identify the *largest* number in each column of the payoff matrix, and then choose the column producing the *smallest* such number.

In the game above, the entry 2 is both the *smallest* entry in its *row* and the *largest* entry in its *column*. Such an entry is called a **saddle point.** (See Figure 1.) As Example 3(c) shows, there may be more than one such entry, but then the entries will have the same value.

Optimum Pure	In a game with a saddle point, the optimum pure strategy for player A is to choose the row containing the saddle point, while the optimum pure strategy for B is to choose the column containing the saddle point.
Strategy	

A game with a saddle point is called a **strictly determined game.** By using these optimum strategies, A and B will ensure that the same amount always changes hands with each play of the game; this amount, given by the saddle point, is the value of the game. The value of the game above is $2. A game having a value of 0 is a **fair game;** the game above is not fair.

The name *saddle point* comes from a saddle. The seat of the saddle is the maximum from one direction and the minimum from another direction.

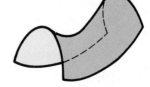

FIGURE 1

EXAMPLE 3

Find the saddle points in the following games.

(a)

$$\begin{array}{c} & \begin{array}{cc} 1 & 2 \end{array} \\ \begin{array}{c} 1 \\ 2 \\ 3 \\ 4 \end{array} & \left[\begin{array}{cc} 2 & 2 \\ 0 & 4 \\ 1 & 6 \\ 3 & 7 \end{array} \right] \end{array}$$

The number that is both the smallest number in its row and the largest number in its column is 3. Thus, 3 is the saddle point, and the game has value 3. The strategies producing the saddle point can be written (4, 1). (A's strategy is written first.)

(b)

$$\begin{array}{c} & \begin{array}{cc} 1 & 2 \end{array} \\ \begin{array}{c} 1 \\ 2 \end{array} & \left[\begin{array}{cc} 6 & 5 \\ 2 & 3 \end{array} \right] \end{array}$$

The saddle point is 5, at strategies (1, 2).

(c)

$$\begin{array}{c} & \begin{array}{cccc} 1 & 2 & 3 & 4 \end{array} \\ \begin{array}{c} 1 \\ 2 \end{array} & \left[\begin{array}{cccc} 4 & 6 & 4 & 12 \\ -8 & -9 & 3 & 2 \end{array} \right] \end{array}$$

The saddle point, 4, occurs with either of two strategies, (1, 1), or (1, 3). The value of the game is 4. (None of the games in parts (a), (b), or (c) of this example are fair games: none had a value of 0.)

(d)

$$\begin{array}{c} & \begin{array}{ccc} 1 & 2 & 3 \end{array} \\ \begin{array}{c} 1 \\ 2 \end{array} & \left[\begin{array}{ccc} 3 & 6 & -2 \\ 8 & -3 & 5 \end{array} \right] \end{array}$$

There is no number which is both the smallest number in its row and the largest number in its column, so that the game has no saddle point. Since the game has no saddle point, it is not strictly determined. In the next section we look at methods for finding optimum strategies for such games. ▨

9.2 EXERCISES

In the following game, decide on the payoff when the strategies of Exercises 1–6 are used.

$$\begin{array}{c} & & \begin{array}{c} \text{B} \end{array} \\ & & \begin{array}{ccc} 1 & 2 & 3 \end{array} \\ \begin{array}{cc} & 1 \\ \text{A} & 2 \\ & 3 \end{array} & \left[\begin{array}{ccc} 6 & -4 & 0 \\ 3 & -2 & 6 \\ -1 & 5 & 11 \end{array} \right] \end{array}$$

1. (1, 1)   **2.** (1, 2)   **3.** (2, 2)   **4.** (2, 3)   **5.** (3, 1)   **6.** (3, 2)

7. Does the game have any dominated strategies?

8. Does it have a saddle point?

Remove any dominated strategies in the games in Exercises 9–14. (From now on, we will save space by deleting the names of the strategies.)

9. $\begin{bmatrix} 0 & -2 & 8 \\ 3 & -1 & -9 \end{bmatrix}$

10. $\begin{bmatrix} 6 & 5 \\ 3 & 8 \\ -1 & -4 \end{bmatrix}$

11. $\begin{bmatrix} 1 & 4 \\ 4 & -1 \\ 3 & 5 \\ -4 & 0 \end{bmatrix}$

12. $\begin{bmatrix} 2 & 3 & 1 & -5 \\ -1 & 5 & 4 & 1 \\ 1 & 0 & 2 & -3 \end{bmatrix}$

13. $\begin{bmatrix} 8 & 12 & -7 \\ -2 & 1 & 4 \end{bmatrix}$

14. $\begin{bmatrix} 6 & 2 \\ -1 & 10 \\ 3 & 5 \end{bmatrix}$

When it exists, find the saddle point and the value of the game in Exercises 15–24. Identify any games that are strictly determined.

15. $\begin{bmatrix} 3 & 5 \\ 2 & -5 \end{bmatrix}$

16. $\begin{bmatrix} 7 & 8 \\ -2 & 15 \end{bmatrix}$

17. $\begin{bmatrix} 3 & -4 & 1 \\ 5 & 3 & -2 \end{bmatrix}$

18. $\begin{bmatrix} -4 & 2 & -3 & -7 \\ 4 & 3 & 5 & -9 \end{bmatrix}$

19. $\begin{bmatrix} -6 & 2 \\ -1 & -10 \\ 3 & 5 \end{bmatrix}$

20. $\begin{bmatrix} 1 & 4 & -3 & 1 & -1 \\ 2 & 5 & 0 & 4 & 10 \\ 1 & -3 & 2 & 5 & 2 \end{bmatrix}$

21. $\begin{bmatrix} 2 & 3 & 1 \\ -1 & 4 & -7 \\ 5 & 2 & 0 \\ 8 & -4 & -1 \end{bmatrix}$

22. $\begin{bmatrix} 3 & 8 & -4 & -9 \\ -1 & -2 & -3 & 0 \\ -2 & 6 & -4 & 5 \end{bmatrix}$

23. $\begin{bmatrix} -6 & 1 & 4 & 2 \\ 9 & 3 & -8 & -7 \end{bmatrix}$

24. $\begin{bmatrix} 6 & -1 \\ 0 & 3 \\ 4 & 0 \end{bmatrix}$

25. When a football team has the ball and is planning its next play, it can choose one of several plays or strategies. The success of the chosen play depends largely on how well the other team "reads" the chosen play. Suppose a team with the ball (team *A*) can choose from three plays, while the opposition (team *B*) has four possible strategies. The numbers shown in the following payoff matrix represent yards of gain to team *A*.

$$\begin{bmatrix} 9 & -3 & -4 & 16 \\ 12 & 9 & 6 & 8 \\ -5 & -2 & 3 & 18 \end{bmatrix}$$

Find the saddle point. Find the value of the game.

26. Two armies, *A* and *B*, are involved in a war game. Each army has available three different strategies, with payoffs as shown below. These payoffs represent square kilometers of land with positive numbers representing gains by *A*.

$$\begin{bmatrix} 3 & -8 & -9 \\ 0 & 6 & -12 \\ -8 & 4 & -10 \end{bmatrix}$$

Find the saddle point and the value of the game.

27. Write a payoff matrix for the child's game *stone, scissors, paper*. Each of two children writes down one of these three words, *stone, scissors,* or *paper*. If the words are the same, the game is a tie. Otherwise, *stone* beats *scissors* (since stone can break scissors), *scissors* beats *paper* (since scissors can cut paper), and *paper* beats *stone* (since paper can hide stone). The winner receives $1 from the loser; no money changes hands in case of a tie. Is the game strictly determined?

28. John and Joann play a finger matching game—each shows one or two fingers at the same time. If the sum of the number of fingers showing is even, Joann pays John that number of dollars; for an odd sum, John pays Joann. Find the payoff matrix for this game. Is the game strictly determined?

29. Two merchants are planning competing stores to serve an area of three small cities. The fraction of the total population that live in each city is shown in the figure. If both merchants locate in the same city, merchant A will get 65% of the total business. If the merchants locate in different cities, each will get 80% of the business in the city it is in, and A will get 60% of the business from the city not containing B. Payoffs are measured by the number of percentage points above or below 50%. Write a payoff matrix for this game. Is this game strictly determined?

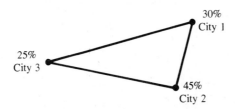

30. Suppose the payoff matrix for a game has at least three rows. Also, suppose that row 1 dominates row 2, and row 2 dominates row 3. Show that row 1 must dominate row 3.

9.3 Mixed Strategies

As we saw earlier, not every game has a saddle point. However, two-person zero-sum games still have optimum strategies, even if the strategy is not as simple as the ones we saw earlier. In a game with a saddle point, the optimum strategy for player A is to pick the row containing the saddle point. Such a strategy is called a *pure strategy,* since the same row is always chosen.

If there is no saddle point, then it will be necessary for both players to mix their strategies. For example, A will sometimes play row 1, sometimes row 2, and so on. If this were done in some specific pattern, the competitor would soon guess it and play accordingly.

For this reason, it is best to mix strategies according to previously determined probabilities. For example, if a player has only two strategies and has decided to play them with equal probability, the random choice could be made by tossing a fair coin, letting heads represent one strategy and tails the other. This would result in each strategy being used about equally over the long run. However, on a particular play it would not be possible to predetermine the strategy to be used. Some other device, such as a spinner, is necessary for more than two strategies, or when the probabilities are not 1/2.

EXAMPLE 1

Suppose a game has payoff matrix

$$\begin{bmatrix} -1 & 2 \\ 1 & 0 \end{bmatrix},$$

where the entries represent dollar winnings. Suppose player A chooses row 1 with probability 1/3 and row 2 with probability 2/3, and player B chooses each column with probability 1/2. Find the expected value of the game.

Assume that rows and columns are chosen independently, so that

$$P(\text{row 1, column 1}) = P(\text{row 1}) \cdot P(\text{column 1}) = \frac{1}{3} \cdot \frac{1}{2} = \frac{1}{6}$$

$$P(\text{row 1, column 2}) = P(\text{row 1}) \cdot P(\text{column 2}) = \frac{1}{3} \cdot \frac{1}{2} = \frac{1}{6}$$

$$P(\text{row 2, column 1}) = P(\text{row 2}) \cdot P(\text{column 1}) = \frac{2}{3} \cdot \frac{1}{2} = \frac{1}{3}$$

$$P(\text{row 2, column 2}) = P(\text{row 2}) \cdot P(\text{column 2}) = \frac{2}{3} \cdot \frac{1}{2} = \frac{1}{3}.$$

The table below lists the probability of each possible outcome, along with the payoff to player A.

Outcome	Probability of Outcome	Payoff for A
row 1, column 1	1/6	−1
row 1, column 2	1/6	2
row 2, column 1	1/3	1
row 2, column 2	1/3	0

The expected value of the game is given by the sum of the products of the probabilities and the payoffs, or

$$\text{expected value} = \frac{1}{6}(-1) + \frac{1}{6}(2) + \frac{1}{3}(1) + \frac{1}{3}(0) = \frac{1}{2}.$$

In the long run, for a great many plays of the game, the payoff to A will average 1/2 dollar per play of the game. It is important to note that as the mixed strategies used by A and B are changed, the expected value of the game may well change. (See Example 2 below.) ■

Let us generalize the work of Example 1. Let the payoff matrix for a 2 × 2 game be

$$M = \begin{bmatrix} a_{11} & a_{12} \\ a_{21} & a_{22} \end{bmatrix}.$$

Let player A choose row 1 with probability p_1 and row 2 with probability p_2, where $p_1 + p_2 = 1$. Write these probabilities as the row matrix

$$A = [p_1 \quad p_2].$$

Let player B choose column 1 with probability q_1 and column 2 with probability q_2, where $q_1 + q_2 = 1$. Write this as the column matrix

$$B = \begin{bmatrix} q_1 \\ q_2 \end{bmatrix}.$$

The probability of choosing row 1 and column 1 is

$$P(\text{row 1, column 1}) = P(\text{row 1}) \cdot P(\text{column 1}) = p_1 \cdot q_1.$$

In the same way, the probabilities of each possible outcome are shown in the table below, along with the payoff matrix for each outcome.

Outcome	Probability of Outcome	Payoff for A
row 1, column 1	$p_1 \cdot q_1$	a_{11}
row 1, column 2	$p_1 \cdot q_2$	a_{12}
row 2, column 1	$p_2 \cdot q_1$	a_{21}
row 2, column 2	$p_2 \cdot q_2$	a_{22}

The expected value for this game is

$$(p_1 \cdot q_1) \cdot a_{11} + (p_1 \cdot q_2) \cdot a_{12} + (p_2 \cdot q_1) \cdot a_{21} + (p_2 \cdot q_2) \cdot a_{22}.$$

This same result can be written as the matrix product

$$\text{expected value} = [p_1 \quad p_2] \begin{bmatrix} a_{11} & a_{12} \\ a_{21} & a_{22} \end{bmatrix} \begin{bmatrix} q_1 \\ q_2 \end{bmatrix} = AMB.$$

The same method works for games larger than 2×2: let the payoff matrix for a game have dimension $m \times n$; call this matrix $M = [a_{ij}]$. Let the mixed strategy for player A be given by the row matrix

$$A = [p_1 \quad p_2 \quad p_3 \cdots p_m],$$

and the mixed strategy for player B be given by the column matrix

$$B = \begin{bmatrix} q_1 \\ q_2 \\ \cdot \\ \cdot \\ \cdot \\ q_n \end{bmatrix}.$$

The expected value for this game is the product

$$AMB = [p_1 \quad p_2 \cdots p_m] \begin{bmatrix} a_{11} & a_{12} & \cdots & a_{1n} \\ a_{21} & a_{22} & \cdots & a_{2n} \\ \vdots & & & \vdots \\ a_{m1} & a_{m2} & \cdots & a_{mn} \end{bmatrix} \begin{bmatrix} q_1 \\ q_2 \\ \vdots \\ q_n \end{bmatrix}.$$

EXAMPLE 2

In the game of Example 1, having payoff matrix

$$M = \begin{bmatrix} -1 & 2 \\ 1 & 0 \end{bmatrix},$$

suppose player A chooses row 1 with probability .2, and player B chooses column 1 with the probability .6. Find the expected value of the game.

If A chooses row 1 with probability .2, then row 2 is chosen with probability $1 - .2 = .8$, giving

$$A = [.2 \quad .8].$$

In the same way,

$$B = \begin{bmatrix} .6 \\ .4 \end{bmatrix}.$$

The expected value of this game is given by the product *AMB*, or

$$AMB = [.2 \quad .8] \begin{bmatrix} -1 & 2 \\ 1 & 0 \end{bmatrix} \begin{bmatrix} .6 \\ .4 \end{bmatrix}$$

$$= [.6 \quad .4] \begin{bmatrix} .6 \\ .4 \end{bmatrix}$$

$$= [.52].$$

On the average, these two strategies will produce a payoff of $.52, or 52¢, for A for each play of the game. This is a little better payoff than the 50¢ found in Example 1. ■

It turns out, however, that B could cause this payoff to decline by a change of strategy. (Check this by choosing different matrices for B.) For this reason, player A needs to develop an *optimum strategy*—a strategy that will produce the best possible payoff no matter what B does. Just as in the previous section, this is done by finding the largest of the smallest possible amounts that can be won.

To find values of p_1 and p_2 so that the probability vector $[p_1 \quad p_2]$ produces an optimum strategy, start with the payoff matrix

$$M = \begin{bmatrix} -1 & 2 \\ 1 & 0 \end{bmatrix}$$

and assume that A chooses row 1 with probability p_1. If player B chooses column 1, then player A's expectation is given by E_1, where

$$E_1 = -1 \cdot p_1 + 1 \cdot p_2 = -p_1 + p_2.$$

Since $p_1 + p_2 = 1$, we have $p_2 = 1 - p_1$, and

$$E_1 = -p_1 + 1 - p_1$$
$$E_1 = 1 - 2p_1.$$

If B chooses column 2, then A's expected value is given by E_2, where

$$E_2 = 2 \cdot p_1 + 0 \cdot p_2$$
$$E_2 = 2p_1.$$

Draw graphs of $E_1 = 1 - 2p_1$ and $E_2 = 2p_1$; see Figure 2.

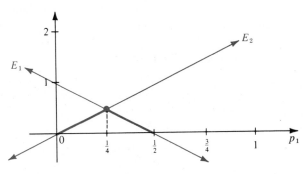

FIGURE 2

As we said, A needs to maximize the smallest amounts that can be won. On the graph, the smallest amounts that can be won are represented by the points of E_2 up to the intersection point. To the right of the intersection point, the smallest amounts that can be won are represented by the points of the line E_1. Player A can maximize the smallest amounts that can be won by choosing the point of intersection itself, the peak of the heavily shaded line in Figure 2.

To find this point of intersection, find the simultaneous solution of the two equations. At the point of intersection, $E_1 = E_2$. Substitute $1 - 2p_1$ for E_1 and $2p_1$ for E_2.

$$E_1 = E_2$$
$$1 - 2p_1 = 2p_1$$
$$1 = 4p_1$$
$$\frac{1}{4} = p_1$$

By this result, player A should choose strategy 1 with probability 1/4, and strategy 2 with probability $1 - 1/4 = 3/4$. By doing so, expected winnings will be maximized. To find the maximum winnings (which is also the value of the game), substitute 1/4 for p_1 in either E_1 or E_2. If we choose E_2,

$$E_2 = 2p_1 = 2\left(\frac{1}{4}\right) = \frac{1}{2},$$

that is, 1/2 dollar, or 50¢. By going through a similar argument for player B, we can find that the optimum strategy for player B is to choose each column with probability 1/2; in this case the value also turns out to be 50¢. In Example 2, A's winnings were 52¢; however, that was because B was not using his optimum strategy.

In the game above, player A can maximize expected winnings by playing row 1 with probability 1/4 and row 2 with probability 3/4. Such a strategy is called a **mixed strategy.** To actually decide which row to use on a given game, player A could use a spinner, such as the one in Figure 3.

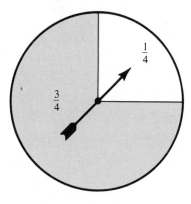

FIGURE 3

EXAMPLE 3

Boll weevils threaten the cotton crop near Hattiesburg. Charles Dawkins owns a small farm; he can protect his crop by spraying with a potent (and expensive) insecticide. In trying to decide what to do, Dawkins first sets up a payoff matrix. The numbers in the matrix represent his profits.

States of nature

		Boll weevil attack	No attack
Strategies	Spray	$14,000	$7000
	Don't spray	−$3000	$8000

Let p_1 represent the probability with which Dawkins chooses strategy 1, so that $1 - p_1$ is the probability with which he chooses strategy 2. If nature chooses strategy 1 (an attack), then Dawkins' expected value is

$$E_1 = 14{,}000p_1 - 3000(1 - p_1)$$
$$= 14{,}000p_1 - 3000 + 3000p_1$$
$$E_1 = 17{,}000p_1 - 3000.$$

For nature's strategy 2 (no attack), Dawkins has an expected value of

$$E_2 = 7000p_1 + 8000(1 - p_1)$$
$$= 7000p_1 + 8000 - 8000p_1$$
$$E_2 = 8000 - 1000p_1.$$

As suggested by the work above, to maximize his expected profit, Dawkins should find the value of p_1 for which $E_1 = E_2$.

$$E_1 = E_2$$
$$17{,}000p_1 - 3000 = 8000 - 1000p_1$$
$$18{,}000p_1 = 11{,}000$$
$$p_1 = 11/18$$

Thus, $p_2 = 1 - p_1 = 1 - 11/18 = 7/18$.

Dawkins will maximize his expected profit if he chooses strategy 1 with probability 11/18 and strategy 2 with probability 7/18. His expected profit from this mixed strategy, $[11/18 \quad 7/18]$, can be found by substituting 11/18 for p_1 in either E_1 or E_2. If we choose E_1,

$$\text{expected profit} = 17{,}000\left(\frac{11}{18}\right) - 3000 = \frac{133{,}000}{18} \approx \$7400. \quad \blacksquare$$

To obtain a formula for the optimum strategy in a game that is not strictly determined, start with the matrix

$$M = \begin{bmatrix} a_{11} & a_{12} \\ a_{21} & a_{22} \end{bmatrix},$$

the payoff matrix of the game. Assume that A chooses row 1 with probability p_1. The expected value for A, assuming that B plays column 1, is E_1, where

$$E_1 = a_{11} \cdot p_1 + a_{21} \cdot (1 - p_1).$$

The expected value for A if B chooses column 2 is E_2, where

$$E_2 = a_{12} \cdot p_1 + a_{22} \cdot (1 - p_1).$$

As above, the optimum strategy for player A is found by letting $E_1 = E_2$.

$$a_{11} \cdot p_1 + a_{21} \cdot (1 - p_1) = a_{12} \cdot p_1 + a_{22} \cdot (1 - p_1)$$

Solve this equation for p_1.

$$a_{11} \cdot p_1 + a_{21} - a_{21} \cdot p_1 = a_{12} \cdot p_1 + a_{22} - a_{22} \cdot p_1$$
$$a_{11} \cdot p_1 - a_{21} \cdot p_1 - a_{12} \cdot p_1 + a_{22} \cdot p_1 = a_{22} - a_{21}$$
$$p_1(a_{11} - a_{21} - a_{12} + a_{22}) = a_{22} - a_{21}$$
$$p_1 = \frac{a_{22} - a_{21}}{a_{11} - a_{21} - a_{12} + a_{22}}$$

Since $p_2 = 1 - p_1$,

$$p_2 = 1 - \frac{a_{22} - a_{21}}{a_{11} - a_{21} - a_{12} + a_{22}}$$
$$= \frac{a_{11} - a_{21} - a_{12} + a_{22} - (a_{22} - a_{21})}{a_{11} - a_{21} - a_{12} + a_{22}}$$
$$= \frac{a_{11} - a_{12}}{a_{11} - a_{21} - a_{12} + a_{22}}.$$

This result is valid only if $a_{11} - a_{21} - a_{12} + a_{22} \neq 0$; it turns out that this condition is satisfied if the game is not strictly determined.

There is a similar result for player B, which is included in the following summary.

Optimum Strategies

in a Non-Strictly

Determined Game

Let a non-strictly determined game have payoff matrix

$$\begin{bmatrix} a_{11} & a_{12} \\ a_{21} & a_{22} \end{bmatrix}.$$

The optimum strategy for player A is $[p_1 \quad p_2]$, where

$$p_1 = \frac{a_{22} - a_{21}}{a_{11} - a_{21} - a_{12} + a_{22}} \quad \text{and} \quad p_2 = \frac{a_{11} - a_{12}}{a_{11} - a_{21} - a_{12} + a_{22}}.$$

The optimum strategy for player B is $\begin{bmatrix} q_1 \\ q_2 \end{bmatrix}$, where

$$q_1 = \frac{a_{22} - a_{12}}{a_{11} - a_{21} - a_{12} + a_{22}} \quad \text{and} \quad q_2 = \frac{a_{11} - a_{21}}{a_{11} - a_{21} - a_{12} + a_{22}}.$$

The value of the game is

$$\frac{a_{11} a_{22} - a_{12} a_{21}}{a_{11} - a_{21} - a_{12} + a_{22}}.$$

EXAMPLE 4

Suppose a game has payoff matrix

$$\begin{bmatrix} 5 & -2 \\ -3 & -1 \end{bmatrix}.$$

Here $a_{11} = 5$, $a_{12} = -2$, $a_{21} = -3$, and $a_{22} = -1$. To find the optimum strategy for player A, first find p_1.

$$p_1 = \frac{-1 - (-3)}{5 - (-3) - (-2) + (-1)} = \frac{2}{9}$$

Player A should play row 1 with probability 2/9 and row 2 with probability $1 - 2/9 = 7/9$.

For player B,

$$q_1 = \frac{-1 - (-2)}{5 - (-3) - (-2) + (-1)} = \frac{1}{9}.$$

Player B should choose column 1 with probability 1/9, and column 2 with probability 8/9. The value of the game is

$$\frac{5(-1) - (-2)(-3)}{5 - (-3) - (-2) + (-1)} = \frac{-11}{9}.$$

On the average, B will receive 11/9 dollar from A per play of the game. ▪

9.3 EXERCISES

1. Suppose a game has payoff matrix

$$\begin{bmatrix} 3 & -4 \\ -5 & 2 \end{bmatrix}.$$

Suppose that player B uses the strategy $\begin{bmatrix} .3 \\ .7 \end{bmatrix}$. Find the expected value of the game if player A uses the strategy

(a) $[.5 \quad .5]$;   (b) $[.1 \quad .9]$;   (c) $[.8 \quad .2]$;   (d) $[.2 \quad .8]$.

2. Suppose a game has payoff matrix

$$\begin{bmatrix} 0 & -4 & 1 \\ 3 & 2 & -4 \\ 1 & -1 & 0 \end{bmatrix}.$$

Find the expected value of the game for the following strategies for players A and B.

(a) $A = [.1 \quad .4 \quad .5]$; $B = \begin{bmatrix} .2 \\ .4 \\ .4 \end{bmatrix}$ (b) $A = [.3 \quad .4 \quad .3]$; $B = \begin{bmatrix} .8 \\ .1 \\ .1 \end{bmatrix}$

Find the optimum strategy for both player A and player B in the games in Exercises 3–14. Find the value of the game. Be sure to look for a saddle point first.

3. $\begin{bmatrix} 5 & 1 \\ 3 & 4 \end{bmatrix}$ 4. $\begin{bmatrix} -4 & 5 \\ 3 & -4 \end{bmatrix}$ 5. $\begin{bmatrix} -2 & 0 \\ 3 & -4 \end{bmatrix}$ 6. $\begin{bmatrix} 6 & 2 \\ -1 & 10 \end{bmatrix}$

7. $\begin{bmatrix} 4 & -3 \\ -1 & 7 \end{bmatrix}$ 8. $\begin{bmatrix} 0 & 6 \\ 4 & 0 \end{bmatrix}$ 9. $\begin{bmatrix} -2 & \frac{1}{2} \\ 0 & -3 \end{bmatrix}$ 10. $\begin{bmatrix} 6 & \frac{3}{4} \\ \frac{2}{3} & -1 \end{bmatrix}$

11. $\begin{bmatrix} \frac{8}{3} & -\frac{1}{2} \\ \frac{3}{4} & -\frac{5}{12} \end{bmatrix}$ 12. $\begin{bmatrix} -\frac{1}{2} & \frac{2}{3} \\ \frac{7}{8} & -\frac{3}{4} \end{bmatrix}$ 13. $\begin{bmatrix} -1 & 2 \\ 3 & 1 \end{bmatrix}$ 14. $\begin{bmatrix} 8 & 18 \\ -4 & 2 \end{bmatrix}$

Remove any dominated strategies and then find the optimum strategies for each player and the value of the game.

15. $\begin{bmatrix} -4 & 9 \\ 3 & -5 \\ 8 & 7 \end{bmatrix}$ 16. $\begin{bmatrix} 3 & 4 & -1 \\ -2 & 1 & 0 \end{bmatrix}$ 17. $\begin{bmatrix} 8 & 6 & 3 \\ -1 & -2 & 4 \end{bmatrix}$

18. $\begin{bmatrix} -1 & 6 \\ 8 & 3 \\ -2 & 5 \end{bmatrix}$ 19. $\begin{bmatrix} 9 & -1 & 6 \\ 13 & 11 & 8 \\ 6 & 0 & 9 \end{bmatrix}$ 20. $\begin{bmatrix} 4 & 8 & -3 \\ 2 & -1 & 1 \\ 7 & 9 & 0 \end{bmatrix}$

21. Suppose Allied Manufacturing Company decides to put its new product on the market with a big television and radio advertising campaign. At the same time, the company finds out that its major competitor, Bates Manufacturing, has also decided to launch a big advertising campaign for a similar product. The payoff matrix below shows the increased sales (in millions) for Allied, as well as the decreased sales for Bates.

Bates

TV   Radio

Allied TV   Radio $\begin{bmatrix} 1.0 & -.7 \\ -.5 & .5 \end{bmatrix}$

Find the optimum strategy for Allied Manufacturing and the value of the game.

22. The payoffs in the table below represent the differences between Boeing Aircraft Company's profit and its competitor's profit for two prices (in millions) on commercial jet transports, with positive payoffs being in Boeing's favor. What should Boeing's price strategy be?*

$$\begin{array}{cc} & \begin{array}{c} \textit{Competitor's} \\ \textit{price strategy} \\ 4.75 \quad 4.9 \end{array} \\ \textit{Boeing's strategy} \begin{array}{c} 4.9 \\ 4.75 \end{array} & \begin{bmatrix} -4 & 2 \\ 2 & 0 \end{bmatrix} \end{array}$$

23. The number of cases of African flu has reached epidemic levels. The disease is known to have two strains with similar symptoms. Doctor De Luca has two medicines available: the first is 60% effective against the first strain and 40% effective against the second. The second medicine is completely effective against the second strain but ineffective against the first. Use the matrix below to decide which medicine she should use and the results she can expect.

$$\begin{array}{cc} & \begin{array}{c} \textit{Strain} \\ 1 \quad 2 \end{array} \\ \textit{Medicine} \begin{array}{c} 1 \\ 2 \end{array} & \begin{bmatrix} .6 & .4 \\ 0 & 1 \end{bmatrix} \end{array}$$

24. Players A and B play a game in which each show either one or two fingers at the same time. If there is a match, A wins the amount equal to the total number of fingers shown. If there is no match, B wins the amount of dollars equal to the number of fingers shown.

(a) Write the payoff matrix.

(b) Find optimum strategies for A and B and the value of the game.

25. Repeat Exercise 24 if each player may show either 0 or 2 fingers with the same sort of payoffs.

26. In the game of matching coins, two players each flip a coin. If both coins match (both show heads or both show tails), player A wins $1. If there is no match, player B wins $1, as in the payoff matrix. Find the optimum strategies for the two players and the value of the game.

$$\begin{bmatrix} 1 & -1 \\ -1 & 1 \end{bmatrix}$$

27. The Huckster† Merrill has a concession at Yankee Stadium for the sale of sunglasses and umbrellas. The business places quite a strain on him, the weather being what it is. He has observed that he can sell about 500 umbrellas when it rains, and about 100 when it is sunny; in the latter case he can also sell 1000 sunglasses. Umbrellas cost him 50 cents and sell for $1; glasses cost 20 cents and sell for 50 cents. He is willing to invest $250 in the project. Everything that is not sold is considered a total loss.

He assembles the facts regarding profit in a table.

$$\begin{array}{cc} & \begin{array}{c} \textit{Selling during} \\ \text{Rain} \quad \text{Shine} \end{array} \\ \textit{Buying for} \begin{array}{c} \text{Rain} \\ \text{Shine} \end{array} & \begin{bmatrix} 250 & -150 \\ -150 & 350 \end{bmatrix} \end{array}$$

---

*From ''Pricing, Investment, and Games of Strategy,'' by Georges Brigham in *Management Sciences Models and Techniques,* Vol. 1. Copyright © 1960 Pergamon Press, Ltd. Reprinted with permission.

†From *The Compleat Strategyst* by J. D. Williams, Published 1966, by McGraw-Hill Book Company. Reprinted by permission of The Rand Corporation. This is an excellent nontechnical book on game theory.

He immediately takes heart, for this is a mixed-strategy game, and he should be able to find a stabilizing strategy which will save him from the vagaries of the weather. Find the best mixed strategy for Merrill.

28. **The Squad Car*** This is a somewhat more harrowing example. A police dispatcher was conveying information and opinion, as fast as she could speak, to Patrol Car 2, cruising on the U.S. Highway: ". . . in a Cadillac; just left Hitch's Tavern on the old Country Road. Direction of flight unknown. Suspect Plesset is seriously wounded but may have an even chance if he finds a good doctor, like Doctor Haydon, soon—even Veterinary Paxson might save him, but his chances would be halved. Plesset shot Officer Flood, who has a large family."

Deputy Henderson finally untangled the microphone from the riot gun and his size 14 shoes. He replied: "Roger. We can cut him off if he heads for Haydon's and we have a fifty-fifty chance of cutting him off at the State Highway if he heads for the vet's. We must cut him off because we can't chase him—Deputy Root got this thing stuck in reverse a while ago, and our cruising has been a disgrace to the department ever since."

The headquarter's carrier-wave again hummed in the speaker, but the dispatcher's musical voice was now replaced by the grating tones of Sheriff Lipp. "If you know anything else, don't tell it. He has a hi-fi radio in that Cad. Get him."

Root suddenly was seized by an idea and stopped struggling with the gearshift. "Henderson, we may not need a gun tonight, but we need a pencil: this is just a two-by-two game. The dispatcher gave us all the dope we need." "You gonna use *her* estimates?" "You got better ones? She's got intuition; besides, that's information from headquarters. Now let's see . . . . Suppose we head for Haydon's. And suppose Plesset does too; then we rack up one good bandit, if you don't trip on that gun again. But if he heads for Paxson, the chances are three out of four that old doc will kill him."

"I don't get it." "Well, it didn't come easy. Remember, Haydon would have an even chance—one-half—of saving him. He'd have half as good a chance with Paxson; and half of one-half is one-quarter. So the chance he dies must be three-quarters—subtracting from one, you know."

"Yeah, it's obvious." "Huh. Now if we head for Paxson's it's tougher to figure. First of all, *he* may go to Haydon's, in which case we have to rely on the doc to kill him, of which the chance is only one-half."

"You ought to subtract that from one." "I did. Now suppose he too heads for Paxson's. Either of two things can happen. One is, we catch him, and the chance is one-half. The other is, we don't catch him—and again the chance is one-half—but there is a three-fourths chance that the doc will have a lethal touch. So the overall probability that he will get by us, but not by the doc, is one-half times three-fourths, or three-eighths. Add to that the one-half chance that he doesn't get by us, and we have seven-eighths."

"I don't like this stuff. He's probably getting away while we're doodling." "Relax. He has to figure it out too, doesn't he? And he's in worse shape than we are. Now let's see what we have."

$$\begin{array}{cc} & \textit{Cad goes to} \\ & \begin{array}{cc} \text{Haydon} & \text{Paxson} \end{array} \\ \textit{Patrol car goes to} \begin{array}{c} \text{Haydon} \\ \text{Paxson} \end{array} & \left[\begin{array}{cc} 1 & \frac{3}{4} \\ \frac{1}{2} & \frac{7}{8} \end{array}\right] \end{array}$$

"Fractions aren't so good in this light," Root continues. "Let's multiply everything by eight to clean it up. I hear it doesn't hurt anything."

$$
\begin{array}{cc}
 & \begin{array}{c} \textit{Cad} \\ \text{Haydon} \quad \text{Paxson} \end{array} \\
\textit{Patrol car} \begin{array}{c} \text{Haydon} \\ \text{Paxson} \end{array} & \left[\begin{array}{cc} 8 & 6 \\ 4 & 7 \end{array} \right]
\end{array}
$$

"It is now clear that this is a very messy business . . ." "I know." "There is no single strategy which we can safely adopt. I shall therefore compute the best mixed strategy."

What mixed strategy should deputies Root and Henderson pursue?

EXTENDED

APPLICATION

Decision Making in the Military

This example has been reproduced with only minor change from the *Journal of the Operations Research Society of America,* November 1954, pages 365–369.* The article is titled "Military Decision and Game Theory," by O. G. Haywood, Jr. This case is presented unedited so that you can get an idea of the type of articles published in the journals.

A military commander may approach decision with either of two philosophies. He may select his course of action on the basis of his estimate of what his enemy *is able to do* to oppose him. Or, he may make his selection on the basis of his estimate of what his enemy *is going to do.* The former is a doctrine of decision based on enemy capabilities; the latter, on enemy intentions.

The doctrine of decision of the armed forces of the United States is a doctrine based on enemy capabilities. A commander is enjoined to select the course of action which offers the greatest promise of success in view of the enemy capabilities. The process of decision, as approved by the Joint Chiefs of Staff and taught in all service schools, is formalized in a five-step analysis called the *Estimate of the Situation.* These steps are illustrated in the following analysis of an actual World War II battle situation.

General Kenney was Commander of the Allied Air Forces in the Southwest Pacific Area. The struggle for New Guinea reached a critical stage in February 1943. Intelligence reports indicated a Japanese troop and supply convoy was assembling at Rabaul (see Figure 1). Lae was expected to be the unloading point. With this general background Kenney proceeded to make his five-step Estimate of the Situation.

Step 1.   The Mission

General MacArthur as Supreme Commander had ordered Kenney to intercept and inflict maximum destruction on the convoy. This then was Kenney's mission.

Step 2.   Situation and Courses of Action

The situation as outlined above was generally known. One new critical factor was pointed out by Kenney's staff. Rain and poor visibility were predicted for the area north of New Britain. Visibility south of the island would be good.

*Reprinted by permission from *Operations Research,* Volume 3, Issue 6, 1954. Copyright 1954 Operations Research Society of America. No further reproduction permitted without the consent of the copyright owner.

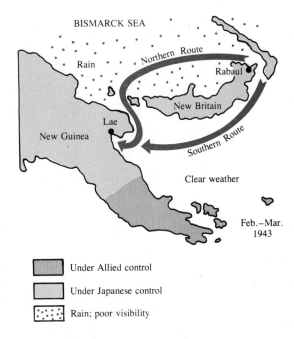

Figure 1 *The Rabaul-Lae Convoy Situation.* The problem is the distribution of reconnaissance to locate a convoy which may sail by either one of two routes.

BISMARCK SEA

Rain

Northern Route

Rabaul

New Britain

Lae

New Guinea

Southern Route

Clear weather

Feb.–Mar. 1943

Under Allied control

Under Japanese control

Rain; poor visibility

The Japanese commander had two choices for routing his convoy from Rabaul to Lae. He could sail north of New Britain, or he could go south of that island. Either route required three days.

Kenney considered two courses of action, as he discusses in his memoirs. He could concentrate most of his reconnaissance aircraft either along the northern route where visibility would be poor, or along the southern route where clear weather was predicted. Mobility being one of the great advantages of air power, his bombing force could strike the convoy on either route once it was spotted.

Step 3. Analysis of the Opposing Courses of Action

With each commander having two alternative courses of action, four possible conflicts could ensue. These conflicts are pictured in Figure 2.

Step 4. Comparison of Available Courses of Action

If Kenney concentrated on the northern route, he ensured one of the two battles of the top row of sketches. However, he alone could not determine which one of these two battles in the top row would result from his decision. Similarly, if Kenney concentrated on the southern route, he ensured one of the battles of the lower row. In the same manner, the Japanese commander could not select a particular battle, but could by his decision assure that the battle would be one of those pictured in the left column or one of those in the right column.

Kenney sought a battle which would provide the maximum opportunity for bombing the convoy. The Japanese commander desired the minimum exposure to bombing. But neither commander could determine the battle which would result from his own decision. Each commander had full and independent freedom to select either one of his alternative strategies. He had to do so with full realization of his opponent's freedom

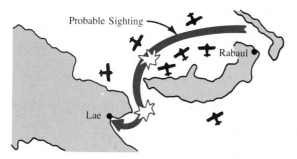

Kenney Strategy: Concentrate reconnaissance on northern route.
Japanese Strategy: Sail northern route.
Estimated Outcome: Although reconnaissance would be hampered by poor visibility, the convoy should be discovered by the second day, which would permit two days of bombing.
TWO DAYS OF BOMBING

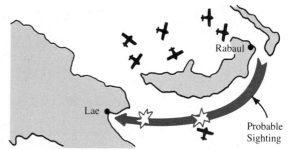

Kenney Strategy: Concentrate reconnaissance on northern route.
Japanese Strategy: Sail southern route.
Estimated Outcome: The convoy would be sailing in clear weather. However, with limited reconnaissance aircraft in this area, the convoy might be missed on the first day. Convoy should be sighted by second day, to permit two days of bombing.
TWO DAYS OF BOMBING

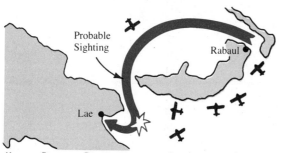

Kenney Strategy: Concentrate reconnaissance on southern route.
Japanese Strategy: Sail northern route.
Estimated Outcome: With poor visibility and limited reconnaissance, Kenney could not expect the convoy to be discovered until it broke out into clear weather on third day. This would permit only one day of bombing.
ONE DAY OF BOMBING

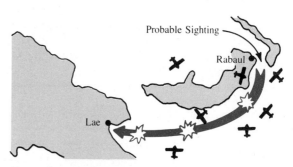

Kenney Strategy: Concentrate reconnaissance on southern route.
Japanese Strategy: Sail southern route.
Estimated Outcome: With good visibility and concentrated reconnaissance in the area, the convoy should be sighted almost as soon as it sailed from Rabaul. This would allow three days of bombing.
THREE DAYS OF BOMBING

Figure 2 *Possible Battles for the Rabaul-Lae Convoy Situation.* Four different engagements of forces may result from the interaction of Kenney's two strategies with the two Japanese from the interaction of Kenney's two strategies with the two Japanese strategies. Neither commander alone can determine which particular battle will result.

of choice. The particular battle which resulted would be determined by the two independent decisions.

The U.S. doctrine of decision—the doctrine that a commander base his action on his estimate of what the enemy is capable of doing to oppose him—dictated that Kenney select the course of action which offered the greatest promise of success in view of all of the enemy capabilities. If Kenney concentrated his reconnaissance on the northern route, he could expect two days of bombing regardless of his enemy's decision. If Kenney selected his other strategy, he must accept the possibility of a less favorable outcome.

Step 5.   The Decision

Kenney concentrated his reconnaissance aircraft on the northern route.

Discussion

Let us assume that the Japanese commander used a similar philosophy of decision, basing his decision on his enemy's capabilities. Considering the four battles as sketched, the Japanese commander could select either the left or the right column, but could not select the row. If he sailed the northern route, he exposed the convoy to a maximum of two days of bombing. If he sailed the southern route, the convoy might be subjected to three days of bombing. Since he sought minimum exposure to bombing, he should select the northern route.

These two independent choices were the actual decisions which led to the conflict known in history as the Battle of the Bismarck Sea. Kenney concentrated his reconnaissance on the northern route; the Japanese convoy sailed the northern route; the convoy was sighted approximately one day after it sailed; and Allied bombing started shortly thereafter. Although the Battle of the Bismarck Sea ended in a disastrous defeat for the Japanese, we cannot say the Japanese commander erred in his decision. A similar convoy had reached Lae with minor losses two months earlier. The need was critical, and the Japanese were prepared to pay a high price. They did not know that Kenney had modified a number of his aircraft for low-level bombing and had perfected a deadly technique. The U.S. victory was the result of careful planning, thorough training, resolute execution, and tactical surprise of a new weapon—not of error in the Japanese decision.

EXERCISES

1. Use the results of Figure 2 to make a 2 × 2 game. Let the payoffs represent the number of days of bombing.

2. Find any saddle point and optimum strategy for the game.

3. Read the rest of the article used as the source for this example and prepare a discussion of the game theory aspects of the Avranches-Gap situation.

KEY WORDS

states of nature	dominated strategy
strategies	optimum strategy
payoff matrix	value of the game
utility	pure strategy
decision tree	strictly determined game
two-person game	saddle point
zero-sum game	mixed strategy

Chapter 9   REVIEW EXERCISES

In labor-management relations, both labor and management can adopt either a friendly or a hostile attitude. The results are shown in the following payoff matrix. The numbers give the wage gains made by an average worker.

$$
\begin{array}{c}
 & \textit{Management} \\
 & \begin{array}{cc} \text{Friendly} & \text{Hostile} \end{array} \\
\textit{Labor} \begin{array}{c} \text{Friendly} \\ \text{Hostile} \end{array} &
\left[\begin{array}{cc} \$600 & \$800 \\ \$400 & \$950 \end{array} \right]
\end{array}
$$

1. Suppose the chief negotiator for labor is an optimist. What strategy should he choose?

2. What strategy should he choose if he is a pessimist?

3. The chief negotiator for labor feels that there is a 70% chance that the company will be hostile. What strategy should he adopt? What is the expected payoff?

4. Just before negotiations begin, a new management is installed in the company. There is only a 40% chance that the new management will be hostile. What strategy should be adopted by labor?

A candidate for city council can come out in favor of a new factory, be opposed to it, or waffle on the issue. The change in votes for the candidate depends on what her opponent does, with payoffs as shown.

$$
\begin{array}{c}
 & & \textit{Opponent} & \\
 & \text{favors} & \text{waffles} & \text{opposes} \\
\textit{Candidate} \begin{array}{r} \text{favors} \\ \text{waffles} \\ \text{opposes} \end{array} &
\left[\begin{array}{ccc}
0 & -1000 & -4000 \\
1000 & 0 & -500 \\
5000 & 2000 & 0
\end{array} \right]
\end{array}
$$

5. What should the candidate do if she is an optimist?

6. What should she do if she is a pessimist?

7. Suppose the candidate's campaign manager feels there is a 40% chance that the opponent will favor the plant, and a 35% chance that he will waffle. What strategy should the candidate adopt? What is the expected change in the number of votes?

8. The opponent conducts a new poll which shows strong opposition to the new factory. This changes the probability he will favor the factory to 0 and the probability he will waffle to .7. What strategy should our candidate adopt? What is the expected change in the number of votes now?

Use the following payoff matrix and decide on the payoff if the given strategies are used.

$$
\left[\begin{array}{cccc}
-2 & 5 & -6 & 3 \\
0 & -1 & 7 & 5 \\
2 & 6 & -4 & 4
\end{array} \right]
$$

9. (1, 1)   **10.** (1, 4)   **11.** (2, 3)   **12.** (3, 4)

13. Are there any dominated strategies in this game?

14. Is there a saddle point?

Remove any dominated strategies in the games in Exercises 15–18.

15. $\left[\begin{array}{cccc} -11 & 6 & 8 & 9 \\ -10 & -12 & 3 & 2 \end{array} \right]$ **16.** $\left[\begin{array}{ccc} -1 & 9 & 0 \\ 4 & -10 & 6 \\ 8 & -6 & 7 \end{array} \right]$ **17.** $\left[\begin{array}{ccc} -2 & 4 & 1 \\ 3 & 2 & 7 \\ -8 & 1 & 6 \\ 0 & 3 & 9 \end{array} \right]$ **18.** $\left[\begin{array}{ccc} 3 & -1 & 4 \\ 0 & 4 & -1 \\ 1 & 2 & -3 \\ 0 & 0 & 2 \end{array} \right]$

Find any saddle points for the games in Exercises 19–24. Give the value of the game. Identify any fair games.

19. $\left[\begin{array}{cc} -2 & 3 \\ -4 & 5 \end{array} \right]$ **20.** $\left[\begin{array}{cccc} -4 & 0 & 2 & -5 \\ 6 & 9 & 3 & 8 \end{array} \right]$ **21.** $\left[\begin{array}{cc} -4 & -1 \\ 6 & 0 \\ 8 & -3 \end{array} \right]$

22. $\left[\begin{array}{ccc} 4 & -1 & 6 \\ -3 & -2 & 0 \\ -1 & -4 & 3 \end{array} \right]$ **23.** $\left[\begin{array}{cccc} 8 & 1 & -7 & 2 \\ -1 & 4 & -3 & 3 \end{array} \right]$ **24.** $\left[\begin{array}{cc} 2 & -9 \\ 7 & 1 \\ 4 & 2 \end{array} \right]$

Find the optimum strategies for each of the games in Exercises 25–28. Find the value of the game.

25. $\begin{bmatrix} 1 & 0 \\ -2 & 3 \end{bmatrix}$ 　　　**26.** $\begin{bmatrix} 2 & -3 \\ -3 & 5 \end{bmatrix}$ 　　　**27.** $\begin{bmatrix} -3 & 5 \\ 1 & 0 \end{bmatrix}$ 　　　**28.** $\begin{bmatrix} 8 & -3 \\ -6 & 2 \end{bmatrix}$

For each of the following games, remove any dominated strategies, then solve the game. Find the value of the game.

29. $\begin{bmatrix} -4 & 8 & 0 \\ -2 & 9 & -3 \end{bmatrix}$ 　　**30.** $\begin{bmatrix} 1 & 0 & 3 & -3 \\ 4 & -2 & 4 & -1 \end{bmatrix}$ 　　**31.** $\begin{bmatrix} 2 & -1 \\ -4 & 5 \\ -1 & -2 \end{bmatrix}$ 　　**32.** $\begin{bmatrix} 8 & -6 \\ 4 & -8 \\ -9 & 9 \end{bmatrix}$

MATHEMATICS OF FINANCE

Karl Gerstner. From the series *Carro 64*, Twenty-one part cycle (Du Clair à l'Obscur à travers le Viol), 1960.

Not too many years ago, money could be borrowed by the largest and most secure corporations for 3% (and home mortgages could be had for 4 1/2%). Today, however, even the largest corporations must pay at least 10% or 12% for their money, and over 20% at times. Thus it is important that both the corporation management and consumers (who pay 21% or more to retailers such as Sears or Wards) have a good understanding of the cost of borrowing money. The cost of borrowing money is called **interest.** The formulas for interest are developed in this chapter.

10.1   Simple Interest and Discount

Interest on loans of a year or less is usually calculated as **simple interest;** simple interest is interest that is charged only on the amount borrowed and not on past interest. The amount borrowed is the **principal,** P. The **rate** of interest, r, is given as a percent per year, and t is the **time,** measured in years. Simple interest, I, is the product of the principal, rate, and time. (To use the formula for simple interest, write the rate r in decimal form.)

Simple Interest

The *simple interest, I*, for t years on an amount of P dollars at a rate of interest r is given by
$$I = Prt.$$

A deposit of P dollars today at a rate of interest r for t years produces interest of $I = Prt$. This interest, added to the original principal P, gives
$$P + Prt = P(1 + rt).$$

This result, called the **future value** of P dollars at an interest rate r for t years, is summarized as follows. (When loans are involved, the future value is often called the *maturity value* of the loan.)

Future or Maturity Value

The *future value* or *maturity value, A*, of P dollars for t years at a rate of interest r is
$$A = P(1 + rt).$$

Find the maturity value for each of the following loans.

EXAMPLE 1

(a)   a loan of $2500, made on June 5; to be repaid in 8 months with interest of 14%

The loan is for 8 months, or $8/12 = 2/3$ of a year. The maturity value is

$$A = P(1 + rt)$$

$$A = 2500\left[1 + .14\left(\frac{2}{3}\right)\right]$$

$$\approx 2500[1 + .09333] \approx 2733.33,$$

or $2733.33. (Here we rounded to the nearest cent, as is customary in financial problems.) Of this maturity value,

$$\$2733.33 - \$2500 = \$233.33$$

represents interest.

(b)   a loan of $11,280 for 85 days at 11% interest

It is common to assume 360 days in a year when working with simple interest. We shall usually make such an assumption in this book. The maturity value in this example is

$$A = 11,280\left[1 + .11\left(\frac{85}{360}\right)\right] \approx 11,280[1.0259722] \approx 11,572.97,$$

or $11,572.97.   ▪

In part (b) of Example 1 we assumed 360 days in a year. Interest found using 360 days is called *ordinary interest,* while interest found using 365 days is *exact interest.*

Present Value   A sum of money that can be deposited today to yield some larger amount in the future is called the **present value** of that future amount. Let P be the present value of some amount A at some time t (in years) in the future. Assume a rate of interest r. As above, the future value of this sum is

$$A = P(1 + rt).$$

Since P is the present value, divide both sides of this last result by $1 + rt$ to get

$$P = \frac{A}{1 + rt}.$$

A summary of present value follows.

Present Value

> The *present value P* of a future amount of A dollars at a rate of interest r for t years is
>
> $$P = \frac{A}{1 + rt}.$$

EXAMPLE 2

Find the present value of the following future amounts.

(a) $10,000 in one year, if interest is 13%

Here $A = 10,000$, $t = 1$, and $r = .13$. Use the formula in the box.

$$P = \frac{10,000}{1 + (.13)(1)} = \frac{10,000}{1.13} \approx 8849.56$$

If $8849.56 were deposited today, at 13% interest, a total of $10,000 would be in the account in one year. These two sums, $8849.56 today, and $10,000 in a year, are equivalent (at 13%); one becomes the other in a year.

(b) $32,000 in four months at 9% interest

$$P = \frac{32,000}{1 + (.09)\left(\frac{4}{12}\right)} = \frac{32,000}{1.03} = 31,067.96 \quad \blacksquare$$

EXAMPLE 3

Because of a court settlement. Charlie Dawkins owes $5000 to Arnold Parker. The money must be paid in ten months, with no interest. Suppose Dawkins wishes to pay the money today. What amount should Parker be willing to accept? Assume an interest rate of 11%.

The amount that Parker should be willing to accept is given by the present value:

$$P = \frac{5000}{1 + (.11)\left(\frac{10}{12}\right)} = \frac{5000}{1.09167} = 4580.14.$$

Parker should be willing to accept $4580.14 in settlement. $\blacksquare$

Simple Discount   It is not an uncommon practice to have interest deducted from the amount of a loan before giving the balance to the borrower. The money that is deducted is called the **discount,** with the money actually received by the borrower called the **proceeds.**

EXAMPLE 4

Exam!

Elizabeth Thornton agrees to pay $8500 to her banker in nine months. The banker subtracts a discount of 15% and gives the balance to Thornton. Find the amount of the discount and the proceeds.

The discount is found in the same way that simple interest is found.

$$\text{discount} = 8500(.15)\left(\frac{9}{12}\right) = 956.25$$

The proceeds are found by subtracting the discount from the original amount.

$$\text{proceeds} = \$8500 - \$956.25 = \$7543.75 \quad \blacksquare$$

In Example 4, the borrower was charged a discount of 15%. However, 15% is *not* the interest rate paid, since 15% applies to the $8500, while the borrower actually received only $7543.75. To find the rate of interest actually paid by the borrower, work as in the next example.

EXAMPLE 5

Find the actual rate of interest paid by Thornton in Example 4.

The rate of 15% stated in Example 4 is not the actual rate of interest since it applies to the total amount of $8500 and not to the amount actually borrowed, or $7543.75. To find the rate of interest paid by Thornton, use the formula for simple interest, $I = Prt$, with r the unknown. Since the borrower received only $7543.75, $I = 956.25$, $P = 7543.75$, and $t = 9/12$. Substitute these values into $I = Prt$.

$$I = Prt$$

$$956.25 = 7543.75(r)\left(\frac{9}{12}\right)$$

$$\frac{956.25}{7543.75\left(\frac{9}{12}\right)} = r$$

$$.169 \approx r$$

The interest rate paid by the borrower is about 16.9%. (This rate actually paid is called the **effective rate.**) ▪

Let D represent the amount of discount on a loan. Then $D = Art$, where A is the maturity value of the loan (the amount borrowed plus interest), and r is the stated rate of interest. The amount actually received, the proceeds, can be written as $P = A - D$, or $P = A - Art$, from which $P = A(1 - rt)$.

Let us summarize the formulas for discount interest.

Discount Interest

If D is the discount on a loan having a maturity value A at a rate of interest r for t years, and if P represents the proceeds, then

$$P = A - D, \quad \text{or} \quad P = A(1 - rt).$$

One common use of discount interest is in *discounting a note,* a process by which a promissory note due at some time in the future can be converted to cash now.

EXAMPLE 6

Jim Levy owes $4250 to Jenny Toms. The loan is payable in one year, at 12% interest. Toms needs cash to buy a new car, so three months before the loan is payable she goes to her bank to have the loan discounted. The bank charges a 16% discount fee. Find the amount of cash she will receive from the bank.

First find the maturity value of the loan, the amount Levy must pay to Toms. By the formula for maturity value,

$$A = P(1 + rt)$$

$$A = 4250[1 + (.12)(1)]$$

$$= 4250\,(1.12) = 4760,$$

or $4760.

The bank applies its discount rate to this total:

$$\text{amount of discount} = 4760(.16)\left(\frac{3}{12}\right) = 190.40.$$

(Remember that the loan was discounted three months before it was due.) Toms actually receives

$$\$4760 - \$190.40 = \$4569.60$$

in cash from the bank. Three months later, the bank would get $4760 from Levy. ■ ★

★ Proceeds

23. $a = P(1+rt)$
$= 7150 + 1 (.16)(11/12)$
$= 1048.6661$

$proceeds =$
$7150 - 1048.6661$
$= 6101.33$

25. $a = P(1+rt)$
$= 358(1+(.216)(183/360)$
$= 40.3084$
$Pro = 358 - 40.3084$
$= 317.6916$

10.1 EXERCISES

Find the simple interest in Exercises 1–6. $I = prt$

1. $1000 at 12% for one year $=1000 (.12)(1)$
2. $4500 at 16% for one year
3. $25,000 at 21% for nine months$=25000(.21)(9/12)$
4. $3850 at 17% for eight months
5. $1974 at 16.2% for seven months $= 1974(.162)(7/12)$
6. $3724 at 14.1% for eleven months

In Exercises 7–12, assume a 360 day year. Also, assume 30 days in each month.

7. $12,000 at 14% for 72 days $=12000(.14) 72/360$
8. $38,000 at 19% for 216 days
9. $5147.18 at 17.3% for 58 days $- 5147.18 (.173)(58/360)$
10. $2930.42 at 13.9% for 123 days

$I = prt$

11. $7980 at 15%; the loan was made May 7 and is due on September 19 $7980 (15) 132/360)$
   Don't count the first day of loan ie. may 7
12. $5408 at 20%; the loan was made August 16 and is due on December 30

In Exercises 13–16, assume 365 days in a year, and use the exact number of days in a month. (Assume 28 days in February.) $I = prt$

13. $7800 at 16%; made on July 7 and due October 25
   $= 7800 (.16)(110/365)$
14. $11,000 at 15%; made on February 19 and due May 31
15. $2579 at 17.6%; made on October 4 and due March 15
   $= 2579 (.176)(162/365)$
16. $37,098 at 19.2%; made on September 12 and due July 30

Find the present value of the future amounts in Exercises 17–22. Assume 360 days in a year. $P = A/ 1+rt$

17. $15,000 for 8 months, money earns 16% $\frac{15000}{1+(.16)(8/12)}$
18. $48,000 for 9 months, money earns 14%

$\frac{5276}{1+(.174)(3/12)}$
19. $5276 for 3 months, money earns 17.4%
20. $6892 for 7 months, money earns 18.2%
21. $15,402 for 125 days, money earns 19.3% $\frac{15,402}{1+(.193)(125/360)}$
22. $29,764 for 310 days, money earns 21.4%

Find the proceeds for the amounts in Exercises 23–26. Assume 360 days in a year.

on top of page.

23. $7150, discount rate 16%, length of loan 11 months
24. $9450, discount rate 18%, length of loan 7 months
25. $358, discount rate 21.6%, length of loan 183 days
26. $509, discount rate 23.2%, length of loan 238 days

27. Donna Sharp borrowed $25,900 from her father to start a flower shop. She repaid him after eleven months, with interest of 18.4%. Find the total amount she repaid.
   $A = P(1+rt)$
   $25,900(1+(.184)(11/12)$
   $= 30,268.47$

28. A corporation accountant forgot to pay the firm's income tax of $725,896.15 on time. The government charged a penalty of 17.7% interest for the 34 days the money was late. Find the total amount, tax and penalty, that was paid. (Use a 365 day year.)

29. Tuition of $1769 will be due when the spring term begins, in four months. What amount should a student deposit today, at 6.25%, to have enough to pay the tuition?
   $P = A/1+rt$
   $\frac{1769}{1+(.0625)(4/12)}$
   $= 1732.90$

30. A firm of attorneys has ordered seven new IBM typewriters, at a cost of $2104 each. The machines will not be delivered for seven months. What amount could the firm deposit in an account paying 15.42% to have enough to pay for the machines?

31. Roy Gerard needs $5196 to pay for remodeling work on his house. He plans to repay the loan in 10 months. His bank loans money at a discount rate of 17%. Find the amount of his loan.

32. Mary Collins decides to go back to college. To get to school she buys a small car for $6100. She decides to borrow the money at the bank, where they charge a 19.8% discount rate. If she will repay the loan in 7 months, find the amount of the loan.

33. Marge Prullage signs a $4200 note at the bank. The bank charges a 17.2% discount rate. Find the net proceeds if the note is for ten months. Find the effective interest rate charged by the bank.

34. A bank charges a 23.1% discount rate on a $1000 note for 90 days. Find the effective rate.

35. Helen Spence owes $7000 to the Eastside Music Shop. She has agreed to pay the amount in 7 months, at an interest rate of 21%. Two months before the loan is due to be paid, the store discounts it at the bank. The bank charges a 23.7% discount rate. How much money does the store receive?

36. A building contractor gives a $13,500 note to a plumber. The note is due in nine months, with interest of 19%. Three months after the note is signed, the plumber discounts it at the bank. The bank charges a 21.1% discount rate. How much money does the plumber actually receive?

Handwritten annotations:

31. ✳ Notice 1 − (.17)
$P = a(1 - r \cdot t)$
$P = A - \text{Discount}$
$5196 = A[1 - (.17)(10/12)]$
$d = 5196$
$1 - (.17)(10/12) = 6053.59$

33. (a) $A = P(1 + rt)$
$= 4200(1 + (.172)(10/12)$
$= 4200 - 603$
$= 3597$
(b) $(1 + i/m)^m - 1$
$(1 + .172/(10/12))^{10/12} - 1$
$= 20.1$
✳ .833

35. $A = 7000(1 + (.21)(7/12) =$
$857.50 + 7000 = 7857.50$
Discount this by a certain amt.
$7857.50(.237)(2/12) =$
$7857.50(.237)$ /6
$P = 7857.50(1 - (.237)(2/12)$
$= 7857.50(1 - .0395)$
$= 7857.50(.9605)$
$= 7547.15$

✳ When doing
$4200(1 + (.172)(10/12$ do $.172 \cdot 10/12$
$4200 + 1 = $ ans

10.2 Compound Interest

Simple interest is normally used for loans of a year or less; for longer periods **compound interest** is used. With compound interest, interest is charged on interest, as well as principal. To find a formula for compound interest, first suppose that P dollars is deposited at a rate of interest i per year. (While r is used with simple interest, it is common to use i for compound interest.) The interest earned during the first year is found by the formula for simple interest:

$$\text{first year interest} = P \cdot i \cdot 1 = Pi.$$

At the end of one year, the amount on deposit will be the sum of the original principal and the interest earned, or

$$P + Pi = P(1 + i). \tag{1}$$

If the deposit earns compound interest, the interest earned during the second year is found from the total amount on deposit at the end of the first year. Thus, the interest earned during the second year (again found by the formula for simple interest), is given by

$$P(1 + i)(i)(1) = P(1 + i)i, \tag{2}$$

so that the total amount on deposit at the end of the second year is given by the sum of the amounts from (1) and (2) above, or

$$P(1 + i) + P(1 + i)i = P(1 + i) \cdot (1 + i)$$
$$= P(1 + i)^2.$$

In the same way, the total amount on deposit at the end of three years is

$$P(1 + i)^3.$$

Generalizing, in j years the total amount on deposit is $P(1 + i)^j$, called the **compound amount.**

Interest can be compounded more than once a year. Suppose interest is compounded m times per year (m *periods* per year), at a rate i per year, so that i/m is the rate for each period. Suppose that interest is compounded for n years. Then the following formula for the compound amount can be derived in the same way as was the previous formula.

Compound Amount

> If P dollars is deposited for n years with interest compounded m periods per year at a rate of interest i per year, the compound amount A is
>
> $$A = P\left(1 + \frac{i}{m}\right)^{mn}.$$

EXAMPLE 1

Suppose $1000 is deposited for 6 years in an account paying 8% per year compounded annually.

(a) Find the compound amount.

In the formula above, $P = 1000$, $i = 8\% = .08$, $m = 1$, and $n = 6$. The compound amount is

$$A = P\left(1 + \frac{i}{m}\right)^{nm}$$

$$A = 1000\left(1 + \frac{.08}{1}\right)^{6(1)} = 1000(1.08)^6.$$

We could find $(1.08)^6$ by using a calculator, or by using special compound interest tables. Such a table is given at the back of this book. To find $(1.08)^6$, look for 8% across the top and 6 (for 6 periods) down the side. You should find 1.58687, thus $(1.08)^6 \approx 1.58687$, and

$$A = 1000(1.58687) = 1586.87,$$

or $1586.87, which represents the final amount on deposit.

(b) Find the actual amount of interest earned.

From the compound amount, subtract the initial deposit.

$$\text{amount of interest} = \$1586.87 - \$1000 = \$586.87 \quad \blacksquare$$

EXAMPLE 2

Find the amount of interest earned by a deposit of $1000 for 6 years at 16% compounded quarterly.

Interest compounded quarterly is compounded four times a year. In 6 years, there are $4 \cdot 6 = 24$ quarters, or 24 periods. Interest of 16% per year is 16%/4, or 4%, per quarter. The compound amount is

$$1000(1 + .04)^{24} = 1000(1.04)^{24}.$$

The value of $(1.04)^{24}$ can be found with a calculator or in the table. Locate 4% across the top of the table and 24 periods at the left. You should find the number 2.56330 with

$$A = 1000(2.56330) = 2563.30,$$

or $2563.30. The compound amount is $2563.30 and the interest earned is $2563.30 - $1000 = $1563.30. ▪

EXAMPLE 3

Find the compound amount if $900 is deposited at 16% compounded semiannually for 8 years.

In 8 years there are $8 \cdot 2 = 16$ semiannual periods. If interest is 16% per year, then 16%/2 = 8% is earned per semiannual period. Use a calculator, or look in the table for 8% and 16 periods, finding the number 3.42594. The compound amount is

$$A = 900(1.08)^{16} = 900(3.42594) = 3083.35,$$

or $3083.35. ▪

The more often interest is compounded within a given time period, the more interest will be earned. Using a calculator with an x^y key, and using the formula above, we get the results shown in the following chart.

Interest on $1000 at 12% per Year for 10 Years

Compounded	Number of Periods	Compound Amount	Interest
not at all (simple interest)	—	—	$1200.00
annually	10	$1000(1 + .12)^{10} = \$3105.85$	$2105.85
semiannually	20	$1000\left(1 + \dfrac{.12}{2}\right)^{20} = \$3207.14$	$2207.14
quarterly	40	$1000\left(1 + \dfrac{.12}{4}\right)^{40} = \$3262.04$	$2262.04
monthly	120	$1000\left(1 + \dfrac{.12}{12}\right)^{120} = \$3300.39$	$2300.39
daily	3650	$1000\left(1 + \dfrac{.12}{365}\right)^{3650} = \$3319.46$	$2319.46
hourly	87,600	$1000\left(1 + \dfrac{.12}{8760}\right)^{87,600} = \$3320.09$	$2320.09
every minute	5,256,000	$1000\left(1 + \dfrac{.12}{525,600}\right)^{5,256,000} = \$3320.11$	$2320.11

As suggested by the chart, it makes a big difference whether interest is compounded or not. Interest differs by $905.85 when simple interest is compared to interest compounded annually. However, increasing the frequency of compounding makes smaller and smaller differences in the amount of interest earned. In fact, it can be shown that even if interest is compounded at intervals of time as small as one chooses (such as each hour, each minute, or each second), the total amount of interest earned will be only slightly more than for daily compounding. This is true even for a process called **continuous compounding,** which can be loosely described as compounding every instant. The interesting topic of continuous compounding is discussed in more detail in calculus.

EXAMPLE 4

Suppose $24,000 is deposited at 16% for 9 years. Find the interest earned by (a) daily, and (b) hourly compounding.

(a)   In 9 years there are $9 \times 365 = 3285$ days. The compound amount with daily compounding is

$$24{,}000\left(1 + \frac{.16}{365}\right)^{3285} = 101{,}264.60,$$

or $101,264.60. The interest earned is

$$\$101{,}264.60 - \$24{,}000 = \$77{,}264.60.$$

(b)   In one year, there are $365 \times 24 = 8760$ hours, while in 9 years there are $9 \times 8760 = 78{,}840$ hours. The compound amount is

$$24{,}000\left(1 + \frac{.16}{8760}\right)^{78{,}840} = 101{,}295.15,$$

or $101,295.15. This amount includes interest of

$$\$101{,}295.15 - \$24{,}000 = \$77{,}295.15,$$

only $30.55 more than when interest is compounded daily.   ▮

Effective Rate   If $1 is deposited at 4% compounded quarterly, we can use a calculator or a table to find that at the end of one year, the compound amount is $1.0406, an increase of 4.06% over the original $1. The actual increase of 4.06% in the money is somewhat higher than the stated increase of 4%. To differentiate between these two numbers, 4% is called the **nominal** or **stated** rate of interest, while 4.06% is called the **effective** rate.

EXAMPLE 5

Find the effective rate corresponding to a nominal rate of 6% compounded semiannually.

Look in the compound interest table for an interest rate of 3% for 2 periods. You should find the number 1.06090. Alternatively, use a calculator to find $(1.03)^2$. By either method, $1 will increase to $1.06090, an actual increase of 6.09%. The effective rate is 6.09%.   ▮

Generalizing from this example, the effective rate of interest is given by the following formula.

Effective Rate

The effective rate corresponding to a stated rate of interest i compounded m times per year is

$$\left(1 + \frac{i}{m}\right)^m - 1.$$

EXAMPLE 6

A bank pays interest of 9% compounded monthly. Find the effective rate.

Use the formula in the box, with $i = .09$ and $m = 12$. The effective rate is

$$\left(1 + \frac{.09}{12}\right)^{12} - 1.$$

Use a calculator with an x^y key to get

$$(1.0075)^{12} - 1 = .0938,$$

or 9.38%. ■

Present Value with Compound Interest The formula for compound interest, $A = P(1 + i/m)^{nm}$, has five variables, A, P, i, m, and n. If we know the values of any four of these variables, we can then find the value of the fifth. In particular, if we know A, the amount of money we wish to end up with, and also know i, m, and n, then we can find P. Here P is the amount that we should deposit today to produce A dollars in n years. The next example shows this.

EXAMPLE 7

Joan Wilson must pay a lump sum of $6000 in 5 years. What amount deposited today at 8% compounded annually will amount to $6000 in 5 years?

Here $A = 6000$, $i = .08$, $m = 1$, $n = 5$, and P is unknown. Substituting these values into the formula for the compound amount gives

$$6000 = P\left(1 + \frac{.08}{1}\right)^{5(1)} = P(1.08)^5.$$

From a calculator or the table, $(1.08)^5 \approx 1.46933$, with

$$6000 \approx P(1.46933)$$

and

$$P = \frac{6000}{1.46933} \approx 4083.49,$$

or $4083.49. If Wilson deposits $4083.49 for 5 years in an account paying 8% compounded annually, she will have $6000 when she needs it. ■

As the last example shows, $6000 in 5 years is the same as $4083.49 today (if money can be deposited at 8% compounded annually.) Recall from the first section that an amount that can be deposited today to yield a given sum in the future is called the *present value* of this future sum.

EXAMPLE 8

Find the present value of $16,000 in 9 years if money can be deposited at 12% compounded semiannually.

In 9 years there are $2 \cdot 9 = 18$ semiannual periods. A rate of 12% per year is 6% each semiannual period. Use a calculator, or look in the table (6% across the top and 18 periods down the side). You should find 2.85434. The present value is

$$\frac{16,000}{2.85434} \approx 5605.50.$$

A deposit of $5605.50 today, at 12% compounded semiannually, will produce a total of $16,000 in 9 years. ■

We can also solve the formula for the compound amount for n, as the following example shows.

EXAMPLE 9

Suppose the general level of inflation in the economy averages 8% per year. Find the number of years it would take for the overall level of prices to double.

We want to find the number of years it will take for $1 worth of goods or services to cost $2. That is, we want to find n in the equation

$$2 = 1(1 + .08)^n,$$

where $A = 2$, $P = 1$, and $i = .08$. This equation simplifies to

$$2 = (1.08)^n.$$

We could find n by using logarithms or certain calculators, but we can find a reasonable approximation by reading down the 8% column of the table. Read down this column until you come to the number closest to 2, which is 1.99900. This number corresponds to 9 periods. The general level of prices will double in about 9 years. ■

10.2 EXERCISES

Find the compound amount when the deposits in Exercises 1–12 are made. $A = P(1 + i)^n$

1. $1000 at 6% compounded annually for 8 years $1000(1.06)$ 2. $1000 at 8% compounded annually for 10 years

3. $4500 at 8% compounded annually for 20 years

4. $810 at 8% compounded annually for 12 years

5. $470 at 12% compounded semiannually for 12 years

6. $15,000 at 16% compounded semiannually for 11 years $= 15000 (1 + \frac{.16}{2})^{(2)(11)}$

7. $46,000 at 12% compounded semiannually for 5 years

8. $1050 at 16% compounded semiannually for 13 years

9. $7500 at 16% compounded quarterly for 9 years

10. $8000 at 16% compounded quarterly for 4 years

11. $6500 at 12% compounded quarterly for 6 years

12. $9100 at 12% compounded quarterly for 4 years

9. $= 7500 (1 + \frac{.16}{4})^{(4)(9)}$

Handwritten at top:
15. $d = 43,000(1+.10/2)(2)(9)$
$I = prt$
$= 43,000(1.05)^{18}$
$ans - 43,000 = i \ earned$

Find the amount of interest earned by the deposits in Exercises 13–18.

13. $6000 at 8% compounded annually for 8 years

14. $21,000 at 6% compounded annually for 5 years

15. $43,000 at 10% compounded semiannually for 9 years

16. $7500 at 8% compounded semiannually for 5 years

17. $2196.58 at 20.8% compounded quarterly for 4 years

18. $4915.73 at 21.6% compounded quarterly for 3 years

Handwritten for 18:
$d = 4915.73(1+.216/4)^{(4)(3)}$
$= 4915.73(6.4)^{12}$
$ans - 4915.73 = i \ earned.$

Find the present value of the sums in Exercises 19–26.

19. $4500 at 8% compounded annually for 9 years

20. $11,500 at 8% compounded annually for 12 years

21. $15,902.74 at 19.8% compounded annually for 7 years   *Handwritten:* $15,902.74 = P(1+(.198)(1)(7))$

22. $27,159.68 at 21.3% compounded annually for 11 years

23. $2000 at 16% compounded semiannually for 8 years

24. $2000 at 12% compounded semiannually for 8 years   *Handwritten:* $2000 = P(1+.12/2)^{(2)(8)}$

25. $8800 at 16% compounded quarterly for 5 years

26. $7500 at 12% compounded quarterly for 9 years

27. If money can be invested at 8% compounded quarterly, which is larger, $1000 now or $1210 in 5 years?   *Handwritten:* $1000 = P(1+.08/4)^{(4)(5)} =$ / $1210 = P(1+.08/4)^{(4)(5)} =$

28. If money can be invested at 6% compounded annually, which is larger, $10,000 now or $15,000 in 10 years?

Find the effective rate corresponding to each of the following nominal rates.   *Handwritten:* $(1 + i/m)^m - 1$

29. 4% compounded semiannually

30. 8% compounded quarterly   *Handwritten:* $(1+.04/2)^2 - 1$

31. 8% compounded semiannually

32. 10% compounded semiannually

33. 12% compounded semiannually   *Handwritten:* $(1 + .12/2)^2 - 1$

34. 12% compounded quarterly

Use the ideas of Example 9 in the text to answer questions 35–37. Find the time it would take for the general level of prices in the economy to double if the average annual inflation rate is   *Handwritten:* level of infl lat 35. / P. 484 Table.

35. 4%

36. 5%

37. 6%.   *Handwritten:* $2 = 1(1+.04)^n$ / $2 = (1.04)^n = 1.94770$ / 17 yrs.

38. **(a)** The consumption of electricity has increased historically at 6% per year. If it continues to increase at this rate indefinitely, find the number of years before the electric utilities would need to double their generating capacity.

(b) Suppose a conservation campaign coupled with higher rates caused the demand for electricity to increase at only 2% per year, as it has recently. Find the number of years before the utilities would need to double generating capacity.

Under certain conditions, Swiss banks pay *negative interest*—they charge you. (You didn't think all that secrecy was free?) Suppose a bank ''pays'' −2.4% interest compounded annually. Use a calculator and find the compound amount for a deposit of $150,000 after

39. 2 years

40. 4 years

41. 8 years

42. 12 years.

Find the compound amount for each of the following deposits.

Handwritten:
39. $A = 150,000(1+(-2.4)(1)(2)$
$150,000(-1.4)^2$

43. $40,552 at 9.13% compounded quarterly for 5 years.

44. $11,641.10 at 10.9% compounded monthly for 8 years.

45. $673.27 at 8.6% compounded semi-annually for 3.5 years.   *Handwritten:* $42. = 150,000(1+(-2.4)(1)(12)$

46. $2964.93 at 11.4% compounded monthly for 4.25 years.   *Handwritten:* $= 15,000(-1.4)^{12}$

10.3 Sequences (Optional)

So far in our discussion of mathematics of finance, we have discussed only lump sums—a lump sum deposit today that produces a lump sum compound amount in the future, or the present value of a lump sum amount in the future. In practice, however, it is very common to deal with a sequence of *periodic payments,* such as a car payment or house payment. We shall develop formulas for these payments in the next sections. To develop these formulas, we need some of the results of this section, on sequences.

A **sequence** is a function whose domain is the set of positive integers. For example,

$$a(n) = 2n, \qquad n = 1, 2, 3, 4, \ldots$$

is a sequence. The letter n is used as a variable instead of x to emphasize the fact that the domain includes only positive integers. For the same reason, a is used to name the function instead of f.

The range values of a sequence function, such as

$$a(1) = 2, \qquad a(2) = 4, \qquad a(3) = 6, \ldots$$

from the sequence given above, are called the **terms** of the sequence. Instead of writing $a(5)$ for the fifth term of the sequence, for example, it is customary to write

$$a_5 = 10.$$

In the same way, for the sequence above, $a_1 = 2$, $a_2 = 4$, $a_8 = 16$, $a_{20} = 40$, and $a_{51} = 102$.

The symbol a_n is often used for the **general** or **nth term** of a sequence. For example, for the sequence 4, 7, 10, 13, 16, . . . the general term is given by $a_n = 1 + 3n$. This formula for a_n can be used to find any desired term of the sequence. For example, the first three terms of the sequence having $a_n = 1 + 3n$ are

$$a_1 = 1 + 3(1) = 4, \quad a_2 = 1 + 3(2) = 7, \quad a_3 = 1 + 3(3) = 10.$$

Also, $a_8 = 25$ and $a_{12} = 37$.

EXAMPLE 1

Find the first four terms for the sequence having the general term $a_n = -4n + 2$.
Replace n, in turn, with 1, 2, 3, and 4. If $n = 1$,

$$a_1 = -4(1) + 2 = -4 + 2 = -2. \qquad \textbf{Let } n = 1$$

Also, $\qquad a_2 = -4(2) + 2 = -6.$ $\qquad\qquad$ **Let** $n = 2$

When $n = 3$, then $a_3 = -10$; finally, $a_4 = -4(4) + 2 = -14$. The first four terms of this sequence are -2, -6, -10, and -14. ◼

Arithmetic Sequences A sequence in which each term after the first is found by adding the same number to the preceding term is called an **arithmetic sequence.**

The sequence of Example 1 above is an arithmetic sequence; -4 is added to any term to get the next term.

The sequence

$$8, 13, 18, 23, 28, \ldots$$

is an arithmetic sequence since each term after the first is found by adding 5 to the previous term. The number 5, the difference between any two adjacent terms, is called the **common difference.**

If a_1 is the first term of an arithmetic sequence and d is the common difference, then the second term can be found by adding the common difference d to the first term: $a_2 = a_1 + d$. The third term is found by adding d to the second term.

$$a_3 = a_2 + d = (a_1 + d) + d = a_1 + 2d$$

In the same way, $a_4 = a_1 + 3d$ and $a_5 = a_1 + 4d$. Generalizing, the nth term of an arithmetic sequence is given by $a_n = a_1 + (n - 1)d$.

nth Term

If an arithmetic sequence has first term a_1 and common difference d, then a_n, the nth term of the sequence, is given by

$$a_n = a_1 + (n - 1)d.$$

EXAMPLE 2

A company had sales of $50,000 during its first year of operation. If the sales increase by $6000 per year, find its sales in the eleventh year.

Since the sales for each year after the first are found by adding $6000 to the sales of the previous year, the sales form an arithmetic sequence with $a_1 = 50,000$ and $d = 6000$. Using the formula for the nth term of an arithmetic sequence, sales during the eleventh year are given by

$$a_{11} = 50,000 + (11 - 1)6000 = 50,000 + 60,000 = 110,000,$$

or $110,000. ■

The formula above gives the nth term of an arithmetic sequence. We can now find a formula for the *sum* of the first n terms of an arithmetic sequence. To find this formula, let an arithmetic sequence have first term a_1 and common difference d. Let S_n represent the sum of the first n terms of the sequence. Start by writing a formula for S_n as follows:

$$S_n = a_1 + [a_1 + d] + [a_1 + 2d] + \cdots + [a_1 + (n - 1)d].$$

Next, write this same sum in reverse order.

$$S_n = [a_1 + (n - 1)d] + [a_1 + (n - 2)d] + \cdots + [a_1 + d] + a_1$$

Now add the respective sides of these last two equations.

$$S_n + S_n = (a_1 + [a_1 + (n - 1)d]) + ([a_1 + d] + [a_1 + (n - 2)d])$$
$$+ \cdots + ([a_1 + (n - 1)d] + a_1)$$

From this,

$$2S_n = [2a_1 + (n - 1)d] + [2a_1 + (n - 1)d]$$
$$+ \cdots + [2a_1 + (n - 1)d].$$

There are n of the $[2a_1 + (n - 1)d]$ terms on the right, making

$$2S_n = n[2a_1 + (n - 1)d],$$

$$S_n = \frac{n}{2}[2a_1 + (n - 1)d].$$

Since $a_n = a_1 + (n - 1)d$, also $S_n = \frac{n}{2}[a_1 + a_1 + (n - 1)d]$, or

$$S_n = \frac{n}{2}(a_1 + a_n).$$

The following box summarizes this work with arithmetic sequences.

Sum of Terms

Suppose an arithmetic sequence has first term a_1, common difference d, and nth term a_n. Then the sum S_n of the first n terms of the sequence is given by

$$S_n = \frac{n}{2}[2a_1 + (n - 1)d]$$

or

$$S_n = \frac{n}{2}(a_1 + a_n).$$

Either of these two formulas can be used to find the sum of the first n terms of an arithmetic sequence.

EXAMPLE 3

Find the sum of the first 25 terms of the arithmetic sequence

$$3, 8, 13, 18, 23, \ldots$$

In this sequence, $a_1 = 3$ and $d = 5$. If we use the first formula from above, we get

$$S_{25} = \frac{25}{2}[2(3) + (25 - 1)5] \qquad \text{Let } n = 25, \quad a_1 = 3, \quad d = 5$$

$$= \frac{25}{2}[6 + 120]$$

$$= 1575. \quad \blacksquare$$

EXAMPLE 4

Find the total sales of the company of Example 2 during its first 11 years.

From Example 2, $a_1 = 50,000$, $a_{11} = 110,000$, and $n = 11$. By the second formula above,

$$S_{11} = \frac{11}{2}(50,000 + 110,000) = 880,000.$$

The total sales for 11 years are $880,000. ▪

Geometric Sequences   In an arithmetic sequence, each term after the first is found by adding the same number to the preceding term. In a **geometric sequence,** each term after the first is found by *multiplying* the preceding term by the same number. For example,

$$3, -6, 12, -24, 48, -96, \ldots$$

is a geometric sequence with each term after the first found by multiplying the preceding term by the number -2. The number -2 is called the **common ratio.**

If a_1 is the first term of a geometric sequence and r is the common ratio, then the second term is given by $a_2 = a_1 r$ and the third term by $a_3 = a_2 r = a_1 r^2$. Also, $a_4 = a_1 r^3$, and $a_5 = a_1 r^4$. The next box generalizes from these results.

***n*th Term**

> If a geometric sequence has first term a_1 and common ratio r, then
> $$a_n = a_1 r^{n-1}.$$

EXAMPLE 5

Find the indicated term for each of the following geometric sequences.

(a) $6, 24, 96, 384, \ldots$; find a_7.

Here $a_1 = 6$. To find r, choose any term except the first and divide it by the preceding term. If we choose 96,

$$r = \frac{96}{24} = 4.$$

Now use the formula for the nth term.

$$
\begin{aligned}
a_7 &= 6(4)^{7-1} \qquad &\text{Let } n = 7, a_1 = 6, r = 4\\
&= 6(4)^6\\
&= 6(4096) \qquad &4^6 = 4096\\
&= 24,576
\end{aligned}
$$

(b) $8, -16, 32, -64, 128, \ldots$; find a_6.

In this sequence $a_1 = 8$ and $r = -2$.

$$
\begin{aligned}
a_6 &= 8(-2)^{6-1} \qquad &\text{Let } n = 6, a_1 = 8, r = -2\\
&= 8(-2)^5\\
&= 8(-32)\\
&= -256 \quad ▪
\end{aligned}
$$

Often we need to find the sum of the first n terms of a geometric sequence. We can find a formula for this sum, just as we did with arithmetic sequences. To find this formula, let a geometric sequence have first term a_1 and common ratio r. Write the sum S_n of the first n terms as

$$S_n = a_1 + a_2 + a_3 + \cdots + a_n.$$

This sum can also be written as

$$S_n = a_1 + a_1 r + a_1 r^2 + \cdots + a_1 r^{n-1}. \tag{1}$$

If $r = 1$, then $S_n = na_1$, the correct result for this case. If $r \neq 1$, multiply both sides of equation (1) by r, obtaining

$$rS_n = a_1 r + a_1 r^2 + a_1 r^3 + \cdots + a_1 r_n. \tag{2}$$

Now subtract corresponding sides of equation (1) from equation (2);

$$rS_n - S_n = a_1 r_n - a_1$$
$$S_n(r - 1) = a_1(r_n - 1),$$
$$S_n = \frac{a_1(r_n - 1)}{r - 1}.$$

or finally

The next box summarizes this result.

Sum of Terms

If a geometric sequence has first term a_1 and common ratio r, then the sum S_n of the first n terms is given by

$$S_n = \frac{a_1(r^n - 1)}{r - 1}, \qquad r \neq 1.$$

EXAMPLE 6

Find the sum of the first six terms of the geometric sequence 3, 12, 48, ... Here $a_1 = 3$ and $r = 4$. Find S_6 by the formula above.

$$S_6 = \frac{3(4^6 - 1)}{4 - 1} \qquad \text{Let } n = 6,\ a_1 = 3,\ r = 4$$

$$= \frac{3(4096 - 1)}{3}$$

$$= 4095 \quad \blacksquare$$

10.3 EXERCISES

In Exercises 1–16, a formula for the general term of a sequence is given. Use the formula to find the first five terms of the sequence. Identify each sequence as *arithmetic, geometric,* or *neither.*

1. $a_n = 6n + 5$ **2.** $a_n = 12n - 3$ **3.** $a_n = 3n - 7$ **4.** $a_n = 5n - 12$

5. $a_n = -6n + 4$ **6.** $a_n = -11n + 10$ **7.** $a_n = 2^n$ **8.** $a_n = 3^n$

9. $a_n = (-2)^n$ **10.** $a_n = (-3)^n$ **11.** $a_n = 3(2^n)$ **12.** $a_n = -4(2^n)$

13. $a_n = \dfrac{n+1}{n+5}$ **14.** $a_n = \dfrac{2n}{n+1}$ **15.** $a_n = \dfrac{1}{n+1}$ **16.** $a_n = \dfrac{1}{n+8}$

Identify each sequence in Exercises 17–32 as *arithmetic, geometric,* or *neither.* For an arithmetic sequence, give the common difference. For a geometric sequence, give the common ratio.

17. 6, 14, 22, 30, 38, 46, . . .   **18.** 40, 46, 52, 58, 64, . . .   **19.** 5, 8, 11, 14, 17, 20, 23, . . .

20. 23, 34, 45, 54, 63, 72, . . .   **21.** 4, 12, 36, 108, . . .   **22.** 7, 14, 28, 56, 112, . . .

23. 2, 5, 9, 14, 20, 27, . . .   **24.** 1, 4, 9, 16, 25, 36, . . .   **25.** 12, 9, 6, 3, 0, −3, −6, . . .

26. 37, 31, 25, 19, 13, 7, . . .   **27.** −18, −15, −12, −9, −6, . . .   **28.** −21, −17, −13, −9, −5, . . .

29. 3, −6, 12, −24, 48, −96, . . .   **30.** −5, 10, −20, 40, −80, . . .

31. −5, 6, −7, 8, −9, 10, −11, . . .   **32.** −12, 9, −6, 3, . . .

In Exercises 33–40, find the indicated term for each arithmetic sequence.

33. $a_1 = 10$, $d = 5$; find a_{13} **34.** $a_1 = 6$, $d = 9$; find a_8

35. $a_1 = 8$, $d = 3$; find a_{20} **36.** $a_1 = 13$, $d = 7$; find a_{11}

37. 6, 9, 12, 15, 18, . . . ; find a_{25} **38.** 14, 17, 20, 23, 26, 29, . . . ; find a_{13}

39. −9, −13, −17, −21, −25, . . . ; find a_{15} **40.** −4, --11, −18, −25, −32, . . . ; find a_{18}

Find the sum of the first six terms for each of the arithmetic sequences in Exercises 41–48.

41. 3, 6, 9, 12, . . .   **42.** 11, 13, 15, 17, . . .   **43.** 88, 98, 108, . . .   **44.** 92, 95, 98, . . .

45. $a_1 = 8$, $d = 9$ **46.** $a_1 = 12$, $d = 6$ **47.** $a_1 = 7$, $d = -4$ **48.** $a_1 = 13$, $d = -5$

Find a_5 for each of the geometric sequences in Exercises 49–56.

49. $a_1 = 3$, $r = 2$ **50.** $a_1 = 5$, $r = 3$ **51.** $a_1 = -8$, $r = 3$

52. $a_1 = -6$, $r = 2$ **53.** $a_1 = 1$, $r = -3$ **54.** $a_1 = 12$, $r = -2$

55. $a_1 = 1024$, $r = 1/2$ **56.** $a_1 = 729$, $r = 1/3$

Find the sum of the first four terms for each of the geometric sequences in Exercises 57–62.

57. $a_1 = 1$, $r = 2$ **58.** $a_1 = 3$, $r = 3$ **59.** $a_1 = 5$, $r = 1/5$

60. $a_1 = 6$, $r = 1/2$ **61.** $a_1 = 128$, $r = -3/2$ **62.** $a_1 = 81$, $r = -2/3$

Sums of the terms of a sequence are often written in *sigma notation* (also used in statistics). For example, to evaluate

$$\sum_{i=1}^{4} (3i + 7)$$

(where Σ is the capital Greek letter *sigma*), first evaluate $3i + 7$ for $i = 1$, then for $i = 2$, $i = 3$, and finally, $i = 4$. Then add the results to get

$$\sum_{i=1}^{4} (3i + 7) = [3(1) + 7] + [3(2) + 7] + [3(3) + 7] + [3(4) + 7]$$
$$= 10 + 13 + 16 + 19 = 58.$$

Evaluate each of the sums in Exercises 63–70.

63. $\sum_{i=1}^{5} (3 - 2i)$ **64.** $\sum_{i=1}^{4} (2i - 5)$ **65.** $\sum_{i=1}^{8} (2i + 1)$

66. $\sum_{i=1}^{4} (-6i + 8)$ **67.** $\sum_{i=1}^{5} i(2i + 1)$ **68.** $\sum_{i=1}^{4} (2i - 1)(i + 2)$

69. $\sum_{i=1}^{4} (3i + 1)(i + 1)$ **70.** $\sum_{i=1}^{5} (i - 3)(i + 5)$

A sum in the form

$$\sum_{i=1}^{n} (ai + b),$$

where a and b are real numbers, represents the sum of the first n terms of an arithmetic sequence. The first term is $a_1 = a(1) + b = a + b$ and the common difference is a. The nth term is $a_n = an + b$. Using these numbers, the sum can be found by using the formula for the sum of the first n terms. Use this method to find the sums in Exercises 71–76.

71. $\sum_{i=1}^{5} (2i + 8)$ **72.** $\sum_{i=1}^{6} (4i - 5)$ **73.** $\sum_{i=1}^{4} (-8i + 6)$

74. $\sum_{i=1}^{9} (2i - 3)$ **75.** $\sum_{i=1}^{500} i$ **76.** $\sum_{i=1}^{1000} i$

Sigma notation can also be used for geometric sequences. A sum in the form

$$\sum_{i=1}^{n} a(b^i)$$

represents the sum of the first n terms of a geometric sequence having first term $a_1 = ab$ and common ratio b. These sums can thus be found by applying the formula for the sum of the first n terms of a geometric sequence. Use this method to find the sums in Exercises 77–82.

77. $\sum_{i=1}^{4} 3(2^i)$ **78.** $\sum_{i=1}^{3} 2(3^i)$ **79.** $\sum_{i=1}^{4} \frac{1}{2}(4^i)$

80. $\sum_{i=1}^{4} \frac{3}{2}(2^i)$ **81.** $\sum_{i=1}^{4} \frac{4}{3}(3^i)$ **82.** $\sum_{i=1}^{4} \frac{5}{3}(3^i)$

83. Joy Watt is hired for $11,400 per year, with annual raises of $600. What will she earn during her eighth year with the company?

84. What will be the total income received by Watt (see Exercise 83) during her first eight years with the company?

85. A certain machine annually loses 30% of the value it had at the beginning of that year. If its initial value is $10,000, use a calculator to find its value (a) at the end of the fifth year, (b) at the end of the eighth year.

86. A certain colony of bacteria increases in number by 10% per hour. After five hours, what is the percentage increase in the population over the initial population?

10.4 Annuities

In the first two sections of this chapter we studied *lump sum* payments; now we study a *sequence* of equal payments. For example, suppose $1500 is deposited at the end of each year for the next six years, in an account paying 8% per year, compounded annually. How much would be in the account after the six years?

A sequence of equal payments made at equal periods of time is called an **annuity.** If the payments are made at the end of the time period, and if the frequency of payments is the same as the frequency of compounding, the annuity is called an **ordinary annuity.** The time between payments is the **payment period,** with the time from the beginning of the first payment period to the end of the last called the **term** of the annuity. The **future value** of the annuity, the final sum on deposit, is defined as the sum of the compound amounts of all the payments, compounded to the end of the term.

Figure 1 shows our annuity of $1500 at the end of each year for six years. To find the future value of this annuity, look separately at each of the $1500 payments. The first of these payments will produce a compound amount of

$$1500(1 + .08)^5 = 1500(1.08)^5.$$

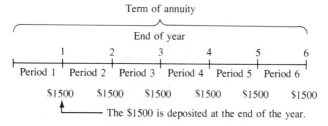

FIGURE 1

Use 5 as the exponent instead of 6 since the money is deposited at the *end* of the first year, and earns interest for only five years. The second payment of $1500 will produce a compound amount of $1500(1.08)^4$. As shown in Figure 2, the future value of the annuity is

$$1500(1.08)^5 + 1500(1.08)^4 + 1500(1.08)^3 + 1500(1.08)^2 + 1500(1.08)^1 + 1500.$$

(The last payment earns no interest at all.) From the compound interest table, this sum is

$$1500(1.46933) + 1500(1.36049) + 1500(1.25971) + 1500(1.16640)$$
$$+ 1500(1.08000) + 1500$$

$$\approx \$2204.00 + \$2040.74 + \$1889.57 + \$1749.60 + \$1620 + \$1500$$

$$= \$11,003.91.$$

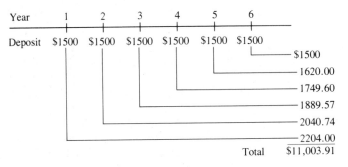

FIGURE 2

To generalize this result, suppose that a payment of R dollars is paid into an account at the end of each period for n periods, at a rate of interest i per period. The first payment of R dollars will produce a compound amount of $R(1 + i)^{n-1}$ dollars, the second payment produces $R(1 + i)^{n-2}$ dollars, and so on; the final payment earns no interest and contributes just R dollars to the total. If A represents the future value of the annuity, then (as shown in Figure 3),

$$A = R(1 + i)^{n-1} + R(1 + i)^{n-2} + R(1 + i)^{n-3} + \cdots + R(1 + i) + R$$

or, written in reverse order,

$$A = R + R(1 + i)^1 + R(1 + i)^2 + \cdots + R(1 + i)^{n-1}.$$

This sum is the sum of the first n terms of the geometric sequence having first term R and common ratio $1 + i$. Using the formula for the sum of the first n terms of a geometric sequence from the previous section,

$$A = \frac{R[(1 + i)^n - 1]}{(1 + i) - 1} = \frac{R[(1 + i)^n - 1]}{i} = R\left[\frac{(1 + i)^n - 1}{i}\right].$$

The quantity in brackets is commonly written $s_{\overline{n}|i}$ (read "s-angle-n at i"), so that

$$A = R \cdot s_{\overline{n}|i}.$$

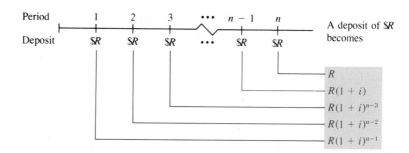

Period
Deposit

A deposit of $R becomes

R

$R(1 + i)$

$R(1 + i)^{n-3}$

$R(1 + i)^{n-2}$

$R(1 + i)^{n-1}$

The sum of these is the amount of the annuity.

FIGURE 3

Values of $s_{\overline{n}|i}$ can be found by a calculator or from the table "Amount of an Annuity," at the back of this book.

To check the result above, go back to the annuity of $1500 at the end of each year for 6 years; interest was 8% per year compounded annually. In the table, these values give the number 7.33593. Multiply this number and 1500:

$$\text{future value} = 1500(7.33593) \approx 11{,}003.90,$$

or $11,003.90. The results differ by 1¢ due to rounding error.

The next box summarizes this work.

Future Value of an Annuity

The future value, A, of an annuity of n payments of R dollars each at the end of each consecutive interest period, with interest compounded at a rate i per period, is

$$A = R\left[\frac{(1 + i)^n - 1}{i}\right], \qquad \text{or} \qquad A = R \cdot s_{\overline{n}|i}.$$

EXAMPLE 1

Tom Bleser is an athlete who feels that his playing career will last 7 years. To prepare for his future, he deposits $22,000 at the end of each year for 7 years in an account paying 6% compounded annually. How much will he have on deposit after 7 years?

His payments form an ordinary annuity with $R = 22{,}000$, $n = 7$, and $i = .06$. The future value of this annuity is (by the formula above)

$$A = 22{,}000\left[\frac{(1.06)^7 - 1}{.06}\right].$$

From the table or a calculator, the number in brackets, $s_{\overline{7}|.06}$, is 8.39384, so that

$$A = 22{,}000(8.39384) = 184{,}664.48,$$

or $184,664.48. ■

EXAMPLE 2

Suppose $1000 is deposited at the end of each six-month period for 5 years in an account paying 16% compounded semiannually. Find the future value of the annuity.

Interest of $16\%/2 = 8\%$ is earned semiannually. In 5 years there are $5 \cdot 2 = 10$ semiannual periods. Find $s_{\overline{10}|.08}$ from the table or a calculator. By looking in the 8% column and down 10 periods, we find $s_{\overline{10}|.08} = 14.48656$, with a future value of

$$A = 1000(14.48656) = 14{,}486.56,$$

or $14,486.56. ▪

Our results so far have been developed for *ordinary annuities*—those with payments made at the *end* of each time period. These results can be modified slightly to apply to **annuities due**—an annuity where payments are made at the *beginning* of each time period. To find the future value of an annuity due, treat each payment as if it were made at the *end* of the *preceding* period. That is, use the table or a calculator to find $s_{\overline{n}|i}$ for *one additional period;* to compensate for this, subtract the amount of one payment.

EXAMPLE 3

Find the future value of an annuity due if payments of $500 are made at the beginning of each quarter for 7 years, in an account paying 12% compounded quarterly.

In 7 years, there are 28 quarterly periods. Look in row 29 $(28 + 1)$ of the table. Use the $12\%/4 = 3\%$ column of the table. You should find the number 45.21885. Multiply this number by 500, the amount of each payment.

$$500(45.21885) \approx 22{,}609.43$$

Subtract the amount of one payment from this result.

$$\$22{,}609.43 - \$500 = \$22{,}109.43$$

The account will contain a total of $22,109.43 after 7 years. ▪

Just as the formula $A = P(1 + i)^n$ can be solved for any of its variables, the formula for the future value of an annuity can be used to find the values of variables other than A. In Example 4 below we are given A, the amount of money wanted at the end, and we need to find R, the amount of each payment.

EXAMPLE 4

Betsy Martens wants to buy an expensive video camera three years from now. She wants to deposit an equal amount at the end of each quarter for three years in order to accumulate enough money to pay for the camera. The camera costs $2400, and the bank pays 12% interest compounded quarterly. Find the amount of each of the twelve deposits she will make.

This example describes an ordinary annuity with $A = 2400$, $i = .03$ $(12\%/4 = 3\%)$ and $n = 3 \cdot 4 = 12$ periods. The unknown here is the amount of each payment, R. By the formula for the amount of an annuity from above,

$$2400 = R \cdot s_{\overline{12}|.03}.$$

From the table or a calculator,

$$2400 = R(14.19203)$$

$$R \approx 169.11,$$

or $169.11 (dividing both sides by 14.19203). ▪

Sinking Fund The annuity in Example 4 is a *sinking fund:* a fund set up to receive periodic payments. These periodic payments ($169.11 in the example) together with the interest earned by the payments, are designed to produce a given sum at some time in the future. As another example, a sinking fund might be set up to receive money that will be needed to pay off the principal on a loan at some time in the future.

EXAMPLE 5

The Stockdales are close to retirement. They agree to sell an antique urn to the local museum for $17,000. Their tax adviser suggests that they defer receipt of this money until they retire, 5 years in the future. (At that time, they might well be in a lower tax bracket.) Find the amount of each payment the museum must make into a sinking fund so that it will have the necessary $17,000 in 5 years. Assume that the museum can earn 8% compounded annually on its money. Also, assume that the payments are made annually.

These payments are the periodic payments into an ordinary annuity. The annuity will amount to $17,000 in 5 years at 8% compounded annually. Using the formula,

$$17,000 = R \cdot s_{\overline{5}|.08}$$

or

$$R = \frac{17,000}{s_{\overline{5}|.08}}$$

$$R = \frac{17,000}{5.86660} \qquad \textbf{From the table}$$

$$R \approx 2897.76,$$

or $2897.76. If the museum deposits $2897.76 at the end of each year for 5 years in an account paying 8% compounded annually, it will have the total amount that it needs. This result is shown in the following table. In these tables, the last payment might well differ slightly from the others because of rounding errors.

Payment number	Amount of deposit	Interest earned	Total in account
1	$2897.76	$0	$2897.76
2	$2897.76	$231.82	$6027.34
3	$2897.76	$482.19	$9407.29
4	$2897.76	$752.58	$13,057.63
5	$2897.76	$1044.61	$17,000.00 ▪

10.4 EXERCISES

Find each of the values in Exercises 1–8.

1. $s_{\overline{12}|.05}$

2. $s_{\overline{20}|.06}$

3. $s_{\overline{16}|.04}$ *21.82453*

4. $s_{\overline{40}|.02}$

5. $s_{\overline{20}|.01}$

6. $s_{\overline{18}|.015}$ *20.48938*

7. $s_{\overline{15}|.04}$

8. $s_{\overline{30}|.015}$

Find the future value of the ordinary annuities in Exercises 9–16. Interest is compounded annually.

A = R sₙ⌐ᵢ

9. $R = 100$, $i = .06$, $n = 10$ *100 S₁₀⌐(.06)*

10. $R = 1000$, $i = .06$, $n = 12$

11. $R = 10,000$, $i = .05$, $n = 19$

12. $R = 100,000$, $i = .08$, $n = 23$ *100,000 S₂₃⌐(.08)*

13. $R = 8500$, $i = .06$, $n = 30$

14. $R = 11,200$, $i = .08$, $n = 25$

15. $R = 46,000$, $i = .06$, $n = 32$ *46000 S₃₂⌐.06*

16. $R = 29,500$, $i = .05$, $n = 15$

Find the future value of each of the ordinary annuities in Exercises 17–22. Payments are made and interest is compounded as given.

18. 12 ÷ 2 = 6%, d = 3700 S₂₂⌐.06
11 × 2 = 22"

17. $R = 9200$, 16% interest compounded semiannually for 7 years

18. $R = 3700$, 12% interest compounded semiannually for 11 years

19. $R = 800$, 12% interest compounded semiannually for 12 years

20. $R = 4600$, 16% interest compounded quarterly for 9 years

21. $R = 15,000$, 12% interest compounded quarterly for 6 years *12÷4=3% , 6×4=24 , 15000(34.42647)*

22. $R = 42,000$, 16% interest compounded semiannually for 12 years

In Exercises 23–26, find the future value of each annuity due. Assume that interest is compounded annually.

use for 12/6 (1+6) = 7 for the years

23. $R = 600$, $i = .06$, $n = 8$

24. $R = 1400$, $i = .08$, $n = 10$

25. $R = 20,000$, $i = .08$, $n = 6$

26. $R = 4000$, $i = .06$, $n = 11$

24. 1400 S₁₁⌐.08 (16.64549)
1400(16.64549) = 23303.686

In Exercises 27–30, find the future value of each annuity due.

Same as 24

27. payments of $1000 made at the beginning of each year for 9 years at 8% compounded annually *1000 S₁₀⌐.08 = 1000(14.48656)* *14486.56 − 1000 = 13486.56* *23303.686 − 1400 = 21903.686*

28. $750 deposited at the beginning of each year for 15 years at 6% compounded annually

29. $100 deposited at the beginning of each quarter for 9 years at 16% compounded quarterly

30. $1500 deposited at the beginning of each semiannual period for 11 years at 16% compounded semiannually *22 yrs. 16/2 = 8%* *A = 1500 S₂₃⌐.08* *Same as 27.*

In Exercises 31–33, find the periodic payment that will amount to the given sums under the given conditions.

31. $A = \$10,000$, interest is 8% compounded annually, payments made at the end of each year for 12 years

32. $A = \$100,000$, interest is 16% compounded semiannually, payments made at the end of each semiannual period for 9 years

33. $A = \$50,000$, interest is 12% compounded quarterly, payments made at the end of each quarter for 8 years *4×8 = 32 i = 3%* *50,000 = r S₃₂⌐.03*

34. Pat Dillon deposits $12,000 at the end of each year for 9 years in an account paying 8% interest compounded annually. Find the final amount she will have on deposit. *1200 Sq⌐.08 ≟ 149850.72*

37. $A = R\left[\dfrac{(1+i)^{n+1} - 1}{i} - 1\right] - R = 2435\left[\dfrac{1.06^{17}-1}{.06}\right] - 2435$

when at beginning use (6+1) 7

1.70985

35. Pat's brother-in-law works in a bank which pays 6% compounded annually. If she deposits her money in this bank, instead of the one of Exercise 34, how much will she have in her account?

12000 597.00 = 137895.84

36. How much would Pat lose over 9 years by using her brother-in-law's bank? (See Exercises 34 and 35.)

149850.72
− 137895.84
11,954.88

✗ 37. Pam Parker deposits $2435 at the beginning of each semiannual period for 8 years in an account paying 12% compounded semiannually. She then leaves that money alone, with no further deposits, for an additional 5 years. Find the final amount on deposit after the entire 13-year period.

annuity due

66,265.86 × 1.79035

$\frac{$10.06}$

38. Chuck deposits $10,000 at the beginning of each year for 12 years in an account paying 8% compounded annually. He then puts the total amount on deposit in another account paying 12% compounded semiannually for another 9 years. Find the final amount on deposit after the entire 21-year period.

39/ 10,000 = a
32 4's 4 %o i
10,000 = R · 5327.04
10,000 / 62.70147 = r

39. Ray Berkowitz needs $10,000 in 8 years. What amount can he deposit at the end of each quarter at 16% compounded quarterly so that he will have his $10,000?

42/ 12,000 = a
8 4's   8 %o i
12000 = r 587.08

40. Find Berkowitz's quarterly deposit (see Exercise 39) if the money is deposited at 12% compounded quarterly.

41. Barb Silverman wants to buy an $18,000 car in 6 years. How much money must she deposit at the end of each quarter in an account paying 12% compounded quarterly, so that she will have enough to pay for her car?

42. Harv's Meats knows that it must buy a new deboner machine in 4 years. The machine costs $12,000. In order to accumulate enough money to pay for the machine, Harv decides to deposit a sum of money at the end of each six months in an account paying 16% compounded semiannually. How much should each payment be?

Recent tax law changes have made Individual Retirement Accounts (IRA's) available to a great many workers. Under these plans, a person can currently deposit $2000 annually, with taxes deferred on the principal and interest. To attract these deposits, banks have been advertising the amount that will accumulate at retirement. Suppose a 40-year-old deposits $2000 per year until age 65. Find the total in the account with the following assumptions of interest rates. (Assume semiannual compounding with payment made at the end of each semiannual period.)

Don't have to times it hereby R
43. 5507.03
45. 5507.65
209.348

43. 6%   **44.** 8%   **45.** 10%   **46.** 12%

Find the amount of each payment to be made into a sinking fund so that enough will be present to pay off the indicated loans.

48. $8500 = R\left[\dfrac{(1.08)^7 - 1}{.08}\right]$

47. loan $2000, money earns 6% compounded annually, 5 annual payments

48. loan $8500, money earns 8% compounded annually, 7 annual payments

49. loan $11,000, money earns 16% compounded semiannually, for 6 years

51. $50,000 = R\left[\dfrac{1.04^{10} - 1}{ }\right]$

50,000 / 12.00610712 = 4164.547

50. loan $75,000, money earns 12% compounded semiannually, for 4 1/2 years

51. loan $50,000, money earns 16% compounded quarterly, for 2 1/2 years

52. loan $25,000, money earns 12% compounded quarterly, for 3 1/2 years

54. 9000 = R 530 7 ⌐15 ⌐ (.015)

53. loan $6000, money earns 18% compounded monthly, for 3 years

54. loan $9000, money earns 18% compounded monthly, for 2 1/2 years

9000 / 37.53868 = 239.75

Find the final amount of the annuities in Exercises 55 and 56.

55. $892.17 a month for 2 years in an account paying 7.5% interest compounded monthly

56. $2476.32 each quarter for 5.5 years at 7.81% interest compounded quarterly.

57. Jill Streitsel sells some land in Nevada. She will be paid a lump sum of $60,000 in 7 years. Until then, the buyer pays 8% interest, quarterly.

   (a) Find the amount of each quarterly interest payment.

   (b) The buyer sets up a sinking fund so that enough money will be present to pay off the $60,000. The buyer wants to make semiannual payments into the sinking fund; the account pays 6% compounded semiannually. Find the amount of each payment into the fund.

   (c) Prepare a table showing the amount in the sinking fund after each deposit.

58. Jeff Reschke bought a rare stamp for his collection. He agreed to pay a lump sum of $4000 after 5 years. Until then, he pays 6% interest, compounded semiannually.

   (a) Find the amount of each semiannual interest payment.

   (b) Reschke sets up a sinking fund so that enough money will be present to pay off the $4000. He wants to make annual payments into the fund. The account pays 8% compounded annually. Find the amount of each payment into the fund.

   (c) Prepare a table showing the amount in the sinking fund after each deposit.

10.5   Present Value of an Annuity; Amortization

As shown in the previous section, if deposits of R dollars are made at the end of each period for n periods, at a rate of interest i per period, then the account will contain

$$A = R \cdot s_{\overline{n}|i} = R\left[\frac{(1 + i)^n - 1}{i}\right]$$

dollars after n periods. Let us now find the *lump sum P* that can be deposited today at a rate of interest i per period which will amount to the same A dollars in n periods.

First recall that P dollars deposited today will amount to $P(1 + i)^n$ dollars after n periods at a rate of interest i per period. We want this amount, $P(1 + i)^n$, to be the same as A, the future value of the annuity. Substituting $P(1 + i)^n$ for A in the formula above gives

$$P(1 + i)^n = R\left[\frac{(1 + i)^n - 1}{i}\right].$$

To solve this equation for P, multiply both sides by $(1 + i)^{-n}$.

$$P = R(1 + i)^{-n}\left[\frac{(1 + i)^n - 1}{i}\right]$$

Use the distributive property; also recall $(1 + i)^{-n}(1 + i)^n = 1$.

$$P = R\left[\frac{(1 + i)^{-n}(1 + i)^n - (1 + i)^{-n}}{i}\right]$$

$$P = R\left[\frac{1 - (1 + i)^{-n}}{i}\right]$$

The amount P is called the **present value of the annuity.** The quantity in brackets is abbreviated as $a_{\overline{n}|i}$, so

$$a_{\overline{n}|i} = \frac{1 - (1 + i)^{-n}}{i}.$$

Values of $a_{\overline{n}|i}$ are given in the table "Present Value of an Annuity," at the back of this text. The next box summarizes the formula for the present value of an annuity.

Present Value of an **Annuity**	The present value, P, of an annuity of n payments of R dollars each at the end of consecutive interest periods with interest compounded at a rate of interest i per period is $$P = R\left[\frac{1 - (1 + i)^{-n}}{i}\right] \quad \text{or} \quad P = R \cdot a_{\overline{n}|i}$$

EXAMPLE 1

What lump sum deposited today at 8% interest compounded annually will yield the same total amount as payments of $1500 at the end of each year for 12 years, also at 8% interest compounded annually?

We want to find the present value of an annuity of $1500 per year for 12 years at 8% compounded annually. Using the table or a calculator, $a_{\overline{12}|.08} = 7.53608$, so

$$P = 1500(7.53608) \approx 11,304.12$$

or $11,304.12. A lump sum deposit of $11,304.12 today at 8% compounded annually will yield the same total after 12 years as deposits of $1500 at the end of each year for 12 years at 8% compounded annually.

Let's check this result. The compound amount in 12 years of a deposit of $11,304.12 today at 8% compounded annually can be found by the formula $A = P(1 + i)^n$. From the compound interest table, $11,304.12 will produce a total of

$$(11,304.12)(2.51817) \approx 28,465.70,$$

or $28,465.70. On the other hand, from the table for $s_{\overline{n}|i}$, deposits of $1500 at the end of each year for 12 years, at 8% compounded annually, give an amount of

$$1500(18.97713) \approx 28,465.70,$$

or $28,465.70, the same amount found above.

In summary, there are two ways to have $28,465.70 in 12 years at 8% compounded annually—a single deposit of $11,304.12 today, or payments of $1500 at the end of each year for 12 years. ▪

EXAMPLE 2

Mr. Jones and Ms. Gonsalez are both graduates of the Forestvire Institute of Technology. They both agree to contribute to the endowment fund of FIT. Mr. Jones says that he will give $500 at the end of each year for 9 years. Ms. Gonsalez would rather give a lump sum today. What lump sum can she give that will be equivalent to Mr. Jones' annual gifts, if the endowment fund earns 8% compounded annually?

Here $R = 500$, $n = 9$, and $i = .08$. The necessary number from the present value table or a calculator is $a_{\overline{9}|.08} = 6.24689$. Ms. Gonsalez must therefore donate a lump sum of

$$500(6.24689) \approx 3123.45,$$

or $3123.45, today. ■

We can also use the formula above if we know the lump sum and want to find the periodic payment of the annuity. The next example shows how to do this.

EXAMPLE 3

A car costs $6000. After a down payment of $1000, the balance will be paid off in 36 monthly payments with interest of 12% per year, compounded monthly. Find the amount of each payment.

A single lump sum payment of $5000 today would pay off the loan. Thus, $5000 is the present value of an annuity of 36 monthly payments with interest of $12\%/12 = 1\%$ per month. We need to find R, the amount of each payment. Start with $P = R \cdot a_{\overline{n}|i}$; replace P with 5000, n with 36, and i with .01. From the table or a calculator, $a_{\overline{36}|.01} = 30.10751$, so

$$5000 = R(30.10751)$$

$$R \approx 166.07,$$

or $166.07. A monthly payment of $166.07 will be needed. ■

 Amortization   A loan is **amortized** if both the principal and interest are paid by a sequence of equal periodic payments. In Example 3 above, a loan of $5000 at 12% interest compounded monthly could be amortized by paying $166.07 per month for 36 months.

EXAMPLE 4

A speculator agrees to pay $15,000 for a parcel of land; this amount, with interest, will be paid over 4 years, with semiannual payments, at an interest rate of 12% compounded semiannually.

(a)   Find the amount of each payment.

If the speculator were to pay $15,000 immediately, there would be no need for any payments at all, making $15,000 the present value of an annuity of R dollars, $2 \cdot 4 = 8$ periods, and $i = 12\%/2 = 6\% = .06$ per period. Using $P = R \cdot a_{\overline{n}|i}$, in our example $P = 15,000$, with

$$15,000 = R \cdot a_{\overline{8}|.06}$$

or

$$R = \frac{15,000}{a_{\overline{8}|.06}}.$$

From the table or a calculator, $a_{\overline{8}|.06} = 6.20979$, and

$$R = \frac{15{,}000}{6.20979} \approx 2415.54,$$

or $2415.54. Each payment is $2415.54.

(b) Find the portion of the first payment that is applied to the reduction of the debt.

Interest is 12% per year, compounded semiannually, or 6% per semiannual period. During the first period, the entire $15,000 is owed. Interest on this amount for 6 months (1/2 year) is found by the formula for simple interest:

$$I = Prt = 15{,}000(.12)\left(\frac{1}{2}\right) = 900,$$

or $900. At the end of 6 months, the speculator makes a payment of $2415.54; since $900 of this represents interest, a total of

$$\$2415.54 - \$900 = \$1515.54$$

is applied to the reduction of the original debt.

(c) Find the balance due after 6 months.

The original balance due is $15,000. After 6 months, $1515.54 is applied to reduction of the debt. The debt owed after 6 months is

$$\$15{,}000 - \$1515.54 = \$13{,}484.46.$$

(d) How much interest is owed for the second six-month period?

A total of $13,484.46 is owed for the second 6 months. Interest on it is

$$I = 13{,}484.46\,(.12)\left(\frac{1}{2}\right) = 809.07,$$

or $809.07. A payment of $2415.54 is made at the end of this period; a total of

$$\$2415.54 - \$809.07 = \$1606.47$$

is applied to reduction of the debt.

By continuing this process, we get the **amortization schedule** shown below. As the schedule shows, the payment is always the same, except perhaps for a small adjustment in the final payment. Payment 0 is the original amount of the loan. ▪

Amortization Schedule

Payment number	Amount of payment	Interest for period	Portion to principal	Principal at end of period
0	—	—	—	$15,000.00
1	$2415.54	$900.00	$1515.54	$13,484.46
2	$2415.54	$809.07	$1606.47	$11,877.99
3	$2415.54	$712.68	$1702.86	$10,175.13
4	$2415.54	$610.51	$1805.03	$8370.10
5	$2415.54	$502.21	$1913.33	$6456.77
6	$2415.54	$387.41	$2028.13	$4428.64
7	$2415.54	$265.72	$2149.82	$2278.82
8	$2415.55	$136.73	$2278.82	$0

EXAMPLE 5

A house is bought for $74,000, with a down payment of $16,000. Interest is charged at 10.25% per year for 30 years. Find the amount of each monthly payment to amortize the loan.

Here, the present value, P, is 58,000 (or 74,000 − 16,000). Also, $i =$ .1025/12 = .0085416667, and $n = 12 \cdot 30 = 360$. We must find R. From the formula for the present value of an annuity,

$$58,000 = R \cdot a_{\overline{360}|.0085416667}$$

or

$$58,000 = R\left[\frac{1 - (1 + .0085416667)^{-360}}{.0085416667}\right].$$

Use a financial calculator, or a calculator with an x^y key to get

$$58,000 = R\left[\frac{1 - .0467967624}{.0085416667}\right]$$

$$58,000 = R\left[\frac{.9532032376}{.0085416667}\right]$$

$$58,000 = R[111.5945249]$$

or

$$R = 519.74.$$

Monthly payments of $519.74 will be required to amortize the loan. ▪

Do 1 - 42 odd. !

10.5 EXERCISES

Use very last page.

Find each of the values in Exercises 1−8.

1. $a_{\overline{15}|.06}$ *9.71225.*   **2.** $a_{\overline{10}|.03}$ **3.** $a_{\overline{18}|.04}$ **4.** $a_{\overline{30}|.01}$

5. $a_{\overline{16}|.01}$ **6.** $a_{\overline{32}|.02}$ **7.** $a_{\overline{6}|.015}$ **8.** $a_{\overline{18}|.015}$
                                                              5.69719.

Find the present value of each ordinary annuity in Exercises 9−16.

9. Payments of $1000 are made annually for 9 years at 8% compounded annually.   *9. A = r a̅ₙ⁷ᵢ*
                                                                                      = 1000 a 9 .08
10. Payments of $5000 are made annually for 11 years at 6% compounded annually.

11. Payments of $890 are made annually for 16 years at 8% compounded annually.

12. Payments of $1400 are made annually for 8 years at 8% compounded annually.

13. Payments of $10,000 are made semiannually for 15 years at 10% compounded semiannually.

14. Payments of $50,000 are made quarterly for 10 years at 8% compounded quarterly.

15. Payments of $15,806 are made quarterly for 3 years at 15.8% compounded quarterly.

16. Payments of $18,579 are made every six months for 8 years at 19.4% compounded semiannually.

In Exercises 17−22, find the lump sum deposited today that will yield the same total amount as payments of $10,000 at the end of each year for 15 years, at each of the given interest rates.   *17. d = 10,000 (a̅15|.04)*

17. 4%, compounded annually   **18.** 5%, compounded annually

19. 6%, compounded annually   **20.** 8%, compounded annually

21. 12%, compounded annually   **22.** 16%, compounded annually

23. In his will the late Mr. Hudspeth said that each child in his family could have an annuity of $2000 at the end of each year for 9 years, or the equivalent present value. If money can be deposited at 8% compounded annually, what is the present value?

24. In the "Million Dollar Lottery," a winner is paid a million dollars at the rate of $50,000 per year for 20 years. Assume that these payments form an ordinary annuity, and that the lottery managers can invest money at 6% compounded annually. Find the lump sum that the management must put away to pay off the "million dollar" winner.

25. Lynn Meyers buys a new car costing $6000. She agrees to make payments at the end of each monthly period for 4 years. If she pays 12% interest, compounded monthly, what is the amount of each payment?

26. Find the total amount of interest Meyers will pay. (See Exercise 25.)

27. What sum deposited today at 5% compounded annually for 8 years will provide the same amount as $1000 deposited at the end of each year for 8 years at 6% compounded annually?

28. What lump sum deposited today at 8% compounded quarterly for 10 years will yield the same final amount as deposits of $4000 at the end of each six month period for 10 years at 6% compounded semiannually?

Find the payment necessary to amortize each of the loans in Exercises 29–36.

29. $1000, 8% compounded annually, 9 annual payments

30. $2500, 16% compounded quarterly, 6 quarterly payments

31. $41,000, 12% compounded semiannually, 10 semiannual payments

32. $90,000, 8% compounded annually, 12 annual payments

33. $140,000, 12% compounded quarterly, 15 quarterly payments

34. $7400, 16% compounded semiannually, 18 semiannual payments

35. $5500, 18% compounded monthly, 24 monthly payments

36. $45,000, 18% compounded monthly, 36 monthly payments

Find the monthly house payment necessary to amortize the loans in Exercises 37–40. You will need a financial calculator or one with an x^y key.

37. $49,560 at 15.75% for 25 years

38. $70,892 at 14.11% for 30 years

39. $53,762 at 16.45% for 30 years

40. $96,511 at 15.57% for 25 years

41. An insurance firm pays $4000 for a new printer for its computer. It amortizes the loan for the printer in 4 annual payments at 8% compounded annually. Prepare an amortization schedule for this machine.

42. Large semitrailer trucks cost $72,000 each. Ace Trucking buys such a truck and agrees to pay for it by a loan which will be amortized with 9 semiannual payments at 16% compounded semiannually. Prepare an amortization schedule for this truck.

43. One retailer charges $1048 for a correcting electric typewriter. A firm of tax accountants buys 8 of these machines. They make a down payment of $1200 and agree to amortize the balance with monthly payments at 18% compounded monthly for 4 years. Prepare an amortization schedule showing the first six payments.

44. When Denise Sullivan opened her law office, she bought $14,000 worth of law books and $7200 worth of office furniture. She paid $1200 down and agreed to amortize the balance with semiannual payments for 5 years, at 16% compounded semiannually. Prepare an amortization schedule for this purchase.

45. When Ms. Thompson died, she left $25,000 for her husband. He deposits the money at 6% compounded annually. He wants to make annual withdrawals from the account so that the money (principal and interest) is gone in exactly 8 years.

(a) Find the amount of each withdrawal.

(b) Find the amount of each withdrawal if the money must last 12 years.

46. The trustees of a college have accepted a gift of $150,000. The donor has directed the trustees to deposit the money in an account paying 12% per year, compounded semiannually. The trustees may withdraw money at the end of each 6-month period; the money must last 5 years.

(a) Find the amount of each withdrawal.

(b) Find the amount of each withdrawal if the money must last 6 years.

Prepare an amortization schedule for each of the following problems.

47. A loan of $37,947.50 with interest at 8.5% compounded annually, to be paid with equal annual payments over 10 years.

48. A loan of $4835.80 at 9.25% interest compounded semiannually, to be repaid in 5 years in equal semiannual payments.

EXTENDED

APPLICATION

A New Look at Athletes' Contracts*

There has been a lot of controversy lately about big-buck contracts with athletes and how this affects the nature of the sports business.

Indeed, the recent headlines of a $40 million contract with Steve Young from Brigham Young University to play football for the USFL has opened Pandora's box. Club owners in all sports are wondering when all of this is going to stop.

To put the issue in its proper perspective, however, it seems to me that the $40 million contract is misleading. Just mentioning dollars misses several points. For one, the USFL has got to be around long enough to pay off. Two, the present value of million dollar payments that stretch 43 years into the future is reduced considerably.

In order to assess the effective value of these kinds of contracts, two important questions must be answered. First, what is the risk of the company to pay off on the periodic principal payments; and second, what is the present value of the return when parlayed into future cash benefits?

Recently, I conducted a survey among a number of sports-minded educators and students here on the campus. The survey was similar to the rating survey conducted by Wall Street rating firms when they evaluate risk of a corporation.

Specifically, the question was: "On a scale of 1 to 10, give me your estimate of the team's ability to continue in business and to meet the commitments of its contracts."

---

*From "A New Look at Athletes' Contracts" by Richard F. Kaufman in *The Sacramento Bee,* April 30, 1984. Reprinted by permission of the author.

I was surprised to find that the baseball teams were rated with the lowest risk; the National Football League teams next; then the National Basketball Association teams; and then the United States Football League teams coming in last.

The cash flows which these athletes receive in the future have a present value today in total dollars based upon about an 8 percent discount factor each year for expected inflation. By determining the expected present value, the average per annum return of Athlete A who receives megabucks in the future can be compared with Athlete B who receives megabucks not so far into the future.

When risk of paying these megabucks is considered, we arrive at a completely different picture than just the dollar signs on the contract portray.

The following chart of the highly paid athletes, recently taken from a newspaper article, shows the athletes' names in sequence according to the best deal when risk and expected yearly return are assessed. A lesser coefficient of variation provides a statistical ratio of lesser risk to the per annum return for each athlete for each dollar of present value.

Notice that these risk assumptions show George Foster of the New York Mets with the best deal. Dave Winfield and Gary Carter are close behind. Steve Young is last, yet it is claimed that he received the most attractive sports contract ever signed.

Some Highly Paid Athletes

	Present Value		Per Annum	
	of Contract (In Millions)	Expected Value	Risk Assessment	Coefficient of Variation
George Foster NL (Mets) $10 million, 5 years	$ 7.985	$1.597	2.3	1.44
Dave Winfield AL (Yankees) $21 million, 10 years	$14.091	$1.409	2.6	1.85
Gary Carter NL (Expos) $15 million, 8 years	$10.775	$1.347	3.0	2.23
Moses Malone NBA (76ers) $13.2 million, 6 years	$10.170	$1.695	5.4	3.19
Larry Bird NBA (Celtics) $15 million, 7 years	$11.157	$1.594	5.2	3.26
Wayne Gretzky NHL (Edmonton Oilers) $21 million, 21 years	$10.170	$ .477	5.8	12.16
Magic Johnson NBA (Lakers) $25 million, 25 years	$10.675	$ .427	5.6	13.12
Steve Young USFL (Express) $40 million, 43 years	$11.267	$ .262	7.2	27.48

It is true that risk is only our perception of the uncertainties of future events, and many times our judgment is wrong. But let's face it. It is the only game in town, unless you are gifted with extrasensory perception or have a crystal ball. In that case, I would appreciate your contacting me because I have work for you.

Anytime we purchase a bond or a like security, we make judgments about the future ability of the firm or municipality to meet its interest and principal payments. We employ expert rating agencies like Moody's or Standard & Poor's to professionally rate these securities. Indeed, the market price of the bond depends upon the judgments of these agencies.

It would seem to me that the time is long overdue for a similar rating system to be implemented to determine the risk of sports organizations—if for no other reason than to help the athlete decide where he would like to hang his hat. But more importantly, to provide a truer financial picture to the fans and broadcasting companies who are asked to pick up the tab. What do you think?

EXTENDED

APPLICATION

Present Value*

The Southern Pacific Railroad, with lines running from Oregon to Louisiana, is one of the country's most profitable railroads. The railroad has vast landholdings (granted by the government in the last half of the nineteenth century) and is diversified into trucking, pipelines, and data transmission.

The railroad was recently faced with a decision on the fate of an old bridge which crosses the Kings River in central California. The bridge is on a minor line which carries very little traffic. Just north of the Southern Pacific bridge is another bridge, owned by the Santa Fe Railroad; it too carries little traffic. The Southern Pacific had two alternatives: it could replace its own bridge or it could negotiate with the Santa Fe for the rights to run trains over its bridge. In the second alternative a yearly fee would be paid to the Santa Fe, and new connecting tracks would be built. The situation is shown in the figure.

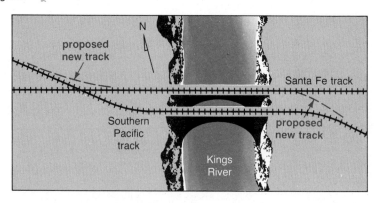

---

*Based on information supplied by The Southern Pacific Transportation Company, San Francisco.

To find the better of these two alternatives, the railroad used the following approach.

1. Calculate estimated expenses for each alternative.
2. Calculate annual cash flows in after tax dollars. At a 48% corporate tax rate, $1 of expenses actually costs the railroad $.52, and $1 of revenue can bring a maximum of $.52 in profit. Cash flow for a given year is found by the following formula.

$$\text{cash flow} = -.52 \text{ (operating and maintenance expenses)}$$
$$+ .52 \text{ (savings and revenue)} + .48 \text{ (depreciation)}$$

3. Calculate the net present values of all cash flows for future years. The formula used is

$$\text{net present value} = \Sigma \,(\text{cash flow in year } i\,)(1 + k)^{1-i},$$

where i is a particular year in the life of the project and k is the assumed annual rate of interest. (Recall: Σ indicates a sum.) The net present value is found for interest rates from 0% to 20%.
4. The interest rate that leads to a net present value of $0 is called the **rate of return** on the project.

Let us now see how these steps worked out in practice.

Alternative 1: Operate over the Santa Fe bridge   First, estimated expenses were calculated.

1976	Work done by Southern Pacific on Santa Fe track	$27,000
1976	Work by Southern Pacific on its own track	11,600
1976	Undepreciated portion of cost of current bridge	97,410
1976	Salvage value of bridge	12,690
1977	Annual maintenance of Santa Fe track	16,717
1977	Annual rental fee to Santa Fe	7,382

From these figures and others not given here, annual cash flows and net present values were calculated. The following table was then prepared.

Interest Rate, %	Net Present Value
0	$85,731
4	67,566
8	53,332
12	42,008
16	32,875
20	25,414

Although the table does not show a net present value of $0, the interest rate that leads to that value is 44%. This is the rate of return for this alternative.

Alternative 2: Build a new bridge   Again, estimated expenses were calculated.

1976	Annual maintenance	$2,870
1976	Annual inspection	120
1976	Repair trestle	17,920
1977	Install bridge	189,943
1977	Install walks and handrails	15,060
1978	Repaint steel (every 10 years)	10,000
1978	Repair trusses (every 10 years, increases by $200)	2,000
1981	Replace ties	31,000
1988	Repair concrete (every 10 years)	400
2021	Replace ties	31,000

After cash flows and net present values were calculated, the following table was prepared.

Interest Rate, %	Net Present Value
0	$399,577
4	96,784
7.8	0
8	−3,151
12	−43,688
16	−62,615
20	−72,126

In this alternative the net present value is $0 at 7.8%, the rate of return.

Based on this analysis, the first alternative, renting from the Santa Fe, is clearly preferable.

EXERCISES

Find the cash flow in each of the following years. Use the formula given above.

1. Alternative 1, year 1977, operating expenses $6228, maintenance expenses $2976, savings $26,251, depreciation $10,778

2. Alternative 1, year 1984, same as Exercise 1, but depreciation is only $1347

3. Alternative 2, year 1976, maintenance $2870, operating expenses $6386, savings $26,251, no depreciation

4. Alternative 2, year 1980, operating expenses $6228, maintenance expenses $2976, savings $10,618, depreciation $6736

KEY WORDS

simple interest	discount interest	common difference
principal	proceeds	geometric sequence
rate	compound interest	common ratio
time	compound amount	annuity
future value	effective rate	ordinary annuity
maturity value	sequence	term of an annuity
ordinary interest	terms	annuity due
exact interest	general term	sinking fund
present value	arithmetic sequence	amortization

Chapter 10   REVIEW EXERCISES

Many of these exercises will require a calculator with an x^y key.

Find the simple interest in Exercises 1–6.

1. $15,903 at 18% for 8 months

2. $4902 at 19.5% for 11 months

3. $42,368 at 15.22% for 5 months

4. $3478 at 17.4% for 88 days (assume a 360-day year)

5. $2390 at 18.7% from May 3 to July 28 (assume 365 days in a year)

6. $69,056.12 at 15.5% from September 13 to March 25 of the following year (assume a 365-day year)

Find the present value of the future amounts in Exercises 7–9. Assume 360 days in a year; use simple interest.

7. $25,000 for 10 months, money earns 17%

8. $459.57 for 7 months, money earns 18.5%

9. $80,612 for 128 days, money earns 16.77%

Find the proceeds in Exercises 10–12. Assume 360 days in a year.

10. $56,882, discount rate 19%, length of loan 5 months

11. $802.34, discount rate 18.6%, length of loan 11 months

12. $12,000, discount rate 17.09%, length of loan 145 days

13. Tom Wilson owes $5800 to his mother. He has agreed to pay the money in 10 months, at an interest rate of 14%. Three months before the loan is due, the mother discounts the loan at the bank. The bank charges a 17.45% discount rate. How much money does the mother receive?

14. Larry DiCenso needs $9812 to buy new equipment for his business. The bank charges a discount of 14%. Find the amount of DiCenso's loan, if he borrows the money for 7 months.

Find the effective annual rate for the bank discount rates in Exercise 15 and 16. (Assume a one-year loan of $1000.)

15. 14%   **16.** 17.5%

Find the compound amounts in Exercises 17–24.

17. $1000 at 8% compounded annually for 9 years

18. $2800 at 6% compounded annually for 10 years

19. $19,456.11 at 12% compounded semiannually for 7 years

20. $312.45 at 16% compounded semiannually for 16 years

21. $1900 at 16% compounded quarterly for 9 years

22. $57,809.34 at 12% compounded quarterly for 5 years

23. $2500 at 18% compounded monthly for 3 years

24. $11,702.55 at 18% compounded monthly for 4 years

Find the amount of interest earned by each deposit in Exercises 25–30.

25. $3954 at 8% compounded annually for 12 years

26. $12,699.36 at 16% compounded semiannually for 7 years

27. $7801.72 at 12% compounded quarterly for 5 years

28. $48,121.91 at 18% compounded monthly for 2 years

29. $12,903.45 at 12.37% compounded quarterly for 29 quarters

30. $34,677.23 at 14.72% compounded monthly for 32 months

Find the present value of the amounts given in Exercises 31–36 if money can be invested at the given rate.

31. $5000 in 9 years, 8% compounded annually

32. $12,250 in 5 years, 12% compounded semiannually

33. $42,000 in 7 years, 18% compounded monthly

34. $17,650 in 4 years, 16% compounded quarterly

35. $1347.89 in 3.5 years, 13.77% compounded semiannually

36. $2388.90 in 44 months, 12.93% compounded monthly

37. In four years, Mr. Heeren must pay a pledge of $5000 to his church's building fund. What lump sum can he invest today, at 12% compounded semiannually, so that he will have enough to pay his pledge?

38. Joann Hudspeth must make an alimony payment of $1500 in 15 months. What lump sum can she invest today, at 18% compounded monthly, so that she will have enough to make the payment?

Write the first five terms for each of the sequences in Exercises 39–42. Identify any which are arithmetic or geometric.

39. $a_n = -4n + 2$ **40.** $a_n = (-2)^n$

41. $a_n = \dfrac{n + 2}{n + 5}$ **42.** $a_n = (n - 7)(n + 5)$

43. Find a_{12} for the arithmetic sequence having $a_1 = 6$ and $d = 5$.

44. Find the sum of the first 20 terms for the arithmetic sequence having $a_1 = -6$ and $d = 8$.

45. Find a_4 for the geometric sequence with $a_1 = -3$ and $r = 2$.

46. Find the sum of the first 6 terms for the geometric sequence with $a_1 = 8000$ and $r = -1/2$.

Find the value of each of the annuities in Exercises 47–52.

47. $500 is deposited at the end of each six month period for 8 years; money earns 16% compounded semiannually

48. $1288 is deposited at the end of each year for 14 years; money earns 8% compounded annually

49. $4000 is deposited at the end of each quarter for 7 years; money earns 16% compounded quarterly

50. $233 is deposited at the end of each month for 4 years; money earns 18% compounded monthly

51. $672 is deposited at the beginning of each quarter for 7 years; money earns 20% compounded quarterly

52. $11,900 is deposited at the beginning of each month for 13 months; money earns 18% compounded monthly

53. Georgette Dahl deposits $491 at the end of each quarter for 9 years. If the account pays 19.4% compounded quarterly, find the final amount in the account.

54. J. Euclid deposits $1526.38 at the beginning of each six-month period in an account paying 20.6% compounded semiannually. How much will be in the account after five years?

In Exercises 55–58 find the amount of each payment to be made into a sinking fund so that enough money will be available to pay off the indicated loan.

55. $6500 loan, money earns 8% compounded annually, 6 annual payments

56. $57,000 loan, money earns 16% compounded semiannually, for 8 1/2 years

57. $233,188 loan, money earns 19.7% compounded quarterly, for 7 3/4 years

58. $1,056,788 loan, money earns 18.12% compounded monthly, for 4 1/2 years

Find the present value of each ordinary annuity in Exercises 59–62.

59. Payments of $850 are made annually for 4 years at 8% compounded annually.

60. Payments of $1500 are made quarterly for 7 years, at 16% compounded quarterly.

61. Payments of $4210 are made semiannually for 8 years, at 18.6% compounded semiannually.

62. Payments of $877.34 are made monthly for 17 months, at 22.4% compounded monthly.

63. Vicki Manchester borrows $20,000 from the bank to help her expand her business. She agrees to repay the money in equal payments at the end of each year for 9 years. Interest is at 18.9% compounded annually. Find the amount of each payment.

64. Ken Murrill wants to expand his pharmacy. To do this, he takes out a loan of $49,275 from the bank, and agrees to repay it at 24.2% compounded monthly, over 48 months. Find the amount of each payment necessary to amortize this loan.

Find the amount of the payment necessary to amortize the loans in Exercises 65–68.

65. $80,000 loan, 8% compounded annually, 9 annual payments

66. $3200 loan, 16% compounded quarterly, 10 quarterly payments

67. $32,000 loan, 19.4% compounded quarterly, 17 quarterly payments

68. $51,607 loan, 23.6% compounded monthly, 32 monthly payments

Find the monthly house payments for the mortgages in Exercises 69 and 70.

69. $56,890 at 14.74% for 25 years

70. $77,110 at 16.45% for 30 years

Prepare amortization schedules for the following loans.

71. $5000 at 10% compounded semiannually, for 3 years

72. $12,500 at 12% compounded quarterly, for 2 years

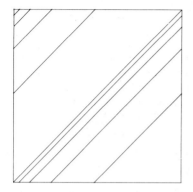 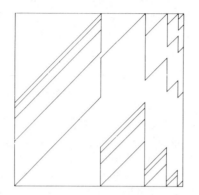 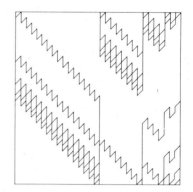

DIGRAPHS AND NETWORKS

Karl Gerstner. Drawings from *Diagon 31*^{2}, *Red/Green*, alterable object, 1956.

453

One area of fairly recent mathematics has found increasing application in social sciences and management. A brief introduction to this branch of mathematics, called **graph theory,** is given in this chapter. We must first mention that the use of the word *graph* in this chapter has no relationship to the word *graph* used earlier, as in "the graph of the equation $y = 2x + 5$." We give the alternate definition of a graph for this chapter in the first section.

11.1   Graphs and Digraphs

In each of the past few presidential election years, one party or the other has had a fairly large number of candidates competing in the presidential primaries held in the various states. Not all the candidates compete in each state. For example, candidates A and B might be the only candidates in one state primary, while another state race might see candidates A, C, and D on the ballot.

Suppose that in one year six candidates, A, B, C, D, E, and F, compete for the presidential nomination. Suppose also that after a few state primaries, the situation is as in the following table.

Candidate	Opponents
A	B, D, and F
B	A and D
C	no one
D	A, B, E, and F
E	D
F	A and D

The information of this table can also be given in a diagram, as in Figure 1, where each candidate is represented by a point, and each line connecting a pair of points represents a primary contest between the two candidates.

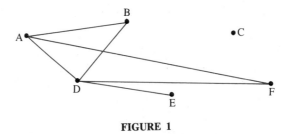

FIGURE 1

The diagram in Figure 1 is called a *graph*; each of the points *A*, *B*, *C*, *D*, *E*, and *F* is a *vertex*, and the lines *AB*, *AD*, *BD*, and so on, are called *edges*. While the edges in Figure 1 are straight lines, this is not at all necessary by definition. (Notice that the point where *DB* and *AF* cross is *not* a vertex.)

Graph

> A **graph** is made up of a finite number of **vertices** A, B, C, . . ., N, together with a finite number of **edges** AB, AC, BC, . . ., each joining a pair of vertices.

As shown in Figure 1, not all vertices have edges; there are no edges ending at vertex C, for example.

In our example of the presidential candidates, it is certainly possible that candidates A and B might run against each other in more than one state primary, so that more than one edge could connect vertices A and B.

EXAMPLE 1

Identify all vertices and edges.

(a)   The graph shown in Figure 2(a) has four vertices, A, B, C, and D, with edges AB, BC, CD, BD, and DB.

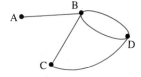

FIGURE 2(a)

FIGURE 2(b)

(b)   The four vertices in Figure 2(b) are M, N, P, and Q; the edges are MQ, QP, PN and NM.   ▧

It could be very useful to modify the graph of Figure 1 so that the *winner* of each election were indicated. Suppose that

A   defeated B and D, but lost to F;

B   defeated D and F, but lost to A;

C   did not run;

D   defeated E, but lost to A, B, and F;

E   lost to D;

F   defeated A and D, but lost to B.

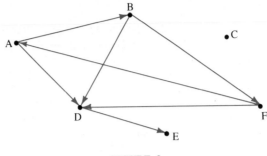

FIGURE 3

This information can be added to Figure 1 by making each edge into a **directed edge,** an edge with an arrowhead. The arrowhead points to the loser of each election. Figure 3 shows the modified graph.

The graph of Figure 3, with directed edges, is a *directed graph,* or *digraph.*

Digraph	A **directed graph,** or **digraph,** is made up of a finite number of vertices, A, B, C, . . ., N, together with a finite number of directed edges, AB, AC, BC, . . ., each joining a pair of vertices.

In a graph, the edge AB is the same as the edge BA. However, in a digraph, the order AB is used to show that the arrowhead points from A to B, so that AB is not the same as BA.

EXAMPLE 2

Identify all vertices and edges in each digraph in Figure 4.

(a) The vertices in Figure 4(a) are A, B, C, and D. The directed edges are AD, DA, AB, CB, and CD.

(b) The digraph in Figure 4(b) has vertices A, B, and C, with directed edges AC and CA. ▨

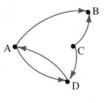

FIGURE 4(a)

FIGURE 4(b)

Matrix Representation of Digraphs   A matrix is a very useful way to represent the information in a graph or digraph. After a matrix is obtained from a digraph, the results of Chapter 2 can be used to obtain further information. A square matrix is obtained from a digraph by placing in row A and column B the number of directed edges from A to B. By the definition of a digraph, there can be only 0 entries in the row 1, column 1 position, the row 2 column 2 position, and so on.

Write a matrix corresponding to each digraph in Figure 5.

EXAMPLE 3

(a)   In Figure 5(a), there are two directed edges from A to C, so the number 2 is placed in row 1, column 3. Place 1 in row 1, column 2, because of the one directed edge from A to B; put 0 in row 2, column 1. Complete the matrix as follows.

$$
\begin{array}{c}
 \\ A \\ B \\ C \\ D
\end{array}
\begin{array}{cccc}
A & B & C & D \\
\left[\begin{array}{cccc}
0 & 1 & 2 & 0 \\
0 & 0 & 0 & 1 \\
0 & 0 & 0 & 1 \\
0 & 0 & 1 & 0
\end{array}\right]
\end{array}
$$

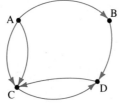

FIGURE 5(a)

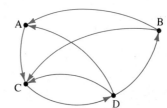

FIGURE 5(b)

(b)   The matrix for the digraph in Figure 5(b) is as follows.

$$
\begin{array}{c}
 \\ A \\ B \\ C \\ D
\end{array}
\begin{array}{cccc}
A & B & C & D \\
\left[\begin{array}{cccc}
0 & 0 & 1 & 0 \\
1 & 0 & 1 & 0 \\
0 & 0 & 0 & 1 \\
1 & 1 & 1 & 0
\end{array}\right]
\end{array}
$$

Note that this matrix contains only 0 and 1 as entries. Such a matrix is called an **adjacency matrix.**

11.1 EXERCISES

In Exercises 1–12, write a matrix for each digraph. Identify any adjacency matrices.

1.

2.
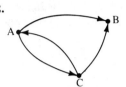

3.

4.
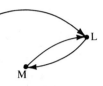

5.
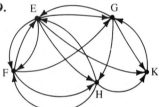

6.
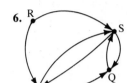

7.
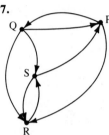

8.
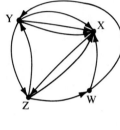

9.
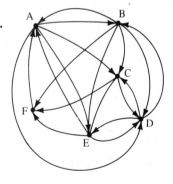

10.
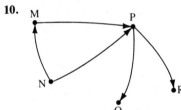

11.

12.
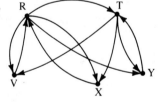

Sketch a digraph for each matrix in Exercises 13–22.

13. $\begin{bmatrix} 0 & 1 \\ 2 & 0 \end{bmatrix}$

14. $\begin{bmatrix} 0 & 1 \\ 1 & 0 \end{bmatrix}$

15. $\begin{bmatrix} 0 & 1 & 1 \\ 0 & 0 & 1 \\ 0 & 0 & 0 \end{bmatrix}$

16. $\begin{bmatrix} 0 & 0 & 1 \\ 1 & 0 & 1 \\ 1 & 1 & 0 \end{bmatrix}$

17. $\begin{bmatrix} 0 & 2 & 0 \\ 2 & 0 & 1 \\ 1 & 2 & 0 \end{bmatrix}$ **18.** $\begin{bmatrix} 0 & 1 & 2 \\ 0 & 0 & 1 \\ 2 & 0 & 0 \end{bmatrix}$ **19.** $\begin{bmatrix} 0 & 0 & 1 & 1 \\ 1 & 0 & 0 & 1 \\ 0 & 1 & 0 & 1 \\ 0 & 1 & 1 & 0 \end{bmatrix}$ **20.** $\begin{bmatrix} 0 & 1 & 0 & 0 \\ 0 & 0 & 1 & 1 \\ 1 & 1 & 0 & 0 \\ 1 & 0 & 1 & 0 \end{bmatrix}$

21. $\begin{bmatrix} 0 & 2 & 0 & 1 \\ 0 & 0 & 0 & 2 \\ 2 & 1 & 0 & 1 \\ 2 & 0 & 0 & 0 \end{bmatrix}$ **22.** $\begin{bmatrix} 0 & 1 & 1 & 2 \\ 0 & 0 & 1 & 0 \\ 2 & 0 & 0 & 1 \\ 0 & 1 & 0 & 0 \end{bmatrix}$

Draw a digraph and write a matrix for each of the following situations.

23. Among the four people, Al, Bill, Cynthia, and Donna, Al can't stand Bill or Cynthia, but likes Donna; Bill can't stand Al, but likes the other two; Cynthia doesn't like Bill or Donna, but likes Al, and Donna doesn't like anyone. No one dislikes himself or herself.

24. In a series of elections, A defeated B and C but lost to D, B defeated D but lost to A and C, C defeated D and B but lost to A, and D defeated A but lost to B and C.

11.2   Dominance Digraphs

The study of **dominance** is an important aspect of sociology and political science. In this study, it is assumed that given a pair A, B (A and B might represent people, or teams, for example) then either A dominates B, or B dominates A, but not both. Dominance would come up when studying prison gang violence, or in a tournament where each team in a league must play every other team exactly once, with no ties allowed.

As an example, the following chart shows the results of a tournament among five teams A, B, C, D, and E, where, for example, *AB* indicates a game between teams A and B.

Game	*AB*	*AC*	*AD*	*AE*	*BC*	*BD*	*BE*	*CD*	*CE*	*DE*
Winner	A	C	D	A	C	B	E	D	E	D

A digraph for this tournament is shown in Figure 6.

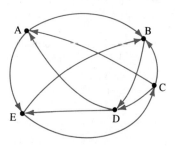

FIGURE 6

Notice that there is no transitive property for dominance. (Recall the transitivity property for "less than," for example: if $a < b$ and $b < c$, then $a < c$.) As shown previously, A dominates (won the game with) B, and B dominates D, but D dominates A.

The matrix corresponding to the digraph in Figure 6 is as follows.

$$
\begin{array}{c c}
& \begin{array}{c c c c c} A & B & C & D & E \end{array} \\
\begin{array}{c} A \\ B \\ C \\ D \\ E \end{array} &
\left[\begin{array}{c c c c c}
0 & 1 & 0 & 0 & 1 \\
0 & 0 & 0 & 1 & 0 \\
1 & 1 & 0 & 0 & 0 \\
1 & 0 & 1 & 0 & 1 \\
0 & 1 & 1 & 0 & 0
\end{array}\right]
\end{array}
$$

As mentioned at the end of Section 11.1, this matrix is an adjacency matrix. A matrix obtained from a dominance situation will always be an adjacency matrix, since either A dominates B, or B dominates A, but not both. Also, if the entry in row i and column j is 0 (where $i \neq j$), then the entry in row j and column i must be 1; if the entry in row i and column j is 1 (where $i \neq j$), then the entry in row j and column i must be 0. Such a matrix is called **asymmetric.** In summary,

> A digraph obtained from a dominance situation leads to a matrix which is an asymmetric adjacency matrix.

EXAMPLE 1

Each of the following matrices comes from a dominance situation. Complete the matrix.

(a)
$$
\begin{bmatrix} 0 & \\ 1 & 0 \end{bmatrix}
$$

Because the matrix obtained from a dominance situation must be asymmetric, the 1 in row 2, column 1 leads to a 0 in row 1, column 2. Complete the matrix as follows.

$$
\begin{bmatrix} 0 & 0 \\ 1 & 0 \end{bmatrix}
$$

(b)
$$
\begin{bmatrix} 0 & 1 & 1 \\ & 0 & 0 \\ & & 0 \end{bmatrix}
$$

The 1 in row 1, column 3 leads to 0 in row 3, column 1, and the 0 in row 2, column 3 leads to a 1 in row 3, column 2. Complete the matrix as follows.

$$
\begin{bmatrix} 0 & 1 & 1 \\ 0 & 0 & 0 \\ 0 & 1 & 0 \end{bmatrix}
$$

EXAMPLE 2

Write a matrix for the dominance situation in Figure 7. List all dominances.

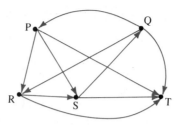

FIGURE 7

The directed edge from Q to P shows that Q dominates P; also, P dominates R, and Q dominates R. Entering 1 for such dominances and 0 for a lack of dominance leads to the following matrix.

$$
\begin{array}{c c c c c c}
 & P & Q & R & S & T \\
\begin{matrix} P \\ Q \\ R \\ S \\ T \end{matrix} &
\left[\begin{matrix}
0 & 0 & 1 & 1 & 1 \\
1 & 0 & 1 & 0 & 1 \\
0 & 0 & 0 & 1 & 1 \\
0 & 1 & 0 & 0 & 1 \\
0 & 0 & 0 & 0 & 0
\end{matrix}\right]
\end{array}
$$

The matrix shows that P dominates R, S, and T; Q dominates P, R, and T; R dominates S and T; S dominates Q and T; and T dominates no one.

Since P dominates R, S, and T directly, as seen in the first row, P is said to have three **one-stage dominances.** Adding the numbers in the second row of the matrix shows that Q has three one-stage dominances; from the third and fourth rows, R and S have two each; from the fifth row, T has none. ■

In Example 2, Q dominated R and R dominated S, but Q did not dominate S. However, Q does have an indirect dominance over S, through R. Because of this, Q is said to have a **two-stage dominance** over S. Also, S has two-stage dominance over P.

Although we shall not prove it, the number of two-stage dominances can be found by *squaring* the adjacency matrix. If we use M for the matrix above, then

$$
M^2 = \begin{bmatrix}
0 & 0 & 1 & 1 & 1 \\
1 & 0 & 1 & 0 & 1 \\
0 & 0 & 0 & 1 & 1 \\
0 & 1 & 0 & 0 & 1 \\
0 & 0 & 0 & 0 & 0
\end{bmatrix}
\begin{bmatrix}
0 & 0 & 1 & 1 & 1 \\
1 & 0 & 1 & 0 & 1 \\
0 & 0 & 0 & 1 & 1 \\
0 & 1 & 0 & 0 & 1 \\
0 & 0 & 0 & 0 & 0
\end{bmatrix}
=
\begin{bmatrix}
0 & 1 & 0 & 1 & 2 \\
0 & 0 & 1 & 2 & 2 \\
0 & 1 & 0 & 0 & 1 \\
1 & 0 & 1 & 0 & 1 \\
0 & 0 & 0 & 0 & 0
\end{bmatrix}.
$$

The 1 in row 1, column 2 of this result shows that P has two-stage dominance over Q (through S), while P has two-stage dominance over T in *two* ways (through R or through S). Adding the numbers in each row of this matrix shows that P has a total of $0 + 1 + 0 + 1 + 2 = 4$ two-stage dominances, while Q has 5, R has 2, S has 3, and T has none. (Notice that matrix M^2 is not an adjacency matrix.)

Adding matrices M and M^2 gives the total number of one-stage or two-stage dominances.

$$M + M^2 = \begin{bmatrix} 0 & 0 & 1 & 1 & 1 \\ 1 & 0 & 1 & 0 & 1 \\ 0 & 0 & 0 & 1 & 1 \\ 0 & 1 & 0 & 0 & 1 \\ 0 & 0 & 0 & 0 & 0 \end{bmatrix} + \begin{bmatrix} 0 & 1 & 0 & 1 & 2 \\ 0 & 0 & 1 & 2 & 2 \\ 0 & 1 & 0 & 0 & 1 \\ 1 & 0 & 1 & 0 & 1 \\ 0 & 0 & 0 & 0 & 0 \end{bmatrix} = \begin{bmatrix} 0 & 1 & 1 & 2 & 3 \\ 1 & 0 & 2 & 2 & 3 \\ 0 & 1 & 0 & 1 & 2 \\ 1 & 1 & 1 & 0 & 2 \\ 0 & 0 & 0 & 0 & 0 \end{bmatrix}$$

The entry 3 in the upper right hand corner of the result shows that P has a total of 3 one-stage or two-stage dominances of T. Also, Q has a total of 2 one-stage or two-stage dominances over both R and S.

The sum of the entries in the P-column of matrix $M + M^2$ gives the number of ways that P is dominated. For example, from the first column, P is dominated in $0 + 1 + 0 + 1 + 0 = 2$ ways, while Q is dominated in 3 ways, R in 4 ways, S in 5 ways, and T in 10 ways. (This dominance is assumed to be in one stage or two stages.)

This process could be continued; finding M^3 would give the number of **three-stage dominances,** M^4 would give the number of **four-stage dominances,** and so on. Generalizing,

> Let M be an adjacency matrix and let k be a positive integer. Then the entry a_{ij} of M^k gives the number of k-stage dominances of i over j. Also, the sum of the entries in row i of the matrix
>
> $$M + M^2 + M^3 + \cdots + M^k$$
>
> is the total number of ways that i can dominate in one, two, . . ., k stages.

EXAMPLE 3

A league is made up of six teams, A, B, C, D, E, and F. In a recent tournament, the teams played each other exactly once, with results as shown in the digraph of Figure 8. (No ties were allowed.)

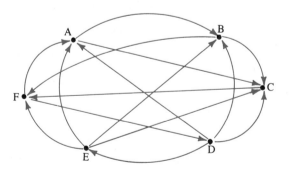

FIGURE 8

The adjacency matrix for the tournament follows.

$$M = \begin{array}{c} \\ A \\ B \\ C \\ D \\ E \\ F \end{array} \begin{array}{c} \begin{array}{cccccc} A & B & C & D & E & F \end{array} \\ \left[\begin{array}{cccccc} 0 & 1 & 1 & 0 & 0 & 0 \\ 0 & 0 & 1 & 0 & 0 & 1 \\ 0 & 0 & 0 & 0 & 0 & 1 \\ 1 & 1 & 1 & 0 & 1 & 0 \\ 1 & 1 & 1 & 0 & 0 & 1 \\ 1 & 0 & 0 & 1 & 0 & 0 \end{array} \right] \end{array}$$

It is not possible to use this matrix to decide on a winner, since both team D and E won four games, while all other teams won fewer games. To help choose a winner, we could calculate M^2 to get two-stage wins for each team. Find M^2 as follows.

$$M^2 = \begin{bmatrix} 0 & 1 & 1 & 0 & 0 & 0 \\ 0 & 0 & 1 & 0 & 0 & 1 \\ 0 & 0 & 0 & 0 & 0 & 1 \\ 1 & 1 & 1 & 0 & 1 & 0 \\ 1 & 1 & 1 & 0 & 0 & 1 \\ 1 & 0 & 0 & 1 & 0 & 0 \end{bmatrix} \begin{bmatrix} 0 & 1 & 1 & 0 & 0 & 0 \\ 0 & 0 & 1 & 0 & 0 & 1 \\ 0 & 0 & 0 & 0 & 0 & 1 \\ 1 & 1 & 1 & 0 & 1 & 0 \\ 1 & 1 & 1 & 0 & 0 & 1 \\ 1 & 0 & 0 & 1 & 0 & 0 \end{bmatrix} = \begin{bmatrix} 0 & 0 & 1 & 0 & 0 & 2 \\ 1 & 0 & 0 & 1 & 0 & 1 \\ 1 & 0 & 0 & 1 & 0 & 0 \\ 1 & 2 & 3 & 0 & 0 & 3 \\ 1 & 1 & 2 & 1 & 0 & 2 \\ 1 & 2 & 2 & 0 & 1 & 0 \end{bmatrix}$$

The sum $M + M^2$ gives the total number of one-stage and two-stage wins for each team.

$$M + M^2 = \begin{bmatrix} 0 & 1 & 1 & 0 & 0 & 0 \\ 0 & 0 & 1 & 0 & 0 & 1 \\ 0 & 0 & 0 & 0 & 0 & 1 \\ 1 & 1 & 1 & 0 & 1 & 0 \\ 1 & 1 & 1 & 0 & 0 & 1 \\ 1 & 0 & 0 & 1 & 0 & 0 \end{bmatrix} + \begin{bmatrix} 0 & 0 & 1 & 0 & 0 & 2 \\ 1 & 0 & 0 & 1 & 0 & 1 \\ 1 & 0 & 0 & 1 & 0 & 0 \\ 1 & 2 & 3 & 0 & 0 & 3 \\ 1 & 1 & 2 & 1 & 0 & 2 \\ 1 & 2 & 2 & 0 & 1 & 0 \end{bmatrix} = \begin{bmatrix} 0 & 1 & 2 & 0 & 0 & 2 \\ 1 & 0 & 1 & 1 & 0 & 2 \\ 1 & 0 & 0 & 1 & 0 & 1 \\ 2 & 3 & 4 & 0 & 1 & 3 \\ 2 & 2 & 3 & 1 & 0 & 3 \\ 2 & 2 & 2 & 1 & 1 & 0 \end{bmatrix}$$

The result shows that team D had a total of $2 + 3 + 4 + 0 + 1 + 3 = 13$ one- or two-stage wins, while all other teams had fewer wins. Based on this result, we would probably declare team D the winner of the tournament. ■

11.2 EXERCISES

For each matrix in Exercises 1–10 that is the matrix of a dominance digraph, find the matrix representing two-stage dominance. Find the total number of people dominated by each person in one or two stages.

1. $\begin{array}{c} \\ A \\ B \end{array} \begin{array}{c} \begin{array}{cc} A & B \end{array} \\ \left[\begin{array}{cc} 0 & 1 \\ 0 & 0 \end{array} \right] \end{array}$

2. $\begin{array}{c} \\ A \\ B \end{array} \begin{array}{c} \begin{array}{cc} A & B \end{array} \\ \left[\begin{array}{cc} 0 & 0 \\ 1 & 0 \end{array} \right] \end{array}$

3. $\begin{array}{c} \\ P \\ Q \\ R \end{array} \begin{array}{c} \begin{array}{ccc} P & Q & R \end{array} \\ \left[\begin{array}{ccc} 0 & 1 & 0 \\ 0 & 0 & 1 \\ 1 & 0 & 0 \end{array} \right] \end{array}$

4. $\begin{array}{c} \\ Z \\ W \\ T \end{array} \begin{array}{c} \begin{array}{ccc} Z & W & T \end{array} \\ \left[\begin{array}{ccc} 0 & 0 & 0 \\ 1 & 0 & 0 \\ 1 & 1 & 0 \end{array} \right] \end{array}$

5. $\begin{array}{c} \\ X \\ Y \\ Z \end{array} \begin{array}{c} \begin{array}{ccc} X & Y & Z \end{array} \\ \left[\begin{array}{ccc} 0 & 0 & 1 \\ 0 & 0 & 1 \\ 0 & 0 & 0 \end{array} \right] \end{array}$

6. $\begin{array}{c} \\ M \\ N \\ P \end{array} \begin{array}{c} \begin{array}{ccc} M & N & P \end{array} \\ \left[\begin{array}{ccc} 0 & 1 & 0 \\ 0 & 0 & 1 \\ 1 & 1 & 0 \end{array} \right] \end{array}$

7. $\begin{array}{c} \\ R \\ S \\ T \\ V \end{array} \begin{array}{c} \begin{array}{cccc} R & S & T & V \end{array} \\ \left[\begin{array}{cccc} 0 & 1 & 0 & 1 \\ 0 & 0 & 1 & 0 \\ 1 & 0 & 0 & 0 \\ 0 & 1 & 1 & 0 \end{array} \right] \end{array}$

8. $\begin{array}{c} \\ P \\ Q \\ R \\ S \end{array} \begin{array}{c} \begin{array}{cccc} P & Q & R & S \end{array} \\ \left[\begin{array}{cccc} 0 & 0 & 1 & 1 \\ 1 & 0 & 1 & 1 \\ 0 & 0 & 0 & 1 \\ 0 & 0 & 0 & 0 \end{array} \right] \end{array}$

9.

$$
\begin{array}{c c c c c c}
 & A & B & C & D & E \\
A & \begin{bmatrix} 0 \\ 0 \\ 0 \\ 1 \\ 1 \end{bmatrix} & \begin{matrix} 1 \\ 0 \\ 0 \\ 1 \\ 0 \end{matrix} & \begin{matrix} 1 \\ 1 \\ 0 \\ 0 \\ 0 \end{matrix} & \begin{matrix} 0 \\ 0 \\ 1 \\ 0 \\ 1 \end{matrix} & \begin{matrix} 0 \\ 1 \\ 1 \\ 0 \\ 0 \end{bmatrix}
\end{array}
$$

$$
\begin{array}{ccccc}
 & A & B & C & D & E \\
A & 0 & 1 & 1 & 0 & 0 \\
B & 0 & 0 & 1 & 0 & 1 \\
C & 0 & 0 & 0 & 1 & 1 \\
D & 1 & 1 & 0 & 0 & 0 \\
E & 1 & 0 & 0 & 1 & 0
\end{array}
$$

10.

$$
\begin{array}{ccccc}
 & X & Y & Z & W & T \\
X & 0 & 0 & 1 & 0 & 1 \\
Y & 1 & 0 & 0 & 0 & 0 \\
Z & 0 & 1 & 0 & 1 & 0 \\
W & 1 & 1 & 0 & 0 & 0 \\
T & 0 & 1 & 1 & 1 & 0
\end{array}
$$

For each digraph in Exercises 11–14, write the corresponding matrix. Find the number of two-stage dominances for A, B, C, and D. List all two-stage dominances.

11.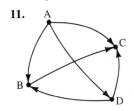

12.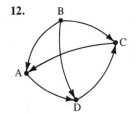

13.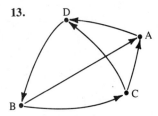

14.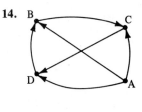

Decide on the winner of the tournaments in Exercises 15 and 16, using two-stage dominance. Here AB represents a game between teams A and B.

15.

Game	AB	AC	AD	AE	BC	BD	BE	CD	CE	DE
Winner	A	C	A	A	C	B	B	D	C	D

16.

Game	AB	AC	AD	AE	BC	BD	BE	CD	CE	DE
Winner	B	C	A	A	B	B	E	C	E	E

Another application of dominance comes from taste- or color-preference tests. For example, a consumer is shown several different colors for a new car, two at a time. The consumer then indicates a preference for one in each pair, for all possible pairs of colors. A "favorite" color can then be selected, using the methods above. In Exercises 17–20, find two-stage dominances and then choose the favorite.

17. Four colors, red, orange, yellow, or green, are under consideration for a new cereal. A consumer is shown samples of the cereal in each color, two at a time. The results are as follows.

Pair of Colors	RO	RY	RG	OY	OG	YG
Choice	R	R	G	O	G	Y

18. A perfume company is considering four possible fragrances for a new perfume, lilac, rose, apple blossom, and gardenia. The results of one consumer preference survey were as follows.

Pair of Fragrances	LR	LA	LG	RA	RG	AG
Choice	R	A	L	R	G	A

19. A wine tasting had a consumer compare five wines, A, B, C, D, and E, with the following results.

Wines	AB	AC	AD	AE	BC	BD	BE	CD	CE	DE
Choice	A	A	D	E	B	B	B	C	E	E

20. A manager made a comparison among five employees of a company, A, B, C, D, and E. The employees were compared two at a time, with the following results.

Employees	AB	AC	AD	AE	BC	BD	BE	CD	CE	DE
Choice	A	A	D	A	C	B	B	C	C	D

Find the number of four-stage dominances for each person in the following matrices.

21. the matrix in Exercise 9

22. the matrix in Exercise 10

11.3 *Communication Digraphs

In our study of dominance digraphs, we found that the associated matrix was asymmetric—if the entry in row i and column j was a 1, say, then the entry in row j and column i had to be 0. However, with *communication digraphs,* the associated matrix turns out to be symmetric. The symmetry of the matrix follows from the nature of communication: if A can communicate with B, then (normally) B can also communicate with A. Communication digraphs arise when studying highway networks, pipelines, airline routes, and telephone links between cities.

A **communication digraph** has the following properties.

Communication Digraph

For any two vertices A and B:
1. The fact that A can communicate with B implies that B can communicate with A.
2. There can be more than one edge between A and B.
3. A can always communicate with B, although not necessarily directly.
4. The associated matrix is **symmetric;** that is, $a_{ij} = a_{ji}$ for all possible values of i and j.

Figure 9 shows the possible routes of communication between cities A, B, C, and D. Arrowheads are used on both ends of the edges to show that communication

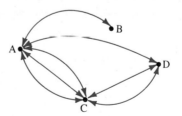

FIGURE 9

is two-way. The associated matrix M for the digraph in Figure 9 is

$$
\begin{array}{c}
 \\ A \\ B \\ C \\ D
\end{array}
\begin{array}{cccc}
A & B & C & D \\
\left[\begin{array}{cccc}
0 & 1 & 3 & 1 \\
1 & 0 & 0 & 0 \\
3 & 0 & 0 & 2 \\
1 & 0 & 2 & 0
\end{array}\right].
\end{array}
$$

Just as in the last section, the matrix M^2 gives the number of communication routes between two cities that go through exactly one other city. Matrix M^2 is

$$
M^2 = \begin{bmatrix}
0 & 1 & 3 & 1 \\
1 & 0 & 0 & 0 \\
3 & 0 & 0 & 2 \\
1 & 0 & 2 & 0
\end{bmatrix}
\begin{bmatrix}
0 & 1 & 3 & 1 \\
1 & 0 & 0 & 0 \\
3 & 0 & 0 & 2 \\
1 & 0 & 2 & 0
\end{bmatrix}
=
\begin{bmatrix}
11 & 0 & 2 & 6 \\
0 & 1 & 3 & 1 \\
2 & 3 & 13 & 3 \\
6 & 1 & 3 & 5
\end{bmatrix}.
$$

The entry 3 in the fourth row of M^2 shows that there are 3 routes connecting C and D that pass through exactly one other city (in this case, all three routes go through A). The entry 5 in the fourth row shows that there are 5 routes connecting city D with itself that go through exactly one other city. (One of these 5 routes goes through city A; the other four go through city C.)

As before, the matrix M^3 would give the number of routes that pass through exactly two other cities. Also, the sum $M + M^2$ gives the number of routes that pass through zero or one cities.

Organizational Communication   The communication digraphs above assumed that any two cities communicate with each other. This assumption is not made in *organizational communication* digraphs. (Mailroom clerks at Exxon probably don't chat with the Chairman of the Board, for example.) Also, we assume that only one method of communication exists between members of an organization. In summary, an **organizational communication digraph** has the following properties.

Organizational	For any two vertices A and B:
Communication	**1.** If A communicates with B, then B communicates with A.
	2. No more than one edge connects A and B.
	3. A does not communicate with A.
	4. The associated matrix is a symmetric adjacency matrix.

A typical organizational digraph is shown in Figure 10. The associated matrix is

$$
\begin{array}{c}
A \\ B \\ C \\ D \\ E
\end{array}
\begin{array}{ccccc}
A & B & C & D & E \\
\left[\begin{array}{ccccc}
0 & 1 & 1 & 1 & 0 \\
1 & 0 & 1 & 1 & 1 \\
1 & 1 & 0 & 0 & 0 \\
1 & 1 & 0 & 0 & 1 \\
0 & 1 & 0 & 1 & 0
\end{array}\right].
\end{array}
$$

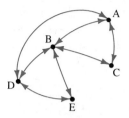

FIGURE 10

While A and E do not communicate directly in the digraph of Figure 10, they can communicate by going through B as an intermediary; alternate communication routes between A and E go through D, or through C and then B, among others. A route from one person to another, perhaps through intermediaries, is a *path*.

Path

> A collection of vertices and edges, with no vertex repeated, leading from one vertex to another, with no vertex repeated, is called a **path.**
> If a path exists between each pair of vertices, the digraph is **connected.**

EXAMPLE 1

(a) The digraph in Figure 11 is an organizational communication digraph.

(b) Two possible paths from *A* to *D* are shown in Figure 12.

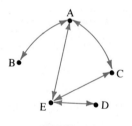

FIGURE 11

FIGURE 12

There is a path connecting each pair of vertices, so the digraph is connected.

(c) The associated matrix for the digraph follows.

$$
\begin{array}{c c}
 & \begin{array}{c c c c c} A & B & C & D & E \end{array} \\
\begin{array}{c} A \\ B \\ C \\ D \\ E \end{array} &
\left[\begin{array}{c c c c c}
0 & 1 & 1 & 0 & 1 \\
1 & 0 & 0 & 0 & 0 \\
1 & 0 & 0 & 0 & 1 \\
0 & 0 & 0 & 0 & 1 \\
1 & 0 & 1 & 1 & 0
\end{array} \right]
\end{array}
$$

We found by inspection that the digraph of Example 1 was connected. This process works well for most simple digraphs, but it is impractical for large ones. For larger digraphs, use the following theorem, which we do not prove.

Theorem

To decide if an organizational communication digraph with n vertices is connected,
1. Find the associated adjacency matrix M.
2. Form the sum

$$M + M^2 + M^3 + \ldots + M^{n-1}.$$

3. The digraph is connected if the matrix found in Step (2) has only positive entries.

EXAMPLE 2

Use the theorem to decide if the following digraphs in Figure 13 are connected.

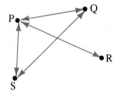

FIGURE 13(a)   FIGURE 13(b)

(a)   For Figure 13(a), first write the associated adjacency matrix M.

$$
\begin{array}{c c}
 & \begin{array}{cccc} P & Q & R & S \end{array} \\
\begin{array}{c} P \\ Q \\ R \\ S \end{array} &
\left[\begin{array}{cccc}
0 & 1 & 1 & 1 \\
1 & 0 & 0 & 1 \\
1 & 0 & 0 & 0 \\
1 & 1 & 0 & 0
\end{array}\right]
\end{array}
$$

Since the digraph involves four vertices, we must find the first $4 - 1 = 3$ powers of M. A calculation gives

$$
M + M^2 + M^3 =
\begin{bmatrix}
0 & 1 & 1 & 1 \\
1 & 0 & 0 & 1 \\
1 & 0 & 0 & 0 \\
1 & 1 & 0 & 0
\end{bmatrix}
+
\begin{bmatrix}
3 & 1 & 0 & 1 \\
1 & 2 & 1 & 1 \\
0 & 1 & 1 & 1 \\
1 & 1 & 1 & 2
\end{bmatrix}
+
\begin{bmatrix}
2 & 4 & 3 & 4 \\
4 & 2 & 1 & 3 \\
3 & 1 & 0 & 1 \\
4 & 3 & 1 & 2
\end{bmatrix}
$$

$$
=
\begin{bmatrix}
5 & 6 & 4 & 6 \\
6 & 4 & 2 & 5 \\
4 & 2 & 1 & 2 \\
6 & 5 & 2 & 4
\end{bmatrix}.
$$

All the entries in this matrix are positive, showing that the given digraph is connected.

(b)   For Figure 13(b), the associated matrix M is

$$
\begin{array}{cccc}
 & A & B & C & D
\end{array}
$$
$$
\begin{array}{c}
A \\ B \\ C \\ D
\end{array}
\begin{bmatrix}
0 & 1 & 1 & 0 \\
1 & 0 & 1 & 0 \\
1 & 1 & 0 & 0 \\
0 & 0 & 0 & 0
\end{bmatrix}.
$$

The sum $M + M^2 + M^3$ is

$$
M + M^2 + M^3 =
\begin{bmatrix}
0 & 1 & 1 & 0 \\
1 & 0 & 1 & 0 \\
1 & 1 & 0 & 0 \\
0 & 0 & 0 & 0
\end{bmatrix}
+
\begin{bmatrix}
2 & 1 & 1 & 0 \\
1 & 2 & 1 & 0 \\
1 & 1 & 2 & 0 \\
0 & 0 & 0 & 0
\end{bmatrix}
+
\begin{bmatrix}
2 & 3 & 3 & 0 \\
3 & 2 & 3 & 0 \\
3 & 3 & 2 & 0 \\
0 & 0 & 0 & 0
\end{bmatrix}
$$

$$
=
\begin{bmatrix}
4 & 5 & 5 & 0 \\
5 & 4 & 5 & 0 \\
5 & 5 & 4 & 0 \\
0 & 0 & 0 & 0
\end{bmatrix}.
$$

The final matrix does not have all positive entries (some entries are 0), showing that the digraph is not connected.   ▨

11.3 EXERCISES

In Exercises 1–8, write the associated matrix for each digraph. Identify any communication digraphs or organizational communication digraphs.

1.
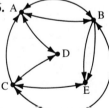

2.
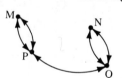

3.

4.
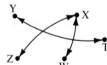

5.
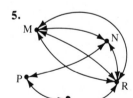

6.
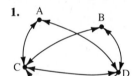

7.
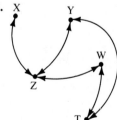

8.
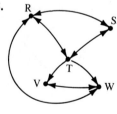

Sketch a digraph for each matrix of a communication digraph in Exercises 9–16. Find all two-stage paths of communication.

9.
$$
\begin{bmatrix}
0 & 1 & 0 \\
1 & 0 & 1 \\
0 & 1 & 0
\end{bmatrix}
$$

10.
$$
\begin{bmatrix}
0 & 2 & 1 \\
2 & 0 & 0 \\
1 & 0 & 0
\end{bmatrix}
$$

11.
$$
\begin{bmatrix}
0 & 0 & 2 \\
0 & 0 & 1 \\
2 & 1 & 0
\end{bmatrix}
$$

12.
$$
\begin{bmatrix}
0 & 1 & 0 \\
1 & 0 & 2 \\
0 & 2 & 0
\end{bmatrix}
$$

13. $\begin{bmatrix} 0 & 1 & 0 & 1 \\ 1 & 0 & 2 & 0 \\ 0 & 2 & 0 & 1 \\ 1 & 0 & 1 & 0 \end{bmatrix}$ **14.** $\begin{bmatrix} 0 & 0 & 2 & 1 \\ 0 & 0 & 1 & 0 \\ 2 & 1 & 0 & 2 \\ 1 & 0 & 2 & 0 \end{bmatrix}$ **15.** $\begin{bmatrix} 0 & 1 & 0 & 2 \\ 1 & 0 & 0 & 1 \\ 0 & 0 & 0 & 1 \\ 2 & 1 & 1 & 0 \end{bmatrix}$ **16.** $\begin{bmatrix} 0 & 1 & 1 & 0 \\ 0 & 0 & 1 & 0 \\ 1 & 1 & 0 & 2 \\ 1 & 0 & 2 & 0 \end{bmatrix}$

Identify all paths from A to D in the organizational communication digraphs in Exercises 17–20.

17.

18.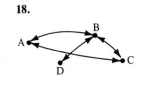

19.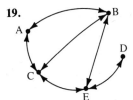

20.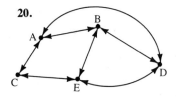

Use the theorem given at the end of the section to prove that the digraphs in Exercises 21–24 are connected.

21.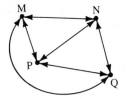

22.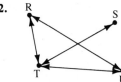

23.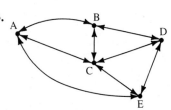

24.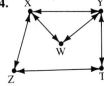

Prove that the digraphs in Exercises 25 and 26 are not connected.

25.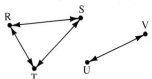

26.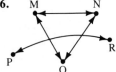

11.4 Networks

Perhaps the single most useful application of graphs comes from the study of *networks*. The interstate highway system is an example of a network: given any city on the system, it is possible to find a route or path from that city to any other city on the system. Formally, as this example suggests, a network is a graph in which a path can be found between any two vertices.

Network

> A **network** is a connected graph.

EXAMPLE 1

The graph in Figure 14(a) is a network, while the one in Figure 14(b) is not. ▧

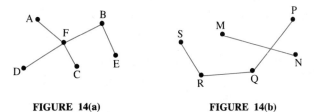

FIGURE 14(a)   FIGURE 14(b)

A path that goes from one vertex back to the same vertex without passing along any edge more than once is called a **cycle.** For example, the graph in Figure 15(a) has five cycles: *PNQP, NMPN, MQNM, QPMQ,* and *PNMQP.* The graph in Figure 15(b) has only one cycle, *WRSTW.*

Graph theory is used to produce the minimum total cost when designing a network, such as a pipeline. For example, in the graph of Figure 15(b), the connection between *W* and *T* isn't really necessary since *T* can be reached from *W* by going through *R* and *S.* (Alternatively, the connection between *W* and *R* could be omitted, with *W* reached from *R* by going through *T* and *S.*) A network with no cycles is called a **tree.** In a tree, there is only one path between any two vertices.

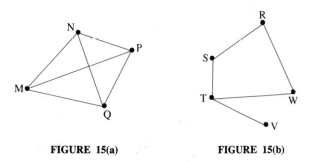

FIGURE 15(a)   FIGURE 15(b)

EXAMPLE 2

The graph in Figure 15(b) is not a tree because of the cycle *WRSTW*. However, the network becomes a tree if we omit edge *WR* or edge *WT*, as seen in Figure 16. ▨

A tree that contains all the vertices of a network is called a **spanning tree.** Think of a spanning tree as a sort of "skeleton" for the graph: the spanning tree includes all the vertices of the graph; any edges that are not really necessary for each vertex to be reachable from all other vertices are omitted.

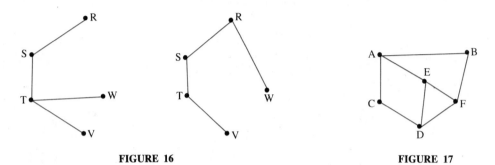

FIGURE 16   FIGURE 17

EXAMPLE 3

Find a spanning tree for the network in Figure 17.

This network contains several cycles, such as *ACDEA*, *ACDFEA*, *AEFBA*, *ACDFBA*, and so on. A spanning tree can contain no cycles, so it is necessary to remove at least one edge from each cycle. Two possible spanning trees are shown in Figure 18. Many others are possible. ▨

In an application, a length or cost is assigned to each edge of a network. For example, lengths might be assigned when designing a new microwave relay network, while costs might be assigned for a pipeline project where some parts go through relatively flat land while other parts involve expensive construction through mountains. In a network, a spanning tree for which the sum of numbers assigned to edges is a minimum is called a **minimum spanning tree.**

EXAMPLE 4

Find the minimum spanning tree for the network in Figure 19.

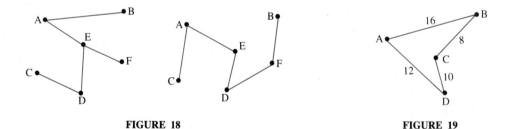

FIGURE 18   FIGURE 19

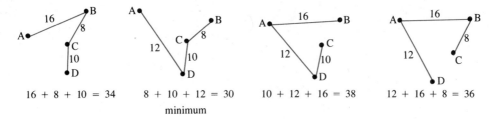

$$16 + 8 + 10 = 34 \qquad 8 + 10 + 12 = 30 \qquad 10 + 12 + 16 = 38 \qquad 12 + 16 + 8 = 36$$
minimum

FIGURE 20

Only four spanning trees are possible for this network; they are shown in Figure 20. In the second spanning tree, the sum of the edge numbers is 30, the smallest of the four sums. This makes *BCDA* the minimum spanning tree. ▪

The minimum spanning tree for Example 4 was found by considering all possible spanning trees. This approach would be much too time-consuming in practice. Instead, find the minimum spanning tree for a network with the following procedure.

Finding the Minimum Spanning Tree	To find a minimum spanning tree for a network with numbers assigned to each edge, **1.** Find the edge with the smallest number (if more than one edge has this number, choose any one of them). **2.** Consider any edge with the next smallest number. If it would form a cycle with the edges already chosen, reject it; otherwise, choose it. **3.** Repeat Step 2 until the number of edges is one less than the number of vertices. Since several edges might have equal numbers, there may be more than one minimum spanning tree.

EXAMPLE 5

A company has branches in Washington, D.C., Charlotte, Nashville, Louisville, and Kansas City. The company wishes to build a private communications line between all these branches and Chicago headquarters. Find the line of minimum distance that will connect all the cities.

The first step is to draw a network showing all possible connections and the corresponding distances. This is done in Figure 21. (The numbers represent straight line distances, but it is not convenient to draw all the edges as straight lines.)

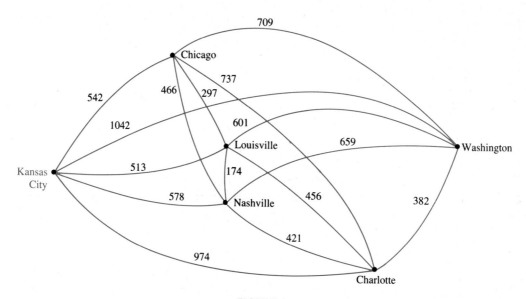

FIGURE 21

To find a minimum spanning tree, start with the edge with the smallest number,

$$\text{Louisville–Nashville} \qquad 174.$$

The next smaller number is associated with the edge

$$\text{Chicago–Louisville} \qquad 297.$$

Next, use the edge

$$\text{Washington–Charlotte} \qquad 382.$$

Now use

$$\text{Charlotte–Nashville} \qquad 421.$$

The next smaller number is Louisville–Charlotte, at 456 miles, but this edge would complete a cycle, so it cannot be used. The next usable edge is

$$\text{Louisville–Kansas City} \qquad 513.$$

The minimum spanning tree is shown in Figure 22. The length of this minimum spanning tree is

$$513 + 297 + 174 + 421 + 382 = 1787 \text{ miles}.$$

Any other spanning tree would produce a greater total mileage.

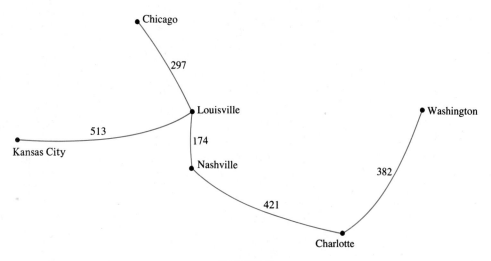

FIGURE 22

11.4 EXERCISES

Identify all cycles in the networks in Exercises 1–4.

1.
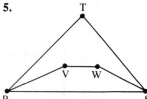

2.
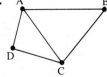

3.
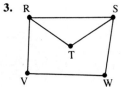

4.
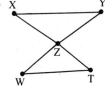

Find all spanning trees for the networks in Exercises 5–8.

5.

6.
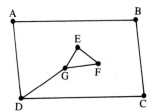

7.
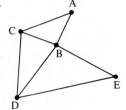

8.
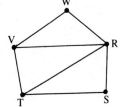

Find a minimum spanning tree for the networks in Exercises 9–12.

9.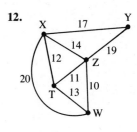

10.

11.

12.

13. The distances between cities A, B, C, D, and E are given in the following mileage chart.

	A	B	C	D	E
A		168	352	152	317
B	168		177	172	296
C	352	177		235	152
D	152	172	235		164
E	317	296	152	164	

Find the minimum spanning tree for this network of cities.

14. The distances between six cities, R, S, T, V, W, and X are given in the following mileage chart.

	R	S	T	V	W	X
R		106	154	194	202	91
S	106		205	274	301	137
T	154	205		82	116	201
V	194	274	82		192	195
W	202	301	116	192		274
X	91	137	201	195	274	

Find the minimum spanning tree for this network of cities.

KEY WORDS	graph theory	asymmetric matrix
	graph	one-stage dominance
	vertex	two-stage dominance
	edge	three-stage dominance
	directed edge	four-stage dominance
	directed graph	communication digraph
	digraph	symmetric matrix
	adjacency matrix	organizational communication digraph
	dominance	network
	path	spanning tree
	cycle	connected digraph
	minimum spanning tree	

Chapter 11   REVIEW EXERCISES

Write a matrix for each graph in Exercises 1–4 that is a digraph. Identify any adjacency matrices.

1.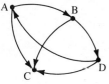

2.

3.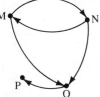

4.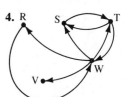

Sketch a digraph for each matrix in Exercises 5–8.

5.
$$\begin{array}{c} \\ A \\ B \\ C \end{array} \begin{array}{ccc} A & B & C \\ \begin{bmatrix} 0 & 2 & 1 \\ 1 & 0 & 2 \\ 0 & 1 & 0 \end{bmatrix} \end{array}$$

6.
$$\begin{array}{c} \\ M \\ N \\ P \end{array} \begin{array}{ccc} M & N & P \\ \begin{bmatrix} 0 & 1 & 0 \\ 1 & 0 & 0 \\ 0 & 1 & 0 \end{bmatrix} \end{array}$$

7.
$$\begin{array}{c} \\ R \\ S \\ T \\ V \end{array} \begin{array}{cccc} R & S & T & V \\ \begin{bmatrix} 0 & 1 & 0 & 1 \\ 0 & 0 & 1 & 0 \\ 1 & 0 & 0 & 1 \\ 0 & 1 & 1 & 0 \end{bmatrix} \end{array}$$

8.
$$\begin{array}{c} \\ X \\ Y \\ Z \\ W \end{array} \begin{array}{cccc} X & Y & Z & W \\ \begin{bmatrix} 0 & 1 & 0 & 0 \\ 1 & 0 & 0 & 1 \\ 1 & 1 & 0 & 1 \\ 1 & 0 & 0 & 0 \end{bmatrix} \end{array}$$

For each matrix in Exercises 9–14 that is the matrix of a dominance digraph, find the matrix representing two-stage dominance. Find the total number of vertices dominated by each vertex in one or two stages.

9.
$$\begin{array}{c} \\ A \\ B \\ C \end{array} \begin{array}{ccc} A & B & C \\ \begin{bmatrix} 0 & 1 & 0 \\ 0 & 0 & 1 \\ 1 & 0 & 0 \end{bmatrix} \end{array}$$

10.
$$\begin{array}{c} \\ M \\ N \\ P \end{array} \begin{array}{ccc} M & N & P \\ \begin{bmatrix} 0 & 0 & 0 \\ 1 & 0 & 0 \\ 1 & 1 & 0 \end{bmatrix} \end{array}$$

11.
$$\begin{array}{c} \\ X \\ Y \\ Z \end{array} \begin{array}{ccc} X & Y & Z \\ \begin{bmatrix} 0 & 1 & 1 \\ 0 & 0 & 1 \\ 1 & 0 & 0 \end{bmatrix} \end{array}$$

12.
$$\begin{array}{c} \\ R \\ S \\ T \end{array} \begin{array}{ccc} R & S & T \\ \begin{bmatrix} 0 & 1 & 0 \\ 1 & 0 & 0 \\ 1 & 1 & 0 \end{bmatrix} \end{array}$$

13.
$$\begin{array}{c} \\ P \\ Q \\ R \\ S \end{array} \begin{array}{cccc} P & Q & R & S \\ \begin{bmatrix} 0 & 1 & 0 & 1 \\ 0 & 0 & 1 & 1 \\ 1 & 0 & 0 & 1 \\ 0 & 0 & 0 & 0 \end{bmatrix} \end{array}$$

14.
$$\begin{array}{c} \\ A \\ B \\ C \\ D \end{array} \begin{array}{cccc} A & B & C & D \\ \begin{bmatrix} 0 & 0 & 0 & 1 \\ 1 & 0 & 0 & 0 \\ 1 & 1 & 0 & 1 \\ 0 & 1 & 0 & 0 \end{bmatrix} \end{array}$$

For each digraph in Exercises 15 and 16, write the corresponding matrix. Find the number of two-stage dominances for A, B, C, and D.

15.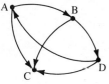

16.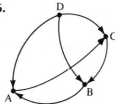

Decide on the winner of the following tournaments in Exercises 17 and 18, using two-stage dominance. Here AB means a game between teams A and B.

17.

Game	AB	AC	AD	AE	BC	BD	BE	CD	CE	DE
Winner	A	C	D	A	B	B	B	D	C	D

18.

Game	AB	AC	AD	AE	BC	BD	BE	CD	CE	DE
Winner	A	A	D	A	B	B	B	D	C	E

Write the associated matrix for each digraph in Exercises 19–22. Identify any communication digraphs or organizational communication digraphs.

19.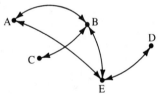

20.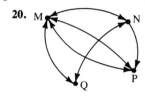

21.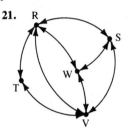

22.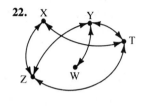

Sketch a digraph for each matrix of a communication digraph in Exercises 23–26. Find all two-stage paths of communication.

23. $\begin{bmatrix} 0 & 0 & 2 \\ 0 & 0 & 1 \\ 2 & 1 & 0 \end{bmatrix}$
  24. $\begin{bmatrix} 0 & 1 & 2 \\ 1 & 0 & 1 \\ 2 & 1 & 0 \end{bmatrix}$
  25. $\begin{bmatrix} 0 & 2 & 1 & 2 \\ 2 & 0 & 0 & 1 \\ 1 & 0 & 0 & 1 \\ 2 & 1 & 1 & 0 \end{bmatrix}$
  26. $\begin{bmatrix} 0 & 2 & 1 & 1 \\ 2 & 0 & 0 & 0 \\ 1 & 0 & 0 & 2 \\ 1 & 0 & 2 & 0 \end{bmatrix}$

Identify all paths from A to D in the digraphs in Exercises 27–28.

27.

28.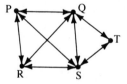

Prove that the digraphs in Exercises 29 and 30 are connected.

29.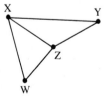

30.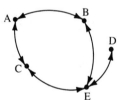

Identify all cycles in the networks in Exercises 31 and 32.

31.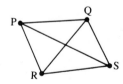

32.

Find all spanning trees for the networks in Exercises 33 and 34.

33.

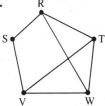

34.

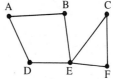

Find a minimum spanning tree for each network in Exercises 35 and 36.

35.

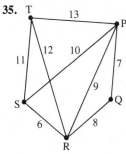

36.

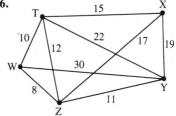

ANSWERS TO SELECTED EXERCISES

Chapter 1   Section 1.1   (page 6)

1. $x = 4$ **3.** $m = 5/4$ **5.** $m = 12$ **7.** $k = -2/7$ **9.** $x = 5$ **11.** $r = -7/8$ **13.** $x = 3$ **15.** $x = 84$
17. $x \le 10$ **19.** $m \le -3/2$ **21.** $k < -5/3$ **23.** $z < -3/11$ **25.** $x \ge 16$ **27.** $t \ge -3/2$ **29.** $p \ge -3/5$
31. $k < 2$ **33.** \$12,000 at 13% and \$8000 at 16%   **35.** \$54,000 at $8\frac{1}{2}$% and \$6000 at 16%   **37.** \$70,000 for the profitable
land; \$50,000 for the unprofitable land   **39.** 400/3 liters   **41.** 4 summers   **43.** (a) 196   (b) $108 + .14x$
(c) $196 < 108 + .14x$; 628.6 miles   **45.** $b - 3a$ **47.** $(3a + b)/(3 - a)$ **49.** $(3 - 3a)/(a^2 - a - 1)$
51. $2a^2/(a^2 + 3)$

Section 1.2   (page 12)

1. $(-2, -3), (-1, -2), (0, -1), (1, 0), (2, 1), (3, 2)$:
range: $\{-3, -2, -1, 0, 1, 2\}$

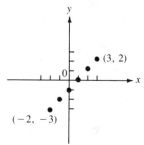

3. $(-2, 17), (-1, 13), (0, 9), (1, 5), (2, 1), (3, -3)$;
range: $\{17, 13, 9, 5, 1, -3\}$

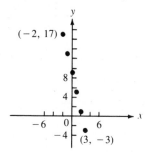

5. $(-2, -3), (-1, -4), (0, -5), (1, -6), (2, -7),$
$(3, -8)$; range: $\{-3, -4, -5, -6, -7, -8\}$

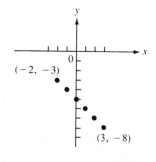

7. $(-2, 13), (-1, 11), (0, 9), (1, 7), (2, 5), (3, 3)$;
range: $\{13, 11, 9, 7, 5, 3\}$

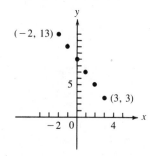

485

9. $(-2, 3/2), (-1, 2), (0, 5/2), (1, 3), (2, 7/2), (3, 4)$; range: $\{3/2, 2, 5/2, 3, 7/2, 4\}$

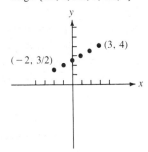

11. $(-2, 2), (-1, 0), (0, 0), (1, 2), (2, 6), (3, 12)$; range: $\{0, 2, 6, 12\}$

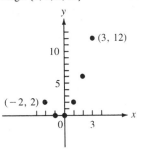

13. $(-2, 4), (-1, 1), (0, 0), (1, 1), (2, 4), (3, 9)$; range: $\{4, 1, 0, 9\}$

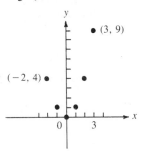

15. $(-2, -13), (-1, -1), (0, 3), (1, -1), (2, -13),$ $(3, -33)$; range: $\{-13, -1, 3, -33\}$

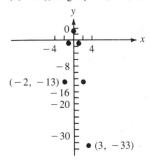

17. $(-2, 1), (-1, 1/2), (0, 1/3), (1, 1/4), (2, 1/5), (3, 1/6)$; range: $\{1, 1/2, 1/3, 1/4, 1/5, 1/6\}$

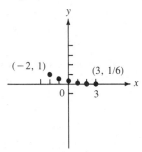

19. $(-2, -3), (-1, -3/2), (0, -3/5), (1, 0), (2, 3/7),$ $(3, 3/4)$; range: $\{-3, -3/2, -3/5, 0, 3/7, 3/4\}$

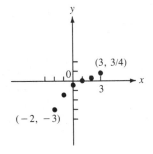

21. $(-2, 4), (-1, 4), (0, 4), (1, 4), (2, 4), (3, 4)$; range: $\{4\}$

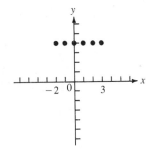

23. Function   **25.** Not a function   **27.** Function   **29.** (a) 14   (b) -7 (c) 2   (d) $3a + 2$ **31.** (a) -12 (b) 2
(c) -4 (d) $-2a - 4$ **33.** (a) 6   (b) 6   (c) 6   (d) 6   **35.** (a) 48   (b) 6   (c) 0   (d) $2a^2 + 4a$ **37.** (a) 5   (b) -23
(c) 1   (d) $-a^2 + 5a + 1$ **39.** (a) 30   (b) 2   (c) 2   (d) $(a + 1)(a + 2)$, or $a^2 + 3a + 2$ **41.** (a) -3 (b) -5
(c) -15 (d) 5   (e) $2a - 3$ (f) $-2r - 3$ (g) $2m + 3$ (h) $2p - 7$ (i) -1 (j) -21 **43.** (a) \$11   (b) \$11   (c) \$18
(d) \$32   (e) \$32   (f) \$39   (g) \$39

Section 1.3   (page 20)

1.
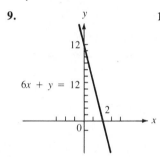
$y = 2x + 1$

3.
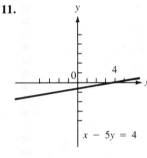
$y = 4x$

5.
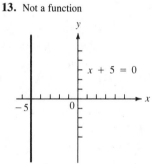
$3y + 4x = 12$

7.
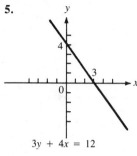
$y = -2$

9.
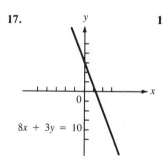
$6x + y = 12$

11.
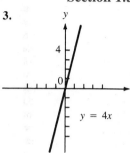
$x - 5y = 4$

13. Not a function
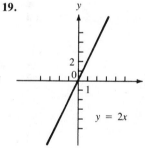
$x + 5 = 0$

15.
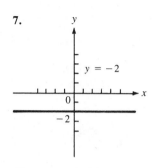
$5y - 3x = 12$

17.
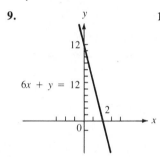
$8x + 3y = 10$

19.
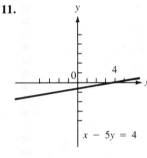
$y = 2x$

21.
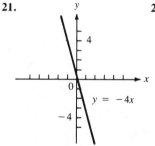
$y = -4x$

23.
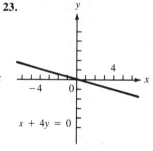
$x + 4y = 0$

25. (a) 16   (b) 11   (c) 6
(d) 8   (e) 4   (f) 0   (g)
(h) 0   (i) 40/3   (j) 80/3
(k) See part (g)   (l) 8
(m) 6

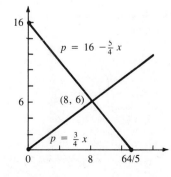
$p = 16 - \frac{5}{4}x$
$(8, 6)$
$p = \frac{3}{4}x$

27. (a)
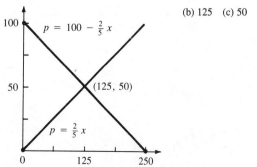
$p = 100 - \frac{2}{5}x$
$(125, 50)$
$p = \frac{2}{5}x$

(b) 125   (c) 50

29. (a) $135 (b) $205 (c) $275 (d) $345 (e)

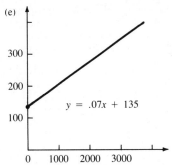

$y = .07x + 135$

Section 1.4 (page 29)

1. $-1/5$ **3.** $2/3$ **5.** $-3/2$ **7.** Undefined slope **9.** 0 **11.** 3; 4 **13.** -4; 8 **15.** $-3/4$; 5/4 **17.** -3; 0

19. $-2/5$; 0 **21.** 0; 8 **23.** 0; -2 **25.** Undefined slope; no y-intercept

27.

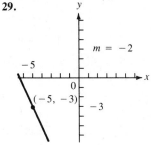

29.

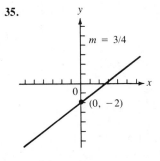

31.

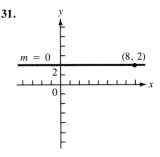

33.

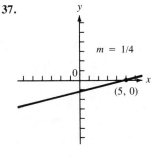

35.

37.

39. $4y = -3x + 16$ **41.** $2y = -x - 4$ **43.** $4y = 6x + 5$ **45.** $y = 2x + 9$ **47.** $y = -3x + 3$
49. $4y = x + 5$ **51.** $3y = 4x + 7$ **53.** $3y = -2x$ **55.** $x = -8$ **57.** $y = 3$ **59.** $y = 640x + 1100$;
$m = 640$ **61.** $y = -1000x + 40,000$; $m = -1000$ **63.** $y = 2.5x - 80$; $m = 2.5$ **65.** (a) $h = 3.5r + 83$
(b) About 163.5 cm; about 177.5 cm (c) About 25 cm

Section 1.5 (page 36)

1. (a) 2600 (b) 2900 (c) 3200 (d) 2000 (e) 300 **3.** (a) 100 thousand (b) 70 thousand (c) 0 (d) -5 thousand; the number
is decreasing **5.** (a) $y = 82,500x + 850,000$ (b) $1,097,500 (c) about $1,510,000 **7.** (a) 480 (b) 360 (c) 120
(d) June 29 (e) -20 **9.** If $C(x)$ is the cost of renting a saw for x hours, then $C(x) = 12 + x$. **11.** If $P(x)$ is the cost
(in cents) of parking for x half-hours, then $P(x) = 35x + 50$. **13.** $C(x) = 30x + 100$ **15.** $C(x) = 25x + 1000$
17. $C(x) = 50x + 500$ **19.** $C(x) = 90x + 2500$ **21.** (a) $97 (b) $97.097 (c) $.097, or 9.7¢ (d) $.097, or 9.7¢
23. (a) $100 (b) $36 (c) $24 **25.** $2000; $32,000 **27.** $2000; $52,000 **29.** $150,000; $600,000 **31.** (a) $20,000
per year (b) $80,000 **33.** (a) $4000; $3000; $2000; $1000 (b) $2500 **35.** $5090.91; $3563.64 **37.** $4171.43; $2085.71

39. 500 units; $30,000   **41.** Break-even point is 45 units; don't produce   **43.** Break-even point is −50 units; impossible to
make a profit here

45. (a)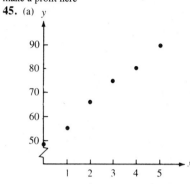

(b)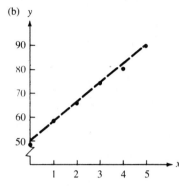

(c) $y = 8x + 50$

(d)

Year	Sales, Actual	Sales, Predicted	Difference
0	$48	$50	−2
1	59	58	1
2	66	66	0
3	75	74	1
4	80	82	−2
5	90	90	0

(e) 106 thousand dollars
(f) 122 thousand dollars

47. (a)

Year	Straight-line	Sum-of-the-years'-digits
1	$1242.80	$2269.45
2	1242.80	2042.51
3	1242.80	1815.56
4	1242.80	1588.62
5	1242.80	1361.67
6	1242.80	1134.73
7	1242.80	907.78
8	1242.80	680.84
9	1242.80	453.89
10	1242.80	226.95

(b)

Year	Straight-line	Sum-of-the-years'-digits
1	$2475.00	$4569.23
2	2475.00	4188.46
3	2475.00	3807.69
4	2475.00	3426.92
5	2475.00	3046.15
6	2475.00	2665.38
7	2475.00	2284.62
8	2475.00	1903.85
9	2475.00	1523.08
10	2475.00	1142.31
11	2475.00	761.54
12	2475.00	380.77

(c)

Year	Straight-line	Sum-of-the-years'-digits
1	$4833.33	$9354.84
2	4833.33	9043.01
3	4833.33	8731.18
4	4833.33	8419.35
5	4833.33	8107.53
6	4833.33	7795.70
7	4833.33	7483.87
8	4833.33	7172.04
9	4833.33	6860.22
10	4833.33	6548.39
11	4833.33	6236.56
12	4833.33	5924.73
13	4833.33	5612.90
14	4833.33	5301.08
15	4833.33	4989.25
16	4833.33	4677.42
17	4833.33	4365.59
18	4833.33	4053.76
19	4833.33	3741.94
20	4833.33	3430.11
21	4833.33	3118.28
22	4833.33	2806.45
23	4833.33	2494.62
24	4833.33	2182.80
25	4833.33	1870.97
26	4833.33	1559.14
27	4833.33	1247.31
28	4833.33	935.48
29	4833.33	623.66
30	4833.33	311.82

(d)

Year	Straight-line	Sum-of-the-years'-digits
1	$17,200.00	$32,250.00
2	17,200.00	30,100.00
3	17,200.00	27,950.00
4	17,200.00	25,800.00
5	17,200.00	23,650.00
6	17,200.00	21,500.00
7	17,200.00	19,350.00
8	17,200.00	17,200.00
9	17,200.00	15,050.00
10	17,200.00	12,900.00
11	17,200.00	10,750.00
12	17,200.00	8,600.00
13	17,200.00	6,450.00
14	17,200.00	4,300.00
15	17,200.00	2,150.00

Extended Application   (page 41)

1. $.1A + 200$ **2.** $.0001A − .3$ **3.** 8000   **4.** 8000   **5.** 800   **6.** $800(10,000) = \$8,000,000$

Extended Application (page 42)

1. 4.8 million units   **2.** Portion of a straight line going through (3.1, 10.50) and (5.7, 10.67)   **3.** In the interval under discussion (3.1 to 5.7 million units), the marginal cost always exceeds the selling price.   **4.** (a) 9.87; 10.22   (b) portion of a straight line through (3.1, 9.87) and (5.7, 10.22)   (c) .83 million units, which is not in the interval under discussion

Section 1.6 (page 51)

1. (a) $60,000   (b) $40,000   (c) 26,667   (d) $17,778

3.

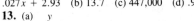

Depreciation in Year	Straight-line	Double Declining	Sum-of-the years'-digits
1	$375	$933	$563
2	375	192*	375
3	375	0	187
Totals	1125	1125	1125

*Only $192 of depreciation may be taken, since the total may not exceed the net cost of $1125.

5. (a) $y' = .3x + 1.5$ (b) $r = .20$ (c) 2.4   **7.** (a) $y' = 1.19x - .84$ (b) 2.4   (c) 3.3   (d) 2.8   (e) .94   **9.** (a) $y' = .027x + 2.93$ (b) 13.7   (c) 447,000   (d) .97   **11.** (a) $y' = .95x + 5.3$ (b) 12.9 million   (c) In 1987   (d) .90

13. (a)

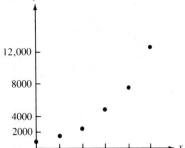

(b) log y

(c) $y = .22x + 3.0$

(d) 4.54; about 35,000

15. $y' = 1.003077x + 8.486716$, $r = .879913$ **17.** $y' = .027980x + 2.489262$, $r = .978365$

Chapter 1 Review Exercises (page 57)

1. $x = 2$ **3.** $k = 3$ **5.** $n = 7$ **7.** $z = 7/5$ **9.** $m \le 5/2$ **11.** $m < -1$ **13.** $k \ge 7/3$ **15.** $x \le 13$
17. $k > 3$ **19.** $12,000 at $8\frac{1}{2}$% and $18,000 at 10%
21. $(-3, -16/5), (-2, -14/5), (-1, -12/5), (0, -2),$
$(1, -8/5), (2, -6/5), (3, -4/5);$
range: $\{-16/5, -14/5, -12/5, -2, -8/5, -6/5, -4/5\}$

23. $(-3, 20), (-2, 9), (-1, 2), (0, -1), (1, 0), (2, 5),$
$(3, 14);$
range: $\{-1, 0, 2, 5, 9, 14, 20\}$

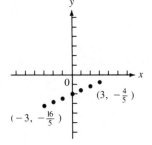

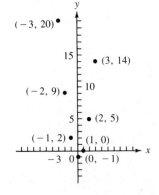

25. $(-3, 7), (-2, 2), (-1, -1), (0, -2), (1, -1), (2, 2),$
$(3, 7)$; range: $\{-2, -1, 2, 7\}$

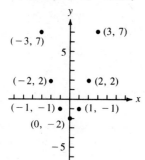

27. $(-3, 1/5), (-2, 2/5), (-1, 1), (0, 2), (1, 1), (2, 2/5),$
$(3, 1/5)$; range: $\{1/5, 2/5, 1, 2\}$

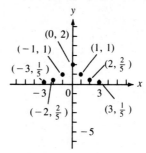

29. $(-3, -1), (-2, -1), (-1, -1), (0, -1), (1, -1),$
$(2, -1), (3, -1)$; range: $\{-1\}$

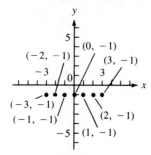

31. (a) 23   (b) -9 (c) -17 (d) $4r + 3$
33. (a) -28 (b) -12 (c) -28 (d) $-r^2 - 3$
35. (a) -13 (b) 3   (c) -32 (d) 22   (e) $-k^2 - 4k$
(f) $-9m^2 + 12m$ (g) $-k^2 + 14k - 45$ (h) $12 - 5p$
(i) -28 (j) -21

37.

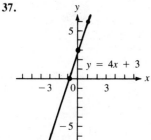

39.

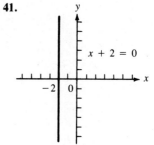

41.

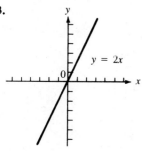

43.

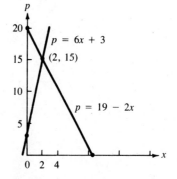

45. (a) 7/6; 9/2   (b) 2; 2   (c) 5/2, 1/2   (d)
(e) 15   (f) 2; 2

47. 1/3   **49.** −2/11   **51.** −2/3   **53.** Undefined slope   **55.** $3y = 2x - 13$ **57.** $5x + 4y = 17$ **59.** $x = -1$
61. $C(x) = 30x + 60$ **63.** $C(x) = 30x + 85$ **65.** (a) 5 units   (b) $200
67.

Year	Straight-line	Double Declining	Sum-of-the-years'-digits
1	$17,000	$39,500	$27,200
2	17,000	19,750	20,400
3	17,000	8750	13,600
4	17,000	0	6800

69. $y' = 3.9x - 7.9$ **71.** .998

Chapter 2   Section 2.1   (page 72)

1. (3, 6)   **3.** (−1, 4)   **5.** (−2, 0)   **7.** (1, 3)   **9.** (4, −2)   **11.** (2, −2)   **13.** No solution   **15.** Same line
17. (12, 6)   **19.** (7, −2)   **21.** (1, 2, −1)   **23.** (2, 0, 3)   **25.** No solution   **27.** (0, 2, 4)   **29.** (1, 2, 3)
31. (−1, 2, 1)   **33.** (4, 1, 2)   **35.** x arbitrary, $y = x + 5$, $z = -2x + 1$ **37.** x arbitrary, $y = x + 1$, $z = -x + 3$
39. x arbitrary, $y = 4x - 7$, $z = 3x + 7$, $w = -x - 3$ **41.** (3, −4)   **43.** No solution   **45.** No solution   **47.** Wife:
40 days; husband: 32 days   **49.** 5 model 201; 8 model 301   **51.** $10,000 at 16%; $7000 at 20%; $8000 at 18%   **53.** $k = 3$;
solution is (−1, 0, 2)

Section 2.2   (page 80)

1. $\begin{bmatrix} 2 & 3 & | & 11 \\ 1 & 2 & | & 8 \end{bmatrix}$ **3.** $\begin{bmatrix} 1 & 5 & | & 6 \\ 0 & 1 & | & 1 \end{bmatrix}$ **5.** $\begin{bmatrix} 2 & 1 & 1 & | & 3 \\ 3 & -4 & 2 & | & -7 \\ 1 & 1 & 1 & | & 2 \end{bmatrix}$ **7.** $\begin{bmatrix} 1 & 1 & 0 & | & 2 \\ 0 & 2 & 1 & | & -4 \\ 0 & 0 & 1 & | & 2 \end{bmatrix}$ **9.** $\begin{bmatrix} 1 & 0 & 0 & | & 5 \\ 0 & 1 & 0 & | & -2 \\ 0 & 0 & 1 & | & 3 \end{bmatrix}$

11. $x = 2$ **13.** $2x + y = 1$ **15.** $x = 2$ **17.** (2, 3)   **19.** (−3, 0)   **21.** (7/2, −1)   **23.** (5/2, −1)
$\ y = 3$ $\ 3x - 2y = -9$ $\ y = 3$
$\ z = -2$

25. No solution   **27.** Same line   **29.** (−2, 1, 3)   **31.** (−1, 23, 16)   **33.** (3, 2, −4)   **35.** No solution
37. (−1, 3, 2)   **39.** (2, 4, 5)   **41.** (0, 2, −2, 1)   The answers are given in the order x, y, z, w.
43. (a) $\begin{bmatrix} 1 & 0 & 0 & 1 & | & 1000 \\ 1 & 1 & 0 & 0 & | & 1100 \\ 0 & 1 & 1 & 0 & | & 700 \\ 0 & 0 & 1 & 1 & | & 600 \end{bmatrix}$; $\begin{bmatrix} 1 & 0 & 0 & 1 & | & 1000 \\ 0 & 1 & 0 & -1 & | & 100 \\ 0 & 0 & 1 & 1 & | & 600 \\ 0 & 0 & 0 & 0 & | & 0 \end{bmatrix}$ (b) $x_1 + x_4 = 1000$; $x_2 - x_4 = 100$; $x_3 + x_4 = 600$
(c) $x_4 = 1000 - x_1$; $x_4 = x_2 - 100$; $x_4 = 600 - x_3$
(d) 1000; 1000   (e) 100   (f) 600; 600
(g) $x_4 = 600$; $x_3 = 600$; $x_2 = 700$; $x_1 = 1000$
45. (4.12062, 1.66866, .117699)   **47.** (30.7209, 39.6513, 31.386, 50.3966)   **49.** 81 kg of the first chemical, 382.286 kg of
the second, 286.714 kg of the third   **51.** 243 of A, 38 of B, 101 of C (rounded)

Section 2.3   (page 89)

1. False; not all corresponding elements are equal.   **3.** True   **5.** True   **7.** 2×2; square   **9.** 3×4 **11.** 2×1;
column   **13.** $x = 2$, $y = 4$, $z = 8$ **15.** $x = -15$, $y = 5$, $k = 3$ **17.** $z = 18$, $r = 3$, $s = 3$, $p = 3$, $a = 3/4$
19. $\begin{bmatrix} 9 & 12 & 0 & 2 \\ 1 & -1 & 2 & -4 \end{bmatrix}$ **21.** $\begin{bmatrix} 5 & 13 & 0 \\ 3 & 1 & 8 \end{bmatrix}$ **23.** Not possible   **25.** $\begin{bmatrix} 1 & 5 & 6 & -9 \\ 5 & 7 & 2 & 1 \\ -7 & 2 & 2 & -7 \end{bmatrix}$

27. $\begin{bmatrix} -12x + 8y & -x + y \\ x & 8x - y \end{bmatrix}$ **29.** $\begin{bmatrix} x & y \\ z & w \end{bmatrix} + \begin{bmatrix} r & s \\ t & u \end{bmatrix} = \begin{bmatrix} x + r & y + s \\ z + t & w + u \end{bmatrix}$ (a 2×2 matrix)
31. $\begin{bmatrix} x + (r + m) & y + (s + n) \\ z + (t + p) & w + (u + q) \end{bmatrix} = \begin{bmatrix} (x + r) + m & (y + s) + n \\ (z + t) + p & (w + u) + q \end{bmatrix}$ **33.** $\begin{bmatrix} m + 0 & n + 0 \\ p + 0 & q + 0 \end{bmatrix} = \begin{bmatrix} m & n \\ p & q \end{bmatrix}$
35. $\begin{bmatrix} 7 & 2 \\ 9 & 0 \\ 8 & 6 \end{bmatrix}$; $\begin{bmatrix} 7 & 9 & 8 \\ 2 & 0 & 6 \end{bmatrix}$ **37.** (a) $\begin{bmatrix} 2 & 1 & 2 & 1 \\ 3 & 2 & 2 & 1 \\ 4 & 3 & 2 & 1 \end{bmatrix}$ (b) $\begin{bmatrix} 5 & 0 & 7 \\ 0 & 10 & 1 \\ 0 & 15 & 2 \\ 10 & 12 & 8 \end{bmatrix}$ (c) $\begin{bmatrix} 8 \\ 4 \\ 5 \end{bmatrix}$

Section 2.4   (page 97)

1. 2×2; 2×2 **3.** 4×4; 2×2 **5.** 3×2; BA does not exist   **7.** AB does not exist; 3×2 **9.** $\begin{bmatrix} -4 & 8 \\ 0 & 6 \end{bmatrix}$

11. $\begin{bmatrix} 24 & -8 \\ -16 & 0 \end{bmatrix}$ **13.** $\begin{bmatrix} -22 & -6 \\ 20 & -12 \end{bmatrix}$ **15.** $\begin{bmatrix} 13 \\ 25 \end{bmatrix}$ **17.** $\begin{bmatrix} -2 & 10 \\ 0 & 8 \end{bmatrix}$ **19.** $\begin{bmatrix} 13 & 5 \\ 25 & 15 \end{bmatrix}$ **21.** $\begin{bmatrix} 13 \\ 29 \end{bmatrix}$ **23.** $\begin{bmatrix} 110 \\ 40 \\ -50 \end{bmatrix}$

25. $\begin{bmatrix} 22 & -8 \\ 11 & -4 \end{bmatrix}$ **27.** (a) $\begin{bmatrix} 16 & 22 \\ 7 & 19 \end{bmatrix}$ (b) $\begin{bmatrix} 5 & -5 \\ 0 & 30 \end{bmatrix}$ (c) No; no (d) No   **33.** (a) P, P, X (b) T (c) I maintains the identity of any 2×2 matrix under multiplication.   **35.** (a) $\begin{bmatrix} 20 & 52 & 27 \\ 25 & 62 & 35 \\ 30 & 72 & 43 \end{bmatrix}$ The rows represent the amounts of fat, carbohydrate, and protein, respectively, in each of the daily meals.

(b) $\begin{bmatrix} 75 \\ 45 \\ 70 \\ 168 \end{bmatrix}$ The rows give the number of calories in one exchange of each of the food groups.   **39.** $\begin{bmatrix} 44 & 75 & -60 & -33 & 11 \\ 20 & 169 & -164 & 18 & 105 \\ 113 & -82 & 239 & 218 & -55 \\ 119 & 83 & 7 & 82 & 106 \\ 162 & 20 & 175 & 143 & 74 \end{bmatrix}$

41. Cannot be found   **43.** No

Extended Application   (page 100)

1. (a) 3 (b) 3 (c) 5 (d) 3   **2.** (a) 21 (b) 25   **3.** (a) $B = \begin{bmatrix} 0 & 2 & 3 \\ 2 & 0 & 4 \\ 3 & 4 & 0 \end{bmatrix}$ (b) $\begin{bmatrix} 13 & 12 & 8 \\ 12 & 20 & 6 \\ 8 & 6 & 25 \end{bmatrix}$ (c) 12 (d) 14

4. (a)

	S	J	NO	H
S	0	1	2	1
J	1	0	1	0
NO	2	1	0	1
H	1	0	1	0

(b) 2 (c) 2 (d) 2

5. (a)

	dogs	rats	cats	mice
dogs	0	1	1	1
rats	0	0	0	1
cats	0	1	0	1
mice	0	0	0	0

$C = $ (as above)

(b) $C^2 = \begin{bmatrix} 0 & 1 & 0 & 2 \\ 0 & 0 & 0 & 0 \\ 0 & 0 & 0 & 1 \\ 0 & 0 & 0 & 0 \end{bmatrix}$ C^2 gives the number of food sources once removed from the feeder. Thus, since dogs eat rats and rats eat mice, mice are an indirect as well as a direct food source.

Extended Application   (page 102)

1. $PQ = \begin{bmatrix} 1 & 2 & 0 & 2 & 1 & 1 \\ 0 & 1 & 0 & 1 & 0 & 0 \\ 1 & 1 & 0 & 1 & 2 & 1 \end{bmatrix}$ **2.** None   **3.** Yes, the third person

4. The second and fourth persons in the third group each had four contacts in all.

Section 2.5   (page 109)

1. Yes   **3.** No   **5.** No   **7.** Yes   **9.** $\begin{bmatrix} 0 & 1/2 \\ -1 & 1/2 \end{bmatrix}$ **11.** $\begin{bmatrix} 2 & 1 \\ 5 & 3 \end{bmatrix}$ **13.** None   **15.** $\begin{bmatrix} 1 & 0 & 0 \\ 0 & -1 & 0 \\ -1 & 0 & 1 \end{bmatrix}$

17. $\begin{bmatrix} 15 & 4 & -5 \\ -12 & -3 & 4 \\ -4 & -1 & 1 \end{bmatrix}$ **19.** None   **21.** $\begin{bmatrix} 7/4 & 5/2 & 3 \\ -1/4 & -1/2 & 0 \\ -1/4 & -1/2 & -1 \end{bmatrix}$ **23.** $\begin{bmatrix} 1/2 & 1/2 & -1/4 & 1/2 \\ -1 & 4 & -1/2 & -2 \\ -1/2 & 5/2 & -1/4 & -3/2 \\ 1/2 & -1/2 & 1/4 & 1/2 \end{bmatrix}$

25. $(-1, 4)$ **27.** $(2, 1)$ **29.** $(2, 3)$ **31.** Same line   **33.** $(-8, 6, 1)$ **35.** $(15, -5, -1)$ **37.** $(-31, 24, -4)$

39. No inverse, no solution for system   **41.** $(-7, -34, -19, 7)$

49. (a) $\begin{bmatrix} 72 \\ 48 \\ 60 \end{bmatrix}$ (b) $\begin{bmatrix} 2 & 4 & 2 \\ 2 & 1 & 2 \\ 2 & 1 & 3 \end{bmatrix} \begin{bmatrix} x_1 \\ x_2 \\ x_3 \end{bmatrix} = \begin{bmatrix} 72 \\ 48 \\ 60 \end{bmatrix}$ (c) 8, 8, 12

In (51) and (53), results are rounded to four decimal places.

51.
$$\begin{bmatrix} -.0047 & -.0230 & .0292 & .0895 & -.0402 \\ .0921 & .0150 & .0321 & .0209 & -.0276 \\ -.0678 & .0315 & -.0404 & .0326 & .0373 \\ .0171 & -.0248 & .0069 & -.0003 & .0246 \\ -.0208 & .0740 & .0096 & -.1018 & .0646 \end{bmatrix}$$

53.
$$\begin{bmatrix} .0394 & .0880 & .0033 & .0530 & -.1499 \\ -.1492 & .0289 & .0187 & .1033 & .1668 \\ -.1330 & -.0543 & .0356 & .1768 & .1055 \\ .1407 & .0175 & -.0453 & -.1344 & .0655 \\ .0102 & -.0653 & .0993 & .0085 & -.0388 \end{bmatrix}$$

55.
$$\begin{bmatrix} .62963 \\ .148148 \\ .259259 \end{bmatrix}$$

57.
$$\begin{bmatrix} .489558 \\ 1.00104 \\ 2.11853 \\ -1.20793 \\ -.961346 \end{bmatrix}$$

Extended Application   (page 113)

1. (a) $\begin{bmatrix} 47 \\ 56 \end{bmatrix}$ $\begin{bmatrix} 0 \\ 130 \end{bmatrix}$ $\begin{bmatrix} 107 \\ 60 \end{bmatrix}$ $\begin{bmatrix} 53 \\ 202 \end{bmatrix}$ $\begin{bmatrix} 72 \\ 88 \end{bmatrix}$ $\begin{bmatrix} -7 \\ 172 \end{bmatrix}$ $\begin{bmatrix} 11 \\ 12 \end{bmatrix}$ $\begin{bmatrix} 83 \\ 74 \end{bmatrix}$ (b) $M^{-1} = \begin{bmatrix} 3/13 & 1/26 \\ -1/13 & 2/13 \end{bmatrix}$

2. $\begin{bmatrix} 39 \\ -98 \end{bmatrix}$ $\begin{bmatrix} -18 \\ 35 \end{bmatrix}$ $\begin{bmatrix} 19 \\ -49 \end{bmatrix}$ $\begin{bmatrix} -25 \\ 49 \end{bmatrix}$ $\begin{bmatrix} 34 \\ -95 \end{bmatrix}$ $\begin{bmatrix} -2 \\ 3 \end{bmatrix}$ $\begin{bmatrix} 5 \\ -24 \end{bmatrix}$ $\begin{bmatrix} 15 \\ -51 \end{bmatrix}$ $\begin{bmatrix} 10 \\ -32 \end{bmatrix}$ $\begin{bmatrix} 33 \\ -85 \end{bmatrix}$ $\begin{bmatrix} 35 \\ -97 \end{bmatrix}$ $\begin{bmatrix} 10 \\ -35 \end{bmatrix}$ $\begin{bmatrix} 39 \\ -105 \end{bmatrix}$ $\begin{bmatrix} 27 \\ -69 \end{bmatrix}$ $\begin{bmatrix} -4 \\ 4 \end{bmatrix}$

3. Santa Claus is fat   **4.** $\begin{bmatrix} 76 \\ 77 \\ 96 \end{bmatrix}$ $\begin{bmatrix} 62 \\ 67 \\ 75 \end{bmatrix}$ $\begin{bmatrix} 88 \\ 108 \\ 97 \end{bmatrix}$ $\begin{bmatrix} 141 \\ 160 \\ 168 \end{bmatrix}$ $\begin{bmatrix} 147 \\ 166 \\ 174 \end{bmatrix}$ $\begin{bmatrix} 105 \\ 120 \\ 123 \end{bmatrix}$ $\begin{bmatrix} 111 \\ 131 \\ 119 \end{bmatrix}$ $\begin{bmatrix} 92 \\ 119 \\ 94 \end{bmatrix}$ $\begin{bmatrix} 75 \\ 93 \\ 79 \end{bmatrix}$ $\begin{bmatrix} 181 \\ 208 \\ 208 \end{bmatrix}$

Section 2.6   (page 118)

1. $\begin{bmatrix} 32/3 \\ 25/3 \end{bmatrix}$ **3.** $\begin{bmatrix} 23{,}000/3579 \\ 93{,}500/3579 \end{bmatrix}$ or $\begin{bmatrix} 6.43 \\ 26.12 \end{bmatrix}$ **5.** $\begin{bmatrix} 20/3 \\ 20 \\ 10 \end{bmatrix}$ **7.** 1079 metric tons of wheat, 1428 metric tons of oil

9. 1285 units of agriculture, 1455 units of manufacturing, and 1202 units of transportation   **11.** 3077 units of agriculture, 2564 units of manufacturing, and 3179 units of transportation   **13.** (a) 7/4 bushels of yams, 15/8 pigs (b) 167.5 bushels of yams, 153.75 pigs   **15.** 33:47:23   **17.** $\begin{bmatrix} 2930 \\ 3570 \\ 2300 \\ 580 \end{bmatrix}$ **19.** $\begin{bmatrix} 1583.91 \\ 1529.54 \\ 1196.09 \end{bmatrix}$

Extended Application   (page 123)

1. (a) $A = \begin{bmatrix} 0.245 & 0.102 & 0.051 \\ 0.099 & 0.291 & 0.279 \\ 0.433 & 0.372 & 0.011 \end{bmatrix}$ $D = \begin{bmatrix} 2.88 \\ 31.45 \\ 30.91 \end{bmatrix}$ $X = \begin{bmatrix} x_1 \\ x_2 \\ x_3 \end{bmatrix}$ (b) $I - A = \begin{bmatrix} 0.755 & -0.102 & -0.051 \\ -0.099 & 0.709 & -0.279 \\ -0.433 & -0.372 & 0.989 \end{bmatrix}$ (d) $\begin{bmatrix} 18.2 \\ 73.2 \\ 66.8 \end{bmatrix}$

(e) $18.2 billion of agriculture, $73.2 billion of manufacturing, and $66.8 billion of household would be required (rounded to three significant digits).   **2.** (a) $A = \begin{bmatrix} 0.293 & 0 & 0 \\ 0.014 & 0.207 & 0.017 \\ 0.044 & 0.010 & 0.216 \end{bmatrix}$ $D = \begin{bmatrix} 138{,}213 \\ 17{,}597 \\ 1{,}786 \end{bmatrix}$ (b) $I - A = \begin{bmatrix} .707 & 0 & 0 \\ -0.014 & 0.793 & -0.017 \\ -0.044 & -0.010 & 0.784 \end{bmatrix}$

(c) Agriculture 195,000 million pounds; manufacture 26,000 million pounds; energy 13,600 million pounds

Chapter 2   Review Exercises   (page 125)

1. $(-4, 6)$ **3.** $(-1, 2, 3)$ **5.** 8 thousand standard, 6 thousand extra large   **7.** 5 blankets, 3 rugs, 8 skirts   **9.** $(-9, 3)$
11. $(7, -9, -1)$ **13.** $x = 6 - (7/3)z,\ y = 1 + (1/3)z,\ z$ arbitrary   **15.** $3 \times 2;\ a = 2,\ x = -1,\ y = 4,\ p = 5,\ z = 7$
17. 3×3 (square); $a = -12,\ b = 1,\ k = 9/2,\ c = 3/4,\ d = 3,\ l = -3/4,\ m = -1,\ p = 3,\ q = 9$
19. $\begin{bmatrix} 5 & 7 & 2532 & 52\frac{3}{8} & -\frac{1}{4} \\ 3 & 9 & 1464 & 56 & \frac{1}{8} \\ 2.50 & 5 & 4974 & 41 & -1\frac{1}{2} \\ 1.36 & 10 & 1754 & 18\frac{7}{8} & \frac{1}{2} \end{bmatrix}$ **21.** $\begin{bmatrix} 8 & -6 \\ -10 & -16 \end{bmatrix}$ **23.** Not possible   **25.** $\begin{bmatrix} 26 & 86 \\ -7 & -29 \\ 21 & 87 \end{bmatrix}$

27. $\begin{bmatrix} 6 & 18 & -24 \\ 1 & 3 & -4 \\ 0 & 0 & 0 \end{bmatrix}$ **29.** $\begin{bmatrix} 15 \\ 16 \\ 1 \end{bmatrix}$ **31.** $\begin{bmatrix} -7/19 & 4/19 \\ 3/19 & 1/19 \end{bmatrix}$ **33.** Not possible   **35.** $\begin{bmatrix} -\frac{1}{4} & \frac{1}{6} \\ 0 & \frac{1}{3} \end{bmatrix}$ **37.** No inverse

39. $\begin{bmatrix} \frac{1}{4} & \frac{1}{2} & \frac{1}{2} \\ \frac{1}{4} & -\frac{1}{2} & \frac{1}{2} \\ \frac{1}{8} & -\frac{1}{4} & -\frac{1}{4} \end{bmatrix}$ **41.** No inverse   **43.** $X = \begin{bmatrix} 3 \\ 4 \end{bmatrix}$ **45.** $X = \begin{bmatrix} 6 \\ 15 \\ 16 \end{bmatrix}$ **47.** (2, 1)   **49.** (−1, 0, 2)   **51.** $\begin{bmatrix} 725.7 \\ 305.9 \\ 166.7 \end{bmatrix}$

Chapter 3   Section 3.1   (page 137)

1.
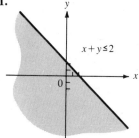
$x + y \le 2$

3.
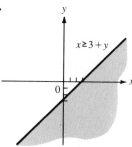
$x \ge 3 + y$

5.
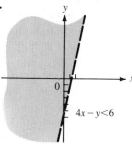
$4x - y < 6$

7.
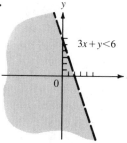
$3x + y < 6$

9.
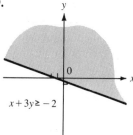
$x + 3y \ge -2$

11.
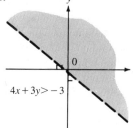
$4x + 3y > -3$

13.
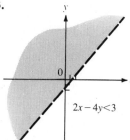
$2x - 4y < 3$

15.
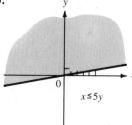
$x \le 5y$

17.
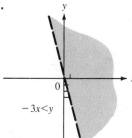
$-3x < y$

19.
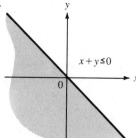
$x + y \le 0$

21.
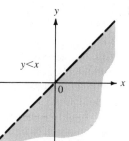
$y < x$

23.
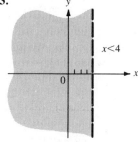
$x < 4$

25.
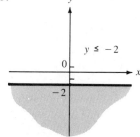
$y \le -2$

27.
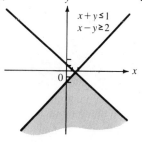
$x + y \le 1$
$x - y \ge 2$

29.
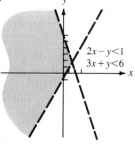
$2x - y < 1$
$3x + y < 6$

31.
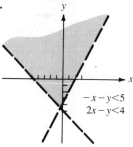
$-x - y < 5$
$2x - y < 4$

33.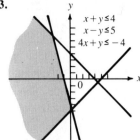
$$x+y \le 4$$
$$x-y \le 5$$
$$4x+y \le -4$$

35.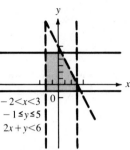
$$-2 < x < 3$$
$$-1 \le y \le 5$$
$$2x+y < 6$$

37.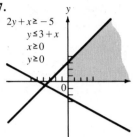
$$2y+x \ge -5$$
$$y \le 3+x$$
$$x \ge 0$$
$$y \ge 0$$

39.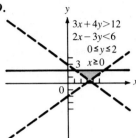
$$3x+4y > 12$$
$$2x-3y < 6$$
$$0 \le y \le 2$$
$$x \ge 0$$

41. (a)

Planter	Number	Wheel	Kiln	Profit Each
Glazed	x	1/2	1	$1.50
Unglazed	y	1	6	$1.50
Maximum Available		8	20	

(b) $(1/2)x + y \le 8$; $x + 6y \le 20$; $x \ge 0$; $y \ge 0$

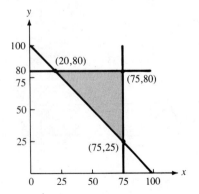

43. (a) $x \ge 1000$; $y \ge 800$; $x + y \le 2400$
(b)

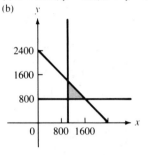

Section 3.2   (page 143)

1. Let x be the number of product A made, and y the number of B. Then $2x + 3y \le 45$.   **3.** Let x be the number of green pills, and y be the number of red. Then $4x + y \ge 25$.   **5.** Let x be the number of pounds of $6 coffee, and y the number of $5 coffee. Then $x + y \ge 50$.

7. Let x be the number shipped to warehouse A and y the number shipped to warehouse B. Then $x + y \ge 100$, $x \le 100$, $y \le 100$, $x \le 75$, $y \le 80$ (these last two constraints make $x \le 100$ and $y \le 100$ redundant); also $x \ge 0$ and $y \ge 0$; minimize $12x + 10y$.

9. Let x be the number of type 1 bolts and y the number of type 2 bolts. Then $.1x + .1y \le 1240$, $.1x + .4y \le 720$, $.1x + .5y \le 160$, $x \ge 0$, $y \ge 0$; maximize $.10x + .12y$. The first two inequalities are redundant; only $.1x + .5y \le 160$ affects the solution.

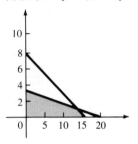

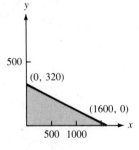

11. Let x be the number of gallons of gasoline (in millions), and let y be the number of gallons of fuel oil (in millions). Then $x \geq 2y$, $y \geq 3$, $x \leq 6.4$; maximize $1.25x + y$ (to find the total maximum revenue; this result must be multiplied by 1,000,000.)

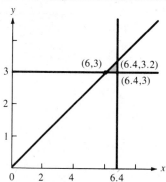

13. Let x be the number of kg of half and half mix, and y be the number of kg of the other mix. Then $x/2 + y/3 \leq 100$, $x/2 + (2y/3) \leq 125$, $x \geq 0$, $y \geq 0$; maximize $6x + 4.80y$.

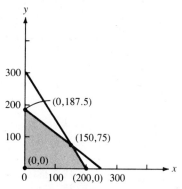

15. Let x be the number of servings of A and y the number of servings of B. Then $3x + 2y \geq 15$, $2x + 4y \geq 15$, $x \geq 0$, $y \geq 0$; minimize $.25x + .40y$.

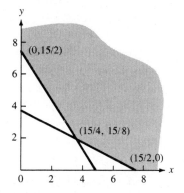

Section 3.3 (page 151)

1. Maximum of 65 at (5, 10); minimum of 8 at (1, 1)   **3.** Maximum of 9 at (0, 12); minimum of 0 at (0, 0)   **5.** No maximum; minimum of 18 at (3, 4)   **7.** $x = 6/5$; $y = 6/5$ **9.** $x = 10$; $y = 5$ **11.** $x = 105/8$; $y = 25/8$ **13.** (a) Maximum of 204; $x = 18$, $y = 2$ (b) Maximum of 117 3/5; $x = 12/5$, $y = 39/5$ (c) Maximum of 102; $x = 0$, $y = 17/2$ **15.** Ship 20 to A and 80 to B; $1040   **17.** 1600 Type 1 and 0 Type 2 for maximum revenue of $160   **19.** 6.4 million gallons of gasoline and 3.2 million gallons of fuel oil, for maximum revenue of $11,200,000   **21.** 150 kg half-and-half mix, 75 kg other mix; $1260   **23.** 3 3/4 servings of A, 1 7/8 servings of B; $1.6875   **25.** (b)   **27.** (c)

Chapter 3   Review Exercises   (page 155)

1.
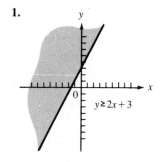
$y \geq 2x + 3$

3.
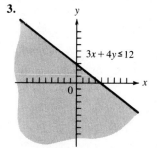
$3x + 4y \leq 12$

5.
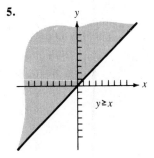
$y \geq x$

7.

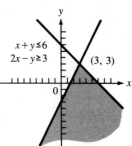

9.

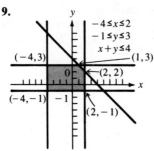

11.

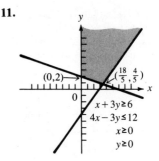

13. Let x = number of batches of cakes and y = number of batches of cookies. Then $x \geq 0$, $y \geq 0$, and $2x + (3/2)y \leq 15$
$$3x + (2/3)y \leq 13.$$

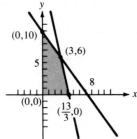

15. Minimum of 8 at (2, 1); maximum of 40 at (6, 7)   **17.** Maximum of 24 at (0, 6)
19. Minimum of 40 at any point on the segment connecting (0, 20) and (10/3, 40/3)
21. Make 3 batches of cakes, and 6 of cookies, for a maximum profit of $210

Chapter 4   Section 4.1 (page 163)

1. $x_1 + 2x_2 + x_3 = 6$ **3.** $2x_1 + 4x_2 + 3x_3 + x_4 = 100$ **5.** (a) 3 (b) x_3, x_4, x_5 (c) $4x_1 + 2x_2 + x_3 = 20$
$$5x_1 + x_2 + x_4 = 50$$
$$2x_1 + 3x_2 + x_5 = 25$$

7. (a) 2 (b) x_4, x_5 (c) $7x_1 + 6x_2 + 8x_3 + x_4 = 118$ **9.** $x_1 = 0$, $x_2 = 0$, $x_3 = 20$, $x_4 = 0$, $x_5 = 15$ **11.** $x_1 = 0$,
$$4x_1 + 5x_2 + 10x_3 + x_5 = 220$$
$x_2 = 0$, $x_3 = 8$, $x_4 = 0$, $x_5 = 6$, $x_6 = 7$ **13.** $x_1 = 0$, $x_2 = 20$, $x_3 = 0$, $x_4 = 16$, $x_5 = 0$ **15.** $x_1 = 0$, $x_2 = 0$,
$x_3 = 12$, $x_4 = 0$, $x_5 = 9$, $x_6 = 8$ **17.** $x_1 = 0$, $x_2 = 0$, $x_3 = 50$, $x_4 = 10$, $x_5 = 0$, $x_6 = 50$

19.
$$\begin{array}{cccc} x_1 & x_2 & x_3 & x_4 \end{array}$$
$$\left[\begin{array}{cccc|c} 2 & 3 & 1 & 0 & 6 \\ 4 & 1 & 0 & 1 & 6 \end{array}\right]$$

21.
$$\begin{array}{ccccc} x_1 & x_2 & x_3 & x_4 & x_5 \end{array}$$
$$\left[\begin{array}{ccccc|c} 1 & 1 & 1 & 0 & 0 & 10 \\ 5 & 2 & 0 & 1 & 0 & 20 \\ 1 & 2 & 0 & 0 & 1 & 36 \end{array}\right]$$

23.
$$\begin{array}{cccc} x_1 & x_2 & x_3 & x_4 \end{array}$$
$$\left[\begin{array}{cccc|c} 3 & 1 & 1 & 0 & 12 \\ 1 & 1 & 0 & 1 & 15 \end{array}\right]$$

25. If x_1 is the number of kg of half-and-half mix and x_2 is the number of kg of the other mix, find $x_1 \geq 0$, $x_2 \geq 0$, $x_3 \geq 0$, $x_4 \geq 0$
so that $(1/2)x_1 + (1/3)x_2 + x_3 = 100$, $(1/2)x_1 + (2/3)x_2 + x_4 = 125$, and $z = 6x_1 + 4.8x_2$ is maximized.
$$\begin{array}{cccc} x_1 & x_2 & x_3 & x_4 \end{array}$$
$$\left[\begin{array}{cccc|c} 1/2 & 1/3 & 1 & 0 & 100 \\ 1/2 & 2/3 & 0 & 1 & 125 \end{array}\right]$$

27. If x_1 is the number of prams, x_2 is the number of runabouts, and x_3 is the number of trimarans, find $x_1 \geq 0$, $x_2 \geq 0$, $x_3 \geq 0$, $x_4 \geq 0$, $x_5 \geq 0$, $x_6 \geq 0$ so that $x_1 + 2x_2 + 3x_3 + x_4 = 6240$, $2x_1 + 5x_2 + 4x_3 + x_5 = 10,800$, $x_1 + x_2 + x_3 + x_6 = 3000$, and $z = 75x_1 + 90x_2 + 100x_3$ is maximized.

$$\begin{array}{cccccc} x_1 & x_2 & x_3 & x_4 & x_5 & x_6 \end{array}$$
$$\left[\begin{array}{cccccc|c} 1 & 2 & 3 & 1 & 0 & 0 & 6240 \\ 2 & 5 & 4 & 0 & 1 & 0 & 10{,}800 \\ 1 & 1 & 1 & 0 & 0 & 1 & 3000 \end{array}\right]$$

29. If x_1 is the number of Siamese cats and x_2 is the number of Persian cats, find $x_1 \geq 0$, $x_2 \geq 0$, $x_3 \geq 0$, $x_4 \geq 0$, $x_5 \geq 0$ so that $2x_1 + x_2 + x_3 = 90$, $x_1 + 2x_2 + x_4 = 80$, $x_1 + x_2 + x_5 = 50$, and $z = 12x_1 + 10x_2$ is maximized.

$$\begin{array}{ccccc} x_1 & x_2 & x_3 & x_4 & x_5 \end{array}$$
$$\left[\begin{array}{ccccc|c} 2 & 1 & 1 & 0 & 0 & 90 \\ 1 & 2 & 0 & 1 & 0 & 80 \\ 1 & 1 & 0 & 0 & 1 & 50 \end{array}\right]$$

Section 4.2   (page 171)

1. Maximum is 20 when $x_1 = 0$, $x_2 = 4$, $x_3 = 0$, $x_4 = 0$, $x_5 = 2$ **3.** Maximum is 8 when $x_1 = 4$, $x_2 = 0$, $x_3 = 8$, $x_4 = 2$, $x_5 = 0$ **5.** Maximum is 264 when $x_1 = 16$, $x_2 = 4$, $x_3 = 0$, $x_4 = 0$, $x_5 = 16$ **7.** Maximum is 22 when $x_1 = 5.5$, $x_2 = 0$, $x_3 = 0$ and $x_4 = .5$ **9.** Maximum is 120 when $x_1 = 0$, $x_2 = 10$, $x_3 = 0$, $x_4 = 40$, $x_5 = 4$ **11.** Maximum is 944 when $x_1 = 118$, $x_2 = 0$, $x_3 = 0$, $x_4 = 0$, $x_5 = 102$ **13.** Maximum is 250 when $x_1 = 0$, $x_2 = 0$, $x_3 = 0$, $x_4 = 50$, $x_5 = 0$, $x_6 = 50$ **15.** 163.6 kg of food P; none of Q; 1090.9 kg of R; 145.5 kg of S; maximum is 87,454.5   **17.** 150 kg of the half-and-half mix; 75 kg of the other; maximum revenue is $1260   **19.** Make no 1-speed or 3-speed bicycles; make 2700 10-speed bicycles; maximum profit is $59,400   **21.** (a) 3 (b) 4   (c) 3   **23.** 6700 trucks and 4467 fire engines for a maximum profit of $110,997

Section 4.3   (page 181)

1. $2x_1 + 3x_2 + x_3 = 8$
$x_1 + 4x_2 - x_4 = 7$ **3.** $x_1 + x_2 + x_3 + x_4 = 100$
$x_1 + x_2 + x_3 - x_5 = 75$
$x_1 + x_2 - x_6 = 27$ **5.** Change the objective function to maximize $z = -4x_1 - 3x_2 - 2x_3$.

7. Change the objective function to maximize $z = -x_1 - 2x_2 - x_3 - 5x_4$.   **9.** Maximum is 480 when $x_1 = 40$ and $x_3 = 16$.
11. Maximum is 750 when $x_2 = 150$ and $x_5 = 50$ **13.** Maximum is 300 when $x_2 = 100$, $x_3 = 50$, and $x_5 = 10$
15. Minimum is 40 when $x_1 = 10$ and $x_4 = 50$ **17.** Minimum is 100 when $x_2 = 100$ and $x_5 = 50$ **19.** 800,000 for whole tomatoes and 80,000 for sauce for a minimum cost of $3,460,000   **21.** 3 of pill #1 and 2 of pill #2 for a minimum cost of 70¢
23. Buy 1000 small and 500 large for a minimum cost of $210   **25.** 2 2/3 units of I, none of II, and 4 of III for a minimum cost of $30.67   **27.** 1 2/3 ounces of I, 6 2/3 ounces of II, 1 2/3 ounces of III, for a minimum cost of $1.55 per gallon

Section 4.4   (page 191)

1. $$\begin{bmatrix} 1 & 3 & 1 \\ 2 & 2 & 10 \\ 3 & 1 & 0 \end{bmatrix}$$ **3.** $$\begin{bmatrix} -1 & 13 & -2 \\ 4 & 25 & -1 \\ 6 & 0 & 11 \\ 12 & 4 & 3 \end{bmatrix}$$ **5.** Minimize $5y_1 + 4y_2 + 15y_3$ subject to $y_1 + y_2 + 2y_3 \geq 4$, $y_1 + y_2 + y_3 \geq 3$, $y_1 + 3y_3 \geq 2$, $y_1 \geq 0$, $y_2 \geq 0$, $y_3 \geq 0$.   **7.** Maximize $50x_1 + 100x_2$ subject to $x_1 + 3x_2 \leq 1$; $x_1 + x_2 \leq 2$; $x_1 + 2x_2 \leq 1$; $x_1 + x_2 \leq 5$; $x_1 \geq 0$; $x_2 \geq 0$.   **9.** $y_1 = 0$, $y_2 = 7$; minimum is 14   **11.** $y_1 = 10$, $y_2 = 0$; minimum is 40   **13.** $y_1 = 0$, $y_2 = 100$, $y_3 = 0$; minimum is 100   **15.** 3 3/4 servings of A and 1 7/8 servings of B for a minimum cost of $1.69
17. 3 of pill #1, 2 of pill #2 for a minimum cost of 70 cents   **19.** (a) Minimize $200y_1 + 600y_2 + 90y_3 = w$ subject to $y_1 + 4y_2 \geq 1$, $2y_1 + 3y_2 + y_3 \geq 1.5$, $y_1 \geq 0$, $y_2 \geq 0$, $y_3 \geq 0$ (b) $y_1 = .6$, $y_2 = .1$, $y_3 = 0$, $w = 180$ (c) $186 ($x_1 = 114$, $x_2 = 48$)   (d) $179 ($x_1 = 116$, $x_2 = 42$)   **21.** Use 81 kg of the first, 382.3 kg of the second, 286.7 kg of the third, for minimum cost of $3652.25.

Extended Application   (page 195)

1. (a) $x_4 = 16.9$, $x_8 = 5.8$, $x_9 = 22.5$, $x_{10} = 1$ (b) $x_2 = 84.8$, $x_8 = 4.3$, $x_9 = 28.2$, $x_{10} = 1$

Chapter 4   Review Exercises   (page 198)

1. (a) Let x_1 = number of item A, x_2 = number of item B, and x_3 = number of item C she should buy   (b) $z = 4x_1 + 3x_2 + 3x_3$
(c) $5x_1 + 3x_2 + 6x_3 \le 1200$ **3.** (a) Let x_1 = number of gallons of fruity wine and x_2 = number of gallons of crystal wine to be
$$x_1 + 2x_2 + 2x_3 \le 800$$
$$2x_1 + x_2 + 5x_3 \le 500$$
made   (b) $z = 12x_1 + 15x_2$ (c) $2x_1 + x_2 \le 110$ **5.** (a) $2x_1 + 5x_2 + x_3 = 50$;   (b)
$$2x_1 + 3x_2 \le 125$$
$$x_1 + 3x_2 + x_4 = 25;$$
$$2x_1 + x_2 \le 90$$
$$4x_1 + x_2 + x_5 = 18;$$
$$x_1 + x_2 + x_6 = 12$$

x_1	x_2	x_3	x_4	x_5	x_6	
2	5	1	0	0	0	50
1	3	0	1	0	0	25
4	1	0	0	1	0	18
1	1	0	0	0	1	12
-5	-3	0	0	0	0	0

7. (a) $x_1 + x_2 + x_3 + x_4 = 90$;   (b)
$$2x_1 + 5x_2 + x_3 + x_5 = 120;$$
$$x_1 + 3x_2 - x_6 = 80$$

x_1	x_2	x_3	x_4	x_5	x_6	
1	1	1	1	0	0	90
2	5	1	0	1	0	120
1	3	0	0	0	-1	80
-5	-8	-6	0	0	0	0

9. (68/5, 0, 24/5, 0, 0,); maximum is

412/5; or (13.6, 0, 4.8, 0, 0); maximum is 82.4   **11.** (20/3, 0, 65/3, 35, 0, 0); maximum is 76 2/3   **13.** Change the objective
function to maximize $z = -10x_1 - 15x_2$ **15.** Change the objective function to maximize $z = -7x_1 - 2x_2 - 3x_3$ **17.** (8,
12, 0, 1, 0, 2); minimum is 62   **19.** None of A; 400 of B; none of C; maximum profit is \$1200   **21.** Produce 36.25 gallons of
fruity and 17.5 gallons of crystal for a maximum profit of \$697.50

Chapter 5   Section 5.1   (page 206)

1. False   **3.** True   **5.** True   **7.** True   **9.** False   **11.** False   **13.** False   **15.** True   **17.** False   **19.** True
21. True   **23.** False   **25.** True   **27.** True   **29.** False   **31.** False   **33.** False   **35.** 8   **37.** 32   **39.** 2
41. 32   **43.** 4   **45.** 3   **47.** 0   **49.** (a) All except $\varnothing$, {s}, {l}, {m}, {s, l}, {s, m}   (b) All except $\varnothing$, {s}, {l}

Section 5.2   (page 210)

1. True   **3.** False   **5.** True   **7.** False   **9.** True   **11.** True   **13.** {3, 5}   **15.** U, or {2, 3, 4, 5, 7, 9}
17. U, or {2, 3, 4, 5, 7, 9}   **19.** {7, 9}   **21.** $\varnothing$ **23.** $\varnothing$ **25.** U, or {2, 3, 4, 5, 7, 9}   **27.** All students in this school
not taking this course   **29.** All students in this school taking accounting and zoology   **31.** All students in this school taking this
course or zoology   **33.** 6   **35.** 5   **37.** 1   **39.** 5   **41.** B' = {stocks having a price to earnings ratio of less than 10};
B' = {ATT, GE, Hershey, Mobil, RCA}   **43.** $B \cap C$ = {stocks having a price to earnings ratio of 10 or more, *and* having a
positive price change}; $B \cap C = \varnothing$ **45.** $(A \cap B)'$ is made up of the stocks that are *not* in the set {stock with a dividend greater
than \$3 and a price to earnings ratio of at least 10}; $(A \cap B)'$ = {ATT, GE, Hershey, Mobil, RCA}   **47.** (a) {s, d, c, g, i, m, h}
(b) {s, d, c}   (c) {i, m, h}   (d) {g}   (e) {s, d, c, g, i, m, h}   (f) {s, d, c}

Section 5.3   (page 215)

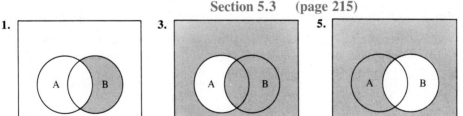

1. $B \cap A'$

3. $A' \cup B$

5. $B' \cup (A' \cap B')$

7. $\varnothing$

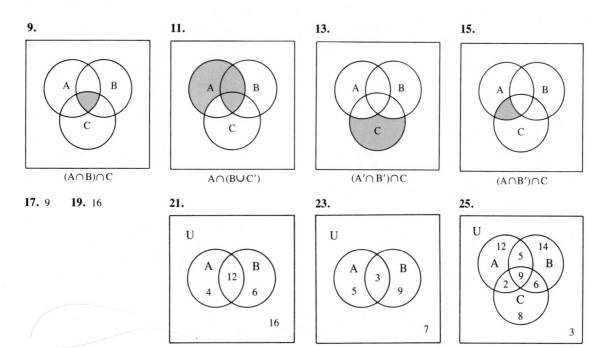

9. $(A \cap B) \cap C$

11. $A \cap (B \cup C')$

13. $(A' \cap B') \cap C$

15. $(A \cap B') \cap C$

17. 9   **19.** 16

21. U, A 4, 12, B 6, 16

23. U, A 5, 3, B 9, 7

25. U, 12, A 5, 14, B, 2, 9, 6, C, 8, 3

27.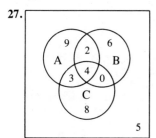

29. Yes; his data add up to 142 people   **31.** (a) 37 (b) 22 (c) 50 (d) 11 (e) 25 (f) 11
33. (a) 50 (b) 2 (c) 14   **35.** (a) 54 (b) 17 (c) 10 (d) 7 (e) 15 (f) 3 (g) 12 (h) 1
37. (a) 40 (b) 30 (c) 95 (d) 110 (e) 160 (f) 65

Section 5.4   (page 225)

1. 12   **3.** 56   **5.** 8   **7.** 24   **9.** 792   **11.** 156   **13.** 2.490952×10^{15} **15.** 240,240   **17.** 352,716
19. 2,042,975   **21.** $\binom{52}{2} = 1326$ **23.** 10   **25.** (a) $5^7 = 78,125$ (b) $9 \cdot 10^5 \cdot 1 = 900,000$ (c) $9 \cdot 10^4 \cdot 1^2 = 90,000$
(d) $1^3 \cdot 10^4 = 10,000$ (e) $9 \cdot 9 \cdot 8 \cdot 7 \cdot 6 \cdot 5 \cdot 4 = 544,320$ **27.** (a) $\binom{8}{5} = 56$ (b) $\binom{11}{5} = 462$ (c) $\binom{8}{3} \cdot \binom{11}{2} = 56 \cdot 55 =$
3080   **29.** $\binom{5}{2} \cdot \binom{4}{1} + \binom{5}{3} \cdot \binom{4}{0} = 40 + 10 = 50$ **31.** (a) $\binom{5}{3} = 10$ (b) 0 (c) $\binom{3}{3} = 1$ (d) $\binom{5}{2} \cdot \binom{1}{1} = 10$ (e) $\binom{5}{2} \cdot \binom{3}{1} =$
30 (f) $\binom{5}{1} \cdot \binom{3}{2} = 15$ (g) 0   **33.** $5 \cdot 3 \cdot 2 = 30$ **35.** (a) $2 \cdot 25 \cdot 24 \cdot 23 = 27,600$ (b) $2 \cdot 26 \cdot 26 \cdot 26 = 35,152$
(c) $2 \cdot 24 \cdot 23 \cdot 1 = 1104$ **37.** $\binom{4}{2} = 6$ **39.** (a) $\binom{7}{2} = 21$ (b) $1 \cdot \binom{6}{1} = 6$ (c) $\binom{2}{1} \cdot \binom{5}{1} + \binom{2}{2} \cdot \binom{5}{0} = 11$
41. (a) $\binom{12}{3} = 220$ (b) $\binom{12}{9} = 220$ **43.** $6! = 720$ **45.** $5! = 120$ **47.** $2 \cdot 26 \cdot 25 \cdot 24 \cdot 10 \cdot 9 \cdot 8 = 22,464,000$
49. (a) $\binom{9}{3} = 84$ (b) $\binom{5}{3} = 10$ (c) $\binom{5}{2} \cdot \binom{4}{1} = 40$ (d) $1 \cdot \binom{9}{2} = 28$ **51.** 2,598,960   **53.** 6.3501356×10^{11}
55. 55,440

Section 5.5   (page 231)

1. $m^4 + 4m^3n + 6m^2n^2 + 4mn^3 + n^4$ **3.** $729x^6 - 2916x^5y + 4860x^4y^2 - 4320x^3y^3 + 2160x^2y^4 - 576xy^5 + 64y^6$
5. $m^5/32 - 15m^4n/16 + 45m^3n^2/4 - 135m^2n^3/2 + 405mn^4/2 - 243n^5$ **7.** $p^{10} + 10p^9q + 45p^8q^2 + 120p^7q^3$
9. $a^{15} + 30a^{14}b + 420a^{13}b^2 + 3640a^{12}b^3$ **11.** $2^{10} = 1024$ **13.** $2^6 = 64$ (This result includes a pizza made with *none* of
the six toppings.)   **15.** $\binom{20}{2} + \binom{20}{3} + \binom{20}{4} + \binom{20}{5} + \binom{20}{6} = 60,439$ **17.** 64

Chapter 5   Review Exercises   (page 232)

1. False   **3.** False   **5.** True   **7.** False   **9.** False   **11.** {6, 7}; 2   **13.** {1, 2, 3, 4}; 4   **15.** $2^4 = 16$
17. {a, b, e}   **19.** {c, d, g}   **21.** {a, b, e, f}   **23.** U **25.** All employees in the accounting department who also have at least 10 years with the company   **27.** All employees who are in the accounting department or who have MBA degrees   **29.** All employees who are not in the sales department and who have worked less than 10 years with the company
31.   **33.**

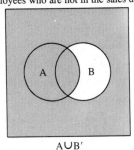

$A \cup B'$

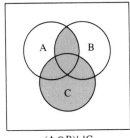

$(A \cap B) \cup C$

35. 52   **37.** 12   **39.** $6! = 720$ **41.** $5 \cdot 4 = 20$ **43.** $\binom{8}{3} \cdot \binom{6}{2} = 840$ **45.** $32m^5 + 80m^4 n + 80m^3 n^2 + 40m^2 n^3 + 10mn^4 + n^5$ **47.** $x^{20} - 10x^{19}y + 95x^{18}y^2/2 - 285x^{17}y^3/2$ **49.** $2^8 - 8 - 1 = 247$

Chapter 6   Section 6.1   (page 241)

1. {January, February, March, · · · , December}   **3.** {0, 1, 2, · · · , 80}   **5.** {go ahead, cancel}
7. {0, 1, 2, 3, · · · , 5000}   **9.** {hhhh, hhht, hhth, hthh, thhh, hhtt, htth, tthh, thth, thht, htht, httt, thtt, ttht, ttth, tttt}
11. {h, th, tth, ttth, tttth, · · ·}   **13.** (a) {(1, 1), (1, 2), (1, 3), (1, 4), (1, 5), (1, 6), (2, 1), (2, 2), (2, 3), (2, 4), (2, 5), (2, 6), (3, 1), (3, 2), (3, 3), (3, 4), (3, 5), (3, 6), (4, 1), (4, 2), (4, 3), (4, 4), (4, 5), (4, 6), (5, 1), (5, 2), (5, 3), (5, 4), (5, 5), (5, 6), (6, 1), (6, 2), (6, 3), (6, 4), (6, 5), (6, 6)}   (b) $F = \{(3, 1), (3, 2), (3, 3), (3, 4), (3, 5), (3, 6)\}$ (c) $G = \{(2, 6), (3, 5), (4, 4), (5, 3), (6, 2)\}$
(d) $H = \varnothing$ **15.** (a) {hh, hth, thh, htth, thth, tthh, ttthh, tthth, thtth, htttth, htttt, thttt, tthtt, ttttht, tttht, ttthht, ttttht, tttth, ttttt}   (b) $E = \{hh\}$ (c) $F = \{hth, thh\}$ (d) $G = \{tttt, ttttt, ttttht, tthtt, thttt, httttt\}$ **17.** (a) Worker is male   (b) Worker has worked five years or more
(c) Worker is female and has worked less than five years   (d) Worker has worked less than five years or has contributed to a voluntary retirement plan   (e) Worker is female or does not contribute to a voluntary retirement plan   (f) Worker has worked five years or more and does not contribute to a voluntary retirement plan   **19.** No   **21.** No   **23.** Yes   **25.** Yes   **27.** No   **29.** (a) E'
(b) $E \cap F$ (c) $E' \cap F'$ or $(E \cup F)'$ (d) $E \cap F'$ (e) $(E \cup F) \cap (E \cap F)'$ (f) $E \cup F$ **31.** {r, s, t}; {r, s}; {r, t}; {s, t}; {r}; {s}; {t}; $\varnothing$

Section 6.2   (page 250)

1. 1/6   **3.** 2/3   **5.** 1/13   **7.** 1/26   **9.** 1/52   **11.** 1 to 5   **13.** 2 to 1   **15.** {2}; {4}; {6}   **17.** {up}; {down}; {stays the same}   **19.** Feasible   **21.** Not feasible; sum of probabilities is less than 1   **23.** Not feasible; $P(s_2) < 0$
25. .12   **27.** .50   **29.** .77   **31.** 6 to 19   **33.** .15   **35.** .85   **37.** .70   **39.** 1/5   **41.** 4/15   **43.** 8 to 7
45. 11 to 4   **47.** 4/11   **49.** .41   **51.** .21   **53.** .79   **55.** Not subjective   **57.** Subjective   **59.** Subjective
61. Not subjective   **63.** Not subjective   **65.** "Odds *in favor* of a direct hit . . ." For 67 and 69 theoretical probabilities are given. Answers using the Monte Carlo method will vary.   **67.** 1/32 = .03125   **69.** .0249995

Extended Application   (page 253)

1. .715; .569; .410; .321; .271

Section 6.3   (page 257)

1. 1/36   **3.** 1/9   **5.** 5/36   **7.** 1/12   **9.** 5/18   **11.** 11/36   **13.** 5/12   **15.** 2/13   **17.** 3/26   **19.** 3/13
21. 7/13   **23.** 1/2   **25.** 3/10   **27.** 7/10   **29.** 1/10   **31.** 2/5   **33.** 7/20   **35.** .88   **37.** .25   **39.** .38
41. .89   **43.** .50   **45.** .09   **47.** .39   **49.** .77   **51.** .951   **53.** .473   **55.** .007   **57.** 3/4   **59.** 1/4
61. 1/4   **63.** .23   **65.** 2/3   **67.** The theoretical answer is 7/8. Answers using the Monte Carlo method will vary.

Section 6.4   (page 264)

1. $\binom{7}{1}/\binom{9}{1} = 7/9$ **3.** $\binom{7}{3}/\binom{9}{3} = 35/84$ **5.** .424   **7.** $\binom{6}{3}/\binom{10}{3} = 1/6$ **9.** $\binom{4}{1}\binom{6}{1}/\binom{10}{3} = 3/10$ **11.** $\binom{52}{2} = 1326$
13. $(4 \cdot 48 + 6)/\binom{52}{2} = 33/221$ **15.** $4 \cdot \binom{13}{2}/\binom{52}{2} = 52/221$ **17.** $\binom{40}{2}/\binom{52}{2} = 130/221$ **19.** $(1/26)^5$ **21.** $1 \cdot 25 \cdot$
$24 \cdot 23 \cdot 22/(26)^4 = 18,975/28,561$ **23.** $4/\binom{52}{5} = 1/649,740$ **25.** $13 \cdot \binom{4}{4}\binom{48}{1}/\binom{52}{5} = 1/4165$ **27.** $1/\binom{52}{13}$
29. $\binom{4}{3}\binom{4}{3}\binom{44}{7}/\binom{52}{13}$ **31.** $1 - P(365, 39)/(365)^{39} \approx .8782$ **33.** 1   **35.** 3/8; 1/4   **37.** $120/343 \approx .3498$
39. $3! = 6$ **41.** $9! = 362,880$ **43.** 1/3

Section 6.5   (page 275)

1. 0   **3.** 1   **5.** 1/6   **7.** 4/17   **9.** 25/51   **11.** $\frac{13}{52} \cdot \frac{12}{51} \cdot \frac{11}{50} \cdot \frac{10}{49} \cdot \frac{9}{48} \approx .00050$ **13.** $9/48 = .1875$

15. $4\left(\frac{13}{52} \cdot \frac{12}{51} \cdot \frac{11}{50} \cdot \frac{10}{49} \cdot \frac{9}{48}\right) \approx .00198$ **17.** $(2/3)^3 \approx .296$ **19.** 1/10   **21.** 0   **23.** 2/7   **25.** 2/7   **27.** The
probability of a customer cashing a check given that the customer made a deposit is 5/7.   **29.** The probability of a customer not
cashing a check given that the customer did not make a deposit is 1/4.   **31.** The probability of a customer not both cashing a check
and making a deposit is 6/11   **33.** 1/6   **35.** 0   **37.** 2/3   **39.** .06   **41.** 1/4   **43.** 1/4   **45.** 1/7   **47.** .049
49. .534   **51.** 42/527 or .080   **53.** Yes   **55.** .05   **57.** .25   **59.** Not very reasonable   **61.** $1 - .000015 = .999985$
63. $1/2000 = .0005$ **65.** $(1999/2000)^a$ **67.** $(1999/2000)^{Nc}$ **69.** $1 - .741 = .259$ **71.** True   **73.** True
75. True   **77.** False   **79.** 0

Section 6.6   (page 283)

1. 1/3   **3.** 2/41   **5.** 21/41   **7.** 8/17   **9.** .146   **11.** .082   **13.** $119/131 \approx .908$ **15.** .824   **17.** $1/176 \approx$
.006   **19.** 1/11   **21.** 5/9   **23.** 5/26   **25.** 72/73   **27.** 165/343

Extended Application   (page 287)

1. .076   **2.** .542   **3.** .051

Section 6.7   (page 292)

1. $\binom{5}{2}\left(\frac{1}{2}\right)^2\left(\frac{1}{2}\right)^3 = 5/16$ **3.** $\binom{5}{0}\left(\frac{1}{2}\right)^0\left(\frac{1}{2}\right)^5 = 1/32$ **5.** $\binom{5}{4}\left(\frac{1}{2}\right)^4\left(\frac{1}{2}\right)^1 + \binom{5}{5}\left(\frac{1}{2}\right)^5\left(\frac{1}{2}\right)^0 = 3/16$ **7.** $\binom{5}{0}\left(\frac{1}{2}\right)^0\left(\frac{1}{2}\right)^5 +$
$\binom{5}{1}\left(\frac{1}{2}\right)^1\left(\frac{1}{2}\right)^4 + \binom{5}{2}\left(\frac{1}{2}\right)^2\left(\quad\quad\binom{5}{3}\left(\frac{1}{2}\right)^3\left(\frac{1}{2}\right)^2 = 13/16\right.$ **9.** $\binom{12}{12}\left(\frac{1}{6}\right)^{12}\left(\frac{5}{6}\right)^0 \approx .0000000005$ **11.** $\binom{12}{1}\left(\frac{1}{6}\right)^1\left(\frac{5}{6}\right)^{11} \approx .269$
13. $\binom{12}{0}\left(\frac{1}{6}\right)^0\left(\frac{5}{6}\right)^{12} + \binom{12}{1}\left(\frac{1}{6}\right)^1\left(\frac{5}{6}\right)^{11} + \binom{12}{2}\left(\frac{1}{6}\right)^2\left(\frac{5}{6}\right)^{10} + \binom{12}{3}\left(\frac{1}{6}\right)^3\left(\frac{5}{6}\right)^9 \approx .875$ **15.** $\binom{5}{5}\left(\frac{1}{2}\right)^5\left(\frac{1}{2}\right)^0 = 1/32$
17. $\binom{5}{0}\left(\frac{1}{2}\right)^0\left(\frac{1}{2}\right)^5 + \binom{5}{1}\left(\frac{1}{2}\right)^1\left(\frac{1}{2}\right)^4 + \binom{5}{2}\left(\frac{1}{2}\right)^2\left(\frac{1}{2}\right)^3 + \binom{5}{3}\left(\frac{1}{2}\right)^3\left(\frac{1}{2}\right)^2 = 13/16$ **19.** $\binom{20}{0}(.05)^0(.95)^{20} \approx .358$
21. $\binom{6}{2}\left(\frac{1}{5}\right)^2\left(\frac{4}{5}\right)^4 \approx .246$ **23.** $\binom{6}{4}\left(\frac{1}{5}\right)^4\left(\frac{4}{5}\right)^2 + \binom{6}{5}\left(\frac{1}{5}\right)^5\left(\frac{4}{5}\right)^1 + \binom{6}{6}\left(\frac{1}{5}\right)^6\left(\frac{4}{5}\right)^0 \approx .017$ **25.** $\binom{3}{1}\left(\frac{5}{50}\right)^1\left(\frac{45}{50}\right)^2 \approx .243$
27. $\binom{10}{5}(.20)^5(.80)^5 \approx .026$ **29.** .999   **31.** $\binom{20}{17}(.70)^{17}(.30)^3 \approx .072$ **33.** .035   **35.** $\binom{10}{7}\left(\frac{1}{5}\right)^7\left(\frac{4}{5}\right)^3 \approx .00079$
37. $\approx .999922$ **39.** $\binom{3}{1}(.80)^1(.20)^2 = .096$ **41.** $\binom{3}{0}(.80)^0(.20)^3 + \binom{3}{1}(.80)^1(.20)^2 = .104$ **43.** .185   **45.** .256
47. $1 - (.99999975)^{10.000} \approx .0025$ **49.** $\binom{12}{4}(.2)^4(.8)^8 \approx .133$ **51.** .795   **53.** 3/16   **55.** 21/256   **57.** 125/23,328
59. $(165(5)^8)/6^{12}$ **61.** 6 teams   **63.** 10 teams   **65.** (a) .000036 (b) .999912 (c) 0   **67.** (a) .148774 (b) .021344
(c) .978656

Chapter 6   Review Exercises   (page 295)

1. {1, 2, 3, 4, 5, 6}   **3.** {0, .5, 1, 1.5, 2, · · ·, 299.5, 300}   **5.** {(3, R), (3, G), (5, R), (5, G), (7, R), (7, G), (9, R), (9, G),
(11, R), (11, G)}   **7.** {(3, G), (5, G), (7, G), (9, G), (11, G)}   **9.** $E' \cap F'$ **11.** 1/4   **13.** 3/13   **15.** 1/2   **17.** 1
19. 1 to 25   **21.** .86   **23.**

	N_2	T_2
N_1	N_1N_2	N_1T_2
T_1	T_1N_2	T_1T_2

25. 1/2   **27.** 5/36   **29.** 1/6   **31.** 1/6   **33.** 2/11

35. .66   **37.** .71   **39.** $\binom{4}{3}/\binom{11}{3} = 4/165$ **41.** $\binom{4}{2}\binom{5}{1}/\binom{11}{3} = 2/11$ **43.** $\binom{5}{2}\binom{2}{1}/\binom{11}{3} = 4/33$ **45.** 25/102
47. 15/34   **49.** 4/17   **51.** 3/10   **53.** 2/5 or .4   **55.** 3/4 or .75   **57.** 19/22   **59.** 1/3   **61.** 1/7   **63.** 5/16
65. 11/32   **67.** $\binom{20}{4}(.01)^4(.99)^{16} \approx .00004$ **69.** .81791 + .16523 + .01586 + .00096 + .00004 = 1.0000
71. (a) 8 wells   (b) 10 wells

Chapter 7   Section 7.1   (page 305)

1. (a)

Number	0	1	2	3	4	5
Probability	0	0	.1	.3	.4	.2

(b)

3. (a)

Number	0	1	2	3	4	5	6
Probability	0	.04	0	.16	.40	.32	.08

(b)

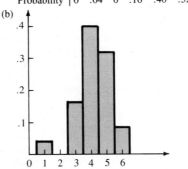

5. (a)

Number	0	1	2	3	4	5
Probability	.15	.25	.3	.15	.1	.05

(b)

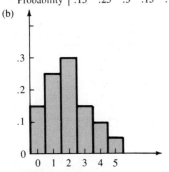

7.

Number of heads	0	1	2	3	4
Probability	1/16	1/4	3/8	1/4	1/16

9.

Number of aces	0	1	2	3
Probability	4324/5525 ≈ .783	1128/5525 ≈ .204	72/5525 ≈ .013	1/5525 ≈ .0002

11.

Number of hits	0	1	2	3	4
Probability	.254	.415	.254	.069	.007

13.

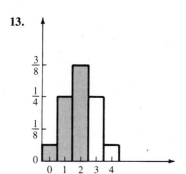

15.

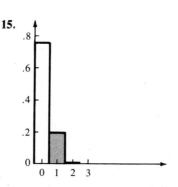

17.

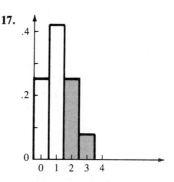

19. E: 18.1%; T: 8.8%; A: 6.2%; O: 4.4%; N: 7.5%; I: 7.1%; R: 5.8%; S: 5.8%; H: 5.8%; D: 2.2%; L: 5.3%; C: 4.9%; U: 4.0%; M: 1.8%; F: 4.0%; P: 1.8%; Y: 1.3%; W: 1.8%; G: 4.0%; B: 0%; V: .4%; K: 0%; X: 0%; J: 0%; Q: 1.3%; Z: 0%

Section 7.2   (page 312)

1. 3.6   **3.** 14.64   **5.** 2.7   **7.** 18   **9.** $-64¢$; no   **11.** $9/7 \approx 1.3$ **13.** (a) $5/3 \approx 1.67$ (b) $4/3 \approx 1.33$ **15.** 1
17. No, the expected value is about $-21¢$.   **19.** $-2.7¢$ **21.** $-20¢$ **23.** (a) Yes, the probability of a match is still 1/2.
(b) 40¢   (c) $-40¢$ **25.** 2.5   **27.** $4500   **29.** 118   **31.** 3.51   **33.**

Account	EV	Total	Class
3	$2000	$22,000	C
4	1000	51,000	B
5	25,000	30,000	C
6	60,000	60,000	A
7	16,000	46,000	B

35. 1.58   **37.** (a) $94.0 million for seeding; $116.0 for not seeding   (b) "Seed"

Extended Application   (page 318)

1. (a) $69.01 (b) $79.64   (c) $58.96   (d) $82.54   (e) $62.88   (f) $64.00   **2.** Stock only part 3 on the truck   **3.** p_1, p_2, p_3
are not the only events in the sample space   **4.** 2^n

Extended Application   (page 320)

1. .9886 million dollars   **2.** $-.9714$ million dollars

Section 7.3   (page 325)

1. $\sqrt{407.4} \approx 20.2$ **3.** $\sqrt{215.3} \approx 14.7$ **5.** $\sqrt{59.4} \approx 7.7$ **7.** Variance is .81; $\sigma = .9$
9. Variance is .000124; $\sigma = 0.011$ **11.** .700   **13.** .745   **15.** (a)   **17.** 2.41   **19.** (a) At least 3/4 (b) At least 15/16
(c) At least 24/25   **21.** (a) Mean is 320; standard deviation is 170.8   (b) 6   (c) 6   (d) At least 3/4   **23.** (a) 12.5   (b) -3.0
(c) 4.3   (d) 3.7   (e) 15.5   (f) 7.55 and 23.45   **25.** Mean is 5.0876; standard deviation is .1065   **27.** Mean is 46.6807;
standard deviation is .9223

Section 7.4   (page 336)

1. 49.38%   **3.** 17.36%   **5.** 45.64%   **7.** 49.91%   **9.** 7.7%   **11.** 47.35%   **13.** 92.42%   **15.** 32.56%
17. -1.64 or -1.65 **19.** 1.04   **21.** 5000   **23.** 4332   **25.** 642   **27.** 9918   **29.** 19   **31.** 15.87%
33. .62%   **35.** 84.13%   **37.** 37.79%   **39.** 2.28%   **41.** 99.38%   **43.** 189   **45.** .0062   **47.** .4325
49. $38.62 and $25.89   **51.** .0823   **53.** 6.68%   **55.** 38.3%   **57.** 82   **59.** 70   **61.** .079614   **63.** .993333
65. .317246   **67.** .152730   **69.** .005107

Extended Application   (page 339)

1. No; yes   **2.** No; yes

Section 7.5 (page 346)

1. (a)

X	0	1	2	3	4	5	6
$P(X)$	.335	.402	.201	.054	.008	.001	.000

(b) 1.00 (c) .91

3. (a)

X	0	1	2	3
$P(X)$	.941	.058	.001	.000

(b) .06 (c) .24   **5.** (a)

X	0	1	2	3	4
$P(X)$	.0081	.0756	.2646	.4116	.2401

(b) 2.8 (c) .92

7. 12.5; 3.49   **9.** 51.2; 3.2   **11.** .1974   **13.** .1210   **15.** .0240   **17.** .9032   **19.** .8665   **21.** .0956
23. .0760   **25.** .6443   **27.** .0146   **29.** .1974   **31.** .0092   **33.** .0001   **35.** .9945
37. For Exercise 30: .029784; for Exercise 31: .068924; for Exercise 32: .110495; for Exercise 33: .028682

Chapter 7 Review Exercises (page 347)

1. (a)

Number	1	2	3	4	5
Probability	.125	.292	.375	.125	.083

(b)

3. (a)

Number	0	1	2	3
Probability	$\frac{1}{8} = .125$	$\frac{3}{8} = .375$	$\frac{3}{8} = .375$	$\frac{1}{8} = .125$

(b)

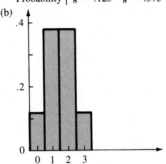

5. (a)

Number	0	1	2	3	4	5
Probability	.1	.1	.2	.3	.3	0

(b)

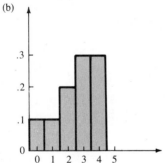

7. .6   **9.** $-28¢$ **11.** \$8500   **13.** 11.87   **15.** 2.6   **17.** \$1.29

19. Variance is 1.64; standard deviation is 1.28   **21.** (a) Diet A (b) Diet B
23. (a) 98.76% (b) Chebyshev's inequality would give ''at least 84%''
25. $z = 1.41$
27. (a)

x	0	1	2	3	4
Probability	.9801	.0197	.0001485	.0000004975	6×10^{-10}

(b) Mean $= .02$, $\sigma = .141$
29. (a) .1019 (b) .0008   **31.** (a) 25.14% (b) 28.10% (c) 22.92% (d) 56.25%

Chapter 8 Section 8.1 (page 358)

1. No   **3.** Yes   **5.** No   **7.** Yes   **9.** No   **11.** Yes   **13.** No   **15.** No   **17.** Yes   **19.** $A^1 = \begin{bmatrix} 1 & 0 \\ .8 & .2 \end{bmatrix}$;

$A^2 = \begin{bmatrix} 1 & .0 \\ .96 & .04 \end{bmatrix}$; $A^3 = \begin{bmatrix} 1 & 0 \\ .992 & .008 \end{bmatrix}$; 0   **21.** $C^1 = \begin{bmatrix} .5 & .5 \\ .72 & .28 \end{bmatrix}$; $C^2 = \begin{bmatrix} .61 & .39 \\ .5616 & .4384 \end{bmatrix}$;

$C^3 = \begin{bmatrix} .5858 & .4142 \\ .596448 & .403552 \end{bmatrix}$; .4142   **23.** $E^1 = \begin{bmatrix} .8 & .1 & .1 \\ .3 & .6 & .1 \\ 0 & 1 & 0 \end{bmatrix}$; $E^2 = \begin{bmatrix} .67 & .24 & .09 \\ .42 & .49 & .09 \\ .3 & .6 & .1 \end{bmatrix}$; $E^3 = \begin{bmatrix} .608 & .301 & .091 \\ .483 & .426 & .091 \\ .42 & .49 & .09 \end{bmatrix}$; .301

25. (a)
$$\begin{array}{c} \\ \text{Small} \\ \text{Large} \end{array} \begin{array}{cc} \text{Small} & \text{Large} \\ \begin{bmatrix} .80 & .20 \\ .60 & .40 \end{bmatrix} \end{array}$$
(b) $[.10 \quad .90]$ (c) $[.724 \quad .276]$ (d) $[.7448 \quad .2552]$ (e) $[.7490 \quad .2510]$ (f) $[.7498 \quad .2502]$

27. (a) $[.53 \quad .47]$ (b) $[.5885 \quad .4115]$ (c) $[.6148 \quad .3852]$ (d) $[.62666 \quad .37334]$ **29.** (a) 42,500; 5000; 2500
(b) 36,125; 8250; 5625   (c) 30,706; 10,213; 9081   (d) 26,100; 11,241; 12,659   **31.** (a) $[.257 \quad .597 \quad .146]$

(b) $[.255 \quad .594 \quad .151]$ (c) $[.254 \quad .590 \quad .156]$ **33.** (a)
$$\begin{array}{c} \\ \text{Single} \\ \text{Multiple} \end{array} \begin{array}{cc} \text{Single} & \text{Multiple} \\ \begin{bmatrix} .90 & .10 \\ .05 & .95 \end{bmatrix} \end{array}$$
(b) $[.75 \quad .25]$ (c) $[68.8\% \quad 31.3\%]$

(d) $[63.4\% \quad 36.6\%]$ **35.** The first power is the given transition matrix;
$$\begin{bmatrix} .2 & .15 & .17 & .19 & .29 \\ .16 & .2 & .15 & .18 & .31 \\ .19 & .14 & .24 & .21 & .22 \\ .16 & .19 & .16 & .2 & .29 \\ .16 & .19 & .14 & .17 & .34 \end{bmatrix};$$

$$\begin{bmatrix} .17 & .178 & .171 & .191 & .29 \\ .171 & .178 & .161 & .185 & .305 \\ .18 & .163 & .191 & .197 & .269 \\ .175 & .174 & .164 & .187 & .3 \\ .167 & .184 & .158 & .182 & .309 \end{bmatrix}; \begin{bmatrix} .1731 & .175 & .1683 & .188 & .2956 \\ .1709 & .1781 & .1654 & .1866 & .299 \\ .1748 & .1718 & .1753 & .1911 & .287 \\ .1712 & .1775 & .1667 & .1875 & .2971 \\ .1706 & .1785 & .1641 & .1858 & .301 \end{bmatrix};$$

$$\begin{bmatrix} .17193 & .17643 & .1678 & .18775 & .29609 \\ .17167 & .17689 & .16671 & .18719 & .29754 \\ .17293 & .17488 & .17007 & .18878 & .29334 \\ .17192 & .17654 & .16713 & .18741 & .297 \\ .17142 & .17726 & .16629 & .18696 & .29807 \end{bmatrix}; .18719$$ **37.** (a) .847423 or about 85% (b) $[.032 \quad .0998125 \quad .0895625 \quad .778625]$

Section 8.2   (page 366)

1. Regular   **3.** Not regular   **5.** Regular   **7.** $[2/5 \quad 3/5]$ **9.** $[4/11 \quad 7/11]$ **11.** $[14/83 \quad 19/83 \quad 50/83]$
13. $[170/563 \quad 197/563 \quad 196/563]$ **15.** $[3/4 \quad 1/4]$ **17.** $[0 \quad 0 \quad 1]$ **19.** $[2/17 \quad 11/17 \quad 4/17]$
21. $[.244 \quad .529 \quad .227]$ **23.** 16/17   **25.** $[51/209 \quad 88/209 \quad 70/209]$ **27.** $[1/3 \quad 1/3 \quad 1/3]$ **29.** 1/2
33. $[.171898 \quad .176519 \quad .167414 \quad .187526 \quad .296644]$ **35.** $[0 \quad 0 \quad .113636 \quad .886364]$

Section 8.3   (page 374)

1. State 2 is absorbing; matrix is that of an absorbing Markov chain.   **3.** State 2 is absorbing; matrix is not that of an absorbing
Markov chain.   **5.** States 2 and 4 are absorbing; matrix is that of an absorbing Markov chain.   **7.** States 2 and 4 are absorbing;
matrix is that of an absorbing Markov chain.   **9.** $F = [2]$; $FR = [.4 \quad .6]$ **11.** $F = [5]$; $FR = [3/4 \quad 1/4]$

13. $F = [3/2]$; $FR = [1/2 \quad 1/2]$ **15.** $F = \begin{bmatrix} 1 & 0 \\ 1/3 & 4/3 \end{bmatrix}$; $FR = \begin{bmatrix} 1/3 & 2/3 \\ 4/9 & 5/9 \end{bmatrix}$ **17.** $F = \begin{bmatrix} 25/17 & 5/17 \\ 5/34 & 35/34 \end{bmatrix}$;

$FR = \begin{bmatrix} 4/17 & 15/34 & 11/34 \\ 11/34 & 37/68 & 9/68 \end{bmatrix}$ **19.** (a) $F = \begin{bmatrix} 3/2 & 1 & 1/2 \\ 1 & 2 & 1 \\ 1/2 & 1 & 3/2 \end{bmatrix}$; $FR = \begin{bmatrix} 3/4 & 1/4 \\ 1/2 & 1/2 \\ 1/4 & 3/4 \end{bmatrix}$ (b) 3/4 (c) 1/4

21. (a) $F = \begin{bmatrix} 20/17 & 240/289 \\ 0 & 20/17 \end{bmatrix}$; $FR = \begin{bmatrix} 145/289 & 144/289 \\ 5/17 & 12/17 \end{bmatrix}$ (b) 144/289   **23.** .8756

25.

p	.1	.2	.3	.4	.5	.6	.7	.8	.9
x_a	.9999999997	.99999905	.99979	.98295	.5	.017046	.000209	.00000095	.0000000003

27. (a) .6 (b) .5

Chapter 8   Review Exercises   (page 376)

1. Yes   **3.** Yes   **5.** (a) $C^1 = \begin{bmatrix} .6 & .4 \\ 1 & 0 \end{bmatrix}$; $C^2 = \begin{bmatrix} .76 & .24 \\ .6 & .4 \end{bmatrix}$; $C^3 = \begin{bmatrix} .696 & .304 \\ .76 & .24 \end{bmatrix}$ (b) .76

7. (a) $E^1 = \begin{bmatrix} .2 & .5 & .3 \\ .1 & .8 & .1 \\ 0 & 1 & 0 \end{bmatrix}$; $E^2 = \begin{bmatrix} .09 & .8 & .11 \\ .1 & .79 & .11 \\ .1 & .8 & .1 \end{bmatrix}$; $E^3 = \begin{bmatrix} .098 & .795 & .107 \\ .099 & .792 & .109 \\ .1 & .79 & .11 \end{bmatrix}$ (b) .099   **9.** $[.453 \quad .547]$; $[5/11 \quad 6/11]$ or
$[.455 \quad .545]$ **11.** $[.48 \quad .28 \quad .24]$; $[47/95 \quad 26/95 \quad 22/95]$ or $[.495 \quad .274 \quad .232]$ **13.** (a) $[.54 \quad .46]$ (b) $[.6464 \quad .3536]$

15. [.428 .322 .25] **17.** [.431 .284 .285] **19.** 2 **21.** .196 **23.** .28 **25.** [.195 .555 .25]
27. [.194 .556 .25] **29.** Regular **31.** Not regular **33.** State 2 is absorbing; matrix is not that of an absorbing Markov chain **35.** $F = [5/4]$; $FR = [5/8 \quad 3/8]$ **37.** $F = \begin{bmatrix} 7/4 & 4/5 \\ 1 & 8/5 \end{bmatrix}$; $FR = \begin{bmatrix} .55 & .45 \\ .6 & .4 \end{bmatrix}$ **39.** State 1, 3, and 6

41. $F = \begin{bmatrix} 5/2 & 1 & 1/2 \\ 1 & 2 & 1 \\ 1/2 & 1 & 5/2 \end{bmatrix}$; $FR = \begin{bmatrix} 11/16 & 1/8 & 3/16 \\ 3/8 & 1/4 & 3/8 \\ 3/16 & 1/8 & 11/16 \end{bmatrix}$

Chapter 9   Section 9.1   (page 382)

1. (a) Buy speculative (b) Buy blue-chip (c) Buy speculative; $24,300 (d) Buy blue-chip **3.** (a) Set up in the stadium
(b) Set up in the gym (c) Set up both; $1010 **5.** (a)

	Better	Not better
Market	50,000	$-25,000$
Don't market	$-40,000$	$-10,000$

(b) $5000 if they market new product, $-$22,000 if they don't; market the new product.

7. (a)

	Strike	No strike
Bid $30,000	-5500	4500
Bid $40,000	4500	0

(b) $40,000 **9.** Emphasize environment; 14.25

Extended Application   (page 388)

1. $E_1 = 18.61M$, $E_2 = 2.898M - 42.055$, $E_3 = .56M - 48.6$
2. $E_1 = 19.7325M$, $E_2 = .054M - 47.973$, $E_3 = .108M - 49.73$ **3.** $E_1 = 19M$, $E_2 = 1.7M - 45$, $E_3 = .6M - 48.5$

Section 9.2   (page 392)

1. $6 from B to A **3.** $2 from A to B **5.** $1 from A to B **7.** Yes **9.** $\begin{bmatrix} -2 & 8 \\ -1 & -9 \end{bmatrix}$ **11.** $\begin{bmatrix} 4 & -1 \\ 3 & 5 \end{bmatrix}$
13. $\begin{bmatrix} 8 & -7 \\ -2 & 4 \end{bmatrix}$ **15.** (1, 1); 3; strictly determined **17.** No saddle point; not strictly determined **19.** (3, 1); 3; strictly determined **21.** (1, 3); 1; strictly determined **23.** No saddle point; not strictly determined **25.** (2, 3); 6

27.
	stone	scissors	paper
stone	0	1	-1
scissors	-1	0	1
paper	1	-1	0

; no **29.** A
	B 1	2	3
1	15	-2	6
2	7	15	9
3	3	-3	15

; no

Section 9.3   (page 402)

1. (a) -1 (b) $-.28$ (c) -1.54 (d) $-.46$ **3.** Player A: 1: 1/5, 2: 4/5; player B: 1: 3/5, 2: 2/5; value 17/5 **5.** Player A: 1: 7/9, 2: 2/9; player B: 1: 4/9, 2: 5/9; value $-8/9$ **7.** Player A: 1: 8/15, 2: 7/15; player B: 1: 2/3, 2: 1/3; value 5/3 **9.** Player A: 1: 6/11, 2: 5/11; player B: 1: 7/11, 2: 4/11; value $-12/11$ **11.** Strictly determined game; saddle point at (2, 2); value is $-5/12$
13. Player A: 1: 2/5, 2: 3/5; player B: 1: 1/5, 2: 4/5; value 7/5 **15.** Player A: 1: 1/14, 2: 0, 3: 13/14; player B: 1: 1/7, 2: 6/7; value 50/7 **17.** Player A: 1: 2/3, 2: 1/3; player B: 1: 0, 2: 1/9, 3: 8/9; value: 10/3 **19.** Player A: 1: 0; 2: 3/4; 3: 1/4; player B: 1: 0, 2: 1/12, 3: 11/12; value 33/4 **21.** Allied should use TV with probability 10/27 and use radio with probability 17/27. The value of the game is 1/18, which represents increased sales of $55,556. **23.** The doctor should prescribe medicine 1 about 5/6 of the time and medicine 2 about 1/6 of the time. The effectiveness will be about 50%. **25.** (a)

		Number of fingers 0	2
Number	0	0	-2
of fingers	2	-2	4

(b) For both players A and B: choose 0 with probability 3/4 and 2 with probability 1/4. The value of the game is $-1/2$.
27. He should invest in rainy day goods about 5/9 of the time and sunny day goods about 4/9 of the time for a steady profit of $72.22.

Chapter 9   Review Exercises   (page 408)

1. Hostile   **3.** Hostile; $785   **5.** Oppose   **7.** Oppose; 2700   **9.** $2 from A to B   **11.** $7 from B to A   **13.** Row 3 dominates row 1; column 1 dominates column 4   **15.** $\begin{bmatrix} -11 & 6 \\ -10 & -12 \end{bmatrix}$ **17.** $\begin{bmatrix} -2 & 4 \\ 3 & 2 \\ 0 & 3 \end{bmatrix}$ **19.** (1, 1); value is -2

21. (2, 2); value is 0; fair game   **23.** (2, 3); value is -3 **25.** Player A: 1: 5/6, 2: 1/6; player B: 1: 1/2, 2: 1/2; value 1/2   **27.** Player A: 1: 1/9, 2: 8/9; player B: 1: 5/9, 2: 4/9; value 5/9   **29.** Player A: 1: 1/5, 2: 4/5; player B: 1: 3/5, 2: 0; 3: 2/5; value $-12/5$ **31.** Player A: 1: 3/4, 2: 1/4, 3: 0; player B: 1: 1/2, 2: 1/2; value 1/2

Chapter 10   Section 10.1   (page 416)

1. $120   **3.** $3937.50   **5.** $186.54   **7.** $336   **9.** $143.46   **11.** $438.90   **13.** $376.11   **15.** $201.46   **17.** $13,554.22   **19.** $5056.06   **21.** $14,434.68   **23.** $6101.33   **25.** $318.69   **27.** $30,268.47   **29.** $1732.90   **31.** $6053.59   **33.** $3598; 20.1%   **35.** $7547.13

Answers in the remainder of this chapter may differ by a few cents depending on whether tables or a calculator is used.

Section 10.2   (page 422)

1. $1593.85   **3.** $20,974.32   **5.** $1903.00   **7.** $82,379.10   **9.** $30,779.48   **11.** $13,213.14   **13.** $5105.58   **15.** $60,484.66   **17.** $2746.51   **19.** $2551.13   **21.** $4490.29   **23.** $583.78   **25.** $4016.21   **27.** $1000 now   **29.** 4.04%   **31.** 8.16%   **33.** 12.36%   **35.** About 18 years   **37.** About 12 years   **39.** $142,886.40   **41.** $123,506.50   **43.** $63,685.27   **45.** $904.02

Section 10.3   (page 429)

1. 11, 17, 23, 29, 35; arithmetic   **3.** $-4, -1, 2, 5, 8$; arithmetic   **5.** $-2, -8, -14, -20, -26$; arithmetic   **7.** 2, 4, 8, 16, 32; geometric   **9.** $-2, 4, -8, 16, -32$; geometric   **11.** 6, 12, 24, 48, 96; geometric   **13.** 1/3, 3/7, 1/2, 5/9, 3/5; neither   **15.** 1/2, 1/3, 1/4, 1/5, 1/6; neither   **17.** Arithmetic, $d = 8$ **19.** Arithmetic, $d = 3$ **21.** Geometric, $r = 3$ **23.** Neither   **25.** Arithmetic, $d = -3$ **27.** Arithmetic, $d = 3$ **29.** Geometric, $r = -2$ **31.** Neither   **33.** 70   **35.** 65   **37.** 78   **39.** -65 **41.** 63   **43.** 678   **45.** 183   **47.** -18 **49.** 48   **51.** -648 **53.** 81   **55.** 64   **57.** 15   **59.** 156/25   **61.** -208 **63.** -15 **65.** 80   **67.** 125   **69.** 134   **71.** 70   **73.** -56 **75.** 125,250   **77.** 90   **79.** 170   **81.** 160   **83.** $15,600   **85.** (a) $1681   (b) $576

Section 10.4   (page 436)

1. 15.91713   **3.** 21.82453   **5.** 22.01900   **7.** 20.02359   **9.** $1318.08   **11.** $305,390.00   **13.** $671,994.62   **15.** $4,180,929.88   **17.** $222,777.26   **19.** $40,652.46   **21.** $516,397.05   **23.** $6294.79   **25.** $158,456.00   **27.** $13,486.56   **29.** $8070.23   **31.** $526.95   **33.** $952.33   **35.** $137,895.84   **37.** $118,667.74   **39.** $159.49   **41.** $522.85   **43.** $112,796.87   **45.** $209,348.00   **47.** $354.79   **49.** $579.65   **51.** $4164.55   **53.** $126.91   **55.** $23,023.98   **57.** (a) $1200   (b) $3511.58   (c)

Payment Number	Amount of Deposit	Interest Earned	Total
1	$3511.58	$0	$3511.58
2	3511.58	105.35	7128.51
3	3511.58	213.86	10,853.95
4	3511.58	325.62	14,691.15
5	3511.58	440.73	18,643.46
6	3511.58	559.30	22,714.34
7	3511.58	681.43	26,907.35
8	3511.58	807.22	31,226.15
9	3511.58	936.78	35,674.51
10	3511.58	1070.24	40,256.33
11	3511.58	1207.69	44,975.60
12	3511.58	1349.27	49,836.45
13	3511.58	1495.09	54,843.12
14	3511.59	1645.29	60,000.00

Section 10.5   (page 442)

1. 9.71225   **3.** 12.65930   **5.** 14.71787   **7.** 5.69719   **9.** $6246.89   **11.** $7877.72   **13.** $153,724.50
15. $148,771.76   **17.** $111,183.90   **19.** $97,122.50   **21.** $68,108.64   **23.** $12,493.78   **25.** $158.00
27. $6698.98   **29.** $160.08   **31.** $5570.58   **33.** $11,727.32   **35.** $274.58   **37.** $663.75   **39.** $742.51

41.

Payment Number	Amount of Payment	Interest for Period	Portion to Principal	Principal at End of Period
0	—	—	—	$4000
1	$1207.68	$320.00	$887.68	$3112.32
2	1207.68	248.99	958.69	2153.63
3	1207.68	172.29	1035.39	1118.24
4	1207.70	89.46	1118.24	0

43.

Payment Number	Amount of Payment	Interest for Period	Portion to Principal	Principal at End of Period
0	—	—	—	$7184
1	$211.03	$107.76	$103.27	$7080.73
2	211.03	106.21	104.82	6975.91
3	211.03	$104.64	106.39	6869.52
4	211.03	103.04	107.99	6761.53
5	211.03	101.42	109.61	6651.92
6	211.03	99.78	111.25	6540.67

45. (a) $4025.90   (b) $2981.93

47.

End of Year	To Interest	To Principal	Total Interest	Total Principal	Balance
1	$3225.54	$2557.95	$ 3225.54	$ 2557.95	$35389.50
2	3008.11	2775.38	6233.64	5333.34	32614.20
3	2772.21	3011.29	9005.85	8344.62	29602.90
4	2516.24	3267.25	11522.10	11611.90	26335.60
5	2238.53	3544.96	13760.60	15156.80	22790.70
6	1937.20	3846.29	15697.80	19003.10	18944.40
7	1610.28	4173.22	17308.10	23176.30	14771.20
8	1255.54	4527.95	18563.60	27704.30	10243.20
9	870.67	4912.82	19434.30	32617.10	5330.39
10	453.07	5330.42	19887.40	37947.50	−0.02

Extended Application   (page 448)

1. $14,038   **2.** $9511   **3.** $8837   **4.** $3968

Chapter 10   Review Exercises   (page 449)

1. $1908.36   **3.** $2686.84   **5.** $105.30   **7.** $21,897.81   **9.** $76,075.85   **11.** $665.54   **13.** $6194.13
15. 16.3%   **17.** $1999.00   **19.** $43,988.32   **21.** $7797.47   **23.** $4272.85   **25.** $6002.84   **27.** $6289.04
29. $18,306.34   **31.** $2501.24   **33.** $12,025.46   **35.** $845.74   **37.** $3137.06   **39.** −2, −6, −10, −14, −18;
arithmetic   **41.** 1/2, 4/7, 5/8, 2/3, 7/10   **43.** 61   **45.** −24   **47.** $15,162.14   **49.** $199,870.32   **51.** $41,208.86
53. $45,569.65   **55.** $886.05   **57.** $3339.86   **59.** $2815.31   **61.** $34,357.52   **63.** $4788.17   **65.** $12,806.37
67. $2806.66   **69.** $717.21

71.

Payment Number	Amount of Payment	Interest for Period	Portion to Principal	Principal at End of Period
0	—	—	—	$5000
1	$985.09	$250.00	$735.09	$4264.91
2	985.09	213.25	771.84	3493.07
3	985.09	174.65	810.44	2682.63
4	985.09	134.13	850.96	1831.67
5	985.09	91.58	893.51	938.16
6	985.07	46.91	938.16	0

Chapter 11   Section 11.1   (page 458)

1.
$$\begin{array}{c} \\ R \\ S \\ T \end{array}\begin{array}{ccc} R & S & T \\ \left[\begin{array}{ccc} 0 & 1 & 0 \\ 0 & 0 & 0 \\ 2 & 1 & 0 \end{array}\right] \end{array}$$

3.
$$\begin{array}{c} \\ X \\ Y \\ Z \end{array}\begin{array}{ccc} X & Y & Z \\ \left[\begin{array}{ccc} 0 & 1 & 0 \\ 1 & 0 & 0 \\ 0 & 0 & 0 \end{array}\right] \end{array}$$; adjacency matrix

5.
$$\begin{array}{c} \\ P \\ R \\ S \\ T \end{array}\begin{array}{cccc} P & R & S & T \\ \left[\begin{array}{cccc} 0 & 2 & 0 & 1 \\ 0 & 0 & 1 & 1 \\ 0 & 0 & 0 & 0 \\ 1 & 0 & 1 & 0 \end{array}\right] \end{array}$$

7.
$$\begin{array}{c} \\ P \\ Q \\ R \\ S \end{array}\begin{array}{cccc} P & Q & R & S \\ \left[\begin{array}{cccc} 0 & 1 & 1 & 0 \\ 1 & 0 & 1 & 1 \\ 0 & 0 & 0 & 1 \\ 1 & 0 & 1 & 0 \end{array}\right] \end{array}$$; adjacency matrix

9.
$$\begin{array}{c} \\ E \\ F \\ G \\ H \\ K \end{array}\begin{array}{ccccc} E & F & G & H & K \\ \left[\begin{array}{ccccc} 0 & 2 & 1 & 1 & 1 \\ 1 & 0 & 1 & 1 & 0 \\ 1 & 0 & 0 & 1 & 1 \\ 1 & 1 & 0 & 0 & 1 \\ 0 & 0 & 1 & 0 & 0 \end{array}\right] \end{array}$$

11.
$$\begin{array}{c} \\ A \\ B \\ C \\ D \\ E \\ F \end{array}\begin{array}{cccccc} A & B & C & D & E & F \\ \left[\begin{array}{cccccc} 0 & 1 & 1 & 1 & 1 & 0 \\ 1 & 0 & 1 & 1 & 1 & 1 \\ 0 & 0 & 0 & 1 & 1 & 0 \\ 0 & 1 & 1 & 0 & 1 & 0 \\ 1 & 0 & 0 & 1 & 0 & 1 \\ 1 & 0 & 0 & 0 & 0 & 0 \end{array}\right] \end{array}$$; adjacency matrix

13.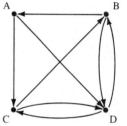

15.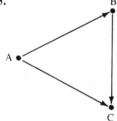

17.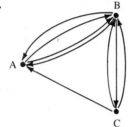

19.

21.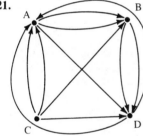

23.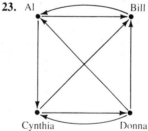

$$\begin{array}{c} \\ A \\ B \\ C \\ D \end{array}\begin{array}{cccc} A & B & C & D \\ \left[\begin{array}{cccc} 0 & 1 & 1 & 0 \\ 1 & 0 & 0 & 0 \\ 0 & 1 & 0 & 1 \\ 1 & 1 & 1 & 0 \end{array}\right] \end{array}$$

Section 11.2   (page 463)

1. $\begin{bmatrix} 0 & 0 \\ 0 & 0 \end{bmatrix}$; A dominates 1 person, B dominates no one

3. $\begin{bmatrix} 0 & 0 & 1 \\ 1 & 0 & 0 \\ 0 & 1 & 0 \end{bmatrix}$;   each dominates 2 people

5. Not the matrix of a dominance digraph

7. $\begin{bmatrix} 0 & 1 & 2 & 0 \\ 1 & 0 & 0 & 0 \\ 0 & 1 & 0 & 1 \\ 1 & 0 & 1 & 0 \end{bmatrix}$; R dominates 5 people, S dominates 2 people, T dominates 3 people, and V dominates 4 people

9.
$$\begin{bmatrix} 0 & 0 & 1 & 1 & 2 \\ 1 & 0 & 0 & 2 & 1 \\ 2 & 1 & 0 & 1 & 0 \\ 0 & 1 & 2 & 0 & 1 \\ 1 & 2 & 1 & 0 & 0 \end{bmatrix}; \text{ all dominate 6 people}$$

11.
$$\begin{array}{c} \\ A \\ B \\ C \\ D \end{array} \begin{array}{cccc} A & B & C & D \\ \begin{bmatrix} 0 & 1 & 1 & 1 \\ 0 & 0 & 1 & 0 \\ 0 & 0 & 0 & 0 \\ 0 & 1 & 1 & 0 \end{bmatrix} \end{array};$$

A has 3 two-stage dominances (*B* through *D*, and *C* through both *B* and *D*), and *D* has 1 two-stage dominance (*C* through *B*)

13.
$$\begin{array}{c} \\ A \\ B \\ C \\ D \end{array} \begin{array}{cccc} A & B & C & D \\ \begin{bmatrix} 0 & 0 & 0 & 1 \\ 1 & 0 & 1 & 0 \\ 1 & 0 & 0 & 1 \\ 0 & 1 & 0 & 0 \end{bmatrix} \end{array};$$

A has 1 two-stage dominance (of *B* through *D*), *B* has 3 two-stage dominances (of *A* through *C* and *D* through both *A* and *C*), *C* has 2 two-stage dominances (of *B* through *D* and of *D* through *A*), and *D* has 2 two-stage dominances (of *A* through *B* and *C* through *B*)

15. *C* won 8 games in one- or two-stage dominance, while *A* won 7. Declare *C* the winner.   **17.** Green has 5 one- or two-stage dominances, while Red has 4. Make the cereal green.   **19.** *B* has 8 while *E* has 7, so wine *B* wins the taste test.

21. *A* dominates *B* in 6 ways, *C* in 4 ways, *D* in 1 way, and *E* in 1 way. *B* dominates *A* in 1 way, *C* in 6 ways, *D* in 1 way, and *E* in 4 ways. *C* dominates *A* in 1 way, *B* in 1 way, *D* in 4 ways, and *E* in 6 ways. *D* dominates *A* in 6 ways, *B* in 4 ways, *C* in 1 way, and *E* in 1 way. *E* dominates *A* in 4 ways, *B* in 1 way, *C* in 1 way, and *D* in 6 ways.

Section 11.3   (page 469)

1.
$$\begin{array}{c} \\ A \\ B \\ C \\ D \end{array} \begin{array}{cccc} A & B & C & D \\ \begin{bmatrix} 0 & 0 & 1 & 1 \\ 0 & 0 & 1 & 1 \\ 1 & 1 & 0 & 2 \\ 1 & 1 & 2 & 0 \end{bmatrix} \end{array}$$
Communications digraph

3.
$$\begin{array}{c} \\ P \\ Q \\ R \\ S \\ T \end{array} \begin{array}{ccccc} P & Q & R & S & T \\ \begin{bmatrix} 0 & 0 & 1 & 0 & 0 \\ 0 & 0 & 0 & 1 & 1 \\ 1 & 0 & 0 & 1 & 0 \\ 0 & 1 & 1 & 0 & 1 \\ 0 & 1 & 0 & 1 & 0 \end{bmatrix} \end{array}$$
Communications digraph

5.
$$\begin{array}{c} \\ M \\ N \\ P \\ Q \\ R \end{array} \begin{array}{ccccc} M & N & P & Q & R \\ \begin{bmatrix} 0 & 1 & 0 & 0 & 2 \\ 1 & 0 & 1 & 0 & 1 \\ 0 & 1 & 0 & 1 & 0 \\ 0 & 0 & 1 & 0 & 1 \\ 2 & 1 & 0 & 1 & 0 \end{bmatrix} \end{array}$$
Communications digraph

7.
$$\begin{array}{c} \\ T \\ W \\ X \\ Y \\ Z \end{array} \begin{array}{ccccc} T & W & X & Y & Z \\ \begin{bmatrix} 0 & 1 & 0 & 1 & 0 \\ 1 & 0 & 0 & 0 & 1 \\ 0 & 0 & 0 & 0 & 1 \\ 1 & 0 & 0 & 0 & 1 \\ 0 & 1 & 1 & 1 & 0 \end{bmatrix} \end{array}$$
Both a communications digraph and an organizational communications digraph

9.
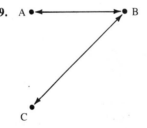
Two-stage paths includes *A* to *A* through *B*, *A* to *C* through *B*, *B* to *B* through *A* and through *C*, *C* to *A* through *B*, *C* to *C* through *B*.

11.
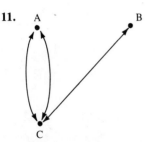
Two-stage paths includes *A* to *A* through *C* in 4 ways, *A* to *B* through *C* in 2 ways, *B* to *A* through *C* in 2 ways, *B* to *B* through *C* in 1 way, *C* to *C* through *A* in 4 ways and through *B* in 1 way.

13. *A* ⟷ *B* (diagram)
Two-stage paths includes *A* to *A* in 2 ways, through *B* and through *D*, *A* to *C* in 3 ways (2 through *B* and 1 through *D*), *B* to *B* in 5 ways (4 through *C* and 1 through *A*), *B* to *D* in 3 ways (2 through *C* and 1 through *A*), *C* to *A* in 3 ways (2 through *B*, 1 through *D*), *C* to *C* in 5 ways (4 through *B*, 1 through *D*), *D* to *B* in 3 ways (2 through *C*, 1 through *A*), and *D* to *D* in 2 ways (1 through *C*, 1 through *A*).

15. 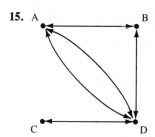 Two-stage paths includes *A* to *A* in 5 ways, *A* to *B* in 2 ways, *A* to *C* in 2 ways, *A* to *D* in 1 way, *B* to *A* in 2 ways, *B* to *B* in 2 ways, *B* to *C* in 1 way, *B* to *D* in 2 ways, *C* to *A* in 2 ways, *C* to *B* in 1 way, *C* to *C* in 1 way, *D* to *A* in 1 way, *D* to *B* in 2 ways, *D* to *D* in 6 ways.

17. *AED*, *ACED*, *ABED*   **19.** *ACBED*, *ABCED*, *ABED*

Section 11.4   (page 475)

1. *ADCBA*, *ACBA*, *ADCA*   **3.** *RTSWVR*, *RSWVR*, *RTSR*

5.

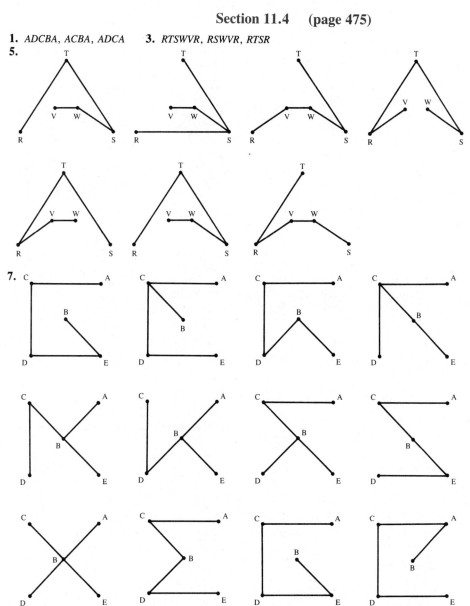

9. Length: 2 + 3 + 4 + 5 = 14

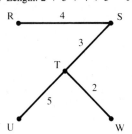

11. Length: 6 + 7 + 12 + 14 = 39

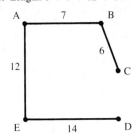

13. Length: 168 + 152 + 164 + 152 = 636 miles

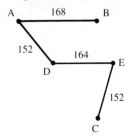

Chapter 11   Review Exercises   (page 477)

1.
$$M\begin{array}{c}M\\N\\P\\Q\end{array}\begin{bmatrix}0 & 1 & 0 & 1\\1 & 0 & 0 & 1\\0 & 0 & 0 & 0\\0 & 0 & 1 & 0\end{bmatrix}$$
Adjacency matrix

3.
$$\begin{array}{c}T\\W\\X\\Y\\Z\end{array}\begin{bmatrix}0 & 0 & 0 & 1 & 1\\1 & 0 & 0 & 1 & 0\\0 & 1 & 0 & 1 & 0\\0 & 0 & 0 & 0 & 0\\0 & 1 & 1 & 1 & 0\end{bmatrix}$$
Adjacency matrix

5.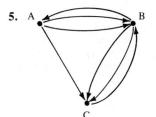

7.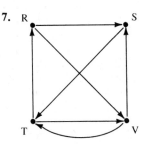

9.
$$\begin{array}{c}A\\B\\C\end{array}\begin{bmatrix}0 & 0 & 1\\1 & 0 & 0\\0 & 1 & 0\end{bmatrix}$$
Total dominances in one- or two-stage dominances: A dominates B and C, B dominates A and C, C dominates A and B

11. Not the matrix of a dominance digraph

13.
$$\begin{array}{c}P\\Q\\R\\S\end{array}\begin{bmatrix}0 & 0 & 1 & 1\\1 & 0 & 0 & 1\\0 & 1 & 0 & 1\\0 & 0 & 0 & 0\end{bmatrix}$$
Two-stage dominances: P dominates R and S, Q dominates P and S, P dominates Q and S. Total dominances: P dominates Q, R, and S; Q dominates P and R once each and S twice; R dominates P and Q once each and S twice; S dominates no one.

15.
$$\begin{array}{c}A\\B\\C\\D\end{array}\begin{bmatrix}0 & 1 & 1 & 0\\0 & 0 & 1 & 1\\0 & 0 & 0 & 0\\1 & 0 & 1 & 0\end{bmatrix}$$
Two-stage dominances: A dominates C and D (1 way each), B dominates A and C in 1 way each, C has no two-stage dominances, D dominates B and C in 1 way each.

17. B wins with 3 + 5 = 8 one- or two-stage dominances, while D has only 3 + 4 = 7.

19.
$$\begin{array}{c}A\\B\\C\\D\end{array}\begin{bmatrix}0 & 1 & 2 & 1\\1 & 0 & 0 & 0\\2 & 0 & 0 & 1\\1 & 0 & 1 & 0\end{bmatrix}$$
Communications digraph

21.
$$\begin{array}{c}R\\S\\T\\V\\W\end{array}\begin{bmatrix}0 & 1 & 1 & 1 & 1\\1 & 0 & 0 & 1 & 1\\1 & 0 & 0 & 1 & 0\\1 & 1 & 1 & 0 & 1\\1 & 1 & 0 & 1 & 0\end{bmatrix}$$
Both a communications digraph and an organizational communications digraph

23.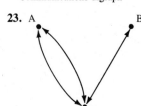
Two-stage paths includes A to A in 4 ways, A to B in 2 ways, B to A in 2 ways, B to B in 1 way, C to C in 5 ways

25. 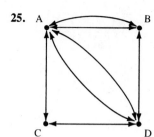 Two-stage paths includes *A* to *A* in 9 ways, *A* to *B* in 2 ways, *A* to *C* in 2 ways, *A* to *D* in 3 ways, *B* to *A* in 2 ways, *B* to *B* in 5 ways, *B* to *C* in 3 ways, *B* to *D* in 4 ways, *C* to *A* in 2 ways, *C* to *B* in 3 ways, *C* to *C* in 2 ways, *C* to *D* in 2 ways, *D* to *A* in 3 ways, *D* to *B* in 4 ways, *D* to *C* in 2 ways, *D* to *D* in 6 ways

27. *ABED, AED*   **31.** *XYZWX, XYZX, XZWX*

33.

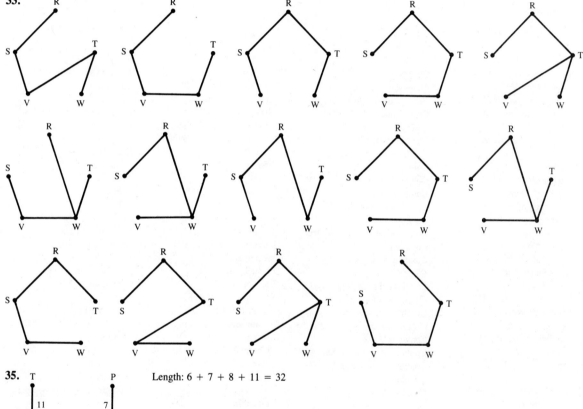

35. 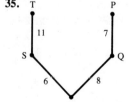   Length: 6 + 7 + 8 + 11 = 32

INDEX

Amount of an Annuity

$$s_{\overline{n}|i} = \frac{(1 + i)^n - 1}{i}$$

n / i	1%	$1\frac{1}{2}$%	2%	3%	4%	5%	6%	8%
1	1.00000	1.00000	1.00000	1.00000	1.00000	1.00000	1.00000	1.00000
2	2.01000	2.01500	2.02000	2.03000	2.04000	2.05000	2.06000	2.08000
3	3.03010	3.04523	3.06040	3.09090	3.12160	3.15250	3.18360	3.24640
4	4.06040	4.09090	4.12161	4.18363	4.24646	4.31013	4.37462	4.50611
5	5.10101	5.15227	5.20404	5.30914	5.41632	5.52563	5.63709	5.86660
6	6.15202	6.22955	6.30812	6.46841	6.63298	6.80191	6.97532	7.33593
7	7.21354	7.32299	7.43428	7.66246	7.89829	8.14201	8.39384	8.92280
8	8.28567	8.43284	8.58297	8.89234	9.21423	9.54911	9.89747	10.63663
9	9.36853	9.55933	9.75463	10.15911	10.58280	11.02656	11.49132	12.48756
10	10.46221	10.70272	10.94972	11.46388	12.00611	12.57789	13.18079	14.48656
11	11.56683	11.86326	12.16872	12.80780	13.48635	14.20679	14.97164	16.64549
12	12.68250	13.04121	13.41209	14.19203	15.02581	15.91713	16.86994	18.97713
13	13.80933	14.23683	14.68033	15.61779	16.62684	17.71298	18.88214	21.49530
14	14.94742	15.45038	15.97394	17.08632	18.29191	19.59863	21.01507	24.21492
15	16.09690	16.68214	17.29342	18.59891	20.02359	21.57856	23.27597	27.15211
16	17.25786	17.93237	18.63929	20.15688	21.82453	23.65749	25.67253	30.32428
17	18.43044	19.20136	20.01207	21.76159	23.69751	25.84037	28.21288	33.75023
18	19.61475	20.48938	21.41231	23.41444	25.64541	28.13238	30.90565	37.45024
19	20.81090	21.79672	22.84056	25.11687	27.67123	30.53900	33.75999	41.44626
20	22.01900	23.12367	24.29737	26.87037	29.77808	33.06595	36.78559	45.76196
21	23.23919	24.47052	25.78332	28.67649	31.96920	35.71925	39.99273	50.42292
22	24.47159	25.83758	27.29898	30.53678	34.24797	38.50521	43.39229	55.45676
23	25.71630	27.22514	28.84496	32.45288	36.61789	41.43048	46.99583	60.89330
24	26.97346	28.63352	30.42186	34.42647	39.08260	44.50200	50.81558	66.76476
25	28.24320	30.06302	32.03030	36.45926	41.64591	47.72710	54.86451	73.10594
26	29.52563	31.51397	33.67091	38.55304	44.31174	51.11345	59.15638	79.95442
27	30.82089	32.98668	35.34432	40.70963	47.08421	54.66913	63.70577	87.35077
28	32.12910	34.48148	37.05121	42.93092	49.96758	58.40258	68.52811	95.33883
29	33.45039	35.99870	38.79223	45.21885	52.96629	62.32271	73.63980	103.96594
30	34.78489	37.53868	40.56808	47.57542	56.08494	66.43885	79.05819	113.28321
31	36.13274	39.10176	42.37944	50.00268	59.32834	70.76079	84.80168	123.34587
32	37.49407	40.68829	44.22703	52.50276	62.70147	75.29883	90.88978	134.21354
33	38.86901	42.29861	46.11157	55.07784	66.20953	80.06377	97.34316	145.95062
34	40.25770	43.93309	48.03380	57.73018	69.85791	85.06696	104.18375	158.62667
35	41.66028	45.59209	49.99448	60.46208	73.65222	90.32031	111.43478	172.31680
36	43.07688	47.27597	51.99437	63.27594	77.59831	95.83632	119.12087	187.10215
37	44.50765	48.98511	54.03425	66.17422	81.70225	101.62814	127.26812	203.07032
38	45.95272	50.71989	56.11494	69.15945	85.97034	107.70955	135.90421	220.31595
39	47.41225	52.48068	58.23724	72.23423	90.40915	114.09502	145.05846	238.94122
40	48.88637	54.26789	60.40198	75.40126	95.02552	120.79977	154.76197	259.05652
41	50.37524	56.08191	62.61002	78.66330	99.82654	127.83976	165.04768	280.78104
42	51.87899	57.92314	64.86222	82.02320	104.81960	135.23175	175.95054	304.24352
43	53.39778	59.79199	67.15947	85.48389	110.01238	142.99334	187.50758	329.58301
44	54.93176	61.68887	69.50266	89.04841	115.41288	151.14301	199.75803	356.94965
45	56.48107	63.61420	71.89271	92.71986	121.02939	159.70016	212.74351	386.50562
46	58.04589	65.56841	74.33056	96.50146	126.87057	168.68516	226.50812	418.42607
47	59.62634	67.55194	76.81718	100.39650	132.94539	178.11942	241.09861	452.90015
48	61.22261	69.56522	79.35352	104.40840	139.26321	188.02539	256.56453	490.13216
49	62.83483	71.60870	81.94059	108.54065	145.83373	198.42666	272.95840	530.34274
50	64.46318	73.68283	84.57940	112.79687	152.66708	209.34800	290.33590	573.77016